ANNUAL REVIEW OF IRISH LAW 1989

Annual Review
of Irish Law 1989

Raymond Byrne
B.C.L., LL.M., Barrister-at-Law
Lecturer in Law, Dublin City University

William Binchy
B.A., B.C.L., LL.M., Barrister-at-Law
Research Counsellor, The Law Reform Commission

THE ROUND HALL PRESS
DUBLIN

The typesetting for this book was produced by
Gilbert Gough Typesetting, Dublin for
The Round Hall Press, Dublin

BRITISH LIBRARY CATALOGUING IN PUBLICATION DATA
Annual Review of Irish law. — 1989 —
1. Ireland (Republic), Law
344.17

ISBN 0-947686-61-4

ISSN 0791-1084

Printed by
Colour Books Ltd, Dublin

Contents

Preface

As with the previous Reviews, the purpose of this volume is to provide a review of legal developments, judicial and statutory, that occurred during the year. In relation to case law, this includes those judgments which were delivered in 1989, regardless of whether they have been (or will be) reported and which were circulated up to the date of this preface.

We would like to thank Mr Justice Brian Walsh (who originated the concept of an annual review of Irish law) for his continuing support and encouragement. Once again, we also are indebted to a number of other people who assisted us in completing this volume. Mr Gary Lynch helped us in the preparation of the text, for which we are extremely grateful. Ms Margaret Byrne and Ms Mary Gaynor, of the Library of the Incorporated Law Society of Ireland, were extremely helpful as always. Mr John Armstrong and Mr Nigel Cochrane, of the King's Inns Library, also helped us with numerous queries. Ms Peggy McQuinn of the Supreme Court Office also assisted our reserach in numerous ways. Ms Jennifer Aston, Librarian in the Four Courts Law Library, provided much needed assistance in sourcing elusive material. Finally, Michael Adams and Martin Healy at Round Hall Press gave us the benefit of their guiding hands and eyes at critical junctures.

One small point on references to judicial decisions in the text. Where a case has been reported in the Irish Times Law Reports (a welcome addition to law reporting in Ireland in 1989), we refer to it thus: Irish Times LR. Where we make reference to an 'ordinary' newspaper report of a case (or other matter reported in a newspaper) we refer to it thus: *Irish Times*.

Raymond Byrne and William Binchy,
Dublin

October 1990.

Table of Cases

Other Tables

CONSTITUTIONAL PROVISIONS

STATUTES

STATUTORY INSTRUMENTS

EUROPEAN COMMUNITY LAWS

Other Tables

ANNUAL REVIEW OF IRISH LAW 1989

Administrative Law

GOVERNMENT FUNCTIONS

Appropriation The Appropriation Act 1989 provided that the appropriation for the year ended 31 December 1989 for supply grants was £6,452,474,000 and for appropriations-in-aid was £619,444,000.

Civil Service In *Reidy v Minister for Agriculture and Food*, High Court, 9 June 1989 O'Hanlon J examined some aspects of the Civil Service Regulation Act 1956. The applicant, an Agricultural Officer in the Department of Agriculture and Food, applied for judicial review of a number of decisions communicated in a letter to him from a principal officer in the Department, after a hearing of certain matters of complaint had been held. The matters of complaint related to certain alleged irregularities in the manner of the applicant's performance of his duties as an Agricultural Officer and in particular whether the applicant had tended to relax the strict requirements of the Beef Premium Scheme in relation to farmers with whom he was acquainted personally. No loss of public money had taken place in any such alleged irregularities. The letter to the applicant had indicated that: (i) an increment 'due on 18 January 1988 will not be paid'; (ii) the applicant would not be allowed to compete for any competitions within or outside the Department for two years; and (iii) the applicant's headquarters were to be changed. In the course of the hearing, certain circulars issued by the Department pursuant to s.17 of the 1956 Act were put in evidence.

On a procedural level, O'Hanlon J considered that the applicant had been fully informed of the case he had to meet so that the requirements of natural justice had been fully complied with in the hearings which the Department had conducted. He then proceeded to deal with the three substantive issues raised.

First, regarding the increment, the judge held that the applicant was entitled to a declaration that the decision made was invalid. This was for the reason that, because of an oversight, the letter did not defer payment for a specified period (subject to review) as was the procedure indicated in the most recent Circular issued by the Department under the 1956 Act. However, O'Hanlon J also stated that it was a matter for the Department to deal with the matter afresh, as there was no bar to withholding an increment even after the date on which it was due to be paid. He stated that it would be lawful to withhold payment of an increment for such reasonable period as was necessary to enable an investigation to be completed.

As to the prohibition on competing for places for two years, he concluded that there was no authority in the 1956 Act or in any Circular issued under it for the imposition of this penalty. He acknowledged that dereliction of duty could be recorded on an officer's file and might count against his application for promotion, but the penalty imposed on the applicant was quite different.

Finally, on the change of the applicant's headquarters O'Hanlon J was satisfied that it had been made bona fide as it was preferable to locate the applicant away from farmers with whom he was personally acquainted. Nonetheless, the decision had not been ratified by the Head of the Department as envisaged in the applicant's Conditions of Service, and it had not been shown that the power to make the decision had been lawfully delegated to the principal officer. On delegation, see the cases cited in the 1988 Review, 7.

National Archives   The National Archives Act 1986 (Commencement) Order 1989 (SI No. 116) brought s.5 of the 1986 Act, which provides for the appointment of a director of the National Archives, into effect on 24 April 1989.

National Parks   The Blascaod Mór National Historic Park Act 1989 established the Park of the Act's title on the Great Blasket Island under the management and control of the Commissioners of Public Works. The Act also allows for the compulsory acquisition of land by the Commissioners. For detailed commentary, with notes of the literary associations with the Island, see Humphries' annotation, *Irish Current Law Statutes Annotated.*

Oireachtas salaries   The Members of the Oireachtas and Ministerial and Parliamentary Offices (Allowances and Salaries) Order 1989 (SI No.203) gives effect to increased salaries and allowances in line with Gleeson Reports.

Semi-State bodies
1 Bord Gáis   The Gas (Amendment) Act 1987 (Section 2(7)) Order 1989 (SI No.162) amends the Schedule to the 1987 Act to allow for changes in the functions of An Bord Gáis.

2 Bord na gCapall: dissolution   The Bord na gCapall (Dissolution) Act 1989 provided for the dissolution of Bord na gCapall and the consequent repeal of the Horse Industry Act 1970. The maintenance of the Irish horse register of stallions has been transferred to the Department of Agriculture and Food.

3 National Authority for Occupational Safety and Health The Safety, Health and Welfare at Work Act 1989 provided for the establishment of the National Authority for Occupational Safety and Health, a semi-State body which now administers and enforces the law on safety, health and welfare in all workplaces in the State: see 379-93, below, in the Safety and Health chapter.

4 Údarás na Gaeltachta The Údarás na Gaeltachta (Amendment) Act 1989 increased to £80 million the maximum aggregate amount which Udaras may advance by way of loan for the development of industry within Gaeltacht areas. The 1989 Act amends s.23 of the Údarás na Gaeltachta Act 1979 accordingly.

SFADCo The Shannon Free Airport Development Company Limited (Amendment) Act 1989 amends the 1970 Act of the same title in order to extend SFADCo's responsibilities to include North Kerry.

Note: the remainder of the chapter deals with judicial review of administrative action.

JUDICIAL REVIEW

This year saw the publication of James O'Reilly and Anthony Collins' major work, *Civil Proceedings and the State in Ireland* (Round Hall Press, 1989). It is a comprehensive and indispensable guide to practice and procedure in all civil proceedings to which the State is party.

Extraneous considerations In *Flanagan v Galway City and County Manager*, High Court, 25 May 1989 (330-1, below, in the Local Government chapter) a planning decision was quashed for taking account of extraneous or irrelevant considerations. In *Pepper v Bofin* (*Irish Times*, 6 March 1989) Gannon J declined to grant judicial review of a decision of the respondent Dublin City Coroner who had refused to hold an inquest into the death of the applicant's infant daughter. Gannon J held that, as the Coroner had taken account of all the relevant factors in the Coroners Act 1962, there were no grounds for the High Court to interfere.

Fair procedures/natural justice
1 Audi alteram partem In *Murtagh v Board of Management of St Emer's National School*, High Court, 27 November 1989, Barron J upheld certain disciplinary decisions made by the respondent board of management. The applicants were the parents of a pupil in sixth class at St Emer's National School, Longford. In the course of a class he wrote the words 'Noleen Bitch

Rooney' on a sheet of paper; Mrs Rooney was a teacher in another class. He was asked to apologise to Mrs Rooney but refused to do so. The next day he left a note on Mrs Rooney's desk which indicated that she was interfering with the running of fifth and sixth classes and that if she wanted to be headmistress she should apply elsewhere. The headmaster continued to require an apology and he subsequently wrote to the applicants seeking a meeting and this took place though they objected to the principal dealing with the matter. The matter was put before a meeting of the board of management who agreed to suspend the pupil for three days. The applicants objected to the procedure and it was agreed that they should attend a meeting of the board, pending which the suspension was lifted. At the subsequent meeting of the board with the applicants present, the suspension was reimposed. Barron J refused on judicial review to quash the decision.

On a preliminary point, he held that judicial review did lie to quash the board's decisions since it operated under Rules formulated by the Department of Education and these were not consensual in nature; and while he accepted that a cause of action might arise from a failure to observe the Rules this did not affect the supervisory jurisdiction of the High Court. Barron J expressed regret at the fact that this kind of preliminary point could be raised at all in spite of O.84 of the Rules of the Superior Courts 1986.

With regard to the procedures adopted in the instant case, Barron J stated that the obligation on the board was to act fairly. In the circumstances he felt that the board and the principal had behaved perfectly properly by giving the applicants opportunities to say why they opposed the suspension. He also rejected the contention that the board had acted with closed minds as this was not a case in which disputed evidence had been ruled on improperly.

Finally, apart from dismissing the principal arguments put forward by the applicants, Barron J added that he would also have refused the relief sought in the exercise of the court's discretion. This was having regard to his view that it seemed more than probable that the real authors of the note which had been left on Mrs Rooney's desk on the day after the original incident were the applicants. This final point made by Barron J may indicate why he did not enter into a fuller discussion of the relevant principles of fair procedures involved in the case. For example, he did not refer to his own judgment in *Flanagan v University College Dublin* [1989] ILRM 469 (see the 1988 Review, 14-5), in which he had cited, *inter alia*, the only other Irish decision on primary school disciplinary procedures, *The State (Smullen) v Duffy* [1980] ILRM 46. It is, perhaps, unfortunate that an assessment of the precise nature of the fair procedures doctrine was not fleshed out given the interesting magesterial/disciplinary dichotomy in the schools context to which Finlay P (as he then was) referred to in the *Smullen* case. Some comparative discussion might include reference to the 'due process' requirements indicated by, e.g.,

Goss v Lopez, 419 US 565 (1975) referred to by Osborough, (1978) 13 *Ir Jur (ns)* 145. Whether such discussion would have mattered to the outcome in *Murtagh* is another matter; the particular circumstances suggest that it would not.

The fairness of the conduct of hearings was also discussed in *Thompson v Minister for Social Welfare* [1989] IR 618 (398, below), *Reidy v Minister for Agriculture and Food*, High Court, 9 June 1989 (3, above) and *O'Flynn and O'Regan v Mid-Western Health Board* [1989] IR 429 (375, below).

2 Bias In *O'Neill v Beaumont Hospital Board* [1990] ILRM 419, the main issue discussed was the importance of the rule that tribunals should not appear to be biased. The applicant had been appointed as a consultant to Beaumont Hospital for a probationary period of one year. Three days before the end of the probationary period, the hospital's chief executive wrote to the applicant, setting out a number of grounds on which his service was not deemed to be satisfactory and informing him that he would cease to hold his appointment as consultant at the end of the probationary period. The applicant instituted proceedings against the hospital, in which Murphy J held that any certificate terminating the applicant's appointment required a decision of the board of the hospital. In light of this judgment, the chief executive of the hospital wrote to the applicant informing him that a meeting of the board had been arranged and that he was invited to attend and speak. The applicant sought an order of prohibition or an injunction restraining the board from meeting on the ground that the chief executive and the board members were biased and would be unable to provide a fair hearing to him. In relation to the board members, the applicant averred that they had placed on record their support for the chief executive's criticism of the applicant's conduct during the probationary period. Murphy J dismissed the applicant's claim, but on appeal the Supreme Court held in his favour.

In the High Court, Murphy J's approach emphasised that the board of the hospital were lay people, not judges, and that the administrative requirements of the hospital should be borne in mind. In essence, therefore, his view was that the doctrine of necessity required some dilution of the normal rule against bias.

He stated firstly that any committee exercising management functions will properly and necessarily have some knowledge of and involvement with the staff of the enterprise they are concerned with; but he stated that while they must exercise their functions fairly they are not expected to emulate the conduct of a judge who must distance himself from any prior knowledge of the matters in issue. Second, he opined that it should not lightly be inferred that a committee with the diversity of backgrounds which the members of the board of the hospital possessed would act otherwise than fairly; and while the applicant's concerns were entitled to respect, Murphy J considered that the board should not be prevented from conducting a hearing in relation to the applicant, though each member of the board should consider whether there was any matter which might preclude participation in the hearing. Finally, while the chief executive of the hospital was intimately connected with the implementation of whatever decision was ultimately reached, and had been instrumental in establishing the management structure in the hospital, Murphy J held that this would not necessarily involve a bias of any description except perhaps a bias in favour of efficiency, and it would not, therefore, be proper to conclude that he would be unable to act fairly at the hearing. It must be said that this approach reflects very closely that taken by the Supreme Court in *McGrath v Trustees of Maynooth College* [1979] ILRM 166, where considerable leeway was allowed by the Court in the circumstances which arose there.

Nonetheless, in the *O'Neill* case, the Supreme Court (Finlay CJ, Walsh and Griffin JJ) on appeal from Murphy J took a slightly different view of the position of the chief executive and the members of the board who had expressed an opinion as to the merits of the chief executive's original decision. There were three elements in the judgment of the Chief Justice which, although it was given ex tempore, reflects the traditional approach to the bias rule in Irish law. First, he stated that there could be no question of the members of the board being in any sense prohibited from conducting a hearing in the present case simply because they might be aware from their management functions of certain information relevant to the case. Second, the real issue was whether there was, from an objective point of view, a reasonable apprehension that the views expressed by the chief executive and two other members of the board would prevent a completely fair and independent hearing. On this point the Supreme Court differed from Murphy J. It found that the particular way in which the two board members had expressed full agreement with the chief executive precluded them from taking part in the deliberations of the board. In accordance with the general rule, the Court expressly pointed out that this conclusion did not in any way cast doubt on the bona fide way in which the chief executive and the other two board members had carried out their functions. The third point made by the Chief Justice involves the clearest statement to date by an Irish court as to the subsidiary nature of the necessity rule in the context of the rule against bias. Having concluded that three members of the board (including the chief executive) were precluded from sitting in the applicant's case, the Supreme Court was not prepared to state that the entire board had become tainted with the views which had been expressed. Finlay CJ stated:

> I think that in relation to this last point regard must be had to the doctrine

of necessity. It is not a dominant doctrine—it could never defeat a real fear . . . of bias or injustice—but it is a consideration in relation to the question of the entire board being prohibited, for if that were to be done there can be no other machinery by which something which is of great importance both to the board of the hospital and to the plaintiff (and I might add to the public who will attend the hospital), namely the continuance or non-continuance of the plaintiff's services in the hospital, can be determined in accordance with the terms of the probationary agreement.

The effect of this view is to preserve the integrity of the decision making process while ensuring that the machinery established is also maintained. Seethe similar view expressed in Hogan and Morgan, *Administrative Law* (Irish Law Texts, 1986), 255-7.

Legitimate expectation   The case law on legitimate expectation (see the 1988 Review, 20-30) continued to grow in 1989. Three High Court decisions dealt with the matter. These were: *Wiley v Revenue Commissioners* [1989] IR 350; *Pesca Valentia Ltd v Minister for Fisheries*, High Court, 6 June 1989 and *Nolan v Minister for the Environment* [1989] IR 357 (discussed in the Local Government chapter, 333, below). In addition, *Finucane v McMahon*, High Court (Divisional), 7 April 1989 (discussed in the Criminal Law chapter, 159, below) referred to the question of estoppel of the State, a connected issue. In none of the cases was the argument as to legitimate expectation accepted, thus indicating the limits to the doctrine. Furthermore, in the *Pesca Valentia* case, the public law aspect of legitimate expectation was emphasised, which appears to indicate further the reluctance of some judges to use the doctrine as an all-purpose remedial device.

In *Wiley v Revenue Commissioners* [1989] IR 350 the doctrine arose in a Revenue context. The applicant suffered from certain physical disabilities which made it impossible for him to drive an ordinary motor vehicle. He had no use in one leg for driving purposes and his left ankle was damaged as a result of extra stress placed on it. In 1983 and 1985 he purchased new motor vehicles in relation to which he obtained certificates of exemption from road tax under s.43(1) of the Finance Act 1968. That section provides that such exemption may only be obtained where the driver 'is wholly, or almost wholly, without the use of each of his legs'. It was clear that, on any reading of s.43(1), the applicant was not entitled in law to the certificates which he in fact obtained. On both occasions, the applicant also obtained refunds on the excise duty payable on the vehicles in accordance with a refund scheme operated by the Revenue Commissioners pursuant to para.12 of the Imposition of Duties (No. 236) (Excise Duties on Motor Vehicles, Televisions and Gramophone Records) Order 1979. The scheme was based on an applicant coming within the terms of s.43(1) of the 1968 Act. In operating the scheme the Revenue granted a refund in 1983 and 1985 on presentation by the applicant of his certificate of exemption from road tax. In 1986 the Revenue Commissioners altered their policy in relation to the excise duty refund scheme, and from that time required a copy of the medical certificate on which the road tax exemption was based. In 1987, when the applicant purchased a new car, and also obtained a road tax exemption under s.43(1) of the 1968 Act, the Revenue Commissioners refused his application for an excise duty refund on the ground that his disability did not come within the terms of the scheme. The applicant applied for judicial review, arguing that he had a legitimate expectation to the excise duty refund. It was conceded on his behalf that he did not come within the terms of the scheme. Blayney J refused the relief sought by the applicant.

The judge cited with approval the statement of the doctrine by Hamilton P in *Duggan v An Taoiseach* [1989] ILRM 710 (see the 1988 Review, 21-4). Blayney J acknowledged that the applicant had an expectation that he would receive a refund on excise duty in 1987, but he did not consider that this could be described as a legitimate expectation. He stated that it could only have been where the applicant had considered himself entitled to the refund when he applied for it in 1987 that such a legitimate expectation could have arisen; whereas in the present case, at best the applicant could claim that he believed he had a good chance of getting it—a reasonable belief in view of the 1983 and 1985 applications—but Blayney J held that this fell far short of being a legitimate expectation.

A second line of argument put forward by the applicant (relying on dicta in *Council of Civil Service Unions v Minister for the Public Service* [1985] AC 374, the GCHQ case) was that the Revenue's conduct towards the applicant prior to 1987, in the two previous applications, should be regarded as an administrative practice which the applicant could expect to continue unless notice of discontinuance was given by the Revenue to affected persons. Blayney J also rejected this point, primarily because the two instances could not be regarded as a practice.

Obviously, the two instances involving the applicant were not isolated events and were part of a wider approach by the Revenue (giving the refund where a certificate of exemption was produced), and so in that sense could be described as a practice. But Blayney J was at pains to point out that the crucial aspect of the case was that the applicant had never been entitled to the refund in the first place. And he added an important rider to drive home that point: if the Revenue had changed its scheme so that persons formerly entitled to a refund were no longer so entitled, a legitimate expectation giving rise to relief by way of judicial review would operate; but that was not the position in the instant case. It may be noted that the statutory provisions in question have since been altered to provide for a more liberal regime for disabled drivers: see the Revenue Law chapter, 367, below.

The second case in which legitimate expectation was discussed in 1989 was *Pesca Valentia Ltd v Minister for Fisheries*, High Court, 6 June 1989. The plaintiff company had instituted proceedings claiming that the Fisheries (Amendment) Act 1983, which introduced new requirements as to the composition of the crews of certain fishing vessels, were invalid as being in violation of European Community law. The company obtained an interlocutory injunction preventing enforcement of the Act pending the decision of the European Court of Justice to which the issue had been referred: [1986] ILRM 68; [1985] IR 193. In January 1988, the ECJ resolved the matter against the company. On remittal to the High Court, the company claimed that, notwithstanding that decision, it was entitled to damages from the defendants. This was put forward on the basis of a legitimate expectation, arising from the conduct of certain semi-State agencies who, the plaintiff claimed, had indicated that any changes in fisheries laws would be gradual, would take account of the plaintiff's special position and would be preceded by consultations with the plaintiff. The defendants denied that any such expectation arose; and counterclaimed damages in relation to the undertaking which the plaintiffs had given on obtaining the interlocutory injunction which had been discharged after the European Court hearing. Neither side received any relief from Keane J.

Keane J cited a number of passages from the speeches in the *GCHQ* case [1985] AC 374, supra, to make the point that the doctrine of legitimate expectation related to the manner in which a decision has been made by a public authority, so that the person affected may have an opportunity to be heard in relation to alterations in a regime, and it does not relate to the nature of the decision itself. In other words, the doctrine related, essentially, to procedural rather than substantive matters. Thus in the instant case the plaintiff company could not rely on the doctrine since it was made aware of, and was consulted in relation to, the proposed change in law which resulted in the 1983 Act. Keane J also resurrected some doubts raised by Murphy J in *Garda Representative Association v Ireland* [1989] ILRM 1 as to whether the doctrine should be recognised as a separate concept in our legal system (alluding to certain dicta of Finlay CJ in *Webb v Ireland* [1988] ILRM 565; [1988] IR 353 in this context). While it would be going too far to suggest that this represents the emasculation of the doctrine, it is a clear indication that its usefulness may be severely restricted by some judges.

This is supported by the 'public law' manner in which Keane J dealt with the connected argument that an equitable estoppel arose in favour of the plaintiff company; it will be remembered that in the *Webb* case legitimate expectation and estoppel were expressly linked. Keane J pointed out that in the instant case the company had not been given an assurance (as opposed to the assuance that had been given in the *Webb* case) that the law concerning fishing would never adversely affect it, so that no equitable estoppel could arise in the circumstances. But, crucially, he was of the view that in any event, had such an assurance been given, it could not conceivably operate to prevent the Oireachtas from legislating or the executive from implementing the legislation when enacted. This view very much reflects that taken by Lardner J in *Devitt v Minister for Education* [1989] ILRM 639 (see the 1988 Review, 26-8) and may place in some doubt the more flexible approach taken by Hamilton P in *Conroy v Garda Commissioner* [1989] IR 140 (see the 1988 Review, 259).

Finally, we may note here the other issue dealt with in the judgment, namely the claim by the State for damages. Although the plaintiff company had given the usual undertaking as to damages when it obtained the interlocutory injunction preventing enforcement of the 1983 Act, Keane J considered that there was no basis on which the Court could measure damages which the State suffered as a result, either by reference to the profits of the company (which could have accrued to another company fishing in accordance with the 1983 Act) or to the penalties which might have been imposed in prosecutions by the State (since none had taken place and the purpose of such prosecutions would have been to deter illegality and not to gather revenue for the State). Thus no order was made in relation to the undertaking, although Keane J noted that this was an unsatisfactory result. We consider this case further below, 194-6.

Practice and procedure

1 Acquiescence In *Browne v An Bord Pleanála* [1989] ILRM 865 (202-4, below, in the European Communities chapter) Barron J held that the applicants had not precluded themselves by their conduct from applying for judicial review. That was a planning permission case in which the applicants had appealed the granting of permission to An Bord Pleanála, and later launched judicial review proceedings challenging the jurisdiction of An Bord in the case. Barron J held that their conduct had not led any person to believe that such judicial review proceedings would not be taken. In applying the views of the Supreme Court in *The State (Gallagher & Co) v de Valera* [1986] ILRM 3, Barron J also drew attention to the more simplified procedure for judicial review in 0.84 of the Rules of the Superior Courts 1986; he stated that the courts would be reluctant nowadays to determine a judicial review on such a preliminary point. See also his view in *Murtagh v Board of Management of St Emer's National School*, High Court, 27 November 1989 (6, above).

2 Costs In *McIlwraith v Fawsitt* [1990] ILRM 1, the Supreme Court confirmed the line of authority that where a judicial review application was not contested it was not appropriate to make an order for costs against the Attorney General. The applicant had been awarded a sum of money by the Employment Appeals Tribunal in his unfair dismissals claim. The employer purported to serve a notice of appeal to the Circuit Court against this determination, but the notice was outside the time limit specified for appeals from the Tribunal. The employer then applied for an extension of time for appealing, and the respondent Circuit Court judge purported to grant such an extension. No such jurisdiction was vested in the respondent, and the applicant applied for judicial review of the respondent's decision. The first respondent did not contest the application, but on the hearing of the motion Barr J made an order, later clarified, that the applicant's costs be recoverable against the Attorney General as indemnifier of the respondent Circuit Court judge. The Attorney General, who had not been a party to the judicial review application, successfully appealed the order for costs to the Supreme Court (Finlay CJ, Walsh and McCarthy JJ).

Delivering the only judgment, Finlay CJ stated that the order for costs made in the High Court was quite contrary to the legal principles applicable in a case of this description. Since the respondent judge had made an order occasioned by the application on behalf of the employer, there was no question of impropriety or *mala fides* but rather an error due to a mistake in relation to the law applicable. In circumstances where the order in question was not contested, the Chief Justice stated, it was not appropriate to order the Attorney General to bear the costs and he quoted with approval the views of Maguire CJ in the unreported decision in *The State (Prendergast) v Rochford*, Supreme Court, 1 July 1952.

Finlay CJ did, however, add an important rider to the decision. He stated that there may be circumstances in which the obligation of the executive to support the judiciary under the Constitution would require the executive to indemnify members of the judiciary in relation to costs which are properly awarded against the judiciary, but since this was not the position in the instant case and no argument had been addressed on the point, he refrained from expressing a view on it. The fact that he raised the point at all (in the absence of any suggestion by counsel during argument) may be taken, perhaps, as an indication that the Court would, in the future, look favourably on such an argument.

3 Declaration/damages The circumstances in which a Court will refuse to grant damages for *ultra vires* action were discussed in *Greene v Minister for Agriculture* [1990] ILRM 364 (99-101, below, in the Constitutional Law chapter).

4 Discretion to refuse   See the reference to this in *Murtagh v Board of Management of St Emer's National School*, High Court, 27 November 1989 (6, above).

5 Master of High Court   In *Elwyn (Cottons) Ltd v Master of the High Court* [1989] IR 14 (78, below, in the Conflict of Laws chapter), O'Hanlon J held that judicial review lies against orders of the Master of the High Court notwithstanding the fact that the Master is an officer 'attached' to the High Court.

6 Severability   The decision in *The State (McLoughlin) v Eastern Health Board* [1986] IR 416 was applied by Murphy J in *Howard v Minister for Agriculture and Food*, High Court, 3 October 1989: see 17, below, in the Agriculture chapter. See also *Greene*, 100, below.

Public law/private law   In *Murphy v Turf Club* [1989] IR 172, Barr J applied well-established case law in holding that judicial review did not lie against a body exercising functions deriving from contract. The respondent Turf Club had purported to suspend the applicant's licence as a racehorse trainer. The applicant instituted proceedings by way of judicial review seeking to quash the suspension on the grounds of failure to observe fair procedures and he also sought damages. The respondent argued that judicial review did not lie in relation to its decisions on the ground that it did not exercise powers of a public law nature but was a private body which exercised control over the racehorse industry. Barr J held for the respondent.

He acknowledged that the courts had, in recent years, extended the scope of the availability of judicial review to bodies which, although not exercising statutory functions, exercised functions of a public nature, and he discussed the decision of the Court of Appeal in *R v Panel on Takeovers and Mergers, ex p. Datafin plc* [1987] QB 815 in this context. However, Barr J felt that the functions exercised by the respondent Turf Club in the instant case derived from contract and were not in the nature of public law functions. Rather they were of a domestic tribunal exercising a regulatory function over the applicant who was an interested person and who had voluntarily submitted to its jurisdiction. He expressly approved the reasoning in the very similar Court of Appeal decision *Law v National Greyhound Racing Club Ltd* [1983] 1 WLR 1302. It may be noted that Barr J also made reference to the decision of the Divisional High Court in *The State (Colquhoun) v D'Arcy* [1936] IR 641 which had held that the Court of the General Synod of the Church of Ireland was not amenable to judicial review. At the end of his judgment, Barr J pointed out that the appropriate course of action for the applicant was to proceed by way of an action for breach of contract against the respondent.

By way of contrast, in *Murtagh v Board of Management of St Emer's National School*, High Court, 27 November 1989 (6, above) Barron J held that the decisions of the respondent Board, acting under Department of Education rules, are subject to judicial review. In this he was taking the same view as that of Finlay P (as he then was) in *The State (Smullen) v Duffy* [1980] ILRM 46.

It may be noted that the question whether judicial review lies was also raised in *O'Neill v Beaumont Hospital Board* [1990] ILRM 419 (7, above), but it was not pursued. When the case came before the Supreme Court, Finlay CJ pointed out that the Court had dealt with the matter on the same basis as it would have in a plenary hearing for injunction. It should be pointed out that the *O'Neill* case was also one of great urgency and so the usual requirements as to judicial review were not strictly applied. For that reason, the concession made by the Court to the parties should not be regarded as setting any precedent for the future.

Reasonableness   In *Hill v Criminal Injuries Compensation Tribunal* [1990] ILRM 36, Lynch J applied the tests on reasonableness set out in *The State (Keegan) v Stardust Victims Compensation Tribunal* [1987] ILRM 202; [1986] IR 642 as applied in *The State (Creedon) v Criminal Injuries Compensation Tribunal* [1989] ILRM 104; [1988] IR 51 (see the 1988 Review, 17, 31).

The applicant in *Hill* was the widow of a man who had been murdered. She applied for compensation to the respondent tribunal under the terms of the non-statutory Scheme of Compensation for Injuries Criminally Inflicted of 1974. At the hearing before the tribunal, the applicant presented actuarial evidence as to the financial loss to the family arising from the death of the applicant's husband. It became clear during the hearing that the estimated figures used by the actuary as to the deceased's weekly contribution to family expenses exceeded the estimated average by a correspondence of 3:2. Accordingly, in calculating the gross figure for financial loss to the dependents as being £108,269, the actuary made the necessary adjustment down, though without taking account of the factors referred to in the Supreme Court decision *Reddy v Bates* [1984] ILRM 197; [1983] IR 131. The tribunal awarded a sum of £65,000, i.e. roughly 40% lower than the actuary's calculation of loss. The applicant sought *certiorari* to quash the award and mandamus to direct the tribunal to rehear the application. Lynch J granted judicial review.

He concluded that the tribunal had mistakenly considered, in making its award, that the sum of £108,269 had been calculated by the actuary on the basis of the original, and excessive, estimated contribution of the applicant's husband to the family expenses when in fact the actuary had already adjusted the figure to allow for this. He also concluded that a further 10% must have been deducted to allow for the decision in *Reddy v Bates*. Lynch J pointed out that the Court would not set aside an award of a tribunal merely on the basis of a mistake made within jurisdiction, it being clear from the terms of cls.2 and 25 of the 1974 Scheme that the Court was not an appeal court. However, he felt that the decision of the tribunal in the instant case was capable of being quashed on judicial review as being unreasonable as it was at variance with reason and common sense, the test laid down in the *Keegan* and *Creedon* cases, above.

In *Pesca Valentia Ltd v Minister for Fisheries*, High Court, 6 June 1989 (11, above), Keane J rejected a claim of unreasonableness for much the same reasons as he had given for rejecting the legitimate expectation claim in that case. See also *Stroker v Doherty* [1989] ILRM 428; [1989] IR 440 (277, below, in the Garda Síochána chapter) and *MacGabhann v Incorporated Law Society of Ireland* [1989] ILRM 854 (401, below in the Solicitors chapter) both of which deal with reasonableness.

Agriculture

ABATTOIRS

The Abattoirs Act 1988 (Commencement) Order 1989 (SI No.150) set 1 September 1989 as the commencment date for the provisions of the 1988 Act which deal with the licensing of abattoirs and the recruitment of local authority veterinary inspectors. The Abattoirs Act 1988 (Section 62(2)) (Repeal of Bye-Laws) Order 1989 (SI No.151) annuls any local authority bye-laws regarding the transport of meat. The Abattoirs Act 1988 (Abattoirs) Regulations 1989 (SI No.152) specify the requirements as to the construction and operation of abattoirs to meet the requirements of the 1988 Act.

ANIMAL DISEASE ERADICATION

BSE The Diseases of Animals Act 1966 (First Schedule) (Amendment) Order 1989 (SI No.60) adds the disease Bovine Spongiform Encephalopothy (BSE, or 'mad cow disease' as it has become known) to those diseases listed in the First Schedule to the 1966 Act. The Diseases of Animals (BSE) Order 1989 (SI No.61) requires the compulsory notification of BSE to the Department of Agriculture and Food and also provides for the destruction of carcases.

Movement permits In *Howard v Minister for Agriculture and Food*, High Court, 3 October 1989, Murphy J held that the Movement Permit provisions in para.13 of the Bovine Tuberculosis (Attestation of the State and General Provisions) Order 1978 were *ultra vires* the Minister's powers under s.20 of the Diseases of Animals Act 1966. He did this on the basis that the scheme adopted in the 1978 Order did not include a procedure for taking possession of diseased animals by agreement, as required by the 1966 Act. He also reached the conclusion, reluctantly, that by virtue of the severability rule in *The State (McLoughlin) v Eastern Health Board* [1986] IR 416 the entire of the 1978 Order was invalid.

No doubt because of the importance of the permit system, the Minister reacted with speed in making the Bovine Tuberculosis (Attestation of the State and General Provisions) Order 1989 (SI No.308) which replaces the 1978 Order. The 1989 Order, as well as setting out the movement permit provisions, sets out the general criteria regarding the certifying of areas as 'disease free'.

DISADVANTAGED MOUNTAIN AND HILL AREAS SCHEME

The question whether the Minister for Agriculture's non-statutory scheme for disadvantaged mountain and hill areas complied with EC requirements as well as Article 41 of the Constitution was considered by Murphy J in *Greene v Minister for Agriculture* [1990] ILRM 364 (99, below, in the Constitutional Law chapter).

EUROPEAN COMMUNITIES

Aside from the particular matters outlined in this chapter, a number of Irish statutory instruments of relevance to agriculture are outlined in the European Communities chapter: 205-7, below.

HORSE INDUSTRY

The Bord na gCapall (Dissolution) Act 1989 dissolved Bord na gCapall and repealed the Horse Industry Act 1970. The maintenance of the Irish horse register of stallions has been transferred to the Department of Agriculture and Food.

INTERVENTION PAYMENTS

In *Clover Meats Ltd v Minister for Agriculture*, High Court, 28 June 1989 Barrington J examined whether bovine disease levies and animal inspection fees could be set-off against intervention sums due by the Minister to the plaintiff company: see 201-2, below.

Commercial Law

ARBITRATION

Discretion of arbitrator In *Grangeford Structures Ltd v S.H. Ltd* [1990] ILRM 277, the Supreme Court affirmed a decision of Costello J ([1988] ILRM 129) in which the actions of an arbitrator had been upheld (see the 1987 Review, 27-8). The matter arose in the following way. The plaintiff company sought to enforce an arbitration award made against the defendant company. The defendant claimed that the award was a nullity on the ground that the arbitrator had acted unreasonably. The arbitrator had set a period of 21 days for the defendant to file an amended defence and counterclaim after a delay of 2 months by the defendant. This was not complied with, and the arbitrator then indicated his intention of proceeding to hearing. Two days before the hearing the defendant gave notice of intention to seek an adjournment to file the counterclaim. At the hearing a short adjournment was granted, but the arbitrator then proceeded in the defendant's absence. Costello J held in the High Court that the arbitrator had acted reasonably and he granted the plaintiff the relief sought. The defendant appealed unsuccessfully to the Supreme Court (Finlay CJ, Griffin and McCarthy JJ).

Delivering one of the judgments in the case, Griffin J stated that in view of the delay between the arbitrator's appointment and the hearing, most of which had been the fault of the defendant, there was no basis for holding that the arbitrator had acted unreasonably or arbitrarily. McCarthy J (with whom Finlay CJ agreed) added that the arbitrator had certain inherent powers to issue directions and was entitled to set a date for hearing the arbitration dispute and to make an award on the basis of the evidence presented to him, even though this did not include the defendant's counterclaim, since such was not before the arbitrator. As in the High Court, the views expressed by the House of Lords in *Bremer Vulkan Schiffbau v South India Shipping Corp. Ltd* [1981] AC 909 were approved in this context.

A more difficult issue, not fully resolved in the Supreme Court, was the precise position of the defendant's counterclaim. The Court expressed no view as to whether the defendant could, in the cicumstances, proceed with its counterclaim. However, McCarthy J (with the concurrence of the Chief Justice, but with Griffin J expressing no view) stated that an arbitrator was not empowered by s.19 of the Arbitration Act 1954 to proceed to dismiss a claim for want of prosecution, and no sanction was possible where a party failed to appear and present his view. It may be noted that it was on this point that the House of Lords had divided in the *Bremer Vulkan* case, the majority taking the view that an arbitrator did have power to dismiss for want of prosecution. The general approval by Costello J of the majority views in *Bremer Vulkan* must now be seen subject to their disapproval on this point by McCarthy J (with Finlay CJ concurring) in the Supreme Court.

Finality of arbitration The decision of the Supreme Court in *Keenan v Shield Insurance Co Ltd* [1988] IR 89 (see the 1988 Review, 43-6) was applied by Carroll J in *McStay v Assicurazioni Generali Spa* [1989] IR 248. The plaintiff was the receiver of a company which had agreed to refer a dispute to arbitration. The arbitrator, in making his award, stated that he had no jurisdiction to award interest on the sum which he declared was due by the first defendant. The plaintiff applied for: (i) an order directing the arbitrator to state a special case for the High Court in accordance with s.35 of the Arbitration Act 1954 or (ii) an order remitting the portion of the arbitration award which related to interest. Carroll J refused the relief sought.

Applying the decision in the *Keenan* case, she held that the power of the Court to direct a special case must be exercised before an award is made, and that once an award has been made the arbitrator is *functus officio*. She went on to conclude that once the parties had agreed, as in this case, to refer all issues of law to the determination of the arbitrator, they were bound by his decision which could include a determination that he had no jurisdiction to award interest, irrespective of the issue whether this part of the award was bad on its face. In this context, she accepted the first defendant's citation of the decision *In re King and Duveen* [1913] 2 KB 32. See also the views of Murphy J in *Hogan v St Kevin's Co.* [1987] ILRM 17.

Carroll J also noted that while there was an arguable case on both sides as to whether the award was bad on its face, any error was not so fundamental, in the sense referred to by the Supreme Court in the Keenan case, as to justify the court interfering with the award.

Stay of proceedings: fraud In *Administratia Asigurarilor de Stat and Ors v Insurance Corporation of Ireland plc* [1990] ILRM 159 O'Hanlon J held that, in a case involving allegations of fraud, an arbitration agreement may have to take second place to court proceedings, notwithstanding s.5 of the Arbitration Act 1980.

The plaintiffs were 14 insurance or reinsurance companies who had entered into reinsurance treaties with the defendant insurance company. The plaintiff companies sought to repudiate liability under the insurance treaties. In correspondence with the defendant the plaintiffs variously alleged fraud as a ground for repudiating liability. In their subsequent pleadings, the plaintiffs alleged misrepresentation and/or fraud. The statement of claim ran to over 80 pages. The defendant denied any fraud or that the plaintiffs were entitled to repudiate liability under the treaties of insurance. The defendant sought to have the disputes referred to arbitration in accordance with the terms of the treaties, and nominated a Queen's Counsel to act as arbitrator. The treaties provided that submission of any disputes to arbitration was a condition precedent to any cause of action. The defendant applied to have the plaintiffs' proceedings stayed pursuant to s.12 of the Arbitration Act 1954, as amended by s.5 of the Arbitration Act 1980. O'Hanlon J refused the stay and ordered the litigation to proceed.

Accepting that the courts were reluctant to interfere with an arbitration process which had been agreed between parties, O'Hanlon J held that the Court retained a discretion under s.39 of the 1954 Act (which was not affected by s.5 of the 1980 Act) to order that any arbitration agreement shall cease to have effect where an allegation of fraud is made. The question that arose, therefore, was as to the level of proof required before it could be said for present purposes that an arbitration agreement should be superceded.

Applying the test laid down in *Workman v Belfast Harbour Commissioners* [1899] 2 IR 234 and *Cunningham-Reid v Buchanan-Jardine* [1988] 2 All ER 438, O'Hanlon J concluded that it was not necessary for the plaintiffs to establish a prima facie case of fraud, but it was sufficient that the allegations are made bona fide. He noted that it was a well-recognised principle that counsel should not sign pleadings containing an allegation of fraud unless satisfied there are substantial grounds for making such allegation, and O'Hanlon J was not prepared to consider that this principle would be disregarded.

Applying this test to the instant case, he said that having regard to the complexity and seriousness of the case and to the fact that the parties would not have envisaged an allegation of fraud at the time of agreeing to arbitration, it was appropriate that the matter be dealt with by the High Court (with the possibility of an appeal to the Supreme Court) rather than by way of arbitration where discovery and points of law might, in any event, have to be referred to the courts. He also concluded that it was more likely that the matter would be dealt with expeditiously by continuing the proceedings in the courts. It is of interest to note that O'Hanlon J also referred to his own decision in *O'Mahony v Lysaght* [1988] IR 29, where he had anticipated the type of exceptional circumstances which arose in the present case: see the 1988 Review, 50.

BANKRUPTCY

Security for costs *Performing Rights Society Ltd v Casey*, High Court, 28 April 1989 involved the question of security for costs in a bankruptcy matter: see the discussion in the Practice and Procedure chapter, 348, below.

FINANCIAL SERVICES

In 1989, fundamental changes to the entire financial services sector in Ireland were effected by the enactment of a number of important Acts. These were the Central Bank Act 1989, the Building Societies Act 1989, the Trustee Savings Banks Act 1989 and the Insurance Act 1989. In total, the legislation has had the effect of liberalising the financial services sector, though with provisions which differ in many respects from those which were introduced in the UK in recent years.

Building societies The Building Societies Act 1989 (Commencement) Order 1989 (SI No.182) set 1 September 1989 as the commencement date for the provisions of the 1989 Act, except for Part IX of the Act.

The Building Societies Act 1989 consolidates and reforms the law on building societies. It enables building societies to provide a far wider range of financial services, modernises the supervisory structure by giving the Central Bank rather than the Registrar of building societies the crucial role, enables building societies to convert from mutual to public limited company status, updates their internal management structure and permits them to operate abroad. The Act is part of the integrated reform of financial institutions of which the Insurance Act 1989, the Central Bank Act 1989 and the Trustee Savings Banks Act 1989 are also parts. For detailed analysis of the Act see Brian Cregan's excellent annotation, *Irish Current Law Statutes Annotated* (1989).

1 Objects S.9 prescribes the permissible and necessary objects of a building society: a society may have as its objects the undertaking of any of the activities permitted by or under the Act and must have as one of its objects the raising of funds for making house loans. The Act does not require that this latter object be the principal one of the society or that any particular minimum proportion of the society's moneys should be devoted to this purpose.

2 Formation S.10 deals with the formation, registration and incorporation of a building society. Any ten or more persons not disqualified under s.64

may form a society by agreeing on its objects, powers and rules for its registration in accordance with the Second Schedule and delivering the memorandum and rules to the Central Bank. The Bank must issue a certificate of incorporation if satisfied that the memorandum and rules are in order, that there is no reason to believe that the society will not be authorised to raise funds under s.17 and that registration would not be prejudicial to the orderly and proper regulation of building societies generally. There is a right of appeal against refusal to the High Court.

3 Membership and liability of members S.16 largely re-enacts s.17 of the Building Societies Act 1976. Everyone holding one or more shares in a society is a member: subs. (1). A society may allow a person to whom a loan is made to be a member without holding a share; his liability can be no greater than if he had been the holder of a share: subs. (2).

4 Powers of a building society Part II of the Act deals with the powers of a building society. These are subject to the approval of the Central Bank on such conditions as it may consider necessary: s.37. It is perhaps worth stressing how important is this scrutiny by the Central Bank: at the end of the day it has the last word on how building societies will develop new powers in forthcoming years.

4(i) Raising funds and borrowing money S.18 involves important innovations. A building society may raise funds including, with the approval of the Central Bank, funds in a currency other that the currency of the State, to be used for the society's objects, by the issue of shares and by borrowing money: subs. (1). The shares must have voting rights attached: subs. (3). A society may give security for money borrowed, including—if the Central Bank approves—the security of mortgages held by the society: subs. (5). The Minister for the Environment, with the consent of the Minister for Finance and after consultation with the Central Bank, may make regulations in relation to the transfer, sale or assignment of mortgages held by a society: subs. (6). The power of Ministerial regulation is also a feature of the Act. We can but wait and see what shape this delegated legislation takes. During the Oireachtas debates, concern was expressed that such wide-ranging functions had thus been delegated as to raise constitutional doubts about the legislation.

4(ii) Holding and developing land Subject to the approval of the Central Bank, a building society may acquire, hold, dispose of, and develop or participate in developing land to be used for residential purposes or other commercial purposes: s.21(1). It must dispose of land thus held, at the direction of the Central Bank: s.21(1).

4(iii) Housing and other loans A building society's power to make loans on the security of a mortgage to its members to enable them to buy or improve a house is of course its traditional *raison d'être*. It is preserved by s.22(1). The power to make these loans includes power to make them on such terms as may be approved by the Central Bank even if the amount due to the society may exceed the value of the security at any time after the loan has been made: s.22(2). The general principle, however, is that a loan made to a member under s.22 must require that the capital element of the mortgage debt is not to exceed the value of the security: s.22(3). A society may not make a loan under s.23 on the security of any freehold estate or leasehold interest or interest which is subject to a prior mortgage unless the prior mortgage is in favour of the society: s.22(4). Contrasting with this limitation s.23 extends the power of building societies to make loans other than housing loans: in future they may make loans to be applied towards the payment of a deposit for the purpose of property that will secure a loan by way of mortgage, up to 15% of the purchase price (or such other percentage as the Central Bank may prescribe): s.23(1)(d).

4(iv) Investment in, and support of, bodies corporate With the consent of the Central Bank, a building society may now invest in bodies corporate and support them with loans, grants, guarantees and the provision of services or property: s.28(1). It may not, however, invest in a body corporate whose objects enable it to carry on activities outside the power of the society or to invest in other bodies corporate, save to the extent that the Central Bank may grant a dispensation on appropriate conditions: s.28(2).

4(v) Financial services With the consent of the Central Bank a building society may provide a wide range of financial services, including investment services, insurance, financing hire-purchase, leasing, foreign exchange, trusteeship, executorship, the sale and purchase of financial obligations, debts and securities, arranging provision of credit, and the issue of drafts, travellers cheques and letters of credit, or other activities of a similar nature that appear to the Central Bank to be financial services other than the making of loans: s.29(1) and (2). A building society is not, however, to carry on insurance business save by a subsidiary or other associated body: s.29(3).

4(vi) Conveyancing services Building societies are now able to provide conveyancing services in accordance with the provisions of regulations made by the Minister for Justice after consulting with the Minister for the Environment and the Central Bank: s.31(1) and (2). The regulations are to be consumer-orientated: they will protect from conflicts of interests those for whom conveyancing services are provided by societies, and ensure that they are adequately protected in the event of negligence or fraud: s.31(4).

The regulations will also deal with the extent to which the services would require the involvement of solicitors and the qualifications and experience personnel generally engaged in their provision, as well as maximum rates of scales of fees: id. Thus it may be possible for lawyers who are not practising solicitors to be employed in this work. Building societies are not to run the conveyancing part of their business at a loss: s.31(12) There was concern among the solicitors' profession that much business would be 'poached' by building societies offering sacrificially low rates for conveyancing. The statutory control may ease some of these fears.

4(vii) Auctioneering services   With the approval of the Central Bank, building societies may now engage in providing auctioneering services in accordance with the Auctioneers and House Agents Act 1947, and other services relating to land: s.32(1). The Minister for Justice, after consulting the Minister for the Environment and the Central Bank, may make regulations in this regard, similar to those in respect of conveyancing services, on such matters as conflicts of interest, negligence and fraud: s.32(3). As with conveyancing, building societies may not use this new facility as a 'loss leader': s.32(5).

4(viii) Power to hedge   Building societies may now enter into contracts for the purpose of reducing the risk of loss arising from changes in interest rates, currency exchange rates or other factors of a similar nature affecting their business: the Central Bank again can specify conditions as with loans: s.34.

5 Central Bank control and supervision   We need not here give a detailed account of Part IV of the Act, which deals with the Central Bank's control and supervision of building societies. These deal with such matters as asset and liability ratios and structures (s.39), inspections and information (s.41 and 44) and the control of advertising (s.42). The High Court has power to prohibit certain contraventions of the Act (s.43). See discussion of the Central Bank Act 1989 below.

6 The management of building societies   Part V of the Act deals with the management of building societies. It requires a society to have a chief executive, who, either alone or with other officers is to be responsible, under the immediate authority of the board of directors, for the conduct of the business of the society: s.49(1). It removes previous restrictions on eligibility for appointment as directors: s.50. It imposes a duty of disclosure on directors to declare their interest if they are 'in any way, whether directly or indirectly, interested in a contract or proposed contract with the society': s.53(1). In this context, and in relation to such matters as substantial property transactions involving directors and connected persons (s.56) or loans to them (s.57), the

Act adopts the models of the Companies (No. 2) Bill 1987. Its civil and criminal sanctions (s.58) are similar to those in the 1987 Bill.

7 Meetings, resolutions, accounts and audit   Part VI and VII deals with the internal procedures of building societies and the accounting and auditing procedures. Henceforth auditors hold office from year to year rather than generally continuing to hold office, save in limited exceptional circumstances: s.83. Again the 1987 Companies Bill provides a model for many of the provisions. As in the Insurance Act 1989 and the Central Bank Act 1989, the auditors to building societies are placed under a duty to report to the Central Bank what they have reason to believe are material defects in accounting records or systems of control: s.89.

8 Disputes and complaints   The Minister for the Environment may make regulations requiring a building society to establish or join in a scheme for the investigation of complaints against the society, its subsidiaries or associated bodies in relation to a prescribed matter of complaint: s.92. The Central Bank has a consultative role, as it has in relation to licensed banks under s.27 of the Central Bank Act 1989.

9 Savings protection   Part IX contains provisions for savings protection similar to those of Chapter V of Part II of the Central Bank Act 1989, which we outline below.

10 Amalgamations and transfers of engagements   Part X provides for controls over amalgamations of societies and transfers of engagements by the Central Bank. In effect, the Central Bank has the last word.

11 Conversion to public limited company   Part XI enables a building society to convert itself into a public limited company (s.101) with the confirmation of the Central Bank (s.104).

12 Winding up   Part XII of the Act deals with winding up of building societies. Its provisions (ss.111-12), regarding the liability of officers of a society where proper accounting methods have not been kept, are modelled on the 1987 Companies Bill.

13 Miscellaneous   Part XIII, which contains miscellaneous provisions, generally deals with necessary changes in legislation brought about by the Central Bank's new role, and the extension of the powers of building societies into a wider financial field. Thus, for example, s.126 extends to building societies the Bankers' Books Evidence Acts 1879 and 1959 and the Bills of Exchange Act 1882.

Central Bank The Central Bank Act 1989 introduced important changes in the manner of regulation of the banking system in Ireland. The Central Bank Act 1989 (Commencement) Order 1989 (SI No.176) specified 12 July 1989 as the commencement date for all provisions of the Act, except for s.28 (commencement on 1 September 1989) and ss.53-73 (commencement on 1 November 1989).

The Central Bank Act 1989 updates and amends the provisions of the Central Bank Acts and strengthens the powers of the Central Bank (referred to below simply as 'the Bank') in relation to the licensing and supervision of banking business. It also introduces a deposit protection scheme for bank depositors. It controls the acquisition of holdings in licensed banks in the State as well as the acquisition by licensed banks of holdings in other corporated bodies. It extends the Bank's supervision to certain companies in the International Financial Services Centre, to financial futures and options exchanges and money brokers. It updates the statute law relating to currency and coinage. Finally, it contains a series of miscellaneous amendments designed to bring the law into line with contemporary commercial and technological realities.

The Bill as initiated was accompanied by a helpful Explanatory and Financial Memorandum, published by the Department of Finance. Timothy Bird has also produced a detailed annotation to the Act, *Irish Current Law Statutes Annotated.* We pirated both these sources for ideas and understanding. The Act has over 140 sections. Our analysis follows the sequence of the Act.

Part I: Preliminary and general In this part, s.2, dealing with commencement, is worthy of note. Chapter VII of Part II, which establishes a new supervisory function in the Bank in relation to certain financial institutions in the International Financial Services Centre, comes into operation on the passing of the Act (9 May 1989). The other provisions come into operation through Ministerial commencement orders: see SI No. 176 of 1989, above.

Part II, dealing with the Central Bank, contains chapters, which we consider in turn.

Chapter I: Preliminary, alteration of penalties and general offence provisions This chapter broadens the scope of offences and penalties under the 1971 Act. (S.8 alters the penalties under the 1942 Act.) The maximum penalty now under the 1971 Act is a fine of £50,000 or imprisonment for five years.

Chapter II: General provisions relating to the Bank Among the general provisions relating to the Bank which are worthy of particular attention is s.13, which removes the obligation on the Minister to appoint banking directors to the Board of the Bank, in view of the wider range of institutions over which the Bank will be exercising supervision. Of greater legal interest is s.16 which defines the parameters of secrecy and disclosure. Employees and former employees of the Bank, as a general principle, are not to disclose at any time any information concerning anyone's business which came to their knowledge by virtue of their employment or concerning the Bank's activities in protecting the integrity of the currency or the control of credit, unless the disclosure is to enable the Bank to carry out its statutory functions: subs. (1). This general obligation of non-disclosure does not apply to seven types of disclosure, those which:

(a) are required by a court in connection with any criminal proceeding;

(b) are made with the consent of the person to whom the information relates;

(c) are made by the Bank, acting as agent for the person to whom it relates;

(d) are made where the Bank considers it necessary for the common good, made to a person charged by law with the supervision of financial institutions and who, in the opinion of the Bank, has obligations concerning that person in respect of non-disclosure corresponding to the obligation under s.16;

(e) are made to a duly authorized equivalent foreign authority;

(f) are made to any European Communities instruction for the purpose of the State's membership of any of the Communities; and

(g) are made to comply with a statutory requirement that a document be laid before a House of the Oireachtas: subs. (2).

Moreover, the non-disclosure rule does not apply, so far as an individual's business is concerned, where the disclosure in question is, in the Bank's opinion, necessary for the protection of depositors or, with regard to the Bank's activities in protecting the integrity of the currency or the control of credit, where the disclosure is made with the Bank's consent and is not prejudicial to the operation of the Bank in any financial market, the issue by the Bank of legal currencies or the integrity of the currency: subs. (3).

Contravention of the non-disclosure provisions is an offence with a maximum penalty on conviction by indictment of a fine of £25,000 or imprisonment for five years: subs. (5).

It is worth considering the constitutional dimension of s.16 in the light of the judicial insistence that the courts are to have the last word in prescribing what may be excluded from evidence on the basis of privilege. It seems clear that the executive has no power to determine this matter: cf. *Murphy v Dublin Corporation* [1972] IR 215. Whether the Oireachtas has such an entitlement, and if so what is the permissible range of legislative prescriptions, are questions which have yet to be resolved: cf. *The People v T*, Court of Criminal Appeal, 27 July 1988, and the 1988 Review, 153. It will be recalled that in *Cully v Northern Bank Ltd* [1984] ILRM 683, O'Hanlon J noted that the question of the constitutional validity of s. 31 of the Central Bank Act 1942, which required employees to take an oath of secrecy, had not been raised in the proceedings. See Casey, *Constitutional Law in Ireland* (1987), 57. Before considering the precise content of s.16 of the 1989 Act, so far as this constitutional issue is concerned, it is worth addressing for a moment the general question of whether the Oireachtas has *any* permissible function to legislate on the matter. We are of the view that it does: the fact that the courts have a duty to ensure that there is no impermissible interference with the judicial function does not require that the Oireachtas should be denied the entitlement to legislate on the law of evidence. Of course, the courts must retain the entitlement to strike down legislation which improperly limits or otherwise interferes with the judicial function; but the separation of powers is not so sharply defined as to leave to the courts the exclusive entitlement of articulating the totality of the rules of evidence.

Having said this, it is perhaps worth noting that the courts have displayed considerable sensitivity at any perceived *ab extra* delimitation on their powers to prescribe the contours of the judicial function and to ensure that the administration of justice in preserved inviolate. In *The State (DPP) v Walsh* [1981] IR 412, this concern went so far as to convince the Supreme Court that the protection of the administration of justice required the un-qualified guarantee of a right to jury trial for a non-minor offence made in Article 38.5 to be set aside in proceedings for criminal contempt of court. (The defendants in *Walsh* had been accused of scandalising the Special Criminal Court.) Henchy J, for the majority, expressed an attitude towards the jury which suggests an extreme anxiety for the Court to retain full control over trials where the protection of the administration of justice is a factor.

As regards the specific features of s.16, it is to be noted that subs. (2) permits disclosure when this is required by a court in connection with any *criminal* proceedings. Whether this limitation is constitutional may be debated.

A person's constitutional rights—for example, to litigate, to own property, to exercise guardianship over his or her children—could all be imperilled, directly or indirectly, by the prohibition on disclosure in non-criminal cases. Certainly, the courts may well take the view that it is for them, rather than the Oireachtas, to take decisions as to disclosure in civil litigation.

Perhaps the best course would have been for s.16 to have been drafted in a manner more deferential to the judicial function. This could have been simply accomplished by permitting disclosure when this is required by a court in connection with *any* proceedings.

S.24 of the Act specifies that the monetary unit of the State is to be the Irish pound. The absence of a reference to a one pound *note* enables the issue of a one pound *coin*. The Minister may vary the general exchange rate of the pound. S.25 provides that references in contracts, bills and other instances to the payments of monies are references to Irish pounds unless the instrument be 'made, executed, entered into, done or had according to a currency other than the currency of the State'. During the Dáil Debates, there was discussions as to whether this allowed contracts to be made in ECUs: cf. Mr Bird's annotation, *Irish Current Law Statutes Annotated*, General note to s.25.

Chapter III: Licensing and supervision of licence holders This Chapter extends the Bank's powers as to the licensing and supervision of banks. The Minister is given power to extend the Bank's statutory licensing and supervision powers to new classes of financial business if he considers it necessary to do so for the protection of the public (or any class of it) from financial loss or for the orderly and proper regulation of financial markets: s.26. The Minister may also by regulations require a licence-holder to establish or join in establishing a scheme or schemes for the investigation of complaints against that holder or an associated company in relation to a prescribed matter of complaint: s.27.

Every licence-holder must notify the Bank of all charges it imposes for any service to the public and any terms or conditions on which the service is provided: s.28(1). As regards banks which are not required to hold a licence, s.30 extends s.7 of the Central Bank Act 1971 by excepting the Central Banks of the other member states of the European Communities. It also provides that, where the Minster is of opinion that it is in the interest of the orderly and proper regulation of banking or of any other financial market, he can, after consultation with the Bank and any other Minister or others as he may consider appropriate, extend or restrict the categories of exempted institutions. The Bank is given power at any time to revoke an exemption as to the use of the word 'bank', 'banking' or 'banker' in a person's title where it is of opinion that the exempted person has in fact carried on banking business or otherwise has held himself out or represented himself as a banker: s.31. The Bank may also exempt any class of person from the requirement to hold a licence where the requirement would arise solely out of the issuing of securities or other obligations to which the definition of 'banking business' relates and the Bank is of opinion that the exemption would not conflict with the orderly and proper regulation of banking: id.

The granting (s.32) and revocation (s.34) of licences is in line with developments in the European Communities: see Bird, op. cit., General notes to s.32 and s.34. As regards revocation, the Bank must obtain the Minister's consent (unless the holder of the licence requests the revocation). The Bank's powers of investigation of the books and records of licence-holders are strengthened (s.36), and its powers to obtain information, not only from licence-holders but also other financial institutions (such as money brokers and investment trust companies), are extended (s.37).

The Bank may give a direction to a licence-holder to suspend for up to six months the carrying on of banking business, the making of payments and the acquisition or disposal of other assets or liabilities which have not been authorised by the bank: s.38 (amending s.21 of the 1971 Act). The grounds for doing so include the Bank's opinion that it is in the public's interest to direct the suspension or its opinion that the licence-holder:

(a) is unable to meet its obligations;

(b) is not maintaining adequate capital resources;

(c) has failed to comply with a condition imposed in relation to the licence under s.10 of the 1971 Act, leading to its stability and soundness being affected;

(d) is conducting business in such a manner as to prejudice the security of deposits in that it is under common control with another enterprise and the common control is not in the interest of persons maintaining deposits with the licence-holder. Either the Bank or the licence-holder may go to court in respect of this direction, and the Court may, on the basis of no specified criteria, uphold or set it aside: see Bird, op. cit., General note to s.38.

The Court has power on summary application to it by the Bank to prohibit the continuation of a breach by a person of one of several obligations specified in the Act, including the keeping of books and records, furnishing information to the Bank, keeping conditions imposed in relation to a licence or directions as to advertising made by the Bank: s.44. The Bank may require a holder to notify it of the name of its proposed auditor; it may direct that this person be not appointed, if of opinion that it would not be in the interests of depositors or of the orderly and proper regulation of banking: s.46. Auditors of licence-holders fall under a reporting duty to the Bank if they have reason to believe that there are material defects in financial systems or controls in accounting records or material inaccuracies in financial returns or if they propose to qualify any certificate or more generally, if they have reason to believe that there exist 'circumstances which are likely to affect materially the holder's ability to fulfil his obligations' to depositors or meet any of his financial obligations under the Central Bank Acts: s.47.

Chapter IV: General provisions relating to winding-up S.48(1) gives the Bank the right to present a petition applying to the Court to have the holder of a licence (a bank) wound up on any of the following grounds:

(a) that it is unable to meet its obligations to its creditors, in the Bank's view;

(b) that it has failed to comply with a direction of the Bank under s.21 of the Central Bank Act 1971;

(c) that the licence has been revoked and the holder has ceased to carry on the business of banking; or

(d) that the Bank considers it in the interests of depositors with the holder that it be wound up.

Where a licence-holder is being wound up *voluntarily* and the Bank has reason to believe that any of these four grounds apply, it may apply to the Court to have the licence-holder wound up by the Court: s.48(3).

The Bank has the right to have an officer or other authorised person attend any meeting of creditors of a licence-holder: s.50(1). Similarly it may have its authorised person as a member of any committee of inspection appointed under s.233 or s.268 of the Companies Act 1963, in respect of a licence-holder (or former holder): s.50(2). S.51 in effect characterises the Irish provisions on the winding up of licence-holders as the same as their foreign equivalents, and applies the provisions of the Central Banks Acts 1942 to 1989 to the winding up of a foreign bank, with such modifications as the Bank may order.

Chapter V: Deposit protection   This Chapter requires the Bank to establish and maintain in the general fund an account to be known as the deposit protection account (s.54), to which licence-holders (banks) are to contribute 0.2% of their Irish pound deposits (excluding interbank deposits and deposits represented by negotiable certificates of deposits) (s.55(2)(6)) or £20,000, whichever is the greater. The idea is to provide a fund for the partial compensation of depositors if the licence-holder becomes insolvent.

When a licence-holder is unable to pay its debts and is being wound up, either voluntarily or by the Court, the Court may, on the application of the liquidator, order that the amount standing in the deposit protection account, plus interest, is to vest in the liquidator: s.58(1). S.59 specifies the mode of calculation of payments from the deposit protection account on insolvency, under s.58. It provides for 80% of the amount of eligible deposits (defined in s.62) up to £5,000, 70% for deposits between £5,000 and £10,000 and 50% for deposits between £10,000 and £15,000. Thus the *maximum* compensation is £10,000 (i.e. £4,000 plus £3,500 plus £2,500). From this must be subtracted the amount paid to the depositor in respect of eligible deposits maintained by him otherwise than in one of funds so vesting; where the amount deposited by a licence-holder under the provisions of Chapter V is not sufficient to pay all that is due under s.59(3)(a), the entire deposit protection account kept by the Bank may be called in aid: cf. s.59(3)(6), s.60 and s.61. Where the Bank is satisfied that a person maintaining deposits with an insolvent licence-holder which is being wound up has directly or indirectly any responsibility or has profited or attempted to profit from it, that person is to be excluded from the compensation system: s.64.

Chapter VI: Acquiring transactions This Chapter deals with acquisitions of shareholdings *in* and *by* banks. It requires the approval of the Bank, and in some instances the Minister, for the first category of acquisition, where the shareholding is of at least 10%. As to the second category of acquisition—of shareholdings in non-banks by banks—it empowers the Bank and the Minister to attach conditions to their approval.

S.75 defines 'acquiring transactions' as meaning, first, an acquisition by a person (or more than one acting in concert) of shares or other interest in a holder of a licence (a bank); excluded are acquisitions falling below the prescribed percentage of shares (i.e. 10%) and, in respect of Irish banks, acquisitions which, together with any other interests already held or controlled, would not confer a right to appoint or remove some or all of the board of directors or committee of management of the bank. Secondly the term extends to any acquisition by a bank of shares or other interest in any other undertaking or business, save one outside the State or one which, together with any other interest already held or controlled, would not confer the right to appoint or remove its board or committee. Moreover, the Bank, subject to such conditions as it sees fit, may exempt all acquiring transactions from the requirements of the Chapter provided it is satisfied that:

(a) the transaction is being or has been entered into by a bank as part of the *bona fide* undertaking of a share issue; or

(b) the interest in shares is not being beneficially acquired by a bank or is being acquired only in the course of its normal business to secure the issue of a loan to be made by the holder in the undertaking or business concerned: s.75(2).

An acquiring transaction is valid only when entered into within a year after the Bank has either given its consent or for a period of six months has neither consented or refused: s.76. In cases of invalidity under s.76, the disappointed vendor may sue the would-be purchaser for damages; but he will not succeed if the would-be purchaser had notified him before the transaction of circumstances which gave rise to the possibility of this invalidity: s.81.

Where a bank proposes to participate in an acquiring transaction and already controls or would control (whether alone or with any subsidiary or associated company) not less than 20% of the total assets in the State of all banks, or where a person proposes to participate in an acquiring transaction which involves the acquisition of shares or other interest in a bank controlling (whether alone or with a subsidiary or associated company) not less than that percentage, the Bank must obtain the prior consent of the Minister before making a decision: s.77(1). The criterion the Minister uses is the interests of the orderly and proper regulation of banking: s.77(2).

The Minister may by order amend the prescribed percentage, up or down, where he is satisfied after consultation with the Bank that it would be in the interest of the orderly and proper regulation of banking to do so: s.79(1). Each House of the Oireachtas must pass a regulation approving of such a draft Ministerial order before it has effect: s.79(2).

The Bank must communicate its approval or refusal to approve a proposed acquiring transaction to the undertaking concerned. If its approval is subject to conditions, it must notify the undertaking of them: s.85(1). An appeal against refusal on a point of law may be made by the undertaking to the High Court within a month: s.86(1). The Minister must be joined if he requests this: s.86(3). No further appeal lies to the Supreme Court: s.86(6).

Contravention of any approval or condition of the approval is an offence; the maximum penalty on conviction on indictment is a fine of £50,000 or imprisonment for up to five years or both: s.87(1).

Chapter VII: Supervision of certain financial institutions in the International Financial Services Centre   This Chapter establishes a new regime whereby certain financial institutions in the International Financial Services Centre must comply with the supervisory and reporting requirements or conditions relating to their business which the Bank considers prudent to impose on them from time to time in the interest of the proper and orderly regulation of themselves as individual entities or as part of a group, or for the purpose of the development of the Area as an International Financial Services Centre: s.92(2). The imposition of these conditions by the Central Bank does not constitute a warranty as to the solvency of any of these institutions and the Bank is not liable in respect of any loss incurred through the insolvency or default of any of them. (We discuss below the question of the interpretation of a similar exemption from liability in s.101(3).) The failure by an institution to comply with a requirement or condition prescribed by the bank may lead to a High Court order prohibiting the continuance of this defiance (s.95) and the submission of a Report by the Bank to the Minister (s.96).

A number of financial institutions do not fall within the scope of Chapter VII, even though they are in the International Financial Services Centre. This is because they already fall under statutory supervision. These institutions are banks holding a licence under s.9 of the Central Bank Act 1971, moneybrokers, building societies, friendly societies and insurance companies: s.90. Moreover, the Minister may by order exclude other institutions if of opinion that they are covered by adequate statutory supervisory and inspection provisions: s.91.

Chapter VIII: Supervision of financial futures and options exchanges   This Chapter gives to the Bank power to supervise financial futures and option exchanges (defined in s.97). After the passing of the Act, no such exchange is to be established unless the Bank has approved the rules proposed to govern its membership and operation: s.99. Existing exchanges must either submit their rules to the Bank for approval or disestablish themselves: s.100. The Bank may make its approval of the rules of an existing exchange subject to conditions or requirements: s.101(1).

The approval by the Bank of rules of or for an exchange does not constitute a warranty as to the solvency of the exchange or any of its members and the Bank is not liable in respect of any losses incurred through the insolvency or default of the exchange or its members: s.101(3). This provision, it should be noted, speaks of warranty rather than of duty of care. Assuming that a plaintiff suing the Bank in negligence in its approval of the rules of or for an exchange could withstand the formidable hurdle of establishing a duty of care (cf. *McMahon v Ireland* [1988] ILRM 610 analysed in the 1987 Review, 24), the question arises as to whether s.101(3) has excluded liability on the part of the Bank. On one view, the exemption from liability to which it refers is merely in the contractual domain; the denial that the approval constitutes a warranty may be seen as setting the context in which the issue of exemption from liability is to be understood. On another view, more likely to commend itself to the Court, s.101(3) seeks to exempt the Bank from *all* civil liability, whether in contract, tort, equity or otherwise, in respect of its approval. At a minimum, the provision would fortify the Court in the view that a duty of care should not be imposed.

The only basis on which the Bank may refuse to approve rules of or for an exchange is that to do so would not be in the interest of the orderly and proper regulation of the exchange: s.102(1). Where the Bank proposes to refuse to approve rules, it must give the exchange an opportunity to make representations in writing to the Minister; the Minister must consider them before deciding to give or withhold his consent, on the same criterion as applied by the Bank: s.102(2). There are specific restrictions on advertising the services of an exchange or the making of any other solicitation in respect of those services, without the Bank's consent: s.104.

The Bank has power to give a direction to an exchange to suspend trading when it is satisfied that it (or a member) has failed to comply with a condition or requirement the Bank gave it. There is a right of appeal to the High Court by the exchange (or its members); the Bank, conversely, may apply in summary manner to the Court to have its direction confirmed by the Court: s.105(2). Powers of revocation of an approval of rules of an exchange are prescribed by s.106. S.107 prescribes offences and penalties for breaches of the provisions of Chapter VIII. The maximum punishment, on conviction on indictment, is a fine of £50,000 or imprisonment for five years or both: s.107(6).

Chapter IX: Supervision of moneybrokers Chapter IX gives to the Bank a supervisory role in relation to moneybrokers similar to that in relation to

financial futures and exchange options. The Bank may grant an authorisation
to those carrying on moneybroking business: s.110(2). It is not to refuse this
unless satisfied that to grant it would not be in the interest of the orderly and
proper regulation of moneybroking or banking: s.110(4). Moneybrokers
must comply with the supervisory and reporting requirements or conditions
which the Bank considers it prudent to impose: s.111. Failure or the threat
of failure to do so may be the subject of High Court injunction ((s.113) or
criminal proceedings (s.116)). The Bank's powers to revoke authorisations
(s.114) are similar to those it has in relation to banks (s.34).

Chapter X: Codes of practice   This single section Chapter empowers the
Bank, in consultation with the Minister, from time to time to draw up, in
relation to any class or classes of licence-holders (or others supervised by the
Bank), a code or codes of practice concerning dealings with any class or
classes of persons: s.117(1). The licence-holders (and others so supervised)
must observe these codes: s.117(2). In drawing up codes of practice the Bank
is to have regard to the interest of customers and the general public and the
promotion of fair competition in financial markets in the State: s.117(3). It
may require licence-holders and others it supervises to provide all relevant
information to enable it to satisfy itself that they or others are complying with
the code: s.117(3)(a). Moreover it may issue a direction to them to comply
with practices specified in the direction where in its view this is necessary to
secure observance of the code: s.117(3)(b). Disobedience is an offence
warranting a fine of up to £1,000 on summary conviction or of up to £25,000
on conviction on indictment: s.117(4)(a). Where a person has thus been
convicted (either summarily or on indictment) and thereafter fails to provide
information or to comply with a direction, as the case may be, he is 'guilty
of contravening this section on every day on which the contravention
continues after that conviction and for each such offence he is liable on
summary conviction to a fine not exceeding £100 or on conviction on
indictment to a fine not exceeding £2,500': s117(4). This provision may one
day be tested in relation to the minor offence doctrine. Is there some point
beyond which the cumulative penalty for a series of separate offences
becomes too large to be handled by non-jury trial? This issue divided the
Supreme Court in *The State (Rollinson) v Kelly* [1984] ILRM 625; [1984]
IR 248. Our own view is that Hederman J's analysis is to be preferred. See
further Casey, *Constitutional Law in Ireland* (1987), 254-5. A narrower
question, specifically related to s.117(4), is whether continuing day-by-day
conduct or omission of the type there envisaged can properly amount to a
separate offence each day (as the subsection provides) or whether it really
constitutes one offence, capable of stretching over a period of days. The tort
of trespass to land with its doctrine of continuing trespass, permitting

enhanced damages for the continuance of wrongful, ongoing possession may suggest that a provision like s.117(4) is satisfactory: cf. *Clarke v MGW Ry Co* [1895] 2 IR 294, at 304-5. But could it not be argued that the real reason for the division of the conduct into separate offences is to coerce the defendant into submission? If this is so, is it permissible for this reason to characterise what in natural perception is one offence as several offences?

The answer to this question may have constitutional implications, since, if Hederman J's approach is accepted, then the same conduct consisting of disobedience for a specific number of days could be summarily prosecuted, consistent with Article 38.5, if characterised as a *multiplicity* of offences, while not being capable of summary prosecution if characterised as a *single* offence.

Chapter XI: Legal tender notes The provisions in this Chapter are, in substance re-enactments of provisions in the Currency Act 1927, which is repealed by the 1989 Act.

Part III: Coinage This part of the Act introduces amendments to the Decimal Currency Act 1969. The Minister, by order, may vary the weight and composition of cupro-nickel or bronze coins: s.125. He may, again by order, provide coins in such metals or mix of metals as he thinks fit: s.126. Under the 1969 Act, the maximum amount of legal tender varied according to the value of the coin. S.127 now provides for a limit of twenty times face value. The maximum penalty on indictment for making or issuing a piece of metal or mixed metal in contravention of s.14(1) of the 1969 Act is raised to a £5,000 fine or 2 years' imprisonment or both: s.128. The same maximum penalty on indictment is prescribed for an offence under s.15 (which now consists of acting in contravention of the section or failing to comply with a condition attached to a licence under it). Moreover, the court may order the articles in respect of which the offence was committed to be forfeited: id. In spite of the general uncertainties regarding the constitutional validity of statutory forfeiture powers, this provision seems clearly capable of withstanding constitutional scrutiny. The court's function in ordering forfeiture is permissive rather than mandatory. It may thus decline to order forfeiture if the case is one raising a constitutional difficulty. If instruments of forgery may not be forfeited then nothing may. On the other hand, if a defendant was in no sense a dishonest person but had merely failed, through negligence or oversight, perhaps, to comply with a condition attached to his licence, the forfeiture of the articles in respect of which the offence was committed might well not be easy to be justified under the Constitution.

Part IV: Miscellaneous provisions relating to financial transactions This Part is a mixed bag designed in large part to bring nineteenth-century legislation in line with contemporary technological and commercial realities. Thus s.5 of the Bankers' Books Evidence Act 1879 is changed to extend the definition of admissible bankers' books and records to computerised and other modern day recording media: s.131. Moreover s.6 of the 1879 Act is amended so that a banker or officer of a bank may not be compelled to produce any banker's book, or to prove the matters it records, unless by order of a judge made for special cause: id. Formerly this limitation applied only where the bank was not a party to the proceedings. S.131 also extends s.7 of the 1879 Act to enable a court or judge to make an order designating a member of the Garda Síochána to be at liberty to inspect and take copies of any entry in a banker's book for the purpose of investigating an offence where satisfied, on application to it made by a member of the Garda Síochána not below the rank of Superintendent, that an indictable offence has been committed and that there is material in the possession of a specified bank which is likely to be of substantial value to the investigation of the offence.

S.132 amends the Bills of Exchange Act 1882 by abolishing days of grace and re-defining non-business days: see Bird, op. cit., General note to s.132. S.133 updates the Cheques Act 1959 by providing that, where a cheque is paid electronically or by other means not involving physical presentment, the collecting banker is deemed to be the banker on whom it is drawn.

S.134 gives the Minister power to suspend certain specified business transactions, in relation to banks, the Stock Exchange, financial futures markets and currency dealers, for example, whenever he considers it necessary in the national interest or to safeguard the currency of the State. S.134 provides that no person is to be compellable to make any payment or do any act on a public holiday which he would not be compellable to make or do on Christmas Day or Good Friday by virtue of any rule of law. S.136 amends s.6 of the Moneylenders Act 1900 and provides for exemptions of persons carrying on a *bona fide* banking business, as well as companies in the International Financial Services Centre. (It will be recalled that D'Arcy J considered the parameters of the concept of carrying on a *bona fide* banking business in *Cripps Warburg Ltd v Cologne Investment Co Ltd* [1980] IR 321.)

S.137 provides that interest bearing deposits with the Central Bank are to be an authorised investment for the purposes of the Trustee Acts. S.138 provides a simpler method of amending the list of authorised trustee investments under the Trustee (Authorised Investment) Act 1958. S.139 allows for the electronic transfer of ownership of certain 'designated securities' (defined in subs. (2)(a)) by computerised means. Finally, s.140 permits the retention in non-legible form of records required to be kept by licence-holders, provided they are capable of being reproduced in a permanent legible form.

Negligence   The issue of negligence by a bank was discussed in *Hazylake Fashions Ltd v Bank of Ireland* [1989] ILRM 698; [1989] IR 624: see 418-21, below, in the Torts chapter.

Trustee Savings Bank: contract   In *Hortensius Ltd v Bishop and Ors (Trustees of Trustee Savings Bank, Dublin)* [1989] ILRM 294 the question for the Court revolved around the legality of a contract having regard to the legislation on Trustee Savings Banks. The defendants were trustees of the TSB Dublin, an unincorporated association formed in accordance with the Trustee Savings Banks Acts 1863 to 1979. In 1983, the trustees entered into a contract in which they agreed to purchase the debts of a commercial bank, Royal Trust Bank (Ireland) Ltd, in consideration of a sum in excess of £5 million. The consideration was drawn by the trustees from funds deposited with the TSB. The plaintiff company had entered into a loan agreement with Royal Trust Bank prior to the 1983 contract with the defendant trustees, and the plaintiff subsequently defaulted on the loan.

In anticipation of proceedings for default by the trustees, the plaintiff company brought the present claim seeking a declaration that the 1983 agreement between the trustees and Royal Trust Bank was void and that the loan agreement between the plaintiff company and Royal Trust Bank was unenforceable by the trustees. The principal argument was that the 1983 agreement was void on the ground that depositors' funds had been used to finance the 1983 contract, in breach of s.15 of the Trustee Savings Banks Act 1863. The trustees argued, *inter alia*, that the contract was valid under s.3 of the Trustee Savings Banks Act 1965 (as amended by s.1 of the Trustee Savings Banks Act 1979) and in particular that the Minister for Finance had given his consent to the contract. They also argued that, even if the contract was prohibited by the Acts, this did not render the loan between the plaintiff and Royal Trust Bank unenforceable at the suit of the trustees. Costello J dismissed the plaintiff company's claims and found for the trustees. It is of interest to note that he did so even though he found that there had been a breach of the relevant statutory provisions.

Costello J found that the 1983 contract was in breach of s.15 of the 1863 Act in that depositors' funds had been used to finance the transaction. He did not think that s.1 of the 1979 Act could be taken as authorising the Minister to consent to the transaction, since the depositors' funds had not been used for the purpose of making a loan but had in fact been employed to purchase loans from the Royal Trust Bank. In any event, Costello J did not consider the evidence as to ministerial authorisation convincing since it appeared to have been given informally and retrospectively. However, that did not end the case; the central issue was whether this illegality tainted the contract and rendered it unenforceable.

The judge held that the contract was not unenforceable under the common law rules as to illegality since s.15 of the 1863 Act did not make illegal the objects of the contract entered into in 1983. In this Costello J followed the well-established line of authority on the matter and he expressly approved the review of the law by Kerr LJ in *Euro-Diam Ltd v Bathurst* [1988] 2 WLR 517. Nor did he consider that the 1863 Act rendered illegal contracts for the purchase of loans, but merely made it illegal for the trustees to enter into such contracts. This important distinction again reflects the views set out by, for example, Lord Devlin (then Devlin J) in *St John Shipping Corp Ltd v J Rank Ltd* [1957] 1 QB 267. See generally, Clark, *Contract*, 2nd ed. (Sweet & Maxwell), 194-8.

In any event, Costello J pointed out that even if the contract had been illegal, this would not have availed the plaintiff company. He noted that the plaintiff's property had passed under the contract and so it was not now open to it to turn around and claim illegality. He applied the views expressed by Lord Denning in the House of Lords decision *Singh v Ali* [1960] AC 167 in that context.

Finally, Costello J addressed the question as to the effect of the transactions. He concluded that since the contract had been completed, the property into which the trust money (the depositors' funds) had been converted (the plaintiff company's debts) became subject to the trust, even though the transaction was entered into in breach of the trust. He approved the view to that effect in Underhill's *Law of Trusts and Trustees* (1987), 751. However, it may be noted that he also added that the position would be otherwise had Royal Trust Bank attempted to resile from the 1983 agreement.

Trustee Savings Banks: statutory regulation   The Trustee Savings Banks Act 1989 updates the legislation governing the operation of TSBs, extends their range of banking activities and gives the central role of supervision to the Central Bank rather than the Minister for Finance. The Act also enables TSBs to convert to corporate status. Except for ss.17 and 18 (which came into effect on 15 March 1990), the Act came into effect on 1 February 1990: Trustee Savings Banks Act 1989 (Commencement) Order 1990 (SI No. 21). It is not necessary here to give minute consideration to the provisions of the Act, as we have already encountered their models in the Central Bank Act 1989 and the Building Societies Act 1989, above.

1 Licensing and financial conditions   As regards the establishment and licensing of TSBs, the Central Bank has the function of granting licences (s.10), subject to such conditions as, in the Central Bank's opinion, are calculated to provide for the proper and orderly regulation of TSBs (s.12(1)). The licensing provisions follow the Central Bank Act 1971 and the European

Communities (Licensing and Supervision of Banks) Regulations 1979. On the exercise of such discretion see *East Donegal Co-Op Ltd v Attorney General* [1970] IR 317. The Central Bank can also give directions as to the maximum borrowings in which a TSB may engage and the terms and conditions on which it may borrow (s.15(2)) as well as fixing rates of interest it may charge on loans and pay on deposits (s.15(1)).

2 Trustees The number of trustees of a TSB must be not less than five and not more than 10 (s.17(1)). The consent of the Central Bank for the appointment of each is necessary (s.17(4)). Retirement is compulsory at the age of 70 (s.18). The payment of hononoria to trustees and the giving of loans to them is subject to the conditions set by the Central Bank (s.20). Disclosure of interest in a company or concern with which the TSB makes a contract is required (s.21).

A trustee is not personally liable for non-fraudulent conduct in carrying out his duties. He will, however, be personally liable for moneys received and not disposed of in accordance with the rules of the bank or for any deficiency (subject to a maximum of £10,000) caused by neglect or omission in complying with the rules or the requirements of the Central Bank in relation to specified matters (s.22). The maximum limit of £10,000, while capable of extension by Ministerial regulations to reflect changes in monetary values (s.22(2)), may raise a constitutional issue of equality. Is it fair to treat a trustee who is actually responsible for a deficiency of £10,000 in the same way as one who is actually responsible for a deficiency of £1,000,000? Presumably the particular social dimensions of the position and of the function of TSBs in general are to taken into account in accordance with Article 40.1, but do these considerations justify such a blunt limitation?

3 Supervision The Central Bank has the supervisory role in relation to TSBs. It may suspend the taking of deposits for a period of up to six months where it is of opinion that it is in the public interest to do so, or that a TSB is or is likely to be unable to meet its obligations to creditors, or is not maintaining adequate capable resources, or has failed to comply with a condition of its licence and the circumstances are such that the Central Bank is of opinion that the stability and soundness of the TSB are affected by the failure. The Central Bank has power to regulate the ratio between assets and liabilities of a TSB (s.31). On Ministerial direction the Central Bank may require the trustees of a TSB to furnish a statement of management expenses (s.28). Trustees must publish annual business statements (s.29) and display in every branch copies of their latest balance sheet and other specified financial information (s.30). Trustees must pay into a special account in the name of the Minister for Finance, or invest in the purchase of Government securities, such proportion of their deposits as may be determined by the Central Bank after consulting with the Minister (s.32). The High Court has power to prohibit certain contraventions of the Act (s.34).

4 Management and administration   Part V of the Act includes detailed provisions relating to the annual appointment of an auditor (s.36(1)) and the auditor's duties and powers (ss.37 and 38). If the auditor comes upon what he or she has reason to believe is wrongdoing, the matter must be reported forthwith to the Central Bank (s.38(1)).

5 Amalgamation   TSBs may amalgamate if each passes a special resolution to this effect and the Minister for Finance approves (ss.47 and 48).

6 Miscellaneous   Of the miscellaneous provisions contained in Part VII of the Act, undoubtedly the most important is s.57, which gives power to the Minister for Finance by order to reorganise TSBs into companies, with the prior approval of the Oireachtas. The new companies thus formed may be under the control of the Minister or some other person. S.60 is also of considerable practical importance. Where a depositor with a TSB dies, the sum on deposit (or part of it, not exceeding such sum as may be fixed from time to time by the Central Bank) may be paid by the TSB, without a grant of representation having necessarily been obtained under the Succession Act 1965, to the person who appears to the TSB to be entitled to receive it, whether as personal representative of the depositor or otherwise. To do this the TSB must be satisfied by evidence contained in a statutory declaration (s.60(1)). The TSB must, as soon as may be, give to the President of the High Court particulars in writing of the payment (s.60(2)).

INSURANCE

Disclosure of information   The year provided another case on the disclosure requirement in insurance contracts: *Keating v New Ireland Assurance Co plc*, Irish Times LR, 17 April 1989 (HC); [1990] ILRM 110 (SC).

The plaintiff and her late husband entered into a contract of life insurance with the defendant company under which the sum of £35,000 would be payable on the death of either of them to the survivor. In the course of the medical examination conducted for the company prior to the completion of the proposal form, the plaintiff's husband disclosed that he had recently attended a cardiologist in a Dublin hospital but he stated that nothing abnormal had been discovered. In fact the plaintiff's husband had been referred to the cardiologist by his own doctor on the doctor's suspicion of angina and this had been confirmed in the tests carried out in the hospital. His discharge note from the hospital, however, read 'Initial report good. Full report to follow.' The defendant company's proposal form stated that the policy was conditional on 'full and true disclosure . . . of all material facts of which the Company ought to have been informed. . . .' On her husband's death the plaintiff sought payment of the sum due under the policy but the company sought to repudiate liability for non-disclosure of the angina. The plaintiff instituted proceedings seeking to enforce the contract. Egan J upheld the plaintiff's claim and this was affirmed by the Supreme Court.

In the High Court, Egan J held that the information which was not disclosed was clearly material from an objective point of view, but on the evidence it could not be held that the plaintiff's husband was aware of his condition at the time of his medical examination, and he considered that non-disclosure could only be relevant to some fact of which the person has knowledge at the relevant time. He concluded that it was not sufficient for the company to establish that the answers given were actually untrue since the policy required disclosure only of information of which the company 'ought' to have been informed.

As already indicated, the company's appeal to the Supreme Court (Finlay CJ, Hamilton P, Walsh, Hederman and McCarthy JJ) was unsuccessful.

On a preliminary point, it was firstly pointed out that the Supreme Court could not disturb the finding of fact by the High Court that the plaintiff's husband was unaware of the angina condition. McCarthy J (with whom Hamilton P concurred) cited *Dunne v National Maternity Hospital* [1989] ILRM 735; [1989] IR 91 in this regard.

As to the substantive point in the case, the Supreme Court held against the company by relying on traditional rules for the interpretation of contracts. In particular, the Court was of the view that the words of the contract could not reasonably be construed as requiring disclosure of information of which the insured was unaware. This reflected very much the approach taken by Egan J in the High Court, who had pointed to the virtually impossible position of an insured if such was the disclosure requirement.

In addition, the Supreme Court did not consider that the company had established by clear and unambiguous language in its contract that it was intended that the plaintiff and her husband warranted the truth of the information supplied in the course of the medical examination. In other words, although the undertaking by the insured was described by McCarthy J as a 'basis of contract' term, it did not amount to a warranty as that term is understood in insurance contract law (the equivalent of a condition in general contract law). This approach of the Supreme Court is, arguably, much more hostile to insurance company contracts than that taken by the Court itself in

Keenan v Shield Insurance Co Ltd [1988] IR 89 (see the criticisms of *Keenan* in the 1987 Review, 39-40 and 1988 Review, 46).

Statutory regulation   The Insurance Act 1989 is a significant legislative provision in connection with the regulation of the insurance industry. The Insurance Act 1989 (Parts I, II, III and V) (Commencement) Order 1989 (SI No.50) brought Parts I, II, III and V of the Act into effect on 20 March 1989.

The Insurance Act 1989 incorporates several changes in the law which had already been achieved by *ad hoc* legislation or regulation; it also gives effect to a number of recommendations of the Final Report of the Committee of Enquiry into the Insurance Industry of 1976 (the O'Donoghue Report) and brings our law into line with some of the requirements of EC directives. We here touch on some of the central provisions in the Act. For an extended and comprehensive analysis, see Martin Hayden's annotation, *Irish Current Law Statutes Annotated.*

Supervision of insurers   Part II of the Act restates and extends the power of supervision of insurers resting in the Minister for Industry and Commerce. Insurers must submit to the Minister returns and documents as prescribed by legislation (s.11). The Minister may make regulations regarding reserves, liabilities, the valuation of an insurance undertaking, assets and several other related aspects of insurance (s.12). He has wide ranging powers to require information (s.16) and direct investigations into undertakings to satisfy himself that they are able to continue to comply with their obligations under the Insurance Acts (s.17). In case of doubtful solvency, he has extensive powers of intervention (s.18), in relation to which he can seek the High Court's approval (ss.18(5) and (6)).

The Minister may scrutinise the qualifications of directors, managers and authorised agents of insurers and take such action as he considers necessary (s.20). He may revoke an authorisation to an insurer if satisfied (*inter alia*) that the insurer has reduced the scale of its business in a class or a part of a class of life or non-life insurance so as to amount in effect to a cessation of the carrying on of business in that class or part of a class (s.21(1)(a)). Where there has been a temporary cessation, he may suspend the authorisation and lay down conditions for the renewal of the suspension. The idea here is to deter insurers from seeking to avoid higher risks: see Hayden, op. cit., General note to s.21.

Reinsurance is now brought within the net of supervision (s.22). The legislative restrictions on group policies, which go back many years, are removed (s.26). The scope of exceptions to the provisions on entering into a contract of assurance with a person who is not the holder of an assurance licence is extended to include a contract with a licensed bank, the Insurance Credit Corporation or Fóir Teoranta, in the course of its business (s.27).

In common with other regulations on insurance matters in 1989, and following on earlier legislation dealing with insurance companies, the Act sets up an Insurance Compensation Fund, involving a 2% levy (s.31). Again echoing other financial legislation in 1989, the Act imposes a duty on an auditor of an insurer who uncovers wrongdoing to report the matter to the Minister (s.35). The Minister also has power to prescribe the qualification and experience of actuaries to insurers (s.34).

Payment of commission by insurers Part III of the Act deals with the payment of commissions by insurers. It largely incorporates into statutory form the terms of the voluntary agreement entered into between the Minister and the insurance companies in 1982. If an insurance intermediary accepts a commission payment in breach of a Ministerial notice under s.37 or order under s.38, he is guilty of an offence (s.41). Where a holder of an authorisation in respect of life assurance is convicted of an offence in respect of contravention of ss.37 or 38, the insured may avoid the contract within a month (s.42). The narrow compass of this entitlement is criticised by Hayden, op. cit., General note to s.42.

Regulation of insurance intermediaries Part IV of the Act regulates insurance intermediaries other than in relation to reinsurance contracts or travel insurance (s.57). S.44 sets out an insurance broker's qualifications. He must be in a position to arrange insurance contracts on behalf of his clients with at least five undertakings. Membership of a recognised representative body of insurance brokers is not essential, contrary to what the O'Donoghue Report had recommended: see Hayden, op. cit., General note to s.44. A person may not act as an insurance agent unless he holds an appointment in writing from each undertaking for which he is an agent, states the names of every undertaking for which he is an agent on his letterheadings and informs any proposer of an insurance contract that he is an agent and of the undertakings to which he is an agent (s.49(1)). He may not hold an appointment from more than four undertakings in the life and non-life insurance cover, respectively (s.49(2)). A tied insurance agent defined in s. 51(3) must state this fact on his letterheads and inform any proposer of an insurance contract (s.49(47)).

The Minister has power to require of insurance brokers or agents to obtain indemnity insurance: s.45. Insurance intermediaries convicted of offences of dishonesty or adjudged bankrupt can carry on business only with the consent of the court (ss.54-55). The task of ensuring that an insurance intermediary (broker or agent) complies with the requirements of the Act falls on the insurance company; the company discharges its obligation if it acts 'to the best of [its] knowledge and belief' in the matter: s.46. An insurance intermediary must, as a general rule, hold a bond to the value of £25,000 as respects his non-life insurance business and to that value of 25% of turnover, as respects his life assurance business (s.47).

S.51 is of crucial importance. It abolishes the traditional rule—capable of working great injustice—that the insurance agent acts for the customer rather than the insurer. Now an insurance agent is deemed to be acting as the agent of the undertaking to whom a proposal for insurance is being made when, for the purpose of the formation of an insurance contract, he completes in his own hand or helps the proposer to complete the proposal. In these circumstances only, the insurer is responsible for any errors or omissions in the completed proposal (s.51)). The O'Donoghue Report recommended this change. Undertakings are responsible for the conduct of their tied insurance agents more widely: they must take responsibility for any act or omission of these agents in respect of any matter pertaining to a contract of insurance offered or issued by the undertakings, as if the agents were their employees (s.51(2)).

As a general rule, an insurance intermediary is not to accept money from a client in respect of a proposal unless it is accompanied by the completed proposal or the proposal has been accepted by the undertaking; nor may he take money from a client in respect of a renewal of a policy unless it has been issued by the undertaking (s.51(1)). The Minister may alter these circumstances (s.52(2)). Where a premium is paid to an insurance intermediary in respect of a renewal of a policy which has been invited by an undertaking or in respect of a proposal accepted by it, the premium is to be treated as having been paid to the undertaking when paid to the intermediate (s.53(1)). This reverses the former position. An undertaking will not be liable for a premium paid to an intermediary in respect of a proposal accepted by an undertaking or a renewal of a policy which has been invited by it, where it has given reasonable notice in writing to the person in question that the intermediary has no authority to collect these premiums on behalf of the undertaking (s.53(2)).

The Minister has power to prescribe codes of conduct to be observed by insurance brokers or agents in their dealings with clients and otherwise (s.56). This may be used in relation to bank managers, for example, to ensure the maintenance of high ethical standards.

Miscellaneous provisions   Among the miscellaneous provisions is s.60, conferring wide-ranging powers on authorised officers, for the purpose of obtaining any information which the Minister may require for enabling him to exercise his functions under the Insurance Acts, to enter 'at all reasonable times' any premises in which they have reasonable grounds for believing that there are any books, documents or records relating to the issue of any insurance policy or the acceptance of any premium in respect of a policy. As Mr Hayden notes (op. cit., General note to s.60), the result is 'to give the Minister effectively an *Anton Piller* injunction without the requirement of obtaining same in court for the purposes of enforcing the obligations under the Insurance Acts.' Of course similar wide-ranging rights of entry are a feature of modern legislation: see McMahon & Binchy, *Irish Law of Torts* (2nd ed., 1990), 450. It should be borne in mind that the absence of reasonable grounds for belief or the choice of an unreasonable time for entry will render the entry unlawful. Moreover, the doctrines of trespass *ab initio* and, more generally, of abuse of rights of entry (cf. *DPP v McMahon* [1987] ILRM 87; McMahon & Binchy, op. cit., 431) protect the occupier. The sanction of exemplary damages should also be an effective control.

Finally, s.61 is worth noting. It enables the Minister, when he thinks it necessary in the public interest and following consultation with the insurance industry and consumer representatives, by order to prescribe codes of conduct to be observed by undertakings in their dealings with proposers of policies of insurance and policy-holders renewing policies of insurance in respect of duty of disclosure and warranties.

INTELLECTUAL PROPERTY

Copyright   In *Radio Telefís Éireann and Ors v Magill TV Guide Ltd and Ors (No.2)* [1990] ILRM 534; [1989] IR 554, Lardner J considered the meaning to be given to the term 'literary work' in ss.2 and 8 of the Copyright Act 1963: see 200-1, below, in the European Communities chapter.

Patent: extension   In *Application of Technobiotic Ltd*, High Court, 14 December 1989, Murphy J granted a full ten-year extension on the term of a patent pursuant to s.27 of the Patents Act 1964. The patent involved was in respect of a pharmaceutical product, known as Flutamide, which was used to treat cancer of the prostate. After many years of research beginning in 1966, the first commercial production took place in 1982.

A crucial issue in an extension application such as this is, of course, whether the applicant/patentee can establish that it has not been sufficiently commercially rewarded by the exploitation of the patent. The Controller argued that the company should have provided the High Court with manufacturing profits for the relevant years. While Murphy J approved the dictum of Whitford J in *Plastic Textile Accessories Limited's Application* [1975] RPC 372 to the effect that such was desirable, Murphy J did not consider that it should be elevated into a statutory condition. He concluded that the evidence of worldwide sales, together with research costs, were sufficient to allow the Court exercise its discretion under s.27 of the 1964 Act.

On the substance of the case, Murphy J approved the factors to be considered in an extension application as set out by Costello J in *JR Geigy AG Irish Patent Extension* [1982] FSR 279, namely, utility, adequate remuneration, and absence of fault by the patentee. On all three items, Murphy J concluded that an extension of at least five years should be granted. He also concluded that an exceptional ten year extention should be granted under s.27(6) of the 1964 Act, having regard to the particular merits of the invention in question as indicated in the evidence to the Court.

Trade marks   The issue of whether a mark is capable of being distinguished from the product with which it is to be connected was again discussed in *The Seven-Up Co. v Bubble Up Co. Inc.* [1990] ILRM 204. The plaintiff company appealed to the High Court against the decision of the Controller of Patents, Designs and Trade Marks to allow registration under the Trade Marks Act 1963 of the first defendant company's mark which included the words 'Bubble Up'. The mark related to a carbonated drink which had, for a number of years, been on sale in the State. The plaintiff company also marketed a carbonated drink, Seven-Up, and a trade mark with the mark 'Seven-Up' had been registered under the 1963 Act.

Evidence was given by way of statutory declaration on behalf of the first defendant that 'Bubble Up' had been marketed in the State for some years without any indications of confusion between it and 'Seven-Up.' It was also indicated that the defendant company had obtained registration of a mark with the words 'Bubble Up' on it in a number of different jurisdictions in which the plaintiff company also traded. On a previous application to the Controller in 1971, he had refused permission to register a mark (which had different features from those on the present mark) which included the words 'Bubble Up'. Murphy J dismissed the plaintiff company's appeal and confirmed the registration of the new mark.

Applying the leading judgment of Kenny J in *Application of Mothercare Ltd* [1968] IR 359, the judge held that while the mark which included the words 'Bubble Up' were marginally descriptive of the goods in respect of which it was sought to be registered, it was less so than the predecessor which had been refused registration in 1971. Murphy J was also mildly critical of shortcomings in the manner by which the evidence as to existing use in the State was presented, but nonetheless concluded that there was sufficient material by which to conclude that the mark did possess the modest but necessary capacity to distinguish within the meaning of s.18 of the 1963 Act. Nevertheless, the use of statutory declarations is clearly not completely satisfactory and this will no doubt be of continuing interest in future litigation.

As to possible confusion, he noted that the plaintiff's and defendant's marks shared only a two letter word ('Up') in common use. Having regard to the absence of any evidence from the plaintiff company that any confusion had in fact arisen between the two products, Murphy J concluded that there was no ground for refusing registration by reference to confusion under ss.19 or 20 of the 1963 Act. He applied *dicta* of Luxmore J in *Aristoc v Rysta Ltd* (1943) 60 RPC 87, which had subsequently been approved by the House of Lords in that case ([1945] AC 68) and by the Supreme Court in *Coca-Cola Ltd v F. Cade & Sons Ltd* [1957] IR 196.

MERGERS AND TAKE-OVERS

The Proposed Merger or Take-Over Conditional Order 1984 (Revocation) Order 1989 (SI No.220) removes the restrictions on the rules of the Irish Civil Service Building Society in view of the commencement of the Building Societies Act 1989: see 22, above.

SALE OF GOODS

Reservation of title *Carroll Group Distributors Ltd v G. & J.F. Bourke Ltd and Anor* [1990] ILRM 285 is the latest Irish decision on reservation of title clauses. The judgment of Murphy J confirms that great care must be taken in the drafting and, more significantly, in the manner of the implementation of such clauses.

The plaintiff company supplied goods to the defendant company on four weeks credit terms, but subject to a reservation of title clause. The clause provided, *inter alia*, that: ownership in the goods would not pass until the sums due to the plaintiff had been discharged in full; that risk transferred on delivery to the defendant; that the defendant acted on its own account, and not as agent for the plaintiff, where the goods were sold by the defendant; and that the proceeds of sale from the goods should be placed by the defendant in a separate account. Crucially as it turned out, no such separate account was opened by the defendant and the defendant in fact placed the proceeds of sale in one of its general bank accounts.

The defendant went into voluntary liquidation. At the time, some goods remained unsold in its premises, and there was a credit of approximately £7,000 in its bank account, after the bank had exercised its right of set-off in respect of another account. A sum in excess of £54,500 was owed by the defendant to the plaintiff in respect of goods supplied. Murphy J held that the reservation of title clause was not operative in the circumstances which were presented to the Court.

First of all, however, he confirmed that the liquidator of the defendant company had acted correctly in returning the goods supplied by the plaintiff and in the possession of the defendant at the time of its liquidation. Then he proceeded to deal with the substance of the plaintiff's argument, namely, whether they could claim all or part of the £7,000 standing to the defendant company's credit. On this aspect of the case, there was little consolation for the plaintiff.

Murphy J referred with approval to the views of McWilliam J in *Frigoscandia Ltd v Continental Irish Meat Ltd* [1982] ILRM 396 where the overall context within which an agreement was made was discussed. Murphy J also stated that the substance of the agreement between the parties, and not merely the form, was of major significance. He referred with approval to the decision in *Re Kent and Sussex Sawmills Ltd* [1947] Ch 177 in this context, where the creation of equitable charges was discussed. Applying these decisions, he concluded that the instant reservation of title clause had in substance, though not in terms, created a charge over the proceeds of sale of the goods supplied by the plaintiff, having regard to the overall context within which the bargain between the parties had been made. Since this charge, as so found, had not been registered in accordance with s.99 of the Companies Act 1963, it was void as against the defendant company and the liquidator. A similar conclusion had been reached by Barron J in *In re W.J. Hickey & Co Ltd; Uniacke v Cassidy Electrical Supply Co. Ltd* [1988] IR 126, and it is regrettable that Murphy J did not appear to have his attention drawn to it.

The absence of reference to Irish authority was, perhaps, more apparent in the context of a *dictum* which Murphy J added towards the end of his judgment. Applying the decision in *Roscoe v Winder* [1915] 1 Ch 62, he stated that even had the plaintiff established a right to trace into the defendant's general account, such right was necessarily defeated when the moneys in the account were dissipated and not replaced by any other asset, after the bank had asserted its right of set-off on the liquidation. The niceties of the extent of the right to trace have never been fully explored in Irish decisions on reservation of title. Should a general right to trace be assumed, and if so how does it apply to a mixed fund such as was in issue in the instant case? Should it make any difference that the party asserting the right to trace made no efforts to ensure that an unmixed fund was established as required by the contract entered into? It is a pity that we are left with a tantalising dictum from Murphy J in the *Carroll* case, particularly in view of some interesting views expressed in *Sugar Distributors Ltd v Monagahan Cash and Carry Ltd* [1982] ILRM 399 in connection with tracing. While the *Carroll* decision clarifies a number of points, some of the nuances remain in doubt. For an informative discussion, with reference to the most recent English decisions as well as that in *Carroll*, see Maguire, (1989) 11 *DULJ (ns)* 40. See also the helpful analysis by McCormack [1990] *Conveyancer (ns)* 275.

Reservation of title: law reform   *The Law Reform Commission's Report on Debt Collection (2): Retention of Title* (LRC 28-1989)   The Commission's Report on Retention of Title is a short document, backed by a larger Research Paper commisioned from Ms Barbara Maguire, LLB. The Report eschews radical wide-ranging reform, such as endorsement of Article 9 of the Uniform Commercial Code would involve, on the basis that this would go far beyond the terms of the Attorney General's requirement to reform the law relating to sheriffs, the collection of taxes and debt collection.

First the Commission propose that a retention of title clause should not be enforceable unless evidenced by a note or memorandum in writing signed by or on the behalf of the buyer; the clause should not be deemed to create any form of charge unless it is expressly so stipulated at the time of the contract for sale.

The Commission justify the latter recommendation on the basis that it is 'most unlikely' that the mass of traders intend to achieve anything more than making the agreement one of conditional sale in which the property in the goods is not to pass to the buyer until payment; in 'far too many cases' artificial inferences have been drawn as to the existence of a charge on the goods.

Next the Commission propose the introduction of a registration system, maintained by the Registrar for Companies at the Companies Office, by which priority should be determined. The proposed regulation would facilitate the registration by suppliers of a single retention of title agreement concerning the repeated supplying of goods over a period not exceeding five years. A retention of title clause intended to secure the payment of a sum not exceeding £500 would be exempt from the registration requirements. Following the model provided by s.106 of the Companies Act 1963, the Commission propose that particulars of retention of title clauses should have to be registered within twenty-one days from the date on which the relevant contract was entered into, subject to a discretionary judicial power of extension.

The Commission accept that the argument against registration requirements is worthy of serious consideration: the only bodies likely to search a register are banks and other financial institutions, who will derive little added protection from it, in view of the manner in which they normally advance funds; moreover, the registration system will not be very enlightening where a 'current account' clause is employed. The Commission consider that these criticisms, so far as they have validity, would apply to the existing register of charges which companies are obliged to retain.

The Commission note the frustration of a judgment creditor who, having spent money in pursuing a judgment debtor to judgment, sends in the sheriff only to find that a large stock of apparently realisable goods belongs to someone else. The option of petitioning for a winding-up or bankruptcy, as far as the judgment creditor is concerned, 'may simply mean throwing more money away'. Accordingly the Commission recommend that, where a contract for the sale of goods contains a retention of title clause and the goods in question are taken by the sheriff, the supplier of the goods may be compelled to elect between abandoning his rights under the clause and petitioning for a bankruptcy or winding-up.

The Commission recommend that the new requirements as to retention of title clauses which they propose should apply to all suppliers, whether companies, partnerships or indiviuals.

The Commission mention that they considered but rejected certain schemes for giving the unsecured creditor more protection, such as (i) a twelve-month moratorium on bankruptcy or winding-up during which the goods could be sold for the general body of creditors, (ii) simply empowering the liquidator or official assignee to dispose of the goods for the benefit of the general body in a manner inconsistent with the clause, or (iii) enabling the receiver, prior to a winding-up order or adjudication in bankruptcy, to apply to the court for an order allowing him to sell the goods in a manner inconsistent with the seller's title. Any such provisions, in the Commission's view, would 'erode the efficacy of retention of title clauses to vanishing point'.

For critical analysis of the Report, see de Lacy, 'Anglo-Irish Retention of Title: The Current Position', (1987) 22 *Ir Jur (ns)* 212, at 224-7.

SUPPLY OF SERVICES

The provisions of s.39 of the Sale of Goods and Supply of Services Act 1980 were adverted to by Costello J in *Capemel Ltd v Lister* [1989] IR 319 (see 125-6, below, in the Contract Law chapter).

TRANSFERRABLE SECURITIES

The European Communities (Undertakings for Collective Investment in Transferrable Securities) Regulations 1989 (SI No.78) provide for the circumstances in which UCITS may operate in an EC context.

Company Law

DIRECTORS' OBLIGATIONS

In *Dun Laoghaire Corporation v Parkhill Developments Ltd* [1989] ILRM 235; [1989] IR 447, Hamilton J addressed the interesting question of the propriety of making orders under s.27 of the Local Government (Planning and Development) Act 1976 against company directors. The case involved an attempt by the applicant corporation to obtain an order under s.27 against one of the directors of an insolvent company (as well as the company) to complete a residential housing development to the applicant's satisfaction.

The President had little difficulty in declining to make the order against the director. Although the director had been in effective control of the company and had failed to comply with ss.131 and 148 of the Companies Act 1963, there was no evidence of fraud, misrepresentation or negligence on his part, nor of any siphoning off or misapplication of the company's funds. Hamilton P thus did not have to resolve the differences of emphasis apparent in earlier judicial analysis of the general question. In *Dublin County Council v Elton Homes Ltd* [1984] ILRM 297, Barrington J (following Finlay P's lead in *Dublin County Council v Crampton Builders Ltd*, High Court, 10 March 1980), expressed the view that '[t]here may be many cases, particularly in the case of small companies, where the most effective way of ensuring that the company complies with its obligations is to make an order against the directors as well as against the company itself. . . . [I]n such a case the order against the directors would be a way of ensuring that the company carried out its obligations. A body corporate can only act through its agents and the most effective way of ensuring that it does in fact carry out its obligations might be to make an order against the person in control of it.' Barrington J refused to make an order against the directors because they were 'fairly small men' who were guilty at worst of mismanagement rather than fraud or siphoning off the assets.

In *Dublin County Council v O'Riordan* [1986] ILRM 104, on the other hand, Murphy J had evinced a more fundamental objection in principle to using s.27 against directors. He accepted that s.27 was a valuable summary remedy to ensure compliance with the terms on which planning permissions are granted but added that:

justice certainly requires that if and in so far as it is to be alleged that

the party against whom such an order is sought has been guilty of fraud
or the misapplication of monies, . . . some form of plenary proceedings
should be instituted in which the party charged with such misconduct
would have the opportunities which the legal system provides for
knowing the full extent of the case being made against him and to have
a proper opportunity to defend himself against it. Similarly, where the
application turns upon the relationship between a director or shareholder
and a company in which he is interested I would anticipate that in most
cases it would be necessary that the relationship should be investigated
in the first instance by a liquidator in accordance with the procedures
provided in the Companies Act for that purpose rather than seeking to
establish all of the relevant facts on proceedings designed to be heard
on affidavit.

There seems to be much to be said for Murphy J's circumspection. A
judicial decision to make an order under s.27 no doubt may have regard to
considerations of efficacy but equally must not let pragmatism occlude its
concern for substantive and procedural justice.

THE RULE IN *FOSS v HARBOTTLE*

In *O'Neill v Ryan, Ryan Air Ltd, Aer Lingus plc, et al.* [1990] ILRM 140, the
plaintiff, the owner of 7.2% of the issued share capital in Ryan Air Ltd,
claimed damages against Aer Lingus plc and all other defendants save Ryan
Air Ltd for breaches of Articles 85 and 86 of the EEC Treaty and for
conspiracy causing damage to him. The essence of the plaintiff's case was
that these defendants had sought to engage in unlawful and anti-competitive
means of confronting competition, which Ryan Air represented, and that this
had resulted in damage to Ryan Air, with a consequent reduction in the value
of his shareholding.

These defendants brought a motion to dismiss or stay the proceedings
against them on the ground that the pleadings disclosed no reasonable cause
of action.

Lynch J dismissed the action. He considered that the rule in *Foss v
Harbottle* (1843) 2 Hare 461 applied. To hold otherwise would mean that:

a holder of 100 shares in a very large public company trading internationally throughout Europe with a capital of one hundred million
shares would be entitled to maintain an action against one or more other
companies large or small if he honestly believed that such other company or companies were seeking to limit his company's international

trade by unfair means contrary to the competition rules of the European Community and/or by conspiring so to do. Many such actions could be brought by individual shareholders even though the directors of the allegedly wronged company, for reasons that seemed to them to be commercially valid, did not consider that any such action should be brought by the company at all.

The plaintiff had contended that the rule in *Foss v Harbottle* did not apply to a course of action based on a breach of the competition rules of the Treaty. Lynch J accepted that it was the duty of national courts to enforce and give effect to directly applicable provisions of the Treaty, such as the competition rules and in particular Articles 85 and 86; but it was also well settled that effect must be given by the national courts in like circumstances and subject to like limitations as would be applied in the national courts to an analogous cause of action in national law, subject to the principle that no limit could be applied which would wholly or substantially negative the enforcement of these Articles in Irish law:

> The rule in *Foss v Harbottle* does not wholly or substantially negative the effectiveness or enforceability of Articles 85 and 86 in Irish law. Breaches of those articles can be challenged by the company which is the victim of the breaches. The rule merely prohibits persons who are not directly affected by the breaches from maintaining an action which is more properly to be maintained, if at all, by the company in which such persons are shareholders. The desirability of avoiding a multiplicity of actions perhaps in many cases contrary to the will of the directors and/or the majority of the shareholders is obviously a major factor in the thinking underlying the rule in *Foss v Harbottle* and demonstrates the sound sense of that thinking.

For consideration of the decision and of the subject in general, see Lyndon MacCann's excellent article, 'The Rule in *Foss v Harbottle*: Recent Developments', (1990) 8 *ILT (ns)* 68.

PRIVACY OF PROCEEDINGS

In *In re R Ltd* [1989] ILRM 757; [1989] IR 126 (analysed in the chapter on Practice and Procedure, below, 351-3) the Supreme Court addressed the question of the proper scope of *in camera* hearings under s.205 of the Companies Act 1963. Subs.(7) of s.205 provides that, '[i]f, in the opinion of the court, the hearing of proceedings under this section would involve the disclosure of information the publication of which would be seriously prejudicial to the legitimate interests of the company, the court may order that the hearing of the proceedings or any part thereof shall be in camera'. The applicant in proceedings in the High Court claiming relief from oppression under s.205 of the 1963 Act set out in his petition and grounding affidavit details concerning the company's accounts, its five-year business plan and the commercial terms of a transaction which it had entered into. The company and one of its directors obtained an *ex parte* order in the High Court under s.205(7) that the proceedings be heard in camera. Having sought unsuccessfully to have that order rescinded, the plaintiff appealed to the Supreme Court. By a 3 to 2 majority (Walsh, Griffin and Hederman JJ; Finlay CJ and Hamilton P dissenting) the appeal was successful.

Walsh J interpreted Article 34 of the Constitution as encapsulating in our fundamental law a principle already accepted in the common law, that judges had no discretion to prevent the public from attending hearings unless they were satisfied that privacy was absolutely necessary to enable justice to be done:

> The primary object of the courts is to see that justice is done and it was only when the presence of the public or public knowledge of the proceedings would defeat that object that the judges had any discretion to hear cases other than in public. It had to be shown that a public hearing was likely to lead to a denial of justice before the discretion could be exercised to hear a case . . . other than in public.

Turning to s.205(7), Walsh J noted that it dealt with proceedings involving a juristic person created by the Companies Acts:

> That puts the case in a quite different category from the private affairs of a human person. It is difficult to see why the disclosure of evidence of this type must necessarily be deemed to be a failure to do justice in the case of a juristic person where it would not be such in the case of a human person or of any unincorporated body of persons. The respondents as well as the applicant are entitled to a fair and public hearing by the courts set up under the Constitution. Is the fact of the statutory condition precedent, namely, a serious prejudice to the legitimate interests of the company, to be regarded as necessarily being equivalent to those exceptional circumstances where public knowledge of the proceedings is likely to lead to an injustice or to defeat the object of the courts in doing justice? I do not think so, even though it might be thought that this appeal proceeded on the basis that it does. While in one sense the quarrels between a shareholder or shareholders in a limited

company and the company itself might be regarded in the nature of a family squabble, it is in no way comparable to family disputes in the true sense. A limited company is the creature of the law and by its very nature and by the provisions of the law under which it is created it is open to public scrutiny.

Walsh J made it clear that he was not contending that there could *never* be circumstances where the public hearings of cases such as the one before the Court would prevent justice being done; but he was of opinion that in the instant case, no such circumstances, 'so far at least', had been shown.

In his concurring judgment Griffin J maintained that it might 'very well be' that the company at trial would be able to establish that there were further circumstances which would justify the trial judge in concluding that the disclosure of some or all of the matters in the pleadings and affidavit would be likely to prevent justice being done in the case. There was agreement among all the judges that s.205(7) could never be availed of to conceal from publication wrongful activities on the part of a company, its directors and officers.

The decision in this case raises a number of questions. First, it may be asked whether the basis on which proceedings are to be heard in private is, or ever was, *the absolute necessity to enable justice to be done*? Unless justice is to be understood in a totally artificial way, it will not provide the explanation for holding legal proceedings in private. The wide-ranging privacy requirements in relation to family litigation are surely inspired by sensitivity for the feelings of those involved, as well as the belief that the public has not a sufficient interest in intruding into the intimate matters of family life. One could no doubt say that it would be 'unjust' to hold these proceedings in public, but this is scarcely the most obvious or convincing rationale. Similarly, the disclosure of military secrets could clearly be undesirable on the basis of the defence of the independence and security of the State; again it would seem odd to explain this exclusion in terms of justice.

The point is of some practical importance, as *In re R Ltd* makes plain, because the Court has, in effect, sucked all vitality out of s.205(7), replacing it by a generic single principle, applicable to *all* litigation, civil and criminal. The implications of this are considerable. It seems that *mandatory* privacy requirements in a statute raise at least the shadow of unconstitutionality.

Walsh J noted that there are several of these provisions and pointedly observed that it was not necessary for the purpose of the case before the Court to consider the interpretation which should be given to them. It is possible that their constitutional validity will be saved by reading into them, contrary to their express language, a discretionary judicial power. If this is not done, the Court *might* hold that, by virtue of the nature of family litigation, for example, and the damage which any disclosure might cause, a mandatory rule of exclusion is permissible.

The real sources of criticism of s.205(7) are that it gives to companies a privilege it denies to ordinary individuals and that this privilege is limited to *Foss v Harbottle* proceedings, when damage to a company's legitimate interests can just as easily occur in other types of litigation.

REDUCTION IN SHARE CAPITAL

In *In re Credit Finance Bank plc*, High Court, 19 June 1989, Costello J addressed a number of issues relating to an application to the court to approve the reduction of share capital which the company had undertaken because of the difficult situation which it had experienced in recent times. A shareholder brought to the attention of the Court certain matters which he argued that the court should consider in deciding whether it should exercise its powers under s.73 of the Companies Act 1963.

The shareholder contended that the proposed scheme was not fair to ordinary shareholders. Costello J thought it of 'considerable significance' that he was the only such shareholder to have made this complaint. Costello J was of the view that the scheme was fair as between the classes of shareholders involved. *Re MacKenzie & Co* [1916] 2 Ch 450 was authority for the proposition that, where there is a class of shareholders entitled to a preferential repayment of capital on winding-up, repayment of these shareholders is permitted. A scheme which recognised this fact was not unfair to other shareholders who had not that right.

WINDING-UP

Courts fees, set off and interest in liquidation   In *In re McCairns (PMPA) plc (In Liquidation)* [1989] ILRM 501, some important issues of general interest in company law arose. The company had been wound up in 1987. One of its main assets was a site of which the bank Hill Samuel & Co (Ireland) Ltd was secured creditor with three charges over it. The bank had consented to the sale of the site by the liquidator. After the sale had been completed, a number of disputes arose as to how much the bank could claim out of the proceeds and the basis on which that claim was sustainable.

The first issue concerned the bank's liability for court fees. In *In re Michael Orr (Kilternan) Ltd* [1986] IR 273, O'Hanlon J had held that fees payable on the sale of mortgaged property in the winding-up of an insolvent company should be paid out of the funds recovered by the liquidator and the amount received by the secured creditors reduced *pro tanto*. Costello J endorsed this approach, rejecting the bank's contention that the total purchase price should be distributed first to the secured creditors and then to the unsecured creditors or, alternatively, that the only asset which the company enjoyed was the equity of redemption and that only it should be subject to the tax payable. Nor did he see any substance in the argument that the liquidator was precluded from claiming anything for the fees by virtue of an agreement he had made with the bank. The correspondence did not support this contention; but, more fundamentally, Costello J did not think that the liquidator would be empowered to enter into an agreement of this type, certainly without the leave of the court:

> The liquidator cannot agree that the mortgagee should be relieved of the legal liability which the law imposes on him as this would place the tax burden on the unsecured creditors and the distribution of the assets would then not have taken place in accordance with law.

The next issue concerned set-off. The liquidator sought a direction as to whether set-off should be operated in respect of the debit and credit balances of the company's three accounts with the bank as at the date of liquidation. The bank sought to resist this on the basis that a wholly owned subsidiary of the company, which had guaranteed the company's performance of its obligation under the mortgage, had not agreed to the set-off of monies received by the bank under the guarantee. Costello J held that the question of the subsidiary's consent did not arise; the bank had been contractually entitled under the guarantee agreement to place moneys it received on foot of the guarantee in an account in the name of the company and credit the company with the sum it had received.

The final issue in the case concerned interest. Costello J examined five options available to a secured creditor in the winding-up of dissolved companies. He may realise his security and, if the sale results in a deficit, prove for the deficit in the winding-up; or secondly, he may value his security and prove in the winding up for the deficit; thirdly, he may surrender his security and prove for the whole debt in the winding-up. In all of these cases, no post-liquidation interest may be claimed: *In re London, Windsor and Greenwich Hotels Co.; Quatermaine's Case* [1892] 1 Ch 638; *In re Burgess* (1888) 23 LR Ir 5. Two other options are to realise his security pursuant to a power of sale outside the winding-up or to allow the liquidator to sell the mortgaged property and agree to release his interest in it on payment of his debt. This last option had occurred in the instant case.

Costello J approached the question by first considering the position without reference to the express statutory incorporation of the bankruptcy rules into the winding-up provisions relating to insolvent companies in the Companies Act 1963. He considered that, if the secured creditor were entitled to post-liquidation interest, this could significantly reduce the amount available for unsecured creditors. He could see no justification for construing the 1963 Act as modifying the contractual obligations so that no post-liquidation interest is payable if the debt is unsecured but not as modifying a similar obligation merely because it is a secured one. Such a distinction would breach the principle of equality and fairness.

Costello J then considered the position under the 1963 Act in the light of the express incorporation by s.284(1) of the bankruptcy rules to deal with the winding-up of insolvent estates. He took the view that this provision should be construed as incorporating only those rules of bankruptcy which are consistent with the provisions of the 1963 Act. No inconsistency could arise by applying to winding-up procedures the *statutory* provisions and rules of court relating to the proof of debts by secured creditors; but if there was a *judge-made* rule in bankruptcy arising from the construction of the bankruptcy code which was inconsistent with a proper construction of the provisions of the 1963 Act, Costello J did not think that the Oireachtas had introduced the incorporation of such a rule. The Act, properly construed, was introduced to modify companies' liability to pay post-liquidation interest, whether the obligation was secured or not. To make this modification depend on whether the debt was secured or not would produce an illogical anomaly as between creditors. If a mortgagee sold at a *deficiency*, he would be debarred from obtaining post-liquidation interest; why therefore should a mortgagee be permitted to claim such interest when he sold at a *surplus*, when this would adversely affect the interests of unsecured creditors?

Mr Seamus Woulfe has criticised the decision as going beyond the accepted canons of interpretation in order to achieve an equitable result: (1989) 11 *DULJ (ns)* 113, at 118-120. He argues that, although incorporation of the applicable bankruptcy rule via s.284 might be seen as producing the anomaly identified by Costello J, 'a statutory anomaly is not altogether uncommon in Irish legislation and is not a sufficient reason for failing to apply a statutory provision.' (id. at 119).

In *In re Hibernian Transport Co. Ltd; Shell International Petroleum Co. Ltd v Gordon* [1990] ILRM 42, a company had gone into liquidation in 1970. The assets now in the hands of the official liquidator were more than sufficient to discharge all its debts ascertained at the commencement of the winding-up and the costs of the liquidation. The surplus had come, not from an unexpected windfall in the realisation of assets, but from the length of time which the liquidation took. An application was brought to the court to determine whether the creditors, or certain classes of them, were entitled to be paid interest on their debts as ascertained and, if so, at what rate and for what period. The secured creditors had long previously been paid off with interest, and the preferential creditors had also been paid. The unsecured creditors comprised those with a contractual claim to interest on their debts (the 'interest creditors') and all others (the 'general creditors').

Carroll J referred to a series of English decisions culminating in *In re Lines Bros Ltd* [1984] BCLC 215, which had treated companies as not having been insolvent at the time of the winding-up, and thus not subject to the rules relating to interest which apply to insolvent companies, where the assets when realised are sufficient to pay all the debts. She did not agree with this approach, but she drew a distinction between those cases and the case she had to decide:

> In the present case the company's surplus does not arise from the realisation of assets but from massive amounts of interest earned over a long period of years. In this it may be unique. In my opinion it would be flying in the face of logic to hold that the company must be treated 'as a company which is and which was and always has been solvent'. ... To my mind there is a significant difference between a company where the assets themselves produce a surplus and a company where interest earned on the realisation of assets produces a surplus.

On this view, she treated the company as falling under s.284 of the Companies Act 1963 which applies the same rules as in bankruptcy to the rights of creditors. By virtue of ss.4 and 86(1) of the Bankruptcy Act 1988 interest was payable at the current rate for judgment debts. After payment of the statutory interest, the contractual creditors would be entitled to be paid the balance of the sum due for contractual interest, giving credit for the amount received for statutory interest.

Finally Carroll J rejected the creditors' argument that the official liquidator is a trustee or *quasi* trustee for the body of the creditors and that, as a matter of equity, the court has inherent jurisdiction to order that the interest should go to the creditors. The rights of the creditor and contributories, she noted, are determined by statute. In ascertaining their rights, it is necessary to interpret the statutory provisions. 'Equity cannot be called in aid to overrule the consequences of a particular statutory interpretation'.

The decision in *Hibernian Transport* is of general interest. It presents some difficult conceptual puzzles, not least that concerning the relationship between the realisation of assets and the generation of assets. Of the nature of things, assets can take some time to realise. Frequently the passage of this time may result in the accumulation of some interest on the proceeds of the assets first realised. So on most liquidations which eventually yield a surplus, that surplus will represent a *combination* of the assets plus the interest. It certainly will not represent one to the exclusion of the other. The question therefore must arise as to when, on Carroll J's test, the retrospective attribution of solvency which she considers appropriate 'where the assets themselves produce a surplus' should be set aside on account of the fact that the interest earned on the realisation has produced the surplus. If the company's liabilities are £1,000,000 and the assets yield £750,000, with interest constituting £250,000, which rule should apply? The facts of *Hibernian Transport*, where the interest was a major explanation for the eventual surplus, might have suggested that a distinction of conceptual credibility can be drawn between a surplus generated by realisation of assets and one generated by the interest. Where the facts are less striking, the conceptual basis fades away.

Carroll J concluded that the case might be 'unique'; if this is so, perhaps her formula for non-application of the retrospective attribution of solvency must be understood as applying only to those cases where the disproportion between the respective contributions of realisation and interest is extreme. As against this interpretation, two difficulties may be mentioned. The first is one of certainty of definition; precisely when is the point reached where the interest is considered to have 'produced' a surplus, by virtue of its constituting a relatively greater proportion than the realisation of the assets? The second difficulty relates to how this interpretation can harmonise with Carroll J's rationale for treating a company as always having been insolvent where 'interest earned on the realisation of assets produces a surplus'. This rationale is that to do otherwise would be 'flying in the face of logic'. But it is also flying in the face of logic if one takes into account even a *small* contribution of interest.

This brings us to a related point. The realisation of assets can sometimes involve a windfall, attributable to factual or legal circumstances occurring after the commencement of the liquidation. For example, a company which owns agricultural land is liquidated. In the course of liquidation a law is passed which renders that land eligible for commercial usage. The liquidation accounts make it plain that the company was completely insolvent until this fortunate change in the law but now has a large surplus. If concern for the fictional quality of a restrospective attribution of solvency is a sufficient reason for declining to engage in this practice where interest has produced a surplus, why should the same concern not also apply to the realisation of the company's assets, especially in a case where there can be no doubt as to the fact that the enhanced value acquired on realisation is attributable exclusively to matters arising after the liquidation has begun?

Payments made after commencement of winding-up The question of the court's discretion under s.218 of the Companies Act 1963 to validate payments made after the commencement of winding-up fell for consideration in a number of winding-up decisions in 1989. They are analysed by Lyndon McCann in (1990) 8 *ILT (ns)* 6 and 113.

In *In re Ashmark (No. 1)* [1990] ILRM 330, the solicitor of the company unsuccessfully sought validation of payments to him made after the commencement of the winding-up in respect of legal costs he had incurred on behalf of the company. These totalled £26,761.42. O'Hanlon J stated succinctly that:

> [t]he general approach has been to allow payments to be validated in certain cases, where it could be shown that the recipient of the payment was unaware that a petition had been presented, and, secondly, to validate payments or dispositions of property made in the course of a transaction which was of benefit to the general body of unsecured creditors.

The payments to the solicitor passed neither of these tests. The solicitor's impression that the company was being allowed a three-month period to wind down its affairs, and his failure to advert to the references in the correspondence to the presentation of the petition were of no avail; in view of the clear statements in the correspondence, he had to be fixed with knowledge of the facts of the petition. Moreover, O'Hanlon J found it hard to envisage a situation where the court would validate a payment in full made after the commencement of a winding-up, in respect of services rendered or goods sold or other obligations incurred by the company prior to the winding-up, when similar treatment could not be accorded to the general body of unsecured creditors. He thus rejected the solicitor's argument that payment should be validated because the services rendered by him as solicitor with an intimate knowledge of the affairs of the company, and the legal costs incurred in the process, were rendered and incurred in the best interests of the company and were beneficial for all creditors of the company.

In *In re Ashmark Ltd (No. 2); Ashmark Ltd v Nitra Ltd* [1990] ILRM 455 two questions arose for consideration: first, whether the drawing of a cheque in favour of a creditor, which the creditor lodged in its bank before the commencement of a winding-up, operated as a 'disposition of the property' of the company which was wound up, and secondly, if it did not, whether the court, in the exercise of the powers under s.218 of the Companies Act 1963, should validate the payment thus made.

Blayney J was quite satisfied that the drawing of the cheque did not amount to a disposition: 'The cheque was no more than an unconditional order by the company to its bankers to pay [the creditor] the sum named in it. Until [the bank] made the payment in accordance with the order there was no disposition'.

The question therefore was one of discretion under s.218. The circumstances of the transaction were that the company, which was in financial difficulties, had for many years been the distributor of Zanussi electrical appliances. The company had instituted proceedings seeking to restrain Zanussi from presenting a petition for its winding-up. These proceedings had been compromised on 4 July 1988 by an agreement whereby Zanussi was entitled to present its petition forthwith, but would not advertise the hearing for three months, the company would not trade from 4 July 1988, and the company agreed to consent to its winding-up on the hearing of the petition. The company owed over £80,000 to the servicer of its appliances. On 7 July, the company gave the servicer a cheque for £11,898.70, which was lodged into the servicer's account that day and paid by the company's bank on 11 July. Zanussi's petition had been presented on 8 July.

In favour of validating this payment it was argued that it had been beneficial to the company in that the servicing carried out on the appliances sold by the company was responsible for the collection of much of the company's debts. Blayney J rejected this contention; the affidavit in support of it had only averred that the servicer 'would have seriously considered terminating at least temporarily' any further servicing if the payment had not been made. It had not stated that this *would have* happened; even if it had, the interruption would at worst have been only temporary. In these circumstances it was difficult to conclude that it was the payment which was of benefit to the company. What was of benefit, if anything, was the servicing, and it was doubtful if its continuance was induced by the payment.

Blayney also rejected the argument that the disposition had been carried out in good faith in the ordinary course of business at a time when the parties were aware that a petition had been presented. It was not carried on in the ordinary course of business because the company had applied to cease trading on and from a date three days before the cheque was handed over; it was 'extremely doubtful' if it was carried out in good faith, since the person who signed the cheque had been party to the agreement supporting the compromise and must have known that, if the petition had not already been presented, it was about to be. The case involved none of the circumstances for exercising a discretion to validate payment mentioned by Buckley LJ in *In re Gray's Inn Construction Co. Ltd* [1980] 1 WLR 711.

Costs of legal costs accountant   In *In re Castle Brand Ltd (In Liquidation)* [1990] ILRM 97, Carroll J held that the cost of solicitors' employing a legal costs accountant in connection with the taxation of their costs could not be said to be 'properly incurred' by the liquidator, for the purposes of s.281 of the Companies Act 1963, because, under long established law, the cost was one which must be borne by the solicitor. On behalf of the liquidator it was argued that there was an analogy with the position of a successful litigant, where, in taxing party and party costs, it is accepted practice that the fees of the legal costs accountant engaged before the Taxing Master on the taxation of these costs should be paid by the client. Carroll J rejected this suggested analogy; party and party costs were the property of the successful litigant; in the recovery of these costs, a legal costs accountant engaged to appear on taxation would be acting on behalf of the successful litigant and not on behalf of his solicitor.

Priorities The European Communities (Preferential Treatment for Debts in Respect of Levies and Production of Coal and Steel) Regulations 1989 (SI No. 219) amend s.285 of the Companies Act 1963 to prioritise the payment of debts for levies imposed in the ECSC context.

TRANS-COMMUNITY TRADE

The European Communities (European Economic Interest Groupings) Regulations 1989 (SI No. 191) facilitate the creation of EEIGs for the purpose of easing barriers to trade between corporate entities in the EC.

Conflict of Laws

JURISDICTION

Claims for contribution or indemnity   Costello J's decision in *International Commercial Bank plc v Insurance Corporation of Ireland plc* [1989] IR 453, discussed in the 1988 Review, 89-90, was appealed to the Supreme Court without success: [1989] IR 453. Briefly, the case concerned the propriety of adding a third party, a company incorporated in Guernsey, at the request of the defendant, an Irish company, in proceedings brought here by an English plaintiff. The defendant had been given liberty by the High Court to issue a third party notice and serve it out of the jurisdiction. The third party in the instant proceedings sought to have that order discharged. It pointed to the fact that it had instituted proceedings in England against the defendant in relation to the same cause of action before the defendant obtained liberty here to serve the third party notice on it. Costello J held against the third party and the Supreme Court dismissed the appeal.

The first issue requiring disposition was whether O. 11, r.1(4) of the Rules of the Superior Courts 1986 applied to a third party claim made by a defendant. Finlay CJ, delivering the judgment of the Court, had no doubt that it did. He was satisfied that there was nothing in the terms of the provision which excluded such claims. Moreover justice frequently required that, as far as possible, a party against whom a claim has been made and who has legal rights against another which may relieve him from some or all of the consequences of that claim should be entitled to have the issue of his liability and of his consequential rights determined in a single set of proceedings and as far as possible at the same time. If the decision of the English Court of Appeal in *McCheane v Gyles* [1902] 1 Ch 287 could not be distinguished, its reasoning should be rejected.

The second issue was whether the third party was 'a necessary or proper party'. The Chief Justice had no doubt that it was, notwithstanding the existence of the English proceedings. He was 'therefore satisfied' that the third party had been properly added. The Chief Justice did not here address the question of the court's discretion whether to decline to make an order for service out of the jurisdiction on the basis of what in effect may be the application of the *forum non conveniens* or *lis alibi pendens* doctrines. It would be quite open to the court, accepting that the third party was indeed 'a necessary or proper party', nonetheless to decline to make an order for service out of the jurisdiction. Costello J had addressed this aspect of the case in some detail. He concluded that in the circumstances, 'as the possible disadvantage which the third party may suffer is self-inflicted and as the possible disadvantage which the defendant may suffer could be very serious indeed and is not of its own making, if its claim is valid . . . the balance of conflicting interests lies in favour of the defendant'. The Supreme Court dealt with this issue as a coda. The Chief Justice was satisfied that 'the vital matter which must affect any question of a discretionary stay is the position in which the defendant is in this jurisdiction. It has been sued on a claim for judgment in a liquidated sum in this jurisdiction. It is necessary to ensure that as soon as may be after the determination of the issue arising in that claim and by the same tribunal the issue between it and the third party is disposed of'.

The third issue addressed by the Supreme Court was whether the 1968 Judgments Convention, the 1971 Protocol and the 1978 Accession Convention applied to the third party proceedings so as to make it mandatory for the High Court on the facts of the case to decline jurisdiction in favour of the English High Court. The whole thrust of the Convention is to avoid clashes of jurisdiction. Article 21 provides that, where proceedings involving the same cause of action and between the same parties are brought in the courts of different Contracting States, any court other than the court first seized is, of its own motion, to decline jurisdiction in favour of that court. Article 34 of the 1978 Accession Convention provides that the Conventions and Protocol are to apply only to 'legal proceedings instituted . . . after the entry into force of the Convention in the State of Origin . . .'. The High Court order giving liberty to the defendant to issue the third party notice had been made on 2 May 1988; the Conventions had come into force here on 1 June 1988. The Chief Justice was of the view that the third party proceedings had commenced on 2 May 1988. Therefore Article 21 did not apply.

In a future case the Court may have to address more definitively the nature of a claim for contribution or indemnity, for the purposes of service out of the jurisdiction. In *International Commercial Bank*, the litigation between the plaintiff and the defendant was still in progress at the time the defendant's application to bring in the third party was made. The desirability of having a single set of proceedings weighed heavily with the Chief Justice. But what about a case where the defendant seeks contribution or an indemnity after the conclusion of the plaintiff's proceedings against him? He has, after all, two further years in which to make this claim: Civil Liability Act 1961, s.31; *Neville v Morgan Ltd*, High Court, 1 December 1988; McMahon & Binchy, *Irish Law of Torts* (2nd ed., 1990), 839-40, and the 1988 Review, 461-2. The third party may perhaps no longer be considered a 'necessary and proper party'. If not, what is the basis of the entitlement for service out of the jurisdiction? That the defendant's claim is 'founded on a tort' committed

here? Australian courts have held to the contrary: *Gilchrist v Dean* [1960]
VR 266; *Stewart v Honey* [1972] 25 ASR 585, at 592; see Sykes & Pryles,
Australian Private International Law (2nd ed., 1987), 48-9. (Presumably a
similar objection could be made to a claim for contribution or indemnity in
respect of breach of contract or of trust: cf. the Civil Liability Act 1961,
s.2(1).) It may perhaps be best to characterise a claim of this nature as
quasi-contractual rather than delictual: Dicey & Morris, *The Conflict of Laws*
(11th ed., 1987), 1408, are of this view. If such an approach were favoured,
a defendant with a third-party claim would still have to overcome the
traditional reluctance of the Irish courts to extend r.1(e) to obligations akin
to those of a contractual nature arising by way of statute: *Clare County
Council v Wilson* [1913] 2 IR 89; *Killiney UDC v Kirkwood* [1917] 2 IR 614;
Shipsey v British & South American Steam Navigation [1936] IR 65; see
further Binchy, *Irish Conflicts of Law* (1988) 141-2. But the case in favour
of permitting service out of the jurisdiction in respect of contribution or
indemnity seems so strong that one suspects that the courts will not let these
earlier decisions stand in their way.

Order 11, tort and contract In *Campbell v Holland Dredging Co.
(Ireland) Ltd*, High Court, 3 March 1989, Keane J had to deal with the
complexities of O.11. The plaintiff, the widow of a ship's captain who was
drowned at Plymouth docks, had instituted fatal accident proceedings in
Ireland against the first defendants in which she claimed that her husband's
death had been caused by the 'negligence of and breach of duty and breach
of statutory duty' of the defendants. Hamilton P had given her liberty to issue
a concurrent plenary summons against the second and third defendants and
to serve notice of the summons on them at addresses in England and the
Netherlands respectively. The Order recited that the action appeared to fall
within r.1(e) of O. 11. The second and third defendants sought vacation of
this order on the ground *inter alia* that the action was one brought in tort and
thus did not fall within the provisions of r.1(e), which deals with actions for
damages or other relief 'for or in respect of the breach of a contract' which
was made within the jurisdiction, made by or through an agent trading or
residing here on behalf of a principal trading or residing out of the jurisdiction, or one governed by Irish law or breached within the jurisdiction.

Counsel for the plaintiff sought to uphold the order on the basis that an
action against an employer by an employee claiming damages for negligence
can be brought in contract. Keane J accepted that this basic submission was
undoubtedly correct. He saw no reason why this principle, recognised in
Matthews v Kuwait Betchel Corporation [1959] 2 QB 57, should not equally
apply to a fatal accidents claim under Part IV of the Civil Liability Act 1961.
But here, if the order were let stand, 'there would be nothing to prevent the

plaintiff from confining her proceedings to a claim for damages in respect of a tort committed outside the jurisdiction. This would not be consistent with the care which the courts must exercise in assuming a jurisdiction which normally belongs to other States'. Retrospective alteration of an order on foot of which service had already been effected would, in Keane J's view, be wholly irregular. No great loss would befall the plaintiff, since there was still ample time to make further application, under the Rules, to have the second and third defendants joined.

A final aspect of the case is worth noting. Although the President's order had permitted only the service of notice of the plaintiff's summons on the second and third defendants, since they were not citizens of Ireland (cf. O. 11, r.8), it appeared that copies of the summons had been served on them. Keane J observed that this did not affect the validity of the order being challenged and that in any event no point had been taken in relation to it on behalf of these defendants.

The Jurisdiction of Courts (Maritime Conventions) Act 1989   This Act gives effect in Irish law to two international Conventions: the International Convention Relating to the Arrest of Sea-Going Ships, which is generally referred to as the Arrest Convention; and the International Convention on Certain Rules Concerning Civil Jurisdiction in Matters of Collision, which is generally referred to as the Collisions Convention. Both were signed at Brussels on 10 May 1952. The Act also abolishes the local admiralty jurisdiction of the Cork Circuit Court, about which constitutional doubts had been expressed. For a very helpful analysis of the Act's provisions, see Vincent Power's annotation, *Irish Current Law Statutes Annotated*.

The Arrest Convention   The Arrest Convention seeks to encourage uniform rules of law relating to the arrest of seagoing ships. Its central provision is Article 2, to the effect that a ship flying the flag of one of the Contracting States may be arrested in the jurisdiction of any of the Contracting States in respect of any maritime claim but in respect of no other claim. Article 1 defines 'maritime claim' broadly, so as to include seventeen categories, very similar to claims generating *in rem* jurisdiction under previous Irish law: see Binchy, *Irish Conflicts of Law* (1988), 160-2; Yale, 'A Historical Note on the Jurisdiction of the Admiralty in Ireland' (1968) 3 *Ir Jur (ns)* 146; *Cox Ltd v Owners of MV Fritz Raabe*, Supreme Court, 1 August 1974. Thus, for example, claims for damage caused by a ship either in a collision or otherwise, claims for loss of life, personal injury, or damage to goods, salvage, general average, towage, pilotage, goods supplied, wages or Master's disbursements, disputes as to title to or ownership of a ship, and the mortgage or hypothecation of a ship, all come within the definition of 'maritime claim'. S.2 of the Act construes disputes as to title to or ownership of a ship as including disputes as to its possession. It brings within the scope of the mortgage or hypothecation of a ship, the mortgage or hypothecation of *any share in a ship*. 'Arrest' is defined as meaning the detention of a ship by judicial process (cf. Article 4) to secure a maritime claim, but not including the seizure of a ship in execution or satisfaction of a judgment. The High Court has jurisdiction to authorise arrest: s.5(2) of the Act. It should be noted that Article 2 leaves unchanged the right and powers of Governments or their Departments, public authorities and dock or harbour authorities under their domestic laws or regulations to arrest, detain or otherwise prevent the sailing of vessels within their jurisdiction.

Article 3 deals with the arrest of a sister ship, owned by the person in respect of whose ship the maritime claim arose. (Ownership here embraces beneficial ownership (s.2 of the Act) and cases where all the shares in the ships are owned by the same person or persons: Article 3(2). See further Chorley & Giles, *Shipping Law* (8th ed., 1987), 77.) Moreover, the owner of the sister ship at the time of the issue of proceedings against it is deemed its owner: s.2(3)(a) of the Act. As a general rule a sister ship may be arrested only once in any one or more of the jurisdictions of any of the Contracting States in respect of the same maritime claim by the same claimant. It cannot be arrested at all where the claim consists of a dispute as to the title, ownership, mortgage or hypothecation of the other ship, or a dispute between co-owners as to the ownership, possession, employment or earnings of the other ship. A sister ship which is eligible for arrest may be arrested more than once only where the claimant can satisfy the Court or other appointed judicial authority that the bail or other security on the first occasion had been finally released before the subsequent arrest or that there is other good cause for maintaining the arrest: Article 3(3).

As we have seen, the High Court exercises jurisdiction to authorise arrest. It also has the function of permitting the release of a ship on bail or other security, and determining the nature and amount of the bail or security in default of agreement between the parties: Article 5. All questions of whether in any case the claimant is liable in damages for the arrest of a ship or for the costs of the bail or other security are determined by the law of the Contracting State in whose jurisdiction the arrest was made or applied for: Article 6. The rules of procedure relating to the arrest of a ship are also governed by that law: id.

Article 7 is designed to discourage forum shopping. The courts of the country where the arrest was made have jurisdiction to determine the case on its merits if their domestic law gives them jurisdiction or in any of the following cases:

(a) if the claimant has his habitual residence or principal place of business there;

(b) if the claim arose there;

(c) if it concerns the voyage of the ship during which the arrest was made;

(d) if it arose out of a collision;

(e) if it is for salvage;

(f) if it is upon a mortgage or hypothecation of the ship arrested.

If the courts of the country where the arrest was made lack jurisdiction to decide on the merits, they should, when fixing bail or other security, also fix the time within which the claimant is to bring an action before a Court having that jurisdiction. Where the parties have agreed to submit to the jurisdiction of a particular Court or to arbitration, the courts of the country where the arrest was made may fix the time within which the claimant is to bring proceedings. Failure to comply with these time limits entitles the defendant to apply for the release of the ship or of the bail or other security.

As regards ships flying the flag of a non-Contracting State, a Contracting State may arrest them in its jurisdiction in respect of any of the maritime claims to which the Convention applies or of any other claim for which the law of the Contracting State permits arrest: Article 8(2). The Convention does not modify or affect the rules of law in force in the respective Contracting States relating to the arrest of any ship within the jurisdiction of the State of her flag by a person who has his habitual residence or principal place of business in that State: Article 8(4).

Part I of the Act, which fine-tunes the incorporation of the Arrest Convention into our law, contains a number of provisions not already mentioned which are worthy of note. 'Master' includes every person (except a pilot) having command of a ship: s.2(4). 'Salvage' is defined by reference to ss.544 to 546 of the Merchant Shipping Act 1894: id. The Minister for Foreign Affairs may by order declare who are Contracting States and what reservations they have made; this constitutes evidence (though not conclusive evidence) as to the position: s.3. In cases where the High Court stays, declines or dismisses proceedings on the ground that the dispute should be submitted to arbitration or determined by the courts of another country, it may order that the ship arrested, or the bail or other security, be retained for the purposes of satisfying in part or whole any award or judgment given in the arbitration or legal proceedings in respect of the dispute which is enforceable in the State: s.5(4). In taking this course, the Court may attach such conditions to the order as it thinks fit, in particular conditions with respect to the institution or prosecution of the relevant arbitration or legal proceedings: s.5(5). For consideration of the enforceability of foreign *in rem* judgments, see Binchy, op. cit., 585ff; as to the enforceability of foreign arbitrations, see id., 24, 616ff.

When Ireland was negotiating the 1978 Convention of Accession with the Community, it was agreed that the Judgments Convention would not deal specifically with jurisdiction for the arrest of sea-going ships but rather that Ireland would implement the Arrest Convention.

S.6 of the Act deals with the arrest of State ships. It provides that the Convention does not modify the rules of law in force in the State in regard to the arrest of warships or ships owned by or in the service of a state. This is in harmony with the general rules of international law as to State immunity: cf. Binchy, op. cit., 173-66; *The Eolo* [1918] 2 IR 78; *Zarine v Owners of S.S. Ramava* [1942] IR 148; H. Schreuer, *State Immunity: Some Recent Developments* (1988), ch. 2.

S.7 of the Act contains three savings. The Arrest Convention is not to affect s.5 of the Mail Ships Act 1891, which protects mail ships from arrest in certain circumstances; nor does it limit the jurisdiction of the court to refuse to entertain an action for the possession of a ship or for wages by the master or an officer or member of the crew of a ship that is not an Irish ship; nor finally does it affect s.552 of the Merchant Shipping Act 1894, which relates to the power of a receiver of wreck to detain a ship in respect of a salvage claim.

The Collisions Convention   The Collisions Convention seeks to introduce uniform rules relating to civil jurisdiction in matters of collision. Article 1 limits the countries in which an action for collision between seagoing vessels, or between seagoing vessels and inland craft, may be brought. These are:

(a) the country where the defendant has his habitual residence or a place of business;

(b) the country where arrest has been effected of the defendant ship or any other ship belonging to the defendant which can be lawfully arrested, or where arrest could have been effected and bail or other security has been furnished;

(c) the country of the place of collision when the collision has occurred within the limits of a port or in inland waters.

The plaintiff may choose between these three options; if, having chosen one of them, he wishes to bring a further action against the same defendant on the same facts in another jurisdiction, he must discontinue the first action. Article 2 makes it clear that the provisions of Article 1 are not in any way to prejudice the right of the parties to bring an action in respect of a collision before a Court they have chosen by agreement or to refer it to arbitration.

Article 4 extends the range of the Convention to an action for damage caused by one ship to another or to the property or persons on board such ships through the carrying out of, or the omission to carry out, a manoeuvre or through non-compliance with regulations *even where there has been no actual collision*. Article 6 excludes from the scope of the Convention claims arising from contracts of carriage or from any other contracts.

Article 5 contains an express provision that the Convention is not to modify the rules of law in the various Contracting States in regard to collisions involving warships or vessels owned or in the service of a State.

Part II of the Act, which implements the Collisions Convention, contains definitions of 'inland waters' and 'port' (s.9), and a provision similar to s.3, enabling the Minister for Foreign Affairs by order to declare who are Contracting States and what declarations they have made.

Abolition of the Cork Local Admiralty Court S.14 of the Act abolishes the Cork Local Admiralty Court. It had not been used in recent years in view of its low jurisdiction (£2,000) and the doubts as to its consistency with the Constitution. The Jurisdiction of Courts (Maritime Conventions) Act 1989 (Commencement) Order 1989 (SI No. 332) set 17 April 1990 as the date on which the Act came into effect.

JURISDICTION AND RECOGNITION OF FOREIGN JUDGMENTS

Formal aspects of enforcement under EC Judgments Convention

Prior to the incorporation of the EC Judgments Convention into Irish law, the best advice a lawyer might give his or her client threatened with foreign legal proceedings would be to sit tight and take no part in the proceedings. If the client was not resident in the foreign state and had no assets there, the judgment would be of no practical benefit to the plaintiff, since it would not normally be enforceable here: see Binchy, *Irish Conflicts of Law* (1988), 589-98. The Judgments Convention has changed the position fundamentally. It has shifted the crucial time to that when the foreign proceedings are launched, and the crucial issue to that of the jurisdictional competence of the foreign court. It establishes uniform jurisdictional rules. If a defendant does not successfully challenge the jurisdiction of the court in these proceedings or if he does not successfully defend the case on the merits, then there is very little he can do to stop the foreign judgment being enforced against him here. The prudent lawyer now must advise the client, above all, not to ignore foreign proceedings falling within the remit of the Convention.

Rhatigan v Textiles & Confecciones Europeas SA [1989] ILRM 659; [1989] IR 18, affirmed by Supreme Court, 31 May 1990, shows how bare is the Convention's cupboard of technical defences to a foreign judgment. Textiles, a Spanish company, had obtained four judgments, totalling over a million pounds, in respect of dishonoured bills of exchange, against Rhatigan, in English proceedings in which Rhatigan had participated. Rhatigan sought to challenge the enforcement of these judgments here on the grounds (i) that the Master's order had contained no address of the plaintiff for service of process within the area of the jurisdiction of the High Court, (ii) that the order failed to disclose on its face that the judgments in respect of which authorisation of enforcement was sought were judgments of a court of a Contracting State which is a party to the Convention, and (iii) that there had been no evidence before the Master to show that the judgments were ones to which the Convention applied. Blayney J rejected all of these grounds. As to the first, Article 33 of the Convention required merely that, in *applying* for the order authorising enforcement, the applicant must give an address for service; Textiles had done this. *Carron v Germany* [1987] 1 CMLR 838 was not of assistance to Rhatigan because the Court of Justice had there required no more than that the address for service should be 'given sufficiently early to ensure that the proceedings are not improperly delayed and that the rights of the party against whom enforcement is sought are safeguarded'. There was no question in the instant case of Rhatigan's rights not having been safeguarded since he was able to serve his appeal within the period permitted by the Convention.

As to the second ground, though no authority was cited for it, Blayney J was willing to accept as a general proposition that the order should indicate clearly the judgment the enforcement of which it was authorising. It was not necessary to do this, however, in regard to a judgment in a case which had been contested, once the judgment was clearly identified in the order. Here the order had stated the court in which the judgments had been obtained, their title and recorded numbers, the date of the judgments and their respective amounts. The plaintiff 'could have been in no doubt whatsoever' that the judgments were those obtained against him in England, a Contracting State.

Blayney J was also satisfied that there had been evidence before the Master that all the proceedings had been instituted after the Convention had come into force in Britain. In respect of each action, there had been a certificate by a Master of the Supreme Court of Judicature.

Rhatigan's appeal to the Supreme Court was unsuccessful. Griffin J delivered the judgment of the Court. As to the first ground, he interpreted *Carron* as having established three principles:

1. the law of the State in which enforcement is sought governs the entire procedure for making the application for enforcement of which the furnishing by the applicant of an address for service of process forms part;

2. at the latest, notice must be given no later than the date when the decision authorising enforcement is served;

3. the sanction for failure to comply with the requirements of Article 33 must be determined by the law of the State in which enforcement is sought.

Griffin J was of opinion that the finding of the Court of Justice that the address for service of process must be given at the latest when the decision authorising enforcement is served was 'wholly inconsistent' with the submission that it must be stated in the order issued by the Master.

As to the second ground, Griffin J was prepared to assume, without deciding, that there was a procedural requirement in Irish law that the order of the Master should, on its face, have stated that the judgments were those of a Contracting State party to the Convention. On that assumption, the sanction for any failure to comply with that requirement should also be determined by Irish law. The interests of justice overwhelmingly required that the order should be enforceable notwithstanding this breach. All the actions had been fully contested by Rhatigan in the English High Court and Court of Appeal and he could not have been 'under the slightest misapprehension' as to the identity of the judgments.

Finally, Griffin J completely endorsed Blayney J's reasoning in rejecting the third ground.

Rhatigan had sought a reference to the Court of Justice under Article 177. Griffin J rejected this on the basis that there was no question of Community law in respect of which a decision was necessary to enable the Supreme Court to give judgment. The only possible question which could arise concerned the giving of an address for service of process pursuant to Article 33, and the Court of Justice had already determined this in *Carron*. That decision had made it clear that the national law governed the entire procedure for making the application for an enforcement order, and the documentary proofs were matters of procedure.

Does *Rhatigan* give future Irish defendants any crumbs of comfort? Precious few, it seems. The only issue arising in the case which both the High Court and Supreme Court left open was whether an enforcement order which failed to disclose on its face that the judgment was one of a Contracting State party to the Convention could *in any circumstance* be ineffective. Clearly it will not when the defendant participated in the foreign proceedings in question *and* (whether by virtue of the description of the judgment in the enforcement order or perhaps otherwise) the defendant in fact is aware that the judgment is of such a Contracting State. Beyond this, the position is somewhat less certain; but Griffin J's emphasis on 'the balance of justice' and 'the interests of justice' suggests that the Court will have no sympathy for a technical objection based on this ground. It is to be noted that Griffin J assumed, *without deciding*, that it is a procedural requirement of our law that an order of this type should state that the judgment was one of a Contracting State which is party to the Convention. Blayney J made no such assumption; but he was willing to accept rather than assume the general proposition that the order should indicate clearly the judgment the enforcement of which it is authorising. It may well be that this is all that future defendants can demand, and then only when in fact they have no reasonable means of readily identifying the judgment. The question of their having participated in the foreign proceedings should be relevant only to the extent that it throws light on their means of identifying the judgment.

Mareva **injunctions**   The EC Judgments Convention was designed to ensure that those seeking to enforce in one Contracting State a judgment obtained in another Contracting State would have the element of surprise. Thus an application to the Master of the High Court under section 5 of the 1988 Act for the enforcement of a judgment is *ex parte*. By virtue of Article 34, the Master 'is not able to summon the other party. At this stage no contentious proceedings are allowed': *Jenard Report*, 48. See also id., 50, and Advocate General Marco Darmon's opinion in *Firma P v Firma K* [1985] 2 CMLR 271, at 277; cf. *Schlosser Report*, para. 219.

This element of surprise is buttressed by section 11(3) of the Act, which provides as follows:

> Subject to Article 39, an application to the Master of the High Court for the enforcement of a judgment and an application to the High Court for the enforcement of an instrument or settlement referred to in Title IV of the 1968 Convention may include an application for the granting of such protective measures as the High Court has power to grant in proceedings that, apart from this Act, are within its jurisdiction and, where an enforcement order is made in relation to a judgment or such an instrument or settlement, the order shall include a provision granting any such protective measures as aforesaid as are applied for as aforesaid.

Article 39 provides as follows:

> During the time specified for an appeal pursuant to Article 35 and until any such appeal has been determined, no measures of enforcement may be taken other than protective measures taken against the property of the party against whom enforcement is sought.
>
> The decision authorising enforcement shall carry with it the power to proceed to any such protective measures.

In *Elwyn (Cottons) Ltd v Pearle Designs Ltd* [1989] ILRM 162; [1989] IR 9 the plaintiff applied for enforcement in Ireland of an English judgment; the plaintiff also sought an order restraining the defendant from reducing its assets below the amount owing on the judgment pending its enforcement. The Master granted the order for enforcement but refused to give the protective measures sought. The plaintiff appealed to the High Court (Carroll J) which treated it as an appeal under O. 63, r.9. Carroll J granted the protective measures on an interim basis, stating that she would give reasons later. Two days afterwards, she stated that, having considered the matter further, it seemed to her that the appropriate way to deal with the matter was to bring an application for leave to apply for judicial review, seeking an order of mandamus directed to the Master to make the order sought, as the person given jurisdiction to do so under s. 11(3). She noted that there was no provision for an appeal against a refusal to grant protective measures though there was provision for an appeal to the High Court for refusal to grant enforcement and against an order for enforcement.

Carroll J did not, however, dispose of the case without a clear statement of her view of the substantive issue:

> The protective measure sought, namely a *Mareva*-type injunction for the total amount due under the judgment, is a protective measure which the High Court would have power to grant in respect of proceedings within its jurisdiction. That being so, it appears to me that the Master of the High Court was not entitled to refuse the order sought. According to the wording of s.11, subs.3, if the Master of the High Court was satisfied that the protective measure sought was relief which the High Court had power to grant in proceedings within its jurisdiction, then, once the enforcement order was made, it should have included a provision granting the protective measure.

Carroll J noted that the matter had arisen in *Capelloni and Aquilini v Pelkmans* [1985] ECR 3147, where the Court of Justice had stated in its judgment that:

> ... the effect of Article 39 is that a party who has obtained authorisation for enforcement is under no obligation to obtain specific and separate judicial authorisation in order to proceed with protective measures during the period mentioned in that article, even though such authorisation may normally be required by the national procedural law of the court in question. . . .
>
> Th[e] expression ['shall carry with it'] indicates that the right to proceed with such measures derives from the decision allowing

enforcement and therefore that a second decision, which could not in any event undermine that right, would not be justified.

When the application for judicial review came before him (*sub nom. Elwyn (Cottons) Ltd v The Master of the High Court*) [1989] IR 14, O'Hanlon J adopted Carroll J's analysis of the issue relating to protective measures, characterising this as 'the *ratio decidendi* of [her] decision, although in the nature of *obiter dicta*'. He also held that an order for *mandamus* might be granted, echoing Costello J's approach towards the granting of an order for *certiorari* against a taxing master in *The State (Gallagher, Shatter & Co.) v de Valera*, High Court, 9 December 1983. He reserved his conclusion, however, on the question whether O. 42A of the Rules of the Superior Courts, adopted in 1989, was a comprehensive code of procedure for enforcement of judgments under the 1988 Act, thereby excluding the conventional appeal procedure under O. 63, r.9.

The decision provokes some consideration since there would be something odd about the Master (or the High Court, where the enforcement of an authentic instrument or court settlement is in question) being obliged, on the enforcer's demand, to give the enforcer whatever protective measures he specifies, without there being any need for these measures, in circumstances where the granting of protective measures will be oppressive on the defendant. Perhaps the answer to this difficulty lies in the nature of protective measures. It would seem undesirable to approach the matter by drawing up a list of protective measures available in a Contracting State's legal system and then concluding that the enforcer has merely to ask for any or all of these in order to be granted them. The better approach would surely be to eschew a simplistic identity between the *names* of the categories of these protective measures and the applicant's entitlement to orders for each of these measures. In other words, the concept of a protective measure should be individuated to the particular case. An applicant would be entitled to a particular protective measure *if, and only to the extent that, this protective measure may serve an actual protective function in the case in question*.

At first sight, this interpretation may appear to be inconsistent with Professor Jenard's contentions that the power to proceed to protective measures under Article 39 'arises automatically', and that '[e]ven in those States whose law requires proof that the case calls for prompt action or that there is any risk in delay the application will not have to establish that either of those elements is present; power to proceed to protective measures is not a matter for the discretion of the court': *Jenard Report*, 52. It may be argued that the apparent conflict is illusory. There is a fundamental difference between an automatic right to protective measures without having to qualify under some discretionary hurdle placed by the law of a particular Contracting

State and a right to what in the particular case are not protective measures because, though falling within the category of a particular remedy carrying the name 'protective measures', they are measures serving a different function in the particular case. At the base of this issue is the fact that the essential notion of a protective measure is one that must embrace only measures serving a protective function. If they go outside or beyond this function, then, regardless of how they are described in the legal system of the Contracting State where enforcement is sought and obtained, they may not be availed of by the applicant for enforcement.

This analysis explains why an applicant may not seek excessive protective measures: cf. the excellent analysis of Gerard Hogan (who acted as counsel for the plaintiff in *Elwyn (Cottons)*): 'The Judgments Convention and *Mareva* Injunctions in the United Kingdom and Ireland' (1989) 14 *European L Rev* 191, at 202, fn 38. There thus would appear to be imposed on the Master (or the High Court, where appropriate) the duty to be satisfied that the measures sought by the applicant are in fact protective measures, in the sense that that concept has to be understood under the Convention. This does not mean, of course, that the Master has to approach applications for *Mareva* injunctions in the same way as under Irish law: on the contrary, as Professor Jenard makes clear, it would be quite wrong for the Master to proceed on the basis that he was obliged to subject the question of the plaintiff's entitlement to a protective measure under Article 39 to the particular judicial discretion appropriate to a case arising in non-Convention proceedings. But this does not mean that the Master must blindly hand out *Mareva* injunctions at the demand of the applicant even in cases where they serve no protective function. On the general subject, see further Hogan, 'Protective Measures and the Judgments Convention—A Practical Guide', in Moloney & Robinson eds., *The Brussels Convention on Jurisdiction and the Enforcement of Foreign Judgments* (ICEL, 1989), 77.

DAMAGES

In *Baker Perkins Ltd v C.J. O'Dowd Ltd*, High Court, 13 April 1989, the defendants, an Irish company, purchased bakery equipment from the plaintiffs, an English company. A clause in the contract provided that the contract 'shall in all respects operate and be construed in accordance with English law'. The contract, in another clause, provided that '[t]he measure of damages shall be any loss or expense of any nature incurred by seller arising out of disposal of goods'.

In an action for damages for the defendants' failure to complete the contract, Blayney J addressed the question of the appropriate measure of damages. He accepted the submission of defence counsel, which counsel for the plaintiffs had not contested, that the measure specified in the contract should be applied rather than what was set out in s.50 of the English Sale of Goods Act 1979.

It is worth identifying the proper law of the contract. The clause as regards the contract's operation and construction in accordance with English law was almost certainly sufficient to constitute a choice of English law as the proper law. If this is so, then the question would arise as to why the other clause, relating to quantum of damages, was applied in preference to s.50 of the English Act. Blayney, J appeared to perceive a *conflict* between the two. In fact s.50 operates as a supplement, rather than in opposition, to a contractual specification of the measure of damages. In truth, if English law was the proper law, and if the proper law was considered to be the appropriate law to determine the damages, then the question of determining the relationship between English statutory provisions and the terms of the contract was a matter for English law to resolve; cf. *D'Almeida Aranjo Ltd v Becker & Co. Ltd* [1953] 2 QB 329. It may be, however, that Blayney J considered that the clause in the contract relating to English law was one merely of *incorporation* of English rules of construction, rather than amounting to an express choice of English law as the proper law; cf. *Griffin v Royal Liver Friendly Society* [1942] Ir Jur Rep 29; Binchy, *Irish Conflicts of Law* (1988), 523-4. On this approach, the terms in the contract—whose proper law, assessed objectively, *may* have been Irish—might be considered appropriate to determine the measure of damages. Certainly s.50 could have no possible claim to attention.

FOREIGN ADOPTIONS: LAW REFORM

In their Report on the *Recognition of Foreign Adoption Decrees* (LRC 29-1989), the Law Reform Commission recommend that Ireland should *not* ratify the Hague Convention on Jurisdiction, Applicable Law and Recognition of Decrees Relating to Adoption (1964). Instead the Commission propose an entirely new system of recognition of foreign adoption orders based on designation of specified countries by the Minister for Health.

Under Irish law, adoption has the effect of completely extinguishing the legal relationship between the parents and their child. Adoption by consent is (subject to an exception relating to legitimated children whose birth has not been re-registered) limited to children who are orphans or whose parents have not married each other. In the latter case, only the consent of the mother is required, unless the father has been made guardian under s.6A of the Guardianship of Infants Act 1964 (as amended): see *K v W* [1990] ILRM 121 considered below, 248-57. Compulsory adoption, under the Adoption Act 1988, is limited to cases where both parents have failed in their duty and are likely to continue to do so until the child reaches full age; furthermore, they must also have abandoned all their parental rights with respect to the child.

Poverty is not a ground for adoption under the Act. If there are other persons suitable and available to act *in loco parentis* to the child—relations or friends of the parents, for example—an adoption would not be authorised as the intervention of the State would be 'unnecessary and, therefore inappropriate'. The unmarried father appears to be completely excluded from the process: he is not the 'parent' of his child (Adoption Act 1952, s.3) even where he is entitled to exercise guardianship rights under the Status of Children Act 1987; possibly he would be considered to be a 'person concerned', under s.3(1) of the 1988 Act, whose rights would have to be considered by the court. Whether such a claim would depend on his having displayed an interest in playing a parental role is not clear. See generally the 1988 Review, 246-52.

Adoption is far from a univocal concept internationally. See Johnson, 'Is Adoption Outmoded?' (1985) 6 *Otago L Rev* 15; Hoggett, 'Adoption Law: An Overview', ch. 8 of P. Bean (ed.), 'Adoption: Essays in the Social Policy, Law and Sociology' (1984). In some countries, the adoption process is child-centred; in others, and increasingly in western societies, it pays attention to perceived claims of those seeking to adopt. In some countries, compulsory adoption ranges far more widely than here: poverty and power-lessness can afford the basis for adoption against the wishes of the parents. A trend is also apparent (again often with a view to accommodating the desires of those wishing to adopt) of making adoption a less final step. The idea here is to encourage mothers to hand over babies for adoption on the basis that they are not cutting off all ties with their children in doing so: see Amadio & Deutsch, 'Open Adoption: Allowing Adopted Children to "Stay in Touch" with Blood Relatives' (1983) 22 *J of Family L* 59, at 70-2.

Irish private international law rules on the recognition of foreign adoptions lack a body of reported case law: see generally Binchy, *Irish Conflicts of Law* (1988), ch. 17. Prior to the introduction of adoption into our domestic law in 1952, Irish judges gave short shrift to the claims based on a foreign adoption order: *In re Tamburrini* [1944] IR 508. Since 1952, there has been no reported decision setting out the circumstances in which a foreign adoption order may be recognised; however, some statute law (e.g. the Status of Children Act 1987, ss.3(1)(b) and 92(1)(b)) proceeds on the assumption that recognition principles exist.

Recognition rules in other common law jurisdictions concentrate on a domicile-based test or a reciprocity principle based on the similarity or identity of jurisdictional criteria as between the country where the adoption takes place and that where its recognition is sought. Where the domicile-based test is applied, the difficult question immediately arises as to *whose* domicile should count. One solution would be to look to the domicile of the child. The argument in favour of this approach is that the law from which the child is withdrawn and which provides the existing framework of his legal relations should have some say in the change: O'Connell, 'Recognition and Effects of Foreign Adoption Orders' (1955), 33 *Can Bar Rev* 635, at 641. The fact that the child in most cases will not be old enough to protect his own interests is a further reason for giving emphasis to the child's *lex domicilii*: Binchy, op. cit., 374. Nor should one ignore the interests of the child's parents, since, if the adoption is recognised, their rights in relation to their child will no longer be recognised: O'Connell, op. cit., at 641.

The principal argument in favour of selecting the adoptive parents' *lex domicilii* is that in most cases the child, when adopted, will be living in the country of their domicile; to attribute to the child a connection with a system of law with which he may have had no point of contact since his earliest months 'might be considered artificial': O'Connell, op. cit., at 642. The analogy with custody proceedings has been pressed, on the basis that one should have regard to the best interests of the child by looking to the future rather than the past: cf. E. Scoles & P. Hay, *Conflict of Laws* (1982), 543. See, however, Baade, (1962), 40 *N Car L Rev* 691, at 703-4.

A solution which some may consider to be more sensitive is to require that recognition of a foreign adoption be based on a cumulative test, requiring compliance with the *leges domicilii* of the child and the adoptive parents. This approach has the support of some courts: see *Re Wilby* [1956] 2 WLR 262 (Barnard J); *Re Wilson* [1954] Ch 733 (Vaisey J); *Perpetual Trustee Co. Ltd v Montouri* [1982] 1 NSWLR 710, at 716-7 (Rath J). Commentators are divided as to its merits: see Jones (1956) 5 *Int & Comp LQ* 207, at 209; Mann (1941) 57 *LQ Rev* 12, at 123-4; O'Connell, op. cit., at 638, 641.

Thus far, the relationship between the Constitution and rules of recognition of foreign adoptions has not been mentioned. We will address this important dimension presently.

The Hague Convention deals, not only with recognition of foreign adoptions, but with the prior questions of jurisdiction and applicable law. It applies only to adoptions with a foreign element: it has no application to wholly 'internal' adoptions, where the adopter or adopters and the child all possess the same nationality and are habitually resident in the State of which they are nationals.

The Convention seeks a *via media* between nationality and domicile as connecting factors—a useful goal in view of the historical differences between civil law and common law countries on this question. It vests jurisdictional competence to grant an adoption in the authorities of the State of habitual residence or nationality of the adoptive parent or parents: Article 3. The child must be unmarried and under the age of eighteen, possessing the nationality of one of the contracting States and habitually resident in one of them (not necessarily the one of which he or she is a national): Article 1.

As regards choice of law, the authorities who have jurisdiction based on the habitual residence of the adopter (or adopters) must apply their internal law to the conditions governing an adoption: Article 4. However, they must apply the national law of the child relating to consents and consultations, other than those in regard to an adopter, his or her family or his or her spouse: Article 5. Moreover, they must respect any provision prohibiting adoption contained in the national law of the adopter (or, in the case of an adoption by spouses, any such provision of their common national law) if the State of nationality of the adopter (or adopters) has made a declaration, when signing, ratifying or acceding to the Convention, specifying the provisions of its internal law prohibiting adoptions founded on:

(a) the existence of descendants of the adopter or adopters;

(b) the fact that a single person is applying to adopt;

(c) the existence of a blood relationship between an adopter and the child;

(d) the existence of a previous adoption of the child by other persons;

(e) the requirement of a difference in age between adopter or adopters and the child;

(f) the age of the adopter or adopters and that of the child;

(g) the fact that the child does not reside with the adopter or adopters: Article 13.

The authorities having jurisdiction to grant an adoption under Article 3 must not do so 'unless it will be in the interest of the child': Article 6. Before granting an adoption they must carry out, through the agency of the appropriate local authorities, a thorough inquiry in relation to the adopter or adopters, the child and his or her family: id. As far as possible this inquiry must be carried out in cooperation with private organisations qualified in the field of intercountry adoptions and the help of social workers having special training or particular expertise concerning the problems of adoption: id. The authorities of all the contracting States are required promptly to give all the assistance requested for the purposes of an adoption governed by the Convention: id.

Jurisdiction to annul or revoke an adoption governed by the Convention is vested in the authorities of (a) the contracting State of habitual residence of the adopted person at the time of the application for annulment or revocation; (b) the State of habitual residence of the adopter (or adopters) at the time of this application, and (c) the authorities of the State which granted the adoption: Article 7. An adoption may be annulled (a) on any ground permitted by the internal law of the State which granted the adoption, or (b) in accordance with the national law of the adopter (or adopters) at the time when the adoption was granted in a case where one of the prohibitions contemplated in Article 13 is alleged to have been breached; or (c) in accordance with the national law of the person adopted at the time when the adoption was granted in cases where the application to annul is based on failure to obtain a consent required by the law.

Article 8 deals with recognition. It provides that every adoption, and every annulment or revocation of an adoption, to which relevant Articles of the Convention apply 'shall be recognised without further formality in all contracting States'. Moreover, if any question arises in a contracting State with respect to the recognition of such an adoption, annulment or revocation, the authorities of that State, in considering the jurisdiction of the authority which granted the adoption or made the annulment or revocation, 'shall be bound by the findings of fact on which that authority based its jurisdiction'. Article 15 of the Convention is worthy of particular note: it is to the effect that the provisions of the Convention may be disregarded in contracting States 'only where their observance would be manifestly contrary to public policy'. For consideration of this Article, see Morris in *Festschrift for Mann* (1977), 241, at 251, and de Nova [1961] 1 *Rec des cours* 68, at 85.

The Commission, in their recommendations on the subject of recognition of foreign adoptions, first dispatch the Hague Convention summarily. They note three 'limitations' in particular:

(a) the Convention does not apply to wholly 'internal' adoptions;

(b) it does not extend to the incidents and effects of an adoption recognised by another State;

(c) it deals only with adoptions by a single adopting parent, or by spouses, of children under the age of eighteen who have not been married.

The Commission note further that the practical utility of Ireland's ratifying the Convention is 'significantly reduced' by the fact that it has been ratified by only three countries—Australia, Britain and Switzerland. They go on to state—apparently as a factor against ratification—that the Convention 'may be superseded, in part at least, by the Convention on the Adoption of Children Coming from Abroad which it is hoped to adopt at the seventeenth session in 1993'. These factors lead the Commission to conclude that Ireland should not ratify the 1964 Convention.

Perhaps this analysis might have been broadened somewhat to examine the implications of the 'limitations', rather than to treat them as insurmountable obstacles. The fact that a Convention, for sound reasons of international *realpolitik*, limits its scope so as to encourage a lowest common denominator of accord in no way prevents individual countries from legislating more broadly when implementing the Convention. There would be nothing to be lost by Ireland's ratification of the Convention, in the context of wide-ranging legislation dealing with such matters as the recognition of wholly 'internal' adoptions and the incidents and effects of adoption.

Casting its shadow over the entire subject of recognition of foreign adoptions is the Constitution, with its vision of natural rights inhering in families and individual family members by virtue of their human dignity. The idea that these rights are the *creation* of legislatures is specifically rejected by the Constitution; this dimension is of considerable importance in relation to adoption, since in some countries the termination of family rights operates on the basis of racist and socially discriminatory legal criteria. Under Article 41, the poverty of the parents does not justify the compulsory adoption of their children. In many other countries, State intervention of this kind is quite permissible. The precise ambit of protection afforded by the Constitution to families with little connection with Ireland is a matter of some uncertainty, but it is clear that the mere fact that there is a foreign dimension to a family will not necessarily suffice to exclude the application of the Constitution's protection to them. *Fajujonu v Minister for Justice* [1990] ILRM 234 appears (*per* Walsh J) to accept that residence here will suffice. It is equally clear from Finlay CJ's analysis that a child who is an Irish citizen may call on the fundamental rights protection of the Constitution.

In making their recommendations for reform, the Commission emphasise (para. 47) the importance that recognition principles should be explicit and clear, since numerous legal consequences flow from the recognition or non-recognition of an adoption order. The need for an individual to be confident as to his legal status, and for administrative officials to be able to make such determinations is also important. Moreover, the Commission consider that new recognition principles should not have the effect of retrospectively rendering invalid adoption orders which, under existing law, might be entitled to adoption. The problem of 'limping' adoptions (valid in some countries but not others) and the spectre of Ireland's becoming 'something of a haven for certain disaffected parents' are also factors identified by the Commission as weighing against too broad an application of Article 41 in this context. The fact that recognition cases quite often arise many years after the adoption order was made, 'and at a time when the application of Constitutional principles may serve little practical purpose', is also noted by the Commission.

In the light of these and other considerations, the Commission take the view (para. 47) that:

> it would be wrong to lay down a general principle in legislation explicitly mandating non-recognition of foreign adoptions on Constitutional grounds. It should be possible for Judges, within the context of a general principle allowing non-recognition for reasons of public policy, to distinguish between cases where the application of Constitutional principles is appropriate from those where it is not.

One may wonder whether this is in fact the best approach. The constitutional provisions protecting families under Article 41 cannot be wished away by the Oireachtas. To take the course that the legislation can safely provide for grounds of recognition that either generally or in specific cases are in defiance of Article 41, on the basis that the courts can invoke public policy as the channel through which all constitutional protection must flow, could place the legislation at serious risk of being struck down by the courts. Against this view, it could perhaps be argued that the Maintenance Orders Act 1974 adopted a legislative approach whereby the constitutional protection of the family was channelled through a public policy proviso; but that legislation at no stage sought to provide expressly for the recognition or enforcement of orders which, on their face, were in opposition to the protection afforded by Article 41.

In paras. 49 to 55 of their Report, the Commission outline the regime of recognition which they would prefer. This is largely modelled on the proposals made by the Review Committee on Adoption Services in its Report published in 1984. Briefly, the proposals envisage the enactment of legislation giving the Minister for Health power to designate countries or jurisdictions whose adoption orders would be recognised in Ireland. If this approach were favoured, 'a valid adoption order made in England or France, for example, would be recognised here, if these were designated countries, with our conflicts rules laying down no requirements as to the domicile, nationality or residence of the child or the natural or adoptive parents'. The effect of this recommendation would be that the adoption in England of a child of Irish nationality or residence would be recognised here, provided English jurisdictional requirements had been fulfilled. The link between the parents and the child could be severed on legal grounds which would offend Article 41. Clearly there is a significant constitutional dimension here. The courts might take the view that such a wide-ranging basis for recognition offended against Article 41 and was not saved by the inclusion of a mere public policy proviso.

The Commission go on to recommend that recognition should be confined to adoption orders made in respect of persons below the age of 18, and to adoptions effected under legislative provisions only. An adoption order made in a designated country should be regarded as having the same consequences as an adoption order made under the Adoption Acts. An important matter which Irish (or indeed other common law) courts have yet to address is how to deal with legal systems where adoption does not involve a complete severance of legal ties with the natural parents. These systems, embracing *adoptio minus plena* (or 'simple adoption') are prevalent in countries with a civil law tradition. However, it would be fair to say that there are trends in some common law countries in this general direction. For an excellent comparative analysis see van Loon, *Report on Intercountry Adoption,*

(Hague Conference on Private International Law, 1990), 99ff. Characterisation strategies may go some way towards resolving the private international law issues, but just as in the case of polygamy, for example, ultimately the courts (and the Oireachtas) have to go deeper than mere nominalist solutions and address the troublesome underlying policy questions. Yet again in the Irish context, the Constitution raises its own distinctive issues: most obviously, in the case of *adoptio minus plena*, who are the parents for the purposes of Article 41's protection?

On the question of the relationship between the broad ground for recognition of foreign adoption orders which they propose and the public policy proviso, the Commission recommend that the proviso should operate as a right on the part of a court in a particular case to refuse recognition on this basis. They completely reject the idea that the Minister, in assessing which countries to put on the list of recognised adoptions, should have the function of assessing whether, in regard to the particular country, the possible constitutional difficulties are such as to make it undesirable for him to exercise his powers. Their reason for doing so is intriguing:

> Under such a provision the Minister might feel obliged to refuse to designate any country whose adoption law contains any provision, no matter how little used, which might be regarded as constitutionally suspect. The Minister might indeed find it difficult under such a provision to designate any country. It seems preferable to allow the Minister to designate those countries whose adoption laws have a broadly similar purpose as our own, leaving the courts with the discretion to refuse recognition in particular cases on grounds of public policy.

The Commission go on to recommend that, in addition to the Ministerial power of designation as a basis for recognition, the legislation should also provide, for the avoidance of doubt, that an adoption order made in a country or jurisdiction in which either or both of the adopting parents was or were domiciled should be recognised; moreover, an adoption *recognised* in such a country or jurisdiction should also be recognised. The Commission recommend the introduction also of a recognition test based on the adoption having been made in the country of the habitual residence of either of the adopting parents or that it is *recognised* 'in the country where the adopting parents had their habitual residence'.

Some puzzling anomalies (which may be the result of nothing more serious than a certain informality of expression) arise in respect of this latter recommendation. Why should recognition be afforded to an adoption decree recognised in the *country* (e.g. France) but not *jurisdiction* (e.g. Ontario) where the adopting parents had their habitual residence? And why in such circumstances (in contrast to cases where the adoption order is *made* in the country or jurisdiction of habitual residence of *either* or both of the adopting parents) should it be necessary that the recognition be 'in the country where the adopting parents had their habitual residence'? This can mean only that recognition in the country of the habitual residence of *one* parent will not suffice. Moreover the literal interpretation rule suggests that it means also that recognition will not be afforded to an adoption decree recognised in both the respective countries of habitual residence of each of the adopting parents where the adopting parents have their habitual residence in different countries. It is difficult to envisage what policy would warrant such discriminations. An interesting parallel may perhaps be drawn with the rules for recognition of foreign divorces contained in s.5(4) of the Domicile and Recognition of Foreign Divorces Act 1986: cf. Binchy, op. cit., 283-4.

Finally the Commission recommend that, to meet the difficulties which administrative officials may have regarding the recognition of foreign adoptions, the High Court should be given jurisdiction to make a declaration that the applicant is or is not the adopted child of a named person by virtue of a foreign adoption. The declaration should be available only on the application of the person whose adoptive status is in question and the applicant would have to be either domiciled or habitually resident in the State at the time of the application. The Commission do not seek to resolve the vicious circle which will inevitably arise here as to the child's domicile. As long as the child's domicile remains one of dependency, there will be no logical way of attributing to the child an Irish domicile until the issue in question — the validity of the foreign adoption order — has been determined. It would thus seem advisable for the legislation to provide for the attribution of a proleptic domicile, on the assumption 'without prejudice', as it were, that the child's domicile is Irish.

DOMICILE

In the 1988 Review, 73-80, we discussed at some length Barr J's decision in *M(C) v M(T)* [1988] ILRM 456 where he held that the domicile of dependency of married women offended against the Constitution. In a later decision on other issues arising in the case, delivered after further legal argument on 30 November 1989, Barr J returned to this theme.

Barr J noted that, in his judgment in *BL v ML* [1989] ILRM 528, he had had occasion to consider in some depth the constitutional implications of the rights of married women in matrimonial property: see the 1988 Review, 213-21 and below, 240-2. He had no doubt that the domicile of dependancy of married women was 'contrary to the spirit and intent' of Article 41 of the Constitution. The court would be 'failing in its duty to interpret and develop the law in a way which is in harmony with the philosophy of Article 41 as to the status and rights of married women' if it upheld the constitutional validity of this doctrine. He recalled that in the Supreme Court decision of *W v Somers* [1983] IR 122, at 126, McCarthy J had specifically adverted to this obligation when he had said that '[t]he judicial branch of government of the State must . . . recognise its duty under Article 41 and seek to achieve the objectives as set out in that Article'.

In Barr J's view the doctrine of dependent domicile of a wife, which in given circumstances might have particularly unjust consequences for her, also offended the principle enshrined in Article 40.1, that all citizens are to be held equal before the law. Moreover, Article 40.3.1 was relevant:

> The old doctrine of dependent domicile clearly militated against a married woman by depriving her on marriage of domiciliary rights which she enjoyed as a single woman by obliging her to acquire and retain the domicile of her husband in all circumstances while the marriage subsisted. In my view a married woman's right to an independent domicile, now specifically recognised by statute, is a fundamental personal right within the ambit of Article 40.3.1, which the State has an obligation by its laws to respect, defend and vindicate. I cannot see any 'practicable' difficulty in the way of upholding that right and declaring that the old doctrine of dependent domicile of a wife was unconstitutional.

The judgment provokes a number of comments. First it seems clear that Barr J held that the domicile of dependency of married women offended against at least *three* provisions of the Constitution—Articles 40.1, 40.3 and 41. He had stated as much in his earlier judgment: [1988] ILRM 456, at 470. The inclusion of Article 41 is important: if the wife's capacity for an independent domicile is attributable in part to Article 41, this suggests an answer to the question, which we raised in the 1988 Review, 112, as to divorces obtained before 2 October 1986 (the date the Domicile and Recognition of Foreign Divorces Act 1986 came into effect). Concern for the family and for the protection of marriage would best be reflected in a rule of recognition of foreign divorces which requires that the divorces should have been obtained (or recognised) in the country (or countries) of the *actual* domicile of *both* spouses. The old doctrine of dependent domicile attributed the husband's domicile, quite artificially, to the wife. Once that artificiality is removed, then the actual reality of the wife's domicile should be taken into account. To transform the rule into one basing recognition on the fact that the divorce was obtained in the country of the domicile of only *one* of the spouses clearly expands the range of recognition very widely. It would mean, for example, that a wife domiciled in Ireland whose deserting husband divorced her in England, where he had acquired a domicile, would lose her status as spouse and, consequently, her entitlements to succession and under the Family Home Protection Act 1976, for example. That this result might be challenged on constitutional grounds was noted by Walsh J in *Gaffney v Gaffney* [1975] IR 133, at 152. Indeed a dark constitutional shadow falls over s.5 of the Domicile and Recognition of Foreign Divorces Act 1986 on this account. If, as Barr J holds, Article 41 is part of the explanation for the abolition of the domicile of dependency of married women, it must operate in a way that buttresses rather than subverts marriage.

Barr J went on to consider whether the wife was entitled to retain her rights under the Family Law (Maintenance of Spouses and Children) Act 1976. He held that the doctrine of 'divisible divorce' (as to which see Binchy, *Irish Conflicts of Law* (1988), 303-4) did not apply, since the wife had sought to participate in the English proceedings, but that, in the light of Articles 40 and 41, s.5 of the 1976 Act should be construed as not meaning that a maintenance order automatically lapsed on the granting of a foreign divorce decree capable of recognition under Irish law, since this 'might result in unjust hardship for those in whose interest the order was made'. It was not difficult to envisage 'many instances of serious injustice, not least to deserted women and children', if the section were so interpreted.

The potential in this approach for transforming Article 41 into actual meaningful protection for families is significant. It is surely only a matter of time before the courts investigate the constitutional validity of the Domicile and Recognition of Foreign Divorces Act 1986, which removes the status of wife from a married woman deserted by a husband who divorces her abroad in the country of his new domicile.

Constitutional Law

ADMINISTRATION OF JUSTICE

Interference with judicial process   Four cases in 1989 concerned alleged interference with the judicial process which, pursuant to Article 34.1 of the Constitution, is given exclusively to judges: *Cashman v Clifford and Attorney General* [1990] ILRM 200; [1989] IR 121; *O'Mahony v Melia* [1990] ILRM 14; [1989] IR 335; *Wheeler v Culligan* [1989] IR 344; and *Shelly v Mahon*, High Court, 31 October 1989; Supreme Court, 8 March 1990.

In *Cashman v Clifford and Attorney General* [1990] ILRM 200; [1989] IR 121 Barron J held invalid certain provisions of the Betting Act 1931 as being an impermissible interference with the judicial process. The applicant was an objector to an application for a bookmaker's licence made under the Betting Act 1931. Upon refusal of the bookmaker's licence, the person applying for the licence appealed to the District Court in accordance with s.13 of the 1931 Act. Pursuant to s.13(5)(a) of the 1931 Act, the relevant Superintendent of the Garda Síochána and the Revenue Commissioners 'and no other person' was entitled to be heard on such appeal. The applicant applied to be heard on the appeal but the respondent Justice refused, and the applicant then sought judicial review.

The applicant argued, inter alia, that the restriction in s.13(5)(a) of the 1931 Act constituted an impermissible interference with the judicial process and was thus invalid. The respondents sought to uphold the restriction on the basis that, since there was no constitutionally guaranteed right of appeal, the Oireachtas was free to restrict the number of appearances permitted. Barron J held, however, in favour of the applicant and granted him a declaration that s.13(5)(a) was invalid.

Barron J distinguished s.13(5)(a) from the provision which was upheld in *The State (McEldowney) v Kelleher* [1985] ILRM 10; [1983] IR 289. He held that, under s.13, there was a *lis* before the District Court but that s.13(5)(a) amounted to an interference with the judicial process in that it restricted the District Court from dealing with the matter before it in accordance with the law applicable to it. In this respect he considered that the provision came within the decision of the Supreme Court in *The State (C.) v Minister for Justice* [1967] IR 106.

Barron J concluded, however, that the offending words 'and no other person' were capable of being severed from the remainder of s.13(5)(a) of the 1931 Act, since this preserved the right of the local superintendent and the Revenue Commissioners to be heard on the appeal. Although Barron J did not cite *Maher v Attorney General* [1973] IR 140 or *King v Attorney General* [1981] IR 233, he would appear to have taken a quite liberal approach to the 'legislative intention' test which is relevant here. He then remitted the case to the District Court for the respondent Justice to exercise his discretion as to whether to permit the applicant to appear on the hearing of the appeal.

The second case on Article 34.1 was *O'Mahony v Melia* [1989] IR 335. In this case, the power of Peace Commissioners to determine bail applications was held to be unconstitutional. The applicants, husband and wife, had been charged in a Garda station before the respondent Peace Commissioner with certain offences under the Misuse of Drugs Acts 1977 and 1984. When the arresting Garda objected to bail, the respondent remanded the applicants in custody overnight pursuant to s.15 of the Criminal Justice Act 1951 (as substituted by s.26 of the Criminal Justice Act 1984). At the sitting of the District Court the next day, the applicants were again remanded in custody. The applicants sought judicial review of the respondent's order remanding them in custody overnight and a declaration that s.15 of the 1951 Act (as substituted by s.26 of the 1984 Act) was invalid for breach of Article 34.1 of the Constitution. Keane J granted the relief sought.

He held, first, that the applicants had *locus standi* to challenge s.15 of the 1951 Act since, although the effects of any declaration of invalidity would be a matter for their trial judge, their constitutional rights could be said to be threatened if the legislation were invalid. On this basis, Keane J held that the applicants fell within the general standing rule in *Cahill v Sutton* [1980] IR 269.

As to the main issue put forward, Keane J quoted with approval the *dicta* of Walsh J in *The State (Lynch) v Ballagh* [1987] ILRM 65; [1986] IR 203. Converting the doubts of Walsh J as to the propriety of Peace Commissioners exercising bail powers into a constitutional condemnation, Keane J held that the determination by the respondent under s.15 of the 1951 Act (as substituted by s.26 of the 1984 Act) was clearly in the nature of a judicial, not an administrative, act. Accordingly it was, to that extent, invalid having regard to the provisions of Article 34.1. As well as the *dicta* in *The State (Lynch) v Ballagh*, the conclusion arrived at could have been supported by the analysis of the Supreme Court in the *Senezio* case, *The State (Clarke) v Roche* [1987] ILRM 309; [1986] IR 619. It is less likely that the *O'Mahony* case will lead to the level of litigation which resulted from *Senezio* (as to which see the 1987 Review, 78-82 and 1988 Review, 184-8).

The third case in this area in 1989 was *Wheeler v Culligan* [1989] IR 344. In this case the role of the Attorney General under the Extradition (Amendment) Act 1987 was upheld. The Extradition Act 1965 provides that an extradition warrant issued in the United Kingdom requires the endorsement of the Garda Commissioner before any further steps in the extradition procedure can take place. The 1987 Act amended the terms of s.44 of the 1965 Act by requiring the Attorney General to examine such extradition warrants. The Attorney is empowered by the 1987 Act to give a direction to the Commissioner not to enforce the warrant. The Attorney is required to form an opinion as to whether: (a) there is a clear intention to prosecute the person named in the warrant for the offence specified in it and (b) the intention to prosecute is founded on sufficient evidence. The applicant was ordered to be extradited to England on foot of a number of extradition warrants which had been endorsed by the Garda Commissioner in accordance with the 1965 Act as amended by the 1987 Act. The applicant challenged the constitutional validity of the 1987 Act on the ground that the Attorney was exercising the judicial power contrary to Article 34.1. Costello J dismissed the claim.

He concluded that the Attorney General was not determining a judicial controversy or making an adjudication in exercising his powers under the 1987 Act, and was thus not exercising a power which the courts alone could exercise. In coming to this conclusion, Costello J cited passages from the well-known decisions in *Lynham v Butler (No. 2)* [1933] IR 74 and *McDonald v Bord na gCon* [1965] IR 217.

Costello J backed up his conclusion by assessing the impact of the Attorney's role in the extradition process. He opined that the functions exercised by the Attorney are procedural and not judicial in nature, and are similar to those exercised by the Garda Commissioner under the 1965 Act. He pointed out that the constitutionality of the Commissioner's powers had been upheld by the Supreme Court in *Shannon v Ireland* [1985] ILRM 449; [1984] IR 548. He also held that they were also comparable to the Attorney's function in determining whether to prosecute in cases where he is the prosecuting authority.

Costello J made one final point of note. He said that the judicial determination of the matter remained exclusively a matter for the courts, as the Supreme Court in *Shannon* had required. That would certainly appear to be the case where the Attorney decides to endorse a warrant. What of the situation where the Attorney declines to endorse for stated reasons? It need hardly be said that not all decisions in adjudicative settings amount to the exercise of the judicial power. However, the type of decision made by the Attorney under the 1987 Act in the *Fr Ryan* case (see *Irish Times*, 14 December 1988 discussed in the 1988 Review, 155-6) seems to be different in nature to the procedural role of the Garda Commissioner, or of that of the Attorney, as described by Costello J in *Wheeler*. It may be that this still falls short of a judicial determination but it is of more substantive significance than perhaps Costello J ascribed to it.

The fourth decision in this area was *Shelly v Mahon and Anor*, High Court, 31 October 1989; Supreme Court, 8 March 1990. In this case the courts declined to give an unconstitutional meaning to the Courts (No. 2) Act 1988. The background to the passing of the 1988 Act and the instant case were as follows.

The first respondent had been appointed a temporary, and later permanent, District Justice. He had initially given his date of birth as January 1919 whereas in fact it was January 1920. The error was not noticed in the Department of Justice although the respondent had, after his appointment, forwarded his birth certificate with the correct date of birth. Under the Courts of Justice (District Court) Act 1949, a District Justice may be continued in office on reaching the normal retiring age of 65, pursuant to warrants issued on a yearly basis by a Committee sitting under the Act. In January 1984, when the respondent reached 65 years of age, a warrant continuing him in office pursuant to the 1949 Act was not issued owing to the fact that the Department Justice were still under the impression that the respondent had not yet reached 65 years of age. In 1985, a warrant was issued under the 1949 Act on the assumption that the respondent was 65 (he was, of course, 66 at this stage) and further warrants were issued in 1986 and 1987. It was accepted in the instant proceedings that these three warrants were of no effect. It was not until 1988 that the error as to the respondent's age was discovered.

The Courts (No. 2) Act 1988 was passed by the Oireachtas and it purported to provide that warrants could be issued by the Committee which operated under the 1949 Act to validate any orders made by a Justice in the position of the respondent. The applicant had been convicted by the first respondent in 1987 of an offence under the Road Traffic Acts, and he sought to quash the conviction on the ground that the first respondent was not, at the time, a validly appointed Justice. Blayney J, whose decision was affirmed by the Supreme Court, granted the relief sought.

Blayney J held that the applicant's purported conviction was null and void since there had been no trial in due course of law by a validly appointed judge as required by Articles 34.1 and 38.1 of the Constitution. He noted that since s.1(3) of the 1988 Act had made any validation subject to any constitutional rights, it was clear that the 1988 Act could not have the effect of validating a matter which would be in conflict with the applicant's constitutional rights, and so his conviction was quashed.

On appeal by the respondents the Supreme Court (Walsh, Griffin, Hederman and McCarthy JJ; Costello J dissenting) upheld Blayney J's decision. The four judges in the majority held that the 1988 Act could not have the effect contended for by the State. This was primarily because such a construction would involve the Oireachtas in an unconstitutional infringement of the judicial function by the retrospective validation of a conviction of the applicant at a time when he had been tried by a person who was not a judge appointed in accordance with Article 34 of the Constitution and whose conviction was a nullity. The majority were saying, therefore, that the interpretation contended for by the State would permit the Oireachtas to impose a punishment on the applicant. Only Costello J, in dissent, was prepared to take the view that the State's argument did not involve this conclusion.

The majority had no difficulty in holding that the effect of s.1(3) of the 1988 Act was clear in that it made any validation of orders subject to any conflict with constitutional rights at the time that such orders were made, and not simply at any time subsequent to the enactment of the 1988 act itself as had been contended for by the State.

The applicant in *Shelly* might be regarded as being fortunate in some senses in that neither the High Court or the Supreme Court raised any preliminary objections to hearing the case. The judges might have objected that the applicant had acquiesced in the unconstitutional trial before the respondent and therefore was now debarred from raising the infirmity in the trial. That was what the Supreme Court unanimously decided in relation to the jury trial which was challenged in *The State (Byrne) v Frawley* [1978] IR 326. Or the Court could have stated that, for reasons of public policy, it was now too late, two years after the original trial, for the matter to be investigated by way of judicial review; that it was too late to unscramble the egg and that the common good required that relief be refused, as was decided in *Murphy v Attorney General* [1982] IR 241. It might also have been said that, in the circumstances, the applicant was not entitled to certiorari *ex debito justitiae*. As the Chief Justice stated in *DPP (Nagle) v Flynn* [1987] IR 534, 540, where one side relies on a purely technical point unrelated to the merits or justice of the case, the other side is equally entitled to raise a technical point. Whether the courts in the *Shelly* case considered any of these matters is now, of course, a moot point but they might be used in any other application related to the 1988 Act. It would appear therefore (as with the *O'Mahony* case, discussed above) that the *Shelly* case will not cause the kind of difficulties which arose in the light of the decision in *The State (Clarke) v Roche*.

Imposition of penalties The question whether certain penalties should be categorised as criminal in nature, thus requiring a judicial determination under Article 34, was discussed in a revenue context in *McLoughlin v Tuite* [1989] IR 82: see 370, below. The point was also raised, but not discussed, in *O'Connor v Giblin* [1989] IR 583: see 375, below, in the Safety and Health chapter.

Public hearings The requirement in Article 34.1 that justice be administered in public was considered by the Supreme Court in *In re R Ltd* [1989] ILRM 757; [1989] IR 126 (see 55-8, above, in the Company Law chapter.

DAMAGES

The circumstances in which damages for breach of constitutional rights may be awarded were considered in *Greene v Minister for Agriculture* [1990] ILRM 364 (see 101, below).

DWELLING HOUSE INVIOLABILITY

The admissibility of evidence obtained in breach of Article 40.5 of the Constitution was considered in *The People v Kenny (M.)*, Court of Criminal Appeal, 15 June and 30 November 1989; [1990] ILRM 569 (SC) (see 145-9, below, in the Criminal Law chapter).

EQUALITY

The provisions of Article 40.1 loomed large in *MacMathuna v Ireland* [1989] IR 504, an unsuccessful challenge to provisions of the income tax and social welfare codes. The *MacMathuna* case could be said to be in the line of authority going back to *Murphy v Attorney General* [1982] IR 241, and that decision was the basis for much of the substantive argument in the case.

The plaintiffs were a married couple with nine children. The wife had given up paid employment on getting married and the husband's income was the sole family income. The plaintiffs challenged two aspects of the income tax code and one aspect of the social welfare code as being in conflict with Articles 40.1, 41 and 45 of the Constitution. The first claim related to s.138A of the Income Tax Act 1967, as inserted by s.4 of the Finance Act 1979, which provided for a tax-free allowance in respect of single parents, namely, widows, widowers, separated married parents and unmarried mothers. The plaintiffs claimed that this was invalid since they, being married, were not eligible for this allowance whereas an unmarried mother was so eligible. The second claim related to the former tax-free allowances available for children under s.141 of the Income Tax Act 1967, which was abolished by s.4 of the Finance Act 1986 and replaced by an allowance for incapacitated children only. While the former allowance was replaced by increased social welfare children's allowances, the plaintiffs claimed that, pursuant to Article 45, they had a personal right to provide for family members from their own earnings rather then to have a State social welfare payment. They also claimed that in any event the children's allowance had not kept pace with inflation. The third claim related to the introduction in s.8 of the Social Welfare Act 1973 (consolidated in s.197 of the Social Welfare (Consolidation) Act 1981) of a new form of social assistance for unmarried mothers who, in the case of a woman with nine children, would be entitled to more than the plaintiff wife as a married woman. Carroll J dismissed the plaintiffs' claim.

Her judgment dealt with a number of preliminary issues raised by the case. First, citing the views of Keane J in *Somjee v Minister for Justice* [1981] ILRM 324, she pointed out that the Court was not empowered to decide that the plaintiffs were entitled to anything in the nature of tax reliefs or social assistance, since this was entirely a matter for the Oireachtas, even if such reliefs or assistance were considered desirable by the Court. This cautious approach reflects the view expressed in the seminal decision *Ryan v Attorney General* [1965] IR 294. In the taxation context, O'Hanlon J had also been emphatic on this point in *Madigan v Attorney General* [1986] ILRM 136. The second preliminary point raised in *MacMathuna* concerned severability. Carroll J held that the Court could not approach the validity of s.4 of the Finance Act 1986 by declaring that the new allowance for disabled children remained intact but that the repeal of s.141 of the Income Tax Act 1967 did not take effect, since to do so would be to re-write the intention of the Oireachtas, which the court was not empowered to do. She cited the decision in *Maher v Attorney General* [1973] IR 140 in this context. The third preliminary point was in connection with *locus standi*. In considering the plaintiffs' claim viz-a-víz an unmarried mother, Carroll J pointed out that she could not take into account assumptions or hypotheses outside the facts or circumstances of the action before her. Carroll J cited *dicta* of the Supreme Court in *Madigan v Attorney General* [1986] ILRM 136 to that effect.

Then Carroll J proceeded to deal with the substantive issues raised in *MacMathuna*. The arguments in the case were based largely on those raised in *Murphy v Attorney General* [1982] IR 241, namely breach of the equality provisions of Article 40.1 and those regarding the family in Article 41. As in *Murphy* Article 40.1 proved of little value to the plaintiffs, and Carroll J was able to use the proviso against the plaintiffs' arguments.

As to the single parents' tax free allowance under s.138A of the Income Tax Act 1967 (as inserted by s.4 of the Finance Act 1979) Carroll J considered that it was a justifiable discrimination under the proviso to Article 40.1 having regard to the difficulties associated with a single parent bringing up children as opposed to the position pertaining to two parents. The relevant passages from *Murphy v Attorney General* [1982] IR 241 (where the proviso was also used extensively) were approved in this context.

As to the social assistance for unmarried mothers, Carroll J held that since the tax-free allowance under s.138A of the 1967 Act was only available to a person with an income, the State was justified in making provision for child support for a woman on her own with no earnings. This had been done through the allowance introduced by s.8 of the Social Welfare Act 1973 (consolidated in s.197 of the Social Welfare (Consolidation) Act 1981), and she also held that this was justified under Article 40.1. Nor did she consider apt the comparison suggested in argument between the position of the unmarried mother and the plaintiff wife. Once again, the strength given to the Article 40.1 proviso is very clear.

As to the argument based on Article 41, Carroll J held that the plaintiffs had failed to establish that the existence of the benefits to the unmarried constituted inducements not to get married. She found it impossible to accept that a woman would choose, in preference to marriage, to have a baby so that she could draw the unmarried woman's allowance. Carroll J was particularly influenced by the evidence put forward by the State that an unmarried mother would not be allowed to cohabit if she claimed the allowance and that she would have to qualify for the means test imposed under the social welfare code. These points were sufficient to distinguish the instant case from the position in *Murphy v Attorney General* [1982] IR 241 where Article 41 had been used to strike down the relevant provisions of the Income Tax Act 1967 on aggregation of incomes of married couples.

Finally, the plaintiffs had also raised the question of Article 45 of the Constitution, which contains the Directive Principles of Social Policy. Carroll J held that the plaintiffs were not entitled to rely on Article 45 in the instant case in view of the prohibition in it against using any of its provisions where an Act of the Oireachtas was impugned. In that respect, therefore, Carroll J was able to distinguish *Murtagh Properties Ltd v Cleary* [1972] IR 330, where Article 45 had been successfully used to obtain an injunction. See also *Parsons v Kavanagh* [1990] ILRM 560 (discussed in the 1988 Review, xv-xvi). In any event, however, Carroll J held against the plaintiffs on this point by returning to the separation of powers argument mentioned earlier in her judgment. She pointed out that the right claimed under Article 45 was not well founded in view of the power of the Oireachtas to legislate for the nation's finances pursuant to the Constitution. She also held that it was within the competence of the Oireachtas to decide to choose a system of social welfare allowances in lieu of tax-free allowances (reflecting her previous reference to the *Somjee* case, as to which see above), as had been done by s.4 of the Finance Act 1986. Finally, she rejected the plaintiffs' claim that there was any constitutional right that social welfare allowances keep pace with inflation.

FAIR PROCEDURES/NATURAL JUSTICE

The case law on the requirements of Article 40.3, regarding fair procedures in adjudicative hearings, are dealt with in the Administrative Law chapter, above, 5-9.

FAMILY

In *Greene and Ors v Minister for Agriculture and Ors* [1990] ILRM 364, Murphy J returned to an issue which he had previously examined in *Lawlor v Minister for Agriculture* [1988] ILRM 400 (see the 1987 Review, 92-4), that is, the meaning to be given to Article 29.4.3 of the Constitution. In particular he explored the extent to which membership of the European Communities supercedes the provisions of the Constitution. In the instant case, he was satisfied that Article 41 was relevant to the determination of the issues before him. The case arose in the following way.

The plaintiffs were farmers in certain disadvantaged hill areas who had been refused payments under a number of non-statutory schemes introduced by the Minister in purported compliance with the 1975 EEC Directive on Mountain and Hill Farming (75/268/EEC). The 1975 Directive required the member States to introduce mechanisms for the purpose of maintaining reasonable incomes for farmers in disadvantaged hill and mountain areas as well as for the purpose of conservation of such areas. Article 6 of the Directive conferred a discretion on the member States to impose additional or restrictive conditions for granting the payments over and above those laid down in the Directive itself.

The schemes introduced by the Minister laid down a means test for farmers by reference to 'off farm income combined with that of their spouses.' The plaintiffs had all been refused payments under the schemes on the basis that their off farm incomes, combined with their spouses, exceeded the limits laid down by the schemes. The plaintiffs sought declarations and damages on the ground that the schemes were, inter alia, *ultra vires* the 1975 Directive, were outside the discretion conferred by the Directive, were discriminatory and failed to protect the institution of marriage. Murphy J granted the plaintiffs the declarations they had sought but not damages.

He first examined the 1975 Directive and concluded that it was intended both to conserve the environment and to provide a reasonable income for farmers, and having regard to the latter objective the Minister was entitled to employ a means test. Although the scheme as drafted led to some anomalies he held that this was not a sound reason for condemning its validity.

Having rejected the claim on this front, the next crucial step was as to whether ther plaintiffs could rely on Article 41 of the Constitution. This in turn depended on the meaning to be attributed to Article 29.4.3, the Third Amendment of the Constitution under which provisions of the Constitution may not be invoked to invalidate any step 'necessitated' by membership of the European Communities. Was the Minister's scheme 'necessitated' by the terms of the 1975 Directive? Murphy J answered in the negative. He applied the view he had put forward in *Lawlor v Minister for Agriculture* [1988] ILRM 400, without feeling required to discuss some of the difficulties which might be associated with his formulation of that test: see the 1987 Review, 93.

Murphy J acknowledged that while some scheme was 'necessitated' to implement the 1975 Directive within the meaning of Article 29.4.3, it did not follow that every such scheme was so necessitated. While some flexibility was to be allowed to the member States, he considered that there was a point where the discretion conferred by a Directive and exercised by the member State was so far-reaching that it could not be said to have been 'necessitated'. He concluded that the Minister's scheme had passed that point. In particular, Murphy J held that the 1975 Directive did not require anything in the nature of a provision dealing with the income of farmers or their spouses, and so the exclusion in Article 29.4.3 was not applicable to the instant case.

This conclusion allowed Murphy J to rely on the case law arising from Article 41 of the Constitution and in particular *Murphy v Attorney General* [1982] IR 241, as explained in *Muckley v Ireland* [1986] ILRM 364; [1985] IR 472. In the light of these decisions, he concluded that the provisions dealing with incomes of farmers and their spouses did not conflict with Article 40.1 as being discriminatory. Although he appeared to concede the point made by counsel for the plaintiffs that this constituted a narrow view of Article 40.1, he felt constrained by the *Murphy* decision to steer clear of any wider interpetation suggested by Professor Kelly in *The Irish Constitution* (1980), 347 (expanded in the 2nd ed. (1984), 446ff).

However, also applying the *Murphy* case, he held that there was a clear failure to uphold the institution of marriage within Article 41, since there was a burden imposed on married couples living together which was substantially different from the burden placed on unmarried couples living together. Taking his lead from the *Muckley* decision, Murphy J noted that there was no need for there to be an increasing burden in this context. He also referred with approval to the decision of Barrington J in *Hyland v Minister for Social Welfare* [1989] ILRM 196 (later upheld by the Supreme Court: [1990] ILRM 213; [1989] IR 624: see 264, below).

Murphy J then examined the consequences of his findings. Applying the severance test in *The State (McLoughlin) v Eastern Health Board* [1986] IR

416, he held that the plaintiffs were not entitled to a declaration of severance of the offensive conditions from the remainder of the schemes since to do so would be to operate a very different scheme from that intended. Neither, he concluded, were the plaintiffs entitled to damages arising from the *ultra vires* action of the Minister (even assuming such action sounded in damages) since it could not be presumed that, if the scheme had operated without the offensive conditions, money would have been available from the government for payment of the sums now being claimed by the plaintiffs. While he accepted that the Minister had failed to protect the institution of marriage it had not been shown that the plaintiffs' personal rights had been infringed, unlike the plaintiffs in *Pine Valley Developments Ltd v Minister for the Environment* [1987] ILRM 747; [1987] IR 23. Accordingly he held that the plaintiffs were entitled to declaratory relief only.

Finally, Murphy J made an important comment on the representative nature of the instant case. He noted that, in addition to the named plaintiffs, there were a further 1,390 farmers whose names had been transmitted by agreement to the defendants and he concluded that it was clear from the evidence that they had all authorised the proceedings on their behalf and in their name. Murphy J, acknowledging that his comments were not necessarily relevant in view of the conclusions that he had reached on damages, made the point that these 1,390 farmers would have been entitled to the benefit of any decision which had awarded damages. Thus, while Irish law does not confer any legal standing on the phrase 'test case' the procedure adopted in the instant case comes very close to giving full effect to such an idea. It also has the effect of avoiding the 'no retrospection' rule established in *Murphy v Attorney General* [1982] IR 241.

The provisions of Article 41 were also considered in *MacMathuna v Ireland* [1989] IR 504 (98, above).

Further case law on Article 41 is discussed in the Family law chapter, below.

INJUNCTION

In *Grange Developments Ltd v Dublin County Council (No.4)* [1989] IR 377, Murphy J confirmed the view that the initiation of a constitutional action does not in itself entitle the plaintiff to an injunction preventing enforcement of the legislative provisions under challenge. He referred to the similar view taken by the Supreme Court in *Cooke v Minister for Communications*, Irish Times LR, 20 February 1989. For discussion of the principles involved, by which an injunction might be granted, see Kelly, *The Irish Constitution*, 2nd ed., Supplement (1987), 72-5.

INTERNATIONAL RELATIONS

The provisions of Article 29.4.3, as they apply to membership of the European Communities, were considered by Murphy J in *Greene v Minister for Agriculture* [1990] ILRM 364: see above, 100.

LIBERTY

The extent of the inquiry authorised by Article 40.4 of the Constitution was discussed in *McGlinchey v Ireland*, High Court, 8 June 1989 (see 178, below in the Criminal Law chapter).

LIFE OF UNBORN

In 1989, the Supreme Court dealt with two more cases arising from Article 40.3.3 of the Constitution. In *Society for the Protection of Unborn Children (Irl) Ltd v Coogan and Ors* [1990] ILRM 70; [1989] IR 734, the Supreme Court affirmed the right of the plaintiff Society to seek injunctive relief without the need for the intervention of the Attorney General (see below in the Locus Standi section).

Further procedural issues were discussed in *Society for the Protection of Unborn Children (Irl) Ltd v Grogan and Ors* [1990] ILRM 350; [1989] IR 753. However the members of the Court also took the opportunity to indicate their views on the substantive content of Article 40.3.3. The plaintiff Society applied for interlocutory injunctions against the defendants preventing the publication or distribution by them of information calculated to inform persons of the identity and location of and the method of communication with clinics where abortions are performed contrary to Article 40.3.3 of the Constitution. The defendants were members of the Union of Students of Ireland, the Student's Union of University College Dublin and the Students' Union of Trinity College Dublin. In the High Court the defendants asserted a right to distribute such information by virtue of the Treaty of Rome. Without expressing a final view on the merits of that asserted right, Carroll J made an order referring certain questions arising from the assertion to the Court of Justice of the EC pursuant to Article 177 of the Treaty of Rome. She declined to make an order in relation to the application by the plaintiff for an interlocutory injunction. The course adopted by Carroll J was to be subjected to some criticism in the Supreme Court.

On appeal by the plaintiff Society, the Court (Finlay CJ, Walsh, Griffin, Hederman and McCarthy JJ) unanimously granted the interlocutory injunction sought. Although the Court did not interfere with the Article 177 reference, the judgments contain some important comments on the relationship between Article 40.3.3 and Article 29.4.3 of the Constitution.

The defendants argued strongly that the Supreme Court did not have jurisdiction to entertain the appeal at all. First, it was argued that to do so would affect the Article 177 reference, and second the High Court had not actually refused to grant an interlocutory injunction and so there was no order or determination of the Court against which to appeal. Both points were rejected by the Supreme Court. As to the first point, it was held that while the order of the High Court did not expressly refuse an interlocutory injunction, this was in reality a separate issue from the reference of questions to the Court of Justice of the EC and the Supreme Court thus had jurisdiction to entertain an appeal from the High Court without affecting the reference. On this basis, therefore, the Court was able to stand by its own decision in *Campus Oil Ltd v Minister for Industry and Energy* [1983] IR 82 by which it held that Article 177 references by the High Court were not, in general, appealable. For criticism of the allegedly self-imposed discipline of the *Campus Oil* case see the articles cited in McMahon and Murphy, *European Community Law in Ireland*, 228. As to Carroll J's silence on the application for interlocutory injunction, the Supreme Court held that the deferral or postponement of a decision on this was, in effect, to decline or refuse to make an interlocutory injunction. Having regard, therefore, to the appellate jurisdiction of the Supreme Court pursuant to Article 34.4.3 the plaintiff had a right of appeal to the Supreme Court on the issue of whether an injunction should be granted.

The Supreme Court then turned to the substantive issues raised by the application. All five judges held that it was clear that the activities of the defendants were unlawful having regard to the provisions of Article 40.3.3 of the Constitution. In argument on the defendants' behalf, it had been suggested that the instant case was distinguishable from the activities which had been prohibited by the Court in *Attorney General (SPUC Ltd) v Open Door Counselling Ltd* [1989] ILRM 19; [1988] IR 593. In *Open Door*, it was suggested, there was the additional element of individualised non-directive counselling as well as publication of information. In the instant case, there was publication of information only and this was already available prior to the application for the injunction and so the interlocutory relief should be refused. This point of distinction was accepted by Carroll J as the basis for her decision to refer the case to the Court of Justice, but the Supreme Court rejected the argument. Finlay CJ stated:

It is clearly the fact that such information is conveyed to pregnant women, and not the method of communication, which creates the unconstitutional illegality, and the judgment of this Court in the *Open Door Counselling* case is not open to any other interpretation. This application for an interlocutory injunction, therefore, consists of an application to restrain activity which has been clearly declared by this Court to be unconstitutional and therefore unlawful and which could assist — and is intended to assist — in the destruction of the right to life of an unborn child, a right acknowledged and protected under the Constitution.

That constitutionally guaranteed right must be fully and effectively protected by the courts.

Having regard to the questions of the *status quo* and the balance of convenience, the Court went on to hold that the interlocutory injunction should be granted. As to the deferral by Carroll J of a decision on this question, Walsh J was particularly critical, categorising it as amounting to a suspension of the provisions of Article 40.3.3 of the Constitution for an indefinite period. He added: 'It is not open to any judge to do anything which in effect suspends any provision of the Constitution for any period whatsoever.'

The judgments in the Supreme Court adverted to one other important matter: the fact that the case had been referred to the Court of Justice of the EC. Finlay CJ (with whom Griffin and Hederman JJ agreed), having made it clear that under Irish constitutional law the impugned conduct was unconstitutional, contented himself with stating that if and when the Court of Justice of the EC rules that some aspect of EC law affects the activities of the defendants, the consequence of such decision would fall to be considered having regard to Article 40.3.3 of the Constitution. A different plurality of the Court, comprising Walsh, Hederman and McCarthy JJ (Hederman J agreeing both with the judgment of the Chief Justice and that of Walsh J), made some very strong comments indicating their view of the relationship between Articles 29.4.3 and 40.3.3. McCarthy J noted the possibility that in enacting Article 40.3.3 in 1983 the People of Ireland may have acted in breach of Article 29.4.3 which had been approved in 1972. Walsh J rejected in trenchant terms the possibility that the right to life of the unborn could in any circumstances be subordinated to the requirements of membership of the European Communities. Walsh J also pointed out that Article 40.3.3 had been enacted after Article 29.4.3. Finally, both Walsh and McCarthy JJ were clear that in the last analysis the Supreme Court had the final say on what the domestic effect of constitutional provisions were to be, though Walsh J, as already indicated, made clear his view as to what the Supreme Court should decide if the Court of Justice were to hold in favour of the defendants in the instant case.

Some interesting questions remain in this light. The Supreme Court appear to have decided that, under Irish constitutional law (including its European dimension), Article 40.3.3 prevails over any European Community norm. In contrast, from the standpoint of Community law, it must be questioned whether it is permissible for the Supreme Court to hold, in effect, that the Court of Justice has no jurisdiction to decide that the ECJ's view of Community law should take priority over the Supreme Court's view of Article 40.3.3. On the other side, does the Court of Justice have jurisdiction to hold that the right to life of the mother (which is given an 'equal' standing to that of the right to life of the unborn in Article 40.3.3 but whose effect has not been fully explained in Irish courts) may validate the information's being supplied by the defendants? Could it be argued that in 1983 the People of Ireland, in enacting Article 40.3.3, must have taken account of Community membership and thus accepted that Article 40.3.3 could be subordinated to EC law (rather than modifying the terms of Article 29.4.3 as suggested by McCarthy J)? This might be a difficult argument to sustain, on the basis of how the public debate unfolded. In approving the terms of the Single European Act in 1987 (and further amending Article 29.4.3) did the People modify any previously made amendments to the Constitution, including Article 40.3.3, in order to take account of the expanding nature of the Community? Again, this would seem hard to establish, in the light of assurances given by proponents of the change. The decision of the Court of Justice on the Article 177 reference may provide some answers to these questions. It seems clear from the Supreme Court's decision, however, that whatever the Court of Justice may have to say the answer is determinable ultimately according to Irish constitutional norms, on which the Supreme Court, rather than the Court of Justice, is reserving the last word. The prospect of a conflict between the two is in theory very real, though one may suspect that, on such a sensitive issue as abortion, the Court of Justice will be circumspect about provoking such a fundamental clash.

LOCUS STANDI

Attorney General Further comments on the role of the Attorney in asserting constitutional rights were made in Society for the *Protection of Unborn Children (Irl) Ltd v Coogan and Ors* [1990] ILRM 70; [1989] IR 734 (discussed below).

Exceptions to usual standing rule   The Supreme Court's view of the uniqueness of Article 40.3.3 of the Constitution continued in *Society for the Protection of Unborn Children (Irl) Ltd v Coogan and Ors* [1989] ILRM 526 (HC); [1990] ILRM 70 (SC); [1989] IR 734. The plaintiff Society sought an interlocutory injunction preventing the publication or distribution of a booklet entitled *Welfare Guide UCD 88/89*. The defendants were eight elected officers of University College Dublin Students' Union, a printer and UCD itself. The plaintiff argued that the contents of the Guide would constitute an undermining of the right to life of the unborn guaranteed protection in Article 40.3.3.

In the High Court Carroll J held that the plaintiff had no *locus standi* to seek the injunction: see the 1988 Review, 117. The plaintiff appealed to the Supreme Court, and in the course of the hearing the Court sought and obtained the views of the Attorney General as to his role and function. The Attorney disclaimed any exclusive claim to assert constitutional rights. In effect, the Supreme Court (Finlay CJ, Walsh, Griffin and Hederman JJ; McCarthy J dissenting) agreed with the argument put forward by the Attorney. The Court allowed the plaintiff's appeal and remitted the injunction proceedings to the High Court.

The four judges of the majority held that the plaintiff Society had sufficient *locus standi* to maintain the proceedings having regard to two factors in particular: its previous involvement in similar proceedings regarding Article 40.3.3 and, more generally, its proximity to or interest in the protection of the particular constitutional right which it was sought to protect, namely, the right to life of the unborn.

Walsh J made the additional point that circumstances could very well arise in which it would be entirely inappropriate for the Attorney General to be regarded as to the sole person with power to assert constitutional claims. He instanced possible conflicts of interest in which State institutions might be alleged to be in breach of Article 40.3.3. He stated that it would be intolerable to expect the Attorney General both to defend the actions of the State institution and at the same time be the sole person with standing to challenge that institution. In such situations, it was important for ordinary citizens to exercise their right of access to the courts. He cited *dicta* from the Supreme Court decision in *The State (Ennis) v Farrell* [1966] IR 107 on the necessity for the continuation of the private prosecutor as support for this view.

McCarthy J dissented on a relatively narrow point. He noted that when the Attorney General had been consulted on the hearing of the appeal, he had offered to consider converting the proceedings into a relator action. The plaintiff Society declined to take up this offer, and in such circumstances McCarthy J did not consider that the plaintiff could be regarded as having the requisite standing.

It may be noted that the same 4-1 breakdown later emerged in the Court when the question of costs was dealt with: *Society for the Protection of Unborn Children (Irl) Ltd v Coogan and Ors (No. 2)*, Supreme Court, 20 March 1990. The majority held that the plaintiff Society was entitled to its costs of the Supreme Court appeal. For the majority, Finlay CJ pointed out that there were no grounds for departing from the usual principle that costs follow the event, and that it would require very substantial reasons of an unusual kind before the Court would depart from that principle. McCarthy J was again the lone dissentient. He was of the view that the application for costs was premature and should await the final outcome of the case.

It would appear that these proceedings have, in effect, been superceded by the fresh injunction proceedings brought by the plaintiff: *Society for the Protection of Unborn Children (Irl) Ltd v Grogan and Ors* [1990] ILRM 350; [1989] IR 753 which is discussed above (102-5).

Rights threatened   In *O'Mahony v Melia* [1990] ILRM 14; [1989] IR 335, Keane J held that the plaintiffs' rights were threatened by the statutory provisions being challenged: see 92, above. A similar view was taken by Costello J in *McGlinchey v Ireland (No. 2)*, High Court, 6 December 1989: see 151, below, in the Criminal Law chapter.

Third party claims excluded   The usual rule precluding the use of third party arguments was applied by Carroll J in *MacMathuna v Ireland* [1989] IR 504 (97, above).

NAME OF STATE

The correct designation of the State (Ireland) was discussed by the Supreme Court in *Ellis v O'Dea* [1990] ILRM 87; [1989] IR 530 (see 160-1, below, in the Criminal Law chapter).

OIREACHTAS

Dáil dissolution   *O'Malley and Anor v An Taoiseach and Anor* [1990] ILRM 461 raised some difficult — and highly publicised — issues as to the validity of the 1989 General Election. It might also serve as a useful study on the distinction between the *ratio decidendi* of a case and the concept of *obiter dicta*. The case arose on the eve of the 1989 election.

The plaintiffs sought an interlocutory injunction restraining An Taoiseach from dissolving Dáil Éireann unless and until further legislation was passed

by the Oireachtas to revise the Dáil constituencies to ensure compliance with
Article 16 of the Constitution. Article 16.2 requires the Oireachtas to revise
the constituencies 'at least once in every twelve years'; that the ratio between
each Dáil deputy and the population shall be between 20,000 to 30,000; and
that the ratio in each constituency, as ascertained at the last preceding census,
'shall, so far as is practicable, be the same throughout the country.' At the
date of the present application, the last revision of constituencies had been
effected by the Electoral (Amendment) Act 1983, and the most recent census
had been held in 1986. The plaintiffs adduced evidence from the Dáil Éireann
Constituency Commission Report 1988, whose Report (Pl. 5984) had not
been implemented because of the lack of consensus in Dáil Éireann on the
thrust of its recommendations and also because the then government lacked
the majority to vote through amending electoral legislation. The 1988 Report
indicated substantial variations from the national average in the ratio of Dáil
deputies to the population and more substantial variations as between
particular constituencies.

Hamilton P (who had chaired the 1988 Constituency Commission)
dismissed the plaintiffs' claim. The structure of his judgment is of interest.
First, he dealt with all the substantive points raised by the plaintiffs, and it
was only towards the end of his judgment that he dismissed the application
on the grounds that the courts had no jurisdiction to intervene in the situation
which presented itself. Arguably, therefore, some of the President's
judgment could be categorised as *obiter*. This was to give rise to debate in
the days immediately after he had given judgment.

On the substance of the plaintiffs' claim, Hamilton P held that it was clear
from the evidence that the ratio between the number of members to be elected
from each of the constituencies as they stood to the population as ascertained
at the last Census were not the same, so far as was practicable, within the
meaning of Article 16.2. He cited a number of instances from the 1988
Constituency Commission Report to support this point. In a crucial passage
he stated:

> No revision has taken place since the last Census in 1986 and I am
> satisfied that the Oireachtas is in breach of its constitutional obligation
> to revise the constituencies, particularly when the Census discloses a
> major change in the distribution of population, and the fact that the ratio
> between the number of members to be elected at any time for each
> constituency and the population of each constituency as ascertained at
> the last preceding Census is not so far as is practicable . . . the same
> throughout the country.

Hamilton P then went on to say that it was 'against this background' that the plaintiffs sought the relief applied for. For students of the *ratio decidendi/obiter dictum* distinction, it might be said that this appears to put in context the rest of the President's judgment and could thus be regarded as part of the *ratio decidendi* of the decision (as indicated below, this was not the view subsequently taken by the judge himself). On this reading, the passage quoted could amount to a judicial determination that the 1989 general election had been held on the basis of unconstitutional constituencies. Does this make the election itself invalid? Professor Kelly has so suggested in *The Irish Constitution*, 2nd ed.,109. However, Professor Casey has pointed out that if this is the case then a constitutional impasse would result since there is no mechanism to overcome the situation, and that it was more likely that the courts would adopt a 'common good' approach to uphold the validity of such elections: *Constitutional Law in Ireland*, 94. The latter view would seem to be the more likely to find favour (Professor Casey citing *In re the Electoral (Amendment) Bill 1961* [1961] IR 169 and *de Burca v Attorney General* [1976] IR 38). This point was not addressed by Hamilton P in his judgment.

He held, quite simply, that the courts had no jurisdiction to place any impediment between the President and An Taoiseach in relation to the dissolution of Dáil Éireann. He quoted the terms of Article 13.2 and 13.8 of the Constitution in support of this conclusion. In view of the urgency of the matter, it is not surprising that his judgment does not contain a list of precedents to support this conclusion. In any event, the Supreme Court decision in *Finn v Attorney General* [1983] IR 154 confirms this general reluctance to interfere with the functions of the Oireachtas.

Despite this strong indication that the courts would not intervene in the situation which presented itself, there was public discussion in the days after the *O'Malley* decision as to whether the impending General Election was constitutionally valid. This gave rise to an application on behalf of counsel for the Taoiseach and the Attorney General as to the status of the President's comments in his judgment rejecting the injunctive relief sought. Hamilton P is reported to have stated (see *Irish Times*, 26 May 1989 and [1990] ILRM 465n) that the reasons for dismissing the application were clearly stated in his judgment and that any other statement made or view expressed was *obiter*. He pointed out that, since the application had been for interlocutory relief, the full case was still before the courts and that it would not therefore be appropriate to make a final ruling on the substance of the issues raised. This clearly corresponds with the decision of the Supreme Court in *Irish Shell Ltd v Elm Motors Ltd* [1984] ILRM 596; [1984] IR 200. Nonetheless, it is unusual for a judge to be able to state that certain parts of his judgment should be regarded as *obiter*; ordinarily, it falls to other judges to make the *ratio/obiter* distinction.

The substantive issues in the *O'Malley* case were not litigated, and no election petitions emerged in the aftermath of the June General Election. There had been suggestions that such petitions might emerge from unsuccessful candidates in constituencies, such as those identified by Hamilton P in his *O'Malley* judgment, which diverged from the average population-to-seats ratio: see *Irish Times*, 26 May 1989. Had such cases emerged, the courts might in any event have taken the 'common good' approach to the validity of the elections, as suggested by Professor Casey (see above).

Dáil failing to elect Taoiseach   The result of the 1989 general election gave rise to another constitutional debate, arising from the initial failure of the reassembled Dáil to elect any person to the post of An Taoiseach. When the Dáil first voted on 29 May 1989, Mr Haughey, the outgoing Taoiseach, failed to command a majority of the votes in the Dáil. Since the other two candidates for the position, Mr Dukes and Mr Spring, also failed to secure a favourable vote, the Dail had reached the situation for the first time in its history that it had failed to elect a person to the Taoiseach's position after a general election. The question which then arose was whether Mr Haughey was required to resign immediately by Article 28.10 of the Constitution. Mr Haughey announced to the Dáil that he had been advised by the Attorney General that he was not required to resign immediately and that he proposed to adjourn the House to facilitate further consultations between the political parties. After some apparent disagreement between the Opposition as to what the correct approach should be the Dáil was adjourned for some hours. On the resumption of the Dáil later that night, Mr Haughey stated that, although he did not consider it necessary to do so, he was resigning as Taoiseach. Under Article 28.11 of the Constitution, the government continued to carry out its functions under what became known for the next days as the 'caretaker Taoiseach.' After further discussions, in particular with the Progressive Democrats Party, a Fianna Fáil/Progressive Democrats programme for Government was drawn up and Mr Haughey was elected Taoiseach.

The Article 28.10 issue did not, therefore, require resolution in any formal sense since Mr Haughey resigned without conceding the validity of the advice he had been given by the Attorney General. No doubt the text of Article 28.10 states that the Taoiseach 'shall' resign on losing the support of Dáil Éireann, but the argument put forward was that the Constitution does not state 'shall immediately resign.' Whether such an argument would be accepted is now moot, but the decision in *Weekes v Revenue Commissioners* [1989] ILRM 165 might be of interest in this context: see the 1988 Review, 367-8. On the role of the 'caretaker Taoiseach' see Morgan, *Irish Times*, 1 July 1989, and his *Constitutional Law of Ireland*, 2nd ed. (1990).

Election legislation The Electoral (Amendment) Act 1989 amended s.91 of the Electoral Act 1963 to allow for the holding of the Údarás na Gaeltachta election on the same date (15 June 1989) as the general election and the election to the European Parliament. The 1989 Act was given effect to by the European Parliament, Dáil Election and Údarás na Gaeltachta Election Regulations 1989 (SI No.128).

Election petition The European Parliament election in 1989 gave rise to an election petition arising from an extremely close result in the Leinster constituency. In *Bell v Tehan and Fitzsimons, Irish Times*, 25 November and 6 December 1989 Hamilton P dismissed the petition by the applicant who claimed, inter alia, that the respondent Returning Officer had wrongly excluded certain ballot papers as spoiled votes. The European election had, as we have seen already, been held on the same date as the general election and the petitioner argued that some electors who had voted 1, 2, 3 etc. in the general election had continued their preferences 10, 11, 12 etc. for the European election. It appeared that such European votes were deemed spoiled by the Returning Officer in the Leinster constituency. The petitioner claimed that there should be a recount involving the votes which had been deemed spoiled. It emerged during the course of the petition that other Returning Officers in the European election had taken a different approach to that adopted in the Leinster constituency in connection with such 'continuation' preferences.

Hamilton P ordered a *de bene esse* recount of all the votes cast in the election, including the votes which had been excluded. As a result of the recount the second respondent, who had been elected just ahead of the petitioner, held a slightly increased margin. Arising from this, the President was able to conclude that the exclusion of the disputed papers had not materially affected the outcome of the election. He therefore declined to rule on the validity of the decision made by the Returning Officer in the instant case to exclude the disputed papers. He was reported as saying that he was 'expressing no opinion, good, bad or indifferent, on the issue as to whether the returning officer was correct.' It might be speculated that Hamilton P made such a clear disavowal of comment in the light of the political controversy which his comments in the *O'Malley* case had provoked earlier in the year in the general election context: see above. A more likely explanation is the practice in election petitions to avoid substantive issues where there has been no material effect on the result: see *Dillon-Leetch v Calleary*, Supreme Court, 31 July 1974.

Legislation: expression of principles The nature of the exclusive power of the Oireachtas to legislate was raised in dramatic form in *McDaid v Sheehy* *and Ors* [1989] ILRM 342. In the wake of the (arguably *obiter*: see the discussion below) comments of Blayney J in the case, grave disquiet was expressed in Dáil Éireann as to the constitutional validity of central aspects of the annual tax-raising mechanisms employed under the Imposition of Duties Act 1957. It may be noted that substantial doubts as to the constitutional validity of the 1957 Act had already been expressed by Hogan, (1985) 7 *DULJ (ns)* 134. The conclusions arrived at in *McDaid* reflect closely the analysis in that note on the Act.

The disquiet which emerged in the light of *McDaid* arose against a somewhat modest legal background. The applicant in *McDaid* had been convicted in the District Court with the offence of keeping in his vehicle certain hydrocarbon oil chargeable with an excise duty on which a rebate of duty had been allowed under the Imposition of Duties (No.221) (Excise Duties) Order 1975, contrary to s.21 of the Finance Act 1935, as amended, *inter alia*, by the 1975 Order. The conviction was upheld by the respondent Circuit Court judge. The 1975 Order was made pursuant to s.1 of the 1957 Act, by which the government are empowered to impose customs duties, by statutory order, with or without qualifications or limitations 'of such amount as they think proper on any particular description of goods imported into the State.' S.2 of the 1957 Act provides that any such excise order shall have effect only until the end of the calendar year in which it is made, unless it is confirmed by Act of the Oireachtas. The 1975 Order had been confirmed by s.46 of the Finance Act 1976, and the applicant had been convicted in respect of an offence alleged to have been committed in 1984.

The applicant sought judicial review of his conviction on the ground that the 1957 Act permitted the government to exercise the legislative power contrary to Article 15.2.1 of the Constitution, and that the 1975 Order was thus invalid. The respondent argued that the delegation of power to the government was permissible and that, in any event, the Order had been confirmed by the 1976 Act. Ultimately, Blayney J held against the applicant on the basis of the validation of the 1975 Order by the Finance Act 1976, but he made some important comments before coming to that conclusion.

It might be appropriate at this point to raise a preliminary objection to the manner in which Blayney J tackled the issues raised in the case. The first sentence of his judgment reads:

This application for judicial review raises for consideration an important issue of constitutional law, namely whether the Imposition of Duties Act 1957 is invalid having regard to the provisions of the Constitution.

In the light of his findings that the applicant's conviction should stand because of the validation of the 1975 Order by the Finance Act 1976, this statement by Blayney J would not appear to be entirely accurate. Since the case was, ultimately, disposed of in the manner indicated, might it not be argued that the constitutional question did not, in fact, arise and thus should not have been alluded to at all? The general rule that 'constitutional issues should be reached last' would appear to apply here. Recent decisions of the Supreme Court would seem appropriate: see *Murphy v Roche* [1987] IR 106 and *Brady v Donegal County Council* [1989] ILRM 282 (discussed in the 1988 Review, 125-6). If this is the correct view, then the comments of Blayney J on the constitutional question might be regarded as *obiter*. Be that as it may, the judgment deals with important issues of constitutional law, and the following discussion takes place in that light.

Blayney J took as his starting point on the constitutional question the leading decision of the Supreme Court in *Cityview Press Ltd v An Chomhairle Oiliúna* [1980] IR 381. In that case the Court acknowledged that the authorisation of secondary legislation was a part of most Acts of the Oireachtas. The crucial point made by the Court was that the Oireachtas, to accord with Article 15.2.1 of the Constitution, must provide a scheme of principles and policy in the primary legislation so that the vires of the secondary legislation may be tested. In the absence of such a scheme of principles and policy, the authorisation by the Oireachtas is unconstitutional.

Applying this test to the 1957 Act, Blayney J was of the view that the powers given to the government by the 1957 Act allowed for more than mere implementation of principles and policies. This was for the simple reason that there were no principles and policies in the 1957 Act; the government were given the power to legislate, since they were free to determine what imported goods were to bear a customs or excise duty and to determine the amount to be levied, and this was not a question of filling in details. In effect, the 1957 Act amounted to a blank cheque to the government, something the Oireachtas was not empowered to give under Article 15.2.1. On this basis, Blayney J concluded that s.1 of the 1957 Act was invalid as was the 1975 Order at the time it had been made. However, this did not end the matter for the applicant, as Blayney J went on to consider the effect of the confirmation of the 1975 Order by the Finance Act 1976.

On this point, he held that the confirmation of the 1975 Order by s.46 of the 1976 Act indicated that the Oireachtas intended to give legislative effect to the 1975 Order. And while it was possible, he acknowledged, to interpret s.46 as having no effect (the 1975 Order being invalid) s.46 was capable of a construction which indicated that the 1975 Order was to have legal effect without infringing the prohibition on retrospective criminal laws contained in Article 15.5. For this reason there was no defect in the applicant's conviction. Blayney J relied on the views of Henchy J, speaking for the Supreme Court, in *Doyle v An Taoiseach* [1986] ILRM 693. In that case,

Henchy J cast doubt on the views of Barrington J in the High Court who had indicated that an invalid Order could not be validated by a subsequent Act.

The *Doyle* case is of interest for another reason. In the High Court, Barrington J had sought the views of the European Court of Justice on certain aspects of the case. When the case ultimately reached the Supreme Court, the matter was resolved on a domestic law point. Henchy J made it quite clear that, as in constitutional issues, the courts should not address a Community law if the case can be dealt with on another basis. It is a pity that this aspect of *Doyle* was not adverted to in the *McDaid* case.

For further discussion of Article 15.2.1 of the Constitution, see *Harvey v Minister for Social Welfare* [1990] ILRM 185 (394-5, below, in the Social Welfare chapter).

Legislation: suspension by government   The decision in *Purcell v Attorney General*, High Court, 14 November 1989 is remarkable for the fact that Barron J held that the Farm Tax Act 1985, which has not been repealed, no longer represented the will of the Oireachtas and was therefore not to be enforced. This conclusion arose from the decision announced by the government in the Minister for Finance's 1987 Budget speech that it would cease to operate the 1985 Act. As Barron J noted in the *Purcell* case, the effects of that decision had already been dealt with by Hamilton P in *Duggan v An Taoiseach* [1989] ILRM 710 in which it was held that the government had acted *ultra vires* in purporting to 'suspend' the 1985 Act without a repealing Act passed by the Oireachtas: see the 1988 Review, 21-4.

The position in the *Purcell* case was that the applicant had been assessed under the Act for 1986, that is, before the government decision to 'suspend' the 1985 Act. Proceedings to recover the sum assessed were initiated in the District Court and the applicant applied to the High Court for an order of prohibition. Barron J acceded to the application. In a crucial passage, Barron J indicated his view:

> If there had been amending legislation, then either from the terms of that legislation or from the provisions of the Interpretation Act [1937], it would have been possible to construe the intention of the Oireachtas as to the extent to which the remaining provisions of the Farm Tax Act should continue to be applied. There is, however, no such amending legislation. An approach to the problem might be to seek to ascertain the intention of the Oireachtas in the events which have happened. But it could never have been contemplated that what has occurred would occur. Legislation is enforced because it is the will of the Oireachtas. If legislation is interfered with unlawfully, then what remains cannot be

the will of the Oireachtas. In that event, it ceases to be enforceable not only for the future, but for the past also.

The conclusion reached by Barron J seems difficult to justify at a general level. Does it indicate that a government statement to one House of the Oireachtas can have the effect of suspending the operation of legislation? It seems clear that such a statement would be incapable of having this effect since it would conflict with the law-making function of the Oireachtas under Article 15.2.1 of the Constitution. That certainly was the view taken by Hamilton P in the *Duggan* case, to which Barron J referred. However, to conclude that the government statement should be given legal force in judicial proceedings seems very different from condemning the government's failure to bring forward amending legislation, as Hamilton P concluded in *Duggan*. To take the view that an unconstitutional action can have legal force might be objected to even had Barron J confined this to an indication that the Budget statement operated prospectively only, that is, for the future (as the 1987 statement itself appeared to envisage). But to conclude that the diktat of the executive may also, in effect, retrospectively annul an Act of the Oireachtas is open to severe objection. In effect, the conclusion in *Purcell* appears to apply a contract-frustration model to the Farm Tax Act 1985, that is, because what occurred (the 1987 Budget statement) was not contemplated by the Oireachtas in 1985, the Act must be deemed not to be enforceable. This method of constitutional interpretation is not soundly based. It might, indeed, have the effect of encouraging unconstitutional action. Where the executive finds itself, as in 1987, in a situation where it could not command a ready majority in Dáil Éireann the *Purcell* case appears to give the green light to executive 'suspension' of legislation without the need to go through the requirement of amending legislation in the Oireachtas. The decision would thus appear to be in direct conflict with the maxim *jura eodem modo destituuntur quo constituuntur*.

RETROSPECTIVE EFFECT OF DECISIONS

In *Murphy v Attorney General* [1982] IR 241, the Supreme Court adopted a non-retrospection rule in constitutional matters, which has been followed since that time. While no decision has expressly cast doubt on *Murphy*, it is of interest to note that one of the planks underpinning its rationale was the decision of the Court of Justice of the EC in *Defrenne v Sabena* [1976] ECR 455. The Court of Justice has since indicated, in *Barra v Belgium* [1988] 2 CMLR 409, that the non-retrospection approach may be the exception rather than the rule: see *Carberry v Minister for Social Welfare*, High Court, 28

April 1989, discussed in the Social Welfare chapter, at 395, below. This may cast some doubt on the continued validity of the *Murphy* line of authority, though for many practical reasons the courts might prefer to continue with the *Murphy* approach.

SEVERABILITY OF UNCONSTITUTIONAL PROVISIONS

The difficult question as to whether the courts may sever unconstitutional provisions from the remainder of statutory provisions was dealt with in three cases in 1989: *MacMathuna v Ireland* [1989] IR 504 (97, above); *Cashman v Clifford and Attorney General*, [1990] ILRM 200; [1989] IR 121 (91-2, above); and *Greene v Minister for Agriculture* [1990] ILRM 364 (100-1, above).

SOCIAL POLICY PROVISIONS

In *MacMathuna v Ireland* [1989] IR 504 (98, above), Carroll J pointed out that the plaintiffs were precluded from invoking Article 45 of the Constitution where statutory provisions were under challenge in a constitutional claim.

TRIAL OF OFFENCES

Minor offence   The categorisation of detention in a reformatory school as a punishment which would indicate that the offence involved was minor or on-minor was discussed in *J. v Delap and Attorney General* [1989] IR 167: see 186-8, below, in the Criminal Law chapter.

Offence: definition   In *McLoughlin v Tuite* [1989] IR 82 (discussed in the Revenue chapter, 370, below), the Supreme Court affirmed the view taken by Carroll J ([1986] ILRM 304; [1986] IR 235) that penalties recovered under s.500 of the Income Tax Act 1967 were not in the nature of criminal penalties and were thus not offences within Article 38.1.

Contract

IMPLIED TERMS

In *Burke v Dublin Corporation*, High Court, 13 July 1989, reversed in part by the Supreme Court, 26 July 1990, important issues of tort and contract arose. Briefly, the Dublin Corporation, in response to the rapid increase in the price of oil in the early 1970s, had sought to find a less expensive means of heating houses it provided in the exercise of its duties under the Housing Act 1966. After making extensive inquiries, it found what appeared to be the answer—a solid fuel warm-air heater. It had this installed in houses in Tallaght. The heater turned out to be quite unsatisfactory, leading to the development of an asthmatic or bronchial condition in a number of people living in these houses. Of three plaintiffs who pursued their claim at the hearing, the first, Mrs Hickey, was a tenant of the corporation; the second, Mrs Tinkler, was originally a tenant but bought her house pursuant to s.90 of the 1966 Act two years after the heater was installed; and the third, Ian Burke, was the three-year-old son of tenants who was born shortly after they moved into the house where the heater had already been installed.

The plaintiffs' case centred on a breach of warranty of fitness for human habitation and on negligence. It will be recalled that in *Siney v Dublin Corporation* [1980] IR 400, the Supreme Court had imposed liability on the Corporation on both these grounds where they let a newly built flat (also in Tallaght) which was so humid and damp as to injure the plaintiff.

With regard to Mrs Hickey's claim in respect of the warranty, Blayney J had no hesitation in rejecting the idea that any distinction with *Siney* could be drawn on the basis that her claim related to a house which was not newly built. A more substantial issue was as to whether the concept of unfitness for human habitation should be determined by s.66(2) of the 1966 Act, which requires the housing authority in considering whether a house is so unfit to have regard to the extent (if any) to which it is deficient as respects twelve different matters set out in the Second Schedule. Blayney J declined to interpret the concept so narrowly. The opinion of the housing authority was not the issue; the Court was required to form its own view on the question. The twelve-point list might be of some assistance as a guide but had no binding force. Blayney J confessed to having had 'enormous difficulty' in deciding whether Mrs Hickey's house, at the time it was let to her, was unfit for human habitation but held that it was unfit.

As regards Mrs Tinkler's claim, Blayney J, '[n]ot without considerable hesitation', held that the warranty applied to the sale to her under s.90. If a warranty were not to be implied 'that would amount to saying that the housing authority was entitled to disregard the responsibilities cast upon it by the Act which authorised the building and selling of the house'. The defendants had submitted that Mrs Tinkler could succeed only if she could show that the house she had agreed to buy was defective because of some latent defect.

Blayney J thought it unnecessary to consider whether or not this was correct because the principal defect of which she complained—the noxiousness of the fumes and dust from the heater—was something of which she was unaware though she was fully conversant with the objective manifestation of the defect. In her case the evidence was that, although she had had a bronchial condition for a number of years before initiating her action, she had not apparently been aware of its provenance until relatively recently. (Fortunately for all the plaintiffs, in the light of the Supreme Court decision in *Hegarty v O'Loughran* [1990] ILRM 403, no issue of limitation of actions was raised in *Burke v Dublin Corporation*.)

Turning to Ian Burke's claim, Blayney J held that his asthmatic condition had been aggravated rather than caused by the heater. He rejected his case based on implied warranty of fitness for human habitation, stating that it had been conceded on his behalf that, as he was not a party to the tenancy agreement, he could not rely on the warranty. (As we shall see, counsel for this plaintiff had not in fact made such a concession.) The case thus was limited to one of negligence, which Blayney J rejected because the Corporation could not reasonably have foreseen that their choice of the heater would be likely to injure any of the occupants of their houses in Tallaght. '[S]ince they could not reasonably have foreseen any injury, they had no duty to take care to avoid it, and in the absence of such a duty there could be no breach of duty and so no negligence'. The onus was on Ian Burke to prove that the defendants could have foreseen that a want of care on their part in relation to the heater would result in an aggravation of his asthma. There was, in Blayney J's view, no evidence on which he could make such a finding.

On appeal, the Supreme Court upheld the verdicts in favour of Mrs Hickey and Mrs Tinkler, and held that Blayney J should not have dismissed Ian Burke's claim on the basis which he had done. In endorsing Blayney J's rejection of the narrow interpretation of s.66(2) suggested by the defendants, Finlay CJ (O'Flaherty J concurring) echoed *Siney's* emphasis on the nature of the statutory duty imposed on housing authorities by the 1966 Act, which was to provide suitable and fit accommodation for those without accommodation or living in sub-standard accommodation, who had not the capacity out of their own resources to provide fit and proper accommodation for themselves. The Chief Justice was 'quite satisfied that such a statutory duty must necessarily involve the provision of accommodation capable of being healthily, safely and properly heated and that such a fundamental series of faults in a heating system as [here] must lead to the conclusion that the defendants were in breach of the implied warranty of fitness for human habitation'.

This passage is of interest in that it relies on the paternalistic thrust of a statute to generate not an enforceable statutory duty in tort or a duty of care in negligence, but rather a *contractual warranty*. This course had been set in *Siney*, where the Supreme Court based liability on such a warranty (as well as negligence) and expressly rejected a claim for breach of statutory duty, on the basis that the statutory duties imposed by the 1966 Act were for the benefit of the public, enforceable only by the Minister under s.111. That solution worked in *Siney* where no problem of privity of contract arose. In *Burke*, however, the warranty rationale gave Mrs Hickey and Mrs Tinkler a remedy but posed problems in relation to Ian Burke in view of the privity of contract doctrine—a matter to which we return. It may be suggested that a straight-forward application of the conventional principles of liability in tort for breach of statutory duty would have been the more satisfactory course for the court to have adopted. To regard these duties as being for the benefit of the public rather than for those who need housing seems to involve an unconventional interpretation of the legislation.

In endorsing Blayney J's holding in favour of Mrs Tinkler, the Chief Justice expressed the view that the power of a housing authority to sell a house to a tenant by *instalments* greatly strengthened its similarity with a letting. The requirement in s.106(1) that, before selling a dwelling under s.90 to a tenant, the housing authority had to ensure that it was in good structural condition was 'quite inconsistent with the application to such a transaction of the ordinary rule of *caveat emptor*, and . . . quite consistent with the existence of the implied warranty of fitness for human habitation'. (The Chief Justice did not refer to *Coleman v Dundalk UDC*, 17 July 1985, where the Supreme Court had rejected an argument seeking to base a distinction on the fact that *Coleman* involved a long lease whereas in *Siney* a weekly tenancy was in question.)

Finlay CJ saw no merit in a distinction between patent and latent defects such that Mrs Tinkler would have lost her case based on the warranty if she had been aware of the danger to her health which the heater posed at the time she bought the house. This consideration was not material. The essence of the warranty of fitness for habitation was that 'it is an absolute guarantee by the housing authority of the condition of the house, and it is not dependent upon proof that some defect in the house was by them discoverable'.

Perhaps this analysis is not the last word of the question of patent dangerous defects. It is worth noting that, whereas Blayney J was concerned exclusively with the patency or latency of the defect relative to the *purchaser*, the Chief Justice's remarks considered the question of patency or latency in the context of the *Corporation*. It is possible to envisage cases where the purchaser might be aware of a danger of which the Corporation could not reasonably have knowledge, as well as other cases where the position is reserved.

At a more fundamental level, it may be argued that the question of patency of a defect is indeed of potential relevance to the question of the warranty of fitness for habitation. In some cases, the patency of a defect will 'defuse' what would have been a breach of the warranty, just as a warning, again only in *some* cases, could discharge the occupier's duty of care to an invitee under the old law of occupier's liability: *Long v Saorstat and Continental Steamship Co. Ltd* (1953) 93 ILTR 137. An all-or-nothing approach to the issue of patency can prove unsatisfactory, as the English decision of *London Graving Dock Co. Ltd v Horton* [1951] AC 737 makes plain.

Apart from the cases where the patency of a defect may, on any view, ensure that there is no breach of warranty of habitability, the question arises as to the extent to which the public statutorily-imposed social context of the warranty reduces the centrality of the element of contract from the relationship between the parties. In a contract for the sale of a house, there is, even today, no general implied warranty of habitability: *Curling v Walsh*, High Court, 23 October 1987, analysed in the 1987 Review, 333; see also McMahon & Binchy, *Irish Law of Torts* (2nd ed., 1990), 232-5. In a case where the warranty does arise, the question whether it may be excluded by express agreement would have to be confronted. It seems clear enough from the Chief Justice's analysis that he perceives the warranty arising from the 1966 Act as being incapable of exclusion by agreement, by virtue of the underlying public policy. In truth, the notion of warranty here is fictional, designed to give effect to a desirable social policy by means of the unlikely conceptual machinery of the law of contract. Contract is possibly the least harmonious legal body of thought to use for this purpose, in view of its ideological background which concentrates on individual autonomy at the expense, on occasion, of socially progressive policies.

If, as may well be the case, the implied warranty of habitability under the housing legislation overrides the normal rules as to express exclusion, perhaps it is also capable of dispensing with conventional privity requirements? As we have seen, Blayney J thought not, on the basis of what he understood to be a concession to this effect by counsel representing Ian Burke. On appeal, counsel for Ian Burke told the Supreme Court that they had not made such a concession, but had contended that Ian Burke was a party to the tenancy agreement in the sense that it was made for his benefit. Counsel also sought to argue a point that had not been made to Blayney J, based on s. 8(1) of the Married Women's Status Act 1957. The defendants did not object as they were anxious to have the question of law determined.

Finlay CJ rejected both arguments. As to the first, it was true that in *Jackson v Horizon Holidays Ltd* [1975] 3 All ER 92, the English Court of Appeal had awarded damages to a man whose holiday was spoilt, not only for the discomfort and vexation which he had suffered but also for the same damages which his wife and children had suffered, the man having entered into the contract for the provision of the holiday on behalf of all the family. However, *Jackson* was distinguishable on its facts. The defendant was expressly aware of the persons for whose benefit the contract was made and whose position was at risk if the contract were broken; in *Burke*, by way of contrast, at the time the parents entered the contract of tenancy, Ian Burke had not been born. Moreover, Lord Wilberforce had subjected *Jackson* to persuasive adverse comment in *Woodar Investment Ltd v Wimpey Construction Ltd* [1980] 1 All ER 571, suggesting that it should be confined in effect to a decision on the measure of damages or possibly as a species of a type of contract calling for special treatment, examples of which are persons contracting for family holidays, ordering meals in restaurants, or hiring a taxi for a group.

As to the argument based on s.8(1), which renders enforceable by a wife, husband or child of a contracting party a contract 'expressed to be for [his or her] benefit . . . or [which] by its express terms purports to confer a benefit upon [him or her]', Finlay CJ rejected the plaintiff's contention that the contract of tenancy could be so construed on the basis that it provided for a differential rent, calculation of which would take into account the number of their dependent children at any time. Such an interpretation would give much wider implied effect to the section than its terms would warrant.

In a crucial passage, the Chief Justice gave a pointer to the future:

> It is attractive to view as a disturbing disparity and unnecessary discrimination a significant difference between the parties entering into a tenancy agreement of a house provided by a housing authority and other members of the family enjoying the same *de facto* rights and privileges who are not parties to that agreement. An argument based on this wider problem of equality before the law was not made in this case and I express no view about it.

Why should the Chief Justice have gone to the length of mentioning this argument if he did not see considerable force in it? The suggestion underlying it is surely that the constitutional principle of equality is capable, in the circumstances of Ian Burke's case, of overriding the doctrine of privity of contract. If this is so, the implications for the law of contract are profound.

The privity doctrine frequently involves injustice in its application. An effective answer scarcely lies in the conceptually unconvincing palliative of the contractual trust: see Flannigan, 'Privity—The End of an Era (Error)' (1987) 103 *LQR* 564, and the 1987 Review, 113-4. A restatement of the doctrine of privity of contract would improve rather than weaken the structure of the law of contract, as experience in the United States has shown. The best way of doing this, we suggest, is for the Supreme Court simply to recognise the claims of intended beneficiaries of contractual obligations. This would be a good deal less radical a step than might at first appear in view of the contractual trust doctrine. It would, in effect, be a more convincing restatement of the law, rather than a completely new formulation of legal principles.

As to the Chief Justice's reference to the constitutional norm of equality, it is interesting to recall that in the Supreme Court decision of *Hanrahan v Merck Sharp & Dohme (Ireland) Ltd* [1988] ILRM 629, at 636 (see the 1988 Review, 463-6) Henchy J spoke of the relationship between constitutional law and tort law:

> So far as I am aware, the constitutional provisions relied on have never been used in the courts to shape the form of any existing tort. . . . The implementation of those constitutional rights is primarily a matter for the State and the courts are entitled to intervene only when there has been a failure to implement or, where the implementation relied on is plainly inadequate to effectuate, the constitutional guarantee in question. . . . A person may of course, in the absence of a common law or statutory cause of action, sue directly for breach of a constitutional right . . .; but when he founds his action on an existing tort he is normally confined to the limitations of that tort. It might be different if it could be shown that the tort in question is basically ineffective to protect his constitutional right.

The question arises as to whether a similar approach should apply to the relationship between constitutional law and the law of contract. The core of contract law is the *enforcement of promises*; outside this central principle, the law of contract, in conjunction with equity and tort law, gives effect to the *reliance* principle. In the 1987 Review, 114, we speculated as to whether the philosophy of *Webb v Ireland* [1988] ILRM 565; [1988] IR 353, with its emphasis on promissory estoppel based on reasonable expectations, might lead to the eclipse, or at least substantial modification, of the privity rule. What Finlay CJ in *Burke* appears to have in mind rests on neither promise nor reliance (since Ian Burke was not a party to the tenancy agreement and, at three years old, certainly did not rely on the Corporation in any way.)

Let us get back to basics. If A enters a contract with B, then, according to conventional contractual theory, A may sue B for B's breach if A suffers damage, because (i) A is a party to the contract and (ii) A has provided consideration. If C complains about A's breach, then, even though C may have suffered injury from the breach, his claim in contract will normally be rejected because he neither was a party to it nor provided consideration. (Of course, if B's breach of contract is also a tort, C may have a right of action, in tort, and will not be nonsuited because B's wrong was also a breach of contract relative to A. The days of *Winterbottom v Wright* (1842)10 M & W 109; 152 ER 402 and *Corry v Lucas* (1868) IR 3 CL 208 are long gone.) If C complains of unequal treatment, because he cannot mount an action in contract, one might have expected the court to tell him that a general rule allowing outsiders to hold parties to their contracts would be worthy of criticism on several grounds, not least its *unfairness* and the damage it would cause to *freedom of contract*. Such a rule would be unfair because an outsider has no business complaining where the contract was not designed to confer a benefit on him; moreover he paid nothing for it. Allowing the outsider sue would also inhibit contractual freedom in that, having entered a contract, A and B might be loathe to vary its terms or to discharge it by agreement lest they be sued by C for consequent loss to him. (This, incidentally, is a problem in respect of s.8(1) of the Married Women's Status Act 1957; see Binchy, *A Casebook on Irish Family Law* (1984), 318.)

Having mentioned these obvious difficulties with an equality-based rule which would let all non-parties sue for breach of contract, it is necessary to focus on what the Chief Justice probably had in mind. It is inconceivable that he was suggesting that such a broad argument would have any prospect of success. Instead, he was surely raising the possibility that a somewhat narrower argument might be successful. One attractive explanation would be that the Chief Justice was endorsing the principle that a person *for whose benefit* a contract was made should not be defeated by the absence of privity. Another, more contextual, explanation may also be considered. In *Burke*, as we have suggested, the implied warranty of habitability operated as a useful means of imposing what is in essence liability for breach of statutory duty rather than involving in any credible sense the application of a conventional contractual norm. If this is so, then it would be reasonable that the range of enforceability should not be restricted by reference to privity and consideration. To do so would leave remediless non-parties, or parties who had provided no consideration, when quite clearly the court would wish that they also should have a right of action. Is there not something disingenuous about a judicial process of imposing liability on a judicial basis (contract) which the court does not really believe is appropriate, and then having to invoke the Constitution to fill in the gaps so as to ensure that the unstated policy (based, it is suggested, on the principle of breach of statutory duty) can be fully effectuated?

Whatever damage this process may do to the law of contract, it is surely regrettable that the Constitution should be used for such a pragmatic purpose.

In this context it is worth nothing the different emphasis of McCarthy J's concurring judgment, where the true basis of the court's holding peeps through:

> The relevant section of the Housing Act 1966 extends to all the community in need of housing, including the children of the tenants of housing authorities. There is no limitation related to date of birth. Such right of action of the named tenant or tenants may derive from the combined effect of the contract of tenancy and the operation of the Act. Such a contention may enter the equation if and when this court has to consider an argument such as that to which the Chief Justice refers [in relation to equality].

This emphasis on the statutory purpose as a factor in moulding the warranty and the range of those entitled to sue upon it is reminiscent of McCarthy J's judgments in *Ward v McMaster* [1989] ILRM 400; [1988] IR 337 (as to which see the observations in the 1988 Review, 430) and in *Sunderland v Louth County Council*, Supreme Court, 4 April 1990.

On the question of negligence in relation to Ian Burke, the Supreme Court held that Blayney J was wrong to have dismissed the action on the ground that he had done. The Corporation's duty of care did not end when they provided their tenants with a heater. There was a continuing obligation on them to render the houses they provided for their tenants fit for human habitation if the fact of unfitness was established to them or they ought to have discovered it. This was a duty, said the Chief Justice, which 'must as a matter of law be taken to continue during the course of the letting.' Since the issue whether there had been a breach of such a continuing duty had not been dealt with in Blayney J's judgment, the Supreme Court directed a re-trial on the question whether Ian Burke's mother had complained to the officials of the Corporation regarding the condition of the heater.

This aspect of the case is perhaps somewhat more complicated than might at first appear. The idea that the supplier of a product is automatically free from a duty of care when he later learns that it is dangerous has for long been rejected in tort law. Clearly a lessor or hirer of a product may fall under a duty of care; but courts have increasingly been willing to impose such a duty on manufacturers also: see, e.g., *Rivtow Marine Ltd v Washington Iron Works* (1973) 40 DLR (3rd) 530. The manner in which that duty is to be discharged can be a question of some difficulty. Withdrawal of the offending product may suffice, while in some cases a mere warning, whether to each recipient or to the public at large, may be enough. What is called for will depend on

several factors, including, of course, the precise risk of injury, the gravity of
the threatened injury and the difficulty in providing adequate notification.

In the present case, the Corporation would surely have discharged its duty
of care by replacing the heater; it is far less clear that a mere warning as to
the danger to health which it involved would have sufficed, since that might
foreseeably have left the occupants of the houses in a position where, on
account of lack of financial resources, they would be obliged to try and make
do with the dangerous heater.

The manner in which the Chief Justice dealt with the issue is interesting.
He stated that the housing authority, if they discovered, or ought to have
discovered, that a dwelling provided for a tenant under the 1966 Act was
unfit for human habitation, would be under an obligation 'to render it fit'.
There is here a conjoining of tort and contract law which may lead to
complications.

The issue of the Corporation's liability in negligence, whether at the
beginning or during the currency of a tenancy, does not depend on any
contractual notion of implied warranty of fitness for habitation, in the sense
that the existence and scope of the warranty can dictate the nature and scope
of the duty of care in negligence. The point is of some considerable practical
significance: if the warranty were to have such effects, then Ian Burke might
well not succeed in his action in negligence because the duty of care might
be considered to be owed only to his parents and not to him: *Palsgraf v Long
Island Railroad Co.* (1928), 248 NY 339; 126 NE 99; *Hay (or Bourhill) v
Young* [1943] AC 92; McMahon & Binchy, *Irish Law of Torts* (2nd ed.,
1990), 98-100. The truth of the matter is that, while the warranty should not
be ignored in the determination of the Corporation's duty of care, both at the
commencement and during the currency of the tenancy, the nature and scope
of the duty of care should be fashioned in the light of the Corporation's
statutory functions untrammelled by any limitations (or, indeed, extension)
of liability which the warranty might involve.

INTERPRETATION

In *Capemel Ltd v Lister* [1989] IR 319 Costello J had to interpret the following
clause in an employer's liability insurance policy: 'The assured shall give to
underwriters immediate notice in writing, with full particulars of the
happening of any occurrence which could give rise to a claim under this
insurance, or of the receipt by the assured of notice of any claim or of the
institution of any proceedings against the assured'.

The plaintiff company, which had taken out this policy, had failed to give
immediate notice in writing of the occurrence of an accident involving an

employee who later sued the company. The underwriters purported to repudiate liability on the basis of this failure. The plaintiff sought a declaration that the underwriters were not entitled to do this.

Costello J made the requested declaration. Following Gannon J's judgment in *Gaelcrann Teo v Payne* [1985] ILRM 109, he held that the obligations were disjunctive. The insured was entitled to give notice in writing in any of the events specified in one clause, which had to be strictly construed against the insurers. This did not produce an absurd result, in Costello J's view.

Of course, a person with business experience, reading the clause, would tend to the view that the insurers had intended that the clause be read as subject to the words: 'whichever is the earliest of these events'; but these did not appear in the clause itself.

EXEMPTION CLAUSES

In *Regan v Irish Automobile Club Ltd t/a Royal Irish Automobile Club*, High Court, 3 November 1989, the plaintiff, who was officiating as a flag marshal at a motor race in the Phoenix Park, was injured when one of the racing cars went out of control and left the track. She sued the defendants for negligence in their organisation and control of the race and the track.

The defendants, who denied negligence, argued that the plaintiff had agreed to waive her rights; she had, they said, entered into a written contract with them under which she agreed to act as a marshal, and, in consideration of the organising club's having effected a personal accident policy for her benefit, she agreed to absolve all persons connected with the meeting from liability 'arising out of accidents howsoever caused, resulting in damage and/or personal injury to any person and/or property'. To this the plaintiff sought to assert a fundamental breach of the contract. Matters came before Lynch J by way of trial on preliminary issues. The first issue facing him was whether the words of the exemption clause were sufficient to exclude liability for accidents caused by negligence. He held that they were. He was:

> satisfied that it is not fanciful or unreal to envisage accidents happening without negligence on the part of anyone at an event such as that at which the plaintiff was officiating. Therefore while accidents usually occur due to some carelessness or other on the part of someone and a reference to 'accidents' would usually imply negligent accidents, however, I have to give effect to the words used and the word 'accidents' is not left unqualified. It is qualified by the words 'howsoever caused' and these words are obviously wide enough to embrace negligent

accidents for which someone is responsible in law. In addition the use of the word 'liability' presupposes some form of wrong. A pure accident for which no one is responsible would create no liability in anyone and therefore the reference to liability necessarily brings within the ambit of the clause accidents resulting from the wrongful or negligent conduct of others.

It is unfortunate that, in support of his conclusion, it would appear that Lynch J's attention was not drawn to the decision of McMahon J in *Alexander v Irish National Stud Co. Ltd*, High Court, 10 June 1977 where the word 'accident' had been left unqualified in an exemption clause.

The next issue was whether, assuming all allegations made by the plaintiff were established, they amounted to such a fundamental breach of the agreement by the defendants as to disentitle them from relying on the exemption clause. Lynch J held that they did not. His discussion of the details of the case was brief, but in essence he appears to have concluded that the defendants' failure to provide solid protection for the plaintiff in the form of a skip filled with two or three tons of sand did not constitute negligence of such a character as to amount to a fundamental breach. The plaintiff had received this level of protection at motor races at another venue.

Lynch J concluded his judgment by expressly reserving his response to the proposition that a fundamental breach of contract would necessarily have the results submitted on behalf of the plaintiff having regard to cases decided since *Clayton Love & Sons (Dublin) Ltd v British & Irish Steam Packet Co. Ltd* (1966) 104 ILTR 157.

FRAUD

In *Smyth v Tunney*, High Court, 6 October 1989, Murphy J held that allegations and counter-allegations of fraudulent conduct in one form or another were not sustainable on the evidence of the case, which concerned a dispute as to the terms of an agreement between a lessor and a lessee of a hotel. The essence of the plaintiff's case was that there had been an alteration in one of the terms. The essence of the defendants' case was that the plaintiff's proceedings amounted to fraudulent or malicious abuse of civil proceedings or of the process of the courts: see below, pp. 444-5. The judgment makes fascinating reading: certainly there was a lack of mutual trust between the parties in the course of negotiations.

We are not concerned with the particular facts: our interest here is limited to Murphy J's invocation of Henchy J's analysis of the onus of proof in *Banco Ambrosiano Spa v Ansbacher & Co.* [1987] ILRM 669, at 701-2. Henchy J there rejected the argument that the onus of proof in civil cases where fraud is alleged should lie somewhere between that of the balance of probabilities and proof beyond reasonable doubt. This would introduce 'a vague and uncertain element, just as if, for example, negligence were required to be proved in certain cases to the level of gross negligence'. (It may here be interjected that courts in North America evinced no particular difficulty in applying the standard of gross negligence in adjudicating 'guest passenger' litigation—now abandoned after constitutional and policy attacks.) Henchy J had gone on to argue that there was no cogent reason for singling out civil cases of fraud for this higher degree of proof. It was of course true that fraud usually carried with it a high degree of moral condemnation which might have serious consequences for the person so condemned; but similar consequences could arise in a negligence action, for example, against a doctor who failed for no good reason to go out to attend a patient to whom he had been summoned, so that the patient died. In Henchy J's view, where the allegation of fraud rested on an inference from established facts '[t]he received inference must, of course, not be drawn lightly or without due regard to all the relevant circumstances, including the consequences of a finding of fraud. But the finding should not be shirked because it is not a conclusion of absolute certainty. If the court is satisfied, on balancing the possible inferences open on the facts, that fraud is the rational and cogent conclusion to be drawn, it should so find'.

This passage gives rise to an ambiguity which should be isolated and resolved. Henchy J's statement that the required inference 'must, of course, not be drawn . . . without due regard to all the relevant circumstances, *including the consequences of a finding of fraud*' (emphasis added) raises the question whether the court's assessment of different consequences of a finding of fraud in two different cases could lead to a different holding in respect of (let us assume) identical evidence. Such a result is surely unsustainable in justice, from the standpoint of equality and objectivity. The court's proper function is not to alter its *verdict* in accordance with what it perceives the outcome of that verdict may be for the defendant (or, indeed, the plaintiff, since a finding of no fraud may have consequential implications for the plaintiff's moral or professional reputation).

Henchy J's consequentialist propensity was evident also in the Supreme Court decision on nullity in *N. (K.) v K.* [1986] ILRM 75; [1985] IR 733, where, in dissenting as to the scope of duress as a ground for annulment, he emphasised that the court should have regard to the implications on the child of the union of a decree, since the child would thereby lose [his] legitimate status. Whatever merit there may be in assessing consequential considerations in the context of an adjudication of status, where third parties' status is indirectly but inevitably affected, this approach has no place in the sphere of tort, where the question of liability for fraud should be determined without regard to its consequences.

ILLEGALITY

In *Hortensius Ltd v Bishop et al, Trustees of the Trustee Savings Bank Dublin* [1989] ILRM 294 Costello J addressed a number of issues relating to the question of illegality of contract. The plaintiffs, who owed money on a mortgage forming part of a loan portfolio of a mortgagee which was sold to the defendant, sought a declaration that the purchase was contrary to the Trustee Acts, and constituted an *ultra vires* or illegal contract, so far as the defendant was concerned, and that thus no money was owing to the defendant. Costello J held that the plaintiffs were correct in asserting that the purchase was contrary to the Trustee legislation (cf. below, 197-8); but he rejected their argument that the contract was either *ultra vires* or illegal.

As to the question of *ultra vires*, he held that this doctrine applied only to the acts and contracts of public authorities and companies. The defendant bank was not a company but an unincorporated association; its trustees had breached their statutory duty but there was no question of there being an *ultra vires* contract.

Costello J went on to consider the notion of illegal contracts at common law and under statute. In the present case, there was a statutory provision (s.15 of the Trustee Savings Banks Act 1863) which prohibited the parties from entering a contract of the type they had in fact done, not a provision which made illegal the objects of the contract they had entered into. Thus, the plaintiff could not rely on the common law rules relating to the unenforceability of illegal contracts as these, so far as they related to statutory provisions, caught only contracts which could not be performed without a breach of the criminal law.

As to the position under the statute itself, Costello J noted that statutes can have various effects on contracts, from rendering them null and void (but not illegal) to prohibiting and penalising the making of certain contracts while remaining silent as to the civil rights of the parties to them. In the latter case, it then became a question of the construction of the statute as to whether the contract should be regarded as an illegal one. S.15 had prohibited the trustees from entering into contracts for the purchase of loans, but had not made these contracts illegal.

In Costello J's view, if the defendant had sought specific performance of the contract for the purchase of the loans, it would have failed because the courts of equity will not give relief to a trustee acting in breach of trust. But it was well established that, if a trustee has actually acquired property in breach of trust, the wrongfulness of his act would not render the transaction void. Public policy had never required that trustees should be deprived of the right to enforce proprietary claims over property acquired in breach of trust. Moreover, even if the contract in question had been an illegal one, once property had been delivered under it the fact that by reason of the illegality the trustees could not originally have enforced the agreement did not mean that the property in the interests they acquired had not passed to them. The trustees could thus enforce the rights they had acquired by virtue of the contract against the plaintiffs. See also 39-40, above.

FRUSTRATION

In *William Neville & Sons Ltd v Guardian Builders Ltd* [1990] ILRM 601 an important, simple issue relating to the doctrine of frustration of contract fell for consideration. The plaintiff sought specific performance of a building contract whereby they agreed to develop a site owned by the defendants and acquire title to the houses they erected for a specific consideration. The site was at the date of the contract effectively landlocked but both parties assumed that Dublin County Council, as the owner of a crucial slip of land between the site and the road, would facilitate the development and thus enable the contract to be performed. This did not in fact happen, for reasons connected with the process of planning permission in the area.

Murphy J was of the view that the contract had been frustrated. The argument in favour of frustration was in many respects far stronger than that which had succeeded in the famous Coronation case of *Krell v Henry* [1903] 2 KB 740, 'because here the change in expectation did not defeat the purpose of the agreement but effectively the only means of performing it short of requiring one or other of the parties to do something not merely different from what he had agreed to do but something which he had not agreed to do at all'.

Murphy J rejected the argument that the doctrine of frustration applied only at common law and had no application where equitable relief was sought. Such a distinction could not be maintained: if a contract was discharged through impossibility, then clearly no court could compel its performance. Nor did he consider that the plaintiff was entitled to specific performance of so much of the agreement as could be performed and either to waive performance of the remaining terms or to be compensated for this breach. Such a position would arise in an appropriate case but not in the circumstances facing the court:

> The problem in performing the contract as a whole is not due to any breach of any of its terms by the defendants. The defendants did not

agree to secure access to the site. If they had done so or if the
unwillingness of the County Council was due to the default of the
defendants then indeed a claim—at least a claim for damages—would
lie and the defendants could not rely on the doctrine of frustration.

Nevertheless Murphy J conceded that it did seem an impertinence to say
to the plaintiffs: 'You are mistaken in seeking to implement this contract.
You cannot gain access to the site as matters stand and accordingly it cannot
be performed by you.' The plaintiffs believed that alternative arrangements
could be made by making the County Council a satisfactory offer; but
Murphy J considered that to proceed on that footing 'would be to impose
entirely new terms on one or other of the parties'. He thought the real extent
of the problem could best be seen by considering what would happen if the
plaintiffs rather than the defendant were seeking the declaration that the
agreement had been frustrated. No court could compel the plaintiffs to build
houses on land to which they could not gain access as a matter of right. It
seemed to him, on this basis, that performance of the contract had been
frustrated and, 'somewhat regretfully', he dismissed the plaintiffs' claim.

This result is unfortunate. The doctrine of frustration is of course capable
of applying where the frustrating event destroys an underlying assumption
of the contract in such a way as to make it unjust to enforce the contract
against *either* party; but it also can apply where its enforcement against *one*
of the parties would involve no injustice. It is difficult to see what injustice
would have befallen the defendant if it had been held to its bargain. Its
reasonable expectations, *so far as its obligations and the rights of the other
party were concerned*, would have been given full effect. That the plaintiffs
should have no right to specific performance may indeed be considered
regrettable. As against this, the mutuality doctrine in specific performance
suggests a basis for declining to grant specific performance. It is interesting
to note that the absence of mutuality was a reason identified by Murphy J,
not for declining specific performance by reference to the restrictions limiting
that remedy but for doing so by reference to the doctrine of frustration itself.

'SUBJECT TO CONTRACT'

In *Silver Wraith Ltd v Siúicre Éireann CPT*, High Court, 8 June 1989, Keane
J confronted the troublesome issue of 'subject to contract' correspondence.
The defendants were negotiating with the plaintiffs' agents for the lease of
the defendants' premises. The defendants' agent wrote to the plaintiffs' agent
a letter which said: "Further to your correspondence and subsequent
discussions . . . the following terms are acceptable subject to full lease being

agreed'. Was this sufficient to bind the parties? Certainly, a line of judicial authority has established that, where the parties are agreed in fact, the inclusion of the expression 'subject to contract' does not vitiate that agreement. Keane J did not consider that these cases were determinative of the issue. He observed that the phrase 'subject to a full lease being agreed' had to:

> be carefully distinguished from the phrase 'subject to contract' which is dealt with in the authorities here and in England. Those authorities have been concerned with situations where parties, usually lay parties or estate agents, had settled the terms of a purchase of property and then went to their solicitors and asked them to carry through the sale; and the solicitors, conscious of the fact that it might be dangerous for their clients to be bound by a purely oral contract, would write to their opposite number a letter headed 'subject to contract' and go on to say: 'We confirm the sale of this property etc.'.
>
> Now, even in those circumstances it has sometimes been held that that is sufficient to prevent a sufficient note or memorandum to come into existence to satisfy the Statute of Frauds. But if one looks at the authorities, one finds that in those cases there had been a complete agreement, that the parties to the transaction had not in mind anything at all about it being subject to contract. It was their solicitors who subsequently put the phrase into the correspondence.
>
> However, in this situation it is totally different. If these letters reflect (as . . . it is virtually agreed that they do) the actual state of mind of the parties at the time, then the coming into existence of a full lease is unquestionably a condition of the agreement and there is no question here of the phrase being subsequently inserted by a party in order to protect himself from an agreement already arrived at. That, I think, is the only inference that can be drawn from the use by [the defendants' agent] in his letter of the phrase 'subject to full lease being agreed' because [he] is the person concerned; he is a layman; he is not a solicitor coming into a deal which has already been concluded between others and saying: 'Well, I must protect these people because they have entered into an oral agreement. I will ensure that no note or memorandum comes into existence by heading the letter "subject to contract".' Here is a lay person writing his understanding of the situation as he sees it and he uses this phrase which in my opinion is only consistent with an intention to ensure that a contractual liability does not arise until a full lease has been agreed. That seems to me to be the weight that has to be attached to those words.

This distinction between solicitors and other negotiators is a useful one. Of course it can be no more than a rule of thumb and must depend very much on the facts of the particular case, since on some occasions a negotiator who is not a solicitor may insert the expression 'subject to contract' after a true agreement has in fact been reached.

On the evidence in the instant case, Keane J found that the parties, apart altogether from the phrase 'subject to full lease being agreed', had not reached a concluded agreement. Such matters as personal guarantees, the deposit to be paid on the signing of the lease and the exact identity of the lessee were still 'up in the air'. Cases of sale could be distinguished from those of lease. Once a person who was selling property had got his money, that was the end of it as far as he was concerned; he 'could not care less who he has sold it to or what the purchaser does with the property'. In contrast a landlord was very much concerned with the identity and solvency of his tenant: 'the more valuable the property, the more exposed the landlord is to comment or criticism. If the lessor is a public body or a semi-state body, it is most important that it should be known who the lessee is'.

Having held that there was no concluded agreement between the parties, Keane J, in deference to the arguments of counsel, went on to consider the moot question of whether the note or memorandum was fatally vitiated by the phrase 'subject to full lease being agreed'. He was of the view that it was, because he could discern no significant difference between it and the phrase 'subject to contract', which had 'in so many instances been held to be fatal to the existence of a note or memorandum'. If the note or memorandum appeared to deny the existence of a concluded agreement, 'then that is fatal to its being a sufficient note or memorandum'. We find here no mention of the Supreme Court decision of *Kelly v Park Hall School Ltd* [1979] IR 340, which Keane J had in *Mulhall v Haren* [1981] IR 364, at 389 sought to distinguish as 'a special [case] decided on particular facts . . .'.

Apart from this, Keane J considered that the letter did not constitute a sufficient note or memorandum because it failed to specify the parties. The earlier correspondence mentioned two or more potential lessees.

Finally, on the question of part performance, the plaintiffs had failed to establish that certain expenditure they had incurred 'was unequivocally referrable to the type of contract alleged'. See further R. Clark, *Contract* (2nd ed., 1986), 55-6.

RECTIFICATION

In *Irish Life Assurance Co. Ltd v Dublin Land Securities Ltd* [1989] IR 253, the Supreme Court addressed the question of the circumstances in which rectification of a contract should be ordered. In *Lucey v Laurel Construction Co. Ltd*, High Court, 18 December 1970, Kenny J had followed the lead of Denning LJ in *Rose Ltd v Pim Ltd* [1953] 2 QB 450, at 46, in taking the view that the court would not rectify a document unless it was preceded by a *concluded oral contract*. Denning LJ had rejected the approach which would base rectification on the existence of a shared intention between the parties; he thought that '[t]here could be no certainty at all in business transactions if a party who had entered into a firm contract would afterwards turn around and claim to have it rectified on the grounds that the parties had intended something different'.

Kenny J had failed to refer to the decision of the English Court of Appeal in *Joscelyne v Nissen* [1970] 2 QB 86, where Russell LJ had repudiated Denning LJ's approach, in favour of one requiring proof of *some outward expression of accord*. In the Northern Ireland decision of *Rooney and McParland Ltd v Carlin* [1981] NI 138, at 146, Lowry LCJ summarised the principles clarified by Russell LJ as follows:

1. there must be a concluded agreement antecedent to the instrument which is sought to be rectified; but

2. the antecedent agreement need not be binding in law (for example, it need not be under seal if made by a public authority or in writing and signed by the party if relating to a sale of land) nor need it be in writing: such incidents merely help to discharge the heavy burden of proof; and

3. a complete antecedent concluded contract is not required, so long as there was prior accord on a term of a proposed agreement, outwardly explained and communicated between the parties, as in *Joscelyne v Nissen*.

In the *Irish Life Assurance* case, the Supreme Court adopted what was said by Russell LJ and Lowry LCJ as representing the law on the subject in this jurisdiction.

Applying these principles to the facts of the case, the Court, affirming Keane J, held that rectification should not be ordered. The plaintiff had sold its large ground rents portfolio to the defendant. The plaintiff's property manager had told the defendant's agent that 'a significant holding of land the subject of a C.P.O. at Palmerstown' was not being included in the contract. The draft contract did, however, include this land, through an error on the part of the plaintiff's legal department. The defendant's solicitor, in ignorance of this whole dimension, had on the day when contracts were to be exchanged indicated his unhappiness about doing so since he was not satisfied that all the properties to which his client would become entitled were included in the draft. The plaintiff's lawyer had responded with an ultimatum to exchange contracts that day or else the deal was off. Later the error about the Palmerstown holding was discovered. Griffin J (with whose judgment Finlay CJ and McCarthy J concurred) was quite satisfied that the case was one of unilateral rather than common mistake. Assuming, without deciding, that the knowledge obtained by the defendant's agent could be imputed to the defendant, Griffin J was of the view that the evidence fell very far short of establishing a common intention that the vacant lands at Palmerstown, or any part of them, should be excluded from the sale. The plaintiff's property manager's reference to these lands 'completely lacked the precision necessary to enable a court to conclude what was the common intention of the parties'. There were in fact two compulsory purchase orders on parts of the land, one by Dublin County Council, the other by the Corporation. Together they did not exhaust the total area of the land in Palmerstown. The giving of the ultimatum to the defendant's solicitor encouraged Griffin J to the view that, were the claim for rectification to succeed, it would be unjust to the defendant.

DAMAGES

In *Baker Perkins Ltd v C.J. O'Dowd Ltd*, High Court, 13 April 1989, a contract for the sale of bakery equipment contained detailed provisions for interest charges in the event of a delay in completion by the purchaser. It was provided that in the event of failure to complete, the measure of damages should be 'any loss or expense of any nature incurred by seller arising out of disposal of the goods'.

Blayney J held that the vendors, in suing for damages for non-completion, could not claim for loss of profit:

> The loss of profit claim is the profit that the plaintiffs would have made if the defendant had completed the contract. It seems to me that this loss resulted from the defendant's refusal to pay for the goods and did not arise out of the disposal of the goods. In refusing to pay for the goods, the defendant deprived the plaintiffs of their profit. So the plaintiffs' loss was suffered at that stage which at the latest occurred . . . when the plaintiffs terminated the contract by reason of the defendant's breach. And it was only then that the question of the disposal of the goods arose. But the loss of profit, having already been suffered, could not have arisen out of that disposal. It preceded it and was caused by the defendant's breach of contract.

The message of this decision is clear: when drafting clauses for the measure of damages for non-completion it is of course sensible to address the matter of the disappointed vendor's disposition of the goods, but this might be done in such a way as to preserve the vendor's right to damages for loss of profit which would have been made if the defendant had completed the contract.

Criminal Law

ARREST

Access to solicitor   The decision of the Supreme Court in *The People v Healy (P.)*, Supreme Court, 5 December 1989 represents a significant shift in emphasis in the judicial exegisis of the nature of the right of access to a solicitor for persons in Garda custody. The accused had been arrested under s.30 of the Offences against the State Act 1939 in connection with an armed robbery. In the course of his detention, he began making an inculpatory statement at approximately 3.40 p.m., which he concluded at 4.30 p.m. approximately. At 4 p.m. a solicitor retained by a member of the accused's family had arrived at the Garda station where the accused was detained and had asked a Garda superintendent to see the accused. This was refused by the Garda in charge on the basis that the accused was in the course of being interviewed. At the trial of the accused in the Central Criminal Court, Egan J ruled that the inculpatory statement was inadmissible in evidence and he directed the jury to return a verdict of not guilty. On appeal by the Director of Public Prosecutions against the acquittal (see *The People v O'Shea* [1983] ILRM 549; [1982] IR 384) the Supreme Court (Finlay CJ, Walsh, Griffin, Hederman and McCarthy JJ) unanimously dismissed the appeal and upheld the ruling of Egan J.

Delivering the leading judgment, Finlay CJ (with whom Walsh and Hederman JJ agreed) noted the limit to the issue before the Court. It did not extend to the right of access to a solicitor as a general right; and so the question whether a detained person has a right to be informed of the right of access by a member of the Garda Síochána or the question of any possible right to the presence of a solicitor during interrogation did not arise in the instant case. He pointed out that the right in issue was that of the detained person to have access during his detention to a solicitor whose attendance he has requested or whose attendance has been requested on his behalf by other persons bona fide acting on his behalf. The Chief Justice noted that such right could be defeated either by failure to convey the request in the first instance or by failing to inform the detained person or to allow access in the second instance.

The crucial point in the case was the nature of the right: was it constitutional in origin, or, as the prosecution contended, merely part of the common law and subject to whatever statutory restrictions might be imposed on it from time to time. If the latter, then its standing would be greatly reduced. The Court held that what it termed 'the right of reasonable access' of a detained person to a solicitor was constitutional in origin. Finlay CJ quoted the views of Walsh J in *The People v Conroy* [1988] ILRM 4; [1986] IR 460, in which the right was regarded as constitutional in origin, and *dicta* of Griffin J in *The People v Shaw* [1982] IR 1 in which he had discussed the issue of fairness of procedures in the context of Garda custody. The Chief Justice continued:

> The undoubted right of reasonable access to a solicitor enjoyed by a person in detention must be interpreted as being directed towards the vital function of ensuring that such person is aware of his rights, and has the independent advice which would be appropriate in order to permit him to reach a truly free decision as to his attitude to interrogation or to the making of any statement, be it inculpatory or exculpatory. The availability of advice form a lawyer must, in my view, be seen as a contribution at least towards some measure of equality in the position of the detained person and his interrogators.
>
> Viewed in that light, I am driven to the conclusion that such an important and fundamental standard of fairness in the administration of justice as the right of access to a lawyer must be deemed to be constitutional in its origin, and that to classify it as merely legal would be to undermine its importance and the completeness of the protection of it which the courts are obliged to give.

The issue which thus arose was whether, if a breach of the right occurred as a result of a conscious and deliberate act by a member of the Garda Síochána, there was a causative link between that breach and the obtaining of the evidence. The Chief Justice was of the view that the right of reasonable access means in the event of the arrival of a solicitor at the Garda station an immediate right of the detained person to be told of the arrival and, if the detained person requests it, an immediate access, subject only to an objectively justifiable reason from the point of view of the detained person's welfare for refusing access. It is hardly surprising that he took this view in *Healy*, as he had come to the same conclusion when President of the High Court in *The State (Harrington) v Garda Commissioner*, High Court, 14 December 1976.

The issues which then arose was whether the breach of the right occurred as a result of a deliberate and conscious act by a member of the Garda Síochána and, finally, whether there was a causative link between the breach and the statements made in the instant case. As to the 'deliberate and conscious act', Finlay CJ rejected the argument that the test of whether the refusal to allow access to the solicitor in the instant case was a deliberate and conscious act was to be based on the Garda superintendent's subjective belief. This was a crucial point which was deal with more fully in *The People v Kenny (M.)*, Court of Criminal Appeal, 15 June and 30 November 1989; Supreme Court, 20 March 1990 (145, below). The Chief Justice stated that the fact that the Superintendent may not have appreciated that his refusal was a breach of a constitutional right was 'immaterial'. As McCarthy J stated in concurrence: 'If it were otherwise, there would be a premium on ignorance.' This dictum echoes the similar comment by Walsh J in *The People v Shaw* [1982] IR 1, at 33, where he commented on the suggestion that, under *The People v O'Brien* [1965] IR 142, admissibility of evidence in this context depended on the state or degree of the violator's knowledge of constitutional, or ordinary, law. In *Shaw*, Walsh J commented:

> To attempt to import any such interpretation of the decision [in *O'Brien*] would be to put a premium on ignorance of the law. The maxim *ignorantia legis neminem excusat* does not permit an intentional and deliberate act or omission to be shorn of its legal consequences.

In *Healy*, Finlay CJ also rejected the argument that sought to justify refusing access for the purpose of completion of a statement; the least that should be done would be to inform the detained person of the arrival of the solicitor and to ask whether he wished to suspend the making of the statement in order to have access to the solicitor.

In all the circumstances the Court concluded that there had been a deliberate and conscious violation of the accused's constitutional right. And applying the usual rules as to the function of an appellate court (see e.g. *The People v Kelly (No. 2)* [1983] IR 1) the Court did not interfere with the conclusion of fact by the trial judge that he could not be satisfied that the incriminating statement was made prior to the arrival of the solicitor. In that light the trial court judge's ruling was upheld and the Director's appeal was dismissed.

Finally, there was what might be described as a brief skirmish between Griffin and McCarthy JJ, both of whom delivered concurring judgments. McCarthy J adverted to the apparently unending discussion as to whether certain comments of Griffin J in *The People v Shaw* [1982] IR 1 (in which he questioned some views expressed in *The People v O'Brien* [1965] IR 142) could be described as *obiter*. It is hardly surprising that in *Healy*, Griffin J was of the view that his comments in *Shaw* should not be considered as mere *obiter dicta*. For previous discussion of this point, see Casey, (1981) 16 *Ir Jur (ns)* 271.

Offences against the State: extension order   *The People v O'Shea (G.),* Court of Criminal Appeal, 28 July 1989 concerned the information available to a Chief Superintendent when making an extension order under s.30 of the Offences against the State Act 1939. The applicant had been arrested under s.30 of the 1939 Act on suspicion of having committed a scheduled offence, namely an offence under the Firearms Act 1925. An order extending the time for his detention under s.30 for a further period of 24 hours was made by a Chief Superintendent of the Garda Síochána. The applicant was subsequently charged with robbery. At the applicant's trial, the Chief Superintendent gave evidence that he had had discussions with the officers involved in the interrogation of the applicant and had formed the opinion that it would be necessary to detain him for the second 24 hour period. He stated that he had been satisfied that this was necessary in the interests of the progress of the investigation. The Special Criminal Court ruled that the extension order made by the Chief Superintendent was valid and the court subsequently convicted the applicant. The Court of Criminal Appeal (Finlay CJ, Barron and Blayney JJ) dismissed the applicant's leave to appeal against conviction.

The Court held that the Chief Superintendent was entitled to rely on the information and opinions of his subordinate officers with regard to matters which had given them a suspicion as to the commission of an offence by the detained person and as to the progress of the investigation of the crime. In the instant case, the Court was satisfied that it was clear from the Chief Superintendent's evidence at the applicant's trial that he retained, at the time he made the extension order, a real suspicion of the guilt of the applicant of the crime of the use of firearms. To that extent, therefore, the circumstances in the instant case are distinguishable from those in *The People v Byrne* [1987] IR 363 (see the 1987 Review, 117-18).

One further point of interest was mentioned in the judgment of Finlay CJ for the Court. It arose in the context of the burden of proof. As the Court stated there is, in general, an 'unqualified' onus of proof on the prosecution in a criminal trial and so there can never be an onus on the defendant to establish any particular matter. However the Court added that in the instant case the Chief Superintendent had given clear answers which had a plain, reasonable meaning attaching to them. In that particular context, it was for counsel for the accused to raise or establish an alternative meaning to those answers. To that extent, therefore, the particular evidential burden (as opposed to the burden of proof, which remains on the prosecution) required to establish the lack of the necessary information grounding the extension order was on the defence.

Rearrest   The circumstances in which a person may be rearrested having been held under s.30 of the Offences against the State Act 1939 were discussed in *Finucane v McMahon*, High Court (Divisional), 7 April 1989 (see 7-9, below).

DELAY IN ISSUING AND PROSECUTING CHARGES

Delay between commission and charge In *O'Flynn and Hannigan v Clifford* [1990] ILRM 65; [1989] IR 524, the Supreme Court affirmed the decision of Gannon J in the High Court that delays between the commission of an offence and the bringing of charges were to be treated quite differently from delays after the charges have been brought: see the 1988 Review, 147-50.

To recapitulate on the circumstances of the case, the applicants had been charged in February 1988 in relation to offences alleged to have taken place in August 1986. Around the time of the alleged offences, they had been arrested under s.30 of the Offences against the State Act 1939 but were released without charge. The respondent District Justice, who had conducted the preliminary examination of the case under the Criminal Procedure Act 1967, considered that the delay involved had been inexcusable. However, he entered into the preliminary examination and he returned the applicants for trial in accordance with s.8 of the 1967 Act. The applicants sought judicial review of the return for trial, grounded on reasons connected with the delays. In the High Court, Gannon J refused the relief sought: [1988] IR 740. The Supreme Court (Finlay CJ, Walsh and Griffin JJ) dismissed the applicants' appeals.

The judgment of Walsh J for the Court placed great emphasis on the constitutional context, as had Gannon J in the High Court. Walsh J made it clear that it could not be claimed that any person had the right to be charged with an offence of which they are suspected. This was so since to charge a person without sufficient evidence would be highly prejudicial to that person, and it was therefore a matter for the prosecuting authorities to decide whether to prosecute taking account of the sufficiency of evidence and the complexity of the case. This reflects very much the analysis of Gannon J in the High Court: see the passage quoted in the 1988 Review, 148.

Walsh J went on to paint quite a different picture once it has been decided that charges should be brought. Drawing on the leading decision of the Court itself in *The State (O'Connell) v Fawsitt* [1986] ILRM 639; [1986] IR 362, he stated that once it was decided that there was sufficient evidence to charge a person, that decision should be given effect to without unreasonable delay and should be prosecuted in a manner which did not lead to undue prejudice to the accused person. In the instant case, the Court concluded that there was no evidence to indicate that the applicants' right to a fair trial had been prejudiced by the delay, and so their applications were dismissed.

It is of interest to note that the Supreme Court 'reached back' to before the actual initiation of criminal charges in requiring what might be described as all reasonable speed in the processing of charges. The effect of the decision appears to be that prosecuting authorities may be subject to judicial review if, being aware that there is sufficient evidence to charge a person, they do not take reasonable steps to proceed to charge. As pointed out by Gannon J in the High Court, and affirmed by the Supreme Court, an individual may not have the 'right' to be charged, but prosecuting authorities have a clear obligation to proceed with charges where there is enough evidence to proceed to the judicial phase of the criminal process. The distinction is a fine one; it seems to reflect the approach that, while the courts will not interfere in a wide-ranging way with an arm of the executive branch of government, judicial review will lie where the judicial process is likely to be tainted with unconstitutionality.

Warrants   Further discussion of the issue of delays in the criminal process took place in *Dutton v O'Donnell* [1989] IR 218. The applicant had been convicted in the District Court in June 1987 of a number of offences and was sentenced to nine months detention in St Patrick's Institution. He was granted bail pending his appeal to the Circuit Court, which was not heard until January 1988 when he withdrew his appeal and his sentences were confirmed. In the meantime, the applicant had been convicted of other offences in December 1987 and sentenced to six months detention in St Patrick's Institution, which detention commenced on the date of sentence. The Court in question had not been informed of the applicant's then pending appeals to the Circuit Court in respect of the June 1987 convictions. Nor was the Circuit Court informed in January 1988, when affirming the June 1987 sentences, that the applicant was at the time serving a sentence of detention in St Patrick's Institution on foot of the December 1987 convictions. No warrants for his arrest were issued by the Circuit Court in January 1988. In March 1988, the applicant was released from St Patrick's Institution on temporary release. Because the Circuit Court had not issued warrants for his arrest in January 1988, the matter was remitted to the District Court, which issued warrants in April 1988. The applicant claimed that the failure to issue the warrants between January and April 1988 was in breach of Rule 198 of the District Court Rules 1948 which requires that such warrants issue 'forthwith' and that the failure was also in breach of his constitutional right to fair procedures. Barron J granted the relief sought.

He held that the issuing of the warrants in April 1988 in respect of a conviction which had been affirmed by the Circuit Court in January 1988 could not be described as having been done 'forthwith'. While Rule 198 of the District Court Rules 1948 did not require that the warrant be issued forthwith, he held that it must be implied as a matter of fair procedures (Barron J not expressly referring to Article 40.3 of the Constitution) that action would be taken promptly. In the circumstances of the instant case, he found that the delay involved was inordinate.

As to the consequences of the delay, Barron J was of the view that the important period was between affirmation of sentence and arrest on foot of the warrants. The question in each case, he felt, was at what point in time should the line be drawn between excessive delay and delay which was excusable, applying dicta of Egan J in *Cunningham v Governor of Mountjoy Prison* [1987] ILRM 33 to that effect. He also distinguished the instant case from the circumstances which arose in *The State (Flynn and McCormack) v Governor of Mountjoy Prison*, High Court, 6 May 1987 (in which he had given judgment: see the 1987 Review, 121-2). Pointing out that delay could result in prejudice, he concluded that in the absence of an explanation for the delay in the instant case, the delay was excessive.

Arising from the difficulties which had arisen in the instant case, Barron J proferred some guidance as to what might be appropriate in future cases. He stated that in circumstances such as arose here, the Circuit Court must be informed of the fact that the person whose sentences are affirmed is already in custody so that a warrant can issue immediately, so that the injustice which can result from the delay in issuing a warrant from the District Court can be avoided.

EVIDENCE

Accomplice evidence: warning   *The People v Murtagh*, Court of Criminal Appeal, 27 July 1989 was a case on the need for a warning in connection with accomplice evidence. The appellant had been convicted of subornation of perjury and of an attempt to pervert the course of justice. At his trial in the Circuit Criminal Court, a central piece of evidence was given by a woman who stated that she had been asked by the appellant to make a false statement to the effect that the appellant had been assaulted while in Garda custody, and that she had made this statement. The appellant was sentenced to two years imprisonment on both counts. He applied for leave to appeal, the application was granted and he was admitted to bail pending his appeal.

The Court of Criminal Appeal (Finlay CJ, Costello and Johnson JJ) allowed the appeal. In relation to both counts, the Court pointed out that the person who had made the false statements in question was an accomplice of the appellant in the two offences alleged against him. For this reason the trial judge should have given a warning to the jury on the dangers of convicting on the evidence of an accomplice, and in the absence of such warning the convictions should be set aside. The decision of the Court underlines the strictness with which the courts continue to deal with cases of accomplice evidence. For a case which approved a charge to a jury on accomplice evidence see the Court of Criminal Appeal decision in *The People v McGinley* [1987] IR 342 (1987 Review, 123).

Burden of proof v evidential burden   The distinction between these matters was raised in *The People v O'Shea (G.)*, Court of Criminal Appeal, 28 July 1989 (140, above).

Confessions: Judges' Rules   In *The People v Buckley*, Court of Criminal Appeal, 31 July 1989 the question raised was the effect of a breach of the Judges' Rules on the admissibility of a statement made later during interrogation. The applicant had been convicted of robbery in the Special Criminal Court. He had been arrested pursuant to s.30 of the Offences against the State Act 1939, and while detained in Garda custody he had been asked to 'tell the truth' in relation to a robbery with firearms. He made a verbal admission which was ruled inadmissible at his trial for breach of Rule 8 of the Judges' Rules. A second admission was made by the applicant shortly afterwards and this was also ruled inadmissible by the trial court on the ground that a fresh caution should have been administered pursuant to the Judges' Rules. A further admission was later made by the applicant, after a caution had been administered to him, and the trial court ruled this statement to be admissible. The applicant sought leave to appeal against conviction on the ground that the last statement should not have been admitted in evidence as it was tainted by the previous inadmissible statements. The Court of Criminal Appeal (Finlay CJ, Carroll and Johnson JJ) dismissed the application.

Delivering the Court's judgment, the Chief Justice stated that a court should have regard to the circumstances surrounding the giving of previously inadmissible admissions where such previous admissions had been made by virtue of threats or inducements (citing, inter alia, *The People v Galvin* [1964] IR 325). But, he added, very different considerations applied where the previous admissions were ruled inadmissible for breach of the Judges' Rules. The Court concluded that, having regard to the fact that a caution was properly administered before the making of the final admission, the trial court had been correct in ruling the admission was admissible in evidence.

Confessions: law reform   In early October, the Director of Public Prosecutions for England and Wales announced his intention not to contest the convictions of the Guildford Four, and they were subsequently released when their case came before the Court of Appeal on referral by the British Home Secretary. While the decision of the Director did not hinge directly on the fact that persons could be convicted solely on the basis of a confession, public disquiet on this count had repercussions in this State. It is clear, of course, that many convictions in criminal cases rest solely on the basis of confessions and many trials involve challenges to their admissibility. Before the Guildford Four and Birmingham Six cases, however, the political agenda did not include the alteration of the existing rules to require, for example, independent corroboration of confessions. As was pointed out by Paul Carney SC (*Irish Times*), 19 October 1989, the current law, through detention powers in s.30 of the Offences against the State Act 1939 and s.4 of the Criminal Justice Act 1984, facilitates questioning in police custody and the admissibility of confessions without further corroboration. In late October, the Labour Party introduced its Private Member's Bill, the Criminal Justice Bill 1989. The Bill proposed that independent corroboration of a confession be required to secure a conviction. The Bill also proposed empowering the Minister for Justice to refer a conviction to the Court of Criminal Appeal in much the same way as facilitated the release of the Guildford Four in England. It seems unlikely that the 'independent corroboration' rule will become law, at least in the near future. In December, the Minister for Justice established a Committee To Enquire into Certain Aspects of Criminal Procedure, chaired by Judge Frank Martin. The terms of reference were two-fold. First to examine whether there was a need for a 'reference' procedure and if so what form it should take. The second term of reference precluded recommending a 'corroboration' requirement for confessions. It stated: 'given that uncorroborated inculpatory admissions made by an accused to the Garda Síochána can be sufficient evidence to ground a conviction, to examine whether additional safeguards are needed to ensure that such admissions are properly obtained and recorded and to made recommendations accordingly.' The Committee reported in 1990 and recommended a reference procedure and also the recording of interviews with accused persons. The government indicated that it accepted the recommendations in principle. The Report will be discussed in the 1990 Review.

Confessions: voluntariness This point was raised in *The People v Egan* [1989] IR 681 (175, below).

Constitutional rights: deliberate and conscious violation *The People v Kenny (M.)*, Court of Criminal Appeal, 15 June 1989 and 30 November 1989; [1990] ILRM 569 (SC) is, without doubt, worthy of being described as a landmark decision in Irish constitutional and criminal law. The Supreme Court held that evidence obtained by means of an action by a member of the Garda Síochána, and which violated a constitutional right of an accused person, was inadmissible regardless of whether the Garda Síochána who obtained the evidence was aware that a right had been violated. The case clarifies, therefore, the meaning of the phrase 'deliberate and conscious violation' which first appeared in the Supreme Court decision in *The People v O'Brien* [1965] IR 142. An indication of the direction the Supreme Court was taking was given in *The People v Healy (P.)*, Supreme Court, 5 December 1989 (137, above), but the *Kenny* decision addressed the issue in full. The decision of the Supreme Court is of such significance that it is discussed in outline here, but a fuller discussion will be made in the 1990 Review.

The background to the case was as follows. The appellant had been charged in the Circuit Criminal Court of offences under the Misue of Drugs Acts 1977 and 1984. The principal evidence against him consisted of quantities of controlled drugs which had been found in his flat pursuant to a search warrant obtained by the Garda Síochána under s.26 of the 1977 Act, as amended by the 1984 Act. The Garda applying for the search warrant had sworn an information stating that he suspected that controlled drugs were in the flat in contravention of the 1977 Act, as amended. The Peace Commissioner who granted the warrant acted on the sworn information without further evidence. At the appellant's trial, the trial judge ruled admissible the evidence obtained on foot of the search warrant, and the appellant was subsequently found guilty of the offences charged. The appellant unsuccessfully appealed to the Court of Criminal Appeal, but on further appeal pursuant to s.29 of the Courts of Justice Act 1924 his conviction was set aside by the Supreme Court.

As to the invalidity of the search warrant, there was no disagreement between the courts. In its judgment delivered on 15 June 1989, the Court of Criminal Appeal (McCarthy, O'Hanlon and Lardner JJ) approved the decision of Hamilton P in *Byrne v Grey* [1988] IR 31 (see the discussion in the 1987 Review, 85-6 and the 1988 Review, 192-4). In line with that decision, the Court concluded that the search warrant was invalid since the Peace Commissioner had acted purely on the say-so of the Garda who applied for the warrant and had failed to exercise any independent judicial discretion as required by s.26 of the 1977 Act, as amended by the 1984 Act. The Court was of the view, however, that this did not determine the admissibility of the physical evidence obtained in the appellant's house. The Court therefore invited further submissions from counsel on the admissibility question.

This involved a full consideration by the Court of the effect of the exclusionary rule first referred to in *The People v O'Brien* [1965] IR 142.

There have been a number of decisions since then, both of the Court of Criminal Appeal and of the Supreme Court, which have demonstrated a clear division of opinion among the judges as to how that exclusionary rule works: see the informative discussion by O'Connor, (1982) 17 *Ir Jur (ns)* 257. Much of the disagreement centres on the meaning of the phrase 'deliberate and conscious violation of constitutional rights', the litmus test of admissibility in *O'Brien*. Is evidence inadmissible under this test only where a member of the Garda Síochána engages in an intentional violation of a constitutional right? Yes said the Court of Criminal Appeal in *Kenny*; no said the Supreme Court.

The answer to this question is not simply a matter of a dictionary definition of the words 'deliberate and conscious'; it involves important policy issues concerning the purpose of the exclusionary rule. This has been a major discussion point in the United States Supreme Court where a strict exclusionary rule had been introduced many years prior to the *O'Brien* decision. Through a number of decisions in the 1960s, the US Supreme Court had explained that the rule was intended to deter unlawful activity by the police. The 'penalty' was to exclude unconstitutionally obtained evidence. By the 1980s, with a differently constituted Supreme Court, there was a degree of drawing back from the exclusionary rule. The decision in *United States v Leon*, 468 US 897 (1984) is representative of this change of heart by the United States Supreme Court. The question thus posed in the *Kenny* case was whether the Irish exclusionary rule was intended as a deterrance against unlawful police conduct. The Supreme Court decision has made it plain that its primary purpose is quite different: the vindication of constitutional rights.

Returning to the Court of Criminal Appeal in *Kenny*, in a second judgment delivered on 30 November 1989, it held that although the entry into the appellant's dwelling was unlawful, there had been no deliberate and conscious violation of the appellant's constitutional right under Article 40.5. The judgment conceded that where no justification could be put forward by the prosecution witnesses for failure to observe a clearly established rule of law, the considerations which applied were clear, and evidence obtained in such circumstances would be ruled inadmissible. But the Court held that different considerations applied where, as with the procedure for obtaining search warrants, the law had been generally interpreted and applied in a particular way without challenge over a substantial period of time, but then in *Byrne v Grey* [1988] IR 31 there was a change in the judicial interpretation of what was accepted as lawful. In such circumstances, the Court held, there is no deliberate and conscious violation of constitutional rights and the courts should not apply the exclusionary rule in relation to evidence thereby obtained (for a similar kind of argument, but which was rejected, see *Finucance v McMahon*, High Court (Divisional), 7 April 1989: 158 below).

Significantly, the Court of Criminal Appeal expressly approved the views put forward by White J, delivering the majority decision of the United States Supreme Court, in *United States v Leon*, 468 US 897 (1984).

The Court concluded that, in the instant case, the admissibility of the evidence was a matter for the trial judge's discretion and since no miscarriage of justice had occurred the Court dismissed the appeal in accordance with s.5(1)(a) of the Courts of Justice Act 1928. The Court did, however, grant a certificate of leave to appeal to the Supreme Court pursuant to s.29 of the Courts of Justice Act 1924. In an unusual move, the Supreme Court admitted the appellant to bail pending the appeal: see Irish Times LR, 19 March 1990. As already indicated, the Supreme Court gave its decision on 20 March 1990. By a 3-2 majority the Court (Finlay CJ, Walsh and Hederman JJ; Griffin and Lynch JJ dissenting) allowed the appeal and quashed the appellant's conviction. The 1990 Review will contain a fuller discussion of the decision, but a brief account is appropriate here in view of its importance.

Delivering the leading judgment, Finlay CJ held that the exclusionary rule should be based on an approach which would be likely to provide a stronger and more effective defence and vindication of constitutional rights. He pointed out that to exclude evidence only where a person knows or ought reasonably to know that he is invading a constitutional right would be to impose a negative deterrent. However, to exclude evidence on the basis of what the Chief Justice described as the absolute protection rule of exclusion (that is in circumstances where there is a conscious and deliberate violation of rights without regard to the state of knowledge of the policeman) incorporates, he said, an additional positive encouragement to those involved in crime prevention and detection to consider in detail the effects of their powers on the personal rights of the citizen.

He acknowledged that although the absolute protection rule of exclusion might lead to anomalies in its application, and might hinder the capacity of the courts to arrive at the truth and thus to administer justice effectively, this could not outweigh the obligation to protect personal rights pursuant to Article 40.3. Accordingly the courts must rule inadmissible evidence obtained in violation of constitutional rights unless the act constituting the breach was committed unintentionally or accidently, or there are extraordinary excusing circumstances justifying its admissibility. To the extent that the majority decision in *The People v Shaw* [1982] IR 1 appeared to be in conflict with this approach, the Chief Justice stated that he would not be prepared to follow it. And the rationale for the exclusionary rule put forward in *United States v Leon*, 468 US 897 (1984) was expressly disapproved. The Court's decision in *The People v Healy (P.)*, Supreme Court, 5 December 1989 was, as indicated earlier, followed.

In conclusion, the majority held that since the acts of the Gardaí in the instant case were neither unintentional or accidental and there were no extraordinary excusing circumstances present, the evidence obtained was inadmissible even though the Gardaí had no knowledge that they were invading the constitutional rights of the appellant. Accordingly the appellant's conviction was quashed. In dissent, Griffin and Lynch JJ considered that the acts of the Gardaí could not be regarded as amounting to conscious and deliberate violations of the appellant's constitutional rights. They both analysed the case law in detail, and this will be discussed in the 1990 Review.

Disclosure of material by prosecution   On the changed instructions from the Director of Public Prosecutions arising from the *nolle prosequi* entered in *The People v Morris* (*Irish Times*, 21 November 1989), see 177, below.

Imputation of character   In *The People v McGrail*, Court of Criminal Appeal, 18 December 1989 an important interpretation was provided of the circumstances in which the accused's 'shield' from being questioned as to previous character might be put in issue. S.1(f)(ii) of the Criminal Justice (Evidence) Act 1924 provides that the accused's previous bad character may not be put in evidence unless the conduct of the defence has involved imputations on the character of the prosecutor or witnesses for the prosecution.

The appellant had been charged with firearms offences. The principal evidence against him was a number of verbal statements which were alleged to have been made by the appellant to members of the Gardai. At his trial the appellant repudiated the verbal statements, and in cross-examination of the Gardai it was argued that the statements had never in fact been made. Counsel for the prosecution applied to the trial judge for leave to cross-examine the appellant as to his previous character on the basis that the character of the Gardai had been put in issue by the defence. Leave was granted, and the appellant stated in his direct examination that he had previous convictions which concerned cars. The appellant was convicted and sentenced to a total of 12 years imprisonment. The Court of Criminal Appeal (Hederman, Egan and Barr JJ) quashed the conviction.

Delivering the Court's judgment, Hederman J stated that the trial judge had erred in concluding that the appellant's 'shield' had dropped as a result of the conduct of the defence in the instant case. He pointed out that in every criminal trial an accused might argue that prosecution witnesses were not to be believed; but this did not bring into effect the terms of s.1(f)(ii) of the Criminal Justice (Evidence) Act 1924. While acknowledging that the conduct in the instant case did involve an imputation of character in one sense, the provisions of s.1(f)(ii) would only become operative where the imputation of character arose independently of the facts of the particular case. Otherwise, the Court stated, an accused person would be intimidated from presenting a full defence to the trial court. The Court of Criminal Appeal concluded by noting that principles of fair procedures required the interpretation it had placed on s.1(f)(ii), and it expressly disapproved of recent English decisions to the contrary.

Newspaper reports   In *Society for the Protection of Unborn Children (Irl.) Ltd v Grogan and Ors* [1990] ILRM 350; [1989] IR 753 (see 102, above, in the Constitutional Law chapter) an issue which arose in the High Court was the degree of proof required to found a conviction for contempt of court. Carroll J rejected the view that in a criminal trial newspaper reports, which were attached to affidavits filed on the plaintiff's behalf, could be regarded as sufficient evidence on which to attach the defendants for contempt. While the contempt in this case would appear to have been civil contempt, as opposed to criminal contempt (for the distinction see *Keegan v deBurca* [1973] IR 223), Carroll J appeared to treat the matter as one requiring proof beyond reasonable doubt. This approach receives support from authorities in other common law jurisdictions: see Miller, *Contempt of Court* (2nd ed., 1989), 27-9. Carroll J stated ([1989] IR 753, at 759): 'I am not prepared to find that someone is guilty of breaking a court order on newspaper reports. . . . It is not prima facie proof; it is hearsay and nobody should be committed to prison on hearsay.' She rejected the view that *The State (Lynch) v Cooney* [1983] ILRM 89; [1982] IR 337 was authority for the proposition that newspaper reports could be relied on in a contempt motion. Had the matter not been dealt with *ex tempore*, she might also have supported her conclusion by reference to the decision of the Court of Criminal Appeal in *The People v McGinley* [1987] IR 342 (see the 1987 Review, 123-4). It should be noted, of course, that on the other aspect of the case, that is, whether an interlocutory injunction should have been granted, the use of newspaper reports is permissible: that was the view taken by the Supreme Court in *Society for the Protection of Unborn Children (Irl.) Ltd v Coogan and Ors* [1990] ILRM 70; [1989] IR 734.

EXTRADITION

There were a large number of High Court decisions in the extradition area in 1989. Two of these, the *Finucane* and *Carron* decisions, dealt with the political offence exception in s.50 of the Extradition Act 1965. What is of particular interest is that these two decisions (along with that in the *Clarke* case, which had been dealt with on quite a different basis in the High Court, as to which see below) were reversed on appeal by the Supreme Court in March and April 1990. This has produced a dramatic reversal of the recent trend in the case law on the topic. 1989 also saw the first case to discuss the Extradition (Amendment) Act 1987.

Arrest safeguards In *McGlinchey v Ireland (No.2)*, High Court, 6 December 1989 Costello J rejected a number of challenges to the constitutional validity of Part III of the Extradition Act 1965. It will be recalled that the plaintiff had previously instituted proceedings challenging various aspects of his extradition: *McGlinchey v Governor of Portlaoise Prison* [1988] IR 671 (see the 1987 Review, 109-10). In the instant case, the defence raised two preliminary objections to the proceedings.

First, it was argued that the plaintiff had no *locus standi* to bring the proceedings, on the basis that since he had already been extradited to Northern Ireland and been returned any arguments were now moot. However, Costello J held that since the plaintiff remained apprehensive that he might be extradited again, he was prepared to accept that this was sufficient to bring him within the decision in *Cahill v Sutton* [1980] IR 269. The second preliminary point was that the issues raised were *res judicata*, but Costello J was of the view that the issues had not in fact been determined in the previous decision reported in [1988] IR 671.

Costello J then turned to the substantive issues raised. He accepted that, on the basis of the expert evidence presented, the Northern Ireland warrants under which the plaintiff had been arrested in 1982 had not been validly issued. However, he did not consider that this rendered Part III of the 1965 Act unconstitutional since the plaintiff was still entitled to institute proceedings under Article 40.4 of the Constitution which would challenge the legality of his detention. And, Costello J added that the procedures introduced by the Extradition (Amendment) Act 1987 provided additional safeguards under which further irregularities might be brought to light by the Attorney General, as to which see *Wheeler v Culligan* [1989] IR 344, (91, above) in the Constitutional Law chapter. Finally, Costello J did not consider that the backing of warrants from Northern Ireland was prohibited by Article 2 or 3 of the Constitution, since the courts had accepted that the recognition of the status of Northern Ireland was constitutionally valid. He relied in particular on the decision of the Supreme Court in *In re the Criminal Law (Jurisdiction) Bill 1975* [1977] IR 112 in this context. He also referred with approval to the decision of Barrington J in *McGimpsey v Ireland* [1989] ILRM 209; [1988] IR 567. While some of the *dicta* in the *Criminal Law (Jurisdiction) Bill* case were put in doubt by the subsequent Supreme Court decision in *McGimpsey* in March 1990 ([1990] ILRM 440), the conclusion reached by Costello J in *McGlinchey* would not appear to be affected. The *McGimpsey* decision will be discussed in full in the 1990 Review.

Attorney General's role   In *Wheeler v Culligan* [1989] IR 344, the High Court upheld the constitutionality of the Attorney General's role under the Extradition (Amendment) Act 1987: see 91, above, in the Constitutional Law chapter.

Correspondence of offences   A number of important issues on correspondence of offences were raised in *Sey v Johnson* [1989] IR 516. The respondent Justice ordered the extradition of the applicant to Scotland on foot of warrants issued by a Scottish sheriff. The warrant specified two counts against the applicant: (i) making false representations to the police and to an insurance company that his house had been broken into and property stolen therefrom, as a result of which compensation was paid to him; and (ii) receiving a cigarette lighter for safekeeping and appropriating it to his own use and stealing it. The respondent Justice's order under s.47 of the Extradition Act 1965 stated that the first count in the warrant corresponded to offences under s.10 of the Criminal Justice Act 1951 and s.6 of the Forgery Act 1913, though the order did not specify the precise offences. As to the second count, the respondent's order stated that this corresponded to fraudulent conversion under s.20 of the Larceny Act 1916. The applicant sought judicial review claiming that the counts alleged did not correspond to offences under Irish law and that, in relation to the second count, the delay of six years in bringing the charge precluded the courts form granting the request. On judicial review O'Hanlon J refused to quash the respondent's order.

O'Hanlon J agreed that the first count corresponded to an offence under s.10 of the Criminal Justice Act 1951. Although he was also of the view that the respondent may have been in error in considering that there was also a correspondence with s.6 of the Forgery Act 1913, O'Hanlon J relied on dicta in *The State (Furlong) v Kelly* [1971] IR 132 to conclude that this did not invalidate the order once correspondence had been established. Citing dicta in *Wyatt v McLoughlin* [1974] IR 378, O'Hanlon J went on to say that while it was preferable that the respondent should have specified the nature of the offences which he considered to correspond with those in the warrants, such failure was not fatal once correspondence was in fact established in the High Court.

On the second count against the applicant, O'Hanlon J did not consider that he should come to a final determination one way or the other as to whether that count did or did not have a corresponding offence under Irish law. This was because, in accordance with the decision in *Molloy v Sheehan*

[1978] IR 438, there was no need to do so since it was sufficient, to validate the warrant requesting extradition, that one of the offences specified correspond with an Irish offence. No doubt the *Molloy* decision remains a sound precedent in this context, but see the constitutional issues raised by Walsh J in *Ellis v O'Dea* [1990] ILRM 87; [1989] IR 530 (160, below). Finally, it may be noted that the applicant's appeal to the Supreme Court was withdrawn on the date of the hearing and O'Hanlon J's order was affirmed: [1989] IR 523n.

The question of correspondence was also raised in *McDonald v McMahon*, High Court, 13 January 1989 (163, below).

Delay in extradition applications In *Sey v Johnson* [1989] IR 516, above, O'Hanlon J also rejected the suggestion that delay by the prosecuting authorities could constitute a ground for refusing an extradition request. O'Hanlon J relied on dicta of Henchy J in *Hanlon v Fleming* [1982] ILRM 69; [1981] IR 489 in which he had stated: 'For the Courts in this State to recognise delay as such a ground, it would be necessary to read into the [1965 Act] something which has been omitted, presumably on purpose.' Whatever about the propriety of speculating on the intention of the Oireachtas in this context, it may be noted that the comments of Henchy J were made before the courts in this State had developed a fully articulated jurisprudence on delay in criminal proceedings. The case law has only emerged since the mid-1980s: see the discussion above, 141.

To rely on *dicta* from a decision in 1980, therefore, might appear to have given this argument shorter shrift than it deserved. In addition, in the specific context of extradition hearings, the courts have also in recent years emphasised whether the person whose extradition is requested will be subjected to fair procedures. The decision of the Supreme Court in *Ellis v O'Dea* (which post-dated O'Hanlon J's judgment in *Sey*) reflects this recent development. The argument as to fair procedures, of course, arises from constitutional requirements and is not a matter explicitly referred to in the Extradition Act 1965. One could, of course, speculate as to whether this ground was also 'omitted, presumably on purpose' by the Oireachtas from the 1965 Act.

Description of State In *Ellis v O'Dea* [1990] ILRM 87; [1989] IR 530 the Supreme Court discussed whether extradition warrants from Great Britain correctly described the State: see 161, below.

High Court's function The limit of the High Court's function in an extradition hearing was the main issue addressed in the judgment of Costello J in *Clarke v McMahon*, High Court, 28 July 1989. As indicated above, however, when the case was decided by the Supreme Court in March 1990 the decision turned on other issues. These will be dealt with in the 1990 Review. For present purposes, the discussion deals solely with the argument as to the type of inquiry undertaken by the High Court under s.50 of the Extradition Act 1965.

The applicant had been convicted in 1979 in Northern Ireland of attempted murder and other offences. The evidence against the applicant was contained in statements made by him while in police custody. The applicant did not contest the admissibility of the statements at his trial and the trial judge ruled them admissible. In 1983, the applicant escaped from custody in the Maze Prison. In 1988, the District Court ordered his extradition to Northern Ireland, on foot of a number of warrants relating to the offences of which he had been convicted and also to the escape from the Maze prison. The applicant claimed, inter alia, that he should not be extradited on the ground that the statements obtained from him while in police custody were the result of inhuman and degrading treatment and were untrue. Costello J refused the application.

He held that the Court could not properly conduct an investigation as to whether the applicant's conviction over 10 years ago had been based on inadmissible evidence, particularly having regard to the fact that the point was not raised at the original trial and that it would not be consistent with the purpose underlying the terms of s.50 of the 1965 Act. Costello J quoted with approval the views of Finlay P (as he then was) in *Archer v Fleming*, High Court, 31 January 1980, where the present Chief Justice had indicated that the courts should not become involved in an inquiry into the merits of the charges being alleged against a person whose extradition was sought. Although Costello J acknowledged that the court had an inherent jurisdiction to protect the constitutional rights of persons, a fair adjudication of the applicant's complaint was not possible and to attempt it would amount to an unconstitutional exercise of the court's judicial powers.

As already indicated, the *Clarke* case took quite a different turn when it reached the Supreme Court, but the general comments made by Costello J were held to continue to reflect the general approach of the High Court to its functions under s.50 of the Extradition Act 1965.

Identification evidence   *Crowley v McVeigh* [1990] ILRM 220; [1989] IR 73 was a case stated to the High Court which arose from a well-publicised decision in the District Court in 1988: see the 1988 Review, 155. The respondent had appeared before the District Court in an application under the 1965 Act seeking his extradition to England. The warrant seeking his extradition named him as 'Patrick McVeigh, of Portlaoise Prison, County Laois, formerly of 18 Forest Street, Belfast, Northern Ireland.' The respondent's name was Patick McVeigh, and at the time that the warrant for his extradition was drafted he was serving a sentence of imprisonment in Portlaoise Prison and was the only person of that name serving a sentence. He had also given his address as 18 Forest Street, Belfast prior to his imprisonment. The District Justice hearing the application for the respondent's extradition was not satisfied that the respondent had been sufficiently identified as the person named in the warrant seeking his extradition, as required by s.47(1) of the Extradition Act 1965, and therefore ordered his release. On a case stated to the High Court Blayney J remitted the matter to the District Court, and held that the identification had, in fact, been sufficient.

On a preliminary point as to service of documents, Blayney J held that although the respondent had not been served with the notice of the appeal as required by s.2 of the Summary Jurisdiction Act 1857, nonetheless where as in the present case every possible effort was made to serve the respondent and where service was then effected on the solicitor who had acted for him in the District Court proceedings, there was sufficient compliance with the 1857 Act to confer jurisdiction on the High Court. Blayney J approved the views of Palles CB to that effect in *Clarke v Maguire* [1909] 2 IR 681.

On the substantive issue raised, he held that the District Justice was incorrect in coming to the conclusion that the respondent was not the person named in the warrant within the meaning of s.47(1) of the 1965 Act, having regard to the uncontested evidence heard in the District Court and the extent of the correspondence between the warrant and the facts known about the respondent. He concluded that where, as here, the evidence in the District Court had been uncontested, the High Court had authority to reach a different conclusion from that in the District Court. He thus distinguished the instant case from the situation which had arisen in *Director of Public Prosecutions v Nangle* [1984] ILRM 171.

Minister for Justice's role In *Kane v McMahon and Shields*, High Court (Divisional), 16 March 1989 the applicant challenged the validity of orders made by the second respondent District Justice for the delivery of the applicant into the custody of the Northern Ireland authorities pursuant to warrants requesting his extradition under the Extradition Act 1965. The principal grounds of challenge to the orders were that the respondent Justice did not have before him any sufficient evidence that the Minister for Justice had considered each of the warrants pursuant to s.44 of the 1965 Act before endorsement by the first respondent. The Divisional Court (Hamilton P, Ganon and Costello J) dismissed the applicant's claim.

The Court held that ss.47, 48 and 49 of the 1965 Act, which prescribed that limited judicial functions of a procedural nature be carried out by the

District Justice hearing the extradition application, did not require the Justice to inquire whether the Minister for Justice had considered the warrant pursuant to s.44 of the Act. The Court cited with approval *dicta* in *The State (Holmes) v Furlong* [1967] IR 210 in this context. As to the nature of the powers given to the Minister under ss.44 and 50 of the 1965 Act, the Court held that these allowed the Minister to intervene in certain instances, but not to make the form of inquiry which was more suited to the courts in exercising the functions conferred by the Act. Finally the Court held that the provisions of ss.45 to 50 of the 1965 Act provided adequate protection and vindication of the applicant's constitutional rights by establishing a procedure by which the validity of the order in the District Court could be challenged. The applicant did not pursue an appeal to the Supreme Court from this decision. He applied to the Minister under the 1965 Act to have his extradition refused, but the Minister declined to overturn the orders made in the courts. This would appear to reflect the view of the Minister's powers expressed by the Divisional High Court. The applicant was subsequently extradited to Northern Ireland: see *Irish Times*, 31 March and 14 April 1989.

Political offence   Two decisions of the Divisional High Court in 1989 endorsed the view taken by the Supreme Court in *Russell v Fanning* [1988] ILRM 333; [1988] IR 505 which had cut down substantially on the availability of the political offence exception. The effect of the Supreme Court decisions in 1990, on appeal from the High Court, has been to overrule the *Russell* decision. While the Supreme Court decisions will be discussed in full in the 1990 Review, the High Court decisions raised some points which are of separate interest, and are discussed here for convenience.

    In *Carron v McMahon*, High Court (Divisional), 16 March 1989 the applicant was arrested and brought before the District Court on foot of warrants for his arrest issued in Northern Ireland, and endorsed by the respondent Deputy Garda Commissioner. The Court ordered his extradition to Northern Ireland. The warrants alleged that the applicant had, on a particular date, in his possession specified arms and ammunition with intent to endanger life. The applicant sought an inquiry pursuant to Article 40.4 of the Constitution, in which he put forward a number of grounds challenging the validity of the order extraditing him. These included, *inter alia*, that the offences with which he was to be charged were political offences or offences connected with political offences and that, if returned to Northern Ireland he faced the risk of ill-treatment or of being killed. The Divisional Court (Hamilton P, Gannon and Costello J) refused the relief sought on all grounds put forward. We may note here, however, that on both the arguments mentioned (the political offence exception and the risk of ill-treatment) the Supreme Court reversed the High Court in March 1990.

Relying on the majority Supreme Court decision in *Russell v Fanning* [1988] ILRM 333; [1988] IR 505 (which had in turn affirmed the view in *Quinn v Wren* [1985] ILRM 410; [1984] IR 322), the Divisional Court held that the offence could not be regarded as one connected with a political offence pursuant to s.50 of the 1965 Act, since the applicant stated they were carried out to further the objectives of the IRA and thus amounted to an attempt to undermine the Constitution and the institutions of State (including the judiciary) established by it. The Court also rejected the argument as to the risk of ill-treatment if he were to be returned to Northern Ireland. Both these points will be dealt with in the 1990 Review.

Finally, the High Court held that the District Justice who heard the application for extradition was not required to inquire whether the Minister for Justice had exercised his powers under s.44 of the Extradition Act 1965. In this the Court followed its decision given on the same day in *Kane v McMahon*, High Court (Divisional), 16 March 1989 (as to which see above, 155).

The second decision of the High Court on the political offence issue raised more extensive issues for discussion. In *Finucane v McMahon*, High Court (Divisional), 7 April 1989, the applicant had been convicted in Northern Ireland in 1982 of possession of firearms with intent to endanger life and was sentenced to 18 years imprisonment. In 1983, he escaped from custody. In October 1987 a number of warrants seeking his extradition were issued in Northern Ireland, and these were indorsed by the respondent Deputy Garda Commissioner on 25 November 1987 on which date the applicant was arrested on foot of the warrants. The applicant had been arrested on 23 November 1987 by the Gardaí under s.30 of the Offences against the State Act 1939 in the course of a nationwide search for arms and ammunition. The arrest under s.30 was made on suspicion that the applicant was a member of a proscribed organisation, the IRA. On the expiry of the detention period under s.30, the applicant was immediately arrested on foot of the extradition warrants without having left the Garda station in which he had been detained under s.30. He was brought before the District Court which subsequently ordered his extradition to Northern Ireland. He challenged the validity of the extradition orders on a number of grounds.

The Divisional High Court (Hamilton P, Gannon and Costello JJ) refused the relief sought under all the grounds put forward. On the political offence issue, the Court (as in its *Carron* decision) followed the majority view in *Russell v Fanning* [1988] ILRM 333; [1988] IR 505. In *Finucane*, the Court held that the averment by the applicant that the acts which he carried out on behalf of the IRA were not aimed at the overthrow of the Constitution were not sufficient to attract the protection of s.50 of the Extradition Act 1965, having regard to the fact that the IRA was a proscribed organisation under s.18 of the Offences against the State Act 1939. It may be noted, briefly, that it was on this point that the Supreme Court reversed the High Court decision, and the mere fact that a person is a member of a proscribed organisation is not now sufficient to deny them the opportunity to avail themselves of s.50 of the 1965 Act. Whether the person can successfully avail himself of s.50 is, of course, another matter. This point will be dealt with in more detail in the discussion of the Supreme Court decision in *Finucane* in the 1990 Review. We will also deal with the argument that the applicant would have been subjected to ill-treatment if returned to Northern Ireland, an argument again rejected by the High Court in *Carron* but which was to prove decisive in the Supreme Court.

There were, as indicated, a number of other points of interest raised in the High Court in *Finucane* and these are dealt with here. The applicant had raised the point that, at the time of the commission of the offences in question, he had believed that they would be regarded as political offences within s.50 of the 1965 Act were he to face an extradition hearing (the offences having predated the decision of the Supreme Court in *McGlinchey v Wren* [1983] ILRM 169; [1982] IR 154). This argument received relatively short shrift from the High Court, which relied on a traditional analysis of the nature of judicial decisions. The Court pointed out that the issue as to whether an offence was a political offence was a mixed question of law and fact, and the court would determine that issue by reference to its understanding of the law at the date of the hearing and not by reference to judicial pronouncements at the date of the commission of the alleged offence. In effect, the Court held to the traditional view that judicial decisions do not make law but merely explain its effect as best the court can in the light of prevailing insight into the meaning of the law.

This view has, of course, a knock on effect, since the 'insight' which courts display may change dramatically from one decision to the next. This is certainly the position with the political offence exception in the 1965 Act. The courts have moved from saying in the early 1970s that all offences committed on behalf of the IRA should be regarded as political offences; to saying in the early 1980s that only activity regarded by civilised persons as political activity should attract the 'political offence' label; to saying in the mid 1980s that a member of a proscribed organisation, such as the IRA, could never claim the benefit of s.50; to saying in March 1990 that the issue must be dealt with on a case by case basis by reference to a number of factors. In *Finucane*, the applicant argued that this change in direction was in breach of Article 40.1 of the Constitution; this was also rejected by the Divisional Court. It held that for a court to follow an authoritative ruling on the question whether an offence was not of a political nature may involve some citizens losing an exemption from extradition which previously appeared to arise, but such consequence did not involve discriminatory treatment contrary to Article 40.1 of the Constitution. Relying on *McMahon v Leahy* [1985] ILRM 423; [1984] IR 525, the Court also rejected the argument that the concept of estoppel could be extended to involve an implied representation by the State that extradition for certain offences would not occur in the future.

The High Court also dealt with arguments arising from the applicant's arrest under s.30 of the Offences against the State Act 1939. As regards the timing and circumstances of the applicant's arrest under s.30 of the 1939 Act, the Court held that, on the evidence, the version of events given by the Gardaí was to be preferred where any inconsistency arose with the version given by the applicant. In this light, the Court held that there was evidence to indicate that the arrest was not merely a device to hold the applicant pending the arrival of extradition warrants from Northern Ireland, and that the Gardai had investigated the question whether the applicant was a member of a proscribed organisation. For difficulties in using s.30 as a 'colourable device' see the 1988 Review, 142-4.

Finally, the Court held that it was lawful for a person to be arrested immediately at the cessation of an arrest under s.30 of the 1939 Act, and there was no legal requirement that the applicant should have been released from custody. The Court relied on *dicta* of Davitt P in *In re Ó Laighléis* [1960] IR 93 and of the Court of Criminal Appeal in *The People v Kehoe* [1986] ILRM 690 in this context.

Presumption of validity of warrants   Two cases considered the effect of s.55 of the Extradition Act 1965, which provides that, in an extradition hearing in the District Court, a document appearing to be a warrant for extradition issued by a judicial authority of the requesting State shall be admitted in evidence as such warrant 'unless the court sees good reason to the contrary'.

In *McMahon and Prenty v McClafferty* [1990] ILRM 32; [1989] IR 68, during the District Court hearing in which the respondent's extradition was sought, evidence was given by a Queen's Counsel practising in Northern Ireland and the District Justice took this evidence as indicating that the fiat of the Attorney General for Northern Ireland was required before proceedings could be commenced seeking extradition. The District Justice held that, in the absence of evidence that such fiat had been granted, the respondent's extradition could not be ordered. On a case stated by the applicants to the High Court Costello J held that the District Justice had erred in law.

First, Costello J dealt with a preliminary point. He held that although the District Justice had not signed the case stated within the six month time period specified in r.200 of the District Court Rules 1948, as inserted by r.17 of the

District Court Rules 1955, this was not a mandatory requirement and the High Court had jurisdiction to hear the appeal. He applied the views of Davitt P in *Prendergast v Porter* [1961] IR 440 in this context. See also the discussion of this point in the 1988 Review, 320.

On the main issue arising, he held that the District Justice had misconstrued the terms of s.55 of the Extradition Act 1965. The Justice was required to accept that the warrants on which the request was based had been duly issued in Northern Ireland, and the existence of a preliminary legal requirement whose fulfilment was necessary before a warrant could be issued was not a good reason for refusing to act on the assumption of validity contained in s.55, in the absence of additional evidence which might suggest non-compliance with such pre-condition.

In the light of this finding Costello J felt that it was not necessary to determine whether the District Justice was required to hear additional evidence as to whether the fiat was in fact a preliminary requirement, counsel for the applicants having indicated that such evidence was available in court.

Costello J returned to s.55 in the second case on this area, *Ellis v O'Dea* [1990] ILRM 87; [1989] IR 530, where his decision was unsuccessfully appealed to the Supreme Court. The applicant sought an order of prohibition preventing the further hearing of an extradition hearing in the District Court until he was furnished with copies of the sworn informations alleging that he committed offences upon which the warrants seeking his extradition under the 1965 Act were based. The applicant had stated in the District Court that English solicitors had been instructed to seek, and had sought, copies of the informations from the Crown Prosecution Service but that no reply had been received. Costello J refused to grant an order of prohibition, holding in effect that the application was premature. This was also the view taken in the Supreme Court.

Costello J held that there was nothing to suggest that the District Court was not going to follow the procedures laid down in s.55 of the Extradition Act 1965. In the absence of a challenge to the constitutionality of s.55, he concluded that the applicant had not shown that his constitutional rights of access to the court or to fair procedures were being infringed.

On appeal by the applicant to the Supreme Court (Finlay CJ, Walsh and McCarthy JJ) the constitutional dimension was addressed full square. In the leading judgment, Walsh J stated:

As the Extradition Act 1965 is a post-constitutional statute it must be construed as not permitting persons appearing before our courts to be by order of our courts subjected to or exposed to any judicial process or procedures, inside or outside this jurisdiction, which in this jurisdiction would amount to a denial or an infringement of the constitutional right to fair procedures. Any statute which would expressly seek to do so, or which by necessary implication would give rise to such a single interpretation, must necessarily be unconstitutional. There is nothing in the Act of 1965 which could be construed as purporting to permit to be exposed any person, the subject of extradition proceedings, to procedures which the Constitution would not tolerate. In other words there must be not only a correspondence of offences but also a correspondence of fair procedures.

The second last sentence clearly indicated that, while the Court was concerned to ensure fair procedures, there was nothing in the instant case to suggest that the District Justice could not enforce production of the information sought by the applicant if he considered that its production was required to ensure compliance with fair procedures. The Court therefore held that the application for prohibition should be dismissed.

Walsh J did, however, raise a point concerning the use of a conspiracy charge in the warrants requesting extradition (neither Finlay CJ or McCarthy J expressing a view on this aspect of the case). He noted that a general conspiracy charge had been joined to a substantive offence. He bluntly commented: 'For many years judicial authorities have condemned the joinder of a conspiracy charge when there is a charge for the substantive offence.' He pointed out that the 'elastic' rules which apply in conspiracy prosecutions could operate 'most oppressively' by, for example, allowing the conviction of a person on the untrue admissions of a co-accused. Drawing on the fair procedures argument he had already made in the passage quoted above, he warned:

> [I]f the courts of this country should at some future time decide that these special rules of evidence [in conspiracy trials] were such as to fall foul of the constitutional guarantees of fair procedures it is obvious that no court here could extradite a person from the protection of this jurisdiction to another where such protection would not be enjoyed.

Clearly, these comments have implications not just for extradition applications but also for criminal procedure in this State. While the practice in Ireland is that conspiracy charges are used rarely (for an example see *The People v Healy (N.)*, Court of Criminal Appeal, 12 July 1989, discussed at 183, below), the views of Walsh J, if taken up by other members of the judiciary, could result in their abandonment entirely. That, however, remains a matter for the future.

Walsh J made one final comment arising from the description of the State in the warrants. In this he was joined by McCarthy J, but Finlay CJ expressly reserved his view since it had not been raised in argument. Walsh J stated that it was impermissible for requesting courts to refer to the State as anything other than 'Ireland', when referring to it in the English language, as provided for in Article 4 of the Constitution. He warned that any warrants requesting extradition in the future which did not refer to the State as 'Ireland' should not be backed under the 1965 Act. Walsh J appeared to be of the view that the misstatement of the State's name was due to factors other than inadvertance.

Without wishing to minimise the importance of this point (it received a large amount of publicity in the immediate aftermath of the decision: see *Irish Times*, 6 December 1989), it could be argued that this State's Republic of Ireland Act 1948 itself may be a source of confusion. Of course, if the 1948 Act is *ultra vires* Article 4 of the Constitution, then it may be declared invalid, though it is unlikely that this point will be litigated. Walsh J adverted to the 1948 Act and, applying what amounted to a presumption of con-stitutionality, noted that any attempt to change the name of the State would require a constitutional amendment. The 1948 Act raises the distinction between a name and a description. Professor Casey considers that the distinction is 'elusive': *Constitutional Law in Ireland* (1987), 34. No doubt the 1948 Act may be explained as purporting to explain the type of political structure created by the Constitution: it is thus informative in a way that a name need not be.

Another source of confusion is Article 4 itself. *The Report of the Committee on the Constitution* (1967, Pr. 9817), para.14, drew attention to the unusual wording of the English language version of Article 4: 'The name of the State is Éire, or in the English language, Ireland'. The Preamble contains the even more confusing phrase 'We, the people of Éire'. Is this aspect of the Preamble easy to harmonise with Article 4?

It may also be that, while communications between the governments of Ireland and of the United Kingdom at the high diplomatic level referred to by Walsh J correctly reflect the true nomenclature of the State (Walsh J pointing out that accreditation of ambassadors is not to the President of the Republic of Ireland) communications at the level which arise in the extradition process may fall short of the ideal by reason of time constraints or other factors. Nonetheless, once the matter has been drawn to the attention of the authorities, it may be that one entry in a word processor will remedy this particular problem in the extradition field.

Indeed, it is to be hoped that the comments of Walsh J in *Ellis* will not fall on deaf ears, as has happened in the context of similar comments made by our judges in connection with domestic Irish criminal procedure. For example, in *The People v Bell* [1969] IR 24, Walsh J criticised the description of the High Court as the Central Criminal Court in s.11 of the Courts

(Supplemental Provisions) Act 1961, having regard to the sole description given to the High Court in the Constitution. It may be noted, however, that no declaration that s.11 was invalid was given in that case. Many Irish judges continue to use the term the Central Criminal Court. Even Walsh J himself appeared to have resigned himself to the s.11 description: *The People v Shaw* [1982] IR 1, 26. In the light of *Ellis*, however, could it be argued that a trial on indictment in the High Court could be challenged where an order returned an accused person to 'the Central Criminal Court'? Another point arises in this context. Some Irish judges, following the practice of those involved in drawing up indictments, continue to refer to proceedings brought in the name of the People of Ireland as 'Director of Public Prosecutions v [defendant].' As was pointed out by Griffin J in *The People v Roddy* [1977] IR 177, in proceedings on indictment the Director does not prosecute in his own right but on behalf of the People of Ireland. Are the indictments drawn up under current practice to be regarded as invalid having regard to the warning given in *Roddy*?

Revenue offences In *McDonald v McMahon*, High Court, 13 January 1989 the plaintiff unsuccessfully argued that his alleged conspiracy to provide Irish passports was a Revenue offence. The plaintiff's extradition under the Extradition Act 1965 Act was requested by the English authorities. The charges related to alleged conspiracy to provide Irish passports to various persons while the plaintiff was a Passport Officer in the Irish embassy in London (as to other preliminary issues arising from the extradition request, see *McMahon and Reynolds v McDonald*, High Court, 3 May 1988, discussed in the 1988 Review, 156-8). The warrants alleged, inter alia, that the conspiracy was contrary to s.1 of the Prevention of Corruption Act 1906. The plaintiff brought an application under s.50 of the Extradition Act 1965 claiming that the order made for his extradition was unlawful on the grounds: (a) that the offences charged were revenue offences within s.50 of the 1965 Act and (b) that they did not correspond to offences under Irish law. Lardner J dismissed the plaintiff's claim.

The judge accepted the argument put forward by counsel for the respondent that the mere fact that the Irish government collected a fee in respect of the issuing of Irish passports did not render such a revenue collecting device. He also accepted the argument that, in any event, the definition of 'revenue offence' in s.3 of the 1965 Act referred to the revenue laws of any country or place outside the State, reflecting the practice and principle that the Irish courts do not aid the collection by another country of its revenue, as held by the Supreme Court in *Buchanan Ltd v McVey* [1954] IR 89. See Binchy, *Irish Conflicts of Law* (1988), ch. 9.

On the question of correspondence of offences, Blayney J held that there was a clear statement of the offences alleged against the plaintiff in one warrant and this was sufficient to establish correspondence (a view also taken in *Sey v Johnson* [1989] IR 516, 152 above). In addition, he held that the charge of conspiracy was, in the circumstances, one which corresponded to offences under s.1 of the Prevention of Corruption Act 1906 (the same statute under which the offence arises in England) and that the other charge also corresponded to an offence under s.10 of the Criminal Justice Act 1951.

Treaties A number of statutory instruments in 1989 gave effect to important changes in our extradition arrangements with countries other than the United Kingdom. The Extradition Act 1965 (Part II) (No.23) Order 1989 (SI No.9) applies Part II of the 1965 Act to countries specified in s.2 of the Order, and it replaces all previous orders concerning the application of the European Convention on Extradition 1957. The Extradition Act 1965 (Part II) (No.24) Order 1989 (SI No.48) applies Part II of the 1965 Act to Australia. The Extradition Act 1965 (Part II) (No.25) Order 1989 (SI No.10) applies Part II of the 1965 Act to the countries specified in the First Schedule to the Order, and was made pursuant to the Hague Convention for the Suppression of the Unlawful Seizure of Aircraft 1970 and the Montreal Convention for the Suppression of Unlawful Acts against the Safety of Civil Aviation 1971. The Extradition (European Convention on the Suppression of Terrorism) Act 1987 (Designation of Convention Countries) Order 1989 (SI No.115) specifies the States who are parties to the European Convention on the Suppression of Terrorism 1977. The Convention came into force on 22 May 1989.

GAMING AND LOTTERIES

In *Flynn v Denieffe and Ors* [1990] ILRM 391; [1989] IR 722, Murphy J held that the Independent Newspapers 'Scoop' game constituted a lottery within the meaning of ss.2 and 21 of the Gaming and Lotteries Act 1956.

The 'Scoop' card containing a four digit number had been distributed free of charge to every postal address in the State. A board-type game was printed in the newspapers published by Independent Newspapers plc with numbered sections. A person with a 'Scoop' card could participate in the game by moving along the numbered sections which corresponded with the numbers on the card. If the person landed on a designated square, they became entitled to a prize provided they answered correctly a question printed in the newspaper. It was not necessary to purchase a newspaper in order to participate in the game. Despite these arrangements, Murphy J held that the game fell foul of the terms of the 1956 Act.

Murphy J referred with approval to a number of previous decisions in this area, and in particular those in *Bolger v Doherty* [1970] IR 233, *Attorney General v Best's Stores Ltd* [1970] IR 225 and *Reader's Digest Association Ltd v Williams* [1976] 2 All ER 737. Applying these decisions, he pointed out that the essential feature of a lottery is that winning or losing depends on chance. In the instant case, he felt that the participant would win the prize offered on the basis of the chance that the numbers on the 'Scoop' card resulted in landing on the designated spot. This matter of chance was not altered by the simple question posed in the newspaper which, Independent Newspapers had argued, involved an element of skill. Murphy J also pointed out that there was no measure of skill in influencing the outcome of the game, since this was dependent on the numbers on the 'Scoop' card. Essentially, therefore, he discounted the question posed in the newspaper and looked at the main feature of the game in assessing it for the purposes of the 1956 Act.

Apart from this analysis of the game, Murphy J also stated that a game of this type will be defined as a lottery if the participants make some form of monetary contribution to participation, whether direct or indirect. It was not necessary that anything in the nature of a ticket be bought to participate in the lottery. In the instant case, although the rules stated that it was not necessary to purchase a newspaper to participate, Murphy J concluded that the reasonable inference was that the vast majority of people would purchase a newspaper and that this, indeed, was one of the main purposes of the game itself.

INSANITY

In *The People v Ellis* (*Irish Times*, 29 July 1989), O'Hanlon J dealt with an application to release a person who had been found 'not guilty but insane' on a charge of murder. At the applicant's trial, evidence had been given by a consultant psychiatrist that, at the time of the killing in question, the applicant had been in an 'automatous state'. The evidence on the application for release was that the applicant was not mentally ill. O'Hanlon J ordered that the applicant be released into the care of his family for a period of six months, pending further medical evidence. For a full statement on the psychiatric evidence given in the case see *Irish Times*, 31 July 1989. When the case was referred back to O'Hanlon J, he delivered a reserved judgment holding that he had no jurisdiction to order the applicant's release and that the appropriate authority to seek an order for release was the Minister for Justice. This decision was reversed by the Supreme Court, which remitted the matter to the High Court: *The People v Ellis (No.2)*, High Court, 9 February 1990; Supreme Court, 15 June 1990. In the meantime, Keane J held, in *The People v Neilan*, High Court, 23 April 1990, that certain provisions of the Trial of Lunatics Act 1883 were inconsistent with the Constitution in purporting to confer a residual power of release on the Minister for Justice. These decisions will be discussed in full in the 1990 Review.

LEGAL AID

The Courts-Martial (Legal Aid) Regulations 1989 (SI No.25) specify revised fees for courts-martials. The Criminal Justice (Legal Aid) (Amendment) Regulations 1989 (SI No.129) specify revised fees for work done pursuant to the Criminal Justice (Legal Aid) Act 1962, and provide for parity in the fees payable for defence and prosecution work.

MINOR OFFENCES

The question whether a punishment of detention in a reformatory school should be regarded as constituting an offence as minor or non-minor was discussed in *J. v Delap and Attorney General* [1989] IR 167: see 186, below.

OFFENCES

The nature of a criminal offence in Article 38.1 of the Constitution was discussed in *McLoughlin v Tuite* [1989] IR 82: see 370, below, in the Revenue chapter.

Blasphemy The international controversy over Salman Rushdie's *The Satanic Verses* surfaced briefly in Ireland in 1989. There was some discussion whether the word as used in Article 40.6 was confined to the traditional meaning associated with respect for Christianity: see *Irish Times*, 1 March 1989 for the suggestion that protection for Islam might be given in the light of Article 44.

Conspiracy The constitutional propriety of conspiracy charges was raised by Walsh J in *Ellis v O'Dea* [1990] ILRM 87; [1989] IR 530 (161, above).

Conspiracy to corrupt public morals The decision in *Attorney General (Society for the Protection of Unborn Children (Irl) Ltd) v Open Door Counselling Ltd* [1987] ILRM (HC); [1989] ILRM 19 (SC); [1988] IR 593 to recognise the common law crime of conspiracy to corrupt public morals (see the 1987 Review, 134-5) is criticised in O'Malley (1989) 7 *ILT* 243.

Incitement to hatred The Prohibition of Incitement to Hatred Act 1989, when introduced as a Bill in 1988, was designed to achieve two goals: to enable Ireland to ratify the United Nations Covenant on Civil and Political Rights and to deal with the periodic problem of the preparation in Ireland of racist material for publication or distribution outside the State. The legislation facilitates both these highly desirable goals.

Article 20, para. 2 of the Covenant provides that: '[a]ny advocacy of national, racial or religious hatred that constitutes incitement to discrimination, hostility or violence shall be prohibited by law'. This Article was the basis of the legislative proposals when initiated.

During the Second Stage in the Seanad, Senator Nuala Fennell and Professor John Murphy proposed that members of the travelling community should be specifically mentioned as being entitled to protection. The Minister for Justice, Mr Collins's initial stance was not supportive. Senator Fennell also expressed regret that the Bill did not extend to homosexuals. The Minister responded by stating:

> Once you begin to add to th[e] grouping [of race, nationality and religion] the list becomes open-ended and we would wind up with a new general category of offences in criminal law. The combined wisdom of the national representatives who drafted this provision in the UN Covenant obviously did not think that this was necessary in our circumstances. We have inquired as far as possible as to the legislation in other countries which implemented this provision of the Covenant and, so far as we can find, the only ratifying States who made specific mention [of] sexual orientation in their legislation relating to the provision of the Covenant were some of the Scandinavian countries. [121 Seanad Debates, cols. 864-5]

At Committee Stage in the Seanad, the Minister adopted the same position (121 Seanad Debates, cols. 1006-7) in response to an argument for extension of the legislation to homosexuals made by Senator Norris.

This position was maintained until Recommittal Stage in the Dáil, on 15 November 1989, when the new Minister for Justice, Mr Burke, put forward an amendment, extending the legislation to the ground of membership of the travelling community or sexual orientation.

Mr Burke said that he had been impressed with the arguments put forward in both Houses that homosexual persons needed the protection afforded by the Bill: 'I am prepared to accept the view that it is of little or no benefit to these people merely to say that I sympathise with them when they are verbally attacked if I am not prepared to do something about it when the opportunity arises' (393 Dáil Debates, col. 583).

The core provisions of the Act are ss. 2 to 4. S.2(1) makes it an offence to publish or distribute written material, or to use words, behave or display written material outside (or heard or seen outside) a private residence, or to distribute, show or play a recording of visual images or sounds, if 'the written material, words, behaviour, visual images or sounds, as the case may be, are threatening, abusive or insulting and are intended or, having regard to all the circumstances, are likely to stir up hatred'.

It is a defence, in a case where the accused person is not shown to have intended to stir up hatred, for him to prove that he was not aware of the content of the material or recording concerned and did not suspect, and had no reason to suspect, that the material or recording was threatening, abusive or insulting: s.2(2)(a).

Broadcasts are covered in detail in s.3, and s.4 makes it an offence to prepare or possess material likely to stir up hatred.

The maximum penalty on indictment for these offences is a fine of £10,000 and two years' imprisonment; on summary conviction the maximum is £1,000 and six months imprisonment: s.6. Where a person is charged with one of these offences, no further proceedings in the matter (other than any remand in custody or on bail) are to be taken except by or with the consent of the Director of Public Prosecutions: s.8. Powers of search and seizure, arrest and forfeiture are prescribed by ss.9 to 11.

It is of course s.3 which has occasioned the greatest scrutiny. Clearly it will catch the racist demagogue and the publisher of racist propoganda designed to provoke violence. How much broader is its range? Some particular aspects of the section are worth noting.

First the offence is based, not on intent or recklessness, but on what might be characterised as negligence: a person may be convicted if his conduct (as defined in the section) is likely to stir up hatred, provided—and this is a most important qualification—that it is also threatening, abusive or insulting. Thus, as Michael Freeman has noted in respect of legislation in England drafted in the same terms on this point: 'no offence is committed by a sophisticated propogandist who uses restrained language or a semi-academic style. . . .' (annotation to section 70 of the Race Relations Act 1976, *Current Law Statutes Annotated*).

It is interesting to note that in New Zealand, s.25(1) of the Race Relations Act 1971 also includes the requirement that the words be 'threatening, abusive or insulting'. This requirement, in the view of the Law Reform Commission of Western Australia, 'probably excludes most statements of fact and most political debate which touches on racial issues': Issues Paper,

Incitement to Racial Hatred (1989), para. 3.32. The Commission go on to quote in this context an extract from Sperling and Mason's *Racism in the Media: If Legislation, What Kind?* (1988) Migration Monitor 16, at 18:

> Simply to report high Aboriginal rates of imprisonment, for example, might excite racial hostility . . . but unless some conclusion denigrating Aboriginal people were drawn, or factual material were presented in an insulting way, such a report would not be 'threatening, abusive or insulting' matter. This formulation means that some publications, which in fact increase racial tension, would not be covered. . . .

It is worth recalling Lord Reid's remarks in *Brutus v Cozens* [1973] AC 854, at 862, speaking of the same formula of words:

> Parliament had to solve the difficult question of how far freedom of speech or behaviour must be limited in the general public interest. It would have been going much too far to prohibit all speech or conduct likely to occasion a breach of the peace because determined opponents may not shrink from organising or at least threatening a breach of the peace in order to silence a speaker whose views they detest. Therefore vigorous and it may be distasteful or unmannerly speech or behaviour is permitted as long as it does not go beyond any one of the three limits. It must not be threatening. It must not be abusive. It must not be insulting. I see no reason why any of these should be construed as having a specially wide or a specially narrow meaning. They are all limits easily recognisable by the ordinary man. Free speech is not impaired by ruling them out.
>
> But before a man can be convicted it must be clearly shown that one or more of them has been disregarded.

See also Bindman (1982) 132 *New LJ* 299, at 300.

A second point worth noting about the Act is that the truth of what is published does not, it seems, afford a defence to a charge under s.2(1). This may perhaps seem odd until it is remembered that, in criminal libel, the truth does not in all cases afford a defence. Moreover, it would seem possible in all cases to tell the truth in language that is not threatening, abusive or insulting.

Thirdly, the Act does not define 'hatred'. It is true that s.1(1) provides that 'hatred' means: 'hatred against a group of persons in the State or elsewhere on account of their race, colour, nationality, religion, ethnic or national origins, membership of the travelling community or sexual orientation'. This definition, of course, throws no light on the meaning of 'hatred' but only clarifies the *objects* of hatred who fall within the scope of the Act's provisions.

The word 'hatred' is not defined in British legislation (save also in terms of the objects of hatred). Nor is it defined in the Canadian Criminal Code. It seems that one can do no more than look to the dictionary meaning, which embraces 'active dislike, detestation, enmity, ill-will, malevolence'.

It should be noted that the Act does not require any more than likelihood of the stirring up of hatred; it does not require that the possibility of such hatred should engender a likelihood, or indeed any risk, of physical attacks on persons or property. That hatred does not *necessarily* have such a consequential likelihood seems to have been the opinion of the Law Reform Commission of Canada when it observed in its Working Paper 50, *Hate Propaganda*, in 1986: 'Promoting enmity is clearly dysfunctional to society. It stirs up hatred among social groups. It can even lay the foundation for physical attacks upon persons or property. Preventing such harm justifies the use of the criminal law'.

Next it is worth noting that the Act does not define 'sexual orientation'. Clearly a homosexual or heterosexual orientation is included; but does the term include what might be called species of these two genera? Does it, for example, include a homosexual or heterosexual paedophile? Does it include sadists? The question is far from academic. At the heart of the legislation, so far as it extends beyond race, religion and ethnicity into the realm of sexual orientation, is the question of the relationship between orientation on the one hand and conduct on the other.

It would of course be quite wrong to subject any person—including a sadist or paedophile—to moral criticism for having an orientation. To do so would be contrary to any self-respecting moral code. It is, of course, a separate matter to express moral disapproval of certain objective conduct, such as a sadistic sexual assault. In other words there is an obvious distinction between conduct and orientation. If the effect of criticism of conduct were that the listener thought less of the wrongdoer, that would not be a matter that falls within the scope of the Act. If the listener's response were to experience enmity to the wrongdoer for his or her conduct, that again would fall outside the Act's scope. If the listener's likely response were to have enmity for persons with a sadistic orientation—where his response springs from a strong moral condemnation of sadistic conduct or, perhaps, from fear that some of them might engage in sadistic conduct—then it could be argued that this likelihood would fall within the scope of the Act. As has been noted, however, it would not involve the speaker in criminal liability unless his words, as well as having this likely effect, were also threatening, abusive or insulting.

To turn to a general homosexual orientation, which clearly falls within the scope of the Act, the position appears to be that, in order to amount to an offence, the words must be threatening, abusive or insulting and intended or likely to stir up hatred against a group of persons of homosexual orientation, rather than on account of the conduct in which they, or any of them, may engage. Some key questions therefore arise.

First, what are the minimum constituent elements of 'a group' here? Must it be the group comprising all homosexuals (as opposed to the group comprising heterosexuals) or can a group be localised? If it can, is it possible for two persons to constitute a group? Does stirring up hatred against an individual come within the scope of the legislation? On a literal interpretation it does not. As against this, if hatred is stirred up against an individual on account of his sexual orientation, it is in one sense because of his membership of the group of homosexuals that the hatred is directed at him.

Secondly, homosexual orientation differs from race, colour, nationality, ethnic or national origins and membership of the travelling community (though not religion) in that it may or may not be accompanied by conduct which offends against moral norms underlying, and given practical effect by, the Constitution. To hate a group for engaging in conduct is something different from hating them on account of their orientation. Very often the line between orientation and conduct is not clearly drawn, in speech or in thought. A person who speaks threateningly, abusively or insultingly about homosexual conduct thus must take care that the likely effect of his words is not to stir up hatred against persons of homosexual orientation even if he is clear in his own mind about the distinction. Where intention is not an issue, the test is one of the *likely effect* of the words on *others*; so even if the defendant can convince the court that he bears no ill will towards persons of homosexual orientation, this will not afford a defence if the threatening, abusive or insulting words are likely to stir up hatred in others.

Thirdly, the question arises as to the *extent* of likely hatred which it is necessary for the prosecution to prove. Is it sufficient to show that a few cranks would be likely to be thus stirred up, or must the words have a more wide-ranging potency so as to be likely to stir up hatred among the majority of the listeners? We suspect that the courts will not adopt an unduly doctrinal approach to this question and will prefer to resolve it by a formula which lacks specificity, ranging somewhat more widely than that of a few cranks. It would be mistaken for the court to invoke the standard of the hypothetical juror. Although this was the text adopted by Devlin in a related but not identical context (*The Enforcement of Morals* (1965) ix), it is not appropriate to the present legislation, which contains no suggestion that those likely to be stirred up be blessed with the qualities of sobriety and rationality.

It is worth noting the possible analogy here with the test of 'right thinking members of society' in the law of defamation, which is concerned with whether the impugned statement subjected the plaintiff to hatred, ridicule or contempt. In defamation our courts have been equivocal as to whether the reference to 'right thinking' members is of normative or sociological import: see *Quigley v Creation Ltd* [1971] IR 269, at 272; *Youssoupoff v Metro Goldwyn Mayer Pictures* (1934) 50 TLR 581; McMahon & Binchy, *Irish Law of Torts* (2nd ed., 1990), 625-6. One suspects that, under the 1989 Act, the test is unequivocally sociological; otherwise the object of hatred would fail to be protected by the Act to the extent that the prejudices of the public deviated from reasonableness and fairness.

Let us now turn to the question of religion. Could it be argued that religion, in contrast to all other factors, such as race, nationality and sexual orientation, presents a difficulty in that in principle it is possible for the norms or tenets of a religion to be so odious as to warrant hatred, and that it might in some cases be understandable that hatred for these norms or tenets should embrace one who subscribes to the religion in question? To take a hypothetical case: if Hitler, in preaching National Socialism, had claimed a divine mandate, would it have been wrong to incite hatred against his disciples? Reverence and respect for religion scarcely requires one to deny the fact that there are religions and religions: some embracing value systems of profound ethical depths, others embracing norms which it is difficult to see any person of good will following. In *H v H*, High Court, 4 February 1976, Parke J observed that '[i]n hearing cases as to the custody of children the Court is not one of comparative religions. The Court is not to prefer one religion to another'. It remains to be seen whether such neutrality is to apply to the 1989 Act. At the end of the day, the courts may say that, however deficient a particular religion may appear to be from the standpoint of ethical depth, the Constitution requires respect for all religions, at least to the extent of not *hating* the followers of any religion.

Larceny   S.2 of the Larceny Act 1916 provides in part that:

> Stealing for which no special punishment is provided under this or any other Act for the time being in force shall be simple larceny and a felony punishable with penal servitude for any term not exceeding five years.

In *Director of Public Prosecutions v Cassidy* [1990] ILRM 30, the accused had taken goods the property of his employer, without the employer's authority or consent, intending at the time permanently to deprive his employer of them. He had been charged with, and convicted of, an offence under s.2. The District Justice stated a case for the High Court as to whether this was legally permissible notwithstanding that the accused might on the same facts be charged with, and convicted of, an offence under s.17(1)(a).

Gannon J had no hesitation in answering the question in the affirmative. He observed that, '[i]f the offence does not fall under the other section of the Act it can be punished under s.2, but it does not follow that, if it does fall under one of the other sections, . . . it cannot be punished under s.2'.

Gannon J emphatically rejected what Davitt J had said, to the contrary, in *The People v Mills* (1955), 1 Frewen 153 and, by implication, adopted the view taken in *The State (Foley) v Carroll* [1980] IR 150; see McCutcheon, *The Larceny Act 1916* (Round Hall Press, 1988), 41.

The question of larceny from supermarkets presents distinct conceptual difficulties, resulting form the changing practices and conventions in relation to the purchase of goods. No longer is there a single transaction, of limited duration, in which the customer indicates his or her wishes to a shop assistant who gives the requested items to the customer in exchange for payment. Matters now take longer; the customer does the selection; and the sales points are decentralised—to such an extent that in some stores it is difficult for a customer to know where the management actually intended payment to be made. Against the background of rapidly changing shopping practices, it is no longer easy to apply notions of 'taking and carrying away' and of consent, actual or implied. For consideration of these issues of nearly twenty years ago, when practices were beginning to change, see Binchy, 'Supermarkets and the Law of Theft' (1971) *ILT & SJ* 273.

In *Director of Public Prosecutions v Keating* [1989] ILRM 561, Lynch J adopted a robust attitude to the question of consent. On an appeal by way of case stated from a dismissal for larceny, based on the view that larceny could be established only where the defendant had left the supermarket premises, Lynch J was:

> clearly of opinion that there is no such rule of law or fact. The case should be decided on the intention of the respondent at the time when he took the clothing, such intention to be ascertained by the District Justice from the evidence given before him. It is quite possible that a person could be convicted of stealing from a supermarket even before he went near the cashier's desk much less past it. If the conduct of a person was such as to make it clear that when he took the goods he did so fraudulently then he could be convicted on the evidence without having to wait for him to go near the cashier's desk. Each case would depend on its own facts but a possible example might be a person who entered the supermarket, took a supermarket trolley, put into it a number of cheap items and then was observed to take possession of some expensive items but not put them in the trolley but instead secret[e] them in an inside pocket in a large coat. That would certainly be evidence of fraudulent intent which, if accepted by the court, could lead to a

conviction in the absence of a plausible explanation. . . . Where a person takes goods from racks or shelves with fraudulent intent permanently to deprive the supermarket owner of such goods there can be no basis in fact or in law or in commonsense for implying that the owner of the supermarket intends to give any form of possession whatsoever of such goods to such a person. The proposition that the supermarket owner must be assumed to consent to that person's possession of such goods so long as that person remains on and does not leave the supermarket premises is quite untenable in law or in fact.

Lynch J did not directly address the more troublesome question of the liability of a shopper who, having taken an item with the intention of paying, gives in to the temptation to steal it and puts it in his or her pocket. Is this a case of larceny by a bailee?

It is interesting to note that in England, the courts have struggled with similar problems, which have to be addressed in terms of 'appropriation' rather than 'taking'. It seems that, on the question similar to that raised in the case stated, they would also impose criminal liability: *R v McPherson* [1973] Crim LR 191. See generally E. Griew, *The Theft Acts 1968 and 1978* (5th ed., 1986), paras. 2-55, and McCutcheon, op. cit., 27.

PARTIES

Accessory before the fact	In *The People v Egan* [1989] IR 681 the question before the Court of Criminal Appeal was whether the applicant had, by his admission to the Garda Síochána, indicated that he had been an accessory before the fact to an armed robbery.

The applicant had been convicted of robbery by a jury in the Circuit Criminal Court and not guilty of receiving stolen goods (having been directed by the trial judge that the charges were alternative ones). He was then sentenced to 7 years imprisonment. The only evidence against him was a statement made by him while in Garda custody pursuant to s.30 of the Offences against the State Act 1939. In the course of his statement, the applicant indicated that he had been asked to make available his garage to leave a van in it for what the applicant said he thought was a 'small stroke.' When the van arrived, the applicant said that he realised only then that the men in the van had been involved in an armed robbery on a jewellery shop. The statement also described how, after the armed men left, the applicant had found a bag of jewellery in the garage and how he had disposed of its contents. The statement had been made after the applicant had been in custody for 30 hours and after he had seen, at various times, his wife and son. During a 'trial within a trial' the applicant stated that he had been abused and threatened by the Gardaí and it was also argued at his trial that the effects of the meetings with his wife and son had been to break down his will. The trial judge rejected the claim that the admission was not voluntary. The applicant sought leave to appeal against conviction on the grounds that the admission should not have been admitted in evidence and, alternatively, that the admission did not disclose sufficient evidence on which the applicant could have been convicted of robbery. The Court of Criminal Appeal (Finlay CJ, Costello and Johnson JJ) dismissed his application.

As to the admissibility of the confession, the Court held that the trial judge had been entitled to find that the admission had been made voluntarily, and that the visits made by his wife and son, which the applicant had requested, had not affected the decision of the applicant to make the admission. The Court thus took the usual approach that, where there is evidence to support the primary factual findings of a trial judge, these will not be interfered with by the Court of Criminal Appeal.

On the issue of the effects of the admissions made, the Court considered that the prosecution was able to establish that the applicant knew before the incident in question had taken place that a crime was to be committed, that it involved the theft of goods and that he assisted in this crime by making his garage available to the principal offender.

The Court then went on to examine the case law on accessories, in particular the decision of the Court itself in *The People v Madden* [1977] IR 336 and also the decision in *R. v Maxwell* [1978] 3 All ER 1140. Applying these authorities, the Court held that where goods are stolen, it is not necessary for the prosecution to establish that a person (who has aided the principal offender prior to the actual commission of the the crime) is aware of any of the following: the means to be employed or the place from which the goods are to be stolen or the time at which the theft is to take place or the nature of the goods to be stolen. It is sufficient, the Court concluded, for the prosecution to show that the accused who gave assistance to the principal before the crime is committed knows the nature of the crime intended, namely the theft of goods. Accordingly, on the evidence in the instant case, it was open to the jury to conclude that the applicant was an accessory before the fact of the crime. On this basis, his conviction stood.

PROCEDURE

Adjourned hearing: absence of counsel of choice In *Dawson v Hamill* [1990] ILRM 257; [1989] IR 275 Lynch J held that the respondent Justice had acted in excess of jurisdiction in convicting the applicant in the absence of the applicant's counsel of choice. The fact that counsel of the applicant's choice was not present arose in unusual circumstances.

The applicant had been involved in two incidents on 4 December 1986 while driving his motor lorry. The first incident involved an allegation that he overtook a line of traffic on a continuous white line at a hill. The second incident was alleged to have occurred about a mile and a half further along the road in which there was a fatal injury involving a collision between the applicant and others. Arising from the first incident, the applicant was served with a summons alleging dangerous driving which was grounded on a complaint made one day before the six month time limit for making the complaint had expired. No previous indication was given to the applicant that a charge would be brought arising from the first incident. The hearing of this summons was adjourned pending the disposal of the charges arising from the fatal accident. The applicant was subsequently acquitted in the Circuit Criminal Court on all charges arising from the fatal accident.

The summons for the first incident then came before the District Court in June 1988. The main evidence was from a witness who gave evidence that the applicant had passed a long line of traffic on a continuous white line. At the end of the evidence, lengthy submissions were made as to whether the applicant could be convicted having regard to the requirements of the Road Traffic Acts 1961 to 1984 as to notice of intention to prosecute. The respondent Justice indicated that he would reserve his decision to the following day. Counsel for the applicant indicated that he would be unable to appear the next day and the respondent excused him on the basis that he would be delivering reserved judgment only. After the hearing had concluded, the witness in the case approached the prosecution and indicated that he had later come across the second incident and remonstrated with the applicant for having earlier overtaken him. On the following day, the prosecution sought to have this evidence introduced. The respondent allowed the new evidence over the objections of the pupil of the applicant's counsel. The applicant was convicted. On judicial review of the conviction, Lynch J quashed the conviction and remitted the case to the District Court for a further hearing.

As to whether the respondent should have re-opened the case at all, Lynch J held that the respondent had jurisdiction to allow the prosecution to do so, having regard to the obligation to be impartial as between both sides. He went on to hold, however, that the respondent had acted in excess of jurisdiction by hearing the additional evidence in the absence of the applicant's counsel of choice, having regard to the specific fact that counsel had been excused by the respondent from appearing at the adjourned hearing. Lynch J referred to the general obligation to comply with the constitutional requirement of fair procedures as set out in *The State (Healy) v Donoghue* [1976] IR 325.

Although Lynch J quashed the conviction, he concluded that it was appropriate to remit the matter to the District Court pursuant to O.84, r.26(4) of the Rules of the Superior Courts 1986, and on this aspect of the case he felt that it was relevant to consider the merits of the case. In this light he held that the courts were required to have regard to the rights of the people of Ireland in seeing criminal charges being proceeded with, and he considered that the applicant would not be in any worse position so far as meeting the charge against him. Lynch J also stated that the matter could be heard by the respondent or by any other Justice assigned to the District in question, and he rejected as without substance the suggestion that justice would not be seen to be done if the case was to be heard by the respondent.

Adjournment: refusal In *Flynn v Ruane* [1989] ILRM 690, Gannon J held that the respondent Justice had acted in excess of jurisdiction in refusing to allow an adjournment to the applicant in order for him to obtain legal representation. Although Gannon J stated that the refusal had been within jurisdiction, the circumstances in which it was made resulted in an order which was not grounded on a valid exercise of jurisdiction. Gannon J emphasised the constitutional dimension to the case by drawing attention to the decision in *The State (Healy) v Donoghue* [1976] IR 325 as to the importance of professional representation.

Book of evidence: witness statements In *The People v Morris (Irish Times*, 21 November 1989) a *nolle prosequi* was entered in a firearms case arising from what was reported as a 'material alteration of a serious sort' in a statement contained in the book of evidence. The Circuit Criminal Court was told that the alteration 'could have led to a serious miscarriage of justice.' It appeared that two statements made by a witness had been entered in the book of evidence as one. Counsel for the defence accepted that there was no mala fides involved in the preparation of the statements. It was later reported that the Director of Public Prosecutions was preparing new guidelines on the preparation of material for inclusion in the book of evidence in accordance with the requirements of the Criminal Procedure Act 1967: *Irish Times*, 22 November 1989. On the judicial approach to such issues see *The People v Kelly (E.)* [1987] IR 596 (1987 Review, 127-8) and *Murphy v Director of Public Prosecutions* [1989] ILRM 71 (1988 Review, 172-3). See also O'Connor, (1989) 7 ILT 158.

Comments by judge in previous trial In *McGlinchey v Ireland and Ors*, High Court, 8 June 1989 an application was made on behalf of the applicant under Article 40.4.2 of the Constitution for an inquiry into his detention. The applicant had been convicted in the Special Criminal Court on a number of charges. On a previous application, the High Court and Supreme Court had rejected a number of complaints made by the applicant regarding that conviction: *McGlinchey v Governor of Portlaoise Prison* [1988] IR 671 (see the 1987 Review, 109-10 and 118 and the 1988 Review, 142). In the present application the applicant raised a new point that, in a previous trial in the Special Criminal Court, which concerned the same incident in relation to which the applicant had been ultimately convicted, the presiding judge had made some comments regarding the role of the applicant in that incident. The applicant alleged that such comments prejudiced his trial and that his conviction was thus invalid. O'Hanlon J dismissed the application.

He held that it could not be said, as had been argued, that the Court which tried the applicant was the same Court which had dealt with the previous trial in which the comments had allegedly been made. This was clear from s.40 of the Offences against the State Act 1939 which clearly envisaged that different judges might be appointed to sit in a Special Criminal Court, and the judges who sat in the applicant's trial were in no way disqualified from sitting.

As to the extent of the enquiry under Article 40.4.2 and having regard to the previous application by the applicant, O'Hanlon J felt that he would not investigate matters which were being raised in the present application but which had been previously raised, and rejected, by the High Court and Supreme Court. This view conforms with established practice.

Court of Criminal Appeal's appeal function   The limits of the Court of Criminal Appeal's appellate jurisdiction were discussed in *The People v O'Brien (P.)*, Court of Criminal Appeal, 21 July 1989. The applicant was convicted of having unlawful sexual intercourse with three girls under the age of 15 years. The complaints against the applicant were made one month after the incident in question and the trial took place over 2 years later. At the applicant's trial, medical evidence was given which indicated that the three complainants were found to be virgins. The trial judge, in his direction to the jury, drew attention to the weakness of the prosecution case and of the danger of convicting on uncorroborated evidence. The applicant unsuccessfully sought leave to appeal against his conviction.

Counsel for the applicant sought to raise the 'lurking doubt' jurisdiction referred to in *R v Cooper* [1969] 1 QB 267, which had been rejected in *The People v Mulligan* (1980) 2 Frewen 16 and *The People v Kelly (No. 2)* [1983] IR 1. The Court of Criminal Appeal (McCarthy, Barrington and Lardner JJ) held that while there might be cases in which the Court would use the wide powers granted it by s.12 of the Courts (Supplemental Provisions) Act 1961 to interfere with the verdict of a jury in a case where there was evidence to support a verdict, this was not such a case. Having regard to the exemplary manner in which the trial was conducted and the express warnings given to the jury, the Court concluded that it was for the jury to assess the evidence tendered and to arrive at the verdict which they did. While the Court of Criminal Appeal did not actually close the door completely on a residual 'lurking doubt' jurisdiction, the door was firmly closed in *The People v Egan*, Court of Criminal Appeal, 13 December 1989; Supreme Court, 30 May 1990. The Court of Criminal Appeal again rejected the *Cooper* decision but certified the issue raised as a point of law of exceptional public importance. In the Supreme Court, the traditional approach as reflected by the Court of Criminal Appeal in *O'Brien* was affirmed. The *Egan* case will be dealt with fully in the 1990 Review.

Cross-examination *Ó Broin v Ruane* [1989] ILRM 732; [1989] IR 214 concerned the practical issue of the limits of cross-examination permissible in a Road Traffic Acts prosecution. The applicant had been charged with an offence under the Road Traffic Acts 1961 to 1984. In the course of the trial before the respondent Justice, the applicant's solicitor inquired of the prosecuting Garda as to what procedures had in fact been followed in the Garda station under s.21 of the Road Traffic (Amendment) Act 1978. The prosecuting solicitor objected to what was termed 'a fishing cross-examination' and the respondent upheld the objection and refused to allow the cross-examination to proceed. The respondent referred to the presumption contained in s.21(4) of the 1978 Act that the terms of that section have been complied with unless the contrary is shown.

The applicant sought judicial review on the ground that the 1978 Act precluded a fair trial. In the course of the application, the Court was informed that the applicant did not have any specific instructions as to non-compliance with procedural requirements. Lynch J refused judicial review but made some important comments in the process.

He held that the respondent had been wrong not to allow a general enquiry by the applicant's solicitor, and the applicant was not confined to asking specific questions. However, he considered that the respondent's error had been within jurisdiction and was not so gross as to oust the jurisdiction of the Court, so that the applicant was left to his remedy of appeal to the Circuit Court, the State authorities having indicated that they would not object to having the appeal heard out of time. While this conclusion might not have been as satisfactory to the applicant as an order of certiorari, the decision has important implications for similar prosecutions in the future, since the leeway allowed to defence lawyers has been clarified.

Indictable offence: District Court changing view on jurisdiction In *Feeney v Clifford* [1988] IR 499 (HC); [1989] IR 668 (SC), Barr J had upheld the decision of the respondent District Justice who had at first accepted jurisdiction in an indictable offence and then later decided to send the case forward for trial on indictment: see the 1988 Review, 173-4. On appeal by the applicants to the Supreme Court (Finlay CJ, Hederman and McCarthy JJ), the decision of Barr J was reversed.

The applicants had appeared before the respondent Justice in February 1988 charged with unlawful possession of two motor vehicles as well as malicious damage to one of them. Having heard evidence of the circumstances of the offences, the respondent decided pursuant to s.2 of the Criminal Justice Act 1951 that the charges were minor and fit to be tried summarily. The applicants agreed to this course and pleaded guilty. When the respondent was informed that the applicants were then serving sentences, including one of 2 years imprisonment imposed in July 1987, he indicated that, as he had intended to impose 2 years imprisonment on the applicants but that this was not possible in the circumstances arising, he would send the applicants forward for trial in the Circuit Court. As already indicated, Barr J refused judicial review of the order sending the applicants forward for trial.

The Supreme Court, somewhat reluctantly, came to the conclusion that the order sending the applicants forward for trial should be quashed. It held that if a District Justice has concluded that an offence is fit to be tried summarily pursuant to s.5 of the Criminal Justice Act 1951, and the accused person then pleads guilty, the Justice is precluded from going back on this decision once he embarks upon an enquiry as to the penalty appropriate to the offence. The Court made the point that there is no such thing in law as a provisional conviction, and in the result the respondent had acted in error and his decision was therefore quashed on certiorari. It was the fact that the respondent in the instant case had, in effect, recorded a conviction that distinguished it, in the eyes of the Court, from *The State (McEvitt) v Delap* [1981] IR 125, a decision which had been relied on by Barr J in the High Court.

However, as noted, the Supreme Court reached this conclusion with reluctance. For the Court, McCarthy J noted that the effect of the decision was to create a procedural lacuna in such cases. The result is that the accused can, in effect, prevent the holding of a trial on indictment in the particular circumstances which arose in the instant case. He concluded his judgment by stating that consideration should be given to amending the Criminal Justice Act 1951 to allow the Director of Public Prosecutions to object to a trial proceeding in such circumstances. Undoubtedly, any such change in the 1951 Act would of necessity be hedged around with procedural protections to ensure that no undue prejudice resulted from a change in the trial venue. It may be, however, that no change will be made in the present arrangements since it could result in longer sentences being handed down in the Circuit

Court. With the present difficulties in connection with prison accommodation, this may be another suggested legal reform which is not taken up.

Indictable offence dropped: remaining summary offences   In *O'Neill v Director of Public Prosecutions* [1989] ILRM 881, the applicant had originally been charged with obstructing police officers in the execution of their duty, contrary to s.38 of the Offences against the Person Act 1861, and had elected for trial before a judge and jury. The Director later added three charges of assault contrary to common law, arising out of the same event as the s.38 charges but involving different parties. The Director sought to have the common assault charges tried summarily but the District Justice declined to accept jurisdiction. The Director then withdrew the s.38 charges and the District Justice, on a subsequent date, determined that the common assault charges could be heard summarily. The applicant sought orders of prohibition and *certiorari* seeking to prevent the common assault charges being disposed of summarily. Barrington J refused the relief sought.

He held that the District Justice was entitled to come to the conclusion that the common assault charges were minor in nature and could be disposed of summarily. He went on to say, however, that had the District Justice taken the view that the common assault charges were inextricably bound up with the s.38 charges then she could not have accepted jurisdiction merely because the s.38 charges had been dropped. However, in the particular circumstances which had arisen, he was satisfied that the common assault charges could proceed in the District Court.

Judicial review: quash or remit   In *Singh v Ruane and Minister for Labour* [1990] ILRM 62; [1989] IR 610 the High Court dealt with the question whether to remit a prosecution to the District Court after quashing a conviction on *certiorari*. The applicant was charged with an offence under s.10(3) of the Industrial Relations Act 1969. In the District Court hearing before the first respondent the applicant's defence was that the offence had been committed by a limited liability company of which he was managing director. The first respondent, who was hearing the case, refused to allow production of the certificate of incorporation of the company. The applicant was subsequently convicted of the offence. In his application for judicial review of the conviction, the applicant argued that the conviction should be quashed on *certiorari* and that this should have the effect of an acquittal so that the matter should not be remitted to the District Court. Barron J granted *certiorari* but remitted the matter to the District Court.

He discussed the leading decision on the matter, *The State (Tynan) v Keane* [1968] IR 348 and in particular the judgment of Walsh J. He also referred to the more recent decision of Lynch J in *The State (Keeney) v O'Malley* [1986]

ILRM 31. In the light of these decisions, Barron J held that in the instant case there had been no valid adjudication before the respondent Justice, and thus the conviction was void *ab initio*. Thus he held that the situation was different from those cases where autrefois convict can be pleaded since there the accused might have been subjected to a lawful punishment within jurisdiction. In the instant case, Barron J considered that the respondent Justice had taken himself outside his jurisdiction.

For another decision remitting a prosecuton to the District Court see the decision of Lynch J in *Dawson v Hamill* [1990] ILRM 257; [1989] IR 275 (175, above).

Jurisdiction of court   The question whether illegality prior to appearance in court deprives the Court of jurisdiction was considered in *McElhinney v Special Criminal* [1989] ILRM 411 (185, below) and *Keating v Governor of Mountjoy Prison* [1989] IR 286; Supreme Court, 10 July 1990 (185, below). The issue was also dealt with by Judge Sheridan in *Director of Public Prosecutions v Hennessy* (1989) 8 ILT 102. In all these cases, the courts held that alleged illegality prior to appearance in court will not affect the jurisdiction of the District Court to hear criminal charges. In the *Hennessy* case, it may be noted that the defect complained of was that a complaint had been made to a District Court clerk rather than to a District Justice. Judge Sheridan held that this procedural defect did not affect the jurisdiction of the District Court to hear the criminal charge.

Pre-condition to prosecution   In *Director of Public Prosecutions v Cunningham* [1989] IR 481, Lardner J rejected the argument that it was necessary to have evidence of certain matters in court for a prosecution in a Revenue matter to proceed: see 369, below, in the Revenue chapter.

ROAD TRAFFIC

Careless driving: endorsement   In *Director of Public Prosecutions v O'Brien* [1989] IR 266, the defendant had been convicted of careless driving under s.52 of the Road Traffic Act 1961, but no disqualification order was made under the Act in consequence thereof. In the Circuit Court, a case was stated for the Supreme Court as to whether it was mandatory under s.36(1) of the 1961 Act, as amended by s.6 of the Road Traffic Act 1968, for an endorsement to be made on the defendant's licence in view of the fact that the conviction in question was the third such conviction under the Act. The Supreme Court (Finlay CJ, Walsh, Griffin, Hederman and McCarthy JJ) answered in the affirmative. Speaking for the Court, McCarthy J held that the Circuit Court judge was correct in taking the view that such endorsement was mandatory under s.36(1) of the 1961 Act, as amended. He did note that this result was produced by a somewhat complex and complicated manner in terms of interpretation, but that otherwise s.36(1) would have no real meaning. McCarthy J also pointed out that a similar conclusion had been reached by Butler J in *Attorney General v Maguire*, High Court, 18 July 1973.

Procedure: cross-examination   The decision in *Ó Broin v Ruane* [1989] ILRM 732; [1989] IR 214 is discussed above, 179.

SENTENCING

Alternatives to prison   An interesting address by District Justice Gillian Hussey, as President of the Medico-Legal Society, was reported in (1989) 7 *ILT* 74.

Co-accused   *The People v Healy (N.)*, Court of Criminal Appeal, 12 July 1989 raised again the rationale for disparity of sentences between co-accused. The applicant had pleaded guilty to conspiracy to commit false imprisonment and conspiracy to rob, and was sentenced to two concurrent terms of 8 years imprisonment. Three co-accused had been sentenced in respect of the same event, and had received sentences of 2 years, 2 years and 4 years, respectively. The sentencing judges who imposed these sentences had taken account of the fact that the applicant's co-accused were, by the time of the imposition of the sentences for the conspriacy to rob, serving lengthy terms of imprisonment for other offences, in respect of some of which they had been free on bail at the time of the conspiracy. The applicant sought leave to appeal against the severity of sentence imposed on him. The Court of Criminal Appeal (McCarthy, Carroll and Barron JJ) dismissed his application.

Applying the oft-quoted views of Walsh J in *The People v Poyning* [1972] IR 402, the Court stated that disparity in sentence was not a ground on which the Court of Criminal Appeal would, necessarily, intervene with the sentence imposed by a trial judge. In the instant case, the Court concluded that the sentence of 8 years imprisonment was in no way excessive or founded on any error of principle, having regard to the characters and antecedents of the different persons who had been convicted. For that reason, the Court did not interfere with the sentence imposed on the applicant. For a successful invocation of the disparity argument, see *The People v Conroy (No. 2)* [1989] ILRM 139; [1989] IR 160 (1988 Review, 181).

Offence committed on bail   The correct application of s.11 of the Criminal Justice Act 1984 was also adverted to by the Court of Criminal Appeal in the *Healy* case. S.11 provides that a judge shall impose consecutive sentences in respect of a crime committed while on bail. The Court noted that, although s.11 of the 1984 Act was not relevant to the instant cases (as the offences had been committed before it came into effect), it appeared that the sentencing judges had taken account of its provisions. The Court thus felt it should take the opportunity to indicate how s.11 should be approached. The Court stated that, where s.11 applies, the sentencing judge should determine the sentence appropriate to the offence without regard to the fact that it must be a consecutive sentence. Having indicated that this is the first step in the judicial sentencing approach, the Court of Criminal Appeal also added that in a grave offence this first step would not preclude the sentencing court from adjusting the sentence downwards where not to do so would impose a manifestly unjust punishment on the accused.

SUMMONSES

In *Director of Public Prosecutions v Howard*, High Court, 27 November 1989 Barron J provided clarification of certain dicta of Finlay CJ in *Director of Public Prosecutions v Roche* [1989] ILRM 39 as to the effect of the Courts (No.3) Act 1986. In *Roche*, the Chief Justice had made reference to the six month time limit in the 1986 Act for applying for summonses. He added: 'No other time limit arises except in the case of certain statutory offences where shorter time limits might apply.' In the 1988 Review, 185-6, it was pointed out that the Chief Justice would appear not to have considered the existence of longer time limits in certain special statutory provisions. We suggested that such longer time limits could be adapted for the purposes of the 1986 Act, having regard to s.1(7)(a) of the Act. That was, in fact, the approach taken by Barron J in the *Howard* case.

The Director had applied for the issue of a summons under the 1986 Act against the accused pursuant to s.39(1) of the Finance Act 1985, which specifies a one year time limit for excise offences. The accused argued that such application must be made within six months, while the Director argued that s.1(7)(a) of the 1986 Act allowed for application to be made within a year. Barron J accepted the Director's argument. He accepted that a literal interpretation of the Chief Justice's comments in the *Roche* case might lean towards the accused, but he concluded that the Chief Justice had not intended to exclude the possibility of longer statutory time limits being adapted to the terms of the 1986 Act. Adapting s.39(1) of the Finance Act 1985, Barron J held that procedure by way of complaint was still open as a means of prosecuting offences; but that where an application was made under the 1986 Act, the time allowed was the same as that for making a complaint in respect of the alleged offence.

TRIAL OF OFFENCES

Appearance before Special Criminal Court In *McElhinney v Special Criminal Court* [1989] ILRM 411, the Supreme Court (Finlay CJ, Walsh, Griffin, Hederman and Murphy JJ) held that once a person was before the Special Criminal Court on a lawful arrest warrant for a scheduled offence under the Offences against the State Act 1939, the Court had jurisdiction under s.43 of the Act to try the accused for non-scheduled offences. See further the 1988 Review, 188-9.

Unlawful remand in custody In *Keating v Governor of Mountjoy Prison* [1989] IR 286 (HC); Supreme Court 10 July 1990, the question arose as to whether an unlawful remand could affect the jurisdiction of the trial court dealing with the issue.

The applicant had been arrested in relation to larceny charges and was then detained in custody under s.4 of the Criminal Justice 1984, during which time he was alleged to have made certain statements to the Gardaí relating to the offences. At the remand hearing in the District Court, his solicitor had raised the legality of the applicant's detention in Garda custody under s.4 of the 1984 Act as a ground for refusing to remand the applicant in custody. The District Justice declined to enter into the question of the validity of the applicant's detention under the 1984 Act, and proceeded to remand him in custody. On an inquiry under Article 40.4.2 of the Constitution it was argued that once the issue of the applicant's detention under the 1984 Act had been raised the District Justice was obliged to consider the matter. Barrington J did not accept this point.

He applied the well-known decisions in *The State (Attorney General) v Fawsitt* [1955] IR 30 and *Attorney General (McDonnell) v Higgins* [1964] IR 374 in stating that the issue which arose in the instant inquiry under Article 40.4 was the legality of the applicant's detention under the order remanding him in custody. It was therefore irrelevant, in relation to the jurisdiction of the District Court to remand him in custody, whether the applicant was lawfully or unlawfully before the District Court. He noted that the District Court was thus in a different position from the Special Criminal Court, citing the decision in *McElhinney v Special Criminal Court* [1989] ILRM 411 in support (see above). It may be noted that the decision of Barrington J was upheld by the Supreme Court on 10 July 1990; this decison will be dealt with in the 1990 Review.

Barrington J did note, at the end of his judgment, that the validity of the applicant's detention under s.4 of the 1984 Act might have repercussions in other aspects of the proceedings, or at his trial. To that extent, he opined that the provisions of s.4 of the 1984 Act should not be regarded merely as administrative safeguards provided by the law, as had been suggested by counsel for the respondent. Barrington J referred with apparent approval to dicta of Walsh J in *The People v Lynch* [1981] ILRM 389; [1982] IR 64, who had pointed out that the District Court was obliged to uphold the constitutional right to liberty under Article 40.4 of the Constitution in the same manner as any other judge appointed under the Constitution. From Barrington J's perspective, however, this appears to be a matter for a trial judge.

The approach taken by Barrington J in *Keating* is quite similar to that of Hamilton P in *Byrne v Grey* [1988] IR 31 (see the 1987 Review, 22). It may be contrasted with that taken by Keane J in *O'Mahony v Melia* [1990] ILRM 14; [1989] IR 335 (92, above), where all the issued raised were determined without directly dealing with the evidential consequences of those matters.

YOUNG OFFENDERS

Nature of detention in reformatory school In *J. v Delap and Attorney General* [1989] IR 167, the applicant, then 15 years of age, was undergoing a period of detention in a reformatory school, Trinity House in Lusk, when he and some others climbed on to the roof of the school and did malicious damage. He and his companions were charged with an offence under s.51 of the Malicious Damage Act 1861. When brought before the respondent District Justice, the applicant's case was treated as a minor offence and the respondent ordered the applicant to be detained in Trinity House until he attained the age of 19 in June 1991, this order amounting to a period of detention of three years and four months. Under ss.57 and 65 of the Children Act 1908, as amended, the Justice is empowered, upon conviction of a young person of a criminal offence, to order detention in a reformatory school for a period between two and four years. The applicant sought judicial review on the ground, inter alia, that the order of detention amounted to an unconstitutional sentence of imprisonment, contrary to Article 38.5. It was conceded that, if the order amounted to a sentence of imprisonment, the matter could not be regarded as a minor offence. Barr J, however, refused the relief sought by the applicant.

He emphasised that Trinity House was a school under the aegis of the Department of Education, and although detention there could amount to a form of punishment, the primary purpose of the detention order was to provide long term training and educational facilities to assist young offenders in making a new start in life rather than to punish them for having committed a criminal offence. On this basis, therefore, he concluded that the respondent's order did not amount to a sentence of imprisonment. He thus distinguished the position of Trinity House from that of St Patrick's Institution and in that way avoided the implications of the decision of the Supreme Court in *The State (Sheerin) v Kennedy* [1966] IR 379.

Barr J relied on a passage from the judgment of Walsh J in *Sheerin* to bolster the conclusion he arrived at in the instant case. As already noted, Barr J reasoned that the purpose of Trinity House was far removed from a penal institution as such. In *Sheerin*, Walsh J had made a comparison between St Patrick's Institution and Borstal Institutions; he made no comparison with reformatory schools. Indeed, it is worth recording that in *Sheerin*, Walsh J had stated (at 395) that his decision as to the constitutionality of the impugned section would have been the same even if the objects of St Patrick's Institution had been declared in the same terms as those of Borstal Institutions. He also stated his view that there was 'no essential difference between detention and imprisonment'. In this light, *Sheerin* does not support the proposition that detention for beneficial purposes can transform what would otherwise be a non-minor offence into a minor offence, as Barr J appears to view it. It may be said that the judgment of Walsh J does not provide direct support for the drawing of any distinction between detention in St Patrick's (or prison) and detention in a reformatory school.

This alternative view of the *Sheerin* decision does not, of course, necessarily indicate that the decision in *J.* is incorrect. It is certainly legitimate to point to the differences in structure, management and philosophy between St. Patrick's Institution and reformatory schools. But the hurdle presented by *Sheerin* is that it identifies detention (regardless of certain beneficial purposes) with imprisonment. At the heart of the matter is the question of the nature of 'punishment' or 'penalty' for the purposes of the definition of 'minor offence'. Here we find that there is an entangled mass of competing philosophies to be applied at the sentencing stage: retribution (proportionality), deterrence (whether of the particular offender or of others), rehabilitation and, possibly, protection of society (for example, from a violent recidivist). It is, in truth, impossible to reconcile each of these goals, and in most instances a judge will in any given case engage in a trade-off between them at the expense, perhaps, of overall intellectual consistency. What is clear is that none of these goals has been given ultimate prominence over the others.

What implications does this have for the decision of Barr J in the instant case? It may be argued that the term 'punishment' for the purposes of determining what is or is not a minor offence should not be confined to those circumstances in which the punishment merely serves retributive and deterrent goals. Punishment that serves a rehabilitative, or a predominantly rehabilitative, goal is nonetheless punishment for the purposes of the minor offence doctrine. Where a court sentences a defendant to imprisonment for a short spell for rehabilitative purposes—so that the defendant can be sure to obtain certain medical assistance or therapy to cure an addiction, for example—the punishment is no less punishment. Certainly, no judge in any of the cases dealing with the minor offence issue prior to *J.* sought to limit the conspectus of punishment to cases of retributive or deterrent punishment as opposed to punishment with the goal of rehabilitation.

Defence Forces

COURTS-MARTIAL

The Courts-Martial (Legal Aid) Regulations 1989 (SI No.25) specify revised fees for appearances before a court-martial hearing.

DUTY OF CARE

Ryan v Ireland [1989] IR 177 (SC); High Court, 19 October 1989 was a significant case on the liability of the State towards members of the defence forces while they are on active service: see 410-8, below, in the Torts chapter.

Education

DISCIPLINE

The decision in *Murtagh v Board of Management of St Emer's National School*, High Court, 27 November 1989 is discussed at 5-7, above.

UNIVERSITIES

The University of Limerick Act 1989 and the Dublin City University Act 1989 provided for the conferring of university status on the two former National Institutes for Higher Education at Limerick and Dublin. It is the first time since 1922 that universities have been established in the State. The 1989 Acts amend the National Institute for Higher Education Limerick Act 1980 and the National Institute for Higher Education Dublin Act 1980, respectively, in order to give effect to the change in status. The Acts came into force on 22 June 1989: see the University of Limerick Act 1989 (Commencement) Order 1989 (SI No.147) and Dublin City University Act 1989 (Commencement) Order 1989 (SI No.148).

S.3 of both Acts allow the Universities to confer awards in their own right; previously many of the degrees obtained in the Universities were conferred by the National Council for Educational Awards. S.4 of both Acts substitute the title 'President' for 'Director' for the chief executive of the Universities, though it might be noted that, in practice, the title 'President' had been adopted by both chief executives some time prior to the initiation of the 1989 Acts. S.7 of the University of Limerick Act 1989 and s.6 of the Dublin City University Act 1989 have (seemingly without prior consultation of the publishing industry) the effect of conferring copyright library status on the libraries of both Universities, and these sections amend s.56 of the Copyright Act 1963 accordingly.

Two important amendments were made to the Acts in Dáil Éireann. The first concerned the functions of the Universities. As introduced, s.3 of both Bills provided that as part of the pursuit of learning and the advancement of knowledge, there should be collaboration with 'business, professional, cultural and other bodies.' This was amended to read collaboration with 'educational, business, professional, trade union and other bodies.' The other amendment was to s.5 of the Acts. It is now provided that membership of the respective governing bodies shall include not less than three representatives of the student body of the University.

Finally, it may be noted that, both in the Dáil and Seanad the enactment of the Acts provided opportunities for Deputies and Senators to consider the general standing of University education in the State: see 390 Dáil Debates cols. 1261-1409 and 122 Seanad Debates cols. 2177-2317.

Electricity and Energy

MINERALS DEVELOPMENT

Designated area   The Continental Shelf (Designated Areas) Order 1989 (SI No.141) specifies designated areas for the purposes of mineral exploration and exploitation.

Licence fee   The Minerals Development (Amendment) Regulations 1989 (SI No.44) provide for an increase in the fee payable in an application for a mineral prospecting licence.

PETROLEUM

The Petroleum Oils (Regulation or Control of Acquisition, Supply, Distribution or Marketing) (Continuance) Order 1989 (SI No.345) continued for 1990 the regime outlined in the 1988 Order of the same title: see the 1988 Review, 198.

Equitable Remedies

INJUNCTIONS

In *Capemel Ltd v Lister (No. 2)* [1989] IR 323, Costello J dealt with an unusual application for a mandatory injunction. In earlier proceedings in the case (considered in the Contract chapter, above 125-6), he had made a declaration that the defendant underwriters were not entitled to repudiate liability to the plaintiff company under a policy insuring the plaintiff against liability as an employer. At that time an employee's action for damages was well advanced. Some weeks later, the employee's action was settled, on counsel's advice. The company was unable to pay the amount agreed. There was a reasonable apprehension that it would go into liquidation unless the insurers made good their liability. In the meantime, however, the insurers had appealed Costello J's earlier decision to the Supreme Court.

Costello J was quite satisfied that, had he been requested to make an order that the insurers pay any damages properly payable to the employee, he would have done so. Moreover, although it was not stated in the original order, liberty to apply was inherent in the situation that existed. Instead, however, the plaintiff had issued new proceedings claiming interlocutory relief.

In the special circumstances, Costello J did not think he should approach this claim on the normally applicable basis, 'particularly the very stringent principles on which the Court would give interlocutory relief of a mandatory sort'. While he could have treated the application as one to re-enter the earlier proceedings and make a new order in them, he thought it more appropriate to make the order on the interlocutory motion, freed from the very strict rules which normally applied in relation to mandatory relief.

Accordingly Costello J directed the insurers to make payment of the sum agreed in the settlement plus costs, putting a four-week stay on the order so that the matter could be brought before the Supreme Court at the earliest possible opportunity should the defendants decide to go on with the appeal. If this order had not been made, the company would have gone into liquidation; on the other hand, without a stay, the order would have meant that the insurers might have been unable to recover the sum if there was an appeal to the Supreme Court in the earlier action.

Costello J's willingness to depart from the test laid down by the Supreme Court in *Campus Oil Ltd v Minister for Industry and Energy (No. 2)* [1983]

IR 88 has been evidenced in previous cases, including *Benckiser GmbH v Fibrosol Service Ltd*, High Court, 13 May 1988 and *Three Stripe International v Charles O'Neill & Co. Ltd* [1989] ILRM 124; [1988] IR 144, both analysed in the 1988 Review, 199-201. This disposition to treat *Campus Oil (No. 2)* as not involving a test of universal application finds support in the House of Lords decision of *American Cyanamid Co. v Ethicon* [1975] AC 395, which greatly influenced the Supreme Court in *Campus Oil (No. 2)*.

Pesca Valentia Ltd v Minister for Fisheries [1985] IR 193 is a leading decision on the power of the courts to grant an injunction against the implementation of legislation whose constitutional validity or conformity with EC law has been challenged. See Keane, *Equity and the Law of Trusts in the Republic of Ireland* (1988), para. 15.28; Casey, (1985) 7 *DULJ* 123 and the 1987 Review, 169-171. The sequelae to the case are also worthy of interest. On 19 January 1988, the Court of Justice answered the two questions which Keane J had referred to it for a preliminary ruling in favour of the defendants. The case was then re-entered by the defendants, who sought to have the proceedings dismissed as well as an assessment of the damages payable by the plaintiffs on foot of their undertaking when they had sought the interlocutory injunction. Keane J ordered a hearing in the ordinary way rather than disposing of the case on the pleadings in the light of the Court of Justice's ruling: High Court, 6 June 1989.

The plaintiffs argued that the doctrine of legitimate expectation or the operation of equitable estoppel applied. Keane J interpreted the doctrine of legitimate expectation in England as giving relief by way of judicial review to a person affected by a decision where he had not been given some rational ground for alterations in a regime to which he has become accustomed and an opportunity to be heard in relation to them before they were implemented. If these principles represented the Irish law on the subject, the plaintiffs could not complain since they had been informed of the proposed changes in the general legal framework affecting their right to fish, and had availed themselves of the invitation to make representations to the Minister; these representations appeared to have been successful to the extent that their licences, for the first year of operation of the new regime, had not been subject to the condition as to the nationality of employees which the legislation envisaged.

Keane J went on to refer to Murphy J's interpretation, in *Garda Representative Association v Ireland* [1989] ILRM 1; [1989] IR 193, of Finlay CJ's analysis of the 'legitimate expectation' doctrine in *Webb v Ireland* [1988] ILRM 565; [1988] IR 353. There Murphy J had expressed the view that the Chief Justice had expressed his reluctance to recognise the doctrine as a new or separate concept in our legal system. Keane J thought it unnecessary to consider this aspect of the matter further, since it clearly could not avail the plaintiffs. See Administrative Law chapter above.

Keane J was satisfied that the Minister's conduct did not fail the *ultra vires* test of 'unreasonableness or irrationality' articulated by Henchy J in the Supreme Court case of *The State (Keegan) v Stardust Victims Compensation Tribunal* [1987] ILRM 202; [1986] IR 642. The gradual manner in which he had introduced the new regime weighed against any holding of *ultra vires*.

As to equitable estoppel, Keane J considered that it was premised on 'at least a representation' of the part of the defendant. He rejected the interpretation of *Webb* which would regard the assurance given by the Director of the National Museum as not essential to that decision. In the instant case, while the plaintiffs had undoubtedly been encouraged in their project by the semi-State bodies, they had not been given any assurance that the law regulating fishing would never be altered so as adversely to affect them, nor, if such an assurance had been given, could any legal rights have followed from it:

> No such 'estoppel' could conceivably operate so as to prevent the Oireachtas from legislating or the executive from implementing the legislation when enacted.

One wonders whether *Webb* supports this bold statement. If, as the Supreme Court in *Webb* plainly preferred, the Oireachtas were to enact legislation on national treasures such as the Derrynaflan Hoard, and if the Director of the National Museum of the day were at some future time to make the same assurance to the finder of a national treasure as was made to Mr Webb, why should this legislation be impervious to an estoppel argument when the constitutional entitlement of State sovereignty on which the legislation would be based proved incapable in *Webb* of withstanding an estoppel argument? This is not, of course, to suggest that the courts should easily suspend or modify the operation of a legislative provision on the basis of the doctrine of equitable or promissory estoppel; but it would seem to be going too far to say that the courts can *never* do so.

The question of quantifying the damages flowing from the plaintiffs' undertaking presented some interesting problems. Counsel for the defendants argued that the Court should assess the loss by reference to the profits which the plaintiffs had made during the period of the fishing (over two and a half million pounds) or, alternatively, by reference to the maximum fines that would have been imposed and the value of the catch that would have been confiscated had the prosecutions restrained by the injunction proceeded (around thirty thousand pounds).

Keane J rejected both suggested tests. As to the first, if the plaintiffs had not made these profits some other fishing enterprise would have. In any event Ireland had not been bound by the injunction and there was 'clearly a problem in awarding damages to a defendant on foot of an undertaking given by a plaintiff in respect of an injunction by which that defendant is not bound'. Moreover, the fish, until they swam into the plaintiffs' nets, were animals *ferae naturae* which did not belong to anyone. Had they been caught by a vessel, Irish or otherwise, which was fishing lawfully in these waters, they would have become the property of the vessel's owner. The second suggested test presented equally insurmountable problems. The primary functions of penalties imposed in respect of criminal offences were deterrence and punishment; the raising of revenue for the State was no more than an incidental by-product. The real loss was the inability to police the lawfully established fishing regime; to award damages on the basis of what the plaintiffs might have been fined would be imposing a penalty on them which, in the absence of an actual criminal trial before a judge and jury, seemed 'constitutionally suspect in the highest degree'.

Accordingly, while recognising that it was unsatisfactory that the undertaking as to damages should have proved incapable of implementation, Keane J declined to make any order as to damages in its regard.

We have already noted (above 101) that, in *Grange Developments Ltd v Dublin County Council (No. 4)* [1989] IR 377, Murphy J confirmed the view that the initiation of a constitutional action does not in itself entitle the plaintiff to an injunction preventing enforcement of the legislative provisions under challenge.

TRUSTS

Resulting trusts In *Daniels v Dunne* (1989) 8 *ILT* 35, the question of resulting trusts fell for consideration. The deceased, 'a very discontented and unhappy man', had been treated kindly by the defendant. This was at least a partial motivation for the deceased's opening a deposit bank account in the joint names of himself, the defendant or the survivor. On the first page of the deposit account book, the words 'payable to either or survivor' appeared. The customer history card, however, signed by the deceased, stated that withdrawals were to be *signed by the deceased only or his survivor.* Judge Sheridan had no doubt that the latter document accurately represented the true position: the deceased had retained in law total dominion over any sums paid into the account until the date of his death. He had made no withdrawals; the defendant had never participated in the account; at the time of the death of the deceased, the account had risen from £3,000 to over £8,000.

The defendant, whom the Judge described as clearly 'a most honourable man', sought a judicial ruling on the position. Judge Sheridan applied the former Supreme Court's decision in *Owens v Greene* [1932] IR 225 in holding that no presumption of advancement arose. The deceased, in retaining complete dominion over the funds until he died, retained the beneficial interest. The only case where the survivor had succeeded notwithstanding that the deceased had dominion over the moneys during his lifetime was *Diver v McCrea* (1907) 42 ILTR 249, which the Supreme Court in *Owens v Greene* had expressly stated was not good law.

Neither could a *donatio mortis causa* be established. Although the deceased had from time to time expressed himself to be in poor health, the lodgement in the account was certainly not in contemplation of his death; nor had there been actual or constructive delivery of the book to the defendant before the death of the deceased.

It is worth noting that in *Lynch v Burke*, High Court, 16 January 1990, O'Hanlon J evinced considerable reluctance to follow the reasoning in *Owens v Greene* and did so apparently from fidelity to the hierarchical system of precedent. He noted that the Supreme Court's judgment had not received the support of the High Court of Australia in *Russell v Scott* (1936) 55 CLR 44 nor the English High Court in *Re Figgis; Roberts v MacLaren* [1969] 1 Ch 123. In the earlier English decision of *Young v Sealey* [1949] Ch 278, Romer J had expressed a preference for *Owens v Greene* but felt bound by earlier English authorities to follow a different approach. Mr Justice Keane, extra-judicially, has given a vote of confidence to *Owens v Greene: Equity and the Law of Trusts in the Republic of Ireland* (1988), para. 12.08.

Purchases in contravention of Trustee Savings Bank legislation In *Hortensius Ltd v Bishops et al. Trustees of the Trustee Savings Bank, Dublin* [1989] ILRM 294, the plaintiffs, who owed moneys on a mortgage forming part of a loan portfolio of a mortgagee which was sold to the defendant, sought a declaration that the purchase was contrary to the Trustee Acts, and consequently void. The contractual aspects of the case are discussed in the Contract chapter, above, 129-30. Here we consider the argument relating to breach of statute.

In an extended judgment Costello J discussed the nature and purpose of the relevant legislation. A crucial provision was s.15 of the Trustee Savings Banks Act 1863, which restricted the power of the trustees of savings banks to make investments only in the Bank of England and Bank of Ireland. The trustees' powers had been expanded by later legislation. S.3 of the Trustee Savings Banks Act 1965 enabled the trustees, with the consent of the Minister for Finance, to undertake any business which was, in the Minister's opinion, 'calculated to encourage thrift and within the financial capacity of the Bank'. S.1 of the Trustee Savings Banks Act 1979 amended s.3 of the 1965 Act to enable the trustees, with the Minister's consent, to undertake any business, 'including, notwithstanding anything in the Acts, the making of loans (whether secured by mortgages of land or any interest in land or otherwise) and the using, for the purpose of making the loans, of money deposited with the bank by depositors', which, in the Minister's opinion, was calculated to encourage thrift and was within the bank's financial capacity.

A question of fact arose in the case as to whether the Minister had given his consent to the purchase of the loan portfolio. Clearly he had given consent to the granting of loans, including house mortgage loans, but the evidence as to his consent for the purchase of the loan portfolio was based on an initial informal meeting with an official of the Department followed by a memorandum indicating that consent would be forthcoming provided the portfolio did not contain a loan of a 'highly commercial nature'. No ministerial consent was obtained before the contracts for the purchase of the loan portfolio were signed. However, Costello J was willing to conclude that it should be implied from later correspondence that the Minister, by his officials, 'albeit in a most informal manner and retrospectively', had purported to consent to the 'business' thus undertaken by the trustees.

Costello J noted that the trustees had in this transaction *purchased* rather than *made* loans; they thus could not claim to fall within the ambit of the 1979 amendment. He did not contest the argument made by the defendant that he could not go behind the Minister's conclusion that the business was 'calculated to encourage thrift', but he considered that, even if this was so, the Minister had no authorisation to give his consent to a business, even one encouraging thrift, which involved the use of depositors' funds in a manner prohibited by the 1863 Act. Nothing in s.3 of the 1965 Act authorised the use of over £5 million of depositors' funds for making the purchase of the loan portfolio. The trustees had thus contravened s.15 of the 1863 Act.

Nevertheless, for reasons we discuss in the Contract chapter, 129-30, above, Costello J held that the plaintiffs were not entitled to repudiate their liability under the mortgage which had been transferred to the defendant. The trustees' breach of statutory duty did not render the purchase of the loan portfolio illegal.

The Trustee Savings Banks Act 1989   We briefly analyse this Act, above, 40-2.

Charitable trusts   In *In re Prescott; Purcell v Pobjoy*, High Court, 23 November 1989, a testatrix had by will in 1985 purported to devise and bequeath her house in Dublin 'unto the Holy Protection Parish Dublin of the Russian Orthodox Church abroad under the jurisdiction of Metropolitan Vhilaret and the Synod of Bishops of . . . New York'. She directed that the house was to be used as a residence for 'clergy of the said Russian Orthodox

Church abroad' (excluding a named individual), and that it 'should only be sold if and when there are no parishioners or members of the said church living in Ireland'. She also directed that, in the event of such sale, the proceeds should be applied 'for the general purpose of the said Russian Orthodox Church abroad in England'. The testatrix died in 1987.

The evidence disclosed that there had been a parish in Dublin to care pastorally for the Russian exiles settled in the city, but that the resident priest had died in 1977; the members of the faithful had dwindled and in 1983 the bishop of the diocese had informed the community that they could no longer be regarded as a parish but as an *obschima*. There was no church, dues were not paid, no decrees were made, nor did church records exist. There were, however, a few members of the community, not all elderly, and they were visited from England by a priest irregularly.

MacKenzie J held that, at the time the testatrix made her will, the Holy Protection Parish had ceased to exist. Counsel for the church argued that, although the parish had lost its status as a parish canonical, it was nevertheless a parish; if it had ceased to exist, the gift should not lapse as the parish should be construed as synonymous with the community. Even if the testatrix's directions could not be carried out, and the gift lapsed, it should not fall into residue.

MacKenzie J rejected this argument. It was 'against reason' to hold that a parish existed at the date of the will or the date of the testatrix's death. The gift lapsed because it was one to a body which did not exist at the relevant times. The gift over, being dependent on the validity of the bequest to the parish, also lapsed. It was, moreover, void for uncertainty, since '[t]he mind of God can only direct' how long there would continue to be members of the Church living in Ireland.

MacKenzie J also declined to find a general charitable intent, to which the doctrine of *cy pres* might be engrafted. He accepted that there were cases of single gift where the court could find such an intent, 'but here . . . the recipient did not exist at the time of the will and death'. One can perhaps regard this conclusion as open for discussion. The parish, the intended recipient, may not have existed, on account of the fact that the death of the priest and dwindling numbers of the community by then had led to its reduction to the status of an *obschima*. But the members of that community continued to exist, and its communal religious dimensions, which must have been of crucial significance to the testatrix, also had vitality, albeit lacking in sufficient structure and quality to merit the status of a parish. A strong argument may be made that a charitable intent existed in this case.

European Communities

ABUSE OF DOMINANT POSITION

The use of Articles 85 and 86 of the Treaty of Rome in a domestic context was in issue in *Radio Telefís Éireann and Ors v Magill TV Guide Ltd and Ors (No. 2)* [1990] ILRM 534; [1989] IR 554.

The first plaintiff was the well-known statutory broadcasting authority in the State established by the Broadcasting Authority Act 1960. It published a weekly magazine, the *RTE Guide*, which contained, inter alia, a complete schedule of its programmes for the week in question. The vast majority of the sales of the magazine were within the State. The plaintiff also entered into agreements with newspapers and magazines by which they were permitted to publish details of its programme schedules for the day of issue of the publication, as well as permitting publication of listings for Saturday and Sunday. The plaintiff was, however, the only organisation which published a full weekly list of schedules. The other plaintiffs were publishers of similar weekly magazines containing lists of schedules for programmes broadcast by the BBC and ITV. They also had agreements with newspapers and magazines which were similar in many respects to those entered into by the first plaintiff.

The first defendant was the publisher of a listing guide to broadcast programmes, and it had entered into an agreement to publish limited extracts from the plaintiffs' schedules. For the week 31 May to 6 June 1986, however, the defendant published the full week's listing. The plaintiffs then instituted proceedings for injunctions preventing the defendant from publishing any listing except in accordance with the terms of the licences entered into. The defendant denied the plaintiffs' claim to copyright, and counterclaimed that the plaintiffs were acting in breach of Articles 85 and 86 of the Treaty of Rome in not permitting the defendant to publish a full listing guide. The plaintiffs obtained interlocutory relief from the High Court in 1986: [1988] IR 97. On the trial of the action Lardner J also granted the plaintiffs the perpetual injunctive relief which they sought.

Lardner J dealt, firstly, with the copyright issue. He said that, in interpreting the phrase 'literary work' in ss.2 and 8 of the Copyright Act 1963, the Court must take a broad view, and the phrase should be taken to mean any written or printed composition which was an original composition that involved labour, time and skill in its compilation. Since the times and titles of programmes were not matters within the public domain but had originated from the plaintiffs, and their compilation had involved considerable labour, time and skill, they were entitled to claim copyright in them. It was the labour, time and skill point which allowed Lardner J to distinguish the instant situation from that in *Educational Co. of Ireland Ltd v Fallon* [1919] 1 IR 62.

Lardner J then went on to deal with the arguments arising from Articles 85 and 86 of the Treaty of Rome. He agreed with the defendants that there was a degree of similarity in the licensing terms which each of the plaintiffs had entered into with newspapers and magazines. However, he did not consider that this involved the type of co-ordination which would amount to a concerted practice between them within the meaning of Article 85 of the Treaty of Rome, as expounded by the Court of Justice in *Imperial Chemical Industries Ltd v Commission* [1972] ECR 619. In addition, he concluded that the defendants had failed to establish that, insofar as any agreements made by the plaintiffs had any effect on trade outside the State, there was any significant distortion of the market within the Community within the meaning of Article 85.

As to the Article 86 argument, Lardner J refered to the fact that issues arising from the present case relating to Article 86 of the Treaty were pending before the Court of Justice on appeal from the Commission. In those circumstances, Lardner J felt constrained to limit his findings to ones of fact without expressing a view on them. Despite this limitation, he considered that the defendant had not established in evidence that the matters complained of would have a significant effect on trade between member states within the meaning of Article 86 of the Treaty, again as explained by the Court of Justice itself in *BRT v SABAM (No. 2)* [1974] ECR 313.

COMMON AGRICULTURAL POLICY

The right of the Minister for Agriculture to set-off sums due to him under animal disease eradication schemes against intervention payments due from the Minsiter was discussed in *Clover Meats Ltd and Anor v Minister for Agriculture*, High Court, 28 June 1989.

The plaintiff companies were both in receivership and insolvent, but there was due and owing to them from the defendant Minister various sums by way of intervention payments pursuant to the Guidance and Guarantee Fund established by Council Regulation 729/70/EEC. The Minister was designated the Intervention Agent for the Fund by the European Communities (Common Agricultural Policy) (Market Intervention) Regulations 1973. The Minister was also responsible in this State for the collection of levies and fees under the Bovine Disease Eradication schemes as well as under specific pieces of legislation. In that capacity the Minister was owed various sums by the plaintiff companies. The companies instituted proceedings seeking payment of the sums due to them under the Guidance and Guarantee Fund, but the Minister sought a set-off of the sums due to him by the companies in respect of the schemes and legislation referred to.

Barrington J held that the Minister was entitled to the set-off claimed since there was a certain overlap between his two capacities as Intervention Agent and National Minister. Barrington J also pointed out that the Minister and all companies involved in the intervention trade had entered into an agreement regarding the guaranteeing of payments under the Fund by which the Minister had reserved his right of set-off in respect of any future payments due to the companies from the Fund. Finally, he rejected the argument made that there was any threat in the circumstances to the integrity of the Fund. In the context of the overlap between the Minister's functions, Barrington J referred to the decision of the Court of Justice on this point in *Continental Irish Meat Ltd v Minister for Agriculture* [1985] ECR 3441, modifying the decision of McMahon J: [1983] ILRM 503.

DIRECTIVES: IMPLEMENTATION IN IRISH LAW

Browne and Ors v An Bord Pleanála [1989] ILRM 865 received widespread publicity, and may very well have as much long-term significance as any court case in recent years. This is not, perhaps, because of the direct outcome of the case but more because of its part in placing environmental matters on the Irish political agenda.

The applicant farmers and members of the Womanagh Valley Protection Association were objectors in an application for planning permission to Cork County Council in respect of the construction of a pharmaceutical plant by a company, Merrell Dow. Permission was granted, subject to certain conditions, and this was confirmed on appeal by the respondent Bord. The applicants sought judicial review of the permission on the ground, inter alia, that the County Council had failed to comply with the requirements of Council Directive 85/337/EEC on the assessment of the impact of certain projects on the environment. In particular they submitted that Merrell Dow had omitted from its environmental impact study certain data required by the Directive. The Council argued that the Directive had been complied with in the planning application. Merrell Dow, in addition, argued that the Directive was not part of Irish law and was thus not relevant to the application. It was agreed that a Circular letter had issued from the Department of the Environment in July 1988 which stated that it was 'for giving effect' to the

Directive. The Circular stated that planning authorities should give 'adequate consideration' to the environmental aspects of a development, and that the planning authority should use their discretionary powers under reg.26 of the Local Government (Planning and Development) Regulations 1977 accordingly. Barron J refused to quash the planning permission and, in effect, rejected all the arguments put forward by the applicants.

First of all, however, he dealt with a preliminary objection put forward by the respondent Bord. He held that the applicants were not estopped from seeking judicial review since (adopting the approach in *The State (Gallagher & Co.) v de Valera* [1986] ILRM 3) their conduct in appealing to the Bord did not lead any person to believe that they would not apply for judicial review. And, following the approach which he has consistently taken to arguments of this kind, he said that the courts would be slow to determine a judicial review on such a preliminary point, in view of the simplified procedures for judicial review which have been recently implemented in the Rules of the Superior Courts 1986: see also his judgment in *Murtagh v Board of Management of St Emer's National School*, High Court, 27 November 1989 (6, above).

Barron J then went on to deal with the substantive issues arising in the case. On the question as to whether the 1985 Directive had the direct force of law in Ireland, he referred to the decision of the Court of Justice in *McDermott and Cotter v Minister for Social Welfare* [1987] ILRM 324; [1987] ECR 1453. From this he concluded that the principles contained in an EEC Directive do not normally have the direct force of law in the Member States of the Community and will usually require a legislative process to be legally binding. In some instances, of course, he pointed out that the Directive can have direct effect between the Member State and its citizens, by which the Member State will be estopped from denying the effect of the Directive and will be bound by the law not as it is but as it should be. It was this reference to an estoppel between the State and its citizens which was to prove crucial in Barron J's judgment.

He went on to refer with approval to another Court of Justice decision, *Foster v British Gas plc* [1988] 2 CMLR 697; [1988] ECR 584. Barron J held that the respondent Bord could not be held responsible for the failure, if there was such a failure, by the State to implement the terms of the Directive, since An Bord Pleanála could not be regarded as falling within the province of a government Department.

Then Barron J turned to the Department of the Environment Circular which purported to implement the Directive. He followed the decision of the Court of Justice in *Commission v Belgium* [1988] 1 CMLR 248 in concluding that the Circular did not have the force of law and could not be deemed to have incorporated the terms of the Directive into Irish law. Examining its contents, he held that the terms of the Circular did not impose a mandatory obligation on a planning authority in relation to the contents of an environmental impact study. Thus, the failure to include any particular information in such a study would not, under the terms of the Circular, be fatal to the present planning application.

As he knew that the case might go further, Barron J added his view that, even if the Directive had been brought into effect in Irish law, the procedures followed by the planning authority in the instant case would have been sufficient compliance with its terms, since the Directive was intended primarily to ensure that information was available to the public, and this had occurred in the instant application. Nor did he consider that there any justification for the claim that the need for specific information in the environmental impact study was a condition precedent to a valid application for planning permission, since he felt that the study was merely part of the documentation required. The documentation, he stated, was separate from the decision to grant permission under s.26 of the Local Government (Planning and Development) Act 1963, which was solely a matter for the planning authority, as was the adequacy of the information contained in the study.

All the issues in the case might very well have been debated in full by the Supreme Court because the applicants did indeed lodge an appeal against Barron J's decision. However, they subsequently withdrew the appeal after it became clear that Merrell Dow had decided not to go ahead with the construction of the pharmaceutical plant. It is outside the scope of this Review to examine the reasons for that decision; it is sufficient to draw attention to the fact that the *Browne* case prompted a number of prominent public figures to question whether we were 'getting the right balance' between environmental concern and the need to obtain more employment. The case certainly has had a major effect on the wider policy front in that sense. One of the immediate issues in the case, that is, implementation of the EEC Directive involved was dealt with later in the year. The European Communities (Environmental Impact Assessment) Regulations 1989 implemented the terms of the 1985 Directive in Irish law with effect from 1 February 1990: see 373, below.

ENFORCEMENT OF JUDGMENTS

The developing Irish case law on the Jurisdiction of Courts and Enforcement of Judgments (European Communities) Act 1988 is discussed in the Conflict of Laws chapter, 73-9, above.

FISHERIES

Pesca Valentia Ltd v Minister for Fisheries and Forestry, High Court, 6 June 1989 involved discussion of the legitimate expectation doctrine in the context of changes in the fisheries laws required by membership of the Communities: see 11-12, above, in the Administrative Law chapter.

IRISH REGULATIONS

The following regulations and orders were made in 1989 pursuant to the provisions of s.3 of the European Communities Act 1972 (or other statutory powers) involving implementation of Community law obligations. Where the title of an instrument does not speak for itself, a brief description of its content is given.

Air Navigation (Eurocontrol) (Route Charges) Regulations 1989 (SI No.362): specify the ECU, rather than US dollar, as the preferred unit of currency for payment of Eurocontrol fees.

Air Pollution Act 1987 (Sulphur Content of Gas Oil) Regulations 1989 (SI No.168): provide for the maximum permissible level of sulphur in gas oil in accordance with EC approximation of content levels.

European Communities (Additives in Feedingstuffs) Regulations 1989 (SI No.49): place limits on the use of additives in feedingstuffs.

European Communities (Agricultural or Forestry Tractors Type Approval) Regulations 1989 (SI No.288).

European Communities (Cancellation of Contracts Negotiated away from Business Premises) Regulations 1989 (SI No.224): provide, *inter alia*, for a "cooling off" period in such contracts.

European Communities (Classification, Packaging and Labelling of Pesticides) (Amendment) Regulations 1989 (SI No.149).

European Communities (Customs) (Revocation of Statutory Instruments) Regulations 1989 (SI No.177): revoke certain Regulations which have become obsolete by virtue of EC obligations.

European Communities (Dangerous Substances) (Classification, Packaging and Labelling) (Amendment) Regulations 1989 (SI No.228): amend previous regulations.

European Communities (Electrically Operated Lifts) Regulations 1989 (SI No.227): specify EOLAS as the certifiying authority for such lifts.

European Communities (Environmental Impact Assessment) Regulations 1989 (SI No.349): see above, in the discussion of *Browne v An Bord Pleanála* [1989] ILRM 865 and 373, below.

European Communities (Establishment and Provision of Services in

Architecture) Regulations 1989 (SI No.15): provide for the mutual recognition of architecture qualifications and also provide for the right of establishment.

European Communities (European Economic Interest Groupings) Regulations 1989 (SI No.191): provide for the creation of EEIGs.

European Communities (Feeding Stuffs) (Tolerances of Undesirable Substances and Products) Regulations 1989 (SI No.216): amend various requirements as to the permitted levels in connection with feedstuffs.

European Communities (Fresh Meat) (Amendment) Regulations 1989 (SI No.66): impose requirements in connection with sliced bovine livers and additional requirements on the storage of frozen meat.

European Communities (Introduction of Organisms Harmful to Plants or Plant Products) (Prohibition) (Amendment) Regulations 1989 (SI No.92).

European Communities (Introduction of Organisms Harmful to Plants or Plant Products) (Prohibition) (Temporary Provisions) Regulations 1989 (SI No.252).

European Communities (Introduction of Organisms Harmful to Plants or Plant Products) (Prohibition) (Temporary Provisions) (No.2) Regulations 1989 (SI No.253).

European Communities (Lawnmowers) (Permissible Noise Levels) Regulations 1989 (SI No.102).

European Communities (Licensing of Drivers) Regulations 1989 (SI No.287): amend the Road Traffic Act 1961 to allow for the introduction of new licensing provisions: see 447, below, in the Transport chapter.

European Communities (Major Accident Hazards of Certain Industrial Activities) (Amendment) Regulations 1989 (SI No.194) amend 1986 Regulations on precautions to be taken in certain large chemical plants: see 379, below, in the Safety and Health chapter.

European Communities (Marketing of Fertilizers) Regulations 1989 (SI No.180).

European Communities (Milk Levy) (Amendment) Regulations 1989 (SI No.47): provides for the reallocation of milk quotas to certain special category producers from a national reserve set up by the Minister for Agriculture and Food.

European Communities (Motor Vehicles Type Approval) Regulations 1989 (SI No.35).

European Communities (Pesticide Residues) (Fruit and Vegetables) Regulations 1989 (SI No.105): provide for maximum permissible pesticide residue levels in fruit and vegetables.

European Communities (Preferential Treatment for Debts in Respect of Levies on Production of Coal and Steel) Regulations 1989 (SI No.219): prioritise the payment of debts for levies imposed in the ECSC context in a winding up or bankruptcy, and amend the provisions of s.285 of the Companies Act 1963 and s.81(1) of the Bankruptcy Act 1988.

European Communities (Preservatives in Food) (Purity Criteria) Regulations 1989 (SI No.262).

European Communities (Pressure Vessels) Regulations 1989 (SI No.59): provide for a conformity of design of pressure vessels to be approved by EOLAS.

European Communities (Protection of Workers) (Exposure to Asbestos) Regulations 1989 (SI No.34): see 378, below, in the Safety and Health chapter.

European Communities (Protection of Workers) (Exposure to Chemical, Physical and Biological Agents) Regulations 1989 (SI No.251): see 378, below in the Safety and Health chapter.

European Communities (Quality of Bathing Water) (Amendment) Regulations 1989 (SI No.99): amend the 1988 Regulations.

European Communities (Quality of Surface Water Intended for the Abstraction of Drinking Water) Regulations 1989 (SI No.294): lay down minimum standards.

European Communities (Retirement of Farmers) Regulations 1989 (SI No.157): increase the annuity payable under the retirement scheme.

European Communities (Sampling and Analysis of Fertilisers) Regulations 1989 (SI No.179).

European Communities (Sampling and Analysis of Fertilizers) (No.2) Regulations 1989 (SI No.202).

European Communities (Scheduled Air Fares) Regulations 1989 (SI No.207): establish the criteria for approval of air fares within the EC.

European Communities (Seed of Fodder Plants) (Amendment) Regulations 1989 (SI No.173): revise the fees payable.

European Communities (Sharing of Passenger Capacity and Access to Scheduled Air Service Routes) Regulations 1989 (SI No.208).

European Communities (Surveillance of Certain Textile Products, Footwear and Tableware Imports) Regulations 1989 (SI No.301).

European Communities (Undertakings for Collective Investment in Transferable Securities) Regulations 1989 (SI No.78): impose requirements in connection with UCITS.

European Parliament Election, Dáil Éireann and Údarás na Gaeltachta Election Regulations 1989 (SI No.128): provided for the holding of the three elections on the same date.

Health (Preservatives in Food) (Amendment) Regulations 1989 (SI No.263) amend the 1981 Regulations of the same title by allowing potassium bisulphate (E228) as a permitted preservative. The Regulations give effect to Council Directive 85/585/EEC.

Merchandise Marks (Prepacked Goods) (Marking and Quantities) (Amendment) Order 1989 (SI No.23): gives effect to a Directive on the approximation of quantities and capacities permitted for prepacked knitting yarns.

Merchandise Marks (Prepacked Goods) (Marking and Quantities) (Amendment) Order 1989 (SI No.284): deals with sparkling wine.

Plaice (Restriction on Fishing) Order 1989 (SI No.215): made in accordance with EC obligations.

NECESSITATED BY MEMBERSHIP

The extent to which the terms of the Constitution must cede priority to Community law pursuant to the 'necessitated' test in Article 29.4.3 was considered in *Greene v Minister for Agriculture* [1990] ILRM 364: see 99-100, above, in the Constitutional Law chapter. The same issue was touched on in *Society for the Protection of Unborn Children (Irl) Ltd v Grogan and Ors* [1990] ILRM 350; [1989] IR 753: see 104-5, above, also in the Constitutional Law chapter.

PAY

The extent to which the Anti-Discrimination (Pay) Act 1974 reflected Community requirements was discussed in *An Chomhairle Oiliúna Talmhaíochta v Doyle and Ors* [1989] ILRM 21; [1989] IR 33: see 283, below, in the Labour Law chapter.

REFERENCE TO COURT OF JUSTICE

The position of the Supreme Court once the High Court has decided to make a reference to the Court of Justice pursuant to Article 177 of the Treaty of Rome was discussed in *Society for the Protection of Unborn Children (Irl) Ltd v Grogan and Ors* [1990] ILRM 350; [1989] IR 753: see 103, above, in the Constitutional Law chapter.

RETROSPECTION

In *Carberry v Minister for Social Welfare*, High Court, 28 April 1989, Barron J followed the Court of Justice decision in *Barra v Belgium* [1988] 2 CMLR

409 in holding that a Directive having direct effect in domestic law may be immediately enforceable despite domestic legislation which purports to postpone its implementation: see further 395, below, in the Social Welfare chapter.

SOCIAL WELFARE

Aspects of Community social welfare equality requirements were discussed in *Carberry v Minister for Social Welfare*, High Court, 28 April 1989 and *Hyland v Minister for Social Welfare* [1990] ILRM 213; [1989] IR 624: see 393 and 264, respectively, below.

Family Law

NULLITY OF MARRIAGE

In 1989 the law of nullity of marriage provoked an important judicial debate, going to the heart of the philosophical basis of the present law. We find on the one hand Keane J completely rejecting the rationale of several earlier High Court decisions dealing with relational incapacity and on the other hand O'Hanlon J applying these decisions in an expansive manner. The Supreme Court's affirmation of the earlier High Court decisions will be analysed in detail in the 1990 Review.

Central to the debate is the understanding of marriage in Irish law. Rightly or wrongly, the Irish Constitution recognises and applies a definite philosophy of marriage and the family. Unlike many countries which regard marriage and 'marriage breakdown' as *events*, to be *recorded* by the State, Irish law regards marriage as involving a *commitment* in the moral order—mutually made, of permanence and irrevocably binding on the parties making this commitment. Our law perceives the generality of human beings as having free will and the capacity to make binding commitments, even one so profound as that of marriage. This perception of human capacity is central to a proper understanding of nullity law; for it follows inexorably from it that, in order to marry, the parties must be able to make the necessary commitment freely.

The question of what constitutes the lowest common denominator of performative capacity is, of course, open to debate; but it is beyond argument that impotence is a ground that may render a marriage invalid. Mental incapacity tended formerly to be defined according to an intellectual rather than a performative criterion: the courts enquired whether a party had sufficient capacity to *understand* the nature of marriage and its obligations: *In the Estate of Park; Park v Park* [1954] P 112. (The parallel with the approach towards insanity at criminal law, under the *M'Naghten rules*, is an obvious one.)

In recent years a number of High Court decisions have sought to supplement the intellectual test for matrimonial incapacity with one referable to performative capacity. In *RSJ v JSJ* [1982] ILRM 263, Barrington J was prepared to entertain as a ground for nullity the fact that a party 'through illness, lacked the capacity to form a caring or considerate relationship with the other party'. Two years later, in *D v C* [1984] ILRM 173, Costello J, invoking *RSJ*, gave a decree for annulment because the respondent 'at the time of the marriage was suffering from a psychiatric illness and as a result was unable to enter into and sustain a normal marriage relationship with the petitioner'.

The possible distinction between a 'caring or considerate relationship' and 'a normal marriage relationship' need not here detain us. The issue is analysed by the Law Reform Commission in their *Report on Nullity of Marriage* (LRC 9-1984), 26-8.

Not all decisions subsequent to *RSJ* and *D v C* have required proof of illness as the source of the functional incapacity. See, e.g., *M (otherwise O) v O*, High Court, 24 January 1984; *W v P*, High Court, 7 June 1984; *BD v MC (otherwise MD)*, High Court, 27 March 1987 and *F v F* High Court, Barron J, 22 June 1988, discussed in the 1988 Review, 224-7.

In *UF (formerly known as UC) v JC*, High Court, Keane J, 24 May 1989, reversed by Supreme Court, 11 July 1990, the petition was based on the homosexual orientation of the respondent. The parties had had a normal sexual relationship before and after the marriage, but four years after the marriage it transpired that the respondent was of homosexual orientation, and that he had engaged in homosexual conduct for many years. He had married in the misplaced hope that this orientation 'would go away'. The parties separated and the petitioner later obtained an annulment in the ecclesiastical courts of the Catholic Church.

Keane J refused to grant a decree of nullity. He reasoned as follows. The ecclesiastical courts of the Church of Ireland had acted with considerable caution in hearing nullity petitions, demanding a high degree of proof. S.13 of the Marriage Law (Ireland) Amendment Act 1870 had preserved this approach when the matrimonial jurisdiction was transferred to the civil courts. Moreover, the underlying public policy which precluded the courts from granting lax declarations of nullity was 'emphatically reinforced' by Article 41.3 of the Constitution. Thus, McCarthy J was mistaken (in Keane J's view) in having stated in *N (otherwise K) v K* [1986] ILRM 75; [1985] IR 733 that the burden of proof was that of the balance of probability. Keane regarded *N (otherwise K) v K* as 'authority . . . for the proposition that, in the particular context of consent, the court must bear in mind the special and irrevocable nature of the status conferred by the contract of matrimony when a case based on want of consent is made'.

After a review of *RSJ* and its progeny, Keane J came to the conclusion that all of these decisions were wrong. He stated that: 'To formulate new grounds for nullity in the manner suggested constitutes an impermissible assumption of the legislative function which Article 15.2.1° of the Constitution vests exclusively in the Oireachtas'.

This conclusion is difficult to support and was rejected by the Supreme Court on appeal. S.13 of the 1870 Act required the civil court to proceed on principles which in its opinion 'shall be as nearly as may be conformable to the principles and rules on which the Ecclesiastical Courts of Ireland have heretofore acted and given relief'. If s.13 had the effect of *completely* tying the hands of judges—and the language of the section falls well short of this—it surely could not have survived the promulgation of the 1937 Constitution which contains a very clear philosophy of marriage. Keane J appears to concede as much in respect of 'the particular context of consent', but the question inevitably arises as to why the Constitution should succeed in eclipsing s.13 in one context and not in others.

The truth of the matter is that the Constitution recognises marriage as involving a freely-made, life-long commitment, based on capacity and consent. As Costello J observed in *Murray v Ireland* [1985] ILRM 542; [1985] IR 532, at 535-6, 'the Constitution makes clear that the concept and nature of marriage which it enshrines are derived from the Christian notion of a partnership based on an irrevocable personal consent, given by both spouses which establishes a unique and very special life-long relationship'. This echoes Costello J's remarks in *D v C* [1984] ILRM 173, at 188-9, as well as Kenny J's identification, in *Ryan v Attorney General* [1965] IR 294, at 313, of the right to marry as a personal right guaranteed by Article 40.3, following from the Christian and democratic nature of the State. Whether one approaches the matter from the standpoint of an incapacitated party or that of the party who goes through a ceremony of marriage with one who is incapacitated, it seems clear that the constitutional understanding of marriage, as well as constitutional justice, must demand the presence of capacity and free consent as ingredients to the lifelong commitment that marriage involves.

Keane J's comments as to the merits of the *RSJ* approach are worth recording. He felt that the analogy with impotence was not very helpful. In impotence the function of the court was narrow and precise, but with the *RSJ* approach '[w]e move from the cold objectivity of ascertainable clinical findings to the elusive and impalpable area of the emotions'. It was not clear how the court could decide the meaning of Barrington J's and Costello J's test in any particular case. The evidence of psychiatrists could not resolve the issue, which remained one for the court alone to determine.

Keane J had another objection:

> It is, I think, also of importance that, in contrast to cases of impotence, it is extremely difficult in cases such as those under consideration for the court to determine whether the person was incapable of entering into the necessary commitment (to use convenient short-hand) *at the time of*

the marriage. The judge trying the case, no matter how conscientiously he may endeavour to direct his mind to the central issue i.e. the respondent's state of mind at the time of the marriage, will inevitably be influenced by the conduct of the spouse, whose marital capacity is in issue, *after* the marriage. Thus, the enquiry he conducts is in sharp contrast to the enquiry normally conducted in impotence cases where there is usually little difficulty in ascertaining what the physical capacity or incapacity of the parties was at the time of the marriage. The enquiry in cases where the new ground is relied on is far more akin to the enquiry conducted by a court hearing a petition for a judicial separation under the present law.

The problem with this analysis is that it appears to see some objection in principle to examining conduct after the marriage ceremony in nullity cases. In fact such an examination may be essential in order to throw light on the position at the time of the marriage. In impotence cases, it may extend quite a considerable period after the marriage ceremony; more frequently this examination occurs in duress petitions, since it is usually necessary to test the allegation of duress against the post-ceremony conduct of the allegedly affected party.

Keane J's third objection to the *RSJ* approach related to the question whether the functional incapacity should be attributable to mental illness. There was, he noted, no unanimity among High Court judges on this question. If mental illness was not a precondition for a decree, then Keane J considered that 'a specific ground of this nature for a nullity decree can no longer be founded on the dictum of Kenny J in *S v S* [1976-7] ILRM 156 on which so much else is founded'.

This was the aspect of Keane J's judgment that differed most fundamentally from the approach of the Supreme Court on appeal. (We will examine the Supreme Court judgment in detail in the 1990 Review.) In *S v S*, Kenny J had stated that the courts in nullity proceedings 'must recognise that the great advances made in psychological medicine since 1870 make it necessary to frame new rules to reflect these'. Clearly this dictum extends to psychological advances in relation to mental illness; but the Supreme Court thought it equally clear that it is capable of embracing psychological advances in the understanding of behaviour and capacity *falling outside the label of mental illness*. Thus, for example, our understanding of homosexual orientation has greatly increased over the past century. The idea that the application of Kenny J's dictum in *S v S* should depend on whether homosexual orientation is now (or, to complicate matters, was in 1870) characterised as an illness seems less than fully helpful to the development of legal principle. It would be naive also to ignore the political and ideological elements in the characterisation of certain orientations as mental illnesses. Homosexuality itself has given rise to much debate on this very question: see Kamery, 'Gay Liberation and Psychiatry', ch. 5 of H. Ruitenbeet, *Homosexuality: A Changing Picture* (1973), Goldstein, Comment, 'History, Homosexuality and Political Values: Searching for the Hidden Determinants of *Bowers v Hardwick*' (1988) 97 *Yale L J* 1073, at 1086-9.

In an important passage, Keane J articulated his concern about how to formulate the criteria for annulment recognised in *RSJ* and its progeny:

> People have been married for centuries, if not millennia, in conditions where one can readily say that they lacked the capacity to form a proper relationship with the other spouse. Long before such celebrated and relatively modern instances as Oscar Wilde and Andre Gide, homosexuals entered into marriages, frequently with the hope . . . of establishing a normal life in the heterosexual culture. There must, moreover, have been many habitual heterosexual lechers throughout history whose promiscuous habits, if continued after matrimony, would have been almost as grave an obstacle to a happy marriage as homosexuality and who might, with the virtues of hindsight, be said to have lacked the capacity to enter into the normal interpersonal relationship referred to by Costello J [in *D v C*]. The same could be said of the heavy drinker, the person of violent temperament, the fortune hunter, the cold and the selfish, the frivolous and unstable, the emotionally weak and immature. No doubt advances in human knowledge have given us a greater understanding of how these various features of the human psyche arise in the first place and everyone is aware of the therapies which psychiatric medicine has developed for alleviating the distress which some of them cause. But they are aspects of the human condition which are as old as recorded history, as literature throughout the ages amply demonstrates. It was presumably the acknowledgement of human frailty and of the suffering to which it gives rise—and not any animus against the institution of marriage as such—that prompted the enactment in other countries of the sort of divorce legislation which our Constitution so resolutely outlaws. Be that as it may, no one has pointed to any decision of the courts prior to 1982 which lends any support to the existence of the ground of nullity for which counsel now contends. Nor has it been suggested that there has been any similar development in any common law jurisdiction exercising a nullity jurisdiction of the same nature as ours.

This passage provokes a number of comments. First, it represents a necessary and desirable warning against letting nullity law slip free from its moorings and float without direction into the wake of a divorce philosophy.

Secondly, while Keane J was wise to sound a warning note about the dangers of slipping into a divorce frame of mind, the clarity of his analysis may be the subject of debate. Of the examples he chose, promiscuity and heavy drinking are often the result of *free moral choice* rather than a *lack of capacity*. The courts have no business granting nullity decrees in respect of freely chosen post-marital conduct; but they do have a role in addressing incapacity that exists at the time of the marriage ceremony. The distinction between conduct that is freely chosen and conduct that springs from incapacity is of course a matter of controversy; thus, the question whether in any case heavy drinking results from a physical or mental illness or moral weakness is a source of ongoing and changing debate. But that does not mean that courts should shirk the troublesome obligation of addressing these issues: our Constitution, premised on the perception of free will as integral to the generality of human decisionmaking, requires a consideration in each individual case of whether a person's conduct is attributable to choice or incapacity. According to a deterministic philosophy, addressing questions such as this is a waste of time.

Thirdly, Keane J's reference to the fortune hunter was perhaps an unfortunate one in the development of his argument. Even countries with liberal divorce laws have been willing to consider whether extreme instances of fortune-hunting may be a ground for nullity, though not usually, of course, on the basis of *incapacity*. For enlightened discussion see Wade, 'Limited Purpose Marriages' (1982) 45 *Modern L Rev* 159; Irvine, 'Sham Marriages' (1963) *Scottish L Times* 93; Bromley, 'The Validity of "Sham Marriages" and Marriages Procured by Fraud' (1969) 15 *McGill LJ* 319; Bates, 'Limited and Extraneous Purpose Marriages—A Problem of Definition and Policy in the Law of Nullity' (1975) 4 *Anglo-American L Rev* 69. (We again consider the subject of 'sham marriages', below, 234-5.)

O'Hanlon J's judgment in *PC v VC*, High Court, 7 July 1989 is at the other end of the judicial spectrum from that of Keane J in *UF (UC) v JC*. In *PC v VC*, the petitioner sought a decree of nullity on the basis that *both* parties were unable to enter into a normal, functional, life-long marital relationship with each other. The evidence disclosed that, during the engagement, serious divisions manifested themselves on such matters as whether the parties should take a pre-marriage course and whether the respondent should have a key for the intended matrimonial home. Shortly before the wedding, the petitioner went to the respondent's home seeking to convince her mother that the respondent had to make a break from her own family: the respondent's mother was reduced to tears and her father took considerable exception to this approach.

After the wedding, the respondent spent most of her time in her parents' home. (The petitioner, an accountant, calculated that 87% of her time was spent there.) When the respondent became pregnant, the petitioner's reaction, instead of being one of joy or happiness, was to become incensed by the fact that the respondent had told her mother the news before telling him. He ceased to trust the respondent from then on, apparently raising a doubt as to whether she and her mother had been truthful as to the identity of the doctor who had confirmed the fact that she was expecting a baby.

During the early months of pregnancy, the respondent was very ill and went back to live with her mother. The petitioner visited her, but declined her mother's invitation to live with the family while the respondent was with them. Gradually the relationship between the parties seriously deteriorated to the point that the respondent was actively seeking a legal separation. When the baby was born there was a dispute about who should pay for the semi-private room at the hospital. The respondent continued to live with her parents, the petitioner visiting her and the baby fairly regularly.

A process of reconciliation then took place 'on a stop-start basis', with the parties living together again. This did not prove successful: the petitioner complained that the respondent had fixed ideas about sex roles, and that she virtually excluded him from any of the chores in looking after their baby. The petitioner's attitude to the respondent's mother remained hostile, and the parties suffered a 'cat-and-dog' existence with no atmosphere of peace or harmony or love developing in the home. Sexual relations, which at all stages had been 'at a low ebb', came to an end shortly afterwards.

A serious incident occurred when the respondent moved into her own bedroom and tried to bring the baby with her. A fracas resulted with each parent struggling for possession of the baby. The Gardai were called. Their advice was to 'cool down'. The respondent's father, 'a near-septuagenarian', committed a very minor assault on the petitioner. The petitioner brought a court case against the father 'which went to the door of the court and ended in the humiliation of an undertaking being given by the [respondent's parents] not to enter the matrimonial home . . . again, save in dire emergencies'. O'Hanlon J considered that these court proceedings were 'quite unwarranted and symptomatic of an exaggerated sense of hostility and resentment' which the petitioner felt towards the respondent's parents.

Two months later, the respondent, whose parents were away on holidays, confessed to feeling lonely and wanted to resume sexual relations with the petitioner. His response was that this could happen only if it came about through counselling. O'Hanlon J considered that this was the turning point in the parties' relationship. The respondent 'had eaten humble pie, at what cost to her pride one can only surmise', and the petitioner had responded with a rebuff. Although the parties continued living under the same roof 'the atmosphere can be gauged from the fact that the [petitioner] said that he kept his bedroom door locked at night for fear that the [respondent] would come in and knife him in his sleep'. For her part the respondent said that 'she felt the presence of the devil' in the matrimonial home and it crossed her mind that the petitioner might be possessed. Even while living with each other in the same house, the parties took legal proceedings against each other: the petitioner sought decrees of nullity in the civil and ecclesiastical courts, and the respondent took proceedings for divorce *a mensa et thoro* against him. Ten months after the respondent had been rebuffed by the petitioner, she left the home taking the baby with her, never to return.

Access arrangements gave rise to a good deal of friction. Evidence given by a priest friend of both parties who had officiated at the marriage was to the effect that the petitioner appeared to have inherited provincial and rural values and attitudes from his parents, in contrast the respondent, who had inherited Dublin and suburban values. The evidence of the psychiatrist was to the effect that, in spite of the respondent's close relationship with her mother, this 'did not inhibit [her] capacity to form the new relationship with [the petitioner], or to enter into a valid marriage'. In his view, there was not such a degree of immaturity as to interfere with her ability to form the marriage contract. He conceded, however, that the couple 'did not have the ability to resolve problems between them — perhaps because of their make-up, their psychological profile from childhood'. While the respondent had the ability to meet the emotional needs of the former, she was 'unable to do so because of [his] difficulties'. He accepted that two persons could have such opposing personalities that they could not live together and meet each other's needs in marriage. The second psychiatrist described the petitioner as intelligent, competent, somewhat lacking in ability for open, spontaneous affection; undoubtedly a strong personality; very assertive with a point of view and very persistent in pursuing it; somewhat inflexible and rigid. He felt that there was a communication difficulty on the petitioner's part, in listening openly and sympathetically to what his partner was saying. In marriage he wanted a traditional home-maker: someone more subservient than the respondent was willing to be. In the psychiatrist's words, the petitioner 'could be O.K. with a person willing to have a dominant husband'.

As regards the respondent, this psychiatrist formed the impression that she was a quiet and gentle person, not a strong personality, who dealt with rows by retreating back to her family of origin. He considered that she had had a sheltered and over-protective upbringing and had thus failed to emancipate herself emotionally. She had found herself 'unable to change in relation to this marriage, whereas she might have succeeded with a spouse who was more mature, gentler, more emotionally expressive'.

In a key passage in the judgment, O'Hanlon J summarised further aspects of the psychiatrist's evidence as follows:

[The psychiatrist] described the relationship between the parties as a 'dysfunctional relationship' in which neither was able to satisfy the emotional needs of the other. While the presence of arguments and conflicts in marriage was not at all abnormal, the ability of the partners to adapt and adjust was an essential factor without which a workable relationship could not be achieved. 'Here neither showed the ability to adapt. Both adhered rigidly to their own perceived role. [The petitioner] was blind to what he was doing and couldn't change it. [The respondent] was incapable of changing her role and retreated back to an area of unconditional love and support, inappropriate for an adult'.

[The psychiatrist] concluded that the marriage had broken down because of personality weaknesses each partner had brought into the marriage, and an inability to adapt to a functional degree. Then love was replaced by tension, and suspicion, and the relationship in such a situation becomes a threat to the personal and psychological health of the partners, and a danger to the welfare of any children of the marriage.

[The psychiatrist] took the view that he was here dealing with a marriage which had not worked at all, not with one which had broken down. He felt the question which should be asked was as follows

'Have the parties sustained a normal marriage relationship to any significant degree?'

in distinguishing between a marriage which never existed, and one which did exist but has broken down.

O'Hanlon J proceeded to review the earlier High Court decisions on the subject, including *BD v MC (otherwise known as MD)*, 27 March 1987. In that decision Barrington J had held that the respondent had suffered from such a degree of emotional immaturity as to preclude the formation of a normal marriage relationship. He had admitted to being uncertain as to whether the respondent's condition could be described as an illness; it was apparently a 'disorder', which required and might be susceptible to psychotherapy. But, whether an illness or a disorder, Barrington J had considered it 'equally incapacitating so far as the formation of a marital relationship is concerned'. In granting a decree of nullity Barrington J had taken into consideration not merely the respondent's incapacity but also 'the respective states of mind and mental conditions' of both parties.

O'Hanlon J noted, as a distinguishing feature, that in the case before him, while there were elements of emotional immaturity and psychological disorder in both sides such as to lead him to conclude that they prevented the formation of 'a normal, viable relationship with each other', these features and traits of character were much more marked in the case of the petitioner than in the respondent. The question thus arose as to whether the petitioner could rely on what was in large measure his own want of capacity where the respondent had not repudiated the marriage contract.

O'Hanlon J concluded that the petitioner could do so, primarily because of the fact that the want of capacity existed 'to some extent' on both sides; but if necessary he would also have inclined to the view that 'as both parties entered into the marriage contract innocently, in the sense that they were unaware that by reason of factors connected with the personality and psychology of each partner, it would be impossible for them to sustain a normal marriage relationship for any length of time, the petitioner should not be denied a decree of nullity because the respondent wishes to hold him to the marriage bond'. He considered that there was 'a good deal of substance' in the criticism expressed by Alan Shatter in his excellent book on family law (2nd ed., 1981), 73-5, concerning the principle that a petitioner cannot be heard to rely on his or her own want of capacity, physical or psychiatric, in reaching a decree of nullity (see also the third edition, 1986, 127-30). O'Hanlon J commented:

> Whereas the law in respect of want of capacity has developed by analogy with the law applicable in cases of physical impotence, it has resulted in the development of a new concept, and it appears to me to call for the re-examination of the applicability of the principle stated by Hanna J in *McM v McM* [1936] IR 177 in such cases. Such re-examination has already been undertaken by the Court of Appeal in England in the case of *Harthan v Harthan* [1949] P 115. Their conclusion was that, even in the case of want of capacity resulting from physical impotence, unknown to the impotent spouse at the time of the marriage, a decree of nullity should be granted on his (or her) application, without requiring evidence of repudiation of the marriage by the other spouse.

O'Hanlon J emphasised that had the matter been one calling for resolution in the case before him he would have tended to follow *Harthan's* lead.

Nor did O'Hanlon J consider that the petitioner had approbated the marriage by delay in applying for a decree of nullity: both parties had been in a state of confusion and unhappiness, over a long period, as to what course they should follow, and the abortive period of attempted reconciliation 'was probably necessary to get across the message firmly' to both parties that they could not survive together in married union.

O'Hanlon J was conscious of the fact that temperamental incompatibility is not a ground for nullity. Moreover, he accepted that some of the recent decisions had 'tended to blur' the distinction between cases where divorce *a mensa et thoro* might be the appropriate and legitimate remedy, and 'the much more extreme cases' where a decree of nullity was called for. With some hesitation he came to the conclusion that what was involved in the case before him went well beyond temperamental incompatibility *simpliciter* and brought into play the other, profounder factors of want of capacity to which he had referred.

On this basis he granted the decree, holding that both parties had been unable to enter into and sustain a normal marital relationship with each other 'by reason of incapacity deriving from lack of emotional maturity, and psychological weakness and disturbance affecting both parties to a greater or lesser degree'. He concluded by noting that the respondent's unhappiness about the effect of the decree on her child's status should be much allayed by the passing of the Status of Children Act 1987, 'which alters, in a radical manner, the legal status and position of the child of a marriage which has been annulled and which was enacted for the specific purpose of giving the child of parents who were not married the self-same status in the eyes of the law as the child of a marriage which has not been determined null and void'.

O'Hanlon J's analysis provokes a number of observations. The most immediate is that, on the facts of the case as stated in the judgment, it is difficult to support the finding of the respondent's incapacity deriving from lack of emotional maturity and psychological weakness and disturbance. (One should, however, bear in mind that this statement of facts was 'necessarily a very curtailed version of a narrative of events which occupied a number of days in court'.)

The psychiatric evidence in relation to her, based on an actual interview with her, was to the effect that in the psychiatrist's view there was *not* immaturity of such degree as to interfere with her ability to form the marriage contract. The evidence of the other psychiatrist was based in part on the account given to him *by the petitioner* and in part on such other evidence as was available to him without having interviewed the respondent. Such evidence, one might have expected, would have to be treated with a degree of circumspection, however competently it was presented. Indeed, the better approach would seem to be to exclude it completely, as Lardner J preferred to do in *RT v VP (otherwise T)*, High Court, 30 July 1989, discussed below, 235-6. The testimony relating to the respondent in *PC v VC* concentrated on the dysfunctional quality of the parties' relationship and, so far as may be gleaned from the judgment, did not include a statement of opinion that the respondent lacked the capacity to form the marriage contract.

Secondly, O'Hanlon J's judgment forces us to consider deeply the meaning of the concept of inability to form a caring and considerate (or normal) marital relationship with the other party where what is alleged is essentially based on an underlying *incompatibility* between the parties. The model of the ground of impotence may be invoked here in order to clarify our analysis.

To establish the ground of impotence it is not necessary to show that the affected party is incapable of sexual intercourse with *anyone*: it is sufficient if he or she is incapable of sexual intercourse *with the other party*. This notion of relative impotence is still referred to as impotence *quoad hunc vel hanc:* see e.g., *S v S* [1976-7] ILRM 156; *McM v McM* [1936] IR 177, at 193-4; *R (otherwise W) v W*, High Court, 1 February 1980. The cause of such relative impotence is usually psychological, but in some circumstances may be physical: *G v G (falsely called K)* (1908) 25 T LR 328.

What analogy may properly be drawn from this notion of relative impotence in the context of incapacity to form a caring or considerate (or normal) marital relationship? If incapacity to have sexual intercourse with the other party is a ground for annulment, why should not incapacity to form a normal marital relationship also be a ground for a decree? In answering that question we have to retain the central general premiss of free will grounding our system of family law, and indeed our constitutional recognition of a wide range of fundamental human rights. A deterministic analysis of interpersonal relationships is not appropriate to nullity proceedings. Of course the psychological, psychiatric and other evidence in a case may establish to the court's satisfaction that a particular person lacked free will, whether on a specific occasion (as where the marriage ceremony was entered into under duress) or on an ongoing basis, provided that condition of incapacity existed at the time of the marriage ceremony. Thus, for example, where a person suffers from a mental illness such as manic-depression, which makes it impossible to enter into a normal marital relationship with the other party, a decree of nullity may be in order: *D v C*, above.

Accordingly, an opinion by the court that parties to a marriage were not suited to each other could not, of itself, be a ground for annulment. The word 'incompatible' is frequently used colloquially in relation to cases where spouses separate; but it must be clear that no decree of annulment may be granted under the *RSJ* line of cases unless it is established that one (or both) of the parties is (or are) at the time of the marriage *incapable* of a normal marital relationship. As O'Hanlon J expressly recognises, 'temperamental incompatibility is not a ground for declaring a marriage null and void'.

It is in this context that one must understand O'Hanlon J's statement that he did:

> not think it . . . any part of my function in these proceedings to apportion blame between the [parties] for the failure of their marriage. Each is possessed of a character and temperament which have been moulded in their own particular family background and environment and, while

there may be weaknesses on both sides, nothing can be gained by a judgmental approach to an assessment of their problems.

Of course judges should be slow to enter into moral condemnations in the course of nullity proceedings: their task is to determine whether a decree of nullity should be granted, not to punish or criticise anyone. But it is as well to point out the dangers of approaching 'dysfunctional relationships' from a deterministic philosophic premiss. In petitions based on the *RSJ* ground, it is essential for the court to examine whether the difficulties in the marital relationship sprang from character weaknesses or from a deeper psychological or psychiatric cause.

This brings us to the question of the extent to which the notion of incapacity *quoad hunc vel hanc* is philosophically defensible in relation to the *RSJ* ground. Clearly it is possible and indeed necessary to speak of *impotence quoad hunc vel hanc*, since, as a matter of scientific fact, a person may be incapable of performing the act of sexual intercourse with the other party though not with other persons. But with incapacity based on the *RSJ* ground matters are not quite so simple.

The real matter of difficulty concerns the question whether cases can arise where it may properly be determined that one party suffers from an incapacity to form a caring relationship with A or B, but not with C or D. If the answer to this question is yes, the implications for our philosophy of human capacity are significant. For it would mean that our capacity to commit ourselves to married life with another person would be subject to the important qualification that we be *compatible* with that person. Such a philosophy devalues human capacity and freedom. If given a free reign it would turn the law of nullity into a system of divorce based on a deterministic interpretation of human nature, inconsistent with that of Article 41. No court has yet granted a decree on this basis, and, if the law of nullity is to preserve its integrity, it is to be hoped that no court in the future will do so. Properly understood, the *RSJ* ground requires a generalised rather than an individuated incapacity. In other words it is necessary that the party suffering from an incapacity must lack what it takes to form a caring and considerate (or normal) marriage relationship with persons of the opposite sex. The odd *obiter dictum* which gives some credence to the notion of incapacity *vel hunc or hanc* in this context should give rise to no expectation that this represents the plan for the future determination of the law. The requirement of a generalised incapacity is entirely consistent with the notion that a party of exceptional qualities of altruism and forbearance might be able to tolerate a marriage with the incapacitated person. Here the analogy with impotence is helpful. The ground of impotence is established even where the other party is willing to live with the impotent person. The question whether a decree should be granted or referred is dealt with separately, by reference to the concept of approbation.

In *RT v VP (otherwise T)*, High Court, 30 July 1989, the petitioner sought an annulment on the ground of the respondent's incapacity, on account of her mental condition, to maintain and sustain a normal marriage relationship. The respondent, who denied such incapacity, supported the claim for a decree of nullity, on the basis that the parties, by reason of incompatible personalities at the time of the marriage, were unable to form and sustain a normal marriage relationship.

The petitioner was a widower, a member of the Church of Ireland, in his forties. The respondent, a Catholic, was his next-door-neighbour, who had lived with a man for some years before his death, bearing him a child. Seven months after the death of the petitioner's wife, the parties began a sexual relationship. They were married, in a Catholic Church, seven months later, in March 1984. After the marriage there was evidence of martial disharmony. The respondent complained that the petitioner had raped her on the wedding night. The respondent continued to work long hours, with much travel. She had an abortion about a month after the marriage, contrary to the wishes of the petitioner. That summer, she spent a period of about two weeks in hospital suffering from fatigue and from depression secondary to stress. For a period when in hospital she developed a paranoid reaction. In April 1985, when the couple went on holidays, the respondent was lethargic. Their relationship deteriorated and they separated in November 1985. Attempts at a reconciliation ultimately proved unsuccessful. Psychiatric evidence indicated that the parties' perceptions of life, lifestyles, work and family life were different and that their temperaments clashed.

Counsel for the petitioner argued that the respondent suffered from a propensity to cyclical mood swings, but submitted that, even without any element of mental disorder, incompatibility is in itself a ground for a decree of nullity. Lardner J understood the concept of incompatibility to mean 'difficulty or inability to get on together—mutual intolerance'. In similar vein, counsel for the respondent submitted on the basis of Kenny J's *dictum* in *S v S*, above, that the institution of marriage depends so much on the compatibility of the parties that, if there is concealed from one or both of the parties before the marriage a quality in one or both or a dynamic between them which would have the effect of destabilising the marriage in a fundamental way and which is such as to amount to an incapacity to maintain a normal marriage relationship, then it is open to the court to give a decree of nullity.

Lardner J reviewed the decisions on nullity over the past decade. He rejected Keane J's view, expressed in *UF (formerly UC) v JC* that such decisions as *RSJ v JSJ* and *D v C* represented an impermissible assumption of the legislative function. He observed:

Historically the common law has developed at least in part by the application of established principles to new cases — to novel facts and circumstances. It has undoubtedly involved the development of the law and novel judicial decisions are not uncommonly referred to as judge-made law. It is a judicial activity which has occurred in Ireland for centuries and has continued in the Superior Courts prior to and since the enactment of the 1937 Constitution. In my view it is not in its proper exercise an impermissible exercise of the legislative function.

Lardner J considered that impotence was recognised as a ground of nullity because it was an incapacity which was fundamental to the marriage contract. *RSJ v JSJ* and *D v C* proceeded on the same principle. Cases relating to incapacity to form a caring marital relationship were bound to involve serious difficulties of proof, but difficulties of this kind could not require the court to lower the standard of proof which was required. Lardner J considered correct the principle he found deducible from *RSJ v JSJ* and *D v C*, that 'where serious incapacity to form and sustain a caring marital relationship is shown to have existed at the time of the marriage it is a proper ground upon which a decree of nullity may be given . . .'. This formula is more compressed than that of *RSJ v JSJ*, where Barrington J spoke of incapacity through illness, to form 'a caring or considerate relationship' with the other spouse; it differs from *D v C*, where Costello J spoke of incapacity through a psychiatric disability 'to enter into and sustain the normal inter-personal relationship which marriage . . . requires'.

Lardner J went on to state that the onus of proof was such that the petitioner had to establish his or her case to a high degree of probability 'or as Lord Birkenhead expressed it [in *C (otherwise H) v C* [1921] P 399, at 400, the petitioner] must remove all reasonable doubt'. He observed: 'As a general rule this will be in cases where a serious mental illness or a serious personality disorder is shown to exist. One cannot say there may never be exceptions where the incapacity is shown in accordance with its heavy onus of proof to exist without serious mental illness or serious personality disorder'.

This is an important passage. It addresses the crucial issue of whether the *RSJ/D v C* ground requires proof that the incapacity to form a caring or considerate (or normal) marital relationship springs from psychiatric or physical disorder. Lardner J treats this, not as a substantive element in the ingredients of the ground, but rather as impinging on the onus of proof. On this view, where a petitioner alleges that the incapacity exists, he or she need not necessarily show that this incapacity springs from such disability; but if he or she seeks to establish the ground without relying on proof of such disability, the task may prove very difficult on account of the heavy onus of proof.

Why should it be more difficult to show that an incapacity to form a caring or considerate (or normal) relationship existed where the incapacity springs from causes other than a psychiatric disorder? The answer must surely lie in the philosophical arena. Many petitioners may allege that the respondent suffered from such an incapacity. Lardner J was prudently cautioning against an easy acceptance by the court of such an allegation, especially in the absence of psychiatric evidence. The psychiatric evidence can add support to the allegation of incapacity, since it may tend to show that the party not only acted in an uncaring manner but also that he or she *could not have* acted otherwise. It is perhaps worth noting here that in the appeal in *U(F) v U(C)*, above, the Supreme Court accepted that the *RSJ/D v C* ground need not be found on proof of a mental or physical illness.

Turning to the facts of the case before him, Lardner J noted that both parties were mature and intelligent and had had previous successful and fulfilling relationships. The psychiatric evidence was to the effect that neither was suffering from any mental illness (let alone a serious one) at the time of marriage.

Their perceptions and judgments, in the view of a psychiatrist whose evidence the judge accepted, were clouded by their previous bereavements and the experience of the happy relationship they shared before marriage. This psychiatrist thought they both had the capacity to form caring marital relationships but not with each other as they were incompatible. Lardner J was not convinced that this latter assessment was correct. In his view this fell 'far short of proving the incapacity necessary to be established' before a decree of nullity could be given. Indeed he was 'not satisfied that any incapacity in regard to each other' had been shown to exist, having regard to the history of their relationship. Accordingly, he dismissed the petition.

The case raises a number of interesting issues. Perhaps the most important is whether Lardner J accepted or rejected the asserted ground of incompatibility of parties as falling within the *RSJ/D v C* rationale. It might be thought that he accepted it in that he did not expressly reject it and that he held, on the facts, that the parties were not incompatible—a seemingly redundant holding if proof of incompatibility would not be a basis for an annulment. Nevertheless, the better view seems to be that Lardner J *rejected* incompatibility as a ground. First, he gave it no express endorsement, having made it clear that he regarded it as a novel assertion. Secondly, he quoted extensively from *RSJ* and *D v C*, and treated these decisions as authoritative; neither decision gives any support for the notion of incompatibility as a ground of nullity.

Finally, we should note that the issue of incapacity under the *RSJ/D v C* ground arose also in the case of *W (otherwise C) v C* [1989] IR 696, which we consider below, 229-35.

Duress   Two cases on duress were circulated in 1989. In *O'S v W (otherwise O'S)*, High Court, 25 July 1989, the petitioner was aged nearly 34 when he went through a ceremony of marriage with the respondent aged 29, after three years' engagement. Before the ceremony, which took place in 1985, the petitioner had expressed to the respondent his desire to call the wedding off. She was very upset with his attitude and insisted that the marriage should take place. She called to his mother and told her that she intended to consult a solicitor if the petitioner did not go ahead. The petitioner (having been told of the respondent's intention) also consulted a solicitor, who told him that his fiancée might have a legal claim against him 'if what he had done had affected her mentally'. This advice is not easy to understand on the basis of the facts stated in the judgment. Breach of promise had ceased to be actionable four years previously (Family Law Act 1981, s.2); there was apparently no suggestion that the petitioner had taken wrongful advantage of the respondent in the sexual or financial spheres. There may, of course, have been good reason for the advice not mentioned in the judgment.

At all events, the petitioner reluctantly decided to go ahead with the marriage, though he told his brother-in-law a few days before the wedding that he did not want to go through with it. His attitude was that he no longer loved the respondent. The marriage was not a success and the petitioner sought an annulment. The petitioner gave evidence that he had gone on with the wedding because he was afraid that otherwise the respondent might kill herself or have a nervous breakdwon. Costello J refused the petition. He quoted from Finlay CJ's judgment in *N (otherwise K) v K* [1986] ILRM 75, at 82, to the effect that consent to marriage must:

> be a fully free exercise of the independent will of the parties. Whilst a court faced with a challenge to the validity of a marriage, based on the absence of real consent, should conduct its inquiry in accordance with defined legal concepts such as duress . . . these concepts and the legal definition of them must remain subservient to the ultimate objective of ascertaining, in accordance with the onus of proof, whether the consent of the petitioning party was real or apparent.

Costello J thought that the evidence in the case fell short of what was required. The petitioner at the time of the marriage was 'a mature intelligent adult'. He suffered from no psychiatric illness or personality disorder. Evidence given on his behalf was to the effect that he tended to have problems with decisions of any importance, changing his mind repeatedly, and often, after taking a decision, resisting it again.

Costello J did not believe that the petitioner had 'to any considerable extent' entertained fears that the respondent might commit suicide or have a mental breakdown if the wedding were called off. There was very little objective evidence to justify either of these fears; nor was there evidence that the respondent was 'a domineering sort of woman'. Whilst the petitioner had taken the threat of legal proceedings sufficiently seriously to cause him to consult a solicitor, the threat 'did not overbear his will to such an extent as to vitiate his ultimate decision'. Refusing to grant a decree of nullity in favour of the petitioner, Costello J said:

> I think his consent was a reluctant one given with considerable misgivings but I cannot hold that either the actions of the respondent or the factual situation in which the petitioner found himself resulted in it being a mere apparent one or a sham.

This decision is to be welcomed, so far as the facts may be gleaned from the judgment. The only issue of substance in the case was whether the petitioner had gone through the ceremony of marriage believing that this was the only way of preventing the respondent from committing suicide or (subject to what is said below) having a nervous breakdown. A close reading of Costello J's judgment indicates that, although he referred to factors in relation to the *objective basis* of the petitioner's fears of these outcomes if he did not go through with the wedding, Costello J's holding depends ultimately on the fact that the petitioner *did not have* such fears to any considerable extent. Had they in fact operated on him, then, in spite of the lack of an objective basis for them, a decree of nullity might have been proper.

In this context it is worth noting that, in the earlier decision of *EP v MC (otherwise P)* [1985] ILRM 34, Barron J took the view that, even in circumstances where a man went through a ceremony of marriage in order to prevent a woman from having an abortion, a decree of nullity could be granted in only narrow circumstances, which did not exist (in his view) on the facts of the case. Barron J had said (at 38):

> Duress must be of such a nature that there is the appearance without the reality of consent. Where consent is procured through fear for the life of another, the party consenting is fully aware that he is giving his consent to a ceremony of marriage but at the same time is in reality consenting to save that life. For this reason, the marriage is a sham. It is merely a device to remove the threat to the life of that other. If the petitioner had given his consent in this case solely for the purpose of saving the life of his unborn child, this would have constituted a ground for a decree of nullity. But the petitioner would have had to establish

that the marriage was such a device to procure this end. If, as in this case, the parties had a normal engagement followed by a normal marriage and held themselves out as being a married couple, it cannot be said that the marriage was a sham.

In a perceptive commentary on this holding, Mr Paul O'Connor has observed:

> Thus, for Barron J, the exclusive object of the consent of the marriage would have had to be directed towards saving the unborn child. Anything less than this apparently would not suffice. If, for example, the dominant, but not the exclusive, purpose was to prevent the abortion the consent would not have been vitiated. Accordingly, the fact that a petitioner, say, in addition to seeking the rescue of his unborn child, sought to spare the respondent the stigma of unwed motherhood, would prevent the marriage from being a sham. In such a situation the consent, while not a complete consent, would still be sufficient for marriage. This result stems from an orthodox and rigid application of the principles of duress. [*Key Issues in Family Law* (1988), 15]

Such an application would undoubtedly be rigid. Whether it would be orthodox may, however, be debated. In *O'S v W (otherwise O'S)*, the threat was one of suicide rather than abortion. There is no reason why a party who marries to prevent another's suicide (or having an abortion) should be prevented from a decree of nullity by reason only of the fact that the heroic party did not intend the marriage to be a sham. (See generally *Hartford v Morris*, 2 Hag Con 423, 161 ER 792 (1776); *Field's Marriage Annulling Bill*, 2 HLC 48, 9 ER 1010 (1848); *Cooper (falsely called Crane) v Crane* [1891] P 369 (Collins J); *Kecsemethy v Magyer*, 2 Fed LR 437 (NSW Sup Ct, Field, J, 1961); cf. *S v O'S*, High Court, Finlay P, 10 November 1978.)

It is interesting that Costello J, like Barron J, referred to the notion of a marriage being 'a sham'; but it would seem quite wrong to infer from this that he was endorsing the restrictions laid down by Barron J in *EP v MC (otherwise P)*.

Finally, it is worth considering the question whether a decision to marry to prevent another's injury or illness (mental or physical) should ever constitute a ground for nullity on the basis of duress. As we have seen, in *O'S v W (otherwise O'S)*, the petitioner's claim based on this ground was rejected on the evidence. While, as a matter of first impression, it is relatively easy to take the position that a threat to *kill* (oneself or another) or a prospect of such killing, should be capable of constituting duress, it is perhaps less easy to say this of a threat of causing injury or illness to oneself and, on first impression, still less easy to say it of a prospect of such injury or illness. As a matter of principle, however, there seems to be no sound basis for distinguishing between a threat and a prospect derived from other means. The question is not so much one of the manner of learning of the prospect, as of the credibility and seriousness of that prospect. The better view would appear to be that a threat or prospect of serious injury or illness to oneself or another is in principle capable of constituting duress. Whether or not it does so will depend on the circumstances: the gravity of the probable injury or illness, its degree of certitude of occurrence and whether other means may be used to prevent it. The analogy with the notion of rescue in tort law may be more helpful than might at first appear. At some stage, the point will be reached where the other party, by marrying, should be considered to have acted without duress. Not every altruistic suitor can be said to have acted under duress. Where the gun is to his or her head (which will be so in some cases of credible threats of suicide or abortion) then the act may often be considered a good deal less free than where there is a prospect that one's fiance or fiancée will suffer some psychological damage from the termination of the engagement.

W (otherwise C) v C [1989] IR 696 is a case with distressing facts. The petitioner, a primary school teacher, went through a ceremony of marriage with the respondent, an accountant, in March 1976, when she was twenty three years old. The couple had been going out together since October 1974. Their relationship was a very uneasy one, consisting 'more an imposition of the respondent's will over the petitioner's than anything else'. He perpetually made derogatory remarks about her, both to her and to others, and seemed to enjoy insulting her in this way. One day in October 1975, the respondent called to the petitioner's digs without arrangement. Notwithstanding her protests he insisted on coming into her flat and notwithstanding further protest insisted upon having sexual intercourse with her. She was at the time a virgin and was extremely upset both by the act itself and by the violence with accompanied it. He called her a whore and treated her as being unclean, forcing her into a bath of disinfectant, whether it was to cleanse her or to prevent her from conception, was not clear. She herself 'was in despair, feeling dirty and used and sure that no one would want her'. She went to the doctor the following day, and was told it was too early to diagnose whether or not she was pregnant. This state was confirmed about a fortnight later.

The petitioner told her brothers and sisters and got them to tell her parents. Their attitude, as expressed by her father, was that she would have to marry the respondent. When the respondent was told, he became even more aggressive towards the petitioner and wanted her to have an abortion. She wanted to keep the child.

The petitioner was employed as a primary school teacher. When the fact of pregnancy began to show, she informed the principal of her school. The principal told her that she could not stay on as an unmarried mother 'and made it quite clear to her that unless she married there was no future for her in the teaching profession'. The petitioner felt obliged to give up her job and she did so. She saw the respondent at weekends. He did not offer to marry her but at the same time he did not get out of her life. She 'was unable to think beyond the fact of her pregnancy and that she had lost the respect of everyone. She felt that unless she married she could not recover her self-respect nor work again in her profession. She decided to marry and the respondent agreed'.

The petitioner made all the arrangements herself. There was a small reception after the wedding (which her parents did not attend) but no honeymoon.

The relationship between the parties totally failed. The respondent was cruel and sadistic, abusive and violent from the start. His behaviour disturbed the other tenants, and the landlord evicted them. They went to live with the respondent's parents. The respondent's conduct there was no better. In sexual matters he was totally repulsive, engaging in forced intercourse, buggery, and injurious conduct after the birth of their son, who was born in June 1976.

The petitioner went back to work two weeks later. The respondent's abuse continued, extending now to compelling the petitioner to hand over her earnings to him and allowing her no more than £2 at a time. The petitioner left the respondent in late 1977 followed by a saga of court orders against the respondent and a suspended prison sentence for abducting the child. The petitioner sought a church annulment in 1980, which she obtained in 1984. It was not until 1987 that she became aware that she could apply for a decree of nullity through the courts. The respondent did not enter an appearance.

Barron J accepted that there was no collusion. He believed the petitioner's evidence, which had been given 'clearly and fairly and . . . without exaggeration', save in regard to dates between Christmas 1975 and March 1976.

Evidence given by a psychiatrist, who had treated the respondent in 1983 and seen him professionally on a number of occasions, was to the effect that the respondent suffered from a gross personality disorder which had been present all his life. He had a complete contempt for authority and saw others only as puppets to be manipulated. He was unable to see any fault in himself and was incapable of changing. In the psychiatrist's opinion, the respondent was unable to form a meaningful relationship with any marriage partner.

The petitioner's case was based on her lack of consent and on the respondent's inability by reason of his personality disorder to sustain 'a proper marriage relationship'. Barron J held in her favour both of these grounds. He was:

> satisfied that the petitioner was unable to see further than her pregnancy . . . [and] that she felt that she was dirty and dishonoured and that she no longer an ordinary member of society. She said that she went around like a zombie at this period and I have no doubt that she did. Her decision in the circumstances to marry the respondent could only be regarded as one brought about by the strain of her circumstances and the lack of ability for normal thought which she was manifesting at that time. In my view there was no element in her decision of a wish to desire to set up a matrimonial home with the respondent.
>
> She married the respondent in order to be able to resume her profession and to resume her place in society. In my view a consent given in such circumstances is not a true consent. It is just as much a sham as a consent solely for the purpose of escaping from a repressive political regime as in *Szechter v Szechter* [1971] P 286 or *H v H* [1954] P 258. The circumstances are not as extreme, but the quality of the apparent consent is the same.

Barron J also considered it clear that the respondent was suffering from a gross personality disorder and that this disorder made him 'incapable of forming any proper marriage relationship', whether with the petitioner or anyone else. Barron J noted that it was sufficient that the respondent was unable to form any proper marriage relationship with the petitioner. (On this question, see above, 222-3.)

The case raises a number of interesting issues. The first concerns the precise nature of the first ground on which Barron J granted the decree. He refers to it exclusively in terms of the absence of valid consent to the marriage. Nowhere does he mention the word duress. As against that, the cases he cites involve judicial analysis expressed in terms of duress. In taking what might be called the generic approach to the issue of consent, Barron J echoes the approach of the majority of the Supreme Court in *N (otherwise K) v K* [1986] ILRM 75. There Finlay J stressed that consent to making the irrevocable commitment which marriage involves must be:

> a fully free exercise of the will of the parties. Whilst a court faced with a challenge to the validity of a marriage, based on an absence of real consent, should conduct its enquiry in accordance with defined legal concepts such as duress or . . . undue influence . . . , these concepts and the legal definition of them must remain subservient to the ultimate

objective of ascertaining, in accordance with the onus of proof, whether the consent of the petitioning party was real or apparent.

Barron J's statement that the alleged consent was 'just as much a sham as a consent solely for the purpose of escaping from a repressive regime . . .' brings to mind two decisions in 1984 where Barron J also expressed the ground of duress partially in terms of 'a sham'. In *JR (otherwise McG) v P. McG*, High Court, 24 February 1984, he said:

> Duress must be such that the apparent consent to marry is not a true consent. It can operate in one of two ways. It can operate so that the party under the duress fails to apply his or her mind to the question of giving consent. In such cases, the duress creates a form of bondage.
> The party concerned may not even be aware that such bondage exists. ... Duress can also operate to compel the party under the duress to make a decision to give his or her consent escape the consequences which will otherwise follow. Such a party knows that his or her consent is not a true consent and is in effect consenting not to being married but to escaping from the threat. Such a marriage is a sham or a device to procure a particular result, i.e., freedom from the particular threat to which he or she is subjected.

In *EP v MC (otherwise P)* [1985] ILRM 34, quoted above, 227-8, Barron J said:

> Duress must be of such a nature that there is the appearance without the reality of consent. Where consent is procured through fear for the life of another, the party consenting is fully aware that he is giving his consent to a ceremony of marriage but at the same time is in reality consenting to save that life. For this reason, the marriage is a sham. It is merely a device to remove the threat to the life of that other. ... If ... the parties had a normal engagement followed by a normal marriage and held themselves out as being a married couple, it cannot be said that a marriage ceremony was a sham.

What emerges from these two decisions of 1984 is the view that a marriage will be 'a sham' only where the party goes through the ceremony of marriage, not in order to become a spouse but to achieve some other goal, such as escaping from a threat or saving another's life. In *W (otherwise C) v C*, there is a similar holding: there was 'no element in [the petitioner's] decision of a wish to desire to set up a matrimonial home with the respondent. She married

[him] in order to be able to resume her profession and to resume her office in society'. This holding may perhaps provoke some debate. In recounting the evidence in the case, Barron J gave no indication that the wife's intention was other than to set up a matrimonial home with the respondent. In fact she did this. The parties lived together (albeit in circumstances involving outrageous behaviour on the respondent's part) for about eighteen months. Barron J records no conduct on the petitioner's part during this period which amounted in any sense to a repudiation of the respondent. All the blame for the wretchedness of their relationship was attributed to the respondent's conduct.

It may be argued that the most convincing basis for duress was the fact that the petitioner's decision to marry sprang, not from a fully rational choice on her part, but from what Barron J in *JR (otherwise McG) v P. McG* characterised as the failure of a party 'to apply his or her mind to the question of giving consent'.

In *W (otherwise C) v C*, Barron J noted that the petitioner 'was unable to see further than her pregnancy', that 'she went around like a zombie' during her pregnancy, and that her decision in the circumstances to marry the respondent 'could only be regarded as one brought about by the strain of the circumstances and the lack of ability for normal thought which she was manifesting at the time'. In short, the true basis of the holding was that the petitioner's apparent consent was that of an unfree, mentally disturbed mind, resulting from the pressure brought about by her circumstances.

If this is a correct analysis of the decision, a difficulty may appear to arise about Barron J's statement that the petitioner married the respondent 'in order to be able to resume her profession and to resume her place in society'. Surely, it may be asked, this analysis appears to be based on the petitioner's having made a *rational*, rather than mentally disturbed, choice? In the light of Barron J's findings as to her mental state, this interpretation seems unconvincing. The reference to resuming her place in society does not imply a cold-blooded, rational plan to re-acquire social prestige; on the contrary it seems more consistent with the despairing act of a person who felt 'dirty and dishonoured', who had 'lost her self-respect' and 'the respect of everyone' and who was 'no longer an ordinary member of society'.

But what of the motive to resume her profession? Was that not in the order of rational career-planning rather than a decision of a disturbed or irresolute mind? It seems clear that the answer must be that it was not. The petitioner was, as we have seen, in a desperate plight, feeling dirty and dishonoured, pregnant, without employment, and lacking the support of her parents. The case, on its facts, gives no support for the general proposition that a decision to marry to preserve or enhance a career vitiates consent and renders a marriage invalid. A man who marries the daughter of the boss, with his eye on the financial advantages which it may confer, is entering a perfectly valid marriage. As Barrington J pointed out in *RSJ v JSJ* [1982] ILRM 263, at 264: '[p]eople have entered into a contract of marriage for all sorts of reasons, and their motives have not always been the highest. The motive for the marriage may have been policy, convenience, or self interest'.

This brings us to the core question concerning Barron J's notion of an apparent marriage being 'a sham'. In all of the cases where he has used this term, the petitioner was arguing, expressly or implicitly, that duress brought about the marriage.

But what of a case where the petitioner freely admits that he or she used the marriage as 'a sham or device to procure a particular result' (to seize on Barron J's words in *JR (otherwise McG) v P. McG)* where a result was a self-interested one—such as to acquire the legal entitlement to reside in a particular country—or an altruistic one—such as to confer a legitimate status or other benefit on a child?

The question raises the subject of marriages for limited purposes (or 'sham marriages'), which has generated much controversy internationally. See above, 215. In England, the view has been taken that such marriages should be regarded as valid: *H v H* [1954] P 258, at 267; *Silver (otherwise Kraft) v Silver* [1958] 1 WLR 728; *Vervaeke v Smith* [1983] AC 145. In most other common law jurisdictions, the same view has been favoured but in the United States some courts have preferred to hold these marriages void: see, e.g., *US v Rubenstein*, 151 F 2d 915 (1945). Scottish law (to the regret the Scottish Law Commission: DP No. 85, para. 3.18 (1990)) favours the same approach as the United States: *Orlandi v Castelli* 1961 SC 113.

Could Barron J's notion of a 'sham' marriage harmonise with the United States approach? The answer seems to be that it could, though it must be admitted that this view is hazarded with some considerable caution. It may be argued that a cool decision to go through a ceremony of marriage, with no intention to commit oneself to a conjugal relationship with the other party, but rather to acquire some independent goal (such as an immigrant status) falls within Barron J's analysis, without the necessity of the inspiration for that decision being such as to amount to duress. A key question which would then follow (and which is in any event relevant even in the context of duress) is the extent to which the choice to accomplish the independent purpose must exclude or occlude the element of conjugal relationship. A person who calculatingly marries for money usually wants the money but also the marital relationship: it is not normally an all-or-nothing choice. If it can be shown that the party who went through a ceremony of marriage with an independent purpose on his or her mind was willing to make *some effort*, however feeble, to make a success of the marriage, is that enough to make the ground inapplicable? From what Barron J said in the two 1984 decisions it would seem that the answer should be yes—that indeed the ground should be inapplicable.

In relation to the second ground, based on the respondent's incapacity, it is interesting to note that this was expressed in terms of an incapacity to form 'any proper marriage relationship' with the petitioner. As we have seen, the expressions which are usually used to describe this ground are incapacity to form 'a caring or considerate relationship' with the other party (*RSJ v JSJ* [1982] ILRM 263), or incapacity to 'enter into and sustain the normal interpersonal relationship which marriage . . . requires' (*D v C* [1984] ILRM 173). It may be argued that the work 'proper' accurately captures the sense of these earlier formulae. In *D v C*, at 189, Costello J observed that 'marriage is by our common law (strengthened and reinforced by our constitutional law) a lifelong union, and that the law should recognise that the lifelong union which the law enjoins requires for its maintenance the creation of an emotional and psychological relationship between the spouses'. The idea here is that a certain minimum core content of relationship is necessary—'proper'—to marriage and that its absence is a ground for a decree of nullity.

Expert evidence in nullity cases In *RT v VP (otherwise T)*, High Court, 30 July 1989, which we have already discussed above, 223-6, Lardner J made a holding on the admissibility of expert psychiatric evidence in nullity cases which is to be greatly welcomed. The petitioner's case was that at the time of the marriage, the respondent was suffering from such disease of the mind that she was incapable of maintaining and sustaining a normal marriage relationship. A psychiatrist called on behalf of the petitioner had never met the respondent; he had, however, been told about the respondent by the petitioner and had read the report of another psychiatrist who had been appointed by the Master of the High Court to conduct a psychiatric examination of the respondent, whose patient she had been at relevant times. The psychiatrist called on behalf of the petitioner gave evidence concerning the respondent. He expressed the judgment that she was incapable of forming a marriage relationship with the petitioner due to his personality; with another person this might not be the case.

Counsel for the respondent submitted that this psychiatrist's opinion was hearsay and inadmissible. He relied on the observation of Lawton LJ in *R v Turner* [1975] 1 All ER 70, at 73 and on the statement of law in *Phipson on Evidence*, 13th ed., 561:

An expert may give his opinion upon facts which are either admitted or proved by himself or other witnesses in his hearing at the trial or are matters of common knowledge as well as upon hypothesis based thereon.

Lardner J accepted this as a correct statement of law and held that the psychiatrist's evidence was inadmissible, being based on hearsay.

This approach may be contrasted with *D v C* [1984] ILRM 73, where Costello J accepted the evidence of the petitioner's psychiatrist derived from information given by the petitioner, as to the mental condition of the respondent, the marriage having been celebrated nine years previously. The petitioner's details of the respondent's moods and behaviour amounted, in the psychiatrist's view, to a classic diagnostic description of a manic depression. The psychiatrist had satisfied himself that the petitioner had not been influenced in her account of events by any reading on the subject she might have undertaken or information about it otherwise obtained. The respondent refused to be examined by this psychiatrist and the respondent's own psychiatrist declined to make any comment about his mental health at the time of his marriage as he considered that it was not possible to make a retrospective diagnosis in the case.

Costello J was satisfied that 'in the particular circumstances of this case' he could not act on the diagnosis of the petitioner's psychiatrist.

It would be best if *D v C* were treated as a case decided very much on its particular facts. It is interesting to note that in *MF McD (otherwise M O'R) v W O'R*, High Court, 24 January 1984, Hamilton P did not appear to derive a great deal of support from the evidence of a psychiatrist based on researches on the subject of homosexuality rather than on having interviewed the respondent. We have seen, however, that, in *PC v VC*, High Court, 7 July 1989, O'Hanlon J was willing to receive evidence of a kind which Lardner J was disposed to reject.

MAINTENANCE OBLIGATIONS

Separation agreements and maintenance obligations   In *D v D*, High Court, 19 December 1989, Barron J was faced with the argument that a husband who, in a separation agreement, had made certain commitments as to the maintenance of his wife, should be entitled to have these commitments reduced because he was no longer able to discharge them on account of a worsening of his financial circumstances. This argument brings into focus the important issue of the relationship between private contractual arrangements between spouses and the social concern that marriage should be backed by effective legal support for the maintenance entitlements of those whose economic welfare is at risk.

Barron J found the source of his resolution of the issue in *HD v PD*, 8 May 1978 (extracted in Binchy, *A Casebook on Irish Family Law* (1984) 313), where the Supreme Court held that a wife was entitled to apply for a maintenance order under s.5 of the Family Law (Maintenance of Spouses and Children) Act 1976 in spite of the fact that a separation agreement had been made between the spouses. Walsh J had referred to s.8 of the 1976 Act, which allows an agreement relating to family maintenance to be made a rule of court if the court is satisfied that it is 'a fair and reasonable one which in all the circumstances protects the interests of both spouses and the dependent children (if any) of the family'. Walsh J had observed that it was clear from this section that a separation agreement entered into after the 1976 Act had come into force did not amount to an election, even if it were possible to forego the benefit of the Act's provisions, but effectively constituted no more than a factor to be taken into account by the court in determining an application brought before it under the Act. Walsh J had gone on to say that, in the case of separation agreements made rules of court under s.8, a provision in them for periodical maintenance payments was not final and there was nothing to prevent the spouse receiving the payments from subsequently applying for a maintenance order if the circumstances changed.

Barron J noted that Walsh J was dealing with the right to *apply for a maintenance order under s.5 rather than a reduction in the agreed payment.* It seemed to him, however, that 'there must be mutuality of rights', and accordingly that the husband was entitled to apply to the Court for an order that the actual sum paid by him to his wife be varied downwards:

> If strict reliance is to be placed upon [the husband's contractual] liability, then the contractual sum must be deducted from the husband's income and added to the wife's. In those circumstances, if she is then seen to be in better financial circumstances than he, he would be entitled to seek a maintenance order under section 5. Whatever way it is looked at, it seems that *HD v PD* is an authority in support of the husband.

It seems that Barron J considered that the proper order was one varying the clause in the contract which had been made a rule of court under s.8 of the 1976 Act, rather than one for the maintenance of the husband under s.5. He may have perceived a certain artificiality, for no particular benefit, in the law's requiring cross-obligations of the same category. If the remedies for breach of these obligations were different, then this solution would have been a good deal less attractive. The effect of s.8 of the 1976 Act, however, is that the maintenance agreements are treated identically with maintenance orders so far as their enforcement is concerned. Thus the party to whom maintenance is contractually promised may seek the assistance of District Court clerks, and the provisions relating to attachment of earnings orders are identical.

Wives and employment   In *B v B*, High Court, 13 March 1989, Barron J rejected the application of a husband for a reduction in the amount of alimony he had to pay his wife. We already discussed this case in the 1987 Review, 192-3 (*sub nom MB v RB* [1989] IR 412), where Barr J dealt with an earlier application, on behalf of the wife, for an increase in the amount of alimony. The husband's reluctance to sell land which was losing money met with no favour from Barron J who assessed his probable income on the basis of what could be obtained if the land was sold and the proceeds invested.

The husband argued that his wife should obtain employment. Barron J disposed of this suggestion as follows:

> It may be that since she is receiving alimony she is not obliged to do so. Nevertheless I think her general attitude is wrong. I appreciate that she makes a good home for her children, but I do not think employment would prevent her from doing this. She points to her bad health. Again I do not think that this is as bad as she thinks. I understand her attitude, and accept that she believes it is totally unreasonable for her to be expected to go out to work. I think for the moment it is reasonable that she continues to make a home for her children.

The case was decided some months before the Judicial Separation and Family Law Reform Act 1989 came into force. S.20 of that Act sets out the criteria to which the Court is to have regard in deciding how it is to exercise its powers as to maintenance and financial provision (see the 1988 Review, 236-7). These are broadly similar to those which are prescribed by s.5(4) of the Family Law (Maintenance of Spouses and Children) Act 1976. It is worth considering the question of spousal roles in relation to maintenance. It is too easy to dispose of the difficult issues involved by simply saying that there is no absolute rule which enables a wife to insist on not working in any circumstances, and that instead it all depends on the circumstances. Reading s.20, one might be tempted to be satisfied by the proposition that it is all a matter of judicial discretion in the light of the particular facts. Such a conclusion fails to come to terms with the more important issues lurking below the surface.

Involved here are *two* issues, which are easy to misrepresent as one. The first concerns the justification for maintenance obligations in support of marriage; the second concerns sex roles. The two are of course connected but need to be separately assessed.

As regards the first, it is worth asking *why* the law imposes maintenance obligations on spouses. The answer touches on a number of factors, moral, social and economic, but of crucial importance is the goal of offering practical support for the option of mutual, irrevocable commitment which marriage involves. There are elements of altruism and risk in marriage: a spouse (often a wife) may sacrifice career prospects and may thus damage his or her economic future. If he or she has the support of the law, in the form of an enforceable maintenance entitlement, this reduces somewhat the risk involved. Of course it will not always ensure that this entitlement will be fully effective in practice: see P. Ward, *The Financial Consequences of Marital Breakdown* (Combat Poverty Agency, 1990). But the law on maintenance may properly be regarded as a necessary buttress to marriage. To the extent, for example, that a deserted spouse would be unjustly forced into employment by the law's failure to provide a maintenance entitlement, the law might be perceived as damaging marriage.

This brings us to the second issue, of sex roles. Formerly, there was a fairly general consensus that children were best reared in the home in which their mother was parent. This consensus has faded in recent years; some argue that both spouses should equally share the day-to-day upbringing of their children, with work-sharing practices to make this possible; others argue that the decision should be one for the couple to make themselves rather than being forced on them by socio-economic realities; others again contend that both parents should work outside the home with the young children being reared during work hours in creches. It seems fair to say that at present in Ireland, while married women are working increasingly outside the home, they are still often in positions of considerably less economic power than those of men, in spite of employment equality legislation. Moreover, many married women, some by choice, others by necessity, continue to work exclusively or predominantly within the home.

How should these two matters—support for marriage and the question of sex roles—affect the court's determination of the issue of maintenance for a wife? It seems clear that merely addressing considerations regarding sex roles is not enough. To do merely this would ignore the crucial function of maintenance entitlements in supporting the option for marriage. It seems equally clear that, provided this function of supporting the option for marriage is secured, the court in the exercise of its discretion ought to have regard to changing attitudes to proper sex roles.

Could it be argued that the 1989 Act envisages a change of policy, involving the *reduction* in the entitlement of married women to periodical maintenance? In favour of this view, it might be suggested that the new facility given to the court to make a wide range of financial orders, including lump sum payments and property transfer orders, envisages the curtailment of the right to maintenance and an introduction of the 'clean-break' philosophy whereby the spouses' mutual relationship, from the financial point of view, is finally 'wound up'. The fact that the court, on granting a decree of judicial separation, may consider whether it should make a property adjustment order *on one occasion* might encourage this view.

It seems, however, that it would be quite mistaken to interpret the Act in this manner. In order to harmonise with the constitutional requirement to protect the family, the 1989 Act has to ensure that the option of marriage is fully buttressed by the orders which the court makes on granting a decree of separation. The 'clean-break' philosophy of divorce has no place in a system of law which is designed to support lifelong marriage.

SPOUSAL PROPERTY ENTITLEMENTS

In the 1988 Review, 213-21, we examined in some detail the important decision in *BL v ML* [1989] ILRM 528, analysed also by Claire Jackson (1989) 11 DULJ 158, where Barr J held that the plaintiff wife was entitled to a half-share in the family home by virtue of Article 41 of the Constitution. He considered that, if the article was to be given flesh and meaning in practical terms, a mother who devoted herself entirely to the family after marriage "has a special place in society which should be buttressed and preserved by the State in its laws'. The judiciary, he thought, had a positive obligation to interpret and develop the law in a way which was in harmony with the philosophy of Article 41 as to the status of women in the home. It was also in harmony with that philosophy to regard marriage as an equal partnership in which a woman who elected to adopt the full-time role of wife and mother in the home might be obliged to make a sacrifice, both economic and emotional, in doing so. In return for that voluntary sacrifice, which the Constitution recognised as being in the interest of the common good, she should receive some reasonable economic security within the marriage. That concept could be achieved, at least in part, by recognising that, as her role as a full-time wife and mother precluded her from contributing directly or indirectly in money or money's worth from independent employment or avocation towards the acquisition by the husband of the family home and contents, her work as home-maker and in caring for the family should be taken into account in calculating her contribution towards that acquisition, particularly as such work was of real monetary value.

In our analysis of that decision, we discussed several issues arising from it: the precise legal nature of the wife's share; how it should be assessed; the relevance of conduct, especially desertion, on the wife's part; how the 'family home and its contents' should be defined; and equality issues as between men and women and between women working in the home, outside the home, and part-time in and outside the home. None of these issues was addressed in the later decision of *EN v RN*, High Court, 27 June 1989, since Barron J, in a threshold analysis, declined to follow *BL v ML*.

In *EN v RN*, the plaintiff sought to establish a beneficial interest in the family home. She had married her late husband in 1964. He was an architect; she was a nurse. On marriage, the wife gave up her profession and devoted herself to looking after the house and the three children of the marriage. Until 1983, she worked in all a total of two months in two temporary jobs. Thereafter she had been employed part-time in her profession.

The family house was purchased in 1966 in the husband's sole name, entirely out of his moneys. With money he later borrowed by way of mortgage, the house was converted into a flat for the family and nine bedsitters. The plaintiff managed these and did all the work in connection with them. The mortgage was paid out of the rents received from the lettings.

The house was later extended, with the financial assistance of an endowment mortgage; this was discharged on the husband's death in 1988. The spouses lived relatively comfortably for some years. In 1984, the husband began to have tax problems. He moved his practice to his home for financial reasons. At the time of his death, the position was such that it was likely that his estate was insolvent. Shortly before his death, the husband discovered that his wife had no claim in the family home. He sought advice as to how to remedy the situation, but his plans came to nothing.

The plaintiff's claim to a beneficial interest in the house rested on two grounds: the constitutionally-based right which Barr J had articulated in *L v L*, and the traditional basis of an indirect financial assistance by virtue of her management of the bedsitters and her part-time work as a nurse.

As we have mentioned, Barron J did not follow *BL v ML*. His brief disposition of the issue may be quoted in full:

> While I see the equity in recognising the contribution made by the plaintiff towards the welfare of her family, there does not seem to me to be anything in Article 41 of the Constitution to support her contention that she should become entitled thereby to a share in the family home or any other property of any member of the family. The Article seeks to protect the family. The right granted is one whereby the State shall 'endeavour to ensure that mothers shall not be obliged by economic necessity to engage in labour to the neglect of other duties in the home'.
>
> Insofar as this provision may be construed as a guarantee of financial reward—and I express no view on this aspect of the matter—it seems to me that it must be a guarantee of reward from outside the family rather than a redistribution within the family.

Several questions arise about this approach. The first is the basic one as to whether Article 41 has any implications for family property law. The answer must surely be that it has. If we imagine a legal regime involving a complete separation of property, with no entitlement to maintenance or to succession in one's deceased spouse's estate, and with no protection of the family home against sale or mortgage by a spouse however vindictive the motivation, could the State, with such a regime be said to have discharged its guarantees under Article 41? Surely not. Such a complete stripping away of legal support for marriage would simply fail to protect the family in its constitution and authority. The exclusive, irrevocable commitment which marriage involves would be subverted if there were no adequate legal scaffolding in support of marriage. The point worth noting here is that this scaffolding includes legally-backed support for an equitable distribution of rights, responsibilities and legitimate expectations *as between the spouses*. Marriage is a commitment generating *moral* entitlements and responsibilities; a spouse who neglects or abandons his or her partner breaks his or her commitment. For the Constitution to guarantee to protect the family in its constitution and authority but to fail to give legal support for the moral entitlements flowing from the commitment of which marriage consists would be a hollow exercise. The argument made here is not that it is *desirable* that family property law should be structured on principles which give practical support to marriage but rather that the constitutional guarantees in Article 41 require the law to be fashioned in these terms.

This is not to suggest that the Constitution requires the introduction of one particular matrimonial property regime; it should be noted that Barr J's decision in *BL v ML*, although widely mentioned in public discussion as involving a holding that 'wives have a constitutional right to a half-share in the home', actually made no such generic finding. It found a half-share on the particular facts of the case.

In *EN v RN*, having rejected the wife's claim based on constitutional grounds, Barr J went on to consider the claim based on traditional grounds. He had no difficulty in recognising her entitlement to a share to the extent that she had contributed indirectly to the payment of the house loan of £5,000 and to the payment of the interest on the second loan. This claim was based on the theory of the resulting trust. As to the plaintiff's claim based on contributions other than to the repayment of loans, Barron J characterised this as being grounded on the theory of the constructive trust. What he had to say on this matter is controversial, and merits quotation *in extenso*:

> As the law stands it is very difficult for a spouse to establish a constructive interest. This is because of the application of the principle that where one person builds on the land of another knowing it to be the land of that other he or she has no right over such land. Save in

exceptional circumstances, the claimant spouse must establish the existence of an agreement that he or she should have an interest in the property of the other. This is illogical because it is recognised that only in exceptional circumstances will couples living happily together discuss such matters. Consequently, it is the exceptional case, where they have done so, which is covered; while the normal case, where no thought has been given to the matter, is ignored.

Acceptance of the principle in contests as between spouses is to be found in the approval in *Heavey v Heavey* 111 ILTR 1 of a passage from the speech of Lord Upjohn in *Pettitt v Pettitt* [1969] 2 All ER 389, at 409 which refers to *Ramsden v Dyson* (1866) LR 1 HL 129 and *Campion v Cotton* (1810) 17 Ves. 263. It seems to me however that these cases are not strong authorities for imposing the principle either as between spouses or on equitable grounds generally. While *Campion v Cotton* did apply the principle as between spouses, the contest was not between the spouses themselves but was between the wife who had received the benefit of the expenditure and the husband's creditors whose claim failed. In *Ramsden v Dyson* a tenant who had built on his holding was refused a new lease. This refusal contrasts with the position of a tenant under a building lease within the meaning of the Landlord and Tenant Acts in present times.

If the Oireachtas can recognise the equity of a tenant who has knowingly built on the land of another in a commercial situation, it can equally recognise that similar equities may arise as between spouses particularly since they are not expected when living happily together to concern themselves with who owns what. Yet until it does so I feel that I must follow what are now established principles notwithstanding my views that they can and do lead to injustice in some cases.

This passage gives rise to a number of comments. First, it appears to involve almost a despair as to the capacity of courts to ensure that justice is done. It recognises as illogical the insistence that a wife's property interest should depend on her having discussed the matter with the husband and it accepts that principles established by the courts 'can and do lead to injustice in some cases'; yet the only perceived solution lies in legislative reform. It might be thought that if the courts develop unjust principles they would be better to abandon them; however, fidelity to the hierarchical system of precedent may explain Barron J's caution. But do the decisions in fact sustain such a narrow interpretation of the role of the constructive trust? It seems not. In *McC v McC* [1986] ILRM 1 the Supreme Court recognised that '[w]hen the wife's contribution has been indirect (such as by contributions, by means of her earnings, to a general family fund) the courts will, in the absence of any express or implied agreement to the contrary, infer a trust in favour of the wife, on the ground that she has to that extent relieved the husband of the financial burden he incurred in purchasing the house'.

THE FAMILY HOME PROTECTION ACT 1976

Section 5 orders   In *O'N v O'N*, High Court, 6 October 1989, the family home was owned by the spouses 'beneficially in equal shares'. The wife had left her husband and children, who remained in the family home. She had later unsuccessfully sought custody of the children and sale of the family home. Thereafter she had borrowed £1,000 from a bank to purchase furniture. She was unable to pay this back, mainly through her inability to retain employment owing to ill health. Again she unsuccessfully sought the sale of the family home. The bank obtained a judgment against the wife in respect of the debt and registered a judgment mortgage against her interest in the family home.

The husband sought an order under s.5(1) of the Family Home Protection Act 1976 transferring his wife's interest in the family home to him. Under s.5(1), where it appears to the court, on the application of a spouse, that the other spouse is engaging in such conduct as may lead to the loss of any interest in the family home or may render it unsuitable for habitation as a family home with the intention of depriving the applicant spouse or a dependant child of the family of his or her residence in the family home, the court may make such order as it considers proper, directed to the other spouse or to any other person, for the protection of the family home in the interest of the applicant spouse or such child.

Also relevant is s.5(2), which deals with a case where damage has already been done rather than merely apprehended. It provides that, where it appears to the court, on the application of a spouse, that the other spouse had deprived the applicant spouse or a dependent child of the family of his or her residence in the family home by conduct that resulted in the loss of any interest in it or rendered it unsuitable for habitation as a family home, the court may order the other spouse or any other person to pay to the applicant spouse such amount as the court considers proper to compensate the applicant spouse and any such child for their loss or make such other order directed to the other spouse or to any other person as may appear to the court to be just and equitable.

The difference between the two subsections, of course, rests on subs.(1)'s requirement of proof of an *intention* to deprive the other members of the family of their residence in the family home. The classic case would be that of a husband, malevolently running up bills in order to have a judgment mortgage registered against the home leading to its eventual sale, or simply not paying the mortgage with a similar vindictive intent. Subs.(2) deals with a situation where, for example, such a malevolent husband actually got as far as engineering the sale of the home or, alternatively, one where an irresponsible or feckless husband, with no such intent, had so misconducted himself as to bring about the sale of the home.

The facts in *O'N v O'N* did not fit in very easily with these types of case. As Barron J noted, the wife had been short of money since she had left the family home. The debt which resulted in the judgment mortgage had not been incurred 'with an express intention' of depriving her husband and children of their residence in the family home. Nevertheless she was putting their residence there at risk since she was making no effort to pay off the judgment mortgage. Barron J added:

> This may be owing to her poor financial circumstances, but does indicate a wish to retain the financial benefit of the loan at the expense of her family. Indeed, it is probable that the same financial circumstances will need her to borrow again. If she does so, there could be no doubt of her intention to obtain a personal benefit at the expense of her family.

Barron J regarded the circumstances of the case as coming within the terms of s.5(1), adding that, as a matter of construction of the provision, he did 'not think that the claimant spouse must wait until there is a fait accompli. If he or she has to, then much of the remedy provided by the subsection would be lost'.

In a central passage of his judgment, Barron J analysed the approach which should be adopted in respect of the order to be made:

> The [sub]section does not require an absolute transfer of the interest of the errant spouse in favour of the claimant spouse or children. Regard must be had to the purpose of the Act. It is to prevent voluntary alienation of an interest in the family home by one spouse to the prejudice of the other or their dependent children. In practical terms, the wife . . . cannot realise her interest until the Court makes an order which in effect permits such a result. This is unlikely to be done before the children cease to be dependent. In the circumstances, it seems to me that the proper relief should be to safeguard this practical situation.
>
> The order should be one which protects the family home for the benefit of the plaintiff and the two children of the marriage. This can be done by transferring the restricted interest which the defendant has in the premises by reason of the provisions of s.3 of the Act. To do so in

reality takes nothing from the defendant, but at the same time achieves the protection which the Act requires.

Barron J made an order requiring the wife to transfer her interest to trustees so that her existing beneficial interest vested in the husband or his personal representatives until such time as she discharged the judgment mortgage or the parties otherwise agreed or a court would, otherwise, have ordered a sale of the premises at the suit of the wife.

The decision provokes a number of observations. First we must examine the element of *intention* required under s.5(1). Barron J's objective approach to the determination of intention in *O'N v O'N* echoes that favoured by him in *CMCB v SB*, on 17 May 1983. There he had held that s.5(1) applied where the defendant husband had 'gone from one financial folly to another and regrettably ... [had] put his obligations to his wife and children at the bottom of his list of priorities, so much so that he ... actively indulged in conduct which could only have been calculated to achieve the end of paying her nothing and ultimately losing his interest in the family home'. Barron J's later reference in that case to allegations that the husband was taking steps to 'endanger deliberately' his interest in the home may suggest a notion of advertent recklessness.

Barron J's approach in these decisions has the support of one commentator, Mr Paul O'Connor, who considers it is warranted by 'the social interest in seeing that a family be secure in the family home': (1983) *ILT (ns)* 132, at 133. It has not, however, received the approval of some judges. In *CP v DP* [1983] ILRM 380, for example, Finlay P favoured a subjective interpretation of intention, so as to exclude implied or imputed intention. Finlay P's approach seems to be directly contrary to that of Barron J in view of the latter's finding in *O'N v O'N* that the wife's bank debt had not been incurred 'with an express intention of depriving her husband and children of their residence in the family home'.

The second aspect to Barron J's decision worthy of comment is that the judgment throws no direct light on the question of matrimonial conduct, but without a doubt that factor must have played an important role in the resolution of the issue facing the court. Barron J made no express finding that the wife had deserted her husband. His only reference to the question of conduct was to record that the marriage had failed and that five years ago 'the wife left the matrimonial home and since then has lived with another man two miles away'. The children were aged five and three at the time of their mother's departure. Barron J, as we have seen, also recorded that the wife had subsequently unsuccessfully sought custody of the children. If we imagine a case where a husband has deserted his wife and the wife borrows £1,000 for furniture, it seems plain that no court would hold that she had breached s.5(1), even where there was a risk of a judgment mortgage. Why, therefore, did Barron J come to the conclusion he did in respect of a wife whose financial embarrassment was as severe? The answer may be that wives who are faithful to their marriage commitments will be treated differently from wives who are not. The same point can be made about husbands, but on account of the general imbalance of financial power as between the sexes, the parallels are not as close as might first be imagined. What is of interest about all this is that s.5(1) provides no express guidance to the court on the question of the relevance of conduct in deciding whether to make an order under it. It gives the court a broad discretion: if the word 'may' in the subsection were interpreted as 'must', this would have the effect of foreclosing the making of distinctions based on conduct.

In this context it is worth considering the position of a *deserting* spouse who makes an application under s.5(1) or (2). Unlike s.4(3), which requires the court to dispense with the consent of a spouse in desertion to a conveyance of an interest in the family home, s.5 contains no express limitation on the rights of an applicant deserting spouse. It seems that he or she would have at least a theoretical entitlement to succeed under s.5(1) or (2), but that the court would have to take into consideration the fact of desertion. Thus, if the only conduct in which the deserted spouse has engaged is to take proceedings under s.4(3), then clearly this course of legitimate action should not be frustrated by an order under s.5(1). But in a case where the deserted spouse 'jumped the gun', as it were, and disposed of the home without seeking a prior dispensation from the court under s.4(3), the court might consider it appropriate to make an order against the deserted spouse. In a case of clear desertion, it is hard to see why the deserting spouse should be entitled to anything more than nominal damages; of course, the interests of the children must also be taken into account and it could well be that the purported disposition of the home amounted to a serious wrong towards *them*, entitling them to damages or such other order as the court might consider just and equitable.

Conveyance of an 'interest' In *Bank of Ireland v Purcell* [1990] ILRM 106, the Supreme Court affirmed Blayney J's holding (9 November 1987), analysed in the 1987 Review, 194-5, in regard to the proper interpretation of s.3(1) of the Family Home Protection Act 1976. The bank held an equitable charge over the defendant's lands, including his family home, by virtue of a deposit of title deeds in 1975 to serve both present and future advances. The defendant's wife had never given her consent to the making of any advances to the defendant in accordance with the provisions of s.3. These advances had been made both before and after the coming into operation of the Act.

The bank claimed that the wife's consent was not necessary because the defendant's interest in his property had passed to the bank by virtue of the deposit of title deeds and that accordingly, when the further advances were made, no further interest could have passed to the court. It relied on Kenny J's statement in *Allied Irish Banks Ltd v Glynn* [1973] IR 188, at 192, that a deposit, as security, of documents of title to land '... gives an equitable estate in the lands' (see also id., at 191).

Delivering the judgment of the (five man) Supreme Court Walsh J stressed the important social purpose of the 1976 legislation in seeking to protect members of a family from having the home sold over their head by a spouse. The Act was 'not to be construed as if it were a conveyancing statute': id., at 108. The purpose of s.3 was to secure the position of the non-owning spouse, who was usually the wife. The extent of the interest conveyed by a mortgage by deposit of deeds depended on the amount which had been borrowed against it. Each time a further advance was made, the interest in the property charged was altered. The 1975 transaction contemplated future charging of the interest in the land in question by way of mortgage. If at any time no moneys were due on foot of the mortgage, 'then, for the purpose of s.3, the property was unencumbered, notwithstanding the deposit of deeds, and the bare equitable interest therein by the deposit of deeds was not the substantive interest in the property contemplated by s.3'.

If some moneys were due on the date the deposit was made, then the family home was encumbered only to that extent. Any interest created after the Act came into force was void as a mortgage though leaving untouched the personal liability of the borrower to the bank.

Walsh J noted that the husband's personal debt might ultimately give rise to the creation of a judgment mortgage. He reserved on the question as to the right of the other spouse in the event of a judgment mortgage's being registered in respect of the advances made after the 1976 Act had come into force.

THE STATUS OF CHILDREN

The subject of illegitimacy raises more subtle issues of social policy than might at first appear. It is very easy to treat questions as black and white when, in fact, they are far more shaded. Moreover, the subject is easily bent by emotions, and by type-casting which can involve gross simplifications of a vast range of people and of the circumstances of their lives.

The subject has gone through stages of public perceptions. Up to recently, sexual relations outside marriage, especially when they resulted in pregnancy, were the source of strong social disapproval. The father, if identified, could be sued for seduction, and also (subject to stringent evidential rules) for maintenance under the Illegitimate Children (Affiliation Orders) Act 1930. Generally he was perceived by the law and in certain sections of society as the primary wrongdoer, even where he might not have been the dominant party. Moreover, if he married under threat of being prosecuted or sued, he could not later have the marriage declared void on the ground of duress: *Griffith v Griffith* [1944] IR 35.

About thirty years ago, the social perception of the unmarried father began to change somewhat. He tended no longer to be regarded as the callous author of the mother's downfall; in cases where he showed an interest in the child, this came to be regarded by many as something which society, and in particular the law, should encourage. This perception was associated with a constitutional challenge to the adoption legislation by an unmarried father, whose consent was not required for the adoption of his child. Mr Nicolaou, who brought this challenge *(The State (Nicolaou) v An Bord Uchtala* [1966] IR 567) was about as deserving a plaintiff as one could imagine, having been left at the altar by the mother, and having shown a continuing interest in his child. He lost his case, because the Supreme Court held that the status of unmarried fathers attracted no specific constitutional rights. Walsh J, for the Court, said:

> When it is considered that an illegitimate child may be begotten by an act of rape, by a callous seduction or by an act of casual commerce by a man with a woman, as well as by the association of a man with a woman making a common home without marriage in circumstances approximating to those of married life, and that, except in the latter instance, it is rare for a natural father to take any interest in his offspring, it is not difficult to appreciate the difference in moral capacity and social function between the natural father and [those entitled under the legislation to veto an adoption or be heard by the Adoption Board].

Walsh J went on to reject the father's argument based on Article 41:

> While it is quite true that unmarried persons cohabiting together and the children of their union may often be referred to as a family and have many, if not all, of the outward appearances of a family, and may indeed for the purpose of a particular law be regarded as such, nevertheless so far as Article 41 is concerned the guarantees therein contained are confined to families based on marriage.

Walsh J also made it clear that the father could not rely on any 'personal right' guaranteed respect, defence and vindication by Article 40.3.1. He considered it:

abundantly clear that the rights referred to in section 3 of Article 40 are those which may be called the natural personal rights and the very words of subs.1, by the reference therein to 'laws', exclude such rights as are dependent only upon law. Subs.3 cannot therefore in any sense be read as a constitutional guarantee of personal rights which were simply the creation of the law and in existence on the date of the coming into operation of the Constitution. . . . It has not been shown to the satisfaction of this Court that the father of an illegitimate child has any natural right, to either the custody or society of that child and the Court has not been satisfied that any such right has ever been recognised as part of the natural law. If an illegitimate child has a natural right to look to his father for support, that would impose a duty on the father but it would not of itself confer any right upon the father. The appellant has therefore failed to establish that any personal right he may have guaranteed to him by Article 40, s.3 of the Constitution has been in any way violated. . . .

About twenty years ago, pressure began to mount in favour of reform of the law relating to illegitimacy. The existing legislation was considered by some to penalise the child for his or her parents' conduct; moreover, the concept of equality suggested that legal distinctions based on the marital status of one's parents could not be justified. The Law Reform Commission in its *Report on Illegitimacy* (LRC 4-1982) made radical proposals for reform, involving, in effect, complete equality as between children, in respect of maintenance, succession, property entitlements and guardianship.

By the time the Commission published its Report, a new consideration had entered the picture. This was the feminist perspective. Some feminists argued that abolishing illegitimacy and equalising the rights of children would extend to *unions libres* the sexual discrimination which they identified as inhering in marriage. Moreover, many single mothers, and the groups representing their interests, were concerned lest conferring joint guardianship status on unmarried fathers could lead to these fathers lawfully 'kidnapping' their children. Indeed, some were of the view that no father should be entitled to exercise any guardianship rights unless the mother agreed.

The fears as to kidnapping may have been largely unwarranted. Moreover, the emphasis on a maternal veto was mother-centred rather than child-centred, unless the controversial thesis could be established that giving the mother the last word on the father's role is *always* in the child's best interests.

The solution eventually adopted by the Status of Children Act 1987 is to equalise rights as to maintenance, property and succession, while retaining a distinction as to guardianship. The mother of a child whose parents have not married each other is (as before) the sole guardian. However, s.12 of the 1987 Act inserts into the Guardianship of Infants Act 1964 a new provision, s.6A(1), which states that, '[w]here the father and mother of an infant have not married each other, the court may, on the application of the father, by order appoint him to be a guardian of the infant'. As may be seen, the new provision gives the court a discretion to appoint the father as a guardian, but gives no guidelines as to the circumstances in which the court should or should not do so. What criteria should the court therefore adopt? The answer, in part or in whole, may be considered to be given by s.3 of the 1964 Act (into which, as we have seen, the 1987 Act is integrated on this matter). S.3 provides that, '[w]here in any proceedings before any court the custody, guardianship or upbringing of an infant is in question, . . . the court in deciding that question shall regard the welfare of the infant as the first and paramount consideration'. Thus, the child's welfare is to be the first and paramount, but not the only, consideration. The question therefore moves to what other considerations may impinge on the decision, and in particular the extent to which the constitutional dimensions to the subject may play a role.

In *K v W* [1990] ILRM 121 the Supreme Court addressed the issue. The applicant was the unmarried father of a child whom the mother had placed for adoption without the father's knowledge. The applicant successfully applied to the Circuit Court to be appointed guardian. On appeal by the mother and prospective adoptive parents to the High Court, Barron J stated a case for the opinion of the Supreme Court as to whether he was correct in interpreting the test under s.6A as being 'whether the natural father is a fit person to be appointed guardian and, if so, whether there are circumstances involving the welfare of the child which require that notwithstanding he is a fit person he should not be so appointed'.

The Supreme Court (Finlay CJ, Walsh, Griffin and Hederman JJ; McCarthy J dissenting) held that this was not the correct test. The Chief Justice (with whose judgment the rest of the majority concurred) identified two errors in this test. First, it presumed a right to guardianship, whereas s.6A created merely a right to *apply* for guardianship. Secondly, a right to guardianship defeasible by circumstances or reasons 'involving the welfare of the child' could not possibly be equated with regarding the welfare of the child as the first and paramount consideration in the exercise by the court of its discretion as to whether or not to appoint the father guardian. The Chief Justice considered that Barron J's construction of s.6A to a large extent sprang from the submission made on behalf of the father that he had a constitutional right, or a national right identified by the Constitution, to the guardianship of the child and that the 1987 Act, by inserting s.6A into the 1964 Act, was thereby declaring or acknowledging that right. In a crucial passage, Finlay CJ said that he was satisfied that this submission was:

not correct and that although there may be rights of interest or concern arising from the blood link between the father and the child, no constitutional right to guardianship in the father of the child exists. This conclusion does not, of course, in any way infringe on such considerations appropriate to the welfare of the child in different circumstances as may make it desirable for the child to enjoy the society, protection and guardianship of its father, even though its father and mother are not married.

The extent and character of the rights which accrue arising from the relationship of a father to a child whose mother he is not married to must vary very greatly indeed, depending on the circumstances of each individual case.

    The range of variation would, I am satisfied, extend from the situation of the father of a child conceived as the result of a casual intercourse, where the rights might well be so minimal as practically to be non-existent, to the situation of a child born as the result of a stable and established relationship and nurtured at the commencement of his life by his father and mother in a situation bearing nearly all of the characteristics of a constitutionally protected family, when the rights would be very extensive indeed.

Accepting that 'the discretion vested in the court on the making of an application must be exercised, regarding the welfare of the infant as the first and paramount consideration', the Chief Justice observed that '[t]he blood link between the infant and the father and the possibility for the infant to have the benefit of the guardianship by and the society of its father is one of many factors which may be viewed by the court as relevant to its welfare.'

These passages provoke a number of comments. *First*, it seems clear that the unmarried father has no constitutional right to guardianship on the basis of his status. The judgment is silent on whether he has a constitutional right to any specific *ingredient* of guardianship, such as access, for example. *Secondly*, the unmarried father apparently has 'rights of interest or concern' arising from the blood link. The precise juridical nature of these rights is not clear. They appear not to have been *conferred* by the Constitution, nor merely derived from statutory benefaction. If they 'aris[e] from the blood link', it might be argued that they should be of unchanging dimensions, as between different unmarried fathers, since the blood link has no necessary connection with the degree of active concern a particular father may evince. This interpretation does not, however, appear to harmonise with the Chief Justice's analysis, which manifestly perceives these rights as of great variability in extent, from 'practically ... non-existent' in the case of a child conceived as a result of a casual intercourse to 'very extensive indeed' where the child is born as a result of a stable and established relationship and nurtured by both parents at the commencement of his life.

It is essential that the juridical nature of these rights should be correctly identified since, if they are indeed natural rights recognised by the Constitution, then the court's decision in *K v W* must surely call into question its earlier analysis of the constitutional issue in *Nicolaou*.

In *Nicolaou*, as we have seen, Walsh J, for the Court, stated that it had not been shown to the satisfaction of the court that an unmarried father had any natural right to either the custody or society of his child, and that the court had not been satisfied that any such right had ever been recognised as part of the natural law. In the light of *K v W* can it be argued that Walsh J's statement in *Nicolaou* amounted to no more than a rejection of the argument as then made to it, and that this rejection was intended to be understood as being of a tentative rather than a final nature. Support for this view can perhaps be gleaned from the repeated reference to the argument's not having been 'shown to the satisfaction of the Court': this may suggest that on a further demonstration the full force of the argument would be capable of being perceived as being stronger than it was in *Nicolaou*. It is, however, odd that the force of an essentially analytic, intellectual argument should, on the court's admission, be capable of being less than fully appreciated by it. As against this it may be replied that the argument contains an important empirical element, on which fuller factual information, or information revised to take account of changing social practices, might be capable of yielding a different answer to the constitutional issue posed in relation to Article 40.3. Undoubtedly there are more unmarried fathers who exercise an active parenting role today in relation to their children than was the position in 1966.

Yet for two reasons it is extremely doubtful that Walsh J's reference to the court's not being satisfied as to the existence of an unmarried father's natural personal right to the custody and society of his child was intended to imply uncertainty or caution in the empirical order. First, the case contained no element of empirical argumentation, no 'Brandeis brief' or its equivalent; nor did the court appear to want such material. Nor, incidentally, did the Supreme Court *In re the Adoption (No. 2) Bill 1987* [1989] ILRM 266; [1989] IR 656 appear concerned to have detailed data on the social position of unmarried parenthood, in spite of O'Higgins CJ's earlier comments in the *In re the Housing (Private Rented Dwellings) Bill 1981* [1983] ILRM 246; [1983] IR 181. Furthermore, it is a central, and essential, feature of natural law theory that rights and duties are rooted in human capacity; identifying the nature of human capacity is not dependent on particular social, economic or political circumstances at a particular time, though of course all information is helpful in assessing the capacity of human beings. In the specific context of the issues raised in *Nicolaou* and *K v W*, natural law theory seeks to identify the mode of interpersonal sexual relationship which is most in harmony with human capacity; it identifies irrevocable mutual commitment as being within the reach of human capacity, save in cases where a particular individual lacks that capacity on account of mental illness, for example. Whether a large or small number of men are unmarried parents, the issue of their natural rights and responsibilities will remain the same.

It is worth noting that in *McGee v Attorney General* [1974] IR 284, where Walsh J addressed the question of the nature and scope of natural law, he noted that the courts should not be asked to choose between the differing views of experts on the interpretation by the different religious denominations of either the nature or extent of the natural rights recognised by the Constitution as being anterior to it, and that 'it falls finally upon the judges to interpret the Constitution and in doing so to determine, where necessary, the rights which are superior or antecedent to positive law or which are imprescriptible or inalienable'. He noted that, in the performance of this 'difficult duty', there were certain guidelines laid down by the Constitution for the judge; these included the notions of prudence, justice and charity (in the Christian sense of mercy). Walsh J observed that '[i]t is but natural that from time to time the prevailing ideas of these virtues may be conditioned by the passage of time; no interpretation of the Constitution is intended to be final for all time. It is given in the light of prevailing ideas and concepts'. Could this analysis support the view that in *K v W*, the Supreme Court has *changed* its interpretation of the natural law on the question of the natural rights of unmarried fathers? We suggest not, for two reasons. First, the court gave no indication in *K v W* that it was seeking to engage in such a radical process. The majority judgment did not even refer to *Nicolaou*. It is stretching credibility to suggest that the court would silently depart from one of its most significant decisions, or that Walsh J would merely concur in a judgment which had such an effect on the judgment delivered for the court in *Nicolaou*. Secondly, and more fundamentally, it may be argued that the elements of variability posited by Walsh J in *Nicolaou* are a good deal more narrow than they have sometimes been interpreted. Closely read, Walsh J's analysis does not suggest that it is the proper function of the judges to make up some theory of natural law of their own, without regard to the corpus of natural law theory which has grown up over many centuries. On the contrary, Walsh J requires that this corpus be the source of judicial decision-making, because the Constitution requires it. Moreover, it is clear that some aspects of natural law theory incorporated by the Constitution are in some respects inconsistent with the ideas of certain thinkers whose thoughts form part of that school of thought. The Constitution's infusion of the elements of prudence, justice and charity further limits and modifies the potential range of thinkers. Walsh J accepts that the prevailing ideas of *these virtues* may be conditioned by the passage of time. Nowhere in his judgment does he suggest that a judge is free to *invent* a new theory of natural law. The judge has to apply natural law theory and this in some cases can involve the function of choosing between theorists on a specific issue, but the judge has not a free hand to write a new moral code, or to reject what is accepted in natural law theory.

This brings us to the *third* point worth noting about the Chief Justice's analysis. Not merely does it not seek to clarify the juridical nature of the unmarried father's 'rights of interest and concern'; it also fails to identify the *object* of those interests. The context indicates that at least some of the constituent elements of guardianship are in issue; but the question whether the right to veto an adoption of the child or, more modestly, to be heard by the Adoption Board in the case of an adoption with the mother's consent, is not addressed. It might be thought that the second question is consequent on the first, since, in cases where the unmarried father is appointed guardian, his consent to an adoption to which the mother consents is essential. But this inter-relationship is the creature of statute (the Adoption Act 1952, s.14) and what the Oireachtas gives, it can take away. It is thus essential to know whether the rights identified in *K v W* extend to the context of adoption; to the extent that they may do, the *Nicolaou* judgment has been modified *sub silentio*. It is curious in this regard that the Chief Justice made no mention of the earlier decision; perhaps Walsh J's concurrence in *K v W* is an indication that he (and the other members of the majority) considered that the 'rights of interest or concern' which the Chief Justice identified were limited to a narrower context.

In the final part of his judgment, Finlay CJ said that:

[i]n a case such as the present case where the application for appoint-ment as a guardian is linked to the application for a present order of custody, regard should not be had to the objective of satisfying the wishes and desires of the father to be involved in the guardianship of and to enjoy the society of his child unless the court has first concluded that the quality of welfare which would probably be achieved for the infant by its present custody which is with the prospective adoptive parents, as compared with the quality of welfare which would probably be achieved by custody with the father, is not to an important extent better.

This proposition may seem at first sight worthy of little comment but in fact it addresses an issue of very considerable complexity. This concerns the relationship between the child's *welfare* and the unmarried father's *'rights of interest or concern'*. Of course in many cases these two elements will overlap: it may well be in the child's welfare to be reared by his or her unmarried father where for example the father and mother are in a stable relationship, and the father's rights of interest or concern may in this case point strongly in the same direction. But what is the position where these two elements pull in separate directions? Where parents have *married* one another, s.3 of the 1964 Act 'must be construed as involving a constitutional presumption that the welfare of the child which is defined in s.2 of the Act in terms identical to those contained in Article 42.1 is to be found with the family unless the court is satisfied on the evidence that there are compelling reasons why this cannot be achieved or unless the court is satisfied that the evidence establishes an exceptional case where the parents have failed to provide education for the child and continue to fail to provide education for the child for moral or physical reasons': *KC & AC v An Bord Uchtala* [1985] ILRM 302, at 317.

If an unmarried father's rights are *not* of any constitutional weighting, then the welfare test should, it seems, be applied as a first and paramount consideration, with no 'gloss' akin to that applying to married parents. If, however, the unmarried father's rights have *some* constitutional weighting, then the question to be resolved is the precise measure of that weighting. Is there to be any presumption, however easily it may be rebutted, that the welfare of the child is to be found within a stable, unmarried family?

This brings us to a further complication. There is judicial authority for the view that a mother who has not married the father of her child has constitutional rights, under Article 40.3.1°, 'which derive from the fact of motherhood and from nature itself'. O'Higgins CJ stated this in *G v An Bord Uchtála* [1980] IR 32, at 55. Walsh and Parke JJ took the same view though Henchy and Kenny JJ did not accept that the mother's rights were of constitutional dimensions. To what extent do the mother's rights outweigh those of the father in a situation of conflict?

McCarthy J's dissenting judgment is also worthy of note. He considered that an unmarried father's application under s.6A should succeed unless he is not a fit person or there are 'circumstances or good reasons' involving the welfare of the child which require that he should not be appointed. He interpreted the second leg of Barron J's test as not departing from the first and paramount consideration test but rather expressing it in a different way. Like the majority, he was of the view that the unmarried father has rights in relation to his child; unlike the majority, he expressly characterised them as natural. S.6A did not, he thought, presuppose a right to guardianship in the unmarried father:

[I]f it does, it is a qualified right—an inchoate right which does not arise unless and until he makes a successful application under s.6A, but such application should succeed unless he is not a fit person or there are circumstances or good reasons involving the welfare of the child which require that he should not be appointed.

THE FAMILY AND THE CONSTITUTION

The international dimension In *Fajujonu v Minister for Justice* [1989] ILRM 234, the Supreme Court had to grapple with the troublesome question of the relationship between the international scope of the protection afforded the family under Article 41 and the social policies underlying the Aliens Act 1935. The first-named plaintiff was a citizen of Nigeria, the second-named plaintiff, his wife, was a citizen of Morocco and the third-named plaintiff, their child, was a citizen of Ireland, born here in 1983. The couple had married before coming here in 1981. They had failed to report to an immigration officer or registration officer when they landed and had failed to obtain permission to remain here after the period of a month had elapsed. Two further children had been born to them since 1983. They were not parties to the litigation. In 1984, the first-named plaintiff had an offer of employment; his prospective employers sought from the Minister for Labour a permit for him to work as an alien. The Minister for Labour consulted with the Department of Justice. The result was the communication to the first-named plaintiff of the refusal of the Minister for Justice to permit him to reside in the State on the ground, among others, that he was unable to support his family without assistance from the State. His dilemma was thus revealed: he could not work as he was an illegal immigrant and he could not stay here without work on the basis of his inability to support his family.

The plaintiffs took legal proceedings against the Minister for Justice, Ireland and the Attorney General seeking four remedies: (a) an order restraining them from prohibiting the plaintiffs or any of them from continuing to reside here or from taking any further action against them under the Aliens Act 1935; (b) a declaration that the plaintiffs were entitled to reside within the State; (c) in the alternative, a declaration that such provisions of the 1935 Act as purported to empower the defendants to deport the plaintiffs or otherwise exclude them from the jurisdiction of the Court were inconsistent with the Constitution; and (d) an order directing the Minister to grant to the first- and second-named plaintiffs a visa entitling them to remain within the State for as long as they were members of the family consisting of themselves and the third-named plaintiff, owing parental duties of care and maintenance to her.

Barrington J dismissed the plaintiffs' claim. The Supreme Court dismissed the appeal (subject to the giving of liberty to apply to the High Court at some future time in the event of certain contingencies).

Two judgments were delivered: by Finlay CJ and Walsh J, with Griffin, Hederman and McCarthy JJ concurring with both judgments. The Chief Justice noted that the argument made on behalf of the plaintiffs on appeal had changed somewhat from that advanced in the High Court: instead of asserting an *absolute* right in the third-named plaintiff, incapable of being affected by the provision of the 1935 Act, counsel had argued that she had a constitutional right of *great importance* which could be restricted or infringed for only very compelling reasons.

Finlay CJ stated as his central conclusion that:

> where, as occurs in this case, an alien has in fact resided for an appreciable time in the State and has become a member of a family unit within the State containing children who are citizens, . . . there can be no question but that those children, as citizens, have got a constitutional right to the company, care and parentage of their parents within a family unit. I am also satisfied that *prima facie* and subject to the exigencies of the common good . . . that is a right which these citizens would be entitled to exercise within the State.
>
> I am also satisfied that, whereas the parents who are not citizens and who are aliens cannot, by reason of their having, as members of their family, children born in Ireland who are citizens, claim any constitutional right of a particular kind to remain in Ireland, they are entitled to assert a choice of residence on behalf of their infant children, in the interest of those infant children.

Having reached these conclusions, the Chief Justice expressed the view that the Minister for Justice, under his powers contained in the 1935 Act, can force the family so constituted to leave the State if, *and only if*, after due and proper consideration, he is satisfied that the interests of the common good and the protection of the State and its society justifies an interference with 'what is clearly a constitutional right'. This discretion, on the Chief Justice's analysis, can be carried out only 'after, and in the light of, a full recognition of the fundamental nature of the constitutional rights of the family'. The reason for exclusion would have to be a 'grave and substantial' one associated with the common good. Barrington J's judgment had not proceeded on the basis that these criteria were appropriate; moreover, matters must necessarily have changed since last investigated in 1984. Accordingly, the Chief Justice considered that the Minister should freshly consider the case 'having due regard to the important constitutional rights which are involved, as far as the three children are concerned, to the question as to whether the plaintiffs should, pursuant to the Act of 1935, be permitted to remain in the State'.

Finlay CJ made it plain that the criteria he had articulated did not prevent the Minister from making an order which had the necessary consequence that, to remain a family unit, the children would have to leave the State with their parents. This did not render the 1935 Act inconsistent with the Constitution. There were no grounds for concluding that the Minister and his officers would carry out their functions under the Act 'otherwise than in accordance with fair procedures and having regard to the rights which have been identified in the judgments of this Court'. The plaintiffs would have liberty to apply to the High Court in the action, challenging any further act or omission on the Minister's part.

In his concurring judgment, Walsh J expressed the view that the *entire family* (comprising the three plaintiffs and the two children who were not parties) constituted a family within the meaning of the Constitution. The three children were entitled to the care, protection and the society of their parents in this family group which was resident within the State. He added that there was 'no doubt' that the family had made its home and residence in Ireland.

Walsh J went on to note that there had been no suggestion that the first two plaintiffs were in any way unfit to maintain the guardianship and custody of their children or that there was any ground on which the State could lawfully separate them either temporarily or permanently from their children. The case was not similar to that of *The State (Bouzagu) v The Station Sergeant, Fitzgibbon Garda Station* [1986] ILRM 98; [1985] IR 426, where the plaintiff, a Moroccan citizen, had had a barring order made against him.

Walsh J noted that the first-named plaintiff was, in effect, not being permitted to support his family within the State because he was not permitted to work. In a crucial part of his analysis he said:

> Such a position could not arise in respect of the support of his family if the parents were citizens, and therefore to that extent the members of the family who were Irish citizens were suffering discrimination by reason of the fact that their parents were aliens. The question which arises, therefore, is whether a family, the majority of whose members are Irish citizens, can effectively be put out of the country on the grounds of poverty. The dilemma posed for the parents by this attitude is [that] they must choose to withdraw their children, who are Irish citizens, from the benefits and protection of Irish law under the Constitution or, alternatively, to effectively abandon them within this State, which would then be obliged to support them.
>
> In view of the fact that these are children of tender age, who require the society of their parents and when the parents have not been shown to have been in any way unfit or guilty of any matter which make[s] them unsuitable custodians to their children, to move to expel the

parents in the particular circumstances of this case would, in my view, be inconsistent with the provisions of the Constitution guaranteeing the integrity of the family.

The Act of 1935 did not in any way contemplate a situation in which infant citizens of this State could be in effect deprived of the benefit and protection of the laws and Constitution of this State. In my view, therefore, the Act is not inconsistent with the Constitution. But it would be *ultra vires* the Act to exercise the powers which had been sought to be exercised by the Minister to disrupt this family for no reason other than poverty, particularly when that poverty has been effectively induced by the State itself.

Walsh J expressed agreement with the Chief Justice that there was nothing to suggest that the Minister had applied his mind to any of these considerations; the Minister would have to reconsider the matter, bearing in mind the constitutional rights involved. In Walsh J's view, the Minister would have to be satisfied that the interests of the common good of the people of Ireland and of the protection of the State and its society were 'so predominant and so overwhelming' in the circumstances of the case that an action which could have the effect of breaking up the family was not so disproportionate to the aim sought to be achieved as to be unsustainable.

The decision in *Fajujonu* raises a number of interesting issues, which we will consider in turn.

Family, citizenship and connection with Ireland   One of the most difficult questions in Irish constitutional theory concerns the proper remit of the protection afforded by the Constitution under Articles 40 to 44. The difficulty springs not from any weakness or oversight in the constitutional provisions themselves but rather on account of more profound jurisprudential reasons. There are traditionally two principal ways of analysing fundamental human rights. The *positivist* approach views rights as capable of generation only within particular legal orders: the right to marry, on this view, is conferred by the legal order in question, and what may be given may be modified or completely taken away. If a right thus conferred is later abolished, in accordance with the proper legal procedures prescribed by that legal order, its abolition may be the source of moral or political criticism but no legal complaint may be made. The *natural law* approach, which grounds our Constitution, rejects the positivist analysis. It seeks to identify the characteristics of human life and conduct which are essential to human flourishing and social order. Having identified these characteristics in general terms, it perceives the law's function as essentially one of trusteeship—to be so structured and administered as to protect the rights, and enforce the responsibilities, necessary to realise these characteristics.

The natural law approach regards fundamental human rights, not as at the gift of the State, but rather as inhering in all human persons, white and black, Irish and otherwise. The idea that the right to life, for example, is the creation of the Irish State is fundamentally opposed to the principles underlying the Constitution. Thus, to speak of the Irish Constitution *conferring* such rights on a certain body of people is to misunderstand the jurisprudential basis of the Constitution. The Constitution recognises *anterior* rights which call for protection as part of the natural law.

Having said this, however, the international facts of life cannot be ignored. Most countries do not adhere so closely of the natural law approach. Some, such as Britain, are fundamentally opposed to it and have traditionally endorsed a rigorously positivist approach. Others, in their Constitutions, endorse a human rights approach which contains the seeds of natural law. Still others favour a direct association between legal and specific religious norms. The fact that the natural law principles grounding the Irish Constitution are universalist in their articulation of human rights does not necessarily commit the Irish courts to the protection of these rights for all citizens of the world.

But where, and according to what principles, is the line to be drawn? One approach would be for the courts to articulate some minimum connection between Ireland and the person seeking the protection of the Constitution (or asserting rights under it). That connection might be residence here, for example, or Irish citizenship. (The Constitution does, after all, direct a number of its crucial guarantees of fundamental rights towards Irish citizens.) The problem with this approach is crudity and insensitivity to context. Is it seriously to be doubted that the courts would deny constitutional protection to the right to life of an American visitor to Ireland on the basis that he has a return ticket to New York in his pocket? Conversely, should mere presence here, however transient, inevitably support a complex argument based on the constitutional right to property? If different constitutional rights have different ranges of application as regards those who may claim their protection, could it also be argued of any particular constitutional right that its range of application as regards those who may claim its protection is a variable rather than a constant? For example, if a right is urgently threatened and a serious violation is foreseeable, this might be considered a reason for a broader approach to the range of claimants: thus a foreign person threatened with torture here might well be able to invoke constitutional rights of health and bodily integrity.

We suggest that the range of claimants should best be determined in a contextual rather than merely categorical manner. There should be no *a priori* requirement of a *constant* minimal connection between the claimant and

Ireland. This seems in practical effect to be the approach which our courts have adopted, most notably in their decisions on guardianship of children.

If the international remit of constitutionally protected *personal* rights is a matter of some uncertainty, the international remit of *Article 41* is understandably a matter of greater uncertainty. There appears to be a difference between the Chief Justice's analysis of this issue in *Fajujonu* and that of Walsh J. The Chief Justice considered that the children, as citizens, had a constitutional right to the company, care and parentage of their parents within a family unit, but he did not include the parents within the range of constitutional protection. It seems that the children's claim was sustainable under Article 41: the Chief Justice mentioned that the Minister's discretion should be exercised 'in the light of a full recognition of the fundamental nature of the constitutional rights of the family', and he later referred to the existence of 'important family rights in the children of this marriage'. Walsh J, on the other hand, made a clear finding that the parents and their three children constituted a family within the meaning of the Constitution. His reason for doing so appears to have been that the family had 'made its home and residence in Ireland'. Thus, for Walsh J, residence here, even if involving breaches of our legislation relating to aliens, sufficed to entitle the parents to claim the protection of Article 41; whereas, for Finlay CJ, their residence had no such effect. The citizenship of the children, rather than the residence of any or all of the members of the family, appeared crucial to his analysis. Two questions arise in this context. First, whether Walsh J would have recognised the claim to protection under Article 41 by alien *children* of spouses who reside here. The language of his judgment suggests that he would. Secondly, whether the Chief Justice would have recognised the claim of foreign parents resident here without any problem under the Aliens Act 1935 is doubtful. Finlay CJ makes no express statement to the effect that it was this particular dimension that prevented the parents' claim to protection under Article 41.

It is worth considering the extent to which, under the Chief Justice's analysis, the *children's* right to call Article 41 in aid falls short of the right, under Walsh J's analysis, of *all* members of the family to do so. It is difficult to see how in any respect it is less extensive. If the children may, under Article 41, assert 'a constitutional right to the company, care and parentage of their parents within a family unit', this would appear to allow them to invoke Article 41 to prevent, for example, their compulsory adoption, or the loss of the guardianship or custody rights of their parents, in any case where a parent could make such a claim on constitutional grounds. There is, however, something artificial about resting this entitlement exclusively on the children. One case where this would be particularly noticeable is where the parents' rights and responsibilities in relation to the education of their children are in issue.

The use by the Chief Justice of citizenship as the criterion of eligibility to assert rights under Article 41 is worthy of comment. If such a test were to be rigorously applied, it would be capable of causing hardship. It is relatively easy to imagine cases where a non-citizen with close and permanent connections with Ireland should be entitled to invoke Article 41. Of course the restriction to citizens of eligibility to seek the protection of Article 41 may be considered to work satisfactorily in respect of the constitutional scrutiny of the Aliens Act 1935; but it may be argued that a more sensitive test should be preferred. There may at first seem to be an inherent contradiction in using distinctively Irish legal principles to assist the claims of persons whose distinguishing characteristic is that they are not Irish; but, for the reasons we have earlier mentioned, this is to misunderstand the nature of fundamental constitutional rights, which are universalist in their projection. Of course there has to be legislation controlling immigration but, as both judgments in *Fajujonu* show, Article 41 should be capable of being called in aid by those with some mimimum connection with Ireland. It is worth noting that neither the Chief Justice nor Walsh J was apparently disposed to recognise any application of Article 41 to the claim of an alien who is neither a citizen nor a resident of Ireland and whose child is neither a citizen nor resident of Ireland. Whether they would be willing to do so in other statutory contexts (such as adoption) remains to be seen.

The Minister's functions   A difference of emphasis may be perceived as between the Chief Justice and Walsh J concerning the functions of the Minister for Justice (and his officials) under the 1935 Act, in the light of constitutional considerations. The Chief Justice favoured an approach involving a degree of scrutiny closely similar to that of *judicial review*: the Minister had a *discretion* to exclude the family, exercisable after due and proper consideration, when satisfied that the interests of the common good and the protection of the State and its society justified an interference with what was clearly a constitutional right. This was a discretion which would 'only be carried out after and in the light of a full recognition of the fundamental nature of the constitutional rights of the family'. If, having conducted the necessary enquiry, and having due regard to the constitutional considerations, the Minister was satisfied that for good and sufficient reason the common good required exclusion, then this was an order he was entitled to make. The Chief Justice's approach thus appears to concede to the Minister a range of discretion, exercisable within stated limits. A decision made within this range could not be overruled by the court, even if the court would not necessarily have come to the same conclusion. Walsh J appeared to endorse the central thrust of the Chief Justice's approach. For Walsh J, however, the stated limits of discretion should be more narrowly drawn. Perhaps at the end of the day his reference to 'predominant' and 'overwhelming' social interests may represent a semantic rather that substantive distinction; but does his express holding that exclusion of parents who are not unfit to have custody of their children is not consistent with Article 41 fly in the face of the Chief Justice's statement that the Minister *is* entitled to make an order the effect of which is necessarily that the family unit will be ruptured if the children do not also leave the State? The technical answer must be that the two judgments are not necessarily in conflict but rather that Walsh J has rendered explicit some specific constitutional principles, by way of application of Article 41, on which the Court of Justice remained silent but in respect of which he ought not necessarily be considered to be in disagreement.

One such express proposition by Walsh J is that it would be *ultra vires* the Act for the Minister for exercise his powers to disrupt the family 'for no reason other than poverty, particularly when that poverty has been effectively induced by the State itself'. This echoes the concern of the Supreme Court in *In re the Adoption (No. 2) Bill 1987* [1989] ILRM 266; [1989] IR 656 to ensure that poverty of parents should not be a ground for compulsory adoption. It remains to be seen whether Walsh J's statement might impinge on a case where alien parents were at risk of losing the custody or care of their children by reason of poverty. Here the risk of disruption would be by virtue of child care proceedings rather than proceedings under the 1935 Act. And that raises the more interesting and radical question: if alien parents in a family receiving the protection of Article 41 are protected from having their poverty invoked as a reason for disrupting the family by exclusion of the parents from the State or, perhaps in child care proceedings, is it possible for a native-born Irish family to insist that difficulties exclusively attributable to poverty should not be invoked by the State in child care proceedings?

Social welfare   In the 1988 Review, 221-3, 382-4, we discussed Barrington J's judgment in *Hyland v Minister for Social Welfare* [1989] ILRM 196; [1989] IR 624, where a provision of social welfare legislation (Social Welfare (No. 2) Act 1985, s.12(4)) was struck down on the basis that it offended against Article 41. The effect of the provision was that the level of unemployment assistance paid to one spouse was reduced if the other spouse with whom the first spouse was living, was in receipt of unemployment benefit, where no similar reduction was made in relation to an unmarried or separated couple. The Supreme Court affirmed: [1989] IR 624.

Finlay CJ, delivering the judgment of the Court, applied *Murphy v Attorney General* [1982] IR 241, as interpreted in *Muckley v Ireland* [1985] IR 472. As in *Murphy*, the court rejected the submission that the benefits accruing to married persons 'could compensate for or justify a failure to guard or protect the institution of marriage in the impugned sub-section of the Act of 1985'. What is not entirely clear about this aspect of the decision is whether it rejects the compensation rationale in the light of the actual quantum of the benefits accruing to married persons (which could, of course, be changed at any time) or whether (as seems more probable) this rejection is made *a priori*, without regard to the question of quantum of benefits.

The Chief Justice rejected the contention that the difference in objectives between taxation statutes and social welfare statutes could affect the constitutional effect of the impugned provision:

> Apart from the special situations provided for in Article 28, s.3, subs.3 and Article 29, s.4, subs.3 of the Constitution, ... if a statutory provision constitutes a breach of a constitutional right or obligation, it is irrelevant what the purpose of the legislation was in purporting to enact it.

If this statement intends to convey the proposition that, in determining the question of the constitutional validity of a statutory provision, the Court is to ignore the objective of the legislation, this is surely too bold a claim. Of course a benevolent or socially advantageous purpose will not save a legislative provision that is unconstitutional, but the prior question is *whether* the provision is unconstitutional. In determining this question the Court must inevitably consider the purpose of the legislation, not on the basis that a good purpose will automatically confer constitutional validity on the legislation but because it is a relevant and necessary ingredient in the determination of the constitutional issue. Therefore the court should have addressed the question of the differing objectives of taxation and social welfare statutes. It must be admitted that it is hard to see how such an examination could have led to a different outcome, but that is a separate issue. It should be noted that the Social Welfare (No. 2) Act 1989 reversed the effect of the *Hyland* decision.

The decision of *Greene v Minister for Agriculture* [1990] ILRM 364 is discussed below, 99-101. *Mac Mathuna v Ireland* [1989] IR 504, is discussed above, 96-8.

CHILD CARE

In *The State (D. & D.) v G (No. 1)* [1990] ILRM 10 and *The State (D. & D. v G (No. 2)* [1990] ILRM 130, the Supreme Court addressed a number of important issues relating to child care legislation. The parents of a child who had been ordered to be committed to the care of the Midland Health Board as a 'fit person' order challenged the validity of the order on procedural and substantive grounds. In the District Court two health board social workers had given evidence of interviews they had had with the child and the parents; a doctor gave evidence of having attempted to make a physical examination of the child, which failed on account of the child's hysteria; two doctors gave evidence that they had physiologically examined the child when she was anaesthesised; and one of these doctors gave evidence concerning a video-recorded interview which she had had with the child, in which she questioned her with the aid of anatomical dolls. This doctor had formed the view that the child had been abused by her father.

The application for a 'fit person' order, brought by a social worker employed by the health board, had been adjourned on the application of the parents' solicitor, who was anxious to obtain copies of the medical reports on which the evidence to be adduced by the health board would be based. Although the District Justice had confirmed his right to these reports, he was not in fact given any report of the joint physiological examination, and was given merely a loan of a copy of the report by the doctor who had interviewed the child. Although he asked for a sight of the video of the interview, he was informed that it was not available at the court. In two telephone conversations, the doctor who had interviewed the child gave the solicitor a summary of her conclusions in the case.

In the High Court Carroll J refused the parents relief. See the 1988 Review, 252-5.

On appeal, the Supreme Court reversed Carroll J. Their grounds for doing so were several, and were stated in two judgments.

First, the Court was satisfied that 'in order to determine with safety, having regard to the nature of th[e] interview [conducted by the doctor with the use of anatomical dolls], such a vital matter as to whether the conclusion reached by the doctor . . . is a sound conclusion which would warrant such a drastic step as the possible long-term removal of the care of a child out of the custody of its parents, it would be necessary for the tribunal before which such evidence of conclusion was given, to have in addition the basic evidence from which that conclusion was reached, namely, the video recording (where it existed), of the interview between the doctor and the child and a demonstration, in addition, of the precise use, and the expert witnesses' belief in the meaning of the use by the child of the anatomical dolls'.

Moreover, for a lawyer representing the parents to be in a fully prepared position to cross-examine the witnesses dealing with this evidence, it would be necessary for him to have had in good time before the trial reports or summaries of the evidence and an examination of the video recording by him and by any medical witnesses he proposed to call. Although no criticism could be laid against the conduct of the District Justice, who had dealt with propriety with the submissions made to him, the combined effect of the inadequacies of the pre-trial procedures and of the trial itself meant that natural justice had not been complied with.

In its further judgment on the issue raised in the case, the court addressed a number of questions relating to the interpretation of the Children Act 1908. We need not examine in any detail the court's discussion of these questions, since the 1908 Act is destined for abolition when the Child Care Bill 1988 (now going into Report Stage in the Dail) becomes law.

The most important holding was that health boards are not 'fit persons' for the purposes of the Act. The result of this holding was the enactment of the Children Act 1989 conferring retrospective entitlement on health boards to act as 'fit persons'.

Another important holding was that the requirement in s.23(1) that the 'fit person' should specify the religious persuasion of the child was mandatory and that its absence made the order incomplete. The Chief Justice went on to express his view that if this had been the only valid ground of challenge to the order, the appropriate way for the court to deal with it would have been to return the matter to the District Court to have the order completed and, if necessary, varied so as to comply with s.23.

It is worth noting the Chief Justice's view that, in a case involving a suspicion of ill-treatment or abuse by one parent only, 'there is a very definite and positive obligation on a court to whom an application is made either under s.24 or s.21 of the Act of 1908 carefully to consider whether the welfare of the child clearly requires its removal from the custody of the innocent parent. A justification for so doing could only be if the innocent parent was unwilling or, as might well be the case, unable to protect the child from the risk of harm from the other parent'. This approach echoes that favoured by the court in *In re the Adoption (No. 2) Bill 1987* [1989] ILRM 266; [1989] IR 656: cf. the 1988 Review, 248-9.

Finally, on the question of letting the parents know of the identity of the 'fit person' and the location of the child's new home, Finlay CJ observed that these facts might in exceptional cases be withheld. Such an exclusion of knowledge 'should not . . . be lightly undertaken, having particular regard for the fact that questions of proper access and communication between such parents and the child may in some instances still be a very necessary ingredient in the welfare of the child'.

In *The State (F) v Superintendent B Garda Station* [1990] ILRM 243, reversed by Supreme Court, 3 May 1990, the applicant took proceedings under Article 40.4 in relation to four of her children who had been taken from her home by two social workers, accompanied by a Garda, who had not told her the basis for this intervention. She had attended the office of one of the social workers on six occasions but was unable to see him. At no time during this period did anyone contact her either on behalf of the health board or the Gardaí nor did she ascertain where her children were. She had been refused legal aid on the basis that her case was not sufficiently urgent. (Barron J considered this to have been 'an unworthy excuse. If, as I am sure was the case, the lawyers attached to the scheme could not accommodate a further case, she should have been told'.) Having independently obtained the services of a solicitor, the applicant established through him that a place of safety order had been made on information sworn by one of the social workers. Her application to the District Court to stay the order pending appeal was refused. The applicant was served with summonses seeking 'fit person' orders. She had two telephone conversations with the social worker, in which he told her that the children were with foster parents. He did not inform her of their names and addresses or of the fact that there were three separate set of foster parents. The applicant was denied permission to have the children at a halloween party on the basis that there was no social worker to accompany them.

Barron J held that the detention of the children was unlawful. He construed ss.20 and 24 as mutually exclusive in their operation: '[c]learly two different types of situations are in contemplation. One or other of the sections may be operated but not both'. Furthermore, it seemed to him that the deprivation of liberty authorised by either section had to be subject to 'at least as stringent safeguards as in the case of persons accused of crime'. The summons following the detention should be issued as soon as possible. A person accused of a criminal offence could not be remanded in custody for more than eight days, and was entitled to see a solicitor during that period. Here the children had been kept in detention without the right to see anyone, since neither the applicant nor her solicitor knew where they were. The behaviour of the Eastern Health Board in failing to give the applicant adequate information within a reasonable time vitiated the detention even if it had been commenced by being lawful.

The Supreme Court reversed. O'Flaherty J (Griffin, Hederman and McCarthy JJ concurring) considered that, while there clearly had been a breakdown in communications, 'this was not due to any deliberate or conscious action on the part of any social worker . . . and it must be said that they were doing their best in the circumstances'. As to the question of not informing the mother of the identity of the foster parents and the location of their houses, this had been addressed in *The State (D & D) v G*, above, where the Chief Justice had said that denial of this information might be justified in exceptional cases.

O'Flaherty J considered that ss.20 and 24 were not mutually exclusive. The power to search contained in s.24(3) did not imply that the need for a search was fundamental to jurisdiction.

Barron J's analogy between s.24 proceedings and criminal proceedings did not commend itself to O'Flaherty J, who observed:

It is true that the word 'detention' is used in both sections [20 and 24], but it is with reference to preserving the life and health of a child or young person and for the purpose of vindicating his constitutional rights. It is in no sense to be construed as meaning a deprivation of liberty or of any of his constitutional rights.

O'Flaherty J considered that, as soon as practicable after the making of the *ex parte* order under s.24 in respect of the children, it was necessary to issue a summons directed to the applicant, seeking the making of a fit person order. The return date for this summons should be 'as short as is reasonable, having regard to the necessity for both the applicant and the respondent under it to have an opportunity of preparing for a proper hearing of the application for the fit person order'.

JUDICIAL SEPARATION

Alimony   In *MB v RB* [1989] IR 412, the question arose as to whether the High Court had power to award a capital sum in favour of a wife in proceedings she had brought for divorce *a mensa et thoro*, under the Matrimonial Causes and Marriage Law (Ireland) Amendment Act 1870. The Supreme Court held that the High Court had no such power. Walsh J, who delivered the judgment of the Court, stressed that alimony was 'by its nature' a periodic payment. It might well be that, when an order for alimony was made, a husband who had no immediate income but had sufficient capital assets might have to dispose of some of these assets to provide the necessary income. But that was a different question. Nor was an order for the payment of alimony *arrears* to be confused with an order for the payment of a capital sum as alimony even though the total sum of arrears might amount to a very considerable amount.

Walsh J observed that, in this jurisdiction, the court in dealing with petitions for divorce *a mensa et thoro* could do all that had formerly been done in relation to matrimonial causes by the ecclesiastical courts of the Church of Ireland, but, in the absence of statutory provisions, could 'do no more'. He contrasted the English Divorce and Matrimonial Causes Act 1857, which had made express provision for the granting of lump sums in proceedings for divorce, but not for judicial separation. In our own jurisdiction there had been no similar provision; nor had any Rule of court so provided, even assuming it could validly have done so.

The approach favoured in *MB v RB* must be examined in the light of *UF (formerly known as VC) v JC*, High Court, 24 May 1989, reversed by Supreme Court, 11 July 1980, where Keane J adopted a somewhat similarly restrictive interpretation of the 1870 Act in the context of nullity of marriage. It seems that *MB v RB* cannot credibly be interpreted as having any implications in relation to the development of the *grounds* for nullity, though it is clear that it does have implications in regard to the *ancillary* jurisdiction of the High Court in nullity proceedings in respect of financial support. The Supreme Court has already involved itself in the development of the grounds for nullity beyond what the ecclesiastical courts of the Church of Ireland had stated in 1870: see, e.g., *S v S* [1976-7] ILRM 156; *N (otherwise K) v K* [1985] IR 733. At the time the Supreme Court handed down its judgment in *MB v RB* all recent High Court decisions reflected the same approach. (Keane J's judgment was not delivered until more than a fortnight later and sought to place no reliance on *MB v RB*, the judgment for which had not by then been circulated.) *MB v RB* says not a word on nullity. The decision of the Supreme Court in *UF* makes it plain that *MB v RB* has no implications in relation to the substantive grounds for nullity.

Having said this, one has still to confront Walsh J's unqualified statement that, in this jurisdiction, the court in dealing with petitions for divorce *a mensa et thoro* 'can do all that was formerly done in relation to matrimonial causes by the ecclesiastical courts but, in the absence of statutory provisions, *can do no more*' (emphasis added). This certainly rules out the possibility of the court's adoption of new and more wide-ranging *ancillary* powers of the financial nature at issue in *MB v RB*. Would it also have prevented the court from developing the grounds for granting a decree of divorce *a mensa et thoro*? The judgment does not address this question expressly. In contrast to nullity of marriage, the courts over the years between 1870 and 1989 did not seek to develop the grounds for divorce *a mensa et thoro*; the only notable decision (apart from Costello J's in *McA v McA* [1981] ILRM 361 dealing with intention to injure the health of one's spouse) was that of *Scovell v Scovell* [1897] 1 IR 162, where Warren P identified as a bar to a decree the fact that the petitioner had, by reckless conduct and wilful neglect, conduced to the respondent's adultery. It is a matter of possibly idle historical speculation as to whether the courts would indeed have been disposed to develop the grounds for divorce *a mensa et thoro*, in the light of the Constitutional guarantees to the Family, had not legislation intervened: the Family Law (Maintenance of Spouses and Children) Act 1976, the Family Home Protection Act 1976 and the Family Law (Protection of Spouses and Children) Act 1981 all had the effect of improving the position for victims of matrimonial misconduct, including desertion and violence. In contrast there was no legislation impinging on nullity of marriage (save for s.1 of the Marriages Act 1972, in the specific context of nonage) prior to the Status of Children Act 1987, whose provisions dealing with nullity are concerned only with the question of the status of a child born of a void or voidable marriage.

It is useful also to place *MB v RB* in its own proper context. The Judicial Separation and Family Law Reform Act 1989, which of course contains detailed provisions for the making of lump sum and property transfer orders, had passed both Houses of the Oireachtas a fortnight before *MB v RB* was handed down.

It is of interest to recall that the Law Reform Commission, in its Report on *Divorce a Mensa et Thoro and Related Matters* (LRC 8-1983), recommended that the court's power to make property transfer orders should be subject to the consent of the spouse whose property is transferred. (Walsh J was, of course, President of the Commission at the time.) The Commission was concerned as to whether a power to make such orders without consent might offend against the Constitution. *MB v RB* makes no reference to the Constitution, perhaps because the holding that there was no power to award lump sum orders made it unnecessary to address this dimension.

Finally it is worth recording a passage from Walsh J's judgment in *MB v RB* in support of his statement that, in the absence of statutory provisions, the court could do no more than what the ecclesiastical courts of the Church of Ireland had done in proceedings for divorce *a mensa et thoro*:

> For example, it cannot bring before it a co-respondent and order him or her as the case may be to pay damages or costs. This point was emphasised by the Oireachtas in recent years when it abolished the action of criminal conversation [in the Family Law Act 1981]. It was always the legislative policy that a spouse, male or female, who sees his or her domestic peace shattered by the intervention of a third party is left without any form of redress. I mention this simply to underline the fact that the Oireachtas has quite intentionally, to date at least, avoided any extension of the jurisdiction in matrimonial causes inherited from the ecclesiastical courts.

It will be recalled that when Walsh J was its President, the Law Reform Commission, in its First Report on Family Law (LRC 1-1981), had recommended the abolition of the torts of criminal conversation, enticement of a spouse and harbouring of a spouse, and their replacement by family actions for damages. The legislature preferred to abolish these torts, leaving nothing in their place. See McMahon and Binchy, *Irish Law of Torts* (2nd ed., 1990), ch. 33. The Commission also proposed the reformulation of the action for loss of consortium as a family action available to either spouse as well as to parents and children. Nothing has come of this proposal thus far (though it is interesting to note that a motion for a legislative initiative on these general lines was carried unanimously at the Fianna Fáil Ard-Fheis in 1988). As we noted in the 1987 Review, 86-8, 198-9, in *Hosford v Murphy* [1988] ILRM

300, (*sub nom. PH v Murphy & Sons Ltd* [1987] IR 621), Costello J declined to recognise the right of children at common law (or under the Constitution) to sue for damages for loss of parental *consortium*; he looked to the Oireachtas as the only way forward. In *McKinley v Minister for Defence*, High Court, 15 November 1989; Irish Times LR, 14 May 1990, discussed below, 442-3, the High Court recognised the right of a *wife* to sue for loss of *consortium*, on constitutional grounds. As we also noted in the 1987 Review, Costello J's remarks in *Hosford* lend themselves to the interpretation that the intentional breaking-up of a family by an outsider might well be grounds for compensation under Article 41 in certain circumstances.

Against this background, *MB v RB* can best be understood as a decision of narrow focus, made at a time where the specific issue raised in the decision had been rendered effectively moot for future cases by the passage of the Judicial Separation and Family Reform Act 1989. No judge has shown a greater willingness than Walsh J, over the years, to investigate the constitutional dimensions of a subject. His failure to do so on this occasion should not be interpreted as evincing a reluctance to become involved in the wider issues of divorce *a mensa et thoro*, torts affecting domestic relations, intentional interference with *consortium* and nullity of marriage. To conclude from *MB v RB* that the Supreme Court had through its silence on these wider issues *implicitly* addressed them would seem naive.

The Judicial Separation and Family Law Reform Act 1989 We examined the main features of the Act in the 1988 Review, 229-42.

Fisheries

CREW COMPOSITION

In *Pesca Valentia Ltd v Minister for Fisheries and Forestry*, High Court, 6 June 1989, Keane J dealt with some outstanding issues connected with the introduction of the Fisheries (Amendment) Act 1983. The 1983 Act implemented EC requirements on the composition of fishing boat crews: see the discussion, 11-12, above.

FISHERY HARBOUR

Van Nierop v Commissioners for Public Works in Ireland and Ors, High Court, 28 July 1989 involved consideration of whether powers of compulsory acquisition can be lost through delay.

The defendant Commissioners determined in 1969 that they would acquire certain lands for the purpose of erecting a boatyard in Killybegs. They inquired of the company which was then believed to be the owner whether the lands in question were available for purchase. A positive reply was received from solicitors acting for the plaintiff in August 1970. In February 1971, the Commissioners wrote stating that arrangements were in train for the compulsory acquisition of the land pursuant to the Fishery Harbour Centres Act 1968. The parties subsequently agreed to put the price of the land to arbitration and a hearing was arranged for April 1974, but this was postponed *sine die* at the request of the Chief State Solicitor. In October 1974 a new set of documents was served under the 1968 Act amending the reference to the size of the land to be acquired. Reminders from the plaintiff's solicitors were sent to the Commissioners between November 1974 and November 1981 but without further progress.

The plaintiff subsequently received an offer for the lands in question and the instant proceedings were instituted seeking to have the notices served declared invalid on the ground that the proposed acquisition of the land had been abandoned by the Commissioners. O'Hanlon J granted the relief sought by the plaintiff.

He referred with approval to the decisions in *Richmond v North London Railway Co.* (1868) LR 5 Eq 352; (1868) 3 Ch App 679 and *Simpsons Motor Sales Ltd v Hendon Corporation* [1962] 3 All ER 75 as authority for the view that it was for the Commissioners to seek to exercise their powers of compulsory acquisition under the Fishery Harbour Centres Act 1968 within a reasonable time from the date of giving notice. Where they did not proceed within a reasonable time (this being a question of fact) he considered that they might well lose their rights to enforce their notice.

Applying that principle to the instant case, he held that on a consideration of all the evidence, it was reasonable for the plaintiff's solicitor to assume that the Commissioners would take the initiative in seeking the appointment of an arbitrator in respect of the 1974 acquisition and notice as had been done for the 1971 proposed acquisition. In the circumstances he concluded that it would be unreasonable for the defendants to seek to rely on the steps taken in 1971 or 1974, having regard to the period of time which had elapsed without any effective steps being taken to pursue the claim and the acquisition must be regarded as being abandoned. Accordingly O'Hanlon J made an order that the notices of 1971 and 1974 were no longer valid or of legal effect and that the powers conferred by the 1968 Act were of no effect for the purpose of compulsory acquisition of the plaintiff's lands. While this decision concerns a relatively little-used power of compulsory acquisition, the approach taken by O'Hanlon J has important implications to other powers of compulsory acquisition, particularly those given to local authorities.

REGISTRATION OF BOATS

The Merchant Shipping (Registry, Lettering and Numbering of Fishing Boats) Regulations 1989 (SI No.344) establish a registry of fishing vessels.

Garda Síochána

COMPLAINTS TRIBUNAL

The Second Annual Report of the Garda Síochána Complaints Tribunal established under the Garda Síochána (Complaints) Act 1986 was published in December 1989. The Report complained of a 'totally unacceptable' backlog in processing complaints, due to staff shortages.

DISCIPLINE

Dismissal: criminal charges   In *McGrath v Garda Commissioner* [1990] ILRM 5; [1989] IR 241 (HC); Supreme Court, 17 July 1990 the question at issue was whether criminal charges brought against a member were such as to justify disciplinary proceedings against him.

The applicant member of the Force had been charged with offences under the Larceny Act 1916 in connection with payments made to him in discharge of court orders imposing fines. The applicant admitted that he had not issued official receipts for any of the payments, thus leaving the persons who had paid their fines to him liable to imprisonment. The applicant was returned for trial before the Circuit Criminal Court, but he was acquitted on all counts. Subsequent to his acquittal, he was served with notices under Reg.9 of the Garda Síochána (Discipline) Regulations 1971 stating that he might have been in breach of discipline as a result of being charged with criminal offences and of appearing before the District Court and the Circuit Criminal Court. He was then served with detailed forms setting out the alleged breaches of discipline. The first three breaches were of conduct prejudicial to the Force, the particulars being the appearances in the District Court and Circuit Criminal Court. The other three breaches alleged were of corrupt or improper practice, the particulars alleging failure to account for the sums of money received by him in the course of his duty which had been the subject matter of the criminal charges. The applicant applied for judicial review seeking to prohibit the holding of an inquiry into the alleged breaches of discipline. Lynch J acceded to the application in part.

He was clearly of the view that the first three alleged breaches of discipline should not be allowed to proceed. He stated that it was untenable that a mere appearance in court to face a criminal charge could amount to conduct prejudicial to the Force within the meaning of the 1971 Regulations. Lynch J pointed out that a disgruntled member of the Force or of the public could bring spurious charges which could cause a member to appear in Court to face such charges.

The remaining charges were, however, in a different category, he concluded. He held that any inquiry could not contradict the finding already made by the jury in the Circuit Criminal Court, namely that the actions of the applicant were not corrupt or dishonest. He stated that the findings of the jury were 'by the court appointed under the Constitution for the determination of such matters and it is not now open to the inquiry to investigate these matters on the basis that there was any element of corruption or dishonesty on the part of the applicant in relation to them.' This conclusion appears to take a very rigid view of the *res judicata* principle (as to which see 358-61, below) as it applies in the instant case. Could it not be argued that the criminal and disciplinary proceedings are quite separate in their intention? The cases referred to in argument, *The State (Murray) v McRann* [1979] IR 133 and *Keady v Garda Commissioner*, High Court, 1 December 1988 (see the 1988 Review, xiii), would appear to posit mutually exclusive hearings. This in the *Murray* case, concerning prison disciplinary decisions, the Court held that a criminal trial did not preclude a disciplinary hearing arising from the same incident. The conclusion of Lynch J in *McGrath* seems to be to the effect that a form of double jeopardy would arise were the disciplinary hearing to go ahead. It may be noted that the Supreme Court upheld this aspect of the High Court decision on the narrow ground that, in the particular cirumstances of the case, it would amount to an unfair procedure to allow the inquiry to proceed under the 'corrupt practice' heading.

But Lynch J added that an inquiry could proceed insofar as the inquiry was confined to an allegation that the applicant's failure to account for the sums he had received was an 'improper' practice, as opposed to a 'corrupt or improper' practice within the meaning of the 1971 Regulations. This aspect of the High Court decision was also upheld by the Supreme Court. The Supreme Court decision will be examined in full in the 1990 Review.

Dismissal: lewd conduct   In *Stroker v Doherty and Ors* [1989] ILRM 428; [1989] IR 440 (HC); Supreme Court, 26 July 1990, the question at issue was whether certain allegedly lewd conduct of the applicant was sufficiently grave to warrant dismissal from the Force.

The applicant had been a member of the Garda Síochána for 14 years when he was involved in an incident in a public house in the rural locality in which he was stationed. It was alleged, *inter alia*, that he made lewd remarks to an acquaintance in relation to his (the applicant's) wife; and that when the licensee of the premises called for the applicant's wife to leave the premises at closing time the applicant failed to assist his wife to leave the premises. The applicant was charged with a number of disciplinary offences under Reg.6 of the Garda Síochána (Discipline) Regulations 1971, being alleged to be conduct prejudicial to the Force. After a disciplinary inquiry under the Regulations and an appeal to an Appeal Board, he was ultimately only convicted in relation to the lewd comments and the failure to assist his wife to leave the licensed premises. The Appeal Board recommended dismissal from the Force and this was implemented by the Garda Commissioner. The applicant sought judicial review, seeking to have the convictions and dismissal set aside, *inter alia*, for unreasonableness. In the High Court, Barron J granted the relief sought.

He held that since the alleged lewd comments in relation to his wife were uttered by the applicant to an acquaintance and were not, on the evidence, overheard by another person or objected to by anybody, the applicant ought not to have been convicted under Reg.6 of the 1971 Regulations on that count.

Barron J went on to hold that it was appropriate for the authorities to take into account that the applicant was stationed in a rural community and the particular locality is relevant to whether a breach of discipline has occurred. In this context, he approved the views to that effect expressed by Gannon J, *ex tempore*, in *Gilmore v Mitchell*, High Court, 18 April 1988 (a decision in which there is no transcript available in the normal way). Applying this approach to the instant case, Barron J held that the failure of the applicant to assist his wife to leave the licensed premises at closing time could have impaired the applicant's ability to enforce the licensing laws in the area in which he was stationed, and in this light he was properly convicted on that count under Reg.6 of the 1971 Regulations.

However, Barron J granted the applicant *certiorari* on the basis that it was not appropriate to take into account the locality in which the applicant was stationed in order for the authorities to impose a more severe penalty than would otherwise have been imposed. He took account of the concession by the respondents that what occurred would not have been a breach of discipline in the case of a Garda stationed in a Dublin suburb. Since no effort had been made to bring the matter to the applicant's attention and to seek his consent to a transfer, Barron J concluded that the dismissal from the Force (effectively preventing him from earning a living by the only means for which he had been trained) was unreasonable, in the sense used in *The State (Keegan) v Stardust Victims Compensation Tribunal* [1987] ILRM 202; [1986] IR 642: see the 1987 Review, 13-4 and the 1988 Review, 31. On that basis, therefore, he quashed the dismissal.

It may be briefly noted here that the decision of Barron J was reversed by the Supreme Court in reserved judgments delivered on 26 July 1990. The decision will be discussed in the 1990 Review.

Regulations The Garda Síochána (Discipline) Regulations 1989 (SI No.94) represent an important code for the regulation of disciplinary matters for the members of the Garda Síochána. The 1989 Regulations replace in full the 1971 Regulations which were at issue in the cases discussed above.

OCCUPATIONAL INJURIES

S.18 of the Social Welfare Act 1989 brought the Garda Síochána within the occupational injuries benefit scheme for the first time. This is in addition to the compensation available under the Garda Síochána (Compensation) Acts 1941 and 1945 for malicious injuries or death.

RETIREMENT

The Garda Síochána (Retirement) Regulations 1989 (SI No.303) specify the terms upon which a member of the Force may retire.

UNITED NATIONS SERVICE

The Garda Síochána Act 1989 enabled members of the Force to serve outside the State for the first time since its establishment. The Act came into effect on its passing on 26 February 1989. The Act was passed for the immediate purpose of allowing for service in the United Nations peacekeeping force in Namibia (UNTAG). The 1989 Act is not, however, confined in its application to that particular UN operation. S.4 of the Act allows for the registration in the State of births and deaths occuring outside the State in connection with service under the Act. The Garda Síochána (Registration of Certain Births and Deaths Occurring Outside the State) Regulations 1989 (SI No.71) give effect to s.4.

Labour Law

UNFAIR DISMISSAL

Procedural requirements In *Halal Meat Packers (Ballyhaunis) Ltd v Employment Appeals Tribunal and Neary* [1990] ILRM 293, the Supreme Court subjected the restrictive regulations in relation to entry of appearance in unfair dismissals cases to a broad equitable gloss. Under Regulation 5 of the Unfair Dismissals (Claims and Appeals) Regulations 1977 (SI No 286 of 1977), a party to a claim or appeal who receives notice thereof under s.8 or 9 of the 1977 Act and who intends to oppose the claim or appeal must enter an appearance by giving to the Tribunal, within fourteen days of receiving the notice, a notice in writing that he intends to oppose the claim or appeal, and containing the 'facts and contentions' on which he will ground his opposition. If he does not adhere to this requirement he will not be entitled to take part or be present or represented at any proceedings before the Tribunal in relation to the claim or appeal unless the Tribunal at its discretion otherwise decides. (This discretionary element was introduced by Regulation 15 of the Maternity Protection (Disputes and Appeals) Regulations 1981 (SI No 357 of 1981).)

In *Halal*, the employee's solicitor had sent a document described as a notice of appearance to the Tribunal merely four days after having received the original notice. The papers were sent back for further particulars, and then a number of mishaps occurred for which 'nobody c[o]uld really be blamed': id., at 306 (*per* Walsh J). These included the non-delivery of letters and the failure of the secretariat of the Tribunal to fully furnish all the documentation which turned out to be necessary for the hearing. At the hearing, the Tribunal, after hearing submissions from both sides, refused to let the employer or its solicitor take part in the proceedings. It decided the case in favour of the employee.

On application for judicial review brought by the employer, Murphy J refused relief (save for one aspect, in relation to the Minimum Notice and Terms of Employment Act 1973, considered below, 282-3). On the central issue he held that the Tribunal had erred within its jurisdiction. The Supreme Court reversed. Walsh J's judgment, delivered a few weeks before his retirement, contains many of the features characterising his approach over three decades: broad, uncomplicated statement of principle, concern for just procedures; and a certain disdain for legislative and regulatory niceties. He set the scene by observing that it was:

> a rather ironic turn in history that this Tribunal which was intended to
> save people from the ordinary courts would [itself] fall into a rigidity
> comparable to that of the common law before it was modified by equity.
>   When we come to deal with what is the main point in the case, as far
> as the High Court decision is concerned, it is the question of 'erring
> within jurisdiction'. I must confess that I am not very impressed by that
> because everything depends on what the error is. However, there is not
> any jurisdiction in any court or tribunal to be unfair. The question here
> is whether what happened was so unfair as to be a fundamental issue in
> the case.

Walsh J referred to the fact that the Tribunal had taken 'a rather rigid view'
as to the eligibility of the employer and its solicitor to be heard, in that the
members of the Tribunal had 'felt that they were precluded from doing
otherwise than to refuse in effect to hear the defence'. It was 'not apparent
that they gave their minds to considering the question of their discretion to
do so. . . . They felt bound to do what they did and in my view they were
erroneous in that'.

In Walsh J's opinion, the rigidity went far beyond 'erring within
jurisdiction':

> [I]t amounted in effect to a refusal to accept jurisdiction to hear half of
> the case. It went even further in refusing the respondent the right to
> cross-examine the case being made against him. It is the duty of all
> adjudicating bodies to act justly. That is a constitutional obligation
> imposed on all tribunals, as on all the courts set up under the Con-
> stitution. By definition, all unfair procedures must necessarily be an
> infringement of the fundamental rights of the citizens to have fair
> procedures in all adjudications determining rights or imposing
> obligations. . . . [T]he procedure adopted led to what [Murphy J]
> described as 'the awesome consequence which completely shut out the
> defendants'.

Walsh J's analysis surely casts a serious constitutional shadow over the
Regulations which can so easily result in the exclusion of a party from
participation in proceedings for unfair dismissal. This may perhaps seem an
unwarranted inference, since all that the case decides is that the Tribunal had
not exercised its discretion properly. Nevertheless the broad expression of
the constitutional requirements suggests that the only way the constitutional
validity of present Regulations may be salvaged is for the Tribunal to

interpret its 'discretion' so widely as to *require* it, save in exceptional cases, to let the employer be heard.

It had been argued that the employers wished to make a defence to the effect that the contract of employment involved a fraud on the revenue, and was thus illegal. Both Walsh and McCarthy JJ were of the view that this would not affect the central issue of the right to be given a fair hearing. Walsh J observed that 't[h]e point in this case is that the employers wish to make a case. It does not matter whether it is a good case or a bad case . . .'. And McCarthy J considered that, '[w]hilst to some it may appear that the raising of the illegality by the employer has a shabby nature to it in making a defence to a man who, if his case is well-founded, has been wrongfully dismissed, that is in no way an answer to the fundamental question as to whether or not fair procedures were used . . .'.

One aspect of Walsh J's analysis is worthy of note in relation to law of evidence. He appeared to assert unequivocally a constitutional right of cross-examination. He said:

> The matter here was a most fundamental one namely, the right of a party to meet the case made against them. . . . One cannot effectively prevent persons from being heard in their own defence, much less prevent them cross-examining the other side's case.
>
> There is a distinction also to be drawn between the right to test your opponent's case and the right to put up a case, as has arisen in this Court several times. Counsel may not be permitted to make points which were not made in the High Court save in exceptional circumstances. But at no time is it envisaged that one is not permitted to try to demolish the arguments of the other side.

On this general theme, the Law Reform Commission's analysis of earlier judicial authorities, in their *Consultation Paper on Child Sexual Abuse*, paras. 7.927ff (1989), may usefully be consulted.

The employers in the case had appealed the case to the Circuit Court, under s.10(4) of the 1977 Act, which provides a right to appeal to the Circuit Court 'from any determination of the tribunal in relation to a claim to redress'. The precise relationship between this right and the right to judicial review was left unresolved by the Supreme Court. McCarthy J observed that he was:

> far from concluding that the existence of a circuit appeal in any circumstances negatives the duty of the High Court and, consequently, this Court to embark on an inquiry as to whether or not an order of an inferior tribunal, District Court or otherwise, was made within juris-diction. The circuit appeal cannot cure a defect that was fundamental to

the procedure itself; I would wait for another day to decide whether or not under any circumstances the existence of an appeal to the Circuit Court can itself be used [to deny] a discretionary order which must ordinarily be made out of the requirements of justice.

Appeals against equality officers' recommendation   In *Board of Management of the Model School Limerick v Culloo*, High Court, 11 May 1989, a procedural question arose concerning an appeal to the Labour Court against a recommendation made by an equality officer under s.19(2) of the 1977 Act directing the Board of Management to pay the plaintiff teacher £11,000 for discrimination arising out of a dispute about the appointment of the school's principal. The Labour Court held that, as a matter of fact, the Board of Management had not decided to lodge an appeal in the case. Under s.21(1), the Board of Management appealed to the High Court, arguing that there had been no evidence before the Labour Court which would justify this conclusion.

Costello J rejected the appeal. On the material before the Labour Court, it was, in his view, entitled to conclude that the notice convening the meeting of the Board of Management shortly after the equality officer's recommendation had been made contained no reference to this matter, that some of the members left when the stated business of the agenda was concluded, that the Board's Chairman had requested three members to remain behind, that they had discussed the matter with him, that no formal decision as to appeal had been then taken or recorded, and that the notices of appeal which were later sent had issued on the direction of the Board's Chairman who was an official of the Department of Education.

Costello J noted that it had not been submitted that the appeal had been authorised by the Minister for Education in the Minister's capacity as patron of the school (the Board's managerial powers not having been terminated) or that a meeting of the Chairman and the three remaining members could have authorised the appeal. It was clear that a decision to appeal could have been authorised only by a properly constituted meeting of the Board's members. The Labour Court thus had evidence on which it was entitled to reach its conclusions of fact.

On the question of costs, Costello J held that since the issue of fact was one which the teacher had a considerable interest in contesting, it would be unjust to deprive her of her costs. It had been open to the Minister to defend the decision of the Labour Court but this had not happened.

Minimum notice   In *Halal Meat Packers (Ballyhaunis) Ltd v Employment Appeals Tribunal and Neary* [1990] ILRM 293, considered in detail above 279-82, Murphy J held that in a case of constructive dismissal, the question of minimum notice could not arise and that thus the element of damages awarded by the Employment Appeals Tribunal under this head should be set aside.

PROTECTION OF EMPLOYEES (EMPLOYER'S INSOLVENCY) ACT 1984

S.6 of the 1984 Act imposes an obligation on the Minister for Labour to make good any shortfall or arrears of normal weekly remuneration, for a period of eight weeks in the event of the insolvency of an employer. In *In re Solus Teo*; *Minister for Labour v O'Toole* [1990] ILRM 180, Murphy J had to decide the scope of the expression 'normal weekly remuneration': did it include trade union dues which were deducted from the remuneration in accordance with a notice from the employee to the employer requesting such deductions, and recognising that they were solely 'as a measure of convenience' to the employee and the union? Murphy J thought that it did. The deduction notice was not an assignment. The union could not sue the employers for the deductions on the basis of the notice, in his view. (The possibility of a contractual trust might here be relevant: see 1987 Review, 113-14; but even this would not serve to convert the notice into one of assignment.) Murphy J also rejected the argument that the deduction notice had operated to divest the employee of the right to recover the moneys: 'It might well have been an inconvenience to reverse some computer programme to enable the respondent to obtain the full amount of her emoluments but *her* emoluments they were. . . . The debt was due to her and to nobody else'.

THE ANTI-DISCRIMINATION PAY ACT 1974

We welcome the publication of Deirdre Curtin's *Irish Employment Equality Law* (Dublin 1989) which comprehensively surveys the application of the 1974 Act and the Employment Equality Act 1977.

In *ACOT v Doyle* [1990] ILRM 21, the claimants, female instructors, employed on a pay scale less than others, who were males, engaged in work which they asserted to be comparable, lodged a claim under the Anti-Discrimination (Pay) Act 1974. The employee with whom the claimants' work was compared had a university degree whereas they had diplomas. The Equality Officer found that there were genuine grounds other than sex for the difference in rates of pay. The Labour Court first held that the distinction was based not on qualifications but on the respective employment records of the two grades. Applying the considerations expressed by the Court of Justice in *Jenkins v Kingsgate (Clothing Productions) Ltd* [1981] ECR 911, it addressed the question whether the policy of paying different rates, although represented as a difference based on employment record, was or was not in reality based on the sex of the workers. It concluded on the evidence that it was. The court considered that the claimants were engaged in like work with those employed on the other grade. It rejected ACOT's argument that the duties of the other employees in relation to agriculture rather than farm house management and poultry-keeping should be considered different in view of the greater economic importance of agriculture and the fact that the two grades were not interchangeable.

ACOT appealed to the High Court under s.8(3) of the 1974 Act on several grounds. Carroll J rejected the argument that there must first be a finding of like work before there can be a finding of whether there are grounds other than sex to justify a different rate of remuneration. The court's finding that there were not grounds other than sex justifying the difference in pay would not have been different if the court had first dealt with the question of like work:

> Therefore, while it was a mistake of law to say in relation to the Equality Officer's investigation that the question of like work does not arise unless and until it is shown that there are not grounds other than sex to justify the difference, it was not a material mistake and there is no basis for setting aside the determination of the Labour Court on this ground.

While one may sympathise with Carroll J's approach, nevertheless an important basis of *principle* exists for ensuring that these questions are not addressed in the wrong order. Confusion of thought may flow from attempting to answer the question whether there were or were not grounds other than sex justifying the difference in pay between the work of a claimant and that of a comparator, without having already addressed, or being in the process of addressing, the question whether the work of the claimant was like work to that of the comparator. If the work was *not* like work, that *has* to be a ground other than sex justifying the difference in pay.

S.2(1) and (3) of the 1974 Act made it plain that the question of grounds other than sex can have relevance only where the case is one of like work. Even if the statute did not expressly so require, the logic of the question to be answered requires that the like work issue is anterior to that of grounds other than sex.

Carroll J went on to hold that the Labour Court would have been wrong to place the burden of proof on ACOT to disprove that like work existed, but that the Labour Court's adjudication, properly interpreted, had not done this. She upheld the test the Labour Court had applied in deciding whether there were grounds other than sex justifying the difference in pay. It had been entitled to have regard to such matters as the demise of diplomas in farm home management or poultry-keeping and the fact that when the requirement for horticultural instructors was raised to degree standard in the past the diploma-holders (all male) had been treated in the same way as degree-holders (all male). Another factor, Carroll J thought, was the policy of the State in paying women less than men for like work before the Accession Treaty. Whether this rationale can withstand the Supreme Court decision in *Aer Lingus Teo v Labour Court* [1990] ILRM 485, reversing Carroll J, may be debated.

Finally, on the question whether the Labour Court had been wrong in law in finding that the claimants were employed on like work with the comparator, Carroll J held that the Labour Court had not had any evidence before it in relation to the claimants and the comparator as to whether there were any differences between the work performed and the conditions under which it was performed so that it could make an appropriate finding of fact on this issue. She remitted the matter to the Labour Court to hear this evidence and make the necessary finding.

EEC LAW

Transfer of undertaking In *Mythen v Employment Appeals Tribunal, Buttercrust Ltd and Joseph Downes & Sons Ltd (in receivership)* [1989] ILRM 844; [1990] ELR 1, the 'very important and difficult' question of law arose as to the relationship between the EEC Directive on the safeguarding of employees' rights on the transfer of undertakings or businesses and the existing common law and statutory provisions for the protection of employees' rights. The Directive (77/187/EEC) was incorporated into Irish law by SI No 306 of 1980.

The applicant had been employed as a checker by the third defendant. The third defendant had gone into receivership and portion of its assets had been sold to the second defendant. His employment had been terminated on the ground of redundancy. He had received a lump sum in respect of this redundancy. He later sued for unfair dismissal before the Employment Appeals Tribunal. The Tribunal interpreted SI No. 306 of 1980 as having no relevance. The applicant took proceedings for judicial review, claiming that the implementation of the Directive had created new employment relationships which the Tribunal was obliged to consider. The central question facing Barrington J concerned the scope of the Directive. On one view, the Directive was not intended to apply to the liquidation of insolvent businesses; if it did apply, it would inhibit the effective realisation of assets, to the detriment of workers in the long term.

The issue had come before the Court of Justice in *Abels* [1985] 1 ECR 649. The argument in favour of the Directive's application to liquidations was essentially based on the concern that companies could engineer bogus liquidations to sidestep the Directive's goals; the Advocate General's rebuttal of this fear is surely satisfactory—that the Directive should not apply to transfers on liquidation and bankruptcy but should apply to transfers made after a court had granted leave to suspend payment under a *surseance van betaling* (broadly similar to the scheme effectuated by the Companies (Amendment) Act 1990).

The reason the Court of Justice considered that the Directive should apply in the latter case was that such a procedure was different from liquidation proceedings 'in so far as the supervision exercised by the court over the commencement and the course of such proceedings is more limited'.

The case which Barrington J had to decide was neither a a liquidation nor the equivalent to a *surseance van betaling* but rather that of receivership. It was true that s.4 of the Protection of Employees (Employers' Insolvency) Act 1984 deemed a company over which a receiver had been appointed on behalf of a debenture holder to be insolvent. Nonetheless, there had been cases in which a receiver had succeeded in turning the company around. More importantly, the appointment of a receiver by a debenture holder was an entirely extra-judicial process, capable of being employed far more easily than a liquidation to defeat the purposes of the Directive. It would therefore be wrong to assume that the Court of Justice would be obliged by its holding in *Abel* to exclude from the remit of the Directive sales by receivers appointed by debenture holders. Barrington J expressed the view that, if the litigation before him continued, it might be necessary to refer this very question to that Court.

Accordingly Barrington J held that the Tribunal had erred in refusing to entertain the applicant's claim. No question of estoppel arose in view of ss.13 and 19 of the Unfair Dismissals Act 1977: s.13 prescribes contracting out of the Act's provisions and s.19 requires an employee who has accepted compensation but is subsequently held entitled to re-instatement to repay the employer what he has received. Moreover, it seemed to Barrington J that the scheme of the Directive contemplated that an employee who had lost his job as a result of a transfer of a business might claim against either the transferor or transferee or both, and that he was not estopped from claiming relief against one because he had claimed relief against the other.

The possible effect of this decision is worth assessing. It may be that it will encourage more liquidations rather than resort to receivership, in order to realise the assets at their greatest value. It seems unfortunate that the fear of abuse should override the more wide-ranging policy objection to application of the Directive to the realisation of the assets of insolvent companies. Our law is well able to control the risk of abuse, through administrative and civil regulation, backed, if considered necessary, by stringent criminal sanctions.

Freedom of movement In *Groener v Minister for Education* [1990] ILRM 335, the question of the proper relationship between freedom of movement for workers and the policy of maintaining and supporting the use of the Irish language fell for consideration. The applicant, a Netherlands national, had fallen foul of the rule in a Ministerial circular requiring that, for certain lecturing posts under the Vocational Education Act 1930, appointees should either hold the Ceard Teastas Gaeilge or have passed a special oral examination in Irish. The position in question was that of lecturer in art at the College of Marketing and Design, Dublin. The circular also contained a provision under which exemption from the linguistic qualification requirement might be granted in a case where there was no fully qualified candidate.

Article 3(1) of Regulation (EEC) No. 1612/68 on freedom of movement provides in the second indent that national provisions or administrative practices of a member state are not to apply where, 'though applicable irrespective of nationality, their exclusive or principal aim or effect is to keep nationals of other member states away from the employment offered. However, the last subparagraph of this provision is not to apply to conditions relating to linguistic knowledge required by reason of the nature of the post to be filled'.

The applicant instituted proceedings for judicial review, maintaining that the linguistic requirement was contrary to Article 48 of Regulation 1612/68. Blayney J referred to the Court of Justice a number of questions under Article 177, the second of which enquired whether, in considering the phrase 'the nature of the post to be filled' in Article 3(1), regard should be had to the policy of the Irish State that persons holding the post should have a competent knowledge of the Irish language, where such language is not required to discharge the duties attached to the post.

Documents before the Court of Justice indicated that the teaching of art, like most other subjects in vocational educational schools, is conducted essentially or exclusively in the English language. It followed, the Court thought, that knowledge of the Irish language was not required for the performance of the duties which teaching of the kind at issue specifically entailed. However, that finding was not sufficient to enable the national court to decide whether the linguistic requirement in question was justified 'by reason of the nature of the post to be fulfilled'. It was necessary to take into account whether the special linguistic requirement in question was justified 'by reason of the nature of the post to be fulfilled'.

The Court had to have regard to the special linguistic situation in Ireland, where, under Article 8.1 of the Constitution, Irish was the first official language, and where the policy followed by successive governments had been designed not merely to maintain but also to promote the use of Irish as a means of expressing national identity and culture. It was for this reason that Irish courses were compulsory for children receiving primary education and optional for those receiving secondary education. The requirement of knowledge of Irish for lecturers in vocational educational schools was one of the measures the government had adopted in furtherance of that policy.

It is useful to quote *in extenso* the crucial passage of the court's answer to the second question:

> The EEC Treaty does not prohibit the adoption of a policy for the protection and promotion of a language of a member state which is both the national language and the first official language. However, the implementation of such a policy must not encroach upon a fundamental freedom such as that of the free movement of workers. Therefore, the requirements deriving from measures intended to implement such a policy must not in any circumstances be disproportionate in relation to the aim pursued and the manner in which they are applied must not bring about discrimination against nationals of other member states.
>
> The importance of education for the implementation of such a policy must be recognized. Teachers have an essential role to play, not only through the teaching which they provide but also by their participation in the daily life of the school and the privileged relationship which they have with their pupils. In those circumstances, it is not unreasonable to require them to have some knowledge of the first national language.
>
> It follows that the requirement imposed on teachers to have an adequate knowledge of such a language must, provided that the level of knowledge required is not disproportionate in relation to the objective pursued, be regarded as a condition corresponding to the knowledge required by reason of the nature of the post to be filled within the meaning of the last paragraph of Article 3(1) of Regulation No. 1612/68.
>
> It must be pointed out that, where the national provisions provide for the possibility of exemption from that linguistic requirement where no other fully qualified candidate has applied for the post to be filled, Community law requires that power to grant exemptions be exercised by the Minister in non-discriminatory manner.
>
> Moreover, the principle of non-discrimination precludes the imposition of any requirement that the linguistic knowledge in question must

have been acquired within the national territory. It also implies that the nationals of other member states should have an opportunity to re-take the oral examination, in the event of their having previously failed it, when they again apply for a post of assistant lecturer or lecturer.

Accordingly, the reply to the second question must be that a permanent full-time post of lecturer in public vocational education institutions is a post of such a nature as to justify the requirement of linguistic knowledge, within the meaning of the last sub-paragraph of Article 3(1) of Regulation No. 1612/68 of the Council, provided that the linguistic requirement in question is imposed as part of a policy for the promotion of the national language which is, at the same time, the first official language and provided that that requirement is applied in a proportionate and non-discriminatory manner.

This answer provokes a number of comments. First, it seems that the Court has given the amber rather than the green light to requirements of competence in the Irish language for employees. The policy of maintenance and promotion of Irish is sufficient to bring within the scope of the last sub-paragraph of Article 3(1) Irish language requirements for posts with no distinctive element of Irish in their course conduct, subject to their being applied in a proportionate and non-discriminatory manner. This was vital for the Irish language; if the last sub-paragraph is not applicable, we are left with the second indent of Article 3(1), which might well mean that an Irish language requirement for educational positions would be contrary to that provision since its principal effect might be considered to be to keep nationals of other member states away from the employment offered.

The answer given by the court leaves entirely unresolved the important issue of what constitutes a *proportionate* and *non-discriminatory* manner of application. As to proportionality, it remains to be seen how the policy of protection and promotion of a language of a member state, constitutionally prescribed as the first official language, is to be balanced against the free movement of workers. The result of a 'proportionality' test might well be the reduction in the scope and effectiveness of the present policy of maintenance and promotion of Irish. The court's answer thus far is somewhat delphic, but one may wonder how the present policy would not collapse completely if its implementation 'must not *encroach upon* a fundamental freedom such as that of the free movement of workers' (emphasis added).

As to the court's insistence that the requirement of linguistic knowledge be applied in a *non-discriminatory* manner, it must be observed that the requirement of knowledge of a language such as Irish almost inevitably discriminates, if by discrimination is meant simply that non-nationals are, by and large, almost certain to have no knowledge of it, in contrast to English,

French, German or Spanish, for example. It is doubtful if that is what is meant. More likely to fall within the notion of discrimination are distinct rules which, apart from the unavoidably restrictive nature of an Irish language requirement, purport to limit the entitlement of non-nationals. The court itself noted that the principle of non-discrimination precludes the imposition of a requirement that the language have been learned within the national territory; moreover it must be sensitive enough to the possible difficulties in learning the language to provide an opportunity to an applicant to re-take the oral examination, if previously failed, when applying again for a post. (It seems that this opportunity may be required, not merely for a second application, but for all subsequent applications.) A question of equality arises in relation to the goal of protecting the languages of different member states. If the court were to accept the argument that, because Irish was less widely known than English, for example, an Irish language requirement is discriminatory where an English language requirement is not, this would treat Irish as a language of less than equal status to English.

Once one moves outside the context of employment in schools, the question of the extent to which the policy of maintenance and promotion of Irish may involve a language requirement for a post becomes more difficult to resolve. It is worth noting that the court placed special emphasis on the importance of primary and secondary education for the implementation of this policy, with teachers having 'an essential role to play' in its regard. The emphasis suggests that the court would not look with similar indulgence on a language requirement for other posts. Even university lecturers would seem to be in a less central position, according to the court's criteria.

Finally, it is worth considering how the present policy of maintaining and promoting Irish might be reconstituted in the light of this case. It seems clear that education *carried out* in the Irish language does not present significant difficulties as regards recruitment, for far as free movement considerations are concerned. If educational policy, instead of requiring a linguistic capacity of teachers which is seldom if ever called on, were to concentrate on how that capacity could best be exercised in practice, the results might be of interest.

CONTRACTS WITH MEDICAL PRACTITIONERS

In *Grehan v North Eastern Health Board* [1989] IR 422, Costello J had to decide what on its face was a simple contractual issue. The plaintiff was a medical practitioner who had entered into a contract of services with the Health Board. This contract contained very detailed terms and conditions, including six paragraphs relating to its termination. These allowed the *plaintiff* to terminate at any time on three months' notice; there would be *automatic* termination if the plaintiff's name was erased from the register, or if she accepted wholetime employment in a specified public post; and the *Health Board* might terminate the agreement on the recommendation of a specified committee or if the plaintiff were to suffer from a permanent incapacity. Finally, the agreement provided that it should terminate on the medical practitioner's reaching the age of seventy years.

The Health Board, having negotiated with the Irish Medical Organisation new terms and conditions on which registered medical practitioners would provide their services, sought to have the plaintiff accept these new terms. The plaintiff, who had never been a member of the Irish Medical Organisation, instituted legal proceedings seeking a declaration that her contract with the Health Board could not be terminated without her consent. The Health Board countered with a claim for a declaration that it could terminate her agreement on reasonable notice.

Costello J had no difficulty in applying the *Moorcock* test to yield a result in favour of the plaintiff. If the contract was one for an *indefinite* period a term might be implied for its termination by reasonable notice. But that was not the position here:

> Looking at the contract which the parties entered into in this case it would, it seems to me, be an abuse of language to say that it amounted to a general hiring of the plaintiff's services for an indefinite period for [it] quite explicitly states that the agreement was to terminate when the plaintiff reached the age of seventy (unless, of course, it had not been previously terminated under one or other of the earlier provisions). Furthermore it will be noted that the provisions relating to termination are very detailed and their comprehensive nature would strongly suggest that an implication of a further term relating to the parties' rights of termination would not be justified.

Costello J went on to address the industrial relations background to the making of the original contract between the parties. The terms of that contract represented the fruits of negotiation between the Minister for Health and the employee representatives in 1972. It was thus open to a party to ask the Court to consider the circumstances surrounding these terms and conditions to see whether a term should be implied in them by reference to these circumstances. In the absence of evidence as to these negotiations, it was 'a matter of elementary common sense' to assume that the final agreed terms had been carefully scrutinised by both sides; the failure to infer a right of termination on the Health Board equivalent to that given to the employee indicated that the negotiating bodies had deliberately decided that the contract would not grant such a right. This inference was strengthened by the fact that these bodies were aware that the contract whose terms they were negotiating was to be offered to medical practitioners participating in existing medical schemes operated by the Health Boards in which they held permanent and pensionable posts; it was probable that it had not been intended to confer an unfettered power to terminate the new contracts by reasonable notice at the discretion of the Health Boards. Moreover, while the *new* contract contained a provision that it was to terminate when the doctor reached the prescribed age, it also permitted alteration in its terms in accordance with the outcome of future reviews of the Minister and the Irish Medical Organisation.

It was, of course, the omission of such a clause which led to this litigation. The effect of this was to allow any doctor to 'hold tight' with the original contract, save to the extent that he or she might be considered to have authorised the Irish Medical Organisation to vary the contract on his or her behalf — a dimension lacking in this case.

FITNESS TO PRACTICE

In *Kerrigan v An Bord Altranais*, High Court, 20 December 1989, the question of the High Court's role under Part V of the Nurses Act 1985 fell for consideration. The Part contains procedures for the holding of an inquiry into an allegation that a nurse is guilty of professional misconduct or is unfit to engage in practice as a nurse. S.28(3) provides that, the inquiry having been held, the Fitness to Practice Committee then expresses an opinion. Under s.39 the Board then decides whether or not the person's name should be erased from the register; the person concerned may apply to the High Court for cancellation of the Board's decision. If no such application is made, the Board may apply *ex parte* to the court for confirmation of the decision, which the court will make unless there is good reason to the contrary.

Costello J considered that the scheme of the Act did not give a complete right of re-hearing to the High Court. The Court should consider the evidence which was before the Fitness to Practice Committee and which was considered by the Board. It should then scrutinise the procedures which these two bodies had adopted. He derived support for his view that the Oireachtas had not intended to give a right of re-hearing from the fact that 'the committee who inquire into these professional matters are well qualified to ascertain whether or not professional misconduct has occurred.'

The applicant was dissatisfied with the decision of the Fitness to Practice Committee and of the Board. Costello J was of the view that the Court 'would consider what arguments and submissions were made in that regard, bearing in mind what documents are adduced before it and the hearing, and would not hear again the allegations which were gone into by Fitness to Practice Committee'. On this view, there was no need for an oral hearing, and the affidavit evidence and the exhibits included in that evidence could be considered by the Court.

Costello J distinguished *In re M, a Doctor* [1984] IR 479, where an inquiry machinery under the Medical Practitioners Act 1978, similar to that under the Nurses Act 1985, had fallen for consideration. There, the doctor had been given no opportunity to be heard before the Council which decided that his name should be erased from the register. In the instant case, the applicant had been represented by counsel before the Fitness to Practice Committee and had had an opportunity to be heard and represented before the Board.

Costello J in his judgment expressed the view that the statutory procedures set out in the 1985 Act regarding recourse to the High Court were 'perfectly constitutional'.

The Supreme Court reversed Costello J. Finlay CJ, delivering the judgment of the Court, saw no reason to depart from his analysis in *In re M*, which had concerned a statutory disciplinary machinery indistinguishable from that in the instant case. In many instances, the issues arising on appeal from disciplinary procedures were not ones of fact but rather 'of propriety, professional conduct, professional standards and the consequences of undisputed facts'. In a small number of instances, however, of which the instant case was one, the issue was of direct fact. The Chief Justice considered that the necessity for vesting in the High Court the function of determining the issue itself arose from 'the constitutional frailty that would attach to the delegation of any such power to a body which was not a court established under the Constitution, having regard to the decision of the former Supreme Court in *Re the Solicitors Act 1954* [1960] IR 239'. For the court to be on effective decision-making tribunal, it was essential that it should make the vital decisions; this would be done only by hearing the witnesses. Were the matter to be tried on affidavit, the High Court would merely be endorsing the procedures of the Fitness to Practice Committee and, of necessity, accepting its finding of the facts.

Land Law

CONVEYANCING

At the beginning of our discussion of aspects of conveyancing, we may give a warm welcome to the publication of Brendan Fitzgerald's *Land Registry Practice* in 1989. The book contains a wealth of detail on the subject, reflecting the author's long experience and wide-ranging knowledge.

Injury to property The problem of the boundaries of liability for the malicious acts of third parties is one that has increasingly confronted the courts in actions for negligence: see e.g. *Smith v Littlewoods Organisation Ltd* [1987] AC 241; *P Perl Exporters Ltd v Camden London BC* [1984] 1 QB 342. In *Bradley v Donegal County Council*, High Court, 14 November 1989, the issue arose in a conveyancing context. The plaintiff had agreed to sell an old church hall to the defendant, clause 26 of the Incorporated Law Society of Ireland's General Conditions of Sale (1978 ed.) prescribing that the property was to be at the sole risk of the purchaser as to any damage howsoever arising after the date of sale, with no claim to be made against the vendor for any deterioration or damage unless occasioned by the vendor's wilful neglect or default. While the copy agreement signed by the vendor was on its way to the purchaser's solicitors, a fire was caused by some youths who broke into the hall and set fire to some of the two hundred and seventy packets of firelighters which were there, along with two hundred cases of disposable nappies.

The defendant resisted specific performance on the grounds that the premises had been inadequately secured against break-ins, and that the vendor was negligent in having introduced onto the premises this large consignment of highly combustible materials without informing the purchaser, at a time when the purchaser was not aware that the vendor had completed the agreement for sale.

O'Hanlon J rejected both contentions on the evidence. The vendor had gone to considerable lengths to padlock the premises and board up the windows. The purchaser must have been aware that large quantities of highly combustible materials were stored in the hall, and, throughout extended negotiations, had made no issue of this practice. The premises were quite suitable for this function, having regard to the facts that the danger of accidental fire was negligible and that such comprehensive steps had been taken to prevent wrongdoers from gaining access and causing damage. The location of the property—in the middle of Buncrana—was some additional guarantee of its safety; the crime rate in the area and the incidence of vandalism in the town were low. Moreover the vendor's supermarket premises were very near the hall, and he and his staff passed it regularly. Clearly the case involves the application of the standard criteria for determining negligence: the *probability* of injury, the *gravity* of the threatened injury, the *social utility* of the defendant's action and the cost of *prevention*: see McMahon & Binchy, *Irish Law of Torts*, 110-19, *Purtill v Athlone UDC* [1968] IR 205, at 212-13; *Callaghan v Killarney Race Co*. [1958] IR 366, at 375.

Thus the present case should be read very much in the context of its particular facts, and would afford no easy defence to the vendor of premises in an urban area where vandalism is a common occurrence.

The Law Reform Commission's Report on Land Law and Conveyancing Law: (1) General proposals (LRC) 30-1989)   On 6 March 1987, the then Attorney General, Mr John Rogers, SC, requested the Law Reform Commission to formulate proposals for the reform of conveyancing law and practice 'in areas where this could lead to savings for house purchasers'. The Commission's first report on this subject was published in June 1989. The Report is helpfully analysed by Gerard Hogan, 11 *DULJ* 238 (1989) and by Patrick McCarthy, *Irish Times*, 2 August 1989.

The Commission had set up a Working Group with Mr John Buckley, Commissioner, acting as Convener. Its members were Miss Justice Carroll (until her appointment as a judge of the Court of the ILO in November 1988), Professor J.C. Brady, Mr George Brady, SC, Ms Mary Laffoy, SC, Mr Ernest B. Farrell, solicitor, and Mr Rory McEntee, solicitor. The Working Group took the view that it would be difficult in practice to separate areas of land law and conveyancing law relating to house purchase from those relating to the transfer of other types of property or interests in property. Accordingly some of its suggestions were of more general effect. The question whether the Report's recommendations *could lead to savings for house purchasers* is not addressed by the Commission. Save in one particular respect, mentioned below, the Report makes no suggestion that implementation of its recommendations would, or should, lead to a reduction in conveyancing tariffs. Possibly it could be argued that simplification of conveyancing (as the Report proposes) must inevitably make the process easier and thus cheaper.

The Report's recommendations are grouped under four headings: (1) removal or modification of archaic doctrines and the simplifying of conveyancing generally; (2) rectification of anomalies arising from modern legislation; (3) amendments to the Statutes of Limitations; and (4) amendments to landlord and tenant law.

1 Removal or modification of archaic doctrines and the simplifying of conveyancing generally

1(i) Reduction of statutory period of title   First the Report recommends that the statutory period of title which must be shown under s.1 of the Vendor and Purchaser Act 1874 be reduced from forty to twenty years. This is based on the perception that the difficulties which presented themselves in nineteenth-century conveyancing have largely disappeared. In England, the period was reduced to thirty years in 1925 and to fifteen years in 1969. Moreover the Survey of the Land Law of Northern Ireland has recommended fifteen years as the appropriate period there.

1(ii) Partial merger of leasehold interests in the reversion   The Commission next recommend that legislation remove doubts as to whether the acquisition by a lessee of the fee simple affects merger of all the various levels of interest in the land. The proposed statutory provision would confirm that, where a person entitled to a leasehold interest in portion only of property held under that lease acquires any superior interest in that property, he should be entitled, if he so desires, to merge the leasehold in the next or all superior interests held by him. This merger would not in any way derogate from the rights of the lessor in respect of any land that might still be subject to the lease.

1(iii) Retention of fee tail estate   The Commission had originally intended to recommend the abolition of the fee tail estate, but ultimately decided to spare it (for the delight of a future generation of law students), on the basis that it 'is not causing harm' and, though rarely used, might prove suitable for some people from time to time. However, the Commission recommend that the sanction of the base fee for failure to enrol a disentailing assurance in the Central Office within six calendar months of its execution should be abolished as being excessive. Instead there should be a requirement that the disentailing deed be registered in either the Registry of Deeds or Land Registry, as appropriate. (Mr Hogan, in a generally sympathetic review of the Report, inveighs against the Commission's failure to recommend the end of the line for the fee tail: 11 *DULJ*, at 239.)

1(iv) Partition of land   Against a background of judicial disagreement as to whether the High Court's power to partition property held by joint tenants or tenants in common survived the repeal of the Act for Joint Tenants of 1542 by the Statute Law Revision (Pre-Union Irish Statutes) Act 1962, the Report recommends that the proposed legislation clarify the matter by restoring the statutory power of partition in express terms. The Report also recommends that the court should have power 'to order a sale of the property in lieu of partition'. This proposal derives from the suggestion made to the Commission (from a source not identified in the Report) that the restoration of the power of partition would not 'of itself solve all the difficulties that present themselves, particularly in the case of matrimonial property, and that the court should also be given the power to order a sale of the property as an alternative to partition'.

1(v) The rule against perpetuities as it affects easements, etc.   Rather than engage in a comprehensive analysis of the rule against perpetuities, the Commission make the narrow recommendation that easements, options, *profits à prendre* and rent charges over land should be removed from the effects of the rule. They mention the difficulty arising on the sale of portion of land to a builder where the landowner wishes to reserve a right of way over roads in the housing estate which are yet to be built: at present a reservation is usually made over such roads as may be built in the next twenty one years. Failure to include such a reference results in the reservation of the right of way being void.

The Commission propose that the change they recommend should be retrospective in its operation. It may be doubted whether this is desirable in terms of social policy; indeed it might well raise constitutional difficulties. It is not clear why the incompetence of lawyers over the years should be the basis of removing a property right from innocent persons.

1(vi) Statutory definitions of certain words in documents connected with interests in land   The Commission propose that certain definitions contained in Part III of the Interpretation Act 1937 should be prescribed for use in documents relating to interests in land. Thus, for example, every word importing the singular is to be construed as if it also imported the plural, and *vice versa*: and every word importing the masculine gender is to be construed as if it also imported the feminine gender. The Commission are of the view that it would be in ease of all parties and might lead to the shortening of some documents if terms such as these could be thus defined.

1(vii) Judgment mortgages   In the wake of the judicial disagreement in *Tempany v Hynes* [1976] IR 101 as to the respective interests of vendor and purchaser between the making of the contract for sale and completion, the Commission recommend that Henchy J's view, rather than that of Kenny J, should prevail, so that, for the purpose of judgment mortgages, the beneficial ownership is treated as having passed to the purchaser from the time the contract was made, subject to the condition subsequent that he complete the sale.

1(vii) Severance of joint tenancies   Hesitating before taking the bold step of recommending the abolition of the Statute of Uses 1535, the Commission recommend that freehold land should be capable of being severed and converted into a tenancy in common by a simple deed between the parties in the same way as a leasehold estate may be severed.

1(ix) Abolition of the rule in Bain v Fothergill   The Commission follow the international trend in recommending the abolition of the rule in *Bain v Fothergill* (1874) LR 7 HL 158. They argue that its underlying rationale has been rendered obsolete by the progressive reductions in the statutory period of title. They reject the argument that the rule should be retained because it protects solicitors by limiting the amount of damages which their clients may recover against them:

> Since . . . a vendor's solicitor is under a duty to investigate or at least to check carefully the title which a vendor is offering in any contract for sale prepared by such solicitor it is difficult to see why the protection of the solicitor should be a valid argument for the retention of the rule.

1(x) Restrictions on convicts disposing of land   Under s.8 of the Forfeiture Act 1870, a convict may not make any disposition of property while in prison. The Commission recommend the repeal of this section. They are understandably of the view that it 'must be very doubtful' whether it is consistent with the Constitution.

Bearing in mind, however, their work on the subject of the forfeiture of the proceeds of crime, on which a report will be issued in due course, the Commission make their proposal to abolish s.8 subject to the possible introduction of a provision conferring a right on a court in particular circumstances to impose a restriction on disposal of individual properties.

2 'Rectification of anomalies'

In a chapter entitled 'Rectification of Anomalies Arising from Modern Legislation', the Commission make a number of uncontroversial proposals, as well as others which, whatever their merits may be, are clearly not mere rectification of anomalies but instead involve radical changes in the law calling for close scrutiny.

2(i) Uncontroversial proposals   Let us dispose of the uncontroversial proposals briefly. The Commission recommend that s.27 of the Local Government (Planning and Development) Act 1976 be amended, first by extending the provisions of s.27(1)(a) to cover development which has been completed without the necessary planning permission and secondly to include in the section a five year limit on the bringing of applications, whether in respect of developments or unauthorised uses. The latter proposal should simplify requisitions on title with no great social cost. The Commission also recommend that s.45 of the Land Act 1965 be amended so that it does not prevent the vesting of an interest in any land which is neither agricultural nor pastoral or is less than two hectares in area and the instrument effecting the vesting contains a certificate to that effect. The rapid extension of urban development into areas formerly agricultural inspires this proposal.

Thirdly the Commission recommend amendments to the Registration of Title Act 1964, to avoid the necessity to register certain titles which at the moment are required to be registered by virtue of s.23, in conjunction with the definition of 'land' in s.3, which includes incorporeal hereditaments and thus rent charges. The Commission note that some titles which involve rent charges or fee farm grants have not in fact been registered because the broad scope of the provisions of the 1964 Act has been overlooked from time to time; where the point has arisen, the effect has been to delay the completion of transactions. Accordingly the Commission recommend that the broad definition of 'land' in s.3 should not apply to s.23 and that this change should, in effect, work retrospectively.

2(ii) Controversial matters (a) Limitation period for s.117 applications
We now turn to the more controversial matters. The first is perhaps not a matter of great debate; however, aspects of the Commission's analysis may provoke discussion. S.117(6) of the Succession Act 1965 requires a child to make an application under the section within a year from the first taking out of representation to the deceased's estate. No extension of time is permitted: *MPD v MD* [1981] ILRM 179. Clearly this rule can work harshly, and may raise constitutional issues—a matter we touch on below. The real question is how reform of the law may best be accomplished—by a specific extension of the period within which an application may be brought, or by giving the court a discretion to extend the present period within which applications may be made? The Commission favour the latter approach, coupled with protection for the personal representatives from any liability for having distributed the estate beforehand.

The Commission recommend against imposing on the personal representatives *any* duty to notify the children of their right to apply. They consider that to do so 'could place an unfair burden on personal representatives in that it could require them to make enquiries of the known next-of-kin as to the possible existence of others'. This is not convincing. Translated into more direct language, the argument is that *no* child should be notified of his or her right to apply under s.117, however clearly the personal representative may be aware of the injustice that will result. One possible rationale for this approach is that a notification requirement might embarrass the known survivors of a deceased person to enquire of them whether they are aware of any children of the deceased born outside marriage. Apart from the fact that personal representatives often ask precisely this question under the Status of Children Act 1987 (cf. the 1987 Review, 183-4), the idea that such a slight consideration could outweigh the opposing claims of justice seems unlikely to commend itself to the courts.

The journey by which the Commission arrive at their conclusions is also worthy of comment. They note that there is 'a distinct possibility' that s.117 would not withstand a constitutional challenge. They invoke *O'Brien v Keogh* [1972] IR 144 in support of their statement that '[s]ince the right of a child to apply under s.117 is undoubtedly a property right, it is difficult to see how the imposition of a one year time limit in the case of an infant child can be other than an unjust attack on that right'. The difficulty with this line of argument is that the Supreme Court appears to have repudiated it in *Moynihan v Greensmyth* [1977] IR 55, when it rejected a constitutional challenge to the two-year *post mortem* limitation period for survival of actions against a deceased person, under s.9 of the Civil Liability Act 1961. The plaintiff, a child, also thought that *O'Brien v Keogh* would carry the day, only to receive the following reply from O'Higgins CJ, delivering the judgment of the Court:

> Bearing in mind the State's duty to others—in particular those who represent the estate of the deceased, and beneficiaries—some reasonable limitation on actions against the estate was obviously required. If the period of infancy were to form part of the period of limitation, as was formerly the case, then the danger of stale claims being brought would be very real and could constitute a serious threat to the rights of beneficiaries of the estate of a deceased. The alternative was to apply a period of limitation which would have general application. It had to be either one or the other; and it does not appear that any compromise was possible.

Now it may be that the Chief Justice's analysis is not beyond criticism: after all, a discretionary extension (albeit no panacea) would be an alternative to the dilemma he perceived. It may also be that *Moynihan v Greensmyth* can be distinguished from the position under s.117(6), where *inevitably* the applicant will be the child of the defendant and in many cases will be an infant. We need not here address these considerations. All that may be noted is that the Commission relegate *Moynihan v Greensmyth* to a footnote where it is cited, not on the relevance of *O'Brien v Keogh* to *post mortem* limitation periods, but on the somewhat esoteric issue, irrelevant to the present context, of the relationship between Article 40.3 and Article 43.

It would be mistaken to think that the only, or indeed primary, attack on the constitutional validity of s.117(6) is one based on the disability of the claimant. Costello J's decision in *Brady v Donegal County Council* [1989] ILRM 282, albeit set aside on appeal [1989] ILRM 282 (see the 1987 Review, 243-6, and the 1988 Review, 125-6), suggests that other grounds may be available. Whether it would be wise to imagine that the Supreme Court is straining at the leash to strike down limitation periods in general may perhaps be debated. *Hegarty v O'Loughran and Edwards* [1990] ILRM 403 indicates otherwise; but the question of protecting doctors from a potentially endless risk of liability is far removed from the policy issues that arise in relation to s.117(6).

(b) Extending s.117 model to intestacies   The Commission go on to propose that s.117 be extended to include applications on an intestacy. They consider that the present position may give rise to injustice:

> For example, a farmer or business person dies intestate (perhaps having deliberately refrained from making a will), predeceased by his or her spouse, and all the children are entitled to an equal share in the estate. One of the children has stayed at home working and looking after the intestate in expectation of a promised inheritance, while the rest of the children have not. At present, such a child would be unable to bring an application [under s.117] on the grounds that the intestate has 'failed in his or her moral duty'.

They go on to argue that the policy underlying the relevant provisions of the 1965 Act 'is that persons with the means to do so should make proper provision for their dependants. Justice and logic both require that this policy should apply whether the person concerned dies testate or intestate. It is difficult to justify a situation in which the child of a testate parent who has been unjustly treated has the means of redress while the child of an intestate parent has none'.

Whether this analysis fully captures the differences between testate and intestate succession may be debated. A will may distribute property arbitrarily or unjustly; intestate succession is based on the principle of equality among children. A will may give the surviving spouse and children little or nothing; intestate succession requires the entire estate to be distributed among them. The specific problem of unfulfilled promises identified by the Commission can be dealt with under existing equitable, contractual and tortious principles, fortified, if needs be, by a specific statutory remedy.

(c) Reducing the protection under the Family Home Protection Act 1976 to five years   The Family Home Protection Act 1976 is undoubtedly a thorn

in the flesh of conveyancers. It requires a good deal of work and the application of some sensitivity and commonsense to the particular facts of the case. Gone are the days when requisitions on title consisted in substantial part of the incantation of set formulae. The 1976 Act is about human realities, with conveyancers playing a vital role in executing the important social policy underlying the Act. They may grumble, but, as the experience in England makes abundantly plain, if they do not do this work, no other system will adequately protect the dependent spouse and children.

The Commission recommend that, where there has been a conveyance of a family home which has been implemented without any objection from the spouse for over six years, the conveyance should no longer be deemed void and that evidence of any consent by the spouse or supporting evidence for any such consent should no longer be required. 'Conveyance' here would embrace only the conveyance of the fee simple estate and assignment or surrender of a leasehold estate or tenancy. The conveyance would be deemed always to have been valid once the six years had elapsed.

The idea behind the Commission's recommendations appears largely to be one of making the lives of conveyancers easier and more productive:

> At present, a great deal of a conveyancer's time is spent obtaining and checking spouses' consents. Our recommendation would simplify the conveyancing process and would therefore reduce the cost for the individual.

This recommendation is puzzling in a number of respects. it seems to be based in substantial part on a degree of doctrinal incomprehension at the notion of a retrospective validation of a void conveyance: while recognising its possibility, the Commission state that it 'is completely foreign to the basic doctrines of the law of property in Ireland under which estates in land must always be vested in some person'. Yet the effect of their own recommendation would be to create an even more complex suspension. Under the 1976 Act, a purported conveyance of any interest in the family home without the prior consent of the non- owning spouse is void, save where the prior dispensation of the court is obtained. Under the regime envisaged by the Commission, a conveyance (defined in the narrow manner proposed by the Commission) *will continue to be void* for the period of six years and then be retrospectively kissed back into life, if it has been implemented 'without any objection' from the non-owning spouse. What is the fate of transactions which occur during this six-year period? If, for example, the 'owner' spouse purports to mortgage the family home in the meantime with the consent of the non-owner spouse, is this transaction retrospectively to be rendered void because of the previous illegal transaction whereby the home was 'sold' by way of void conveyance of the fee simple estate? A proposal that the mortgagee's rights are to be wiped out because of the previous illegality would seem to be of doubtful constitutionality. And what of the case where the non-owner spouse is privy to the illegality? And, more fundamentally from the standpoint of justice, why should a secret vindictive disposition of the family home by one spouse leave the other spouse and the dependent children without a roof over their heads by reason only of the passage of a period of time during which the other spouse could not have discovered the fraud?

3 Limitation periods

3(i) Adverse possession   The present law on adverse possession is in a state of some confusion. The precise effect of the owner's long term intentions as to the use of his property on the capacity of another to acquire possession adverse to the owner is far from clear: see, e.g., *Durack Manufacturing v Considine*, High Court, 27 May 1987, and *Dundalk UDC v Conway*, analysed in the 1987 Review, 231-4. The Commission recommend that the legislation should clarify the law so that the court should not regard the intention of the owner as a decisive factor when considering whether or not he has been dispossessed. Adverse possession should be defined as possession inconsistent with the *title* of the true owner rather that inconsistent with the *intention* of the true owner.

3(ii) Tenancies from year to year   The Commission recommend that the distinction between periodic tenancies in writing and those created orally, contained in s.17(2) of the Statute of Limitations 1957 should be abolished.

4 Landlord and tenant   The Commission recommend that the legislation provide that the benefit of a guarantor's covenant should pass with the transfer of a lessor's interest. This is in line with recent English judicial developments.

Among their other proposals the Commission recommend that s.28 of the Landlord and Tenant (Ground Rents) Act 1978 be amended to limit its operation so that it does not affect covenants which have been entered into with third parties. This proposal is inspired by the fear that s.28 may be too widely drafted to withstand constitutional scrutiny, since 'covenants entered into by a person with another to protect the amenities of that other person's land should not be capable of being abolished without that other person's consent'.

As regards contracting out of the provisions of the Landlord and Tenant (Amendment) Act 1980, prohibited by s.85, the Commission recommend that this should be allowed, so far as it applies to business tenancies, provided that both parties have received independent legal advice. They reject the English solution of judicial authorisation for the exclusion of similar legislation as being pointless, once the parties are in agreement. Of course the strength of this reasoning weakens to the extent that the court actively investigates the possibility of oppression or injustice. It may well be that the balance of convenience lies against involving the court in this process, since the prospects of its uncovering either of these elements must be rated low. It is perhaps worth recalling that in *Bank of Ireland v Fitzmaurice* [1989] ILRM 452, Lardner J's broad interpretation of s.85 of the 1980 Act evinced a judicial concern lest the social policy underlying that provision be subverted by the ingenuity of conveyancers. We analysed *Fitzmaurice* in the 1988 Review, 271-2.

The Commission recommend that if, under s.23 of the Landlord and Tenant (Amendment) Act 1980, the term of a new lease has to be fixed by the court, it should be such a period being not more than thirty-five years and not less than five years as the court should determine. The idea here apparently is to prevent a tenant bringing frequent applications to the court, where the renewal is (as s.23 now permits) for a period of less than five years.

Finally the Commission recommend that the Landlord and Tenant (Ground Rents) Act 1967 be amended by the addition of a provision requiring appeals from the award of a County Registrar to be brought within twenty-one days of the publication of the award to the parties. At present there is *no* time limit: *Tassel Ltd v Kauai Investment Co. Ltd*, High Court, O'Hanlon J, 26 October 1988.

ADMINISTRATION OF ESTATES

In *Bank of Ireland v King*, High Court, 5 December 1989, Costello J had to deal with a case of an unwilling administratrix. The bank had obtained a judgment against the administratrix of a debt she personally owed. The bank had gone on to register a judgment mortgage against her interest in her late husband's lands. As administratrix she had taken no steps to vest her interest in herself.

The bank issued proceedings claiming an order requiring her assent to the vesting, or, alternatively, a limited order for the administration of the estate. Costello J refused the first and granted the second order. He did not consider that a judgment mortgage of lands to which a judgment mortgage is entitled on an intestacy was the 'person entitled', for the purposes of s.52(4) of the Succession Act 1965. However, he considered that a grant limited to a particular purpose, under s.27(4) and (5), could adequately deal with the case. Costello J noted that a question would arise as to whether the assent to the vesting in the judgment mortgage of the share should be subject to a fee from or subject to a charge for the payment of moneys which the personal representative of the deceased might be liable to pay under s.52(2). He therefore ordered that the new limited administrator should advertise for creditors in a local newspaper and that, if no creditors gave notice of a claim, the land was to be vested free from the claims of any creditors or otherwise. If, however, claims were made, then the matter should be relisted to consider whether the limited administration should be widened.

SUCCESSION

At the introduction to our discussion of developments in relation to succession, we must enthusiastically welcome the publication in 1989 of Professor James C. Brady's *Succession Law in Ireland*. It analyses the law with Professor Brady's customary clarity of thought and expression and is a very helpful addition to the practitioner's library.

Interpretation of wills The question of the interpretation of wills arose in two decisions in 1989. In *In re Curtin Deceased; Curtin v O'Mahoney*, High Court, 20 December 1989, Lardner J faithfully applied the Supreme Court decision of *Rowe v Law* [1978] IR 55. The testator had made a will in which he left his dwelling house to a named person absolutely and, in the event of her being deceased, to her husband absolutely. The will went on to state that, '[i]n the event of I [*sic*] selling the dwelling house . . .', the estate both real and personal was to be divided in percentage shares among several legacies. These included legacies for masses, the provision of a headstone to commemorate his wife and himself, and several other charitable legacies. As matters transpired the testator had not sold his house at the time of his death.

Lardner J, predictably, held that the provision in the will, and the provisions relating to the legacies, were perfectly clear, unambiguous, and not contradictory. The failure of the testator to dispose of more than his house meant that the residue should be distributed in accordance with the statutory intestacy rules.

Lardner J accepted the Attorney General's contention that it had not been a sensible thing for the testator to have made the legacies, especially those relating to masses and the headstone, contingent on his having sold the home. Nevertheless, the case was not one in which the admission of extrinsic evidence would be proper, since there was no legitimate dispute as to the meaning and effect of the language used. He considered that the will seemed to have been 'badly thought out and ill-constructed'. It was possible that this was due to the incompetence of the solicitor responsible for drafting it; but it was also possible that it did accord with the testator's instructions, however lacking in good sense.

In *In re Egan Deceased; Dillon v Dillon and A.G.*, High Court, 16 June 1989, an elderly testator, shortly before his death in 1985, made his last will, which contained the following clause:

> I direct my executors to sell all my estate both real and personal not hereinbefore specifically bequeathed and, after payment of all the aforesaid legacies, my lawful debts, funeral and testamentary expenses, to apply the same at the discretion of my executors for masses for the repose of my soul, the soul of my deceased wife and the soul of all my deceased relatives.

Earlier that year, before making this will, he had sold his farm, and lodged the proceeds to his bank account. The deceased also owned a dwelling house, which was sold after his death by the executors.

The next-of-kin argued that the will was unambiguous, and that the testator's mandate to the executors to 'sell' all his estate, both real and personal, which had not been specifically bequeathed and (subject to certain specified deductions) to apply 'the same' at their discretion for masses could apply only to property *still unsold at his death*. This would mean that the proceeds of the sale of the farm, having already been converted into money, would fall into the residue, since money cannot be sold.

Egan J rejected this argument. Constrained by *Rowe v Law* to consider extrinsic evidence under s.90 of the Succession Act 1965 'only when there is a legitimate dispute as to the meaning or effect of the language used in the will', Egan J held that the language in the will before the court *was* ambiguous in that the direction to apply 'same' could 'be construed to mean that all the testator's real and personal estate was to be applied for masses after payment of the specific legacies, debts and funeral expenses'. With the introduction of extrinsic evidence, the matter became a good deal easier to determine. It turned out that in 1979 the testator had made a fairly similar will which gave the same direction. Thus, if he had died before selling his farm his entire estate (subject to the specified deductions) would have been bound to be applied for masses. The testator was, of course, perfectly free to change his mind and in his second will bring about a position where there would be an intestacy as regards the bulk of his estate instead of its being used for masses; but Egan J thought that the testator, an elderly man, had not intended to change his mind in this way. The instructions for the 1985 will had clearly dealt in the main with changing the pecuniary legacies and had not sought to bring about any other drastic change. They had ended up with the very simple direction: 'leave remainder of will as it stands'. Accordingly, the totality of the testator's estate (save for the specified deductions) was to be applied for masses.

This decision is clearly desirable; it ensures that the will was interpreted in the way the testator intended. It again raises the question whether *Rowe v Law* should be modified by legislation. Henchy J made it plain that, if the language of the will is 'clear, unambiguous and without contradiction', then s.90 has no application. If Egan J had considered that no ambiguity attached to 'same', it seems that he would have been obliged to interpret the will in a way which would have frustrated the testator's intent. It is quite possible to allow extrinsic evidence even in cases where the words appear unambiguous without thereby 'empowering the Court to re-write the will', as Henchy J contended. The whole issue is helpfully analysed by Professor Brady, op. cit., 115-18 and by the Law Reform Commission of British Columbia in their *Report on Interpretation of Wills* (LRC 58-1982), 18-25.

S.117 applications   In *The Estate of IAC Deceased; C and F v WC and TC* [1989] ILRM 815, the Supreme Court restated in narrower terms than formerly the principles of interpretation of s.117.

The testatrix, a widow, had died in 1985, leaving two sons and two (twin) daughters, all in their early forties. Each of the children had his or her own difficulties. The elder son was a permanent invalid with brain damage, married with a child, and dependent on a disability pension. The younger son's business, which had been transferred to him by his mother, was in financial difficulties before the time of her death. One of the daughters, C, who married in 1969, had been separated since 1974. She had four children. Her husband was providing £2,880 per annum for the family at the time the testatrix died. This daughter was in steady employment, earning about £6,000 at the time of her mother's death. She owned the home, which was subject to a 'relatively small' mortgage. The other daughter, Ch, separated after her mother's death; there were two young children.

During her lifetime, the testatrix had given all her children benefits of various kinds. She gave her elder son £7,000 in 1983. She injected between £10,000 and £20,000 in her young son's business after she had transferred it to him. She gave a car and cash of a total value of around £18,500 to her daughter C. To her other daughter, Ch, she gave £3,000 as well as £2,400 per annum as upkeep for two years during which the mother lived with Ch (from 1983 to 1985). The net value of the testatrix estate was around £122,000. To her elder son she left a share valued at £30,800, to her younger son a share conservatively valued at £62,900. To C she left a share valued at £12,900 and to Ch. a share valued at about £13,100.

The High Court Judge, Costello J, found that the testatrix had failed to make proper provision for her two daughters. The Supreme Court, allowing the appeal, held that there had been no failure of duty relative to C, but affirmed the finding of failure relative to Ch, as well as the provision made by Costello J for Ch, of a two-ninths share in property of a value of £50,000 bequeathed to the younger son (as part of his share of a total value of £62,900). Thus Ch would be entitled to an extra interest conservatively valued at about £11,000.

The manner which the Supreme Court reached its conclusions is of considerable general interest. Finlay CJ (Griffin and Hederman, JJ concurring) adopted and approved as 'a correct statement of the law' Kenny J's view, expressed in *GM deceased; TM v TAM* (1972) 106 ILTR 82, at 87, that:

> the existence of a moral duty to make proper provision by will for a child must be judged by the facts existing at the date of death and must depend upon
>
> (a) the amount left to the surviving spouse or the value of the legal right if the survivor elects to take this,
>
> (b) the number of the testator's children, their ages and their positions in life at the date of testator's death,
>
> (c) the means of the testator,
>
> (d) the age of the child whose case is being considered and his or her financial position and prospects in life,
>
> (e) whether the testator has already in his lifetime made proper provision for the child.
>
> The existence of the duty must be decided by objective considerations. The court must decide whether the duty exists and the view of the testator that she did not owe any is not decisive.

To this general statement of the applicable principles the Chief Justice added further principles which, he admitted, might to an extent be considered a qualification of it. He was satisfied that the phrase 'failed in his moral duty to make proper provision for the child in accordance with his means' placed a relatively high onus of proof on an applicant for relief under s.117:

> It is not apparently sufficient from these terms in the Section to establish that the provision made for a child was not as great as it might have been, or that compared with generous bequests to other children or

beneficiaries in the will, it appears ungenerous. The Court should not, I consider, make an order under the Section merely because it would on the facts proved have formed different testamentary dispositions. A positive failure in moral duty must be established.

In a case such as is the instant case where evidence has been given of the Testatrix's financial support of her children during her lifetime indicative of a concerned assistance to all the members of her family, and where, as was established to the satisfaction of the learned trial Judge in this case, the relationship between the Testatrix and her children, and in particular, between the Testatrix and her daughters, was one of caring and kindness, the Court should, it seem to me, entertain some significant reluctance to vary the Testatrix's disposition by will. Quite different considerations may apply, as have been established in some of the decided cases under this Section, where a marked hostility between a testator and one particular child is established to the satisfaction of the Court.

Applying these principles to the facts of the case, the Chief Justice took the view that, whilst the bequest made for Ch in the will was probably a proper provision when the will was made, it had ceased to be so by the time the testatrix died four year later. The testatrix was by then aware of the difficulties in Ch's marriage; in the light of this knowledge, and the fact that up to then, of the four children, Ch had received the least financial benefit from her mother by a very considerable margin, a proper provision for her necessarily involved either a further testamentary disposition or a gift *inter vivos*. The Chief Justice added:

> The testatrix by her provision for C. during her lifetime indicated in a very definite fashion her appreciation of the particular problems facing a daughter whose marriage had broken down. The logical consequence of that view would, it seems to me, have been that she should have made some improved provision for her daughter Ch, having regard to the learned trial Judge's finding on the evidence that she was aware of the likelihood of a break-up of that marriage also.

In rejecting C's claim, Finlay CJ pointed out that the evidence appeared to indicate that, at the time of the death of the testatrix, C 'was established, living with her four children in a house subject to a relatively small mortgage, and in a steady, well-paid job, though not at an extravagant salary, and was receiving a reasonable contribution from her husband towards the maintenance of her children'. Moreover, her difficulties from the time of her separation in 1974 to 1985 had been 'substantially aided' by sums totalling just under £20,000.

The Chief Justice did not refer to *B (née M) (otherwise known as SM) v Bank of Ireland Trustee Co.*, High Court, 27 July 1988, where Blayney J expressed a preference for a principle of equality of treatment as between siblings. As we noted in the 1988 Review, 245, it is not entirely clear whether Blayney J considered that this should be a principle of *general* application or merely one that arose in the *particular circumstances of the case.* As can be seen from the Supreme Court decision, Finlay CJ rejected the former approach.

Law Reform Commission's proposals   In the *Report on Land Law and Conveyancing Law (1) General Proposals* (LRC 30-1989), the Law Reform Commission made two important proposals in relation to the law of succession: that a child should be able to bring a s.117-type application in the case of intestacy and that the present limitation period for bringing applications under s.117 be qualified by a power of judicial extension. We examine these proposals in detail, above, 299-301.

JUDGMENT MORTGAGES

Formalities   Practitioners inured to exercising the greatest of caution when registering judgment mortgages will breathe a sigh of relief when they read Costello J's judgment in *Irish Bank of Commerce Ltd v O'Hara*, High Court, 10 May 1989. The plaintiffs had registered a judgment mortgage for three quarters of a million pounds against the defendant's house in Killiney, Co. Dublin. The affidavit described the property by its name and the road on which it was situate, adding 'Killiney, Borough of Dun Laoghaire, Barony of Rathdown and County Dublin'. It thus gave information (as to name and road) more extensive than is required by s.6 of the Judgment Mortgage (Ireland) Act 1850, but failed to mention the parish in which the property was situate, as that section required.

An interesting issue thus arose as to whether this omission invalidated the judgment mortgage. The decisions are not easy to reconcile: see Wylie, *Irish Land Law* (2nd ed., 1986), paras. 13.168ff.

Costello J thought it unnecessary to decide this question because, even if the omission amounted to non-compliance with the section, this would not invalidate the judgment mortgage. The Act did not expressly provide that failure to comply had such a drastic effect. To see whether non-compliance would result in invalidity, the Court should first consider the purpose of the statutory requirement:

> If the . . . affidavit actually filed achieves the purpose which the

legislature sought to achieve then there is no reason why the Court should construe the section as requiring strict compliance with its provisions, particularly in a case like the present one when to do so would be to offend against both common sense and justice.

If non-compliance arose from a misdescription then it was very likely that this would be fatal to the judgment mortgage. But if it arose from a mere omission of a statutory requirement, this would not automatically invalidate the judgment mortgage. The purpose of the requirement relating to the location of the lands was to identify with precision the location of the lands affected by the judgment mortgage and to enable persons subsequently dealing with the judgment debtor and his lands to be warned of its existence:

> The whole affidavit should be looked at, including any additional information it may contain which is not prescribed by the section. If the particulars actually given achieve this purpose then there is nothing in the statute which would require the Court to invalidate the transaction.

Applying this test, the omission in the affidavit did not invalidate the judgment mortgage, since, as a result of the additional information which it contained, the affidavit disclosed the exact location of the property and nobody dealing with it could in any way be misled by the particulars given in it. He added that the need for strict compliance with the provisions of s.6 relating to the locality of the lands was 'considerably diminished' by the fact that the Registry of Deeds had ceased for several years to put entries in the Index of Lands:

> So long as the parties are sufficiently described in the affidavit so that accurate entries can be effected in the Index of Names, this will help to ensure that the statutory purposes are achieved.

Costello J also rejected the submission that a decree for enforcement of the plaintiffs' statutory right should be refused because they had failed to adduce evidence that the judgment mortgage affidavit had been filed in the Central Office. Once it had been established that it had been filed in the Registry of Deeds and that there was a sworn averment that the provisions of the 1850 Act had been complied with, it was not necessary to prove that the affidavit had been filed in the Central Office unless the defendants adduced evidence to suggest that this had not been done. If any such doubt arose, the matter could be dealt with by adjournment rather than a final determination of important proprietary rights in the absence of the true facts of the case.

The case is of considerable general interest, ranging well beyond the specific context of judgment mortgages. Costello J looked behind the details of the formal requirements in order to discern their underlying rationale. Having identified this, he interpreted the formal requirements as being fulfilled where they achieve the underlying policy, rather than insisting on strict compliance. If this principle of interpretation were applied to formal requirements generally it would have radical implications. Formal requirements have, of course, an underlying policy but their very specificity has its own rationale. This is to remove uncertainty in legal, business and personal relationships—witness the formal requirements of marriage, for example—and to avoid leaving matters open to constant debate and repeated appeal to the general underlying policy, which inevitably will leave grey areas. The whole point about formal requirements is to make the position black and white. If this is thought likely to result in undue 'fussiness', the better answer may perhaps be to streamline and improve the relevance of statutory requirements rather than to remove the real advantages which specificity offers.

Contracts of sale   As we noted above, 297, the Law Reform Commission in the *Report on Conveyancing*, have recommended that Henchy J's view in *Tempany v Hynes* [1976] IR 101 should be given legislative effect.

LANDLORD AND TENANT

At the beginning of our discussion of the developments on this subject we must welcome the publication of Professor J.C.W. Wylie's *Irish Landlord and Tenant Law* (1990). Published by Butterworth (Ireland) Ltd, with John Farrell SC in the role of consultant editor, this loose-leaf volume provides a comprehensive, penetrating and scholarly analysis of the law.

Interpretation of terms of lease   In *Hippodrome Night Club Ltd v Sean Quinn Properties Ltd*, High Court, 13 December 1989, Blayney J had to construe the term of an agreement between the proprietors of Parkes Hotel, Stillorgan and the plaintiff licensee, who was given a licence to run a discotheque in the hotel for five years. The agreement enabled the proprietors to sell the hotel during the currency of the licence provided they gave the plaintiff the first option either to purchase or to lease the premises or bar areas. The clause provided that '[t]he lessee will be permitted to exercise such option in writing provided it does so within 14 days of receipt of the notice of the licensor's intention to sell or lease . . . the hotel premises'. The licensors gave

oral notice of their intention to sell. The question thus was whether this form
of notice complied with the requirements of the clause.

Blayney J held that it did. The drafting of the clause left much to be desired,
and the agreement should have provided that the notice was to be in writing,
in view of the value of the hotel—which was sold for four million pounds.
Nevertheless, such a modification could not be implied:

> If the clause had said 'within 14 days of receipt of notice of the licensor's
> intention to sell . . .' it seems to me that it would have been clear that
> oral notice would have been sufficient, and I do not think that the
> addition of the definite article before the word 'notice' is sufficient to
> bring about a change.

In *Hynes Ltd v O'Malley Property Ltd* [1989] ILRM 619 on an appeal
from a case stated by an arbitrator to the High Court, the Supreme Court had
to interpret a rent review clause which required the arbitrator to fix the
amount of the new rent at a sum equal to the yearly rent which, having regard
to the tenor of the lease, might reasonably be expected on a letting of the
demised premises, with vacant possession, on an open market, without
having regard 'to any improvements' lawfully made by the lessee (otherwise
than in pursuance of an obligation under this lease) . . .'. Gannon J had
interpreted this as requiring the arbitrator to determine the market rental value
of the premises at the relevant time, *including* any improvements which the
lessee had lawfully made to them, *without allowance or deduction to the
lessee.*

The Supreme Court reversed. In a succinct analysis, Finlay CJ for the
courts, held that the clause was unambiguous, and led to the following result:

> 1. If a lessee having duly notified and obtained the consent of the lessor
> carries out an improvement to the premises which will on the termina-
> tion of the term be to the advantage of the lessor, he will not be damnified
> by having to pay an increase in his rent on review which is referable to
> that improvement.

> 2. If, however, notwithstanding the fact that an improvement of this
> description is carried out by the lessee and was to the advantage of the
> lessor on the final termination of the term, it was at the time when the
> lease was created part of the burden which the lease imposed on the
> lessee as distinct from imposing them on the lessor he would not be
> freed from having to pay an extra amount of rent in respect of an
> increased rental value due to that improvement. To do so would be to
> relieve him to some extent of a burden which the general provisions of

the lease had imposed on him or, to put the matter in another manner would be to deprive the lessor of an advantage which he had obtained from the obligations on the part of the lessee contained in the original lease.

3. Improvements made in breach of the lease would involve no allowance to the lessee making them.

The interpretation suggested by the lessor would mean that the clause had effected a 'wholly unsatisfactory situation'. The Chief Justice identified two anomalies which would result. First, if the lessee had *lawfully* made an improvement, he would have to pay for its value but, if he made it *unlawfully* or in breach of the terms of the lease, he would not. Secondly, a lawful improvement made *voluntarily* by the lessee would be a factor tending to increase his rent; an improvement made by him *under obligation in the lease* would not. The 'very absurdity' of these consequences militated against this interpretation.

Compensation for disturbance   In *Aherne v Southern Metropole Hotel Company Ltd* [1989] IR 186, the Supreme Court, on a case stated, held that, where the court had refused a new tenancy under s.22 of the Landlord and Tenant Act 1931 in circumstances which entitled the tenant to compensation for disturbance, an offer by the landlord to grant the tenant a new tenancy in the premises on favourable terms would be a factor in fixing compensation under s.23. In this case, the landlord had stated to the High Court judge (on appeal from the Circuit Court) that it was willing to grant the tenant a new 21-year lease *on such terms as might be fixed by the court* in accordance with the original application of the tenant. The Supreme Court held that it was not the function of the court to fix terms of a new tenancy save in the circumstances provided by the legislation; s.23 did not envisage such a power.

The 1931 Act was repealed by the Landlord and Tenant (Amendment) Act 1980. In *Aherne* the notice claiming the new tenancy had been served a few months before the 1980 Act came into force.

***Bona fide* business use**   In *Plant v Oakes*, High Court, 16 March 1989, O'Hanlon J had to determine whether premises had been '*bona fide* used wholly or partly for the purposes of carrying on a business' for a period of at least three years. If the tenant could establish this, he would be entitled to a new lease under s.13(1)(a) of the Landlord and Tenant (Amendment) Act 1980.

The premises in question consisted of a house. Nearby was a garage in which the tenant carried on business. The tenant argued that the diningroom in the house was set aside for use as an office as a necessary adjunct to the garage business. His wife did all the book-keeping and other paper work. The diningroom contained filing cabinets, a typewriter and the materials needed for the Kalamazoo system of book-keeping and accounts. There were telephones in the garage and in the house but with no internal telephone system linking the two. Both telephone numbers were listed in the directory, with the addition of the words 'motor dealers' opposite the garage number only. VAT inspectors who called to check the VAT returns were directed to the house, where they were dealt with by the tenant's wife. She gave evidence confirming that the work she did in the room took place on a few days per week. The description of the contents of the room suggested that it was not used exclusively for office work.

O'Hanlon J held that the house was used partly for the purpose of carrying on the garage business as a necessary adjunct to its operations. He was satisfied that the use made of the house was a means adopted to carry on the business in the most convenient and economic way having regard to the circumstances of the tenant and his family, and was *bona fide* within the meaning of s.13(1)(a). The expression *bona fide* was 'probably intended to exclude a claim based on purported business user which was not genuine but was merely embarked upon as a subterfuge for the purpose of building up a "business equity" as a basis for a claim a new lease under the Act'.

Clearly, the room was being used for the purpose of an office. But what would be the position, in the light of *Plant v Oakes*, if a garage proprietor, fully conscious of the legal position, were to elect to have his office in his home in circumstances where this was a perfectly satisfactory means of conducting his business but not one which he would have chosen if the possibility of deriving a benefit under s.13(1)(a) was not present? In the instant case, the solution of using the diningroom was 'the most convenient and economic way' of carrying on the business; what would have been the position if it had been merely a convenient and economic way of doing so? It is submitted that a tenant may be self interested without his conduct losing its *bona fide* status. Provided the office work is truly carried out in the home, and provided that it is an economically defensible (albeit not necessarily essential) strategy in its own right, it would seem that this should be sufficient to pass the requirements of s.13(1)(a).

O'Hanlon J went on to note that a 'nice question' arose as to whether the tenant had been under an obligation to apply for 'change of user' permission before converting part of his residence to business purposes, under the Local Government (Planning and Development) Acts; the respondent had not relied on this point and O'Hanlon J himself had earlier held in *Terry v Stokes*, 13 March 1986, that it should not defeat the claim to a new tenancy. He adhered to this decision in the instant case.

The Landlord and Tenant (Amendment) Act 1989   We analysed this Act in the 1988 Review, 273, when it was passing through the Oireachtas. Briefly, it amends s.13 of the Landlord and Tenant (Amendment) Act 1980 to enable leases to be made with financial services companies in the Customs House Docks Area without rights to a new tenancy of thirty-five years accruing.

Law Reform Commission's proposals   In chapter 5 of their *Report on Land Law and Conveyancing Law (1) General Proposals*, the Law Reform Commission make some important proposals for change in the law of landlord and tenant. We examine these above, 303-4.

POWERS OF ATTORNEY: LAW REFORM

In their *Report on Land Law and Conveyancing Law (2): Enduring Powers of Attorney* (LRC 31-1989), the Law Reform Commission, following the lead of most other common law jurisdictions recommend the introduction of the concept of enduring powers of attorney into our law. At present, a power of attorney is automatically revoked by the donor's mental incapacity: *Drew v Nunn*, 4 QBD 661; *Younge v Toynbee* [1910] 1 KB 215; *Re Parks, Canada Permanent Trust v Parks*, 8 DLR (2d) 155, at 161 (1957). There is no provision for an enduring power of attorney which would continue in force even where the donor becomes incapable of handling his or her own affairs. As the Commission note,

> [t]he result of this is that a person who is concerned that he or she might become incapable of managing his or her affairs is unable to make provision for that possibility. It appears that the result of the increase in the life expectancy of the population is that there is an increase in the number of people who become senile. We would also be concerned with, for example, people in the early state of Alzheimer's disease.

Of course the wardship jurisdiction of the President of the High Court is available for the management of mentally ill persons' property. The Commission seem not to be greatly impressed by this:

> The form of management by Committee [appointed by the President] is ... fairly passive. A Committee may not, for example, deal in equities and has no power to actively manage an investment portfolio. Stocks and shares of a ward may be bonus issues, for example, an application must be made to the Registrar of Wards of Court who then takes advice from a stockbroker. An attorney, on the other hand, need not have a

passive role and may manage any investments and affairs of the donor in the way the donor would wish.

Several different models of legislation, actual or proposed, are available for consideration in relation to enduring powers of attorney, ranging from those with minimal controls, such as the Uniform Durable Power of Attorney Act (1979) in the United States, to those with elaborative substantive and procedural requirements, such as the Enduring Powers of Attorney (Northern Ireland) Order 1987, which came into force on 10 April 1989.

The Commission's Report tends more towards elaboration but nonetheless some of its recommendations, as we shall see, may prove controversial. Briefly, the Commission recommend that a system of enduring powers of attorney be introduced here; an intention to create such a power should be evidenced in the instrument creating it. The current restrictions on donors concerning ordinary powers of attorney should apply. There should be no limit on the number of attorneys that may be appointed.

The Commission recommend that the instrument creating the power should have to be witnessed. The donor would be capable of acting as witness but neither the attorney nor his solicitor would. The instrument should evidence the fact that the donor has either received independent legal advice or, having been advised of the wisdom of doing so, has declined to take this step. They envisage that a standard form would be used (though they recommend that this should not be mandatory); the form would contain explanatory notes in plain English. The donor should be allowed to limit the duration of the power; if he or she becomes incompetent before the specified time has elapsed, the power would continue until the scheduled moment of termination.

In line with all other law reform agencies save the New South Wales Law Reform Commission in their Working Paper on the subject, the Commission recommend that the donor should not be permitted to waive the protections contained in the legislation for his or her benefit. One of these protections is a special system of regulation for enduring powers of attorney when the attorney has reason to believe that the donor is becoming, or has become, mentally incapable. This system, which is part of the law in England and Northern Ireland, requires the attorney to register the power in the appropriate office of the court, having notified specified relatives of the donor and giving them a chance to object, on the basis that the power was obtained by fraud or undue influence or that the donor is still mentally capable or that the attorney is unsuitable. The Commission recommend the inclusion of a requirement of registration on these lines.

As regards the authority and duties of attorneys, the Commission recommend that, where a general power is conferred, the attorney should be entitled to act so as to benefit himself or any other person to the extent that the donor might be expected to provide for his or that person's needs; he should be under a duty of good faith rather than one of prudent management, which the Commission consider 'too onerous'. As regards accounts, the Commission recommend that the court should be empowered to look for accounts where it appears reasonable to do so. The court should be entitled to terminate a power only where there is evidence that it is not being operated properly.

The Report raises a number of important issues of general public interest. The first is whether it is desirable to supplement wardship, with its strong paternalistic concern for the welfare of mentally incompetent persons, by a privatised system with far fewer controls either as to its creation or day-to-day administration.

The effect of an enduring power of attorney is to transfer effective control over a person's property to another where it is in many cases likely that the donor will become mentally incompetent. It is surely not too pessimistic a judgment of human nature to suggest that this system may tempt some donees either fraudulently or negligently to abuse their trust in the absence of stringent controls. Sadly this has been the experience in some Canadian jurisdictions: see the Alberta Law Reform Institute's Report for Discussion No. 7, *Enduring Powers of Attorney* (1990) 26-8.

Secondly, there is a problem with the *time* at which the donor appoints the attorney. The Report, as we have seen, envisages that people 'in the early stages of Alzheimer's disease' will avail themselves of the facility. If they are already some way down the road towards mental incompetence, it is possible that they may be already too far to exercise a fully informed choice. The reality is that their condition may first manifest itself to *others*; the idea that every donor will have sufficient insight into his or her mental state to be able independently to see the need for appointing an attorney seems naive.

This brings us to a third difficulty. Giving an enduring power of attorney which transfers to the attorney, then and there, power to act over the donor's property may not be what every donor wants. Certainly a person who is not worried about his or her mental capacity might baulk at the prospect of relinquishing control over his or her property (either totally or in part). What may be needed is the ability to appoint an attorney whose powers will come into fruition only at such time as the donor becomes mentally incompetent. The Commission do not address this issue expressly, unless their reference to the duration of the power is intended to embrace the question of the commencement as well as the termination of the power. They extract in the Appendix of the Report, however, the form of explanatory notes which the English legislation prescribes, and this makes clear to a would-be donor that 'you can include a restriction that your attorney(s) must not act on your behalf until they have reason to believe that you are becoming mentally incapable'. This issue has excited much discussion internationally in the past few years. The experience in Canada and the United States has been that, in the absence of clear, specific legislative authority to defer the commencement of the power, third parties are slow to respect instruments conferring a deferred power. This suggests that the matter should be addressed in the legislation; as the Law Reform Commission of British Columbia point out in their *Report on the Enduring Powers of Attorney: Fine-Tuning the Concept* (LRC 110-1989), 13:

> In many cases, whether or not an instrument, in fact and law, confers authority on the attorney is not the critical issue. The issue is whether a person or institution with whom the attorney may wish to deal on behalf of the principal is prepared to accept that the attorney has the authority he claims. If such a person is not satisfied of the attorney's authority, there may be no way to compel him to deal with the attorney. In this way the principal's wishes will be frustrated even if, as a matter of law, the power of attorney was effective.

The problem with the donor's specifying the time he or she becomes mentally incompetent as the trigger for the activation of the attorney's powers is that very often this involves a process rather than an event. Thus there is no clear moment at which this activation should occur. One solution, favoured by New York legislation in 1988, is for the donor to name in the instrument a person whose function it is to declare in writing that a specified contingency (such as the donor's mental capacity) has occurred. On such declaration, the power of attorney takes effect, without regard to whether the specified contingency has in fact occurred.

We have already noted that the Commission rejects the imposition of a duty of prudent management on the attorney as being too onerous, and that a duty of good faith should suffice. The Commission appears to have been convinced by the English Law Commission's similar conclusion in their Report No. 122, *The Law of Incapacitated Principal* (Cmnd. 8977, 1983), 41. The English body was of the view that compliance would be difficult, that the duty would be unrealistic where the attorney was a close, possibly elderly, relative, that it would discourage would-be attorneys from acting, and that the range of the duty to third parties was unclear. It may be useful to record the refutation of this conclusion by the Alberta Law Reform Institute, in their Report for Discussion No. 7, *Enduring Powers of Attorney* (1990), 68-9, published some months after the Irish report:

> In our opinion [the English Law Commission's] arguments do not outweigh the case for imposing a statutory duty to act. We doubt whether such a duty will deter many people from consenting to act as an EPA attorney. Even if it does, it is far preferable that they decline the appointment rather than leave the donor's affairs 'in limbo' after incapacity. Nor do we perceive the duty as onerous, difficult, or unrealistic. . . . Finally, the prospect of the scope of the duty being unclear can easily be addressed in the legislation.

It is interesting to note that s.6 of Newfoundland's Enduring Powers of Attorney Act 1990 (c.15) goes further, in imposing a duty straddling the duty of care and trusteeship. S.11c of Tasmania's Powers of Attorney Amendment Act 1987 goes further still, deeming the donee to be the trustee of the property and affairs of the donor according to the tenor of the power and requiring him under sanction of liability to compensate the donor for loss, to exercise his powers as attorney to protect the interests of the donor.

Finally, it may be worth considering whether the defects which the Commission perceive in the present *wardship* jurisdiction call more urgently for legislative reform. Enduring powers of attorney are clearly not the answer for many people. A recent model for law reform is offered by the Australian Law Reform Commission in their Report No. 52, *Guardianship and Management of Property* (1990).

Law Reform

The Law Reform Commission was busy in 1989. It published a Consultation Paper on Child Sexual Abuse in August. We defer consideration of this theme until the 1990 Review, when we will examine in detail the Commission's final recommendations on the subject, contained in their Report, published in September 1990. The Commission also published two reports on conveyancing and land law. The first, containing general proposals on a wide range of topics, we consider, above, 295-304. The second, proposing the creation of the institution of enduring powers of attorney, we consider, above, 316-20.

In the area of private international law, the Commission recommend against the ratification of the Hague Convention on Adoption, in their Report on the Recognition of Foreign Adoption Decrees. We examine this Report, above, 80-88. Finally we examine the Commission's proposals in relation to reform of the law relating to retention of title, above, 51-2.

Licensing

BOOKMAKERS

District Court hearing: objectors In *Cashman v Clifford* [1990] ILRM 200; [1989] IR 121, Barron J held that the range of objectors who may appear in a District Court hearing in connection with the granting of a bookmaker's licence cannot be restricted to the persons specified in s.13 of the Betting Act 1931: see 91, above, in the Constitutional Law chapter.

Prosecutions: recovery of duty In *Director of Public Prosecutions v Cunningham* [1989] IR 441, Lardner J dealt with a procedural point concerning the recovery of duty payable on bets under the Finance Act 1926: see 369, below, in the Revenue chapter.

INTOXICATING LIQUOR

Transfer of licence In *In the Matter of Thank God It's Friday Ltd* [1990] ILRM 228 Barr J considered the effect of a licence transfer on existing licence holders.

The applicant company sought a declaration that certain premises were fit and convenient to receive a 7-day licence under s.14 of the Intoxicating Liquor Act 1960. The premises from which the licence was to be transferred was one where the maximum capacity was 200 clients, and in which very little food was served. The applicant company sought transfer of that premises' licence to a premises in the immediate vicinity in which the applicant intended to serve hot meals at lunch time and which would be part of a larger leisure complex incorporating bowling and gym facilities. A number of licensees in the neighbourhood objected to the application on the ground that the new premises would have a material adverse effect on their business, in particular having regard to the increased emphasis on meals and the size of the premises. Barr J held that the application for the transfer should be refused.

Applying dicta in *Application of Irish Cinemas Ltd* (1970) 106 ILTR 17, he concluded that, having regard to the nature and size of the premises, it was clear that the application would have a material adverse effect on the businesses in the neighbourhood within the meaning of s.14(1)(c)(ii) of the 1960 Act. See also the cases in the 1988 Review, 239-40.

Limitation of Actions

FATAL INJURIES AND SURVIVAL OF ACTIONS

In *McCullough v Ireland* [1989] IR 484, the question of the relationship between the respective limitation periods for survival of actions and for fatal accidents fell for consideration. The plaintiff's husband sued for damages for personal injuries in 1979. A statement of claim was delivered in 1981. The husband died that year. No steps were taken on behalf of his estate until 1985, when particulars, requested by the defendants during the husband's lifetime in 1981, were eventually furnished.

The plaintiff was substituted as plaintiff. In 1987, she was given liberty by order to amend the proceedings to include a claim under Part IV of the Civil Liability Act 1961. In their defence to the amended pleadings, the defendants relied on s.48(6), which requires the action under Part IV to be commenced within three years after the death of the deceased.

Barron J noted that two causes of action were pleaded. The first, the original cause of action which had been vested in the husband, had arisen within three years prior to the issue of the plenary summons; by virtue of s.7 of the 1961 Act, it survived for the benefit of his estate subject to the provisions of that section (which exclude, for example, damages for pain or suffering or personal injury, and exemplary damages). The second course of action was one vested in the dependants of the deceased, granted by s.48 of the Act. The plaintiff had submitted that the 1987 amendment would normally relate back to the date of the original summons and statement of claim, but that, as it had not arisen at that date, it must be deemed to relate back to the earliest possible date, which was the date of death. Barron J rejected this argument. Clearly, the cause of action had arisen more than three years before that date. The plaintiff's claim under this heading was therefore statute barred.

The infant dependant was in no better position. In *Moynihan v Greensmyth* [1977] IR 55, an infant plaintiff had been held to be barred after two years when bringing proceedings in tort against a deceased tort-feasor by virtue of the provisions of s.9(2) of the 1961 Act. In the instant case, the statutory limitation relied on by the defendants was contained in the same statute and the submissions were the same. *Moynihan v Greensmyth* accordingly governed.

The conclusion in this case that s.48(6) should not be interpreted as 'stopping the clock' during a child's minority seems clearly correct. But it may be argued that this is so on account of the provisions of Part IV, interpreted as a whole, rather than because of an identity of issues as between *Moynihan v Greensmyth* and the instant case.

The purpose of Part IV is to provide a statutory system of compensation, brought in *one action for damages* (cf. s.47(2)), on behalf of all the dependants, with a maximum total sum of £7,500 allowable for mental distress, which has to be apportioned between the dependants as the judge considers reasonable. The idea here is clearly for what is a class action to be taken within three years of the death of the deceased. Dr John White is surely correct in submitting that the requirement that the action be commenced within three years after the death of the deceased 'is the only relevant limitation period': *Irish Law of Damages for Personal Injury and Death*, para. 8.3.08. To subject this action to the extension of the limitation period for minors in general would be contrary to the thrust of the provisions in Part IV, as well as the express language of s.48(6).

Moynihan v Greensmyth was concerned with the somewhat different question of whether a two-year limitation period for actions *against* the estate of deceased person was invalid constitutionally on account of its failure to protect the right of action of an infant plaintiff. The Supreme Court held that the limitation period survived constitutional scrutiny. O'Higgins CJ, delivering the judgment of the Court, said:

> Bearing in mind the State's duty to owners—in particular those who represent the estate of the deceased, and beneficiaries—some reasonable limitation on actions against the estate was obviously required. If the period of infancy were to form part of the period of limitation, as was formerly the case, then the danger of stale claims being brought would be very real and could constitute a serious threat of the rights of beneficiaries of the estate of a deceased. The alternative was to apply a period of limitation which would have general application. It had to be one or the other; and it does not appear that any compromise was possible.

This analysis justifies the constitutionality of a short, absolute limitation period for actions *against* deceased persons; it does not address the separate question of the constitutionality of a short limitation period for a single class action *on behalf of dependants of a deceased person* against a *living* defendant (or, as in the instant case, a defendant incapable of dying). It seems that in *McCullough v Ireland* the question was simply one of statutory interpretation rather than involving a constitutional challenge to the validity of s.48(6).

Nevertheless the presumption of constitutionality would enable for the constitutional dimensions to be addressed to some extent in the case.

REGISTRATION OF TITLE: ADVERSE POSSESSION

In *In re Noone Deceased; Nolan v Monaghan*, High Court, 16 June 1989, Carroll J held that adverse possession was established against the registered owner. The purchaser of a site from the owner had been shown its dimensions by the owner in a way that indicated to him that the area which later formed the subject matter of the litigation would form part of his property. The owner retained a hut and building materials on this spot for some years but eventually in 1972 removed the hut and most of the materials (save for some rubble and steel girders) after repeated requests by the purchaser. The purchaser removed the remaining rubble but left the girders where they were. The purchaser's understanding at the time was that he had a right to the area in question.

Carroll J held that this belief was correct. She did not consider that leaving the girders on the property indicated an *animus revertendi* on the registered owner's part. The fact that the girders were still there indicated that the cost and trouble of removing them was more than they were worth and that they had been effectively abandoned. The purchaser had the requisite *animus possidendi*.

In due course, the purchaser had sold the site to a couple, without specifically mentioning the area in question. He explained this omission to the court on the basis that he had become so used to treating it as his own. The couple treated the area as theirs for a period of at least twelve years. In 1986, when the question of ownership was first closely scrutinised, the couple discovered that the area in question was still registered in the name of the original owner.

Carroll J held that the couple were entitled to be registered as full owners of the disputed area. The registered owner had abandoned it; it could not be said that the plot was incapable of use and enjoyment as it had become absorbed into the garden as a natural completion of the site and occupied by the purchaser and then the couple, who had enjoyed exclusive use of it.

Local Government

BURIAL GROUNDS

In *McCarthy v Johnson* [1989] ILRM 706; [1989] IR 691, the Supreme Court upheld the decision of Hamilton P ([1988] IR 24) on the effect of s.44(2) of the Local Government (Sanitary Services) Act 1948, which prohibits burials other than in approved burial grounds: see the 1988 Review, 295.

The plaintiff was the owner of a dwelling-house within 100 yards of a plot which adjoined a cemetery attached to a church or chapel of the Church of Ireland, of which the defendants were trustees. The trustees had purchased the plot, and had obtained permission from the Minister for the Environment pursuant to s.44(2) of the Local Government (Sanitary Services) Act 1948 to use the plot as a burial ground. The plaintiff sought a declaration that the plot could not be used as a burial ground without his permission. S.174 of the Public Health (Ireland) Act 1878 provides that no ground not already used as or appropriated as a burial ground under the Act shall be appropriated as a burial ground nearer than 100 yards from a dwelling-house without the consent in writing of the owner, lessee and occupier of such dwelling-house. It was agreed that the plot had not been used as a burial ground at any time, but the defendants argued that the plaintiff was not entitled to relief since a cemetery attached to a private church did not fall within the provisions of the 1878 Act. In the High Court [1988] IR 24, Hamilton P held in favour of the defendants, and on appeal by the plaintiff the Supreme Court (Finlay CJ, Walsh and Griffin JJ) affirmed that decision.

Delivering the Court's decision, Walsh J held that s.174 of the 1878 Act dealt only with the situation where a burial ground has been provided by a local authority acting as burial board for its functional area and that section was not, therefore, relevant to the present case. He went on that the 1948 Act was the only relevant statutory provision in the present circumstances. Under s.44(2) of the 1948 Act, Walsh J stated that it was clear that the Minister was given a discretion as to whether to permit the use of a plot as a burial ground; and in the absence of a challenge to the reasonableness of the decision he held that the plaintiff was not entitled to the relief claimed.

As Hamilton P had done in the High Court, Walsh J approved the views of Sergeant J in *Clegg v Metcalfe* [1914] 1 Ch 808 as to restrictions on the building of new cemeteries under the English equivalent of the 1878 Act. Walsh J noted, however, that the 1948 Act had been the first Irish legislative provision which prohibited the burial of a person other than in a recognised burial ground.

COMPULSORY ACQUISITION

Van Nierop v Commissioners for Public Works in Ireland, High Court, 28 July 1989 was an important decision on compulsory acquisition of land, and in particular on the loss of the statutory right to acquire through delay. Although it did not involve acquisition by a local authority, the principles applied by O'Hanlon J are equally applicable: see 272, above.

CONTROL OF DOGS

The Control of Dogs Act 1986 (Guard Dogs) (Amendment) Regulations 1989 (SI No.329) amend the 1988 regulations which introduced a local authority licensing system for guard dogs: see the 1988 Review, 295-6.

EXECUTIVE AND RESERVED FUNCTIONS

The obligation of a County Manager to refuse to give effect to an unlawful decision of a County Council was discussed in *Flanagan v Galway City and County Manager and Anor*, High Court, 25 May 1989 (328, below).

HOUSING

Fitness for habitation The duty on a housing authority under s.66 of the Housing Act 1966 to provide accommodation that is fit for human habitation was considered in *Burke and Ors v Dublin Corporation*, High Court, 13 July 1989; Supreme Court, 26 July 1990 (117-25, above, in the Contract Law chapter).

Homelessness The Housing Act 1988 (Commencement) Order 1989 (SI No.40) brought ss.9, 11 and 20(1) of the 1988 Act into effect on 1 April 1989. These sections deal with the requirement on a housing authority to make an assessment of the housing needs of the homeless: see the 1988 Review, 303. The 1989 Order also repealed s.60 of the Housing Act 1966, s.16 of the Housing (Miscellaneous Provisions) Act 1979 and the Housing Act 1984.

PLANNING

Acquisition notice: open space   S.25 of the Local Government (Planning and Development) Act 1976 empowers a planning authority to serve an acquisition notice on the owners of land where that land is not being maintained as an open space in circumstances where such land was required to be kept as an open space. In *Dublin County Council v Grealy and Ors*, High Court, 7 December 1989, Blayney J held that the section did not operate retrospectively.

The defendants were the owners of a plot of land which was required to be maintained as an open space in accordance with a general planning permission granted in 1957 in connection with surrounding land. The County Council was dissatisfied with the manner in which the defendants were maintaining the plot. In 1985 the Council served a notice under s.25 of the 1976 Act requiring them to 'level, topsoil, seed and maintain' the plot. The notice also indicated that an acquisition notice might also be served if there was no compliance with the notice. The defendants did not comply with the notice and the Council subsequently registered its title to the plot on foot of a vesting order in 1986. The Council then instituted the instant proceedings, an Ejectment Civil Bill, but the case was dismissed by Judge Martin in the Circuit Court. The Council unsuccessfully appealed that decision to the High Court.

Blayney J pointed out that the crucial issue was whether s.25 of the 1976 Act operated retrospectively. Since it involved a potential impairment of the defendants' rights, it would be deemed to be retrospective if it applied, he stated, applying dicta of O'Higgins CJ in *Hamilton v Hamilton* [1982] ILRM 290; [1982] IR 466. But he concluded that s.25 did not in fact operate retrospectively. Drawing on the decisions referred to in the *Hamilton* case, Blayney J noted that the courts lean against retrospection and favour the view that legislation ought to be construed as operating prospectively only unless there was, for example, specific indications to the contrary in the legislation itself. Blayney J found that the language of s.25 supported the conclusion that s.25 was neutral on the question or, at most, perhaps open to a possible interpretation of retrospection. He did not consider this was sufficient to rebut the normal presumption of prospective effect. Accordingly, he held that the Council's vesting order was *ultra vires* and of no legal effect.

Compensation: matters to have regard to   In *Bardun Estates Society Ltd v Dublin County Council*, High Court, 27 June 1989, Barrington J considered an issue connected with the assessment of compensation arising from a refusal of planning permission. The company had been refused planning permission to erect houses on a particular site both by the respondent as planning authority and on appeal by An Bord Pleanála. Refusal was by reference to major road proposals. The company then claimed £1.938 million compensation pursuant to s.55 of the Local Government (Planning and Development) Act 1963 for the alleged reduction in the value of the company's interest in the lands. The company later served a purchase notice for the lands on the Council, which the Council was unwilling to comply with. Since the original refusal of the planing permission, the Council had, by administrative decision, abandoned the road proposals for the land owned by the company, but the proposals remained part of its development plan. An Bord Pleanála subsequently made an order in which it directed that permission should be granted for the company's planning application in the event of an application being made to it. The applicant proceeded to arbitration of its claim for compensation under the 1963 Act. The arbitrator stated a case for the High Court as to whether the direction of An Bord Pleanala could be taken into account in assessing compensation under s.55 of the 1963 Act. During the hearing in the High Court, the Council pointed out that it could not itself grant permission in view of the continuation of the road proposals in its development plan: see *Attorney General (McGarry) v Sligo County Council* [1989] ILRM 768, below.

Barrington J held that the arbitrator was entitled to 'have regard to' the direction of An Bord Pleanála pursuant to s.55 of the 1963 Act, since although s.55 referred to three particular matters which did not arise in the instant cse, this did not preclude the arbitrator from having regard to other matters. He considered that it was clear that it had not been the intention of s.55 of the Act to put the arbitrator in blinkers in assessing compensation. And he did not think that it was for the company to complain that it would be put to expense to bring a further application for permission since it was for the company to prove its entitlement to compensation under s.55 of the 1963 Act. In this, he discussed the decision in *Owenabue Ltd v Dublin County Council* [1982] ILRM 150.

Development plan Two decisions examined the effects of contravention of a development plan.

In *Attorney General (McGarry and Ors) v Sligo County Council* [1989] ILRM 768, the Supreme Court dealt with the effects of a planning decision made in contravention of a development plan. The plaintiffs were residents of Sligo who sought an injunction restraining the defendant Council from giving effect to a decision to use as a refuse dump a quarry adjacent to the megalithic tomb at Carrowmore in County Sligo. The Carrowmore tomb was listed for preservation in the Council's Development Plan made in accordance with the Third Schedule to the Local Government (Planning and Development) Act 1963. The Plan quoted from a report as to the historical value of the tomb, both in Irish and European terms. When the application for an injunction came before the High Court, the plaintiffs undertook to seek the permission of the Attorney General to convert the proceedings into a relator action and such consent was given. McWilliam J (High Court, 21 December 1983) declined to grant the injunction but the Council undertook not to use the site as a dump until further order and until a hydrological report on the site had been commissioned. The plaintiffs appealed the decision to the Supreme Court (Walsh, Hederman and McCarthy JJ) which granted the injunction sought.

Delivering the Court's decision, McCarthy J drew immediate attention to the significance of the Carrowmore tomb, as indicated by the documentation attached to the Council's own development plan. In this light, he stated that the decision to use the area around the tomb was in clear conflict with the Council's Development Plan, and thus in breach of the Council's duty under s.39 of the 1963 Act which precludes it from effecting a development 'which contravenes materially the development plan.'

As to the effect of this in the instant case, McCarthy J distinguished the decision of O'Keeffe P in An *Taisce v Dublin Corporation*, High Court, 31 January 1973. In that case the then President had declined to intervene in connection with a contravention where there was a conflict of views as to the appropriateness of a development: see Keane, *The Law of Local Government in the Republic of Ireland* (1982), 214-15. McCarthy J pointed out that the instant case was not one in which the courts were asked to choose between competing views as to the ecological effect of the dump or as to whether it would constitute an actionable nuisance. Since the situation was clear on this point, the plaintiffs were therefore entitled to the relief sought.

He also said that the plaintiffs would have been entitled to the relief sought on the basis that the Council had failed in its obligation to notify its decision to the Commissioners of Public Works, who were the guardians of the Carrowmore tomb, as required by s.14 of the National Monuments Act 1930.

On a procedural point, McCarthy J doubted if the plaintiffs were obliged in the circumstances (being ratepayers and residents) to have the proceedings converted into a relator action. Finally, the Court later dealt with interest on the costs awarded in the case: see 348, below.

The second case dealing with contravention of a development plan was *Flanagan v Galway City and County Manager and Anor*, High Court, 25 May 1989. This case raised issues similar to those dealt with by the Supreme Court in *P. & F. Sharpe Ltd v Dublin City and County Manager* [1989] ILRM 565; [1989] IR 701 (see the 1988 Review, 296-301), and that decision loomed large in the instant case. The outcome of the case was, however, quite different.

The applicant had been granted planning permission for retention of a development pursuant to a resolution under s.4 of the City and County Management (Amendment) Act 1955 which had been passed by Galway County Council as planning authority. The applicant had previously been given planning permission for the development, provided it was used for non-commercial purposes, but the applicant had sought retention for commercial use. At the meeting of the Council, the proposers and seconders of the motion allowing retention drew attention to the fact that the applicant might be forced to emigrate if retention was not granted, and also that the applicant was employing a number of people who might otherwise be a burden on the State. It emerged that some members of the Council had visited the applicant on the day of the Council meeting. The Council's engineer had recommended against allowing retention on the ground that the development was beside a dangerous part of a national road route and that the Council's Development Plan would be breached. The first respondent declined, as City and County Manager, to implement the decision of the Council.

S.26(1) of the Local Government (Planning and Development) Act 1963 provides that the planning authority is restricted to considering the proper planning and development of its area, having regard to the provisions of its Development Plan. The applicant sought judicial review of the failure of the first respondent to implement the Council's decision. Blayney J refused to grant judicial review. Applying the Supreme Court decision in the *Sharpe* case, above, he held that the Council was restricted by s.26 of the 1963 Act to considering the proper planning and development of its area, and it was also required to act judicially by disregarding any irrelevent or illegitimate factor which might be advanced. In the present case, he held that the Council had taken account of irrelevant factors, including the possibility of the applicant's emigration and the employment provided by him; and the visit by the councillors to the applicant on the day of the Council meeting was also another factor. In those circumstances he held that it would have been virtually impossible for the councillors to have excluded how the plaintiff would be personally affected by their decision, and indeed he noted that the minutes of the meeting indicating that they had in fact not excluded such considerations. For these reasons, he concluded that the Manager had acted correctly in refusing to give effect to the granting of the permission.

Environmental impact assessment   The decision in the Merrell Dow case, *Browne and Ors v An Bord Pleanála* [1989] ILRM 865 is discussed on 201-3, above. The issue posed in the case, namely whether the 1985 EC Directive which requires environmental impact assessments had direct effect in Irish law, was obviated later in the year. In December, the Minister for the Environment signed the European Communities (Environmental Impact Assessment) Regulations 1989 (SI No. 349). The Regulations amend a

number of different statutory provisions, including the terms of the Local
Government (Planning and Development) Acts 1963 to 1982. They require
that an application for planning permission in respect of a scheduled list of
developments must be accompanied by an Environmental Impact Study
(EIS). The regulations came into effect on 1 February 1990.

Exempted development on motorway scheme   In *Nolan and Ors v
Minister for the Environment and Electricity Supply Board* [1989] IR 357,
Costello J discussed a number of points concerning the relationship between
the Local Government (Planning and Development) Act 1963 and the Local
Government (Roads and Motorways) Act 1974.

The respondent Minister had made an order under the 1974 Act approving
a motorway scheme by Dublin County Council. The motorway path included
a number of pylons which the respondent Board sought to remove and
relocate. The Board applied to the Minister pursuant to the 1974 Act for his
consent to the removal and relocation of the pylons. The Minister purported
to grant such consent pursuant to s.10 of the 1974 Act, which states that
consent may be given by the Minister to a statutory undertaker in connection
with excavating any apparatus in the motorway path. The applicants, house-
holders beside which the pylons were to be relocated, sought judicial review
of the Minister's consent on the grounds that it was *ultra vires* in purporting
to permit the respondent Board to perform an illegal act, namely to relocate
the pylons without planning permission under the 1963 Act. They also sought
damages, inter alia, on the ground of breach of fair procedures and breach of
a legitimate expectation that the pylons would not be relocated close to their
houses. Costello J granted the applicants the declaration sought but declined
to award damages.

He held that the respondent Board's relocation of the pylons was not an
exempted development under s.4 of the Local Government (Planning and
Development) Act 1963, nor was it authorised as a development by a
planning authority pursuant to ss.74 and 77 of the 1963 Act or carried out in
accordance with the original planning permission for the pylons. On the
effect of the Local Government (Roads and Motorways) Act 1974, he held
that s.10 of the 1974 Act must be construed as only giving to the Minister
power to consent to development on motorway land where such development
is exempted development. In the instant case he concluded that the consent
given was therefore *ultra vires* the Minister. He thus held that the applicants
were entitled to a declaration to that effect. However, he pointed out that this
construction of the statutory provisions in no way affected the Minister's
power to exempt developments under s.4 of the 1963 Act on land forming
part of a motorway scheme where the consent of the relevant road authority
was present.

On the damages issue, a number of arguments had been put forward by the applicants, but Costello J rejected them all. First, they argued that they had a right to fair procedures pursuant to Article 40.3 of the Constitution in connection with the decision-making process. Costello J held that there could be no constitutional obligation on the Minister to give public notice in relation to the proposed exercise of what he had already decided was an illegal act, so that the applicants were not entitled to such notice as a matter of fair procedures or as an unspecified personal right under Article 40.3 of the Constitution, and so they could not claim damages on this ground.

The applicants also relied on the case law on legitimate expectation emanating from the Supreme Court decision in *Webb v Ireland* [1988] ILRM 565; [1988] IR 353 (see further 9-12, above in the Administrative Law chapter). But Costello J rejected this argument also, noting that in *Webb* Finlay CJ had linked legitimate expectation with promissory estoppel, thus requiring at the very least a representation to the applicants. They had put in evidence certain statements in this regard, arguing that these amounted to representations that the pylons would not be sited near them. Costello J was not convinced. Having reviewed the evidence he concluded that any statements by Dublin County Council or its engineer could not be regarded as a representation or promise to the effect suggested by the applicants, nor was there evidence that they were communicated to or relied on by the applicants. Switching to the 'public law' meaning of legitimate expectation (see the 1988 Review, 21), Costello J held that, in any event, the Minister could not be bound by such statements in the exercise of his statutory powers under s.10 of the Local Government (Roads and Motorways) Act 1974.

Failure to complete In *Dun Laoghaire Corporation v Parkhill Developments Ltd and Anor* [1989] ILRM 235; [1989] IR 447, the applicant planning authority sought orders under s.27 of the Local Government (Planning and Development) Act 1976 compelling the defendants to complete a development. The respondent company had obtained planning permission from the applicant planning authority in respect of a housing development. Construction work was completed without full compliance with the terms of the permission, so the applicant sought an order under s.27 of the 1976 Act. The company was, at the date of the application, insolvent and had ceased trading. The applicant also sought to make the second respondent, a director of the company, personally liable for the failure of the company to complete. The evidence indicated that the company had been controlled by the second respondent, that no annual general meeting had ever been held, that no formal directors meetings had ever been held, no financial reports were issued to shareholders nor were any director's fees paid to the other director of the company. Hamilton P granted the order under s.27 against the company but not against the second respondent.

The President accepted that the second respondent had failed to comply with a number of provisions of the Companies Act 1963, but he also concluded that there was no evidence of fraud, of misrepresentation, of misapplication of company funds or of negligence on the respondent's part. In those circumstances he concluded that it would not be appropriate to deprive him of the benefit of trading with limited liability by making him personally liable for the company's default. In this, he approved the approach taken in *Dublin County Council v Elton Homes Ltd* [1984] ILRM 297 and *Dublin County Council v O'Riordan* [1986] ILRM 104.

Fees   The Local Government (Planning and Development) (Fees) (Amendment) Regulations 1989 (SI No.338) set out the revised fees payable to An Bord Pleanála applicable from 1 February 1990.

Injunction: s.27   In *Furlong v McConnell Ltd and Ors* [1990] ILRM 48, the applicant sought orders under s.27 of the Local Government (Planning and Development) Act 1976 preventing the allegedly unauthorised use of certain lands. Essentially, the case turned on whether the defendants were engaged in use for which no planning permission had been granted. Gannon J held, on the evidence presented, that the first defendant, the owner of the land, was not engaged in an unauthorised development within the meaning of s.3 of the Local Government (Planning and Development) Act 1963, as it had leased the use of the property to the other defendants. The second defendant was held, on the evidence, to have been engaged in use which arose before the appointed day (1 October 1964) under the 1963 Act, and so no unauthorised development had taken place. In relation to the third defendant, Gannon J was satisfied that the use had arisen since 1985 only, and so the development was unauthorised since no planning permission had been obtained for the use, which consisted of storage of fuel oils.

However, adopting the form of order employed by Finlay P (as he then was) in *Dublin Corporation v Garland* [1982] ILRM 104, Gannon J put a 12 month stay on the order to allow the planning authorities and the third defendant to reconsider the planning factors which arose in the case. Gannon J stated that this approach was consistent with the purposes of s.27 of the 1976 Act, which was to assist in the enforcement of the proper development of lands in accordance with planning objectives, and this was different from the factors which might apply in an ordinary lis inter partes. It was therefore important to allow the planning authorities time to consider the full implications of the situation which now presented itself.

Tree preservation order: appeals In *Wicklow County Council v An Bord Pleanála*, High Court, 22 June 1989 the applicant Council, pursuant to powers conferred by s.45 of the Local Government (Planning and Development) Act 1963, made a Tree Preservation Order in 1978 in respect of an area in Coolattin Woodland. In March 1987, a company applied to the Council for consent to selected felling of trees in the area covered by the 1978 Preservation Order. The Council refused four applications but granted a fifth subject to conditions. The company purported to appeal against the four refusals to An Bord Pleanála, and a local group of citizens also purported to appeal the granting of the consent. The Council applied for judicial review seeking to prohibit the Bord from rehearing the appeal. Barrington J granted the relief sought and issued an order of prohibition.

He held that s.45 of the 1963 Act empowered the Council, in making a Tree Preservation Order, to adapt any of the provisions of Part IV of the 1963 Act which related to permission to develop land, and that Part included the provision relating to appeals to An Bord Pleanála. Since this particular Order had, by its terms, excluded s.26(5) of the 1963 Act which dealt with appeals to An Bord Pleanála, no appeal lay against the granting or withholding of a consent under the 1978 Order. On this point of interpretation Barrington J distinguished the instant case from the decision of Murphy J in *The State (Haverty) v An Bord Pleanála* [1988] ILRM 545; [1987] IR 485 (see the 1987 Review, 9-10).

Undertakings The long-running Grange Developments litigation, which culminated in *Grange Developments Ltd v Dublin County Council (No. 4)* [1989] IR 377, was discussed in the 1988 Review, 312-14. Some of the problems associated with this litigation, namely the granting of undertakings by planning authorities to avoid payment of compensation under the 1963 Act, are now likely to be resolved by the Local Government (Planning and Development) Act 1990. See the discussion in the 1990 Review.

ROADS AND MOTORWAYS

The interaction of the Local Government (Planning and Development) Act 1963 and the Local Government (Roads and Motorways) Act 1974 was discussed in *Nolan v Minister for the Environment* [1989] IR 357 (332-3, above).

SANITARY SERVICES

The issue of charges for sanitary services arose again in *Louth County Council v Matthews*, High Court, 14 April 1989. The plaintiff Council had issued District Court proceedings seeking the recovery of £110 from the defendant on foot of a charge for refuse collection levied by the plaintiff under s.2 of the Local Government (Financial Provisions) (No. 2) Act 1983. The defendant had declined to avail of the refuse collection service provided by the Council. The defendant obtained a case stated from the District Justice which raised the questions as to whether the Council was empowered to raise a charge for refuse services and whether the Council was entitled to collect a charge from a person who did not avail of the service provided.

In the High Court, Gannon J was faced with a scrambled egg of legislation to pick through. He first summarised the points of agreement between the parties. It was common ground that: s.52 of the Public Health (Ireland) Act 1878 created a statutory obligation on the Council as rural sanitary authority to provide a service of refuse collection; that by reason of the repeal of s.232 of the 1878 Act by s.4 of the Local Government (Sanitary Services) Act 1948, the Council was precluded from raising a rate in relation to the expense involved in discharging that statutory obligation; and that since the enactment of the Local Government (Financial Provisions) Act 1978 the Council had no statutory authority to recover the expenses involved. Against this complex statutory background, therefore, the Council was empowered to charge for the refuse service since s.2 of the Local Government (Financial Provisions) (No. 2) Act 1983 empowered it to charge for a service which the Council was required to provide under 'any existing enactment' which did not empower it to charge for its provision.

That conclusion, however, did not bring the case very far. The nub of the case was whether the Council could impose a charge on a person, like the defendant, who did not wish to avail of the refuse service. It was on this point that Gannon J held against the Council. In view of the maze of legislation involved, it was not surprising that he was required to invoke the general principles of statutory interpretation laid down by Henchy J in *Inspector of Taxes v Kiernan* [1982] ILRM 13; [1981] IR 117. Gannon J noted that the Council was empowered to impose a charge for a 'service' pursuant to the 1983 Act, and that this appeared consistent with the creation of a contractual relationship. Having regard to the previous withdrawal by the legislature of the authority to raise money by a rate levy, he concluded that it could not have been the intention of the legislature to reintroduce this power through an oblique use of words in the 1983 Act which might be capable in their ordinary use of a different meaning, rather than by expressly conferring a power to impose a levy to meet anticipated expenses. Accordingly, he held that the defendant was not liable to pay the Council in respect of domestic refuse which was not collected by the Council.

VALUATION (RATING)

Case stated: delays   The effect of delays in processing a case stated was considered in *Irish Refining plc v Commissioner of Valuation*, High Court, 25 January 1988; Supreme Court, 4 May 1989: see 343, below, in the Practice and Procedure chapter. See also the *Pfizer* case, immediately below.

Case stated: form   In *Mitchelstown Co-Op Society Ltd v Commissioner of Valuation* [1989] IR 210, Blayney J reiterated some advice on the correct form of a case stated: see 345, below, also in the Practice and Procedure chapter.

Machinery or buildings   *Pfizer Chemical Corp v Commissioner of Valuation*, High Court, 9 May 1989 involved discussion as to whether certain installations on a factory were exempt from rating. The company was the owner and occupier of a large factory premises in Cork in which it manufactured food chemicals and bulk pharmaceuticals. In 1973, it appealed against the Commissioner's valuation for rating purposes of certain installations on the factory site. Further appeals were taken for subsequent years which were heard and determined in the Circuit Court in 1983, when the appeal was dismissed. The company appealed by way of case stated to the High Court. The appeals concerned ten categories of installations on the factory site, and included tanks for the reception of crude beet molasses, tanks for the reception of sulphuric acid, a number of other tanks as well as pipelines (which were in total over 40 miles long) which were used to transmit the molasses and acid to the factory. In addition to claiming that the Commissioner had incorrectly valued the installations for valuation purposes, the company argued that the Commissioner had wrongly categorised them in the Annual Valuation List, and that the Court had no power on appeal to amend the List. Costello J dismissed the company's appeals.

Applying the decision of the Supreme Court in *Roadstone Ltd v Commissioner of Valuation* [1961] IR 239, Costello J first noted that land used for commercial purposes does not fall to be valued under s.11 of the Valuation (Ireland) Act 1852, but must be valued under s.64 of the Poor Relief (Ireland) Act 1838; thus any installation which does not qualify for exemption on the ground that it is 'machinery' but which cannot, on the other hand, be described as 'buildings' is nonetheless a 'rateable hereditament' for the purposes of the Acts.

Taking the ordinary meaning of the word 'machinery', he held that the installations were not 'machinery' within the meaning of s.7 of the Valuation (Ireland) Act 1860, since although it was clear that some of the tanks were not mere receptacles for their contents, he considered that it would do violence to the ordinary meaning of the word to describe them as 'machinery'. Costello J applied dicta in *Cement Ltd v Commissioner of Valuation* [1960] IR 268 and *Beamish & Crawford Ltd v Commissioner of Valuation* [1980] ILRM 149 in this context. Nor could the installations properly be regarded as 'buildings', though they could properly be regarded as rateable hereditaments if the Commissioner had included them in the miscellaneous column of the Valuation List compiled under the Annual Revision of Rateable Property (Ireland) Amendment Act 1860.

This left a problem for the Court: could it amend the Valuation List compiled by the Commissioner? Costello J answered in the affirmative. He pointed out that the Court had power to make such order under s.11 of the Valuation (Ireland) Act 1860 as it 'may seem fit' to the Court. The power thus conferred could not have been wider, he stated, and the Court was accordingly empowered to amend the Commissioner's error in the instant case and would do so, following the decision of Hamilton P in *Siúcre Éireann Cpt v Commissioner of Valuation*, High Court, 5 October 1988.

Costello J made two other comments on the case. In view of the complex web he had had to untangle, it was no surprise that he stated that the rating and valuation code should long ago have been repealed and modernised. He pointed to the ease of passage of the Valuation Act 1986 (which he noted had tackled and hopefully settled the issue which had arisen in the instant case: see the annotation by Ó Caoimh, *Irish Current Law Statutes Annotated*) as indicating that public controversy would not be too aroused by reforming legislation which did not impose new liabilities. On another aspect of the instant case, he suggested that the delay in having the appeals in the case determined, the reasons for which were not made clear, must have been some sort of record in the 150 years history of the rating and valuation code.

Newly reclaimed land   In *Coal Distributors Ltd v Commissioner of Valuation* [1990] ILRM 172; [1989] IR 472, Blayney J affirmed the view that newly reclaimed land could be added to the Annual Valuation List. The appellant company was the owner of two plots of land in Dublin, both of which had been reclaimed from the sea and brought within the County Borough of Dublin for the first time in 1985. One of the plots was held by the company under separate titles. Pursuant to s.4 of the Valuation (Ireland) Amendment Act 1854, Dublin Corporation raised valuations on the plots and the company appealed against these to the Commissioner who confirmed them. On further appeal to the Circuit Court, the judge stated a case for the

High Court as to whether: (a) a valuation could be raised on the plots as part of the annual revision having regard to their being newly reclaimed land; and (b) the plot which was held under separate should have been valued separately, and if so whether the valuation was null and void.

Blayney J held that newly reclaimed land was capable of being valued under the annual revision, since s.4 of the 1854 Act requires a revision of the existing valuation of the entire County, Barony or Poor Law Union as a whole, and in that annual revision it was necessary to include any tenements introduced for the first time into the valuation. Blayney J quoted with approval the views to that effect of Palles CB in *Alma v Dublin Corporation* (1876-7) IR 10 CL 476.

He concluded that the plot which was held under separate titles should have been valued separately by the Commissioner pursuant to s.11 of the Valuation (Ireland) Act 1852, again following dicta of the Chief Baron, on this occasion in *Switzer & Co Ltd v Commissioner of Valuation* [1902] 2 IR 275. However, since the Circuit Court judge had power under s.23 of the 1852 Act and s.6 of the Annual Revision of Rateable Property (Ireland) Amendment Act 1860 to make such order as he thinks fit on appeal from the Commissioner, Blayney J remitted the matter to the Circuit Court for a separate valuation to be placed on that plot. Note that in *Pfizer Chemical Corp v Commissioner of Valuation*, High Court, 9 May 1989, above, Costello J corrected the valuation list under s.11 of the 1860 Act, though that case did not require an actual valuation to be made.

Public purposes In *St Macartan's Diocesan Trust v Commissioner of Valuation*, High Court, 16 June 1989 Gannon J discussed the rating status of a school funded partly by the State. The Trust was the owner of lands and buildings which were used as an agricultural college for young boys. The establishment and upkeep of the college was funded through collections made by the Catholic bishop of Clogher in the 1940s. The Department of Agriculture agreed at the time to provide funding for teachers' salaries for a limited time. In more recent years, Teagasc (the Agriculture and Food Development Authority) funded the salaries of a number of teachers in the college, and the remainder continued to be funded by the Catholic diocese, but admission to the college was on a non-denominational basis. The Trust appealed to the Valuation Tribunal against the refusal of the Commissioner to exempt the buildings and land from rating, but the Tribunal dismissed the appeal. On further appeal by the Trust Gannon J upheld the Tribunal's decision.

He concluded that, while the continued existence of the college was by now dependent on continued State aid, such vicarious State involvement in the college could not reasonably qualify the land and buildings as being dedicated to or used for public service within the meaning of s.63 of the Poor Relief (Ireland) Act 1838, applying the meaning given to 'public service' in *Kerry County Council v Commissioner of Valuation* [1934] IR 527 and *Maynooth College v Commissioner of Valuation* [1956] IR 189. Therefore, with regret, Gannon J concluded that the Trust was not entitled to the exemption claimed.

Practice and Procedure

APPELLATE COURT FUNCTION

Extension of time for appeal   The principles applicable in granting an extension of time were discussed in *Dalton v Minister for Finance* [1989] ILRM 519; [1989] IR 269, below.

Fresh evidence   The question whether the Supreme Court will allow fresh evidence to be led on appeal from the High Court was considered in two decisions in 1989.

In *Dalton v Minister for Finance* [1989] ILRM 519; [1989] IR 269 the plaintiff had been awarded over £55,000 damages in the High Court in a claim against the defendant. The defendant appealed against the order within the prescribed time period, but the plaintiff did not cross-appeal. Almost two years later, the plaintiff obtained medical advice that her condition had deteriorated since the date of the trial of the action, and she applied to the Supreme Court, pursuant to O.58, r.3(4) of the Rules of the Superior Courts 1986, for an extension of time within which to lodge an appeal against the High Court award, based, inter alia, on the deterioration. She also brought a motion pursuant to O.58, r.8 of the 1986 Rules to introduce affidavit evidence of the deterioration. The Supreme Court (Finlay CJ, Griffin and Hederman JJ) dismissed her application.

The Court applied the normal rule as to extension of time established in *Éire Continental Trading Co. Ltd v Clonmel Foods Ltd* [1955] IR 170. The Court held that the plaintiff had not formed an intention to appeal within the time limit specified, nor had there been any misapprehension between her and her legal advisers as to whether she would be allowed to make an argument as to quantum on the defendant's appeal.

Delivering the Court's decision, Finlay CJ pointed out that, if the plaintiff were to be allowed to rely on evidence obtained after a High Court verdict in seeking an extension of time to appeal, then a defendant would also be entitled to seek an appeal on the basis of similar grounds. The Chief Justice commented on this possibility as follows:

> Such a proposition of law is without any authority and is, in my view, wholly unsound in principle. It is of the essence of litigation that subject to a proper right of appeal, as provided by law, the judgment of a court

is a final judgment. In the case of a decision of the High Court, the appeal to the Supreme Court is limited to an appeal based on an assertion either [*sic*] that the learned trial judge in the High Court erred in some issue of law which he determined; erred on some principle in exercising a discretion or assessing damages; or made a finding or findings not supported by the evidence before him. If an order made in the High Court were to be varied or set aside on the basis of events which occurred after the making of that order and which, therefore, neither were nor could possibly be in evidence before the High Court judge, this would be wholly inconsistent with the appellate jurisdiction of [the Supreme] Court.

This passage provides a succinct statement of the appellate jurisdiction of the Supreme Court. In addition the passage clearly establishes that the Court has no discretion to allow the introduction of new evidence in the Court where this was not considered in the High Court. It might be noted, however, that the Chief Justice appeared to refer to the position of the Supreme Court in relation to the High Court when assessing the functions of an appellate court. It is, for example, the case that where the High Court acts as an appellate court from Circuit Court decisions of first instance it may hear any evidence; this is of course a hearing *de novo*, as opposed to an appeal on a point of law. The point, however, is that an appellate court is not always precluded from hearing evidence which had not been considered in the court below. Thus, what appeared to be a principled argument put forward by the Chief Justice in *Dalton* does not appear to be supportable from a practical point of view. There are, no doubt, many arguments in favour of finality of litigation, but even the Chief Justice and the Supreme Court as a whole have moderated that principle in other contexts: see for example *O'Shea v Director of Public Prosecutions* [1989] ILRM 309; [1988] IR 655, *Keenan v Shield Insurance Co. Ltd* [1988] IR 89 (both discussed in the 1988 Review, 319), *Irish Refining plc v Commissioner of Valuation*, Supreme Court, 4 May 1989 (344, below) and *Harvey v Minister for Social Welfare* [1990] ILRM 185 (395, below). See also the cases on *res judicata*, below in this chapter. It may be that the Court felt that the double hurdle of seeking an extension of time as well as the application for leave to introduce fresh evidence was just a leap too far. Indeed, a more flexible approach, albeit with the same result, was evident in the second case on this area before a Court of precisely the same composition which delivered judgment just over five months later.

In *O'Connor v O'Shea*, Supreme Court, 24 July 1989 the plaintiff had been involved in a road traffic accident arising from which he instituted High Court proceedings for damages against the defendant. In the course of the trial, a major portion of the evidence was devoted to addressing the nature and extent of the spinal injuries which the plaintiff was alleged to suffer from. A number of consultants were called on the plaintiff's behalf indicating the circumstances in which the plaintiff might recover full use of his spine, but emphasising the difficulty of so doing. The jury awarded no damages for future pain and suffering. The plaintiff appealed the refusal to award damages for future pain and suffering and, pursuant to O.58, r.8 of the 1986 Rules, brought a motion to have additional medical evidence considered by the Supreme Court in the appeal. In this instance, therefore, it may be noted that the plaintiff was within time in appealing to the Supreme Court. Nonetheless, the Court (again composed of Finlay CJ, Griffin and Hederman JJ) dismissed the application.

But, as indicated above, Finlay CJ was prepared to concede that in certain circumstances the need for finality of litigation could be outweighed by the need to do justice, thus indicating that in some circumstances fresh evidence could be introduced. In line with the *Dalton* case, however, he added that there was a strong presumption against permitting the reopening of a case. Counsel for the plaintiff referred to the 'dramatic alteration' rule discussed in *Mulholland v Mitchell* [1971] AC 666. However, the Chief Justice stated that the Court would refuse to admit the evidence in the instant case as it could not be said to result in a dramatic alteration in the circumstances which were considered in the trial court, and could only be described as a different medical view reached by a different medical practitioner. He said that to admit the evidence would give rise to the disadvantage and mischief which would undermine finality in litigation.

Raising issues de novo In *Harvey v Minister for Social Welfare* [1990] ILRM 185 (394, below, in the Social Welfare chapter) and *Irish Refining plc v Commissioner of Valuation*, Supreme Court, 4 May 1989 (344, below), the Supreme Court dealt with issues which had not been raised in the High Court.

Review of trial court's findings The well-established limitations on the Supreme Court's functions in assessing the findings of a trial court were applied in *Dunne v National Maternity Hospital* [1989] ILRM 735; [1989] IR 91 (421, below, in the Torts chapter) and *Keating v New Ireland Assurance Co. plc* [1990] ILRM 110 (43, above, in the Commercial Law chapter).

CASE STATED

Delays The effect of delay in processing a case stated was dealt with by the Supreme Court in *Irish Refining plc v Commissioner of Valuation*, Supreme Court, 4 May 1989. The applicant company had appealed to the Circuit Court against a valuation of property made by the respondent Commissioner. The matter was dealt with by judgment of the Circuit Court of July 1984. In October 1984, the Commissioner requested the Circuit Court judge to state and sign a case stated for the opinion of the High Court, and this request was within the three month period specified by s.10 of the Annual Revision of Rateable Property (Ireland) Amendment Act 1860, as amended by s.31(1) of the Courts of Justice Act 1936. The 1860 Act, as amended, also provides that the Circuit Court judge 'shall . . . transmit it to the Commissioner of Valuation within twenty-one days . . .'.

The parties were not agreed on the contents of the case stated, and no final draft was presented to the judge. By notice of January 1987, the applicant company sought to have the notice for a case stated set aside for want of prosecution. A draft case stated was presented to the judge by counsel for the Commissioner in March 1987. In June 1987, the applicant company informed the judge of its intention to proceed by way of judicial review to have the notice quashed, and the application on the motion to set aside was then adjourned. Egan J held, High Court, 25 January 1988 that the delay was not a bar to the transmission of the case stated: see the 1988 Review, 319-20. The applicant company appealed to the Supreme Court. Prior to the hearing of the appeal, the Circuit Court judge who had heard the case had retired. The Supreme Court (Finlay CJ, Hederman and McCarthy JJ) dismissed the company's appeal.

Delivering the Court's decision, Finlay CJ held (applying the views of Davitt P in *Prendergast v Porter* [1961] IR 440) that the requirement in s.10 of the 1860 Act that the judge transmit the case stated within twenty-one days was directory in nature, and not mandatory, and thus non-compliance with its provisions did not invalidate a case stated signed and stated subsequent to that period. He pointed out that the contention for the applicant company would leave a person seeking a case stated at the mercy of the judge, and such manifestly unfair or unjust procedure should not be assumed to have been the real intention of the legislature.

The Court allowed the applicant company to argue an additional ground, alleging prejudice resulting from the delay in prosecuting the case stated, in view of the gravity and importance of the point to it and to the County Council. However, on the evidence, the Court concluded that the company had not made out any case of prejudice arising from the delay in the present case.

Finally, adding to recent judicial concern over some difficulties in the case stated procedure (see the 1988 Review, 320-1), the Court indicated that although the transmission of a draft case stated to the judge was not required by legislation but was merely a matter of practice, it might well be desirable that it be obligatory. Changes along these lines have in fact been introduced by the Circuit Court Rules (No.2) 1990: see the discussion in the 1990 Review.

Form of case stated   In *Mitchelstown Co-Op Society Ltd v Commissioner of Valuation* [1989] IR 210, Blayney J reiterated some old advice on the correct form which a case stated should take. The Society appealed by way of case stated to the High Court from a determination of the Valuation Tribunal, which was established by the Valuation Act 1988. This was the first such appeal under s.5 of the 1988 Act, and the Society submitted that the form of the case stated would make it difficult for the High Court to adjudicate upon the case. The form adopted by the Tribunal stated that it accepted the uncontroverted evidence adduced by the Society as to the installations concerned in the valuation appeal, and the entire transcript of evidence was annexed to the case stated. The Tribunal also included the text of its determination in an annex to the case stated. Blayney J remitted the case stated to the Tribunal for amendment.

Blayney J quoted with approval the principles stated by Murphy LJ in *Emerson v Hearty* [1946] NI 35. Adapting those to the instant case, he said that the form of the case stated should include the findings of fact by the Tribunal and that the High Court should not be required to go outside the case stated to discover such findings. And he stated that similar considerations applied to the contentions of the parties, the inferences drawn by the Tribunal from the primary facts and the Tribunal's determinations. While he acknowledged that this might lead to excessively long cases stated, it would also allow the Court to deal with a case more expeditiously. Since the decision reiterates the general principles laid down in the *Emerson* case, it is of much wider application than the rating context in which it arose.

Service on solicitor   In *Crowley v McVeigh* [1990] ILRM 220; [1989] IR 73 (154, above, in the Criminal Law chapter), Blayney J held that where every possible effort had been made, without success, to serve a respondent in a case stated then service on the solicitor who had acted for the respondent in the District Court was sufficient compliance with the Summary Jurisdiction Act 1857.

Signing of case stated   The requirement that a case stated be signed within a certain period, although stated in apparently mandatory language in different statutory contexts, has consistently been held to be directory in nature only. This was confirmed in 1989 in two cases decided within three weeks of each other: *McMahon v McClafferty* [1990] ILRM 32; [1989] IR 68, which dealt with the requirment in r.200 of the District Court Rules 1948 (158, above, in the Criminal Law chapter) and *Irish Refining plc v*

Commissioner of Valuation, Supreme Court, 4 May 1989, which dealt with s.10 of the Annual Revision of Rateable Property (Ireland) Amendment Act 1860 (343 above).

CIRCUIT COURT

Establishment of jurisdiction *Harrington and Anor v Murphy* [1989] IR 207 involved an important point on the proofs required to establish jurisdiction of the Circuit Court. The applicants were defendants in a Circuit Court action in which rights of pasturage had been claimed over certain lands. In the course of the hearing before the respondent Circuit Court judge, the applicants contested the jurisdiction of the Court to hear the case. The respondent rejected the applicants' argument and proceeded to find in favour of the plaintiffs in the action. S.22 of the Courts (Supplemental Provisions) Act 1961, and the Third Schedule thereto, as amended most recently by the Courts Act 1981 (not the non-existent Courts Act 1980, which the report mentions) provides that the Circuit Court's jurisdiction in such actions extends to land with a rateable valuation of £200 or less. On judicial review O'Hanlon J refused to quash the decision of the respondent.

Although O'Hanlon J acknowledged that formal proof of rateable valuation should be given in every case, failure to do so did not deprive the Circuit Court of jurisdiction to determine the case provided that it subsequently transpires that the Court had jurisdiction in fact. Of course, as he pointed out, where the Court was subsequently found not to have jurisdiction any order would be set aside *ex debito justitiae* by the High Court. In the instant case, however, since it had later emerged that the rateable valuation of the land was £13.50, the applicants were not entitled to the relief sought. The effect of the decision is two-fold: where jurisdiction is not formally established, litigants run the risk of having the Circuit Court judge decline to entertain the case; if the judge accepts jurisdiction without formal proof, they run the risk of judicial review proceedings. Thus while the absence of formal proof will not be fatal to proceedings in all circumstances, it remains good practice to establish jurisdiction in advance.

For a similar approach in a different context see the decision of Lardner J in *Director of Public Prosecutions v Cunningham* [1989] IR 481, discussed at 369, below, in the Revenue Law chapter.

COSTS

Appeal from Taxing Master *Crotty v An Taoiseach (No. 2)* [1990] ILRM

617 involved an appeal from the Taxing Master in connection with the plaintiff's costs in his successful constitutional action concerning the Single European Act: [1987] ILRM 400; [1987] IR 713 (see the 1987 Review, 91-2). In the appeal from the Taxing Master, Barr J approved the principles set out by Hamilton J (as he then was) in *Kelly v Breen* [1978] ILRM 63. A number of different items were challenged.

The first group of items concerned fees marked by counsel for drafting and settling various affidavits. The Taxing Master had taken the view that these should not be allowed on the ground that a prudent solicitor would not have expected these to be discharged on a party and party basis. Barr J reversed this finding of the Taxing Master on the basis that it did not appear to have been based on any supporting evidence.

The second group of fees in dispute concerned the various appearances by counsel throughout the constitutional proceedings. Substantial reductions had been ordered by the Taxing Master on these fees, primarily because the fees had been accepted by the solicitor for the plaintiff without exercising any judgment as to whether they were reasonable. Barr J was of the view that the Taxing Master had not made sufficient inquiries of the solicitor for the plaintiff as to why the fees marked had been accepted. However, he accepted that for most of the items in this group 'the Taxing Master correctly assessed counsels' brief fees but for the wrong reason.' Barr J was of the view that the fees marked by counsel for the plaintiff should bear a fair and reasonable proportion to those marked by counsel for the defendants, and in this light the Taxing Master's reductions were allowed to stand. The exceptions to this view by Barr J were the fees marked for settling the statement of claim. The judge accepted that the drafting of the statement of claim had been much more onerous than the drafting of the defence. On that basis, therefore, he reinstated the fees marked by counsel.

The third group of items concerned what Barr J described as 'an extraordinarily large number of consultations' held during the proceedings. He accepted that the Taxing Master had been correct to disallow much of what was claimed in this group.

Finally, Barr J dealt with the solicitor's brief fee. While acknowledging the difficulty of preparing the case, he agreed with the Taxing Master's reduction in the fee claimed. Barr J stated that, in addition to the factors referred to by the Taxing Master, it was relevant to bear in mind that the constitutional action concerned questions of law which were essentially in the domain of counsel. It was, therefore, quite different from the situation in a personal injuries case where much of the burden of preparing the case falls on the instructing solicitor.

Follow the event   In *Society for the Protection of Unborn Children (Irl)*

Ltd v Coogan and Ors (No. 2), Supreme Court, 20 March 1990 the general principle that costs follow the event was applied: see 106-7, above.

Interest: party and party   In *Attorney General (McGarry and Ors) v Sligo County Council (No. 2)* [1989] ILRM 785, the Supreme Court ruled that, in general, interest was not payable on party and party costs. The substantive issues in the case are discussed at 329, above. The Supreme Court (Walsh, Hederman and McCarthy JJ) held that the plaintiffs, who were awarded costs in the substantive action, were not automatically entitled to interest on their party and party costs, bearing in mind that the relevant sums, including fees, might not yet have been paid out by the solicitor and that the principle of indemnity applies to such costs. Since the only sums at issue in this case related to fees, the plaintiffs were not entitled to the order for interest on these costs. This decision is an important exception to the recently established jurisprudence on the area which was applied by the Court itself in *Cooke v Walsh (No. 2)* [1989] ILRM 322: see the 1988 Review, 322-3.

Security for costs: bankruptcy   In *Performing Rights Society Ltd v Casey*, High Court, 28 April 1989 the plaintiff society had obtained judgment against the defendant in the Circuit Court for £584.82 and costs in June 1988. Notice of appeal was lodged by the defendant in the same month. The defendant was adjudicated a bankrupt in August 1988. The defendant's appeal was adjourned to ascertain whether the Official Assignee wished to prosecute the appeal. He indicated that he did not wish to do so, but that the defendant was free to do so provided no funds comprising the defendant's estate were used. The plaintiff applied for security for costs against the defendant. Barron J ordered that security be provided.

He said that it was important to bear in mind that the present case involved an appeal against a determination made and that the liability arose before the bankruptcy; and that while the defendant had an interest in proceeding with the appeal, it was appropriate to order that security for costs be provided bearing in mind that no funds would be available from his estate to meet the plaintiff's costs in the event of the defendant's appeal being unsuccessful. However, he also held that the order for security should be confined to the level which would have been incurred in an appeal from the District Court to the Circuit Court, having regard to the award made. Barron J thus followed the practice indicated by the decision of the Court of Appeal in *United Telephone Co. v Bassano* (1886) 31 Ch D 630.

Security for costs: company   In *Comhlucht Páipéar Ríomhaireachta Teo v Údarás na Gaeltachta and Ors* [1990] ILRM 266, the Supreme Court dealt with an important point on security for costs not mentioned previously in the recent case law on the topic.

After his appointment, the liquidator of the plaintiff company (which was insolvent though with some funds available for unsecured creditors) had instituted proceedings against the defendants under s.286 of the Companies Act 1963 claiming that a loan repaid by the company while it was insolvent amounted to a fraudulent preference. The defendants applied pursuant to s.390 of the Act for an order for security for costs. In the High Court, Costello J refused to make the orders sought on the ground that, in the exercise of his discretion, there were special circumstances which justified such refusal: [1987] IR 684 (see the 1987 Review, 278-9). On appeal by the defendants the Supreme Court (Finlay CJ, Hederman and McCarthy JJ) upheld the High Court order, but for quite different reasons.

Delivering the Court's decision, McCarthy J held that the application for security for costs simply failed *in limine*. This was because where an action is brought by a company after liquidation, the costs of a successful litigant against an insolvent company rank in priority to all other claims under ss.281 and 285 of the Companies Act 1963 where, as in the instant case, there are sufficient funds available to pay the costs of the successful litigant. In this context he approved a passage to that effect in *Halsbury's Laws of England*, 4th ed, vol.7(2), para.1803. He also noted that this might have a negative effect in that the liquidator, faced with so large a prospective claim in priority to all other creditors, might be reluctant to proceed with the action against any or all of the defendants. He did not indicate whether he thought this was a matter which required legislative intervention. There are clearly some difficult policy issues involved here; as has been pointed out in other cases, a company might find itself in liquidation arising from the wrongdoing of persons who the company might wish to sue, but the effect of the Supreme Court decision might be to deter such litigation.

Finally, on the manner in which Costello J had decided the case, McCarthy J offered some comments. He stated that the High Court judge had erred in concluding that there were special circumstances which justified his refusal to make an order against the company; nor did he consider that the strength of the plaintiff's case was such as to indicate that such order should not be made. Thus, in the particular circumstances of this case an order for security would have been made were it not for the provisions of ss.281 and 285 of the 1963 Act.

In *Society for the Protection of Unborn Children (Irl.) Ltd v Grogan and Ors (No. 2)*, Irish Times LR, 12 February 1990 (decided 27 November 1989), Lardner J dismissed an application for security for costs brought by the defendants. The substantive action in this case is discussed above 102-5. It will be recalled that the plaintiff society had applied for an interlocutory injunction to restrain the defendants from distributing information on abortion clinics. In the High Court, Carroll J declined to grant the relief sought and referred certain questions to the Court of Justice of the European Communities. The plaintiff society appealed this decision to the Supreme Court, and pending the hearing of the appeal the defendants applied for the order for security for costs. Lardner J held, applying the principles in the recent case law on this topic, that the defendants were not entitled to obtain an order for security for costs. He had regard in particular to the general circumstances of the case and the fact that the plaintiff society had an arguable case.

DISCOVERY

In *Bord na Mona v J. Sisk & Son Ltd*, High Court, 30 November 1989, Costello J held that documents which were marked 'without prejudice' were privileged. In addition, he held that documents which were privileged for one set of proceedings were also entitled to privilege in respect of other proceedings. In this he followed the decision of the English Court of Appeal in *The Aegis Blaze* [1986] 1 Lloyd's Rep 203.

DISTRICT COURT

Fit person order   The nature of the investigations to be conducted by the District Court when being asked to make a 'fit person' order under the Children Act 1908 was considered by the Supreme Court in *The State (D.) v G. and Ors* [1990] ILRM 10 and [1990] ILRM 130 and in *The State (F.) v Superintendent of B. Garda Station* [1990] ILRM 243 (HC); Supreme Court, 3 May 1990 (see 265-9, above).

ENFORCEMENT OF JUDGMENTS: EUROPEAN COMMUNITIES

The Rules of the Superior Courts (No.1) 1989 (SI No.14), which took effect on 1 February 1989, set out the changes in the 1986 Rules in the light of the Jurisdiction of Courts and Enforcement of Judgments (European Communities) Act 1988. An extremely helpful *Guide to the Changes in the 1986 Rules* by Hogan and O'Reilly was also published under the auspices of the Superior Courts Rules Committee.

For convenience we refer below to the case law on the 1988 Act which occurred during 1989. In *Elwyn (Cottons) Ltd v Pearle Designs Ltd* [1989] ILRM 162; [1989] IR 9 and *Elwyn (Cottons) Ltd v Master of the High Court* [1989] IR 14, the High Court dealt with the granting of protective measures pursuant to the 1988 Act: see 76-9, above. In *International Commercial Bank plc v Insurance Corporation of Ireland plc* [1989] IR 453, the Supreme Court dealt with some of the transitional provisions of the 1988 Act: see 66-8, above. Finally, *Rhatigan v Textiles y Confecciones Europeas SA* [1989] IR 18 (HC); Supreme Court, 31 May 1990 dealt with important formalities which must be complied with in order to obtain judgment under the 1988 Act: see 73-6, above.

IN CAMERA HEARINGS

The decision of the Supreme Court in *In re R Ltd* [1989] ILRM 757; [1989] IR 126 was the first major analysis in recent years of the circumstances in which court hearings may be held other than in public. In an application by a member of the named company under s.205 of the Companies 1963 claiming relief on the grounds of oppression, Costello J made an order under s.205(7) of the Act that the entire of the proceedings be heard otherwise than in public. The applicant member of the company, who had been its chief executive until shortly before the proceedings, had filed a lengthy affidavit, which included some comments and opinions. It also contained descriptions of a five year business plan for the company, details of its accounts and details of the commercial terms of one transaction into which the company had entered. The company claimed that the information in the affidavit would be seriously damaging to the company's interests if made public. Costello J held that it would be impracticable to hold part of the proceedings in public and part *in camera*. On appeal by the applicant the Supreme Court by a 3-2 majority (Walsh, Griffin and Hederman JJ; Finlay CJ and Hamilton P dissenting) allowed the appeal and ordered that the proceedings be held in public.

The leading judgment for the majority was delivered by Walsh J. He pointed out that the discretion given to the trial judge by s.205(7) of the 1963 Act, namely to take account of the commercial impact of hearing the case in public, must be considered in the context of the obligation on the courts under Article 34.1 of the Constitution to administer justice. He went on:

> In seeking to avail of the protection apparently offered by [s.205(7)] the party seeking it must be able to satisfy the court that not only would the disclosure of information be seriously prejudicial to the legitimate interests of the company, but it must also be shown that a public hearing

of the whole, or of that part of the proceedings which it is sought to have heard other than in a public court, would fall short of the doing of justice.

Walsh J noted that it was common case that publication of the information contained in the applicant's affidavit would be seriously prejudicial to the company's legitimate interests. However, Walsh J concluded that the evidence to date did not indicate that a hearing in public would prevent justice being done. On this basis, therefore, the Court reversed the High Court decision.

The majority offered some solace to the company, however. They stated that if the company were to establish that the disclosure of the three matters referred to in the applicant's affidavit would prevent justice being done, this would not necessarily require that the entire of the proceedings be held other than in public, even if this made the trial inconvenient or even troublesome. In any event, the majority was of the view that the judgment of the Court should be pronounced in public.

It may be noted that Walsh J also made reference to a number of statutory provisions which speak of hearings other than in public. He noted that some of these provisions did not appear to give a discretion to a trial judge as to whether a particular type of case should be heard in private. He did not give a definitive ruling as to whether such provisions were constitutionally valid, but he was clearly not prepared to give them a constitutional imprimatur. Walsh J emphasised the primacy of 'doing justice' as the touchstone for deciding whether hearings should be otherwise than in public, and in his reference to the statutory provisions in this area, some of which predated the enactment of the Constitution, he indicated that these had also been motivated by the same objective. Whether this historical analysis is correct may be a moot point, but if it is intended to indicate that 'doing justice' forecloses reference to such considerations as the legitimate commercial interests of a company, it might be open to question. Having regard to the positivist and utilitarian considerations which would have surrounded the enactment of legislation or the development of common law rules by judges in connection with public court hearings, it is difficult to imagine that commercial interests of a company do not form part of the 'justice' matrix. Inevitably, the decision whether to hold a public or in camera hearing will be a matter for discretion; the decision of the Supreme Court in the instant case certainly indicates that the commercial interests of the company can never be the deciding factor: see further, 55-8, above. Finally, Walsh J expressly disapproved of the dictum in *In re Redbreast Preserving Co. Ltd* (1956) 91 ILTR 12, at 23 which suggested that Article 34.1 was always satisfied by the public pronouncement of a decision based on a hearing in private. He commented:

[W]here that is not expressly authorised by a post-Constitution statute [the dictum] is clearly incorrect and ought not to be followed. All evidence in proceedings before a court must be taken in public save where otherwise expressly permitted in accordance with the terms of Article 34 of the Constitution.

From this it is clear that the passage quoted earlier from Walsh J's judgment governs any statutory provision on hearings other than in public. Indeed, the Court was unanimous on the point that any statutory provision which allows for hearings other than in public must be strictly construed in accordance with the requirements of Article 34.1. In the particular context of s.205(7) of the 1963 Act, the word 'proceedings' was taken by all five judges to include pleadings, affidavits and other documents relevant to the trial of the action.

JOINDER OF PARTIES

Centralising an action The circumstances in which parties should be joined to a single set of proceedings were considered in two Supreme Court decisions in 1989.

In *International Commercial Bank plc v Insurance Corporation of Ireland plc* [1989] ILRM 788; [1989] IR 453, the defendant had joined a company registered in Guernsey as third party in proceedings brought in the Irish courts by the plaintiff. The plaintiff claimed in respect of a credit guarantee insurance agreement by which the defendant agreed to repay a certain sum on default of a loan given by the plaintiff to a company. The defendant had entered into a contract of reinsurance with the third party. The defendant denied liability on the basis of a claim of misrepresentation by the plaintiff. The third party claimed, inter alia, that it was not a necessary party to the Irish proceedings within the meaning of O.11, r.1(h) of the Rules of the Superior Courts 1986. In the High Court, Costello J held that the defendant was entitled to join the third party: see the 1988 Review, 89-90. On appeal by the third party the Supreme Court (Finlay CJ, Griffin and McCarthy JJ) upheld Costello J's decision.

Delivering the Court's decision, Finlay CJ stated that, as a general rule the requirements of justice were that a party against whom a legal claim was made was entitled to have the issue of liability determined against him in a single set of proceedings. In such proceedings, any third party who might relieve the other party of all or some of the liability could be joined, and O.11, r.1(h) of the 1986 Rules should be interpreted in that light. Finlay CJ agreed with Costello J that the instant case could be distinguished from that in

McCheane v Gyles [1902] 1 Ch 287, but that in any event the narrow view taken by the English Court of Appeal in that case should not be followed in this State.

Turning to the particular circumstances of the present case, the Chief Justice stated that the third party here was a necessary party to the proceedings within the meaning of O.11, since it was clear that the defendant's defence in the proceedings brought by the plaintiff were to a large extent the same as those which would be put forward by the third party. For these reasons, the decision of Costello J was upheld. It may be noted that the Court also dealt with an issue arising from the Jurisdiction of Courts and Enforcement of Judgments (European Communities) Act 1988: see 66-8, above.

In the second case on joinder of parties, the Supreme Court took a similar view, though without reference to its *International Commercial Bank* decision. In *Tromso Sparebank v Beirne and Ors (No. 3)*, Supreme Court, 15 December 1989 the plaintiff bank had issued proceedings for payment on foot of promissory notes which had been discounted by the plaintiff. The defence filed by a number of defendants, who included the parent bank of the branch which had issued the notes, alleged fraud in the making of the notes. The parent bank, which was registered in England, was joined as defendant under O.11, r.1(h) of the Rules of the Superior Courts 1986. The parent bank appealed against the High Court order joining it as defendant. The Supreme Court (Finlay CJ, Walsh and McCarthy JJ) dismissed the appeal.

McCarthy J delivered the only considered judgment for the Court. He noted that it was clear from the plaintiff's Statement of Claim that it would not have discounted the notes without a certification of validity from the parent bank and it was therefore clear that the parent bank had a direct connection with the proceedings. Echoing the view taken in the *International Commercial Bank* case, he concluded that in view of the desirability of having all issues centralised in one action, there was ample jurisdiction to justify the making of the order under O.11, r.1(h) of the 1986 Rules to join the parent bank. Indeed, McCarthy J stated that it was difficult to see how the High Court judge could have exercised his discretion in any other way.

Time limit   In *Kelly v Board of Governors of St Laurence's Hospital (Staunton, Third Party)* [1989] ILRM 877, the Supreme Court dealt with the requirement that a third party notice be served as soon as is reasonably possible. The plaintiff had successfully brought an action against the defendant hospital for personal injuries sustained while a patient in the hospital. The proceedings had been instituted in 1983, and the hospital had filed a defence in 1984. The trial of the action took place in 1987, and the hospital appealed to the Supreme Court, which dismissed the appeal in 1988:

[1989] ILRM 437; [1988] IR 402 (see the 1988 Review, 410-12 and 417). The hospital had, after the conclusion of the trial of the action, been given leave to issue and serve a third party notice against the named third party, a consultant in the hospital. The consultant had been called as a witness in the plaintiff's action against the hospital but no indication had been given to him that the hospital would claim against him. He appealed to the Supreme Court against the High Court order granting leave to serve the third party notice, and the Supreme Court (Finlay CJ, Hederman and McCarthy JJ) allowed his appeal.

The Court held that s.27(1)(b) of the Civil Liability Act 1961 envisaged the issuing of a third party notice in two circumstances, one of which required that the notice be served as soon as was reasonably possible. Since the application in the High Court under O.16, r.1 of the Rules of the Superior Courts 1986 was clearly made under this provision, the Court held that the trial judge had erred in allowing liberty to serve the notice, it not being as soon as was reasonably possible when notice was served after the conclusion of the trial of the action concerned.

The Court also took the view that s.27(1)(b) of the 1961 Act allowed for a second method of claiming contribution, namely a substantive claim for contribution which could be prosecuted by an action brought by civil bill or plenary summons. Such a claim would, of course, be subject to the question as to whether the delay in bringing such a claim resulted in prejudice or unfairness (under the decision in *Ó Domhnaill v Merrick* [1985] ILRM 40; [1984] IR 151: see the 1987 Review, 250-2); or could also be in breach of the general principle in the 1961 Act that all claims of a similar nature be determined at the same time: see the cases on centralising the action, above. However, as this matter had not been fully argued before the Supreme Court in the appeal, it expressed no view as to what the decision of the High Court would be were the hospital to institute such an action for contribution.

JUDICIAL APPOINTMENTS

The Courts (No.2) Act 1988 arose out of a particular difficulty in connection with the continuation in office of District Justices from 65 years of age to 70 years of age: see the 1988 Review, 337-8. In *Shelly v Mahon*, High Court, 31 October 1989; Supreme Court, 8 March 1990, the effect of the 1988 Act on a conviction entered against the applicant was considered: see 94-5, above.

JUDICIAL SALARIES

The Courts (Supplemental Provisions) Act 1961 (Section 46) Order 1989 (SI No.204) provided for phased increases in judicial salaries in line with the Gleeson Report No.30. Transitional increases were provided, to take effect on 1 July 1989 and 1 April 1990. As from 1 October 1990, the Order provides for the following annual salaries:

Chief Justice:	£72,356
President of the High Court:	£64,927
Supreme Court ordinary judge:	£62,274
High Court ordinary judge:	£57,498
President of the Circuit Court:	£57,498
Circuit Court ordinary judge:	£45,825
President of the District Court:	£45,825
District Justice:	£38,397

NOTARY PUBLIC

In *In re McCarthy* [1990] ILRM 84, Finlay CJ, sitting in the Court of the Chief Justice, affirmed well-established principles as to the circumstances in which a Notary Public is appointed. The applicant in this case was a retired person who carried out the functions of Commissioner for Oaths and Peace Commissioner. It was accepted that he was a person of the highest integrity, but he was not a qualified lawyer. Finlay CJ noted that it was well established that only members of the legal profession should be appointed as a Notary Public, because of the particular requirements associated with the office. The Chief Justice referred with approval to the decision of Ó Dálaigh CJ in *In re McKeon* [1965] Ir Jur Rep 24 in this context. Indeed, Finlay CJ added that, having regard to the expanding role of the Notary in the European Community context, it was appropriate that a solicitor appointed to the office should have a significant number of years experience rather than being a newly-qualified solicitor.

PRECEDENT

High Court decisions While decisions of one High Court judge are not regarded as binding on another High Court judge there is, generally speaking, a great deal of deference to such decisions by the judges of the Court. In 1989 an unusual degree of disagreement broke out, three arising in the Family Law context. In *U.F. v J.C.*, High Court, 24 May 1989 Keane J declined to follow the direction of a number of decisions of his colleagues in the nullity area. In the event the Supreme Court reversed Keane J in a judgment delivered on 11 July 1990. Earlier, Lardner J, in *R.T. v V.P.*, High Court, 30 July 1989 had been inclined to accept the earlier decisions and thus to disagree with Keane J. And in *E.N. v R.N.*, High Court, 27 June 1989, Barron J had refused to follow the decision of Barr J in *L. v L.* [1989] ILRM 528. All these decisions are discussed in the Family Law chapter, above. Finally, in *Carberry v Minister for Social Welfare*, High Court, 28 April 1989, Barron J declined to follow the decision of Hamilton P in *Cotter v Minister for Social Welfare (No.2)*, High Court, 10 June 1988: see the discussion at 395, below, in the Social Welfare chapter.

Ratio decidiendi/obiter dictum In *O'Malley v An Taoiseach* [1990] ILRM 460 (107-9, above, in the Constitutional Law chapter), Hamilton P had the unusual privilege for a judge of being able to describe parts of a judgment which he had delivered one day previously as being *obiter*. We also argued earlier that certain comments by Blayney J in *McDaid v Sheehy* [1989] ILRM 342 were *obiter* (see 111-3, above, also in the Constitutional Law chapter).

RECEIVER BY WAY OF EQUITABLE EXECUTION

The circumstances under which a receiver by way of equitable execution may be appointed were considered by O'Hanlon J in *Ahern v M. O'Brien & Co. Ltd*, High Court, 8 May 1989. The plaintiff had recovered judgment for over £4,000 against the defendant company. He applied to court for the appointment of a receiver by way of equitable execution over certain ground rents payable to the defendant company out of certain properties in respect of which the defendant company held a moiety interest. O'Hanlon J made a conditional appointment.

He stated that while in general a receiver by way of equitable execution will not be appointed over payments to be made in the future, there were exceptional circumstances where this could be done. In the instant case it appeared to him that, prima facie, the moneys payable in favour of the defendant would not be subject to disbursements to third parties (save that tax might be payable to the Revenue Commissioners), so that a conditional appointment could be made subject to an opportunity for the defendant to argue that the order should not be made absolute. O'Hanlon J accepted as correct the decision of the Irish Court of Appeal in *Orr v Grierson* (1890) 28 LR Ir 20, but he distinguished the instant case from that in *Cohen v Ruddy* [1905] 2 IR 56.

RELATOR ACTIONS

In *Attorney General (McGarry) v Sligo County Council* [1989] ILRM 768, McCarthy J doubted whether, in the circumstances in that case, the plaintiffs had been obliged to seek the consent of the Attorney General to convert the case into a relator action: see 330, above, in the Local Government chapter.

REPRESENTATIVE ACTIONS

In *Greene and Ors v Minister for Agriculture* [1990] ILRM 364 (see 101, above, in the Constitutional Law chapter), the names of over 1,390 persons in a similar position to the named plaintiffs had been transmitted by agreement to the defendants. Murphy J accepted that these 1,390 persons had all authorised the proceedings taken on their behalf and he concluded that, had damages been payable to the plaintiffs, the other 1,390 would have been entitled to the benefit of that decision. Although this might appear to be a somewhat tortuous procedural device, it obviously circumvents the 'non-retrospection' problem arising from decisions such as *Murphy v Attorney General* [1982] IR 241.

RES JUDICATA

Two judgments in the same litigation provided some interesting insights into the res judicata principle. *Breathnach v Ireland and Ors* [1989] IR 489 and *Breathnach v Ireland and Ors (No. 2)*, High Court, 14 March 1990 arose out of a criminal prosecution of the 1970s, commonly known as the Sallins Train Robbery case. While three accused persons had been convicted on certain charges by the Special Criminal Court, two of the convictions, including that of the plaintiff in the instant case, were overturned by the Court of Criminal Appeal: see *The People v McNally and Breathnach* (1981) 2 Frewen 43. The third person's conviction was, ultimately, not overturned by the courts: *The People v Kelly (No. 2)* [1983] IR 1. In subsequent civil proceedings brought by him, O'Hanlon J held that the issues raised in the civil case were *res judicata: Kelly v Ireland* [1986] ILRM 318. In his judgment, O'Hanlon J relied on the well-established principles, as set out by the House of Lords in *Hunter v Chief Constable of West Midlands* [1982] AC 529. While the principles are well-established, the House of Lords was adjudicating in what has become known as the Birmingham Six case, a *cause célèbre* on both sides of the Irish sea. The civil litigation of the Birmingham Six has become famous for the dictum of Lord Denning MR that, to reopen the issues decided against the Six in their criminal trials, would present an 'appaling vista'. That dictum has not been relied on by any Irish judge in using the general principles expressed in the *Hunter* case. Nonetheless, it is equally clear that a great deal of emphasis is placed on the principle of finality of litigation, a principle which undoubtedly underlies Lord Denning's dictum.

To return to the *Breathnach* case, which as indicated above arose out of the same criminal prosecution as gave rise to the claim in *Kelly v Ireland* [1986] ILRM 318. The plaintiff instituted proceedings against the State as well as named Gardaí claiming damages for assault and battery, false imprisonment, intimidation, malicious prosecution and failure to vindicate his constitutional rights. The claim arose out of events alleged to have taken place while the plaintiff was in Garda custody in 1976 pursuant to s.30 of the Offences against the State Act 1939. The plaintiff was subsequently charged with armed robbery and convicted in the Special Criminal Court. During his trial, the Court held: (i) no assault or battery took place on him while he was in Garda custody; (ii) the plaintiff's confession had not been signed in fear of assault nor had it been extracted by oppression; (iii) the plaintiff had been falsely imprisoned and wrongfully detained for a period of 48 hours; and (iv) that, on the view most favourable to the plaintiff's evidence at his trial, he had been denied a right of access to a solicitor having requested such. On appeal to the Court of Criminal Appeal, the plaintiff's conviction was overturned only on the basis that the confession obtained from him was not voluntary: (1981) 2 Frewen 43. The Court of Criminal Appeal expressly refused to interfere with the findings of fact by the trial court.

In the plaintiff's civil action, preliminary issues were set down for decision as to whether the four issues dealt with by the Special Criminal Court were now *res judicata* or alternatively whether it would be an abuse of the process of the court to relitigate those issues. A judgment dealing with some issues was delivered by Lardner J in July 1989: [1989] IR 489. A second judgment was delivered by Blayney J on 14 March 1990. It is notable that in the first judgment Lardner J points out that certain matters were not raised by the State as preliminary issues; these were the very points which were contested in the second decision. The other point of interest is that in the second judgment, Blayney J makes no reference whatever to the judgment of Lardner J.

In the first judgment ([1989] IR 489), Lardner J followed the decision of O'Hanlon J in the *Kelly* case by holding that where a clearly identifiable issue had been raised in a criminal trial and determined against a party to those proceedings, such determination raised an issue estoppel against the party in any subsequent civil proceedings in which that party was also involved. In the instant case, he pointed out that the Special Criminal Court had made a clear determination, after a full hearing, that the statements alleged to have been made by the plaintiff were not made as a result of any assaults or illtreatment by the Gardai and this finding had not been disturbed by the Court of Criminal Appeal. Applying dicta in *Reichel v McGrath* (1889) 14 App Cas 665, he concluded that neither justice or fairness required that the matters be reopened, and that accordingly the plaintiff was estopped from raising these issues now. In the second judgment delivered by Blayney J on 14 March 1990, yet another aspect of the plaintiff's claim was closed off. Applying the same principles as Lardner J had (though without referring to his judgment), Blayney J held that the plaintiff was estopped from asserting that the confession had been obtained in fear of assault or from oppression. It seems that, while the defendants had not put this point in issue before Lardner J (a point the judge referred to), they were not to be estopped from raising this point before Blayney J!

It is of interest that, while in the *Kelly* case O'Hanlon J had talked of an issue estoppel being raised in unusual or exceptional circumstances, the practice now seems to be to raise that estoppel in the normal run of events. This severely limits the potential for reopening issues in civil litigation subsequent to a criminal prosecution in which those issues have been determined against the accused-turned-plaintiff. This is particularly significant in the *Breathnach* case where the plaintiff had ultimately been found not guilty. Given that the Court of Criminal Appeal in his case was acting under the constraint of having, in effect, to accept findings of fact made by the Special Criminal Court the creation of an issue estoppel in those circumstances seems somewhat harsh. In the eyes of the law, the plaintiff was found not guilty of a criminal offence and yet is unable to present to court the full circumstances in his civil action.

However, the double-edged nature of the estoppel which arises was brought to the fore in the second judgment, delivered by Blayney J on 14 March 1990. While he ruled out another aspect of the plaintiff's case (see above), he also turned his attention to the Gardaí. He accepted that the Gardaí in the instant civil proceedings could not be regarded as having been a party to the criminal trial, and so they did not fall within the usual *res judicata* principle in *Kelly v Ireland* [1986] ILRM 318 or that in *Shaw v Sloan* [1982] NI 393. However, adverting to another aspect of the House of Lords decision in *Hunter v Chief Constable of West Midlands* [1982] AC 529, he concluded that it would be an abuse of the process of the court for the Gardaí to reopen matters which had been determined in the criminal trial. The Gardaí were thus precluded from denying that the plaintiff had been falsely imprisoned or detained wrongfully for a period of 48 hours, in view of the Special Criminal Court's findings on that aspect of the trial. This holding makes even clearer the overall policy approach now taken, at least by the High Court, in these kinds of cases. In essence, the courts now appear to take the view that, once a decision has been made in a criminal trial, the matter is either *res judicata* or that it would be an abuse of the process of the court to reopen the matter. This conforms with the view taken by the House of Lords in the *Hunter* case, above. Insofar as the Supreme Court has dealt with the issue, the decision in *Dublin Corporation v Flynn* [1980] IR 357 appears to support this view. But note the views expressed by McCarthy J in *McGrath v Garda Commissioner*, Supreme Court, 17 July 1990, which will be discussed in the 1990 Review.

Finally, it may be noted that Blayney J left just one issue to be litigated in the civil action. This was the question whether the plaintiff had been denied access to a solicitor while in custody. This point was not *res judicata* since the Special Criminal Court had not made a final determination on this allegation in the criminal trial.

RULES OF COURT

Appeal to High Court from Circuit Court The Rules of the Superior Courts (No. 2) 1989 (SI No. 20) provide, *inter alia*, for a number of changes in O.61 of the 1986 Rules in connection with appeals from the Circuit Court to the High Court.

Application to High Court from medical tribunals The Rules of Superior Courts (No. 2) 1989 (SI No. 20) provide, *inter alia*, that applications to the High Court in connection with the decisions of disciplinary bodies associated with different branches of medicine shall be by way of special summons, thus amending O.95 of the 1986 Rules.

Bankruptcy The Rules of the Superior Courts (No. 3) 1989 (SI No. 79) provide for the new rules required in consequence of the enactment of the Bankruptcy Act 1988.

Circuit Court: separation The Circuit Court Rules (No. 1) 1989 (SI No.289) set out the forms for proceedings under the Judicial Separation and Family Law Reform Act 1989.

Circuit Court: sitting The Circuit Court Rules (No. 2) 1989 (SI No. 310) amend the 1950 Rules by deleting Bailieborough as a town for the sitting of the Court.

District Court: safety at work The District Court (Safety, Health and Welfare at Work Act 1989) Regulations 1989 (SI No. 275) set out the form of appeal from the making of various enforcement orders by workplace inspectors pursuant to the 1989 Act: see further on the 1989 Act at 377-91, below, in the Safety and Health chapter.

District Court sittings   The District Court Areas (Variation of Days and Hours) Order 1989 (SI No.158) amends the dates for the sitting of certain District Courts.

Enforcement of Judgments   The Rules of the Superior Courts (No.1) 1989 (SI No.14) give effect to the changes in the 1986 Rules consequent on the coming into force of the Jurisdiction of Courts and Enforcement of Judgments (European Communities) Act 1988. For discussion of the case law on the 1988 Act see the Conflict of Laws chapter.

Fees   The Supreme Court and High Court (Fees) Order 1989 (SI No.341) sets out the fees payable from 1 January 1990 in the Supreme Court and High Court. The Circuit Court (Fees) Order 1989 (SI No.342) sets out the fees payable in the Circuit Court from 1 January 1990. The District Court (Fees) Order 1989 (SI No. 343) sets out the fees payable in the District Court from 1 January 1990. The latter two Orders provide that no court fees are payable in family law proceedings.

Interest on judgment debts   The Courts Act 1981 (Interest on Judgment Debts) Order 1989 (SI No.12) reduced the rate of interest on judgment debts from 11% to 8%.

Notice of trial: personal injuries   The Rules of the Superior Courts (No.2) 1989 (SI No.20) provide, *inter alia*, for the setting down of personal injuries cases (and any others referred to in s.1(1) and (2) of the Courts Act 1988) without prior application to Court at the following venues: Cork, Dundalk, Galway, Kilkenny, Limerick, Sligo and Waterford.

Remittal or transfer   The Rules of the Superior Courts (No.2) 1989 (SI No.20) provide, *inter alia*, that an application under O.49, r.7(2) of the 1986 Rules may be made at any time after an appearance is entered and before service of notice of trial. It is also provided that, in a personal injuries action (as defined in s.1(1) of the Courts Act 1988), such application may be made at any time before the commencement of the trial of the action.

Succession   The Rules of the Superior Courts (No.2) 1989 (SI No.20) provide, *inter alia*, for amendments to O.79 and 80 of the 1986 Rules consequent on the enactment of the Status of Children Act 1987.

Wardship The Rules of the Superior Courts (No.2) 1989 (SI No.20) provide, *inter alia*, for an amendment to O.67, r.92 of the 1986 Rules in connection with the jurisdiction of the Court in wardship.

SERVICE OUT

The case law on service out of the jurisdiction pursuant to O.11 of the Rules of the Superior Courts 1986 is dealt with in the Conflict of Laws chapter.

SUPREME COURT

Many issues as to the appellate function of the Supreme Court are dealt with under the Appellate Court Function heading, above, 339-41.

High Court declining to make order The wide jurisdiction of the Supreme Court, on an appeal from the High Court, given by Article 34.4.3 of the Constitution, was discussed in *Society for the Protection of Unborn Children (Irl) Ltd v Grogan and Ors* [1990] ILRM 350; [1989] IR 753. The Court held that, although the High Court had declined to make any order as to whether the plaintiff was entitled to an interlocutory injunction, the Supreme Court had jurisdiction to adjudicate on the issue: see 103, above, in the Constitutional Law chapter.

UNLIQUIDATED CLAIMS

The question of compound interest in an unliquidated claim is discussed by Doyle, (1989) 7 *ILT* 215 and (1990) 8 *ILT* 94.

Prisons

RULES

The Detention of Offenders (Wheatfield) Regulations 1989 (SI No.135) prescribe the different categories of persons who may be detained in Wheatfield Place of Detention, Clondalkin, Dublin. It also prescribes the disciplinary regulations applicable in this recently-opened facility.

TEMPORARY RELEASE (PAROLE)

Long term prisoners: review In December, the Minister for Justice announced the creation of a non-statutory Sentence Review Group, chaired by Dr T.K. Whitaker (who had chaired the Committee of Inquiry into the Penal System, which reported in 1985): *Irish Times*, 2 December 1989. The purpose of the Review Group is to examine whether prisoners serving life sentences in particular should be given definite release dates. A prisoner sentenced to a definite term of imprisonment is given a release date immediately on arrival in prison, but this is not the case with indeterminate sentences such as life. The establishment of this Group came in the light of similar procedures introduced in recent years in Northern Ireland. As with that initiative, the Sentence Review Group in this State is expected to result in release dates being given, *inter alia*, to persons convicted of crimes associated with paramilitary organisations. Christmas temporary release (parole) was arranged for a number of long-term prisoners arising from the first deliberations of the Sentence Review Group: *Irish Times*, 15 December 1989.

Rules The Temporary Release of Offenders (Wheatfield) Rules 1989 (SI No.136) prescribe the conditions under which persons may be granted temporary release from Wheatfield in accordance with the Criminal Justice Act 1960.

TRANSFER FROM ST PATRICK'S INSTITUTION TO PRISON

The Prisons Act 1970 (Section 7) Order 1989 (SI No.85) continued s.7 of the 1970 Act in operation until 26 April 1990. As to s.7, see the 1988 Review, 353.

Revenue Law

As with previous Reviews, this chapter focuses primarily on case law during 1989. A detailed analysis of the terms of the Finance Act 1989 may be found in Kennedy's annotation, *Irish Current Law Statutes Annotated*. As well as providing for the annual revisions of tax provisions, some of the special features of the 1989 Act included: incentives to renovate inner-city housing (s.4); further reduction on the mortgage interest relief (s.7); restrictions on the use of the Business Expansion Scheme (s.9); increasing the amount of relief in respect of motor vehicles (s.12); regulation of UCITS (ss.18 and 19); relief for film investment (s.28); a self-assessment system for gift and inheritance tax (s.74); and a general anti-avoidance provision (s.86).

ADDITIONAL ASSESSMENTS

In *Hammond Lane Metal Co Ltd v Ó Cúlacháin* [1990] ILRM 249, Carroll J held that an assessment to tax which has been agreed to by an Inspector of Taxes may, nonetheless, be subject to an additional assessment at a later time. The appellant company had been assessed for tax due in the year 1974/75 in connection with the deduction from the company's profits of the whole of the premium reserved by a lease into which the company had entered with a wholly owned subsidiary for the letting to the company of premises used by the company in the course of its trade. The assessment was compromised by agreement with an Inspector of Taxes. In 1982 a new Inspector raised an additional assessment, taking the view that the premium should not have been allowed against the computation of the company's profits. The company argued that an assessment which had been compromised could not be reassessed and that, in any event, it was entitled to have the premium deducted in accordance with s.91(1) of the Income Tax Act 1967. Carroll J dismissed the company's argument on the preliminary point but ruled in its favour on the substantive point.

First, she held, in an important general point, that there was no difference in this context between an unappealed assessment and the situation in the instant case. She pointed to the fact that s.416(3)(b) of the 1967 Act provides that, where an assessment is compromised by agreement, the assessment or amended assessment is to have the same force and effect as if it were an unappealed assessment. On this basis, in the absence of a constitutional challenge to s.416, she held that the Inspector was entitled to exercise his power to make an additional assessment pursuant to s.186(1) of the 1967 Act. In this respect, Carroll J applied the approach taken by Kenny J in *W. Ltd v Inspector of Taxes* (1974) ITC Leaflet No.110.

On the substantive issue, Carroll J held that, pursuant to s.91(2)(a) of the Income Tax Act 1967, the company was entitled to make the deduction argued for. She noted that s.91 did not deal with the actuality of the situation as to whether the company was actually receiving the entire premium by way of rent. The general provisions of s.61 of the Act, on which the Inspector had relied, was held to be overridden by the specific provision of s.91. Accordingly, Carroll J concluded that the scheme operated by the company was tax effective.

AVOIDANCE

As mentioned in the 1988 Review, 358, s.86 of the Finance Act 1989 is a general anti-avoidance section which is the government's response to the invitation of Finlay CJ in *McGrath v McDermott* [1988] ILRM 647; [1988] IR 258 to enact just such a provision. As originally drafted, s.86 was subjected to criticisms from various quarters. On the floor of the Dáil, speeches referred to possible constitutional defects in the section, and in particular to the apparent ability of the Revenue Commissioners to make a final determination as to the question of whether a particular transaction fell within the net of s.86. While such a provision might be read subject to judicial review by the High Court, this would be of limited value. In the event, s.86 as enacted provides for the usual appeal mechanisms to operate. Whether s.86 is now effectively sealed from constitutional challenge is another matter. The fact that the Chief Justice invited the enactment of such a provision may prove a weighty consideration in upholding the general thrust of s.86.

CAPITAL GAINS TAX

Multipliers The Capital Gains Tax (Multipliers) (1989-90) Regulations 1989 (SI No.164) set out the multipliers which applied in computing capital gains tax for the year 1989-90 for the purposes of the Capital Gains Tax Act 1975, as amended.

Refund to mortgagee In *Bank of Ireland Finance Ltd v Revenue Commissioners*, High Court, 13 October 1989 the plaintiff bank had obtained a well charging order on certain property over which it held an equitable mortgage on foot of a loan in respect of which there had been default. The bank then obtained a High Court order sanctioning the sale of the property; the bank was authorised to retain the purchase money for the purposes of discharging the debt owed to it. The bank applied to the Revenue to obtain a clearance certificate under the Capital Gains Tax Act 1975. By the time the property was actually sold, however, a clearance certificate had not been issued. It was not argued that this failure arose from breach of any statutory duty by the Revenue. The purchaser of the property retained the sum of £15,000 (out of a total purchase price of £100,000) in respect of capital gains tax liability and remitted it to the Revenue. The plaintiff bank argued that this sum should be returned to it on the ground that it was not liable to capital gains tax on the transaction on the ground that it was beneficially entitled to the sum on foot of the High Court order. Costello J declined to accede to the bank's view.

He stated that, in accordance with the Fourth Schedule to the 1975 Act, the purchaser was clearly obliged to deduct 15% of the purchase price. He also held that s.8(5) of the Act, which deals specifically with disposal by a mortgagee, indicated that the disposal in this case was made by the company (the bank merely being a nominee) and thus the Revenue were entitled to retain the 15% remitted to it as this was due to the company's liability. There was, therefore, no trust in favour of the bank in respect of the money. It may be noted that Costello J pointed out that had a clearance certificate been obtained before the purchase went through then the Revenue would have been left to pursue its claim against the company (as he noted, probably in vain). As it was the bank was left with its claim (also, he noted, probably a hollow entitlement). Finally, Costello J pointed that the terms of s.8(5) of the 1975 Act were altered by the Finance Act 1983, but this did not apply to the transaction in the instant case.

CORPORATION TAX

The Taxation of Companies (Self-Assessment) Regulations 1989 (SI No.178), which took effect on 1 October 1989, brought companies within the self-assessment procedures contained in Chapter II of Part I of the Finance Act 1988.

DISABLED DRIVERS

The Disabled Drivers (Tax Concessions) Regulations 1989 (SI No.340) give effect to the provisions of s.92 of the Finance Act 1989, which liberalise the concessions given to disabled drivers by s.43 of the Finance Act 1968. S.92 of the 1989 Act was introduced after the strictness of the previous concessions were brought to light: see *Wiley v Revenue Commissioners* [1989] IR 350, discussed at 9-10, above.

FARM TAX

The decision in *Purcell v Attorney General*, High Court, 14 November 1989 is remarkable for the fact that Barron J held that the Farm Tax Act 1985, which has not been repealed, no longer represented the will of the Oireachtas and was therefore not to be enforced: see the discussion at 114-5, above.

INCOME TAX

PAYE/PRSI The Income Tax (Employments) Regulations 1989 (SI No.58) allow for the returns for PAYE/PRSI to be made at other than monthly intervals.

Plant: suit In *G v O'C (Inspector of Taxes)*, Circuit Court, 24 October 1989 it was held that, where it was a condition of employment that a suit be worn (in this instance by a tax manager in a firm of chartered accountants), the suit was 'plant' within the meaning of s.241(1) of the Income Tax Act 1967. The Inspector of Taxes expressed dissatisfaction with the decision and it is likely to be appealed by was of case stated to the High Court: see the note in (1989) 4 *Irish Tax Review* 481.

MANUFACTURING

The meaning of the term 'manufacturing process' arose for discussion again in *Irish Agricultural Machinery Ltd v Ó Cúlacháin* [1989] ILRM 478.

The company claimed stock relief in respect of its business which consisted of importing components which it assembled with other materials and then sold to farmers, 55% of sales being made with some dealer involvement. The Finance Act 1975, as amended, provided for stock relief in respect of certain trades, which were defined to mean trades consisting wholly or mainly of, inter alia, the manufacture of goods and the sale of machinery or plant (excluding vehicles for conveying people by road) to persons engaged in farming. In the High Court Murphy J held ([1987] IR 598) that the company was not entitled to the relief sought: see the 1987 Review, 295-6.

On appeal by the company the Supreme Court (Finlay CJ, Griffin and Hederman JJ) reversed Murphy J's decision.

Applying the test it had laid down in *Charles McCann Ltd v Ó Cúlacháin* [1986] IR 196 (the banana ripening case), Griffin J speaking for the Supreme Court held that the company was engaged in a manufacturing process since the finished agricultural machines, which included combine harvesters, were a marketable commodity and quite different from the component parts from which thet were assembled, and were much more than an aggregation of the components. The Supreme Court also referred with approval to the approach taken in *Samuel McCausland Ltd v Ministry of Commerce* [1956] NI 36 and *Prestcold Ltd v Minister of Labour* [1969] 1 All ER 69. It may be noted briefly that s.41 of the Finance Act 1990 has restricted the definition of manufacturing, specifically excluding many of the activities held by the courts to have fallen within the original definition.

PROSECUTIONS

In *Director of Public Prosecutions v Cunningham* [1989] IR 481, Lardner J held that it was not necessary to produce in the District Court an order of the Revenue Commissioners authorising a prosecution.

The defendant was prosecuted by summons in relation to alleged failure to pay duty on bets under the Finance Act 1926 as amended. It was accepted that the charges were proceedings to recover fines and penalties under an Act relating to inland revenue, and that accordingly s.21(1) of the Inland Revenue Regulation Act 1890 applied. It provides that it shall not be lawful to commence such proceedings except by order of the Revenue Commissioners and in the name of the Attorney General for Ireland, now the Director of Public Prosecutions as a result of the Prosecution of Offences Act 1974. During the prosecution's case in the District Court, no evidence was offered that an order had been made by the Commissioners, and the defendant applied for a dismiss on this ground. On a case stated to the High Court Lardner J held that the order need not be produced in the District Court.

He was clearly of the view, however, that the terms of s.21(1) of the 1890 Act required that an order be made by the Commissioners prior to commencement, and the Director was required to be satisfied that such order had been made. However, unless objection is actually made, he held that it is to be presumed that the Director has discharged his duty in this respect, so that the prosecution is only required to prove affirmatively the making of such an order if required by the defendant to do so. In this respect he followed the decision in *R. v Waller* [1910] 1 KB 366.

RECOVERY OF PENALTIES: CIVIL OR CRIMINAL

In *McLoughlin v Tuite* [1989] IR 82, the Supreme Court affirmed the view taken by the High Court that revenue penalties were not in the nature of criminal penalties.

The plaintiff instituted proceedings challenging the constitutional validity of ss.500 and 508 of the Income Tax Act 1967. Pursuant to s.500, a taxpayer who fails to deliver various tax returns referred to in the Act shall be liable to a penalty of £100, together with further sums after a judgment for specific sums has been obtained in a court. S.508 of the Act provides that such penalties are recoverable as a liquidated sum in the High Court. The plaintiff claimed that the penalties imposed under s.500 constituted the imposition of a criminal penalty so that the requirements of Article 38.1 of the Constitution required a trial in due course of law in relation to whether they should be levied. In the High Court [1986] ILRM 304; [1986] IR 235, Carroll J dismissed the claim and, on appeal by the plaintiff, the Supreme Court (Finlay CJ, Walsh, Griffin, Hederman and McCarthy JJ) affirmed this conclusion.

The Supreme Court approached the case on the basis that ss.500 and 508 of the Income Tax Act 1967 must be seen in the overall context of the taxation code. In particular the Court noted that there was a consistent series of provisions designed to ensure that each taxpayer would pay a fair proportion of taxation with promtitude to enable the Central Fund to be established so as to avoid unnecessary short-term borrowing by the State.

While the payment of interest was one method to ensure prompt payment, the Court stated that the imposition of a penalty was another method in the same category of deterrent. In this context, it was clear, the Court stated, that the penalties imposed under s.500 were not in the nature of criminal penalties. The Court here applied the test propounded by Kingsmill Moore J in *Melling v Ó Mathghamhna* [1962] IR 1. It noted that there was no question of a person being brought into custody, or of being charged, or a right to search or examine papers of the taxpayer, or of any risk of being imprisoned, or of any issue of *mens rea*. The Court concluded that the fact that the penalty was in the nature of an involuntary payment was not in itself sufficient to indicate that it was criminal in nature. A similar conclusion in connection with s.128 of the Income Tax Act 1967 had been reached by Barr J in *Downes v Director of Public Prosecutions* [1987] ILRM 665; [1987] IR 139: see the 1987 Review, 295.

One aspect of the *Melling* test was not adverted to by the Supreme Court in the *McLoughlin* case, namely, that a criminal offence is one against the community, rather than against an individual. Carroll J had dealt with this item in her High Court judgment and had suggested that no member of the community would regard failure to fill in a form and send it to the Revenue authorities as an offence. While one might doubt that there would be such a universal social judgment on this point, the view is defensible if it is taken as an indicium of criminality based on objective reasonableness, rather than merely whatever attitude might be current in society at a particular time. If that is so then the act in question is likely to be judged not by reference to a philosophical analysis as to the nature of crime but by how the community regards the conduct instinctively. This approach would place Carroll J in the somewhat unlikely company of Lord Devlin: see *The Enforcement of Morals* (OUP), Chapter 1.

STAMP DUTY

In *Waterford Glass (Group Services) Ltd v Revenue Commissioners*, High Court, 21 June 1989, the issue raised was as to whether the Court should look to the legal form or to the reality of a series of transactions for the purpose of determining the amount of stamp duty payable on a conveyance. Carroll J was firmly of the view that the reality or substance of the transaction was the crucial factor.

The case concerned four agreements between three companies. The first agreement was executed on 14 October 1986, while the remainder were executed the next day. The agreements concerned two parcels of land valued at £3.9 million. The first agreement was between Smiths Engineering Ltd and Waterford (Lightingware) Ltd, by which Smiths agreed to sell the land for £3.9 million, with a deposit of £3.889 million, leaving a balance of £1,000. The contract provided that, on payment of the deposit, Lightingware was entitled to immediate possession. The second agreement was between Smiths and the appellant company. Under this agreement Smiths agreed to sell the same property to the appellant, subject to the first contract, for the sum of £1,000. The third agreement was a transfer of the land from Smiths to the appellant company for £1,000. Under the fourth agreement, the appellant company transferred the land to Lightingware for a consideration of £1,000. The two transfers were submitted to the Revenue Commissioners on the basis that no stamp duty was payable. The Revenue declined to accept this submission, and argued that duty of £234,000 (6% of £3.9 million) was payable by Group Services, the appellant company. Carroll J upheld the Revenue view.

She referred to s.54 of the Stamp Act 1891, which defines a conveyance of sale as including any instrument by which any property or any estate or interest in property is transferred to or vested in a purchaser or any other person on his behalf or by his directions. Crucially, she stated:

> Just because the parties put a particular label on a transaction, the court is not obliged to accept that label blindly. The court will look at the legal effect and the legal rights of the parties resulting from the transaction. . . . The contract of 15 October 1986 . . . was the sale of an empty shell. The entire benefit of the contract of 14 October, except for £1,000, had already been taken by the vendor Smiths. All that was included in the contract of 15 October 1986 and in the subsequent transfer of the same date was the legal estate of the registered owner and an infinitesmal equitable interest represented by £1,000 with no right to possession and with the obligation to transfer on payment of that £1,000. That was in fact done on the following day and the money paid over to Group Services. The same persons signed both contracts on behalf of Ligthingware and shared a common solicitor.

This narrative indicated Carroll J's clear view that the actual nature of the transaction was one which attracted stamp duty in accordance with the Revenue's calculations. She was thus unimpressed with the appellant company's argument seeking a literal construction of s.54 of the Stamp Act 1891, by which duty is payable on an 'instrument' not a transaction. Carroll J considered that it was not possible in the circumstances to separate the 'instrument' from the 'transaction.' It is of interest to contrast her approach in this case with her view on tax avoidance transactions (upheld in the Supreme Court) in *McGrath v McDermott* [1988] ILRM 647; [1988] IR 258: see the 1988 Review, 356-8. See also the 'reality of the transaction' approach applied by Carroll J and the Supreme Court in *Ó Connlain v Belvedere Estates Ltd* [1985] IR 22 (HC); Supreme Court, 28 July 1988: see the 1988 Review, 359-60. For a case where the express terms of statutory language precluded an examination of the reality of the transaction, see *Hammond Lane Metal Co. Ltd v Ó Cúlacháin* [1990] ILRM 249: see 363, above.

Safety and Health

ENVIRONMENTAL SAFETY AND HEALTH

Air pollution   The Air Pollution Act 1987 (Commencement) Order 1989 (SI No.167) set 1 July 1989 as the commencement date for the power to regulate fuels under the Act. The Air Pollution Act 1987 (Sulphur Content of Gas Oil) Regulations 1989 (SI No.168) set out the permissible levels for sulphur in gas oil in accordance with EC approximation requirements. The Special Control Area (Ballyfermot Area B) (Confirmation) Order 1989 (SI No.291) and the Special Control Area (Ballyfermot Area C) (Confirmation) Order 1989 (SI No.292) were made under the Air Pollution Act 1987. The Air Pollution Act 1987 (Authorised Fireplace) (Revocation) Regulations 1989 (SI No.293) revoke the Air Pollution Act 1987 (Authorised Fireplace) Regulations 1988: see the 1988 Review, 372. The Air Pollution Act 1987 (Retail Sale of Fuels) Regulations 1989 (SI No.333) require that, from 1 January 1990, retail outlets selling fuels must have smokeless fuels available. Further regulations made in 1990 prohibit the sale of fuels other than specified smokeless fuels: see the 1990 Review.

Environmental impact assessment   The decision in the Merrell Dow case, *Browne and Ors v An Bord Pleanala* [1989] ILRM 865 is discussed at 201-3, above. The European Communities (Environmental Impact Assessment) Regulations 1989 (SI No.349), which came into effect on 1 February 1990, require that an Environmental Impact Study (EIS) be conducted prior to an application for planning permission in connection with a long list of developments (primarily in the industrial area but also including, e.g., airfields) specified in the Regulations. The Regulations replace and amend, for example, a number of provisions of the Local Government (Planning and Development) Act 1963 in order to incorporate the EIS requirement into the planning process.

FOOD HYGIENE

Enforcement   The Food Hygiene (Amendment) Regulations 1989 (SI No.62) introduced, *inter alia*, important new enforcement mechanisms to ensure compliance with what are now the Food Hygiene Regulations 1950 to 1989. The principal provisions of the 1989 regulations, which came into effect on 1 May 1989, are as follows. First, any premises which operates a food business must keep written records of the persons from whom and the date on which any food, food animals or food material is obtained. The written record must be produced to an environmental health officer upon request. Second, the 1989 Regulations provide for a more efficient method of obtaining a closure order, by substituting a new Article 34 of the 1950 Regulations. This now provides that '[w]henever . . . a chief executive officer of a health board has evidence that there is a grave and immediate danger that food intended for sale for human consumption may become so diseased, contaminated or otherwise unfit for human consumption as to be liable to cause serious illness if consumed', an application for a closure order may be made to the District Court. If the District Justice grants the application, the effect is to prohibit the operation of a food business from the premises in question. Finally, the 1989 Regulations provide for registration with health boards as food premises. In the case of a restaurant, the fee is £100 and in all other cases £200.

Preservatives   The European Communities (Preservatives in Food) (Purity Criteria) Regulations 1989 (SI No.262) set out harmonised standards for preservatives in food. The Health (Preservatives in Food) (Amendment) Regulations 1989 (SI No.263) amend the 1981 Regulations by providing that potassium bisulphate (E228) is a permitted preservative.

HEALTH SERVICES

Eligibility   The Health Services (Amendment) Regulations 1989 (SI No.106) raise the income levels for eligibility for general medical services.

General practitioner's contract: excessive attendance   The method by which excessive attendance by a GP is to be judged was considered by Lardner J in *O'Connor v Giblin and Ors* [1989] IR 583. The plaintiff had entered into an agreement with the Southern Health Board to provide a general medical service pursuant to s.58 of the Health Act 1970. Para.7 of the agreement stated that the plaintiff agreed to provide 'all proper and necessary treatment of a kind usually undertaken by a general practitioner.' Para.15 required the plaintiff to keep attendance records available for inspection by medical officers of the board. Para.23 of the agreement stipulated that where a claim for remuneration by a GP appeared to be excessive, the circumstances shall be investigated by a medical officer of the board, who may refer the matter to an investigating group consisting of three persons. The investigating group is entitled to decide that a deduction be made in the remuneration payable to the GP. The GP is entitled to appeal the decision of the investigating group to a committee appointed under Art.8 of the Health Services Regulations 1972.

Two years after the plaintiff had begun to provide services under the agreement, a medical officer attached to the board carried out an investigation into the plaintiff's rate of attendance of patients, and he referred the matter to an investigating group as provided in para.23 of the agreement. The group considered that the plaintiff's attendance rate was excessive, and reduced his remuneration for the two year period by £8,600. The plaintiff appealed the decision to a committee appointed under the 1972 Regulations. The committee affirmed the investigating group's decision, taking account in particular of the average attendance rates of other doctors in the area. The plaintiff successfully sought a declaration that the decision made was *ultra vires* the committee.

Lardner J held that the committee had acted unreasonably in the circumstances, as that term was defined in *The State (Keegan) v Stardust Victims Compensation Tribunal* [1987] ILRM 202; [1986] IR 642: see the 1988 Review, 31, and also 15, above, in the Administrative Law chapter. He considered that a claim that a GP had made a claim for excessive attendance could only be determined by investigating the medical and other relevant circumstances of the patients on the plaintiff's panel. It was, therefore, irrelevant for the committee to have used as the sole criterion a comparison with the average attendance rates of other doctors in the plaintiff's town or surrounding area. The committee would be required to investigate the needs of individual patients in order to reach a correct judgment on this issue.

Lardner J also indicated that, in any event, where a committee determined that fees previously paid should be disallowed, the proper course was for the the sums in question to be recovered by way of deduction from subsequent remuneration. However, he accepted that, to that extent, the agreement entered into allowed for retrospective deductions from fees already paid.

It may be noted that, in the circumstances, Lardner J did not address a further issue which had been raised, namely as to whether the deduction of remuneration by a committee amounts to the imposition of a fine contrary to Articles 34 or 37 of the Constitution. That remains for a future decision. For a relevant decision in this context see *McLoughlin v Tuite* [1989] IR 82, discussed at 370, above, in the Revenue chapter.

General practitioner's contract: investigation procedure In *O'Flynn and O'Regan v Mid-Western Health Board* [1989] IR 429, Barr J dealt with some procedural aspects of the investigation procedure under the Health Services Regulations 1972.

In 1981, the applicant doctors had entered into agreements to provide a general medical service to the respondent board pursuant to s.58 of the Health Act 1970. In June 1986, a complaint was received by the respondent health board that the applicants were in breach of their contracts in that they allegedly obtained fraudulent payments for pharmaceutical products alleged to have been prescribed for their patients. Between June and October 1986, the board investigated the complaint and then referred the matter to the Garda Síochána. In October 1987, the Gardaí informed the board that the Director of Public Prosecutions had decided that no prosecutions would be brought.

The board subsequently wrote to the applicants informing them under cl.24 of their agreement with the board that it was pursuing the complaint, and setting out in general terms the nature of the complaint. The applicants by letter denied the complaint and requested details of the allegations made against them. By subsequent letter from the board, they were informed that the chief executive officer had requested the Minister for Health to establish a Committee to inquire into the complaint pursuant to the 1972 Regulations. The Minister subsequently established such a Committee. The applicants sought judicial review of the appointment of the Committee on the ground, *inter alia*, that thay had not been given an opportunity to make representations to the chief executive officer of the board prior to his referral of the matter to the Minister as envisaged by para.24 of the applicants' agreement with the board. Barr J granted the judicial review.

He held that para.24 of the agreement between the applicants and the board clearly envisaged a two part machinery for dealing with complaints made to health boards, the first stage being dealt with by the chief executive officer, while the second stage involved the request for the establishment of a Committee under the Health Services Regulations 1972. Barr J considered that the first stage necessarily entailed the chief executive officer informing the doctor fully about the complaint made against him, followed by consideration of any subsequent representations from the doctor, it being clear that a meaningful response to a complaint could not be made if the doctor is not fully informed as to the complaint alleged.

In the instant case, Barr J concluded that the applicants had not been provided with sufficient information with which to make any considered response to the letter informing them of the complaint, and accordingly the chief executive officer was not entitled to request the appointment of a Committee under the 1972 Regulations and so he quashed its appointment.

Barr J also added that unreasonable delay in the appointment of a Committee might give rise in some instances to injustice, and a doctor should be given an opportunity to investigate and answer complaints as soon as reasonably practicable after they have been made to a health board. This seems to fit in with the recent case law on delay in criminal proceedings, as to which see 140-2, above.

General practitioners' contract: termination The question whether a health board could terminate the 1972 general contract with GPs was considered in *Grehan v North Eastern Health Board* [1989] IR 422: see 290, above, in the Labour Law chapter.

Health boards: child custody In *The State (D.) v G.* [1990] ILRM 10; [1990] ILRM 120, the Supreme Court had held that a health board was not a 'fit person' within the meaning of the Children Act 1908, thus precluding it from applying for place of safety orders in connection with the care of children. The Children Act 1989 was enacted in the immediate aftermath of the Supreme Court decision in order to provide that health boards could be deemed to be 'fit persons': see the discussion at 265-9, above, in the Family Law chapter.

Termination of consultant's appointment Procedural aspects of the termination of a consultant's appointment to a hospital were considered in *O'Neill v Beaumont Hospital Board* [1990] ILRM 419: see 7-9, above, in the Administrative Law chapter.

MEDICAL PREPARATIONS

In *United States Tobacco International Inc v Minister for Health*, High Court, September 1987 (the judgment in which was circulated in 1989) the plaintiffs successfully challenged the validity of the Health (Restricted Article) Order 1985, which had been made by the Minister for Health in purported exercise of his powers under s.66 of the Health Act 1947. The 1985 Order had attempted, in effect, to ban the importation of the tobacco product intended for chewing known as 'Skoal Bandits.' The plaintiff put forward a number of arguments as to why the 1985 Order was invalid, and Hamilton P accepted that the 1985 Order was *ultra vires* s.66 of the 1947 Act.

In his judgment, the President pointed out that s.66 allowed the Minister to make an order in respect of any 'substance as respects which he is of opinion that it is likely, when accessible to the general public, to be used for purposes involving risk of serious injury to health or body.' He also noted that the word 'substance' in s.35 of the 1947 Act (as amended by s.39 of the Health Act 1953) was defined by reference to medical preparations. He also had regard to the fact that s.66(3) of the 1947 Act referred to the Minister granting a licence to a medical practitioner in respect of a restricted article. Hamilton P applied the maxim *noscitur a sociis* (which he pointed out had been discussed by the Supreme Court in *Dillon v Minister for Posts and Telegraphs*, Supreme Court, 3 June 1981) and the views of Walsh J in *East*

Donegal Co-Op Ltd v Attorney General [1970] IR 317 as to interpreting statutory provisions in the context of the whole of an Act. Based on these principles, the President concluded that it had not been envisaged by the Oireachtas in enacting s.66 of the 1947 Act that the Minister would have made an order restricting an item such as 'Skoal Bandits.' For this reason he held the 1985 Order invalid. He did not, therefore, consider it necessary to address the other issues raised by the plaintiff, such as whether the Minister had acted contrary to principles of fair procedures in not considering representations from the company prior to making the Order.

OCCUPATIONAL SAFETY AND HEALTH

Arsenic and other agents The European Communities (Protection of Workers) (Exposure to Chemical, Physical and Biological Agents) Regulations 1989 (SI No.251) impose obligations on employers to monitor exposure of employees to arsenic, cadmium, mercury and organic compounds of lead. Adequate information must be provided to employees and their representatives in connection with the dangers which these agents present. In addition, employers must arrange for surveillance to be carried out of the health of employees exposed to organic compounds of lead. These Regulations give effect to Council Directive 80/1107/EEC, which is the Framework Directive on exposure to chemical, physical and biological agents, hence the title of the 1989 Regulations. Three 'daughter' Directives of the 1980 Directive have now been implemented in Irish law: concerning lead, in 1988 (see the 1988 Review, 376); concerning asbestos, in 1989 (below); and concerning noise, in 1990: European Communities (Protection of Workers) (Exposure to Noise) Regulations 1990.

Asbestos The European Communities (Protection of Workers) (Exposure to Asbestos) Regulations 1989 (SI No.34), which apply to all places of work, except air and sea transport, require reduction in the level of exposure to asbestos fibre in the workplace. They set exposure limits for asbestos dust concentrations and establish sampling and measuring methods. In conformity with other EC-based requirements, they provide that employees must have access to an assessment of their state of health arising from any exposure, if the employees so wish. The employer must also provide adequate information to employees and their representatives in connection with the potential risks to health from exposure to asbestos and the precautions to be taken.

Dangerous substances The European Communities (Dangerous Substances) (Classification, Packaging and Labelling) (Amendment) Regulations 1989 (SI No.228) impose additional obligations regarding the labelling of certain substances.

Fire: factory premises   The Fire Services Act 1981 (Prescribed Premises) Regulations 1989 (SI No.319), in conjunction with s.55 of the Safety, Health and Welfare at Work Act 1989, provide that premises used as a factory within the meaning of the Safety in Industry Acts 1955 and 1980 are to be regarded as coming within s.18 of the Fire Services Act 1981. This has the effect that the person having control over factory premises is now subject to the general duty in that section of the 1981 Act. Factory premises may now also be served with fire safety notices under the 1981 Act. The provisions of the 1955 and 1980 Acts on fire safety have been repealed.

General   The Safety, Health and Welfare at Work Act 1989 is discussed separately below.

Seveso Directive   The European Communities (Major Accident Hazards of Certain Industrial Activities) (Amendment) Regulations 1989 (SI No.194) amend the 1986 Regulations of the same title. The 1986 Regulations had implemented the 'Seveso' Directive dealing with certain chemical installations. The 1989 Regulations clarify that the list of processes affected is intended to be indicative and not exclusive; adjust the thresholds under which certain substances must be notified to the National Authority for Occupational Safety and Health; and extend the definition of those activities deemed to be dangerous, including processes connected with and storage of sulphur trioxide and processes involving liquid oxygen.

SAFETY, HEALTH AND WELFARE AT WORK ACT 1989

Because of the importance of the Safety, Health and Welfare at Work Act 1989 we deal with its content under a separate heading, apart from the other statutory provisions in this area. The Act is the most significant development in the statutory regulation of occupational safety and health since the foundation of the State. For the first time, all places of work have been brought within a statutory framework for the prevention of accidents and ill-health at work. All provisions of the 1989 Act (apart from s.4(3), which will be explained below) were brought into effect on 1 November 1989: Safety, Health and Welfare at Work Act 1989 (Commencement) Order 1989 (SI

No.236). For more detailed analysis of the 1989 Act see Byrne's annotation, *Irish Current Law Statutes Annotated.*

Background Up to the enactment of the 1989 Act, it was estimated that only about 20% of the workforce was covered by safety statutes. The most significant of these are the Safety in Industry Acts 1955 and 1980 (the Factories Act 1955 as amended by the Safety in Industry Act 1980), which apply to the manufacturing sector and certain other industrial premises, and whose genesis can be traced back to the early nineteenth Century.

The 1989 Act represents a radical attempt to tackle the high level of accidents and ill-health at work. Between 11,000 and 12,000 employees claim occupational injuries benefit each year, and there are many accidents which give rise to claims based on the employer's duty of care (as to which see the Torts chapter). The toll in human terms is enormous; and in financial terms the cost, shared between the private sector and the State, has been estimated at £650 million annually: see Byrne, *The Safety, Health and Welfare at Work Act 1989: A Guide* (NIFAST, 1990), pp.8-9. Many of the serious accidents occur in those sectors already covered by safety legislation, but other sectors such as agriculture, fisheries, forestry and hospitals also require active preventive regulation.

Barrington Commission Against the background of a perceived failure of existing statutory controls and acknowledging the need for comprehensive statutory regulation, the government established a *Commission of Inquiry into Safety, Health and Welfare at Work* in 1980, under the chairmanship of Mr Justice Barrington. The Commission reported in 1983 (Pl.1868) and made a substantial number of recommendations. The 1989 Act implemented the substance of the Commission's recommendations. The Barrington Commission Report is, therefore, indispensible to an understanding of the main purpose of the 1989 Act.

In essence, the Barrington Commission, whose members represented all the social partners, acknowledged that any new scheme of legislation on safety and health must reflect the fact that management within an organisation have ultimate responsibility for the safety and health of employees. The difficult reality that many accidents and much ill-health at work are due to failure of management to apply known standards of care is borne out by studies in the area: see Byrne, *Guide*, op. cit., 10. It also reflects the approach taken in the UK Health and Safety at Work Act 1974, which is the model for much of the 1989 Act.

Thus, the Barrington Commission recommended that a central feature of the new order in occupational safety and health must be a dynamic management programme setting out clearly defined objectives as to how accidents and ill-health can be prevented at a place of work. This is clearly reflected in the requirement in s.12 of the 1989 Act that management prepare a safety statement based on an indentification of hazards and an assessment of risks at the place of work. Mechanisms for consultation on safety and health issues at all places of work are also set out in s.13 of the Act. In addition, general duties are placed on employers, employees and others by ss.6 to 11 of the Act. Finally, a large portion of the Act is taken up with the new arrangements at national level for enforcement of safety at work legislation. We will discuss that aspect of the Act below.

Developments since 1983   As part of the government's commitment in the 1987 Programme for National Recovery to improve competitiveness in industry, by reducing insurance premiums, undertakings were made to abolish juries in personal injuries actions and to implement the recommendations of the Barrington Commission. The legislative changes were effected by the Courts Act 1988 (see the 1988 Review, 454-6) and the Safety, Health and Welfare at Work Act 1989. Whether these changes will result in reduction of insurance premiums is a more contentious subject.

Another significant development in this area has been the increased role played by the European Communities in the area of safety and health at work. This has been influenced to a large extent by the express reference to health and safety at work in Article 118a of the Treaty of Rome, inserted by the Single European Act. The European Commission has embarked on an ambitious programme to harmonise occupational safety and health laws to coincide with the completion of the single market, and this programme is seen as an important aspect of the Social Dimension to the 1992 Programme. The 1989 Act has taken account of the proposals emanating from the Commission, proposals which had resulted in the approval of six directives in the area by May 1990. These directives deal with: (1) general duties on employers, employees and others; (2) workplaces; (3) machinery safety; (4) personal protective equipment (ppe); (5) visual display screens; and (6) lifting of loads. Further directives are planned by the Commission, and in the meantime Directives from the pre-SEA period continue to be implemented in Irish law. Since the European Community is also involved in setting Community-wide standards for machinery and ppe, it is likely that over the next few years its impact will be felt to a large extent.

The 1989 Act and breach of statutory duty   A significant feature of the duties imposed by ss. 6-11 of the 1989 Act on employers, employees and others is that they are not cognisable in any compensation claim: that is the effect of s.60 of the Act. This is not, however, particularly significant since the common law duty of employers remains intact, and the level of duty imposed by the 1989 Act is limited to those preventive measures which would be regarded as 'reasonably practicable.' This level of obligation is similar to the test now common in employer's liability claims, so the 1989 Act does not add anything new. To exclude the terms of the statutory obligations from pleadings in an employer's liability claim does not, therefore, affect the likelihood of success or failure one way or the other.

What may be of interest to practitioners, however, is that s.60 of the Act only rules out the use of ss.6 to 11 of the 1989 Act in civil proceedings. It would thus appear that s.12 of the 1989 Act, which imposes the obligation on management to write a safety statement, may in some instances be of use in a claim for damages. Where a safety statement identified a problem but this had not been remedied prior to an accident, it is arguable that this could indicate a lack of due care. More significantly, perhaps, where a safety statement failed to identify a particular (foreseeable) risk of injury to an employee, the representatives of an injured employee might point to this as an indication of lack of due care. This possibility was, in fact, identified to by the Barrington Commission in its 1983 Report as an incentive to management to prepare well-structured safety statements.

The 1989 Act as a framework Act: effect on existing legislation   The Safety, Health and Welfare at Work Act 1989 applies, as already mentioned, to all places of work in the State, including those previously dealt with in safety legislation such as factories. It is thus necessary to consider the effect of the Act in such regulated areas as well as in the 'new entrant' sectors (that is, those not previously covered by statutory safety requirements) such as farms and hospitals. It should be noted that the 1989 Act very much reflects the intention behind the UK Health and Safety at Work Act 1974 (on which many of its provisions are directly modelled), which is to replace all existing legislation with a single comprehensive statute, supplemented by any necessary regulations and other quasi-legislative provisions.

This long-term goal is daunting. Looking at the experience in the UK with its 1974 Act, large swathes of its Factories Act 1961 remain in place, supplemented by regulations which, of necessity, only apply in the manufacturing sector. For the foreseeable future, therefore, much of our Safety in Industry Acts 1955 and 1980 are likely to remain in place together with the regulations made under them. It is, however, important to recognise that the 1989 Act has resulted in two significant changes in the manner in which pre-1989 statute law should be examined.

First, by virtue of the coming into effect of the 1989 Act on 1 November 1989, a number of provisions of pre-1989 Act statutory provisions were repealed and replaced by the 'framework' provisions of the 1989 Act. Thus, in factories, the statutory obligation to compile a safety statement was replaced by a much more stringent requirement in the 1989 Act (a requirement which now applies to all places of work, not just factories). But at the same time, the 1989 Act left untouched the strict statutory duties on, for instance, fencing of machinery contained in ss.21-30 of the Factories Act 1955. These remain in place, alongside the general duties imposed on all employers by s.6 of the 1989 Act: see below.

The second major feature of the 1989 Act is that all pre-1989 Act statutory provisions, including for example the unrepealed provisions of the Factories Act 1955 and the Mines and Quarries Act 1965, may be repealed by ministerial order. That is the effect of a combined reading of s.1(2) and s.4(3) of the 1989 Act. S.4(3) states that the enactments listed in Part I of the Second Schedule to the Act (which include the Safety in Industry Acts 1955 and 1980 and the Minies and Quarries Act 1965) 'are hereby repealed.' However, s.1(2) of the 1989 Act also states that the Minister may bring s.4(3) into effect on different days as regards different existing enactments. Thus, the commencement order for the 1989 Act (see above) brought all provisions of the 1989 Act, *except s.4(3)*, into effect from 1 November 1989. The Minister for Labour is thus empowered to repeal by statutory instrument all the primary legislation referred to in Part I of the Second Schedule to the 1989 Act. The first operation of this enormous power of the Minister for Labour came on the same day that the Minister signed the commencement order for the 1989 Act. The Safety, Health and Welfare at Work Act 1989 (Repeals) Order 1989 (SI No.237) could be described as a tidying up Order. It repealed s.55 of the Factories Act 1955 and s.101 of the Mines and Quarries Act 1965, both of which provided for inquests into deaths at work. Since s.56 of the 1989 Act (as part of its framework approach) now contains a provision on inquests which applies to all places of work, the provisions of the 1955 and 1965 Act were now obsolete, and so they were repealed. It might be argued that this repeal should have been done in the body of the 1989 Act, and indeed many other provisions of the 1955 and 1965 Acts were expressly repealed by, for example, s.4(1) of the 1989 Act. What the Repeals Order indicates is that what would ordinarily be a matter for the Oireachtas has now been delegated to the Minister for Labour.

Constitutional infirmities? Whether the power to repeal by Ministerial order a large amount of primary legislation is constitutionally permissible raises difficult issues not directly addressed before. Can it be assumed that the Oireachtas is empowered to grant to the Minsiter for Labour the function of deciding whether to repeal the remaining provisions of the Factories Act 1955? In previous cases which have raised the competence of the Oireachtas to legislate so as to allow another body to promulgate secondary legislation, the courts have not been asked to address the issue as to whether the Oireachtas may allow a Minister to repeal primary legislation.

The power given by the 1989 Act is, arguably, more extensive than that which was found impermissible by Blayney J in *McDaid v Sheehy* [1989] ILRM 342 (see 111, above). In *McDaid*, there was no question of repeal of primary legislation by statutory instrument. The only comparable situation is where primary legislation is repealed in purported compliance with the terms of s.3 of the European Communities Act 1972: see the European Communities (Environmental Impact Assessment) Regulations 1989 (SI No.349), 373, above. It may be that such powers are given the shield of protection of Article 29.4.3 of the Constitution, though even that was doubted by Senator Robinson in the course of the debate on the 1989 Act: 122 Seanad Debates cols.800ff. Perhaps in defence of the power given in the 1989 Act, it may be stated that, in s.4(3) of the 1989 Act, the Oireachtas has already given approval to the repeal in toto of the pre-1989 Act statutory provisions. On this analysis, therefore, it has merely left the 'timetable' for the actual repeal in the hands of the Minister for Labour who must be guided by the overall purposes contained in the 1989 Act itself. Looked at in this light, it may be argued that there has been no real delegation of the power of statutory repeal. No doubt, this is why the particular form of words contained in ss.1(2) and 4(3) of the Act was employed by its drafters. Should the matter ever be litigated, it would only require that a court examining the matter would see things in the same way as those who so carefully drafted these two provisions.

One other provision of the 1989 Act raises a constitutional doubt. S.61 of the Act purports to confer an immunity from suit on the National Authority for Occupational Safety and Health, the primary enforcing body under the Act (see below). This immunity is in respect of any injury to persons or damage to property arising from the failure to perform or to comply with any of its powers or functions under the Act. Such an immunity may be constitutionally suspect: see Hogan and Morgan, *Administrative Law* (Sweet & Maxwell, 1986), 365-9. The provision may also be, for all practical purposes, unnecessary, in view of the high degree of proof required in any claim for damages arising from failure to perform statutory functions: *Pine Valley Developments Ltd v Ireland* [1987] ILRM 747; [1987] IR 23 (see the discussion in the 1987 Review, 24).

Without wishing to ignore the constitutional context, the remainder of this discussion focuses on the provisions of the 1989 Act, and for these purposes it will be assumed that it is constitutionally valid. For the purposes of discussion the Act may be broken into two main segments: provisions dealing with the workplace and those setting out the position at national level, where new important arrangements for enforcement have been made.

General duties at workplace level   Ss.6-11 of the 1989 Act, as previously mentioned, impose duties on employers, employees and others in connection with safety, health and welfare. These duties do not give rise to any cause of action, by virtue of the provisions of s.60 of the Act, also previously discussed. It is of interest to note, however, that each of the duties imposed by ss.6-11 are couched in terms of what is 'reasonably practicable'. It may be, therefore, that the 1989 Act will prove of some use as a 'statutory analogy' to the level of liability in the common law context.

Thus s.6(1) of the Act, which imposes a general duty on all employers towards employees provides:

> It shall be the duty of every employer to ensure, so far as is reasonably practicable, the safety, health and welfare at work of all his employees.

The level of obligation imposed by the phrase 'so far as is reasonably practicable' was raised in the Seanad debate on the Act: 122 Seanad Debates col.809. The Minister for Labour referred the House to the judgment of Asquith LJ in *Edwards v National Coal Board* [1949] 1 KB 704. In that case, the Court was required to interpret a provision in mines and quarries legislation which employed the same phrase. Asquith LJ stated:

> 'Reasonably practicable' is a narrower term than 'physically possible' and seems to me to imply that a computation must be made in which the quantum or risk is placed on one scale and the sacrifice involved in the measures necessary for averting the risk (whether in money, time or trouble) is placed in the other, and that, if it be shown that there is a gross disproportion between them—the risk being insignificant in relation to the sacrifice—the [employers] discharge the onus which is upon them.

See further the discussion in McMahon and Binchy, *Irish Law of Torts*, 2nd ed. (Butterworths, 1990) 119. It would appear, however, that in many instances this test is similar to the test of employer's liability at common law.

Without prejudice to this general duty of employers towards employees, s.6(2) of the 1989 Act spells out ten particular matters to which the employer must have regard. These are: (1) design, provision and maintenance of the place of work in a condition that is safe and without risk to health; (2) design, provision and maintenance of safe means of access to and egress from any place of work under the employer's control; (3) design, provision and maintenance of plant and machinery that are safe and without risk to health; (4) provision of systems of work that are planned, organised, performed and maintained so as to be safe and without risk to health; (5) provision of such information, instruction, training and supervision as is necessary to ensure the safety and health at work of employees; (6) provision and maintenance of suitable protective clothing or equipment to ensure the safety and health of employees (where it is not reasonably practicable to control or eliminate hazards); (7) preparation and revision of adequate emergency plans; (8) ensure safety and prevent risks in connection with the use of any substance or article; (9) provision and maintenance of facilities and arrangements for the welfare of employees; (10) obtaining, where necessary, the services of a competent person, whether under a contract of employment or otherwise, for the purpose of ensuring the safety and health of employees.

Many of these provisions reflect the existing common law duties on employers, but the Barrington Commission felt that such duties should be drawn to the attention of employers in order for them to appreciate the range and extent of their legal obligations. It is also clear, however, that other items, such as (9), above, go beyond what would normally arise at common law. And in terms of the overall preventive purpose of the Act, the ten items constitute a useful checklist in assisting an employer to compile a safety statement pursuant to s.12 of the 1989 Act.

To indicate that, on the other side of the employment equation, individuals also have obligations, section 9 places a number of obligations on employees while at work. The employee must: (1) take reasonable care for his/her own safety, health and welfare and that of others who might be affected by his/her acts or omissions; (2) co-operate with the employer or any other person to enable the employer or other person to comply with statutory obligations; (3) use any suitable appliance, protective clothing, convenience, equipment or other means provided for securing his/her safety, health or welfare; (4) report to the employer or immediate supervisor any defects of which the employee becomes aware in plant, equipment, place of work or system of work which might endanger safety, health or welfare; (5) not intentionally or recklessly to interfere with or misuse any appliance, protective clothing, convenience, equipment or other means provided to ensure his safety, health and welfare. This latter obligation applies, in fact, to any person, not just employees. While most of these obligations reflect the common law duties of employees, the obligation to report defects is new. No doubt, the obligations placed on employees by s.9 of the Act may have implications in, for example, the context of disciplinary matters and dismissal claims.

To emphasise the extensive nature of the obligations on employers, s.7 requires that account be taken of non-employees, such as contractors. S.7(1) requires every employer to conduct the undertaking so as to ensure, so far as is reasonably practicable, that persons not employed but who may be affected by the undertaking are not exposed to risks to their safety or health. Regulations may require the employer to provide certain information to people who might be so affected. This emphasis on what might be described as the environmental impact of premises reflects an approach seen in European Community regulations e.g. the European Communities (Major Accident Hazards of Certain Industrial Activities) Regulations 1986 and 1989, which implemented the 'Seveso' Directive in Irish law. S.8 of the Act overlaps to some extent with s.7. S.8 places obligations on persons responsible for buildings (in effect, occupiers who will also usually be the employers) to ensure, so far as is reasonably practicable, safety and health for contractors and the like in connection with: (a) the place of work; (b) safe access to and egress from the place of work; and (c) the use of articles or substances in the place of work. This is not much different from the obligation which an occupier has under common law.

The 1989 Act also brings self-employed persons into the legislative picture for the first time. S.7(2) states that every self-employed person must conduct his/her undertaking in such a way as to ensure, so far as is reasonably practicable, that s/he and other persons (not being employees) who may be affected by the undertaking are not exposed to risks to their safety or health.

To underline the preventive aspect of the Act and to indicate that some risks are 'imported' into a place of work, there are also obligations placed on other persons.

S.10 of the Act places the following obligations on any person who designs, manufactures, imports or supplies any article for use at work: (1) to ensure, so far as is reasonably practicable, that the article is designed, constructed, tested and examined so as to work safely and without risk to health when used by a person at a place of work; (2) to take steps to ensure that persons using the article are given adequate information about the use for which it has been designed and tested and about any conditions relating to it to ensure that when it is in use, dismantled or disposed of, it will be safe and without risk to health; and (3) to provide revised information for the purposes mentioned in (2), as necessary.

Designers or manufacturers must also conduct research for the purposes of discovering and, so far as is reasonably practicable, eliminating risks to safety and health arising from the design.

Manufacturers, importers or suppliers must also, in relation to substances (a) ensure that the substance is safe and without risks to health; (b) carry out testing of the substance as necessary; and (c) provide information as to the substance's properties to ensure that when in use it will not be a risk to safety or health.

Designers of buildings and those involved in construction are, by s.11, placed under obligations to ensure that, so far as is reasonably practicable, the place of work is safe and without risk to health. This section deals with the structural safety of a place of work, ventilation as well as proposed access and egress points. Again, there is a broad correspondence with the common law duties of, e.g., architects.

Safety statement and safety consultation   S.12 of the Act sets out the obligations as to an employer preparing a safety statement, referred to previously. As indicated, there may be circumstances in which an inadequate safety statement may be of use in a compensation claim. It is particularly important to note in this context that s.12(3) specifies that the safety statement must be 'based on an identification of the hazards and an assessment of the risks to safety and health at the place of work to which the safety statement relates.' Since this statutory requirement now applies to all places of work, whether a factory, shop, office, government department, hospital or farm, the potential for its use is wide. In addition to laying down this general basis for the safety statement, s.12 (4) states that the statement must: (a) specify the arrangements made and the resources provided for safeguarding the safety, health and welfare of employees; (b) specify the co-operation required from employees as regards safety, health and welfare; and (c) specify the names, including names of authorised deputies and job titles where applicable, of the persons responsible for the performance of tasks assigned to them by the statement. It was indicated by the Barrington Commission that this latter requirement would involve the designation of members of line management and supervisory staff with specific functions.

The employer may be directed to revise the safety statement if found to be inadequate by an inspector from the National Authority for Occupational Safety and Health (see below). Finally, the contents of the safety statement must be brought to the attention of employees.

To emphasise that the 1989 Act regards safety and health as part of the normal economic performance of management, s.12(6) also states that the directors' report under s.158 of the Companies Act 1963 must contain a reference to the extent to which the policy in the safety statement has been fulfilled during the period of time covered by the report. At present, this obligation only applies to companies registered in the State.

S.13 of the Act involves another indication of the two-sided approach to safety and health which lies behind the Act. It places a general obligation on an employer to consult with employees and take account of any representations made by the employees for the purposes of giving effect to the employer's statutory duties. But section 13 goes much further than this by providing for the selection by the employees of a safety representative.

The powers and functions of the safety representative under s.13 are: (1) to receive information from the employer as is necessary to ensure the safety, health and welfare of employees; (2) to be informed by the employer that an inspector is on the premises; (3) to accompany the inspector, except where the inspector is investigating an accident; (4) to make oral or written representations to an inspector; (5) to receive advice and information from an inspector; (6) to make representations to the employer as to safety, health and welfare, which the employer is required, where necessary, to 'act upon'; (7) to investigate accidents and dangerous occurrences; (8) to investigate potential hazards to safety or health, after notice to the employer; (9) to carry out inspections, on notice to the employer, who cannot unreasonably withhold permission, and subject to agreement on frequency; (10) time off 'as may be reasonable', without loss of remuneration, for two purposes: (a) to acquire knowledge to carry out his/her functions (e.g. training courses); and (b) to carry out his/her functions (e.g. conducting inspections and making representations). To allay some fears expressed during the Dáil debate, a provision was added which states that the safety representative is to suffer 'no disadvantage' arising out of the performance of his/her duties.

Finally, while there is no specific mention in the 1989 Act of the mixed management/employee safety committees which have operated in factories (and the relevant statutory provisions providing for such committees have been repealed by the 1989 Act), such committees could continue on a voluntary basis as a consultation mechanism within the meaning of s.13.

It may be noted that Guidelines on the implications of ss.12 and 13 of the 1989 Act were published in May 1990 by the National Authority for Occupational Safety and Health, established by the 1989 Act, and to whose nature and function we now turn.

National Authority for Occupational Safety and Health Ss.14 to 26 of the Act relate to the establishment and functions of the new National Authority for Occupational Safety and Health. The Authority, established on 1 November 1989 when the Act itself came into force, is a semi-State body which now has the enforcement functions formerly vested in the Department of Labour, as well as the new functions conferred by the 1989 Act. Thus the Authority now has responsibility for enforcement of the factories and mines and quarries legislation as well as enforcement of the 1989 Act in those sectors, as well as in the 'new entrant' sectors such as farms and hospitals. Enforcement will be through the Authority's inspectorate, in effect the inspectorate formerly attached to the Department of Labour. The Department's staff were, pursuant to s.20 of the 1989 Act, transferred to the Authority in much the same way as occurred with the transfer of staff from the Department of Posts and Telegraphs to An Post and Bord Telecom Éireann under ss.45 and 46 of the Postal and Telecommunications Services Act 1983.

One of the significant features of the Authority is that its executive (part-time) board consists of representatives of employers, employees and government. Three members of the Authority were nominated by employer organisations, three by the ICTU and four others nominated by the Minister for Labour, representing relevant State and other organisations. This very much reflects the recommendations of the Barrington Commission and is in line with the creation of the independent Health and Safety Commission and Health and Safety Executive in the UK under its Health and Safety at Work Act 1974.

Pursuant to s.16 of the Act, the Authority's main functions are: (1) to make adequate arrangements for the enforcement of all legislation on occupational safety; (2) to keep existing legislation under review; (3) to submit to the responsible Minister proposals for amending existing legislation (the actual changes would have to be signed into law by the Minister for Labour); (4) to draw up codes of practice (discussed below); (5) to appoint inspectors to enforce the relevant legislation; (6) to promote, encourage and foster the prevention of accidents and injury to health at work; (7) to encourage and foster activities designed to promote safety, health and welfare at work; (8) to make arrangements for the provision of information and advice; (9) to undertake, promote, sponsor, evaluate and publish research, surveys and studies relating to safety, health and welfare at work; (10) to make arrangements with other bodies (including government Departments) to perform its functions; (11) to submit reports to the Minister for Labour as to how it will carry out its functions; (12) to issue licences in relation to any activities which the Minister considers should be subject to licensing.

Despite the wide-ranging powers of the Authority, the Minister still retains a supervisory function in this area. It is the Minister who retains the power to actually sign regulations into law. In practice, the likelihood is that the Minister would sign regulations which are recommended by the Authority: that is what was envisaged by the Barrington Commission. Finally, the Minister also retains the ultimate budgetary control over the Authority. Nonetheless, on a day-to-day basis, responsibility rests with the Authority as with any other semi-State organisation.

Codes of practice   As part of the new approach envisaged by the Barrington Commission and the 1989 Act, the Authority may, with the approval of the Minister, pursuant to s.30 approve codes of practice which, the section states: 'shall be for the purpose of providing practical guidance with respect to the requirements or prohibitions of any of the relevant statutory provisions.' This provision again reflects the approach in the UK Health and Safety at Work Act 1974. It also is in line with the EC approach to health and safety, which is to back up legal obligations with technical specifications which indicate in a clear manner how the legal obligations are to be carried out.

S.30 also states that the Authority may approve of any code of practice or any part of one which has been drawn up by any other body. This gives the new Authority a wide brief to accelerate the introduction of codes under the Act by, for example, incorporating codes of practice issued by the National Standards Authority of Ireland, the UK Health and Safety Executive or the EC Standards Body, CEN. Thus, in August 1990, the Authority adopted standards from the NSAI on the storage of LPG as codes of practice under the 1989 Act.

As well as providing practical information to those concerned, an approved code of practice may, under s.31, be used in a criminal prosectuion by the Authority. If a code of practice provides practical guidance as to how an employer is to comply with a statutory duty, then failure to comply with the code may be used as 'evidence' in the prosecution. Without shifting the burden of proof on the prosecution, this provision certainly has an impact on the evidential burden in any prosecution. In addition to s.31, s.50 of the Act also affects the onus of proof in general (discussed below).

Powers of inspectors S.34 of the 1989 Act gives powers of entry to Authority inspectors which are modelled on those in, for example, the Safety in Industry Acts 1955 and 1980. The 1989 Act powers apply, of course, to all places of work. The powers are to: (1) enter, inspect, examine and search at all times premises which the inspector has reasonable cause to believe are being used as a place of work; (2) take a member of the Garda Síochána with him/her, where required; (3) bring into the premises any material or person authorised by the Authority; (4) use reasonable force, on foot of a search warrant obtained from the District Court, to enter any premises where s/he has reasonable cause to believe a breach of the legislation has been or is being committed; (5) make any necessary examination or inquiry; (6) require production of any books, registers, records, certificates etc. which must be kept under any of the legislation; (7) require people to give information and to sign a declaration of the truth of information supplied; (8) order places to be left undisturbed; (9) require samples of articles or substances to be given to him/her; (10) cause tests to be made on any article or substance likely to cause injury or danger to health; (11) take atmospheric samples; (12) take any measurements or photographs.

In addition, the Act gives to inspectors important new enforcement powers without the need to bring a prosecution. These powers range from what might be regarded as 'reminders' to a power to order the immediate shutdown of a place of work. S.35 authorises an inspector to issue an Improvement Direction, to which the employer would be required to respond with an Improvement Plan, in relation to activities which the inspector considers may involve risk to safety or health. Under s.36, the inspector may issue an Improvement Notice stating his/her opinion that an employer has broken a legislative provision or regulation, and involving directions as to how the employer can comply with his statutory duties by a specified date. These notices are based on the Fire Safety Notices under the Fire Services Act 1981. An employer may appeal to the District Court within 14 days against the making of an improvement notice to the District Court. Under s.37, an inspector may issue a Prohibition Notice in relation to an activity which the inspector is of opinion has been or is likely to be a cause of serious personal injury to persons at work. The employer has 7 days within which to appeal the making of a Prohibition Notice. Such appeal (unlike that for the Improvement Notice) does not always have the effect of suspending the operation of the Prohibition Notice. The inspector is entitled to declare that the Prohibition Notice is to take effect immediately. The District Court (Safety, Health and Welfare at Work Act 1989) Regulations 1989 (SI No.275) set out the procedure for appealing to the District Court pursuant to ss.36 and 38 of the Act. On a comparative note, it is of interest that appeals under the UK Health and Safety at Work Act 1974 are to industrial tribunals.

In exceptional circumstances, the Authority may apply pursuant to s.39 of the Act to the High Court for an order prohibiting certain activities; this can be obtained on an *ex parte* basis. It might be that such an order would be applied for where there were a number of contractors on a building site who were to be served with orders. Clearly also, the fact that the order can be obtained *ex parte* indicates that it could be employed where an inspector might anticipate difficulty in obtaining compliance with the other powers already mentioned.

Prosecutions and penalties The Act envisages prosecutions by or under the control of the Authority, or other enforcing agency such as local authorities who are still left to enforce certain pieces of legislation. The format of such prosecutions will be as before, but the method of proof alters in two respects. First, s.50 of the Act provides that, where a prosecution relates to a failure to comply with a duty to do something 'so far as is practicable' or 'so far as is reasonably practicable', it is for the accused (the corporate body or individual) to prove that it was not practicable (or not reasonably practicable as the case may be) to do more than was in fact done. This certainly shifts the evidential burden on to the accused person, whether a corporate body or an employee. Second, the effect of s.31 of the Act, in relation to the use of codes of practice, has been outlined above.

Prosecutions have, in the past, been taken against corporate entities only and this is likely to continue in the future. However, experience with the UK Health and Safety at Work Act 1974 indicates that prosecutions of individuals within organisations is also much more likely in the future. Prosecutions of 'ordinary' employees would be under s.9 of the Act. For corporate officers, s.48(19) of the 1989 Act states that where an offence by a corporate body: 'is proved to have been committed with the consent or connivance of, or to have been attributable to any neglect on the part of any director, manager, secretary, or other similar officer . . . he as well as the body corporate shall be guilty of that offence . . .'. This is based on s.37 of the UK 1974 Act. For examples of prosecutions see *Armour v Skeen* [1977] IRLR 310 and *R v Mara* [1987] 1 WLR 87.

The Act also introduces increased penalties for offences under the existing statutory provisions as well as for offences under the 1989 Act itself. For most offences, the fines have been increased to £1,000 for conviction in a summary trial, which would be the procedure for most prosecutions. It is of interest to note that there is no possibility of imprisonment under the 1989 Act on conviction in the District Court.

For trials on indictment, there is no limit on the fine which may be imposed on conviction (the Act as introduced provided for a maximum fine of £15,000). There is also a discretion on indictment to impose a term of imprisonment of up to two years, but this is reserved for three offences only: (a) disobeying the terms of a Prohibition Notice; (b) unauthorised disclosure of information; and (c) breach of a condition attaching to a licence issued under the Act.

Finally, a brief word may be made on prosecution policy. It is unlikely that many prosecutions (in relation to the total level of accidents) will take place. Enforcement policy has been based in the past on 'prosecution as a last resort'. Encouragement and advice is the staple of the inspectors appointed to police compliance with occupational safety and health legislation, and this is unlikely to change dramatically in the future. However, the new enforcement mechanisms referred to above will undoubtedly prove a useful lever for inspectors when they enforce the 1989 Act.

WATER

European Community regulations on quality of bathing water (SI No.99) and of surface water intended for abstracting water (SI No.294) are referred to in the European Communities chapter, above, 206.

Social Welfare

As with previous Reviews, this chapter concentrates on the case law on the social welfare code in 1989. For a detailed analysis of the Social Welfare Act 1989, see Clark's annotation, *Irish Current Law Statutes Annotated*. As well as giving effect to the changes in benefits announced in the 1989 Budget, the 1989 Act altered the arrangements concerning deserted wives' benefit and introduced a new widower's allowance and deserted husband's allowance. The Garda Síochána were also brought into the occupational injuries scheme. The year also witnessed a second Act, the Social Welfare (No.2) Act 1989; this was a direct response to the decision of the Supreme Court in *Hyland v Minister for Social Welfare* [1990] ILRM 213; [1989] IR 624: see 264-5, above, in the Family Law chapter.

BLIND PENSION

In *Harvey v Minister for Social Welfare* [1990] ILRM 185 the Supreme Court dealt with the question as to whether the blind pension was also an old age pension. The applicant received a widow's allowance and a blind pension up to the pensionable age of 66, when the widow's allowance was withdrawn and she was given an old age pension only. The decision was based on Article 4 of the Social Welfare (Overlapping Benefits) (Amendment) Regulations 1979, which states that where a woman who reaches pensionable age would otherwise be entitled to a widow's pension and an old age pension, she is to receive only one of the two. The applicant sought judicial review, contending that the blind pension was not an old age pension and that she did not therefore come within the terms of Article 4 of the 1979 Regulations. She was unsuccessful before Blayney J (High Court, 8 April 1987): see the 1987 Review, 305-6. On appeal to the Supreme Court (Finlay CJ, Hamilton P, Walsh, Griffin and Hederman JJ) her appeal was allowed.

The first point which the Supreme Court dealt with was whether s.75 of the Social Welfare Act 1970, under which the 1979 Regulations had been made, was invalid for breaching Article 15.2 of the Constitution, which gives the exclusive law-making power to the Oireachtas. Applying the test in *East Donegal Co-Op Ltd v Attorney General* [1970] IR 317, the Court held that s.75 of the 1970 Act must be presumed to have been validly enacted, and since it was capable of being operated without a breach of Article 15.2, it had not been shown to be repugnant to the Constitution. However, as we will see below, Article 15.2 was to play a crucial part in the ultimate decision of the Court in the context of the 1979 Regulations.

The Supreme Court supported Blayney J's view that the applicant's blind pension was an old age pension within the meaning of s.6 of the Old Age Pensions Act 1932, notwithstanding the slight change in wording in s.175 of the Social Welfare (Consolidation) Act 1981. The Court noted that 1981 Act, being a consolidation Act, was subject to a rebuttable presumption that no change in the pre-existing law was intended. And the Court went on to say that the question whether a person on reaching 66 years of age should be granted two allowances rather than one was a matter of social policy to be determined by the Oireachtas. Since the blind pension was, under the legislative provisions, an old age pension it was not unreasonable for it to be withdrawn in the manner effected in the instant case.

However, the Court reversed the decision of Blayney J on a point not argued in the High Court. The Supreme Court accepted that this was unusual but it decided to deal with the new issue, taking into consideration that the respondents had had a reasonable opportunity to meet the point. The Court held that Article 4 of the 1979 Regulations was an impermissible exercise of legislative power by the Minister, in contravention of Article 15.2 of the Constitution, since it purported to negative the intended effect of s.7 of the Social Welfare Act 1979, under which the applicant was entitled to retain both allowances, and Article 4 was thus *ultra vires*.

EQUALITY

The question whether the EC Directive on Equal Treatment in Social Security (79/7/EEC) had immediate legal effect in Irish law on the date it was due to be implemented (December 1984), or only from the date it was implemented by the Social Welfare (No.2) Act 1985 (November 1986), had been discussed by Hamilton P in *Cotter v Minister for Social Welfare (No.2)*, High Court, 10 June 1988: see the 1988 Review, 382. In that case the President had limited the immediate impact of the Directive in Irish law, in line with the Supreme Court decision in *Murphy v Attorney General* [1982] IR 241.

In *Carberry v Minister for Social Welfare*, High Court, 28 April 1989 Barron J took a different line and expressly declined to follow the decision of the President in the *Cotter* case. Briefly, the background to the case was as follows.

The EEC Social Security Directive (79/7/EEC) provided that, as from December 1984, there shall be no sex discrimination in the calculation of social security benefits in the national laws of the member States of the

Community. The Social Welfare (No. 2) Act 1985 purported to implement the Directive in Irish law, but the Act did not come into force until November 1986. On a reference under Article 177 of the Treaty of Rome, the Court of Justice held in *McDermott and Cotter v Minister for Social Welfare* [1987] ILRM 324; [1987] ECR 1453 that in the absence of national measures implementing the Directive women were entitled to have the same rules applied to them as were applied to men. On reference back to the High Court, Hamilton P held, in *Cotter v Minister for Social Welfare (No. 2)*, High Court, 10 June 1988 that the applicants were entitled to certain relief, but that such claims could not be fully retrospective to December 1984.

In *Carberry* the applicant was a married woman claiming entitlement to increased disability benefits on the same basis on which her husband could have so claimed under transitional provisions in Article 4 of the Social Welfare (Adult Dependent) Regulations 1986 and Article 6(b) of the Social Welfare (Preservation of Rights) (No.2) Regulations 1986. Barron J granted the applicant the relief she sought.

He held that although the applicant had not actually been in receipt of the adult dependent allowance before implementation of the Directive, she ought to have been, and to refuse her the increase at this stage would be to continue the discrimination notwithstanding that the Directive had been implemented in Irish law.

On the crucial retrospection point, he considered that he could not follow the approach taken by Hamilton P in the *Cotter (No.2)* case. Barron J referred to the decision of the Court of Justice in *Barra v Belgium* [1988] 2 CMLR 409; in that case the Court had held that where, in an Article 177 ruling, the Court does not itself specifically limit the retrospective effect of its decision, a national court is bound, under the Court of Justice's jurisprudence on the matter, to give full retrospective effect to the Directive. Thus the applicant in the instant case was entitled to claim in respect of the period from December 1984 to December 1986. The decision in *Defrenne v Sabena* [1976] ECR 455, which limited retrospective effect in the context of pay equality, may thus be regarded as an exception to the normal retrospection rule. It is of interest to note that in *Murphy v Attorney General* [1982] IR 241, where the Supreme Court developed a non-retrospection rule for con-stitutional decisions, Henchy J for the majority referred with approval to the *Defrenne* decision to support his view. The decision in *Barra* may cast some doubt on whether the *Murphy* decision ought to be applied with the degree of vigour which has been associated with it since 1980.

FAMILY

In *Hyland v Minister for Social Welfare* [1990] ILRM 213; [1989] IR 624, the Supreme Court discussed whether certain provisions of the Social Welfare (No. 2) Act 1985 were in conflict with Article 41 of the Constitution: see 264-5, above, in the Family Law chapter. Note that the Social Welfare (No. 2) Act 1989 reversed the effect of the decision. In *MacMathuna v Ireland* [1989] IR 504, Carroll J considered the validity of a number of provisions of the Income Tax and Social Welfare codes in the context of Article 41: see 96-8, above, in the Constitutional Law chapter.

OCCUPATIONAL INJURIES BENEFIT

The question whether certain benefits under Part II of the Social Welfare (Consolidation) Act 1981 should be taken into account in assessing damages in an employer's liability claim was considered in *Doran v Dublin Plant Hire Ltd*, High Court, 25 April 1989.

REGULATIONS

The following regulations were made in 1989 in relation to social welfare.

Social Welfare (Agreememt with the Republic of Austria on Social Security) Order 1989 (SI No.307)

Social Welfare (Amendment of Miscellaneous Social Insurance Provisions) Regulations 1989 (SI No.188).

Social Welfare (Availability for Employment) Regulations 1989 (SI No.328).

Social Welfare (Collection of Contributions by the Collector-General) Regulations 1989 (SI No.72).

Social Welfare (Collection of Employment Contributions by the Collector-General) Regulations 1989 (SI No.298).

Social Welfare (Collection of Employment Contributions for Special Contributors) Regulations 1989 (SI No.302).

Social Welfare (Commencement of Employment) Regulations 1989 (SI No.339).

Social Welfare (Family Income Supplement) (Amendment) Regulations 1989 (SI No.196).

Social Welfare (Miscellaneous Social Insurance Provisions) (Amendment) Regulations 1989 (SI No.18).

Social Welfare (Modification of Insurance) (Amendment) Regulations 1989 (SI No.74).

Social Welfare (Overlapping Benefits) (Amendment) Regulations 1989 (SI No.279).

Social Welfare (Prescribed Relative Allowance) Regulations 1989 (SI No.361).

Social Welfare (Preservation of Rights) (Amendment) Regulations 1989 (SI No.63).

Social Welfare (Preservation of Rights) (Amendment) (No.2) Regulations 1989 (SI No.186).

Social Welfare (Preservation of Rights) (Amendment) (No.3) Regulations 1989 (SI No.354).

Social Welfare (Rent Allowance) (Amendment) Regulations 1989 (SI No.187).

Social Welfare (Supplementary Welfare Allowances) (Amendment) Regulations 1989 (SI No.200).

Social Welfare (Voluntary Contribution) (Amendment) Regulations 1989 (SI No.75).

Social Welfare (Unemployment Payments) Regulations 1989 (SI No.166).

Social Welfare (Widowers' (Non-Contributory) Pension and Deserted Husband's Allowance) Regulations 1989 (SI No.281).

Social Welfare Act 1989 (Section 6) (Commencement) Order 1989 (SI No.280).

Social Welfare Act 1989 (Section 18) (Commencement) Order 1989 (SI No.73).

SOCIAL WELFARE APPEALS

The need for reform of the social welfare appeals system is discussed in Whyte and Cousins, (1989) 7 ILT 198.

TERMINATION PROCEDURE

Thompson v Minister for Social Welfare [1989] IR 618 concerned the procedure by which the applicant had had his unemployment assistance terminated.

The applicant had been in receipt of unemployment assistance from 1981 to 1987. In September 1987, the applicant attended an interview as part of the National Jobsearch Programme and he was offered a place in a four week Jobsearch Course. A letter to participants indicated that failure to attend the course 'will result in your social welfare entitlement being reviewed.' The applicant refused to participate in the proposed course on the basis that it would be of no assistance to him. In October 1987 the applicant received a letter from his Employment Exchange asking him to explain his refusal, to which he replied that it would be of no benefit to him and that he was available for work. On 23 October 1987, a Deciding Officer notified the applicant of a discontinuance of his unemployment assistance for the period 21 to 27 October. After an interview between the deciding officer and the applicant in November 1987, a further Notification of Disallowance was issued on 5 November 1987. The applicant appealed both decisions, requesting that the Appeals Officer sit with assessors. The Appeals Officer, due to an oversight, sat without assessors in December 1987 and affirmed the October and November decisions. In April 1988, a Deciding Officer made a decision disallowing the applicant's unemployment assistance with effect from 18 December 1987. In evidence this deciding officer stated that he was, to some extent, influenced by the December decision of the Appeals Officer. The applicant successfully sought judicial review of the four decisions.

O'Hanlon J firstly held that the October 1987 decision was invalid for the failure of the Deciding Officer to inform the applicant that his position was being reviewed, the grounds on which he was considering disallowing further payment, and giving the applicant an opportunity to answer the case made against him, however informally this might have been done. Second, he held that the November 1987 decision, which followed the interview with the applicant, was not invalid, since the applicant was fully aware at the time that his entitlement to social assistance was under review. The third decision of the Appeals Officer was invalid for failure to sit with assessors in accordance with s.298(12) of the Social Welfare (Consolidation) Act 1981. Finally, the decision of April 1988 was invalid for being influenced, in part, by the invalid Appeals Officer decision.

O'Hanlon J added, however, that the stand taken by the applicant appeared to him to be wholly unreasonable and indefensible, but he granted the judicial review because the decisions to disallow payments must be based on the rules in the 1981 Act as well as the requirements of natural justice. The applicant's appeal against the critical November 1987 decision was remitted back by O'Hanlon J for decision by an Appeals Officer.

Solicitors

ADMISSION TO LAW SOCIETY SCHOOL

MacGabhann v Incorporated Law Society of Ireland [1989] ILRM 854 was the second case in recent years concerning the Law Society's Final Examination, First Part, sometimes called the Entrance Examination. Although the applicant in the previous case, *Gilmer v Incorporated Law Society of Ireland* [1989] ILRM 590, obtained judicial review of her examination result while the applicant in the instant case was unsuccessful the *MacGabhann* case has had a profound impact on the Law Society's examination rules.

The applicant in *MacGabhann* was a registered solicitor's apprentice who had been unsuccessful in the Law Society's Final Examination, First Part, which had been held by the Society pursuant to the Solicitors Acts 1954 and 1960 (Apprenticeship and Education) Regulations 1975. (As we will see later, these Regulations have since been amended.) The Society's Education Committee, which has overall superintendence in relation to the Examination, had decided that a candidate must achieve 50% in each of the six subjects in the Examination. The Society also operated a compensation system which, after the High Court decision in *Gilmer*, required a student who achieved less than 50% in each subject to attain 50% overall. The applicant, who had previously passed one subject for which he then had an exemption, achieved 50% precisely in three subjects, 51% in one other subject and 46% in his remaining subject in the Examination held in 1986. Under the Society's rules, therefore, he was deemed not to have been successful. The applicant sought judicial review of the Society's decision.

In the course of the hearing, the evidence indicated that, due to space restrictions in the Society's premises where courses were conducted, it was necessary to decide how entrance to the limited places was to be decided. The Education Committee determined that a competitive examination was required—the Final Examination, First Part. Booklets published by the Society stated that 'candidates compete for 150 places.' Between 1981 and 1986, the percentage pass rate of those who sat the Examination went down: from 72% in 1981 to 40% in 1984. At the same time the numbers sitting the examination increased significantly. The applicant argued that the Society applied an annual quota system by which it restricted the numbers who were successful in the Examination. It was also argued that the standard applied by the Education Committee amounted to an unreasonable exercise of power.

Blayney J dismissed the applicant's claim for a declaration that he had reached the required level of performance, but he did grant certain other declarations of importance.

On the claim that a quota had actually been imposed, he held against the applicant. He was of the view that in 1986 it was clear that it had been unnecessary for the Law Society to impose a quota in the circumstances which had arisen. He concluded that those students who were not successful had failed to reach the level of performance required, which was that they reach an aggregate of 50% overall, as laid down in *Gilmer*.

However, of some importance, Blayney J was of the view that it was equally clear that had it become necessary the Society would have imposed a quota of 150 places in view of the space limitations in its premises. He held that such a quota would be *ultra vires* Reg.18(2) of the 1975 Regulations under which an apprentice who had passed the Final Examination, First Part was entitled to admission to the Law School. The applicant, he held, was entitled to a declaration to that effect, and that the Society was thus not entitled to conduct a competitive entrance examination. These declarations were of crucial importance in the developments which the Law Society put in train later in 1989, which are outlined below.

It had also been argued in *MacGabhann* that the Law Society's Education Committee, in laying down the standard in relation to compensation, had acted unreasonably, in the sense laid down in *Cassidy v Minister for Industry and Commerce* [1978] IR 297. A large part of the case comprised a study of the results in the Part I subjects from 1981 to 1986, with evidence given by the Law Society's own examiners as well as by members of the State's university law faculties. Blayney J rejected the argument that the Law Society had acted unreasonably, arbitrarily or partially. Ultimately, he reached this conclusion on the basis that the Law Society operated a fixed standard which applied equally to all candidates. Having heard all the evidence given, he was not prepared to 'second-guess' the Law Society's examiners. He concluded that since the Education Committee had been applying a reasonable standard, he would be substituting his own judgment for the Committee's if he were to hold that the applicant had reached the required standard. On this basis, therefore, the applicant was not entitled to have his result quashed.

There was, however, a final comment by the judge which indicated a certain unhappiness that lines of responsibility had not been as clearly drawn as they might as between the Education Committee and the Law Society's examiners. Blayney J stated that, although the matter did not arise directly in the instant case, the Law Society might consider whether the function of laying down the examination standard should be carried out by the Education Committee and the function of applying that standard should be carried out by the Law Society's examiners only.

As indicated above, while the applicant in *MacGabhann* was unsuccessful in having his examination result quashed, he did obtain certain declarations from Blayney J and the judgment also contained other comments on the procedures adopted by the Law Society. In September 1989, the Law Society stated that it had adopted certain changes in the examination system and these were given effect to in the Solicitors Acts 1954 and 1960 (Apprenticeship and Education) Regulations 1989 (SI No.231). In effect, these regulations now exempt from the Final Examination, Part I those law graduates who have successfully completed the 'core' subjects which they formerly had to sit in the Examination. For those law graduates, therefore, the argument put forward in *MacGabhann* as to a quota now no longer arises. However, for law graduates who have not taken the 'core' subjects in their law degree, and for non-law graduates, the Final Examination, Part I remains, in effect, as the Entrance Examination to the Law Society School. Finally, the Solicitors Acts 1954 and 1960 (Apprentices' Fees) Regulations 1989 (SI No.19) prescribe the fees payable for courses of lectures at the Law Society School.

COMPENSATION FUND

Extent of Law Society's subrogation In *Incorporated Law Society of Ireland v Owens and Ors*, High Court, 11 January 1989 Hamilton P outlined some of the limits to the Law Society's right of subrogation and tracing under s.21 of the Solicitors (Amendment) Act 1960.

The first-named defendant, the County Registrar for Cavan, received an order of *fieri facias* from the High Court together with a certificate of sum due demanding execution for the sum of £26,696 plus interest from the second-named defendant. The second-named defendant, a solicitor, had acted for the third-named defendant in the sale by the third-named defendant of certain lands. The *fi fa* order was in respect of the money due by the second-named defendant to the third-named defendant. The County Registrar decided to execute the *fi fa* order of the High Court, having first notified the Law Society which had no objection to the course proposed. In the course of execution in October 1988, the County Registrar put the Court Messenger and bailiffs into possession of the second defendant's house and offices. On the same date, the second defendant obtained a bank draft payable to the County Registrar in discharge of the *fi fa* order of the High Court. Payment for the draft was drawn on the second defendant's client account.

In November 1988, the Law Society instituted the present proceedings seeking a declaration that the sum drawn on the client account was wrongly paid to the County Registrar on the ground that the second defendant held it in trust for his clients. The Law Society also applied for injunctions requiring the County Registrar to lodge the money held in the second defendant's client account or, alternatively, in Court. In evidence, the Law Society averred that there was a substantial deficit in the second defendant's client account and that there was a likelihood of claims being made on the Law Society's Compensation Fund and that one claim in the sum of £8,500 had already been admitted by the Law Society pursuant to the 1960 Act. Hamilton P granted the declaration sought by the Law Society but refused the injunctions.

On the evidence, the President held as follows: that the second named defendant was indebted to the third named defendant by virtue of the High Court order; that the amount paid out from the second defendant's client account was not the property of the third defendant; that on the date of the payment there was a substantial deficit in the account; and that the money in the client account was held by the second defendant in trust for his clients. Thus, Hamilton P concluded that the second named defendant was not beneficially entitled to that money and was not entitled to draw a cheque on the client account for the purposes of discharging the amount due by him to the third defendant. However, Hamilton P went on that it had not been shown that either the County Registrar, the third defendant or the bank who made payment on the bank draft were aware of the fact that there was a substantial deficit in the second defendant's client account, there being a sum of £67,312 to the credit of the account at the time.

He concluded that the Law Society was entitled to a right of subrogation pursuant to s.21 of the Solicitors (Amendment) Act 1960 only insofar as the Society had made a grant in accordance with the provisions of s.21(4) of the Act. In the instant case this amounted to the sum of £8,500, and the Law Society was subrogated to that right and entitled to maintain the instant proceedings to that extent.

The Law Society was given a declaration that the money held by the second defendant was held in trust for his client and that he had no beneficial interest in the money and was not entitled to use such money to satisfy any personal debts. But, applying the approach taken in *In re Irish Shipping Ltd* [1986] ILRM 518, Hamilton P held that the right to trace ends with a purchaser for value who has no notice of the circumstances which have given right to the right to trace. Since in the instant case the County Registrar, the third defendant and the bank who made payment on the draft had paid consideration thereon and acted in good faith, the Society was not entitled to the injunctions sought. Accordingly, he held that the County Registrar was obliged to pay the sums held by him to the third defendant in accordance with the terms of the *fi fa* order of the High Court.

Solicitor as trustee: fraud In *Trustee Savings Bank v Incorporated Law Society of Ireland* [1989] ILRM 665; [1989] IR 234, the Supreme Court affirmed the decision of Johnson J in an important point on recourse to the Compensation Fund.

The plaintiff bank had granted a loan to a solicitor for the purchase of a house. The loan was on foot of an undertaking from the firm of solicitors, of which the solicitor in question was a partner, and purporting to be signed by one of the other partners in the firm. On default in respect of the loan, it transpired that the signature had been forged by the solicitor who had received the loan from the plaintiff bank. The bank applied for compensation from the fund established by the Incorporated Law Society under s.21 of the Solicitors (Amendment) Act 1960. In the High Court Johnson J had granted the relief sought: [1988] ILRM 541; [1987] IR 430 (see the 1987 Review, 310). The Supreme Court (Finlay CJ, Griffin and McCarthy JJ) dismissed the Law Society's appeal.

Delivering the Court's decision, Finlay CJ stated that there was no warrant for interpreting the unambiguous words of s.21(4) of the 1960 Act other than by reference to their ordinary meaning, pursuant to which 'any person' suffering loss was entitled to make a claim from the fund established by the Law Society. He did not think that this general provision was affected by the special provisions of s.23 relating to the fund established by the Incorporated Law Society of Northern Ireland. Having dealt with that matter, which was the real point in dispute, the Chief Justice concluded that the terms of the arrangement in the instant case involved a clear case of dishonesty within s.21 of the 1960 Act. On this basis, therefore, the plaintiff bank was entitled to have recourse to the Compensation Fund.

It may be helpful to quote a passage from the judgment of the Chief Justice to indicate the apparent scope of the decision in the case. He commented as follows:

> One is aware as a matter of fact and practice that in a great number of instances, whether in associations, clubs or groups or in relation to family matters and affairs, solicitors are chosen to act as trustees, being considered reliable and expert for the tasks imposed upon a trustee, and that they carry out their duties as such, though not acting as solicitors. It is quite practical and realistic to assume that the legislature intended to provide compensation for persons who, having chosen their trustee on those grounds, were damaged by his dishonesty.

Though strictly speaking these comments were *obiter* in the instant case, they clearly reflect the considered views of the Supreme Court and put the profession on notice of the extent of the liability assumed by the fund established under the 1960 Act.

PRACTISING CERTIFICATES

The Solicitors Acts 1954 and 1960 (Fees) Regulations 1989 (SI No.356) specify revised fees for obtaining practising certificates.

Statutory Interpretation

Consolidation Act   The presumption that a consolidation Act does not result in an alteration of the pre-existing law was referred to in *Harvey v Minister for Social Welfare* [1990] ILRM 185: see the discussion in the Social Welfare chapter at 394, above.

'Have regard to'   The meaning to be attributed to a statutory provision by which a person was required to 'have regard' to certain matters was discussed by Barrington J in *Bardun Estates Society Ltd v Dublin County Council*, High Court, 27 June 1989: see 329, above, in the Local Government chapter.

Mandatory or directory   The distinction between mandatory and directory statutory provisions was discussed by the Supreme Court in connection with adjoining sections of the Children Act 1908 in *The State (D.) v G. (No.2)* [1990] ILRM 130 and *The State (F.) v Superintendent of B. Garda Station* [1990] ILRM 243 (HC); Supreme Court, 3 May 1990: see the discussion at 265-9, above (Family Law chapter). The distinction also arose in the context of signing a case stated within a certain period in *McMahon v McClafferty* [1990] ILRM 32; [1989] IR 68 (see 158, above, in the Criminal Law chapter) and *Irish Refining plc v Commissioner of Valuation*, Supreme Court, 4 May 1989 (see 344, above, in the Practice and Procedure chapter).

Noscitur a sociis   This maxim was applied by Hamilton P in *United States Tobacco International Inc. v Minister for Health*, High Court, September 1987: see 377, above, in the Safety and Health chapter.

Oireachtas debates   In *Conaty v Tipperary (NR) County Council* (1987) 7 ILT 222 (not reported until September 1989) Judge Sheridan declined to follow the lead of Costello J in *Wavin Pipes Ltd v Hepworth Iron Co. Ltd* [1982] FSR 32 where Oireachtas debates had been employed to support a particular statutory interpretation. Judge Sheridan took the more traditional line that the meaning of statutory language was to be gleaned from the words of the legislation alone.

Ordinary meaning   The approach by which the judges will avoid interpreting legislation in an oblique manner, not clearly intended by the legislature, was discussed by Gannon J in *Louth County Council v Mathews*, High Court, 14 April 1989: see in the Local Government chapter, 336, above. A similar approach was adopted by Costello J in *Pfizer Chemical Corp v Commissioner of Valuation*, High Court, 9 May 1989: see 337, above, also in the Local Government chapter.

Overall intention   Dicta of Walsh J in *East Donegal Co-Op Ltd v Attorney General* [1970] IR 317 as to interpreting statutory provisions in the light of the whole of an Act were also applied by Hamilton P in the *United States Tobacco* case, above. A similar approach was adopted by Costello J in *In re McCairns (PMPA) plc.* [1989] ILRM 501: see 60, above, in the Company Law chapter.

Prospective effect   In *Dublin County Council v Grealy and Ors*, High Court, 7 December 1989 Blayney J applied the presumption that legislation operates prospectively only: see 328, above, in the Local Government chapter.

Severability   The extent to which a court may sever a valid part from an invalid provision was discussed in *Greene v Minister for Agriculture* [1990] ILRM 364: see 100, above, in the Constitutional Law chapter; and in *Howard v Minister for Agriculture*, High Court, 3 October 1989 (17, above). See also the references on 116, above.

Telecommunications

BROADCASTING

Injunction to prohibit statutory power In *Cooke v Minister for Communications*, High Court, 6 February 1989; Supreme Court, Irish Times LR, 20 February 1989, the Supreme Court refused to grant an interlocutory injunction preventing the operation of s.8 of the Broadcasting and Wireless Telegraphy Act 1988: see the 1988 Review, 406.

Restrictions on broadcasting The Broadcasting Authority Act 1960 (Section 31) Order 1987 Order 1989 (SI No.13) continued in force the terms of the 1987 Order until 19 January 1990. Under the terms of the 1987 Order, spokespersons for certain named and proscribed organisations are prohibited from broadcasting any material on Radio Telefís Éireann, including party political broadcasts. For discussion, see *The State (Lynch) v Cooney* [1983] ILRM 89; [1982] IR 337.

DATA PROTECTION

The Data Protection Act 1988 (Restriction of Section 4) Regulations 1989 (SI No.81), the Data Protection Act 1988 (Section 5(1)(d)) (Specifications) Regulations 1989 (SI No.84), the Data Protection (Access Modification) (Health) Regulations 1989 (SI No.82) and the Data Protection (Access Modification) (Social Work) Regulations 1989 (SI No.83) were discussed in the 1988 Review, 395-6.

POSTAL SERVICES

The Postal and Telecommunications Services Act 1983 (Section 111(1)) Order 1989 (SI No.77) licences An Post to provide a public national telecommunications mail service.

VIDEO RECORDINGS

The Video Recordings Act 1989 was signed by the President in December 1989 but, aside from ss.29 and 30 (which concern the Annual Reports of the Official Censor of Films), it will not come into effect until the Minister for

Justice signs commencement orders. In the 1987 Review, 316-20, we provided an analysis of the terms of the Act when it was the Video Recordings Bill 1987. As indicated there, a significant alteration to the structure of the 1989 Act occurred during the course of its passage by means of the addition of a licensing system for video outlets. A classification system for videos was also added in the course of the Oireachtas debate.

Briefly, the 1989 Act introduces a system for the control and regulation of the importation and supply of video recordings in tandem with the existing system for films which operates under the Censorship of Films Acts 1923 to 1970.

S.3 of the Act sets out the criteria by which the Censor of Films may grant a supply certificate for a video. The Censor must refuse to grant such certificate if, in his opinion, the video is unfit for viewing because it depicts acts of gross violence or cruelty towards humans or animals or else because it (i) would be likely to cause persons to commit crimes; (ii) would be likely to stir up hatred against a group of people in the State on account of their race, colour, nationality, religion, ethnic or national origins, membership of the travelling community or sexual orientation; or (iii) would tend, by reason of obscene or indecent matter, to deprave or corrupt person who might view it. The 'likely to stir up hatred' criterion was added to conform with the terms of the Prohibition of Incitement to Hatred Act 1989 (see 166, above, in the Criminal Law chapter). For the earlier deletion of a less extensive provision in the Bill as initiated see the 1987 Review, 317.

Some of the criticisms of s.3 of the Act as initiated, from the point of view of the Censor's certification function, were allayed by the insertion of a classification system, which is now contained in s.4 of the Act. Videos will be classified in one of four ways: suitable for general viewing, for under 12s in the company of a responsible adult, for those of 15 years or more and for those of 18 years or more. This is similar to the system which exists under the UK Video Recordings Act 1984 and users of Irish video outlets were familiar with the UK classification system prior to the introduction of the 1989 Act.

S.5 of the Act makes it a criminal offence for a person to supply or offer for sale a video recording which has not been given a supply certificate by the Censor, unless the video is 'exempted' under the Act: see the 1987 Review, 318. S.6 makes it an offence to possess an uncertified video work.

Ss.18 to 24 of the Act deal with the licensing of wholesale and retail video outlets and the establishment of an Official Register of licences by the Censor.

Torts

THE DUTY OF CARE

Does the army owe a duty of care in negligence to soldiers to protect them against an unreasonable risk of injury or death? The immediate response might well be that it does not. Of all professions, that of the soldier has an inherent aura of danger. Moreover, the idea that judges should have a role in looking over the shoulder of generals and ordering them not to take certain strategic decisions may seem preposterous.

Nevertheless in *Ryan v Ireland, the Attorney General and the Minister for Defence* [1989] IR 177, the Supreme Court took a different view. The plaintiff was a member of the Defence Forces serving as a volunteer with the United Nations Interim Force in Lebanon. He was seriously wounded by a mortar attack launched by hostile forces on a camp where he and other Irish soldiers were on duty. He alleged that his wounds were due to his having been negligently exposed to unnecessary risk by being placed in an un-protected billet close to a target area consisting of a machine gun, at a time when an attack was apprehended as being imminent. Keane J withdrew the case from the jury on the basis that the plaintiff had failed to establish that the Irish army rather than the United Nations was responsible on the occasion for his safety and welfare. Counsel for the defendants conceded that he could not stand over this ruling as this issue had not been raised in the defence nor at trial until after the conclusion of the plaintiff's evidence. However, he contended that there had been no *prima facie* evidence of negligence and that the plaintiff had voluntarily assumed the risk of injury through the action of hostile forces and waived his legal rights in respect of the injury. More broadly, he contended that under Irish law a member of the Defence Forces could not sue the State for any injury of damage caused to him in armed conflict, even if it were established to have been caused by the negligence of his superior officers.

The Supreme Court dealt with these three arguments in reverse order. On the question of State immunity, Finlay CJ (delivering the judgment of the Court) referred (*inter alia*) to decisions in Australia and the United States which held that the army or Government owed no duty of care to members of the armed forces. He noted that counsel for the State had not sought to defend an all-embracing immunity but had confined his submission to alleged negligence during armed conflict in a theatre of war. The Chief

Justice confessed that the reason for this boundary line was 'not very clear to me, and would appear to be based more on pragmatism than principle'. (Later we will suggest that a limitation of this type has much to be said for it on grounds of both principle and policy.) Finlay CJ noted that, by virtue of s.4 of the Defence (Amendment) Act 1960, a soldier serving with the United Nations Emergency Forces is deemed, for the purposes of the Defence Act 1954, to be 'on active service'. The consequences of this provision largely related to discipline and the punishment for military offences. But, said the Chief Justice, '[t]he provision does not . . . in any way, equate service with the United Nations with war, nor do considerations of the defence of the State arise in such service. No question of a dominant priority for the effectiveness of armed action against an enemy occurs.' He went on to refer to Article 28 of the Constitution which provides 'the most ample and unrestricted powers' of the Oireachtas to legislate to secure public safety and the preservation of the State in time of war, as there defined, or in time of armed rebellion. Nothing in the Constitution may be invoked to invalidate such legislation expressed to be for such purposes.

Finlay CJ stated:

> It is impossible, having regard to these provisions, to accept the application of a common law doctrine arising from the necessity to ensure the safety of the State during a period of war or armed rebellion, which has the effect of abrogating constitutional rights. In so far, therefore, as the principle apparently supporting some of the decisions to which we have referred in the question of the dominant priority in regard to the defence of the State, such decisions would not appear to be applicable and cannot be applied to the question of service with the United Nations peacekeeping force.

This analysis gives rise to a number of comments. First there is the task of understanding precisely its intended import. The argument appears to be that, in the light of the draconian legislative powers conferred on the Oireachtas by Article 28, any common law doctrine of State immunity or the absence of a duty of care based on the necessity to ensure the safety of the State during a period of war or armed rebellion must have evaporated to the extent that it would have the effect of abrogating constitutional rights. Secondly there is the need to assess the merits of this holding. A major difficulty with it appears to be that it begs the question. If, for the purposes of argument, there *was* a common law State immunity based on the need to ensure the safety of the State during such a period, then the question of its status after the promulgation of the Constitution cannot be disposed of without first confronting the issue of whether it was of sufficient potency to withstand competing constitutional considerations. Reference to Article 28 is hardly determinative of this issue: the granting of draconian legislative powers to the Oireachtas in times of war and armed rebellion does not necessarily have the effect of killing the former common law immunity, unless it could be argued that the express granting of this power inevitably wiped away, without saying so, the common law immunity. This would be a hard argument to sustain since there is no necessary conflict or redundancy involved in coexistence between Article 28 and the common law immunity.

The reference to the abrogation of constitutional rights raises the complex question of the relationship between (i) the absence of a duty of care in negligence, (ii) the existence of an immunity from suit on the part of the State, and (iii) the abrogation of constitutional rights. As to the first, our courts have yet to confront in express terms the relationship between such an absence of duty and constitutional rights. For example, it has been assumed up to now that the absence of a duty of care on the part of a lawyer in respect of advocacy under *Rondel v Worsley* [1969] 1 AC 191 would not be constitutionally suspect merely because it abrogated the constitutional right to litigate. If the policy justification for not imposing a duty of care in negligence is sufficient for the purposes of the law of tort, then it should not unthinkingly be 'trumped' by the invocation of a constitutional right. This was surely what Henchy J was seeking to ensure in *Hanrahan v Merck Sharp & Dohme (Ireland) Ltd* [1988] ILRM 629, at 636, when he said that:

> [i]n many torts—for example, negligence . . .—a plaintiff may give evidence of what he claims to be a breach of a constitutional right, but he may fail in the action because of . . . some . . . legal or technical defence. . . . [W]hen [a person] founds his action on an existing tort he is normally confined to the limitations of that tort. It might be different if it could be shown that the tort in question is basically ineffective to protect this constitutional right.

It can scarcely be the case that a serious constitutional doubt affects every instance where the courts have, on policy grounds, held that no duty of care should be imposed in negligence. If this were so, the courts would be engaging in a useless exercise in addressing the duty issue in negligence cases, since, wearing their constitutional hat, they would be obliged to strike down as unconstitutional the exemption from liability which they recognised in tort. The truth of the matter is that, if a court, after due consideration, holds that the defendant who, let us assume, caused admitted harm to the plaintiff, was not under a duty of care to the plaintiff and thus is not obliged to make compensation, this normally does not even raise a *prima facie* constitutional issue. Of course the plaintiff has sustained a loss for which the law gives no remedy but that does not necessarily mean that his or her constitutional right to litigate or right to property has been infringed. The scope of these constitutional rights cannot properly be articulated without regard to the fact that compensation under tort law is (at least in theory) based on the principle of fault rather than of social welfare.

Tort and constitutional law are not antagonistic systems of law: they each respect the other and generally serve to complement rather than confront each other, as Henchy J makes plain.

It is worth considering the difference between State immunity from suit, in general or in particular respects, on the one hand, and the absence of a duty of care on the part of the State, on the other. *Byrne v Ireland* [1972] IR 241 made it clear that the State has no immunity from suit based on a line of succession to the British royal prerogative. (It will be recalled that declaring this line broken led to a somewhat *ad hoc* conceptualisation in *Webb v Ireland* [1988] ILRM 565; [1988] IR 353, to ensure that the State's right to treasure trove—eminently desirable from the social and cultural standpoint—could find a constitutional anchor other than that based on the royal prerogative of treasure trove: see the 1987 Review, 104-6.) In *Byrne* Walsh J noted that, according to constitutional theory in the United States, Governmental immunity was based, not on succession to the recently repudiated royal prerogative, but on public policy.

Could a credible argument be made that the rejection of State immunity based on the British royal prerogative does not commit the Court to rejecting a contemporary argument in support of State immunity on some *other* ground? In the context of the present case, that ground would presumably be that questions of war, peace and army strategy and discipline are so clearly matters for executive rather than judicial resolution that the separation of the powers requires that the courts admit without embarrassment that it is beyond their constitutional authority to decide cases against the State which requir them to tell the generals how to run the army. Such an argument would de little *support* from Walsh J's analysis; but equally importantly, it de appear to have been disposed of by the rejection of a prerogative immunity. It is interesting to note that *Webb* is capable of lendin of the argument, since it recognised a form of State sovereignty on that the Constitution which is not easy to reconcile fully with Walsh that the of sovereignty in *Byrne*. Walsh J's rejection of the view that the sovereignty in Article 5 as amounting to a constitution is not amenable State is above the law is clearly harmonious with W how in *Webb* the declaration as to sovereignty in Article 5 means th ng a specific power or to any external authority for its conduct could tizens) to deprive a finder concept of State sovereignty was capable of entitlement of the State (albeit on behalf of what would otherwise have been a constitutionally-protected right of property in a very valuable item.

Apart from the operation of State immunity, there is the matter of the existence or otherwise of a duty of care in negligence on the part of the army relative to its soldiers. The Court did not address this issue in detail. Had it done so in conventional terms, it would have asked whether there was a sufficient proximity between the parties to warrant the imposition of a *prima facie* duty. Applying Lord Wilberforce's two-step test in *Anns v Merton London Borough Council* [1978] AC 728, at 751, it would then have determined whether there were any considerations which ought to negative or reduce or limit the scope of the duty or the class of person to whom it was owed or the damages to which a breach of it might give rise. Finally, it might have incorporated the *Peabody* appendage of whether it was 'just and reasonable' to recognise a duty of care.

A strong argument may be made on policy grounds that imposing an unqualified duty of care of this type is mistaken. If the cut and thrust of the battle in a court is sufficient to exempt an advocate from a duty of care (*Rondel v Worsley* [1969] 1 AC 191; *Saif Ali v Sydney Mitchell & Co. (a firm)* [1980] AC 198; *Somasundaram v Melchior & Co.* [1988] 1 WLR 1394), and if the fear of 'defensive policing' is a good enough reason to relieve the police from a duty of care in the investigation of crime (*Hill v Chief Constable of West Yorkshire* [1988] 2 All ER 238), then surely the strategic decisions which waging war involves are beyond the proper scrutiny of courts? This is not to suggest that every negligence action by a soldier against the army in respect of an accident taking place during armed conflict or hostilities would inevitably fail. Contrary to what the Supreme Court thought, a distinction *can* be made between battle strategy on the one hand and more domestic or conventional acts of negligence, such as spilling hot soup over an officer, where the military context is largely irrelevant to the commission of the tort. Such a line may be difficult to draw in some cases but it is scarcely more so than that drawn between 'discretionary' and 'operational' decisions made by public authorities: see G. Hogan & D. ⟨r⟩gan, *Administrative Law* (1985), 374-7. See also the analysis by Hogg, *⟨ty of the Crown⟩* (1971), 93-8, largely in harmony with that of the ⟨the⟩ Court.

⟨are likely⟩t of the Court's acceptance that the State owes a duty of care to ⟨though perha⟩ct of operations consisting of armed conflict or hostilities, ⟨owed to a civilia⟩ as to why it should owe any less a duty to civilians who ⟨to be injured by the n⟩ed in the conflict. A soldier, after all, is a volunteer, ⟨⟩ver to the suggestion that *a fortiori* a duty must be ⟨⟩the Court's analysis the soldier does not volunteer ⟨⟩ of the army rather than the inevitable risks of armed conflict. It is interesting to note that, in the pursuit of criminals, police cannot ignore their competing duty to lawful road users: *Priestman v Colangelo* [1959] SCR 615. But is it really the function of the court to say how many civilian casualties are permissible in armed conflict?

Having held that the plaintiff's superior officers owed him a duty of care Finlay CJ went on to consider 'the general nature and, to an extent, the parameters of that duty'. His analysis is worthy of particular attention:

> In broadest terms the duty can be stated to be to take such care for the safety of the plaintiff as is reasonable in all the circumstances of their relationship and the activity in which the carrying out of the task allotted to the forces concerned could involve an unavoidable risk of death or serious injury. In such situations considerations of standards of care drawn from the experience of the workplace may be of little assistance. There could, I think, be no objective in a master and servant relationship which would justify exposing the servant to the risk of serious injury or death other than the saving of life itself. In the execution of military service exposing a soldier to such risk may often be justified by the nature of the task committed to the forces concerned. Furthermore, there can, in relation to armed conflict, be many situations where those in authority must make swift decisions in effect in the agony of the moment. Mere proof of error in such decisions would not in itself establish negligence. Importance may be attached, I am satisfied, in regard to alleged negligence in a military situation, to the question as to whether the role of the soldier at the time of the alleged negligence is one of attack or defence, or, to put the matter another way, whether he is engaged actively in armed operations or is only passively engaged in them.

Where, as occurred in the case before the Court, the plaintiff, while on guard duty, was acting in a defensive role and in effect standing by, the Chief Justice was satisfied that his commanding officer owed him a duty to take such precautions as were reasonable and practical, having regard to the functions which, as a member of the guard, the plaintiff was obliged to perform, 'to try and reduce the risk of his being wounded or killed'.

A number of questions arise in relation to these observations. First, the idea of the superior officer's being under a duty to try to *reduce* the risk of injury or death raises the issue of which points of negligence are being involved. From what level of risk is the officer obliged to seek a reduction? There is no risk in existence independent of the combination of decisions made by the opposing combatants. The plaintiff was at risk in the first place as a result *inter alia* of decisions made by his superior officers. The notion of reducing the risk seems therefore unhelpful unless it connotes an idea that all decisions should involve the maximum amount of safety for soldiers consistent with the needs of the situation.

Secondly, the question arises as to the extent to which the superior officers' duty of care extends to protecting their soldiers from foreseeable aggression from adversaries. Could there be a duty to order a retreat, for example, to save unnecessary casualties? Could there be a duty not to place a soldier in a particular *place* (as opposed to in a building or a particular structure) because of the risk of sniper attack?

Thirdly, the Chief Justice's statement that no objective in a master and servant relationship 'would justify exposing the servant to the risk of serious injury or death other than the saving of life itself' is interesting. The source of the limitation is not stated but is probably the constitutional guarantee of protection for the right to life. Of course the quantum of risk must be a factor: some types of employment, such as mining, transport or security duties, for example, unquestionably expose the employee to a risk of death, probably well in excess of that to which most Irish soldiers have been exposed over the years; but that risk is presumably not in general of such proportions as to fail the Chief Justice's test. (Interestingly, the issue was touched on in *Walsh v Securicor Ireland Ltd*, High Court, 7 April 1989, considered below, 425-7.) The distinction which the Chief Justice seeks to draw between situations of attack and defence suggests that perhaps in relation to the former the Court would hesitate about overruling, in effect, the decisions of the military.

The Court's rejection of the defence of voluntary assumption of risk is also worthy of note. Finlay CJ observed that, to succeed, it would be necessary to establish that the plaintiff, by enlisting and volunteering for United Nations service, had entered into a contract waiving his right to sue if injured by the negligence of his superior officers. No express contract to that effect had been suggested. While the plaintiff had accepted the risks inherent in the possibility of being involved in armed conflict, it could not be implied that he accepted the risk of being unnecessarily exposed to injury by negligence. This analysis treats the engaging by an employee (or soldier) in an inherently risky activity as waiver for the purposes of s.34(2)(b) of the Civil Liability Act 1961 rather than as a matter to be dealt with in terms of a restricted duty of care. The point might seem of no great moment since either waiver or a restricted duty can defeat a plaintiff's case. But a plaintiff will not always have *communicated* his waiver to the defendant: cf. *O'Hanlon v Electricity Supply Board* [1969] IR 75 (on which the Chief Justice here relied). Where waiver is thus not established, the question whether the issue of inherent dangers can be dealt with in terms of a restricted duty of care can thus become crucial: cf McMahon & Binchy, *Irish Law of Torts* (2nd ed., 1990), 100-1, 336-8.

The Supreme Court directed a new trial on all issues. On 19 October 1989,

Barr J, who heard the case, imposed liability. He was of the view, on the evidence, that the declaration of an 'all clear' by the United Nations overall commander after an earlier abortive mortar attack did not imply that there would be no further attack that night. On the contrary, all experienced United Nations personnel were aware at this place that the Christian Militia was a volatile force which lacked proper military discipline, that the high tension had been exacerbated by a shooting of a Militia man that morning, for which no retribution had been obtained, and that there were reasonable grounds for apprehending that at least some Militia men might not obey the cease-fire order. Moreover, since the Militia man had been shot at or near an Irish checkpoint, having been stopped by Irish soldiers, there was an added risk that an attack by way of retaliation was likely to be directed at Irish troops. The plaintiff, in an unprotected portacabin only yards from the Christian Militia, was 'the softest possible target'.

In coming to the conclusion that the plaintiff's superior officers had been negligent in causing or permitting him to return to the billet, Barr J took into account that the decision had not been taken in the agony of the moment but rather at a time when there was sufficient opportunity to consider its implications in full. He also found the defendants negligent in not having the plaintiff's billet protected by sandbags or the side of it exposed to the main road, in view of the possibility of a major attack on the base.

Barr J accepted that, even if the plaintiff had not been sent to the billet, the attack was so severe that the plaintiff would have been at serious risk of personal injury or death; but he rejected this as a defence, since he considered that the risk of injury or death to which he had been subjected was 'substantially greater' than that which would otherwise have applied. This raises the troublesome question of the relationship between negligence, risk and causation. Where a plaintiff would have been more likely than not to have been injured or killed even if the defendant was not negligent, should the defendant be liable for having *caused* the injury or death? The traditional answer is no: *Kuhn v Banker*, 133 Ohio St. 304, 13 NE 2d 242 (1938); *Sykes v Midland Bank Executor & Trustee Co.* [1971] 1 QB 113, criticised by Schaefer, 'Uncertainty and the Law of Damages' (1978) 19 *Wm & Mary L Rev* 719, at 763-5. More recently commentators and courts in the United States have shown an increasing willingness to permit compensation, with damages reflecting the limited prospect of survival which the plaintiff had before the defendant's act: King, 'Causation, Valuation and Chance in Personal Injury Torts Involving Pre-Existing Conditions and Future Consequences', (1981) 90 *Yale L J* 1353; Robinson, 14 *J of Legal Studies* 779 (1985); *Herskovits v Group Health Co-Operative* (1983) 99 Wn 2d 609, 664 P 2d 474 (concurring opinion of Pearson J); *Waffer v United States*, 799 F 2d 911 (1986).

In England, the House of Lords did not exclude the possibility of developing the law on these lines, in *Hotson v East Berkshire Area Health Authority* [1987] 2 All ER 909. In the light of its subsequent decision in *Wilsher v Essex Area Health Authority* [1988] 1 All ER 871, however, it would seem that the plaintiff would have far greater difficulty in succeeding in such a case. *Ryan v Ireland* represents a novel incursion of negligence into an area traditionally considered beyond the remit of the judiciary. The evils of 'defensive medicine' have been described by many commentators. Are we now to have 'defensive warmaking', with judges telling generals when to attack or retreat and granting injunctions against journeys into the valley of death?

LIABILITY OF PUBLIC AUTHORITIES

In *Burke v Dublin Corporation*, High Court, 13 July 1989, reversed in part by the Supreme Court, 26 July 1990, important issues relating to the defendant's duty under, and in respect of, the Housing Act 1966 fell for consideration. We examine the case, so far as both its contractual and tortious aspects are concerned, in the chapter on Contract, above, 117-25.

NEGLIGENT MISSTATEMENT

In *Hazylake Fashions Ltd v Bank of Ireland* [1989] ILRM 698; [1989] IR 601, the plaintiff company, which manufactured children's clothing for the export, market agreed with the defendant Bank that the Bank would advance 90% of the full amount of all bills of exchange falling within the Export Finance Insurance Scheme and presented within the period covered by it, subject to the stipulated limit of revolving credit. The Bank did not agree to discount or make advances against unaccepted bills. Murphy J was satisfied that this change of practice was attributable to an administrative error rather than an express or implied variation of the original agreement.

The error was eventually discovered after fifteen unaccepted bills had been discounted. The Bank told the company that in future only accepted bills would be discounted. (In fact the Bank discounted and three more unaccepted bills, as a result of a decision taken by the Credit Division in Dublin for the purpose and with the effect of clearing the company's overdraft). As a result of cash flow problems, the company ceased manufacturing though it continued to act as agent for the sale of goods to its previous customers.

The plaintiff sued for, *inter alia*, negligent misstatement in that the actions of the Bank in discounting unaccepted cheques shortly after their receipt amounted to an implied statement. Murphy J rejected this contention. He considered that the basis of liability recognised in *Hedley Byrne & Co. Ltd v Heller & Partners Ltd* [1964] AC 465 did not extend to implied statements. Even if it did, it was difficult to extract from the actions of the parties the statement which was said to have been made negligently and caused economic loss. It could not be contended that the Bank had led the company to believe that the bills had been accepted before they were discounted. If it was suggested that the premature discounting of the bills was a representation that this procedure would continue, then effectively the plaintiff was contending that the original contract had been amended, and there had been neither evidence nor argument to support that conclusion:

> The reality of the matter is that the Bank acted negligently in the sense that they failed to take appropriate steps to safeguard their own interests. They did not await notification of acceptance before discounting and they may have lost the protection of the insurance cover as a result. In my view they were making no 'statement', express or implied, to the company. The company was simply the beneficiary of an unfortunate administrative error made within the banking system.

> I accept that the correction of this error on very short notice to the company must have added to the serious financial problems which it was then undergoing but I cannot see that the Bank acted in breach of its duty by making a mistake in relation to the conduct of its own business or in correcting the error when it was identified.

Several comments on the issues raised in this case seem in order. First, the notion of an implied statement is scarcely different in principle from that of an express statement. Court have for long dealt with implied statements in both civil and criminal contexts of fraudulent misrepresentation. In *R v Barnard* 7 C & P 784; 173 ER 342, at 342 (1837), it was accepted that a man in Oxford who wore a student's cap and gown was representing that he was a student. See also *The People v Finkel & Levine* (1951) 1 Frewen 123; and *Brogan v Bennett* [1955] IR 119. Similarly in *Gill v McDowell* [1903] 2 IR 463, the notion of a 'tacit or 'implied' representation was accepted by the Court.

Is there any reason in principle why, if a *fraudulent* representation may be implied rather than expressed, the tort of *negligent* misrepresentation should exclude implied statements? We can see none. The *Hedley Byrne* principle, in its original exposition, required representation and reliance as central elements. Provided these requirements are adhered to, it seems that an implied representation should be capable of generating liability under the *Hedley Byrne* principle. The reliance element is, of course, central to imposition of liability for *fraudulent* misrepresentation; but it is easy to envisage cases where a person might hold himself out as making a proposition, without resort to language, which might induce reliance in circumstances where the implied representation was negligently made. This is not for a moment to suggest that a court should be over-eager to find implied representations inhering in conduct which is either unsupported by any linguistic representations, or indeed, contrary to them. Equally, courts should closely scrutinise claims by plaintiffs that they relied on representations of this type. But this caution extends merely to the application of principle to fact rather than to the acceptability of the principle itself.

Next, it is worth considering whether the plaintiff's argument in *Hazylake* that there had been an implied representation that the procedure of discounting unaccepted bills would continue *necessarily* amounted to a contention that the original contract had been amended. The circumstances in which a contract may be amended do not exactly coincide with those in which a representation inconsistent with that contract may occasion liability in tort. The question of the proper relationship between the law of contract and the tort of negligent misrepresentation is a troublesome one; the crucial point here is that a person may sue for negligent misrepresentation in the context of the performance of contractual obligations without having to base his case on the breach of those obligations or on the misrepresentations' having had the effect of varying any contractual term. To take a more straightforward case than *Hazylake*: if a bank has contractually agreed to discount only accepted bills, and the manager calls in the client and says: 'I know we're not contractually bound to do this, and I'm not wishing to change our contractual position, but I want you to know that we'll discount unaccepted bills for the next year', it is clear that the client can sue for negligent misrepresentation if the manager resiles from this assurance, without being forced to show that the contract had (contrary to the manager's express statement) been varied by his representation.

A striking feature of *Hazylake* is the absence of discussion in the judgment of the principle of *estoppel*. *High Trees* was, after all a case involving the forbearance of one party to stand on his contractual rights, and in *Tool Metal Manufacturing Co. v Tungsten Electric Co.* [1955] 1 WLR 761 the issue concerned the period of grace which must be given when a person decides to reassert contractual rights having not done so for some time. All of this touches on the question whether a bank, having been guilty of an error in providing a service beyond that which it had contractually undertaken, can turn round, on discovering the error, and leave the client to work out the cash flow problems resulting from a withdrawal of the extra service (save to the extent of ensuring that the client's overdraft in the bank is cleared).

The judgment contains no mention of *Webb v Ireland* [1988] ILRM 565;

[1988] IR 353; it is true that the application in private law of the estoppel doctrine recognised administered in *Webb* has not proved popular with the High Court judges: see the 1988 Review, 20-30 and the above, 9-12. Nevertheless, it would have been interesting to see whether that doctrine applies to the facts of *Hazylake*. An attractive argument can be made that these facts fit comfortably with the principle of law stated by Lord Denning MR in *Amalgamated Investments Ltd v Texas Commerce International Bank* [1982] 2 QB 84, at 122, which received the support of Finlay CJ in *Webb*:

> When the parties to a transaction proceed on the basis that an underlying assumption (either of fact or of law, and whether due to mis-representation or mistake, makes no difference), on which they have conducted the dealings between them, neither of them will be allowed to go back on that assumption when it would be unfair or unjust to allow him to do so. If one of them does not seek to go back on it, the courts will give the other such remedy as the equity of the case demands.

MEDICAL NEGLIGENCE

In *Dunne v National Maternity Hospital* [1989] ILRM 735; [1989] IR 91 the jury awarded the plaintiff over a million pounds in a claim in which he had alleged negligence in the management of his mother's labour and of his birth, resulting in his sustaining brain damage. The Supreme Court ordered a retrial on grounds we shall examine below. Of general interest and importance is Finlay CJ's analysis of principles of medical negligence, which he traced to the Court's earlier decisions in *O'Donovan v Cork County Council* [1967] IR 173; *Daniels v Heskin* [1954] IR 73; *Reeves v Carthy* [1984] IR 348; and *Roche v Peilow* [1985] IR 232. He said:

> 1. The true test for establishing negligence in diagnosis or treatment on the part of a medical practitioner is whether he has been proved to be guilty of such failure as no medical practitioner of equal specialist or general status and skill would be guilty of if acting with ordinary care.

> 2. If the allegation of negligence against a medical practitioner is based on proof that he deviated from a general and approved practice, that will not establish negligence unless it is also proved that the course he did take was one which no medical practitioner of like specialisation and skill would have followed had he been taking the ordinary care required from a person of his qualifications.

3. If a medical practitioner charged with negligence defends his conduct by establishing that he followed a practice which was general, and which was approved of by his colleagues of similar specialisation and skill, he cannot escape liability if in reply the plaintiff establishes that such practice has inherent defects which ought to be obvious to any person giving the matter due consideration.

4. An honest difference of opinion between doctors as to which is the better of two ways of treating a patient does not provide any ground for leaving a question to the jury as to whether a person who has followed one course rather than the other has been negligent.

5. It is not for a jury (or for a judge) to decide which of two alternative courses of treatment is in their (or his) opinion preferable, but their (or his) function is merely to decide whether the course of treatment followed, on the evidence, compiled with the careful conduct of a medical practitioner of like specialisation and skill to that professed by the Defendant.

6. If there is an issue of fact, the determination of which is necessary for the decision as to whether a particular practice is or is not general and approved within the meaning of these principles, that issue must in a trial held with a jury be left to the determination of the jury.

Finlay CJ went on to state three further legal principles which had not been expressly mentioned in the earlier decisions:

(a)'General and approved practice' need not be universal but must be approved of and adhered to by a substantial number of reputable practitioners holding the relevant specialist or general qualifications.

(b) Though treatment only is referred to in some of these statements of principle, they must apply in identical fashion to questions of diagnosis.

(c) In action against a hospital where allegations are made of negligence against the medical administrators on the basis of a claim that practices and procedures laid down by them for the carrying out of treatment or diagnosis by medical or nursing staff were defective, their conduct is to be tested in accordance with the legal principles which would apply if they had personally carried out such treatment or diagnosis in accordance with such practice or procedure.

A few points about the principles spelt out by the Chief Justice are in order. First, proposition no. 3 is in harmony with *O'Donovan* and *Roche v Peilow*. It represents a compromise between absolute deference to customary professional practice and what might be considered to be undue intrusion by the courts. By virtue of their traditions, their rules or of self-regulation, and the high intellectual calibre of their members, professions are regarded by the courts as being substantially competent to determine and require a satisfactory standard of care in the performance of professional duties. But if customary practice has inherent defects which ought to be obvious to any person giving the matter due consideration, then the courts consider they can no longer stand idly by. This approach is not immune from criticism.

It may be asked whether the rationales for deference to professional practice are not really smokescreens for a tacit solidarity between lawyers and other professionals. (If the law is kind to doctors, its generosity to barristers is overflowing in that it imposes *no* duty of care in relation to the performance of advocacy functions.) Whether there is any validity in this criticism is a matter for sociological resolution. Certainly, the suspicion of some tacit sense of solidarity finds little support from the decision of *Hughes v J.J. Power Ltd*, High Court, 11 May 1988, where Blayney J considered that the distinct rules of professional negligence should be applied to mechanics, as persons 'exercising and professing to have [a] special skill'. But was not that decision pushing the boundaries of professional negligence very far? See the 1987 Review, 413.

A second point worth noting about the Chief Justice's proposition of law in *Dunne* is the reference, in propositions 1 and 2, to '*no* medical practitioner' of equal specialisation and skill. This might suggest that, if a defendant could dig up a *single* medical practitioner who acted as he or she had done, liability could not be imposed (subject to the 'inherent defects' long-stop). In fact, this is not so, because even that single practitioner, to be of use to the defendant, would have to pass the test of ordinary care. The reference to 'no medical practitioner...' has a long and distinguished pedigree, and, provided it is understood in context, can do no harm.

Thirdly, the reference in proposition no. 4 to an 'honest' difference of opinion between doctors as to which is the better of two ways of treating a patient should not be understood as providing an exemption from liability on the basis of an honest though unreasonable belief as to the desirability of a particular mode of treatment.

Fourthly, the fact that the Courts Act 1988 has abolished juries for personal injuries litigation renders the fourth ground largely otiose; it may still have relevance to the extent that the trial judge may dismiss a case at the conclusion of the plaintiff's evidence.

Fifthly, it is interesting to note that the Chief Justice made no reference to the law relating to informed consent to treatment (which did not arise in *Dunne's* case). Thus it remains a matter of debate as to the extent to which the principles articulated in *Daniels v Heskin* continue to apply. The fact the *Daniels v Heskin* was cited in *Dunne's* case should not lead to the conclusion that on the specific question of informed consent to treatment, as opposed to the general principles of liability for medical malpractice, *Daniels v Heskin* stands as a solid precedent.

The Chief Justice thought it helpful to set out two broad parameters underlining the principles of law stated in his judgement:

> The development of medical science and the supreme importance of that development to humanity makes it particularly undesirable and inconsistent with the common good that doctors should be obliged to carry out their professional duties under frequent threat of unsustainable legal claims.
>
> The complete dependence of patients on the skill and care of their medical attendants and the gravity from their point of view of a failure in such care, make it undesirable and unjustifiable to accept as a matter of law a lax or permissive standard of care for the purpose of assessing what is and is not medical negligence.

These two factors can be regarded from a number of standpoints. They could perhaps be dismissed as no more than a general rhetorical reminder that the law of negligence, in relation to medicine as in relation to any other human behaviour, should be neither unduly oppressive nor permissive. But this is scarcely all that the Chief Justice sought to convey. He was surely isolating medical practice as a *particular* area in which the common good requires that doctors be relieved from the frequent threat of unsustainable legal claims. In contrast to other areas of negligence, where the courts have adopted the strategy of curtailing or excluding the *duty* of care in order to accomplish their policy goals, it seems that, in relation to medical practice, a modified *standard* of care is preferred.

As regards the defendants' appeal in *Dunne*, the Supreme Court held that the trial judge had erred in his direction to the jury in failing to make it clear that *deviation* from general and approved practice would constitute negligence only if no other hospital medical administrator or consultant obstetrician would have so deviated if he were taking the appropriate ordinary care, and that *adherence* to such practice would not involve negligence unless it was one which had inherent defects which should have been obvious on due consideration to a hospital administrator or consultant obstetrician.

The court accordingly ordered a retrial, which later took place before Carroll J sitting without a jury as a result of the 1988 Act. The case was settled for £400,000 plus costs, payable by the hospital. The case was settled without admission of liability. The action against the consultant was dismissed, the hospital paying his costs: 8 December 1989; see *Irish Times*, 9 December 1989.

EMPLOYERS' LIABILITY

Safe system of work In *Walsh v Securicor Ireland Ltd*, High Court 7 April 1989 (ex tempore), Irish Times LR, 29 May 1989, the plaintiff, a driver with a security firm, was ambushed by armed robbers and injured. He had travelled the same route between 10 and 10.30 a.m. every Thursday, delivering large amounts of cash, for at least seven years previously. He sued his employers alleging negligence.

Barrington J imposed liability. The ambush was one which could not have been carried out without knowledge of the movements of the van, which ran 'with clockwork precision' on a high-risk route. He accepted that the single most important factor in security was to have a police or Army escort, and that here there had been a police escort. He also accepted that there was no evidence that either lack of training or staff was a causative factor; nor could the defendants be criticised for not using one of the alternative routes. However, it offended common sense that the same time and route should have been used over a number of years. He rejected the defendant's evidence that it was necessary to adhere rigidly to particular times, and noted that there had been no evidence to suggest that they had ever considered the issue.

The basis of liability here imposed falls under the heading of the negligent failure to provide a safe system of work: see *McMahon & Binchy* (2nd ed., 1990), 329-32. The holding may be contrasted with the English decision of *Charlton v Forrest Printing Ink Co.* [1980] IRLR 331, where the Court of Appeal held a firm not to have been liable in negligence for injuries sustained by an employee who was mugged when collecting wages from a bank. The managing director had emphasised the need for varying the collector and the method and route for collection of the wages, but after some time the practice had developed for the plaintiff to do the task, using the same route. In view of the relatively low amounts of money involved, the managing director's instructions and the plaintiff's own appreciation of the risk, the Court exempted the defendant.

The policy issues underlying the duty of care to protect others against criminal assault are more complicated than might at first appear. It might be considered desirable for the courts to expand the range of this duty as far as possible, in line with a general extension of liability for failure to protect against third party conduct. However, in the American decision of *Boyd v*

Racine Currency Exchange Inc. (1973) 56 Ill. 2d 95, 306 NE 2d 39, the Illinois Supreme Court, by a majority, held that a bank did not owe its customer a duty of care where a robber made, and executed, a threat to kill the customer if the bank teller failed to hand over the money. Justice Ryan, for the majority, said:

> If a duty is imposed on the [bank] to comply with such a demand the same would only inure to the benefit of the criminal without affording the desired degree of assurance that compliance with the demand will reduce the risk to the invitee. In fact, the consequence of such a holding may well be to encourage the use of hostages for such purposes, thereby generally increasing the risk to invitees upon business premises. If a duty to comply exists, the occupier of the premises would have little choice in determining whether to comply with the criminal demand and surrender the money or to refuse the demand and be held liable in a civil action for damages brought by or on behalf of the hostage. The existence of this dilemma and knowledge of it by those who are disposed to commit such crimes will only grant to them additional leverage to enforce their criminal demands. The only persons who will clearly benefit from the imposition of such a duty are the criminals. In this particular case the result may appear to be harsh and unjust, but, for the protection of future business invitees, we cannot afford to extend to the criminal another weapon in his arsenal.

Of course, the facts in *Boyd* were far different from *Walsh* (though sadly they are facts which can very easily be mirrored in the context of the transfer of large amounts of cash). The business of security is one which is inevitably attended by the risk of violent attack. Thus the mere fact that that risk matures in any particular case is no ground for a negligence action by an employee against his employer. What the employee will have to show is the *enhancement of the risk* by his employer's unreasonable conduct or omission. The adherence to the same route for so long offended common sense, being below the level of prudence which a reasonable employer ought to have manifested. In this context it is worth noting *Reilly v Ryan*, High Court, 18 July 1990, where Blayney J held that a pub employee who used a customer as a shield against a robber was not acting in the course of his employment in grabbing the customer. The effect of this decision in relation to security firms would be that the cowardice of one employee would insulate the employer from vicarious liability for the injury to another employee resulting from the cowardly act. This looks very like a revival of the 'common employment' doctrine.

It may be worth considering what are the implications of *Walsh* for security firms in other contexts. Must they provide their employees with masks or protective equipment sufficient to withstand assault or even bullets? What weapons, if any, should they be given to defend themselves? How sturdy should the transport vehicles be? What degree of variability of time and route is necessary to pass Barrington J's test? And, getting closer to *Boyd*, what 'standing orders' should apply to cases where a criminal threatens to kill an employee of the security firm (or a bystander) if the money is not disgorged from the vehicle? It seems that there is little in *Walsh* to suggest that the answers to any of these questions will involve the imposition of an onerous range of liability on security firms. At the end of the day, employers' liability is but one aspect of the law of negligence, rather than a species of strict liability. In this context it is worth recalling Finlay CJ's statement in *Ryan v Ireland* [1989] IR 177, at 183 (considered above, 410-18) that no objective in a master and servant relationship 'would justify exposing the servant to the risk of serious injury or death other than the saving of life itself'. This can scarcely mean that security personnel whose duties are to protect property rather than life would have an automatic right to compensation for injury sustained in the course of their duties; but it would seem to imply the need for an employer in a security firm to take stringent precautions (as, for example, by sending several employees on an assignment or using as effective equipment as possible) to minimise the risk of serious injuries or death for his or her employees.

Competent fellow-employees   In *Barrett v Anglo Irish Beef Producers Ltd* High Court, 6 March 1989, the plaintiff, an employee who drove a fork lift truck, was injured when the truck fell over. He had just taken over from another employee who was inexperienced in the operation of the truck, and who had parked it on a dangerous slope. One of the forks had either been wrongly positioned or allowed to move inwards.

Barr J imposed liability in negligence on the employee, in having caused or permitted the inexperienced co-worker to use the truck and park it in a dangerous place, and in having caused or permitted the fork to be in a dangerous state. He reduced the plaintiff's damages by 25%, however, because the plaintiff had attempted to continue the process of tipping of the load when he could have lowered it and moved the truck to a safer position, as well as checking the forks. Barr J took into account that he was taking over an operation which was nearing completion and had been set up by someone else.

PRODUCTS LIABILITY

The decision of *Burke v Dublin Corporation*, High Court, 13 July 1989, reversed in part by the Supreme Court, 26 July 1990, raised the important question of whether the duty of the defendant as installer of heaters in houses provided to tenants and purchasers under its statutory functions extended beyond the time the heaters were actually installed. We discuss the case, as regards both its contractual and tortious aspects, in the chapter on Contract, above, 117-25.

OCCUPIERS' LIABILITY

A decade and a half after *McNamara v ESB* [1975] IR 1, the Supreme Court has still to hold unambiguously that the duty of care in negligence applies to all entrants. McCarthy J has thus far been alone in nailing his colours to the mast; the majority in *Rooney v Connolly* [1986] IR 572 preferred to reserve their view since the issue had not been debated at trial. We have the unlikely position that the possibility of *absolute* liability attaching to supermarkets in respect of injuries sustained by customers can be seriously canvassed (cf. *Mullen v Quinnsworth Ltd t/a Crazy Prices*, Supreme Court, 28 February 1990, *per* McCarthy J) when the general issue of negligence towards invitees and licensees has yet to be definitively resolved.

In the Circuit Court, Judge Sheridan has had no doubt that the effect of *McNamara* was to apply the *Donoghue v Stevenson* principle in relation to all entrants. He said as much in *Murphy v O'Brien* (1987) 6 *ILT (ns)* 75, analysed in the 1987 Review, 324-5, 331-2, and he said the same again in *O'Neill Garvan v Brennan* (1988) 7 *ILT (ns)* 319. The plaintiff, when visiting the house of her daughter and son-in-law, put her hands on the table 'so as to use it to take her weight as a resting place'. Judge Sheridan commented that this act could readily be criticised 'in that [she] might have used a chair if she wanted to sit down and tables are not designed for [this] purpose. . . . Be that as it may, the defendants never made any complaint of this method being used by the plaintiff and in many houses persons are wont to rest their bodies against a table without expecting that the heavy top of the table will fall down and cause them injury'. This is what befell the plaintiff. The table looked perfectly safe, and had withstood the ravages of the defendants' children for eight years without having given any trouble. It collapsed because it had been glued together without appropriate metal screws or brackets.

The first question concerned the plaintiff's status. Judge Sheridan was inclined to consider her an invitee, as a person who would be on call to help with or mind the children in 'the free and easy relationship which governs such matters between mother and daughter'. In the light of his holding that the duty of care in negligence applied whether she was an invitee or licensee, he did 'not consider that this issue made any difference'. It is worth recalling that in *Shelton v Creane and Arklow UDC*, High Court, 17 December 1987, analysed in the 1988 Review, 424-5, Lardner J held, without discussion on the point, that a neighbour who had arranged to keep an eye on an occupier's four children when their mother was out was an invitee. The controversial decision of *Moynihan v Moynihan* [1975] IR 192 must surely encourage the view that neighbours and relatives who engage in acts of kindness are invitees.

On the question of foreseeability, the plaintiff's action came to grief. While her own conduct in leaning against the table was foreseeable and not 'in any way outside her permission, invitation or licence', the collapse of the table could not reasonably have been foreseen by the defendants. Judge Sheridan noted that '[i]t would be different, of course, if the action was against the manufacturer who would be clearly liable as . . . from his point of view merely using glue for the purpose of affixing the table top base was not sufficient without appropriate metal screws or brackets'.

It is worth considering how the plaintiff would fare under the EC Products Liability Directive. It may be argued that she would have no difficulty in establishing the table's defectiveness under Article 6. It seems that one of the specific circumstances which it mentions—'the use to which it could reasonably be expected that the product could be put'—embraces people leaning against a table: sedateness and prim and proper comportment in the sanctuary of one's daughter's home are not called for.

SCHOOLS' LIABILITY IN NEGLIGENCE

Traditionally, the law of negligence has judged schools leniently. The courts are conscious of the competing demands of protecting children from danger and of encouraging self-reliance. Vaisey J may have gone a little too far when he observed, in *Suckling v Essex County Council*, 26 January 1955, that 'it is better that a boy should break his neck than allow other people to break his spirit'; but there is no doubt that schools are not treated by the courts as *de facto* insurers for injuries sustained by children on their premises. See Binchy, 'Schools' Liability in Negligence' (1984) 78 *Incorp L Soc of Ireland Gazette* 153, 185. Even juries, notorious for stretching liability in negligence to the limit and beyond, especially where the victim was young, displayed a reluctance to bring in verdicts against schools: see e.g., *Smith v Golly*, High

Court, O'Hanlon J with jury, 17-18 May 1984; *Irish Times* 18 May 1984; *Walsh v Bourke*, High Court, Hamilton J with jury, 25 January 1985, *Irish Times*, 26 January 1985.

In *Mapp v Gilhooley*, High Court, 8 November 1989, the question of the proper standard of supervision called for consideration. The plaintiff, aged five, was injured when he fell in the school's playground. At the time there were 223 boys in the yard, most of them around the plaintiff's age. The portion of the yard in which the 161 boys of around the plaintiff's age were playing measured about 30 yards by 15 yards. Two teachers were on duty at the time. The plaintiff gave unsworn evidence that groups of boys of his age had been playing a game of 'trains', each train comprising an 'engine' and nine 'carriages' with one boy holding the next by the waist. Every now and then trains would collide. The plaintiff said that he had been knocked over when a bigger train bashed into his train. He had received injuries to the back of his head. This account was disputed by the teachers who were supervising at the time. One of them said that the game of 'trains' had been played occasionally but that, if she saw it, she would put a stop to it. She did not recall its having been played that day. She believed that, if it had, she would have observed it and prevented it from continuing. The other teacher gave evidence substantially corroborating this account. Barr J preferred the plaintiff's account. He considered that, in the circumstances of the case, with so many small boys running around in a portion of the yard measuring 30 paces by 15 paces, it was 'not surprising that . . . while perambulating as they were, [they] failed to notice two or three "trains" forming and running about before they collided with one another . . .'.

Barr J imposed liability on the school manager. His expression of the standard of care owed by a school authority is worth recording. He stated that, in measuring the duty owed in given circumstances, the Court had to take into account:

> all relevant factors, including the ages of the children in question; the activities in which they are or may be engaged; the degree of supervision (if any) required having regard to the prevailing circumstances and the opportunity (if any) which those in charge of the child or children had to prevent or minimise the mischief complained of. It goes without saying that that duty ought to be measured realistically and should take into account also that children, particularly small boys, are high spirited by nature and some are inclined to be mischievous. In the absence of a regime of draconian servitude, it is impossible to keep very young children under complete control when at play. Disciplinary and supervisory measures required of a school authority should be construed within reasonable bounds.

Barr J did not demur from the Supreme Court's proposition in *Lennon v McCarthy*, unreported 13 July 1966 (extracted in McMahon & Binchy, *A Casebook on the Law of Torts* (1983), 182), that the duty of a schoolmaster is to take such care of his pupils as a careful father would of his children. Authority for this criterion goes back to *Williams v Eady*, 10 TLR 41 (1893). In *Beaumont v Surrey County Council*, 112 *Sol J* 704, at 704 (1968), however, Geoffrey Lane J criticised this reference to a father's negligence as 'unrealistic, if not unhelpful', especially where the number of pupils is high. Not many parents, even during their children's birthday parties, have to cope with 161 young boys. It seems fair to say that Barr J's reference to this test was somewhat less than enthusiastic. He noted merely that it did 'not seem to be at variance with the statement of the law' which he had advanced.

Counsel for the school manager sought to rely on Ó Dálaigh CJ's statement (for the Court) in *Lennon v McCarthy* that 'when normally healthy children are in the playground it is not necessary that they should be under constant supervision'. Barr J distinguished it as 'not [having been] intended to have general application', the boys concerned in that case being about '10 and 12 years of age respectively'. It was not an authority for the proposition that children of the ages and numbers in the school yard on the fateful day did not require some continuous supervision.

The 'crucial aspect' of the case was whether the supervising teachers (or the headmistress, who was in the yard on the occasion) ought to have known that some boys in the junior sector of the yard were playing 'trains' and whether they had had a reasonable opportunity to stop them from doing so before the accident happened. He accepted the plaintiff's evidence that the game had been in progress for a significant period which was sufficiently long to have allowed one or other of the teachers to see what was happening and to stop it if they had been keeping a reasonable watch.

On one view the case involves essentially no more than a conflict of evidence. Nevertheless, if it is meaningful to speak of the 'feel' of the judgment, it evinces less sympathy for the difficulties of schools and the desideratum of encouraging self-reliance among children than some of the earlier cases. Barr J did not hold that the school had been negligent in letting so many young children play in so confined an area. Perhaps that would have been an attractive basis of liability; as we have mentioned, Barr J expressed a consciousness of the difficulty for the supervising teachers in noticing the 'trains' forming and running about on account of the crowded space.

VOLUNTARY ASSUMPTION OF RISK

In *Downey v Limerick Motor Club Ltd and Tynan*, High Court, 28 April 1989, a navigator injured in a road accident during a motor rally sued the organiser's alleging negligence in their failure to indicate in the book containing a map of the course the corner at which the driver came to grief. She claimed that the corner was an intersection, which merited inclusion. Lynch J rejected her claim on the evidence. The topography was not consistent with her characterisation: 'At this particular corner or junction a tarmac road, which was the rally route, went to the left; the telegraph poles indicated that the road would go to the left; the ditches indicated that the road would go to the left. There was a stone and gravel and sand laneway to the right'.

Undoubtedly the bend called for skill in distinguishing the laneway and negotiating the bend, but the failure of the Motor Club to record the bend on the map did not amount to negligence; in this context, Lynch J stressed that the book's main purpose was to ensure that rally participants did not go off the route and drive on open roads, in a manner that would be highly dangerous to non-participants.

The decision is noteworthy for the deferential test by which the question of the organisers' negligence was assessed. Lynch J asked 'whether this was a corner or junction so obviously requiring a warning in the . . . [b]ook that no reasonable organiser of the motor rally would omit it from the . . . [b]ook'. This formula echoes Finlay CJ's judgment in the *Dunne* case, above, 423.

Lynch J was apparently relieved that, in view of the plaintiff's narrow and specific allegation of negligence, he did not have to confront the 'abstruse legal arguments' which could have arisen in respect of the duties of rally organisers to participants, analogous to those relating to the duty of a rally driver to his navigator, which divided the Supreme Court in *McComiskey v McDermott* [1974] IR 75. There the majority (Henchy and Griffin JJ) favoured an individuated circumscribed duty of care; Walsh J, on the other hand, preferred to impose a constant duty on motor drivers relative to other road users (including navigators), leaving the specific relationship of driver and navigator to be modified, if at all, by the defence of voluntary assumption of risk or contributory negligence. The difference in approach is more important in practice than might at first appear: the majority's solution can cut off a plaintiff at the threshold duty stage; Walsh J's approach requires the defendant to prove affirmatively either that the plaintiff was *volens* (not always an easy task in view of the requirement of proof of 'some sort of intercourse or communication between the [parties] from which it could be reasonably inferred that the plaintiff had assured the defendan[t] that he waived any right of action he might have in respect of [his] negligence . . .':

O'Hanlon v ESB [1969] IR 75, at 92). See further McMahon & Binchy, *Irish Law of Torts* (2nd ed., 1990), 368-70.

Although Lynch J was satisfied that the narrow issue of negligence alleged by the plaintiff enabled him to avoid addressing 'abstruse legal arguments', his analysis inevitably reflects a policy choice. To answer the question whether the defendants were guilty of negligence, he had to have an underlying notion of the nature of the duty of care they owed the plaintiff. What he had to say indicates that he favoured the majority's approach in *McComiskey* in defining the duty of care owed by the defendants in individuated, constricted terms. Of course, in *Downey* there was no credible generic category of duty equivalent to that owed by a driver to other road users: map-makers for rallies are not easily comparable with map-makers for general road users. Nevertheless it may be argued that, even in the former case, considerations of safety are important. The idea that omitting to record a particular turn could be justified on the basis that the unmarked bend undoubtedly calls for skill in distinguishing or ignoring the laneway *and negotiating the bend* seems consistent only with the perception of the relationship between the parties as being an individuated one in which the rally driver and navigator may be exposed to a risk which an 'ordinary' map-reading driver would not.

DAMAGES

The year 1989 saw the publication of Ireland's first treatise on damages in torts litigation: Dr John P.M. White's *Irish Law of Damages for Personal Injuries and Death*. This two-volume work contains a detailed analysis of the existing law as well as extracts from a host of decisions, many unreported. Throughout his analysis, Dr White draws on materials from other common law jurisdictions. No practitioner should be without this book.

Loss of earnings In *O'Callaghan v Site Services Ltd*, High Court, 25 January 1989, O'Hanlon J faithfully applied the Supreme Court's requirement, in *Reddy v Bates* [1983] IR 141; [1984] ILRM 197, that some reduction be made to damages for loss of earnings to allow for the fact that there is no guarantee of continuous employment. As is customary in these circumstances, O'Hanlon J did not mention expressly the precise percentage attributable to this factor.

In *Ryan v Ireland, The Attorney General and the Minister for Defence*, High Court, 19 October 1989, discussed on the issue of negligence, above, 410-18, the plaintiff, a soldier, was injured in Lebanon, and some time later discharged from the service. His injuries were such that the best job he could hope for, after retraining, was that of store-keeper or cashier, a gross weekly wage of £150, and net value of £110. This resulted in a differential of £28 per week, the capital value of which, based on an actuary's calculation, amounted to £28,000.

Barr J observed that service in the army constitutes secure employment which, subject to the risk of death, serious injury or serious ill-health, is likely to continue to the age of sixty. The civilian jobs which the plaintiff might find, 'if eventually . . . lucky enough to get one', did not have the same degree of security of tenure. Barr J allowed the plaintiff £24,000 as compensation under this head, 'paying due regard to the principles laid down by the Supreme Court in *Reddy v Bates*' [1983] IR 141; [1984] ILRM 197. Perhaps it might be argued that the plaintiff could have expected more. The insecurity of employment lay, not in the position which he had held before the accident, but in the jobs he might obtain afterwards. Had the plaintiff not been injured, he would not have had to worry about employment (though he would have had to be concerned about the risk of being injured or killed in the line of duty). If £28,000 represented the differential on the assumption that he would obtain and retain a civilian job, then the risk of unemployment in relation to that job might be considered to aggravate his loss.

In *Burke v Blanch*, High Court, 28 July 1989, Costello J held that, in assessing damages under the heading of loss of earnings, he should compute the sum on the basis that the plaintiff, who had suffered spinal injuries resulting in paralysis, would not be employed again. He said:

> Persons suffering from paraplegia are of course capable of earning good wages in a variety of different occupations. But each case has to be decided on its own facts and in this case I am dealing with a young man whose education finished at the age of 16, who was a semi-skilled factory worker before his accident, whose home is now [in a rural area] where the opportunities for employment for disabled persons like the plaintiff are virtually nil. I think his chances of being retrained so that he may obtain gainful employment are also remote. He may well try to start a business using his welding skills from his home . . . but there is no evidence which would justify me in holding on the balance of probabilities he would be able to earn any significant profit from it.

GENERAL DAMAGES

Burke v Blanch, mentioned above, is a decision of radical importance in relation to the computation of general damages in torts litigation. The plaintiff, aged 24, had suffered what Costello J described as 'devastating injuries' in a car accident caused by the defendant's negligence. He had fractured his thoraco-lumbar spine, which resulted in paraplegia.

Costello J awarded the plaintiff around half a million pounds under several heads, such as special damages and loss of earnings. His disposition of the issue of general damages must be quoted in full:

> It requires little imagination to fill in the details of the pain and suffering (physical and mental) which . . . this young [man] . . . must have suffered and will suffer in the future and it is not difficult to comprehend how his life has been shattered by what has happened to him. The Court can compensate him for the pecuniary loss which has followed as a result of the accident (and that I have endeavoured to do) but no award of money can remotely compensate him for his physical and mental suffering, past and future. There are clear legal guidelines laid down by the Supreme Court as to how the assessment of general damages in a case of this sort should be approached (see *Reddy v Bates* [1984] ILRM 197; *Cooke v Walsh* [1984] ILRM 208; *Sinnott v Quinnsworth* [1984] ILRM 523; *Griffith v Van Raj* [1985] ILRM 582) and applying these and in particular bearing in mind that the plaintiff, apart from general damages, will be receiving half a million pounds approximately, I think a fair and reasonable sum for general damages is an additional sum of £100,000.

This passage is worth close scrutiny, in order to unearth its underlying principles. It will be recalled that in *Sinnott v Quinnsworth Ltd*, the Supreme Court imposed a tariff on awards for general damages of £150,000 (1984 values) in relation to a plaintiff whose injuries were broadly similar to those of the plaintiff in *Burke v Blanch*. Why therefore was the plaintiff in *Burke v Blanch* entitled to only £100,000 (1989 values)? The answer appears to be that the Court took into consideration the fact that the plaintiff was receiving around half a million pounds under *other* heads of damages.

There appears to be a difficulty with this approach. A plaintiff is entitled to compensation under the other heads of damages in their own right. The damages awarded represent an attempt to neutralise an economic deficiency inflicted on him: if they achieve this goal, the plaintiff should not be expected to feel grateful, or even happy, but rather relieved that he will not have to pay for an economic loss caused by the defendant's wrong. It is a matter of contingency whether the amount of compensation under these other headings is high or low. The fact that an award under these headings gives the plaintiff money for economic losses which he has not yet sustained may encourage the impression that the plaintiff is receiving a windfall or profit, but this is not so. The largeness of the amount merely reflects the economic damage which he will sustain.

If, in awarding general damages, account were to be taken of the quantum of the award under other heads, then serious inequalities would arise: where two plaintiffs suffered identical devastating injuries, one of them at the time of the accident being unemployed with no job prospects, the other earning £50,000 per annum, it would surely be unjust that the second plaintiff should be awarded less compensation than the first plaintiff *for general damages* on account of the fact that he received (say) half a million pounds compensation for his loss of future employment.

Is there any way of salvaging the principle that general damages, at all events for devastating injuries, should be reduced if the award under other heads is high? One possible avenue might be considered to be that the task of awarding general damages for such injuries is inherently futile—'assaying the impossible', as O'Higgins CJ put it in *Sinnott v Quinnsworth Ltd*—and that thus any figure awarded is necessarily arbitrary. If the plaintiff receives a very large amount of money under other heads of damages, he should be happy. But the difficulty with this, as we have indicated, is that such a plaintiff should be no happier than one who has received a modest award for modest losses under these other heads.

Two other decisions on general damages may be noted briefly. In *Kennedy v Taltech Engineering Co. Ltd*, High Court, 10 February 1989, the plaintiff, a 19-year-old machine operator, suffered a serious injury to the upper part of his right hand. This consisted of an extensive u-shaped deep wound on the outside of the hand. The extensor tendons of both damaged fingers were operated on, and placed in a plaster cast for six weeks. The end result was that the damaged tendons were retethered and tightened, in consequence of which the plaintiff could not extend the index and middle fingers individually (though he could do so in conjunction with the other fingers of the hand). The injured fingers drooped significantly when not stretched on the remaining fingers. There was no prospect of improvement over time.

The plaintiff had difficulty in writing due to the defect in the index finger. It seemed that he would never be able to perform fine work with his right hand nor be able to play the guitar. The appearance of the scar caused the plaintiff some embarrassment. The plaintiff was able to work but Barr J considered that his condition restricted the range of employment prospects open to him.

Barr J awarded the plaintiff £25,000 for pain and suffering to date, continuing disablement and disfigurement in the future.

In *Heffernan v Byrne*, High Court, 11 May 1989, the plaintiff, a 50-year-old private investigator who was injured in an accident caused by the defendant's negligence, suffered from acute mixed endogenous and reactive depression, that is, 'coming partly from within . . . himself, and partly from the effects of the accident and the painful injuries he had sustained'. He also suffered from stiffness in his arms, leg and back, which resulted in an operation involving the removal of a disc and the performing of a bone graft. This improved his condition, enabling him to walk without a stick but he continued to suffer from certain back pain. The prognosis was that the plaintiff would have to continue taking anti-depressants for about a year and a half.

O'Hanlon J awarded him £25,000 general damages for the period before the judgment and £100,000 for the future. The total figure for general damages of £125,000 may be compared to that of £150,000 (1984 values) which the Supreme Court in *Sinnott v Quinnsworth Ltd* ordained in respect of a person suffering from quadriplegia who was fully aware of his plight.

VICARIOUS LIABILITY

In *Kennedy v Taltech Engineering Co Ltd*, High Court, 10 February 1989 the plaintiff suffered injury from 'a most unfortunate, unintended consequence of a light-hearted prank which occurred on the factory floor at the end of the day's work'. The plaintiff, who was still in his teens, was a machine operator employed by the defendants. When he was leaving the factory floor, he put on his jacket from the pocket of which protruded a large crisp bag which he has used for wrapping his lunch but which by then contained only an apple. He was called over by the factory supervisor, who was talking to another employee who was holding a large metal plate with sharp edges.

The plaintiff walked over to the supervisor, who then said, 'give us the crisps'. The plaintiff replied that it was only an apple, to which the supervisor responded, 'Even better', and took the bag from the plaintiff's pocket. The plaintiff 'by way of reflex action' immediately grabbed the bag while it was in mid air. During the incident the bag broke and the plaintiff's hand swung back and hit the metal plate.

Barr J imposed liability on the employers. There was no doubt about the supervisor's negligence; the only issue was 'whether at the time he was acting within or outside the ostensible scope of his employment as supervisor'. Barr J concluded that he was. If the supervisor had been 'merely an ordinary fellow employee' his employers would not have been liable for an isolated prank which they could not reasonably have foreseen. However, the supervisor was a person in authority whom the plaintiff was bound to obey. Though the supervisor had intended to perpetrate an innocent prank, he had used his authority to put his intention into effect. The plaintiff had responded to the supervisor's direction in innocence under 'an obligation as an employee' to do so, since, as far as he knew, it might well have related to a legitimate work matter. In Barr J's view, the entire incident should be regarded as a single entity and it was unreal to break up its constituent elements. This aspect of the case may be contrasted with *Reilly v Ryan*, High Court, 18 July 1990, already mentioned, where Blayney J abstracted the act of a barman in grabbing a customer to act as a shield against a robber from the totality of the circumstances of the raid in a way which resulted in the employer's being exempted from vicarious liability.

SELF DEFENCE AND DEFENCE OF PROPERTY

In *Ross v Curtis*, High Court, 3 February 1989, the question of the scope of self defence and defence of property in tort fell for consideration. This is the first time in many years in which the issue has been addressed in a written judgment in our courts.

The defendant owned a small supermarket in a village in County Meath. He lived beside it, by himself, in a bungalow, which was attached to the supermarket by an internal door. He also owned a public house and a shop in a neighbouring town. Three days before Christmas, he returned at 1.20 a.m. to his dwelling, with the day's takings from all three businesses, amounting to £25,000, most of it in cash. He went to bed, with the monies in the room and a .22 rifle beside him. The premises had a burglar alarm system, comprising an alarm bell and siren outside and another bell in the bedroom.

The plaintiff and three other young men had that night stolen a car and embarked on a campaign of thefts from shops in Counties Dublin and Meath. Their *modus operandi* was to throw missiles through the windows or doors, and then take everything of interest which they could find. They relied on numbers and were indifferent as to whether or not they might be discovered on the premises by the occupiers or whether they might activate an alarm system.

At 4 a.m. they broke into the defendant's supermarket, using major force to break through the thick glass in the door. One of them took cash from the till and the others a cigarette dispenser which they brought to the car. The plaintiff then went back in search of more cash, followed by two of the others; having entered the shop and while still close to the broken door, he was struck in top of his skull by a bullet fired from the defendant's rifle. The plaintiff conceded that at the time of the shooting he saw a man in the shop about thirty feet away from him.

The plaintiff sued in tort. The judgment does not record the grounds but one may assume that they included battery and negligence. The defendant testified that he had been woken by the alarm and had gone to the shop with his rifle. He had stood in the shop close to the internal door and in a position where he was illuminated by a florescent light a few feet away. He had seen the men removing the cigarette machine, one of them looking back in his direction.

He had got a dreadful fright and had frozen where he stood. After they had left, a third man had approached the door to enter the shop. He knew that this man could see him but the man continued to advance, apparently caring nothing for his presence. He believed then that the three robbers were all coming back to attack him. He put the rifle to his shoulder and pointed it upwards at the top of the shop door. He thought that he would fire a warning shot so that they would not attack him. He had no intention of shooting the plaintiff or of injuring him in any way, but only wished to scare away the intruders. In the event the single shot he fired struck the top of the plaintiff's skull. It is worth noting that counsel for the plaintiff specifically accepted that the defendant had not intended to shoot the plaintiff or to injure him.

Barr J considered that the next issue was whether the defendant had acted in reasonable self defence and in defence of his property 'or whether in firing the shot he acted with reckless disregard' for the plaintiff. With hindsight, it might be concluded that the defendant could perhaps have achieved his purpose by firing into the ceiling of the shop or in a direction well away from the plaintiff. But one had to bear in mind the nature of the 'ruthless, vicious crime' in which the plaintiff and his accomplices were engaged. Barr J was satisfied that the defendant had had good reason to fear that he was in imminent personal danger from this man. This entitled him to fire a warning shot in the hope of scaring him away. Unhappily he had not aimed high enough, in the terror of the moment. The defendant had 'acquitted himself reasonably in all circumstances of the case and . . . was not guilty of reckless disregard for the safety of the plaintiff, which is the test appropriate to the circumstances of this case'. Accordingly he dismissed the action.

The issue of the use of force in self-protection or the protection of one's property has given rise to much moral and legal debate. The two defences, though they come together in *Ross v Curtis*, are conceptually severable, since it is quite possible to envisage circumstances where the occupier is not in any physical danger.

The law in relation to self-defence is clear: the test is whether the force one used was of a quantum and kind that was 'reasonable and proper to use': *Dullaghan v Hillen* [1957] Ir Jur Rep 10, at 13. This is what is called a 'question of fact' (though of course it really is one of value). The courts evince a realistic sensitivity to the urgency of the occasion (as Barr J did in his judgment), applying an 'agony of the moment' test which has a parallel in negligence actions: cf. McMahon & Binchy, *Irish Law of Torts* (2nd ed., 1990), 355-6.

In *Chaplin of Gray's Inn's Case* (1400), YB 2 Hen IV, fo. 8, pl. 40, it was stated that a person threatened with assault is 'not bound to wait until the other has given a blow, for perhaps it will come too late afterwards'. In *Gregan v Sullivan* [1937] Ir Jur Rep 64, at 65 (High Court, 1936), O'Byrne J stressed the *via media*: he was 'inclined to agree that we ought not to weigh a method of self-defence on too fine a scale, but steam hammers ought not to be used to crush flies'.

It is the issue of defence of property which raises greater conceptual difficulties. The occupier may use 'reasonable' force to evict a trespasser where either the trespasser refuses to leave or has come onto the property with force and violence. It is easy to see this as a form of self-defence but in truth it is not, since, as we have mentioned, an occupier may be in no personal danger as a result of the trespass, even where it was accomplished with force. A burly landowner may, for example, witness young boys taking apples from his orchard. Such steps as the landowner is entitled to take are not based on any necessary concern for the protection of his bodily integrity, which has not been imperilled by the young boys' trespass.

Another factor of considerable importance historically was that an occupier owed no duty of care in negligence to a trespasser. He did, however, owe the fairly minimal obligation not to injure the trespasser intentionally nor to act with reckless disregard for the trespasser's presence. It is of interest to note that the courts spelt out this obligation in cases involving the causing of injury to trespassers, in defence of property interests, by the use of spring guns: *Bird v Holbrook*, 4 Bing 628; 130 ER 911 (1820). See the interesting analysis in (1971) 56 Iowa L Rev 1219 by Geoffrey Palmer (the present Prime Minister of New Zealand).

One finds in Barr J's expression of the criterion of liability a reflection of this historical test. He twice refers to 'reckless disregard' for the plaintiff or his safety, apparently as another means of expressing the test of reason-ableness. Since the reasonableness test applied, there would be little point in referring to the test of reckless disregard as an *alternative* basis of liability because, from the plaintiff's standpoint, it would be a more onerous test than that of reasonableness, and it seems difficult to envisage conduct which could be characterised as involving recklessness without also being unreasonable.

The gradual restatement of the general obligation of occupiers to tres-passers in terms of straightforward negligence rather than reckless disregard, evidenced by *Purtill, McNamara* and their progeny, suggests that in future it may be best to address the specific question of the use of force in defence of property exclusively by reference to the test of reasonableness (or, of course, intention where intentional battery is in issue).

Finally, it is worth considering the question of the burden of proof. Historically, in actions for battery where the plaintiff proves that he has received a direct physical contact from the defendant, without the plaintiff's consent, the onus rests on the defendant to show that the contact was caused neither intentionally nor negligently: see McMahon & Binchy, *Irish Law of Torts* (2nd ed., 1990), 309. In the United States, New Zealand and, more recently, England (*Wilson v Pringle* [1987] QB 237), the onus remains on the plaintiff throughout. In Canada (*Cooke v Lewis* [1951] SCR 830) and Australia (*Venning v Chin*, 10 SASR 299 (1974)) the older view still prevails, though, in *Hackshaw v Shaw*, 155 C L R 614, at 619 (1984) Gibbs CJ expressed a tentative preliminary preference, *obiter*, for placing the onus fully on the plaintiff.

The issue is one extending beyond academic disputation about the derivation of the action for trespass: it involves important questions of policy. Should people who have been injured by guns have to prove negligence or intention on the part of those who shot them? Is it clear that the policy considerations point in the same direction where the injury is caused by a fist? Thus far, our courts have not examined the policy issues relating to the onus of proof in tort actions in any great detail. The closest they have reached to doing this was in the Supreme Court decision of *Hanrahan v Merck, Sharp & Dohme (Ireland) Ltd* [1988] ILRM 629, where Henchy J analysed the relationship between the onus of proof in nuisance actions (which lies on the plaintiff) and the guarantee, under Article 40.3.1, to vindicate a plaintiff's personal rights. Henchy J rejected the argument that the plaintiff's constitutional rights would not be vindicated if the onus of proof rested on him. He observed that '[t]he same may be said about many other causes of action. Lack of knowledge as to the true nature of the defendants' conduct of course may cause the plaintiff difficulty, but it does not change the onus of proof'.

Whether a constitutional argument might be raised in an action for battery arising from injuries caused by guns is a question worthy of serious consideration. Perhaps the doctrine of *res ipsa loquitur* could assist a plaintiff, if the court accepts that accidents are not usually caused by guns without negligence (or, *a fortiori* intention) on the part of those in charge of them.

LOSS OF CONSORTIUM

If I injure a person and as a result damage that person's relationship with his or her family, should the other members of the family have a right of action against me for their loss? The question, posed today for the first time, might call for an answer in terms of the duty of care in negligence, proximity of relationship and reasonable foresight but the issue is far from new. It was addressed several centuries ago, in terms of the action for loss of *consortium*. The effect of this ancient lineage has not been helpful. Modern courts are understandably cautious about breathing new life into a tort with discredited notions of feudalism and sexism.

The action for loss of *consortium* clearly allows compensation to a *husband* for *total* deprivation of his wife's *consortium*, even where the deprivation is for a limited period: *Spaight v Dundon* [1961] IR 201; *O'Haran v Divine* (1964) 100 ILTR 53. The two principal uncertainties were whether a *wife* might sue, and whether *impairment*, as opposed to total deprivation, of consortium was compensable. In England in 1952, the House of Lords (which at that time (as now!) was disposed to say no to all tort plaintiffs, however deserving) held that the action was so anomalous that there was no good reason to extend the anomaly by recognising a right for wives to sue. The House was divided on the question whether impairment of *consortium* was compensable: *Best v Samuel Fox and Co. Ltd* [1952] AC 716. Subsequently, English courts accepted that impairment sufficed: *Hare v BTC* [1956] 1 WLR 250; *Lawrence v Biddle* [1966] 1 QB 504; *Cutts v Chumley* [1967] 1 WLR 742.

In Ireland, in view of the constitutional guarantee of equality, the wife's claim could not be disposed of so cavalierly. In *McKinley v Minister for Defence*, High Court, 15 November 1989, *Irish Times*, 14 May 1990, the plaintiff sought damages for impairment of her husband's *consortium*. Her husband had been severely injured in an explosion which resulted in a condition of sterility and impotence. The defendants sought an order that the statement of claim be struck out as disclosing no cause of action. Counsel for the defendants made no attempt to defend a distinction between the sexes as to the entitlement to sue; either both could or neither, and Counsel argued that the better conclusion was that the promulgation of the Constitution had killed rather than extended the action. Moreover, counsel contended that there was no right of action for impairment of consortium.

Johnson J refused to grant the order that the action be struck out. He is reported as having said that it was clear that in *Spaight v Dundon* the Supreme Court had held that a right to sue for loss of *consortium* existed for the husband; this had been affirmed in *O'Haran v Divine* and the Oireachtas had recognised the existence of such a right under s.35 of the Civil Liability Act 1961. He had been asked by the defendants to declare unconstitutional the right of consortium and s.35. Had this been argued in full it might not have caused him any difficulty. However, it was not his function to reverse the Supreme Court. Johnson J allowed the plaintiff to continue her action, whether her claim was based on total loss of *consortium* or merely impairment. The extent of that right was a matter for the trial judge to determine.

Johnson J's approach finds support in the decision of the Supreme Court of Canada in *Woelk v Halvorson* (1980) 114 DLR (3d) 385, albeit in the context of interpretation of a specific provision in Alberta legislation rather than on the basis of a re-assessment of the common law principles in isolation. It may be contrasted with Saskatchewan Queen's Bench decision of *Shkwarchuk v Hansen* 30 CCLT 121 (1984), where MacLeod J held that the action for loss of *consortium* was 'an historical anomaly' which had not survived the promulgation of the Canadian Charter of Rights and Freedoms. He left open the question whether the action for loss of *servitium* might apply equally to a husband and a wife.

It will be recalled that in its Working Paper No. 7-1979 and its First Report on Family Law (LRC1-1981), the Law Reform Commission recommended that the Oireachtas enact legislation permitting damages to be recovered by the members of the family of an injured person in respect of the damage to the continuity, stability and quality of the relationship with the injured person. This would, in effect, extend the action for loss of *consortium*, not only to wives but also to parents and children. No action has been taken on this recommendation over the past nine years. The existence of the Report appeared to discourage Costello J, in *PH v Murphy & Sons Ltd* [1988] ILRM 300; [1987] IR 621, from recognising the claim of children at common law. See the 1987 Review, 198-9.

A statutory reform on this basis would be likely to be welcomed by many people. One should, however, be fully conscious of the high insurance premiums for motorists and for employers. It would seem imprudent at present to recommend an open-ended entitlement to recover damages for this type of loss.

Fortunately, there is a useful model for legislation contained in Part IV of the Civil Liability Act 1961, which allows family members of a person who has been killed (as opposed to injured) to claim damages against wrongdoers. The Act (as amended by the Courts Act 1981) places a limit of £7,500 on the amount which can be claimed by all the family members, or a group, for mental distress. Adopting a cautious approach, the legislation could apply the same maximum limit to the total claim of the family of a person who has been negligently injured. In some cases, of course, little or no losses will have occurred under any of these heads. The legislation should make it clear that £7,500 is not to be awarded save in the more serious cases. It might be considered desirable for the legislation to be introduced on an experimental basis of three years, in order to gauge the economic and social effects. If handled sensitively by the courts, this type of legislation could provide justice to families without laying undue demands on motorists, employers or other groups of potential defendants. Recent trends, notably the abolition of juries for personal injuries litigation, do not suggest that any moves in this direction are imminent.

MOTOR INSURERS' BUREAU

In *Bowes v Motor Insurers' Bureau of Ireland* [1990] ILRM 59, the question of the proper relationship between the courts and the Motor Insurers' Bureau of Ireland fell for consideration. The plaintiff had sought a declaration in the High Court that she had sustained serious and permanent disablement as a result of injuries she had suffered and that there was reasonable certainty that this had been caused by the negligent use of a mechanically propelled vehicle whose owner or driver could not be traced. The Agreement made in 1964 between the Bureau was accompanied by a series of notes which were 'not [to] be taken as qualifying the Agreement . . .'. One of those notes contained the statement that the Bureau might make an *ex gratia* payment in certain circumstances which included those asserted in the application for the High Court declaration.

The essence of the applicant's case was that, in the absence of the note's specifying who had to determine the matters asserted in the application, the High Court was the appropriate body to do this. Lardner J did not agree and neither did the Supreme Court.

Finlay CJ, reading the note in conjunction with the other provisions of the Agreement, was quite satisfied that it was for the Bureau rather than the courts to make this determination. Decisions taken by the Bureau in response to claims made pursuant to the note could be reviewed by the courts only if, in accordance with the principles of judicial review, it could be established to the satisfaction of a court that the decision reached or the opinion formed by the Bureau was one which no reasonable body or person could form on the evidence before it.

The Revised Agreement of December 1988, to take account of EC requirements, is analysed by McMahon & Binchy, *Irish Law of Torts* (2nd ed., 1990), 29-31.

ABUSE OF PROCESS

In *Smyth v Tunney*, High Court, 6 October 1989, considered above, 127-9, Murphy J rejected the arguments by the defendants, by way of counterclaim, that the plaintiff's proceedings were a fraudulent attempt to frustrate and delay ejectment proceedings, malicious prosecution or malicious abuse of the process of the Court. The essence of the defendants' argument was that the plaintiff's claim 'was a conscious attempt by him to blackmail' them. Murphy J held that this allegation was without foundation. The plaintiff had maintained his proceedings in the honest but mistaken belief that the defendants had perpetrated a fraud on him.

It is interesting to note that in the recent decision of *Metall und Rohstoff AG v Donaldson Lufkin & Jenrette Inc* [1990] QB 391, the English Court of Appeal, albeit in the absence of full argument on the point, had 'great doubt' (id., at 471) as to whether any general tort of maliciously instituting civil proceedings exists. Echoing its approach in *Speed Seal Products Ltd v Paddington* [1986] 1 All ER 91, the Court accepted that it was 'at least arguable that there could be liability for abuse of process'. For general consideration of the issue, see Wells, 'The Abuse of Process' (1986), 102 *LQ Rev* 9.

Of course, as well as being a tort, misuse of process may amount to a crime, such as attempting to pervert the course of justice, or contempt of court (*R v Weisz, ex parte Hector MacDonald Ltd* [1951] 2 KB 611). Moreover, the court has wide-ranging powers to dismiss proceedings which are frivolous or vexatious: see Rules of the Superior Courts 1986 O. 19, r.28 and *Barry v Buckley* [1981] IR 306. This area of the law is examined in detail by the Australian Law Reform Commission in their *Report on Contempt of Court* (1987), paras. 209ff.

Transport

AIR NAVIGATION

Air routes and fares   The European Communities (Scheduled Air Fares) Regulations 1989 (SI No.207) establish the criteria for approval of air fares within the EC. The European Communities (Sharing of Passenger Capacity and Access to Scheduled Air Service Routes) Regulations 1989 (SI No.208) provide for sharing of access to scheduled air services routes within the EC.

Carriage of munitions   The Air Navigation (Carriage of Munitions of War, Weapons and Dangerous Goods) (Amendment) Order 1989 (SI No.130) allows the Minister to exempt certain aircraft from complying with the requirements of Articles 6 or 7 of the 1973 Order of the same title.

Compulsory acquisition of land   The Air Navigation and Transport (Compulsory Acquisition of Land) Order 1989 (SI No.165) allows for the compulsory acquisition of certain land.

Eurocontrol fees   The Air Navigation (Eurocontrol) (Route Charges) Regulations 1989 (SI No.362) provide that the preferred unit of currency of payment for Eurocontrol charges shall be the ECU rather than the US dollar.

Protection Area   The Air Navigation (Protection Area) Order 1989 (SI No.114) specifies requirements as to areas required for air navigation.

Registration of aircraft   The Air Navigation (Transfer of Certain Functions and Duties of State of Registry of Aircraft) Order 1989 (SI No.322) gives effect to the 1980 Protocol to the Chicago Convention on International Civil Aviation. It transfers certain functions where Irish-registered aircraft are on lease to operators in other countries who are also party to the Convention. Such arrangements have become quite common in recent years.

INTERNATIONAL CARRIAGE OF PERISHABLE FOODSTUFFS

The International Carriage of Perishable Foodstuffs Act 1987 (Commencement) Order 1989 (SI No.51) brought the 1987 Act into effect from 22 March 1989. On the terms of the Act see the 1987 Review, 348-9. The International Carriage of Perishable Foodstuffs Regulations 1989 (SI No.52) give detailed effect to the requirements of the Agreement on the International Carriage of Perishable Foodstuffs and on the Special Equipment to be Used for such Carriage of 1970 (ATP) (Pl.4762). Finally, the International Carriage of Perishable Foodstuffs Act 1987 (Authorised Person) Order 1989 (SI No.53) designates EOLAS as the body authorised to approve transport equipment for the purposes of ATP.

MERCHANT SHIPPING

Fees   The Merchant Shipping (Fees) Regulations 1989 (SI No.101) set out the fees payable in respect of obtaining various certificates of competency.

Light dues   The Merchant Shipping (Light Dues) Order 1989 (SI No.55) amends the level of light dues payable to the Commissioners of Irish Lights by ships who sail into Irish waters.

Passengers   The Merchant Shipping (Passenger Ship Construction) (Amendment) Rules 1989 (SI No.97) specify certain requirements as to access points for passengers on roll on/roll off ships. The Merchant Shipping (Passenger Boarding Cards) Regulations 1989 (SI No.98) make mandatory the issuing of boarding cards for all voyages and also require the retention of records of the numbers of passengers who travel.

Registry of fishing boats   The Merchant Shipping (Registry, Lettering and Numbering of Fishing Boats) Regulations 1989 (SI No.344) establish a registry of fishing vessels.

Weighing of vehicles   The Merchant Shipping (Weighing of Goods Vehicles) Regulations 1989 (SI No.64) require compulsory weighing of goods vehicles over a certain tonnage.

ROAD TRAFFIC

Licensing of drivers   Substantial changes in the regime for licensing of drivers were effected by regulations made in 1989. The Road Traffic (Licensing of Drivers) Regulations 1989 (SI No.285) and the Road Traffic (Licensing of Drivers) (Amendment) Regulations 1989 (SI No.353) revoked and consolidated all previous regulations made under the Road Traffic Act 1961 in connection with the licensing of drivers. The European Communities (Licensing of Drivers) Regulations 1989 (SI No.287) amend the relevant provisions of the Road Traffic Act 1961 in order to allow for the introduction of the new licensing requirements contained in SI No.285, above. The Driving Licences (Repayment of Excise Duties) Regulations 1989 (SI No. 286) deal with the repayment of excise duties under the relevant arrangements.

Index